D1587082

ENGLISH CHURCH PLATE

597–1830

THE RAMSEY ABBEY CENSER
Second quarter of 14th century
Victoria and Albert Museum
H. $10\frac{3}{4}$ in.

ENGLISH CHURCH PLATE

597–1830

BY

CHARLES OMAN

KEEPER OF THE DEPARTMENT OF METALWORK
AT THE VICTORIA AND ALBERT MUSEUM

LONDON
OXFORD UNIVERSITY PRESS
NEW YORK TORONTO
1957

Oxford University Press, Amen House, London E.C.4
GLASGOW NEW YORK TORONTO MELBOURNE WELLINGTON
BOMBAY CALCUTTA MADRAS KARACHI KUALA LUMPUR
CAPE TOWN IBADAN NAIROBI ACCRA

PRINTED IN GREAT BRITAIN

PREFACE

THE need for a book on English church plate was first borne in upon me when, a short time before the late war, I discovered that I could not lay my hands on any up-to-date list of the surviving examples of medieval church plate. I set to work to remedy this and published a list, now itself obsolete, in the 1940 volume of the *Archaeological Journal*. In 1945 I decided to write the present work.

The subject has been curiously neglected in the past. There is a very considerable literature in book or periodical form, dealing with the church plate of this or that county or diocese, but the only attempts to cover the subject as a whole are contained in Wilfred Cripps's *Old English Plate*, 1878 (11th edn., 1926), Sir Charles Jackson's *Illustrated History of English Plate*, 1911, and W. W. Watts's *Old English Silver*, 1924). The first two were primarily writers on old silver, whilst the third, who was much better equipped to deal with ecclesiological matters, unfortunately spared under forty pages for church plate.

My aim has been to try to describe the part which church plate has played in the national life. This wide approach appeared to me to be appropriate for a work published with the aid of a grant from the Pilgrim Trust. It aims at being more than a book on old silver but not a specialized study on liturgical instruments on the lines of Fr. Braun's *Das Christliche Altargerät*. Of course, this book is largely concerned with the developments in the form and decoration of chalices, &c., through the ages, and allusion has had to be made to the changes in ritual which led to the destruction of one type of vessel and the appearance of another. I felt that it was desirable, however, to attempt to give answers to some questions which have never seriously been tackled. Amongst these are the character of the custom which the church extended to the goldsmiths through the ages, and the amount of plate which an average church of a particular grade might be expected to possess in successive periods. Similarly, I have traced in detail the effects of the administrative action which, between 1530 and 1580, resulted in the destruction or the alteration of nearly all the plate in English churches.

Since allusion has now been made to the Reformation, I had better refer to another matter. When discussing this book in 1947 with Mr. Geoffrey Cumberlege, he strongly urged me to include the plate of the English Roman Catholics. I readily fell in with this suggestion, realizing from the first that it would add greatly to the labour. With the exception of one or two articles, nothing had been written on the subject. Consequently, whereas with Anglican plate I was able to take advantage of the work done by many predecessors, with the Roman

Catholic I had to do my own pioneering. I should, therefore, like to remind readers who may find that I have dealt inadequately with this subject, that the time which I have had for searching out examples has been taken almost entirely from my annual leave from the museum at which I work. I have managed to visit many of the great religious centres like Ampleforth, Oscott, and Stonyhurst, but it has simply not been possible to visit stray churches remote from London. Here I should like to record especial thanks to the Rev. E. A. Clark, S.J., of Stonyhurst, and the Rev. R. W. Willson, O.S.B., of Ampleforth, for drawing my attention to many pieces of plate in the churches scattered over England which are served by the Society of Jesus and the Order of St. Benedict. I have found it much more difficult to get information regarding the ancient plate in the churches served by the secular clergy.

The idea of including Anglican and Roman Catholic plate in the same volume has merits which may not have occurred to some readers. A number of Anglican parish churches possess chalices and patens originally made for Recusant use. Some of these have come as gifts after a Recusant family has decided to conform, whilst others have been bought on the open market in recent times. Writers on Anglican plate have almost invariably come to grief when describing such pieces. Similarly, a fine Anglican chalice and cover, made during the Anglican Recusant period (1650–60), now serves as a ciborium in the church of St. Ignatius, Liverpool. There is little sign that the goldsmith's trade was divided on denominational lines, and we shall see that most of the identifiable craftsmen who worked for the Recusants also provided plate for the parish churches. It is well, therefore, that Anglican and Recusant plate should not be treated as entirely separate subjects.

Before proceeding farther, I had better explain how I have limited my subject. Firstly, I have concerned myself with the plate of the old ecclesiastical provinces of Canterbury and York. I have adhered rigidly to the definition of plate as meaning articles made of gold or silver. In medieval times goldsmiths sometimes worked in enamelled copper, copper-gilt, or gilt bronze, but I decided to exclude all such products. If the Gloucester candlestick and the Balfour ciborium were admitted, I should have had to have drawn a more arbitrary line lower down the artistic scale in order to exclude pieces made in the same materials by less competent craftsmen who were not goldsmiths at all.

Next, I have confined myself to plate used in the service of religion to the exclusion of pieces which are really badges of office. No further mention will, therefore, be made of the pastoral staves of William of Wykeham and Richard Foxe, bishops of Winchester, and of James Smith, bishop of Callipolis, nor of the silver mitre of Richard Challoner, Bishop of Debra. This ruling also explains the absence of the more numerous but not artistically very important class of vergers' wands.

I have excluded pieces which, although used for a religious purpose, were originally made for a secular one. By this means we steer clear of the hunting-horns stuffed with relics mentioned in the 1327 inventory of Exeter Cathedral, and of the numerous standing cups and salvers which were presented to churches in order to serve as chalices and patens in the seventeenth and eighteenth centuries. Such pieces are only included in the statistical tables.

I have confined myself solely to pieces of English manufacture. A certain amount of foreign plate has always been in the possession of English churches. A Greek paten was presented to the shrine of St. Cuthbert by Athelstan, whilst other Byzantine pieces are mentioned in the thirteenth-century inventories of St. Paul's. Jocelin of Brakelonde tells how his hero Abbot Samson always brought back to St. Edmund's Abbey some ornament whenever he returned from abroad. A little later on Walter Stapledon, Bishop of Exeter, had pieces of Tours plate, whilst Thomas de Bekynton, Bishop of Bath and Wells, had candlesticks of Paris work. The Reformation did not put an end to the importation of foreign plate. At Bishopstone, Wilts., is a set of plate made at Cologne, used by John Earle, later Bishop of Salisbury, whilst serving as chaplain to an Anglican Royalist colony during the Commonwealth. At Auckland Castle is a chalice used by John Cosin, later Bishop of Durham, whilst serving a similar congregation in Paris at the same period. More Paris plate is to be found at Rushbrooke, Suffolk, and is due to the munificence of Henry Jermyn, Earl of St. Albans, who had it made in 1661 after most of the Royalists had returned to England. At Corpus Christi College, Cambridge, is plate made at The Hague for the private chapel of the future Mary II.

Rather surprisingly, there is much less foreign plate, imported soon after manufacture, to be found in the Roman Catholic churches than might have been expected. An eighteenth-century Arundell of Wardour might return from the Grand Tour with a censer from Paris, or a Weld of Lulworth might bring back a monstrance from Italy, but generally the Catholic Recusants took their chance with English goldsmiths.

On the other hand I have included medieval church plate which has found its way abroad. As we shall see, a large amount of it was sent abroad as a result of the Norman Conquest. There was a regular flow of gifts to the popes at Rome or at Avignon, borne by newly elected abbots and bishops or by ambassadors. English church plate found its way in small quantities to most of the countries of northern Europe, but the Scandinavian market was of real importance to English goldsmiths down to the end of the thirteenth century. It never ceased during the medieval period to absorb English plate, for there is no reason to doubt that the two late-medieval chalices which have turned up in Iceland reached there before the Reformation. It is rather doubtful whether much English plate did in fact go abroad as a result of the spoliation of the

English churches, though the chalice at Calcena in Aragon would appear to be an example.

The export of church plate did not cease at the Reformation, but the direction was changed. The story of the plate supplied to the churches and chapels in the American colonies was outlined by E. Alfred Jones in his *Old Silver of the American Churches* in 1913, though there is still more to be said on the subject. It remains uncertain how much English plate found its way into Irish churches during the Middle Ages, but the Church of Ireland now possesses a considerable quantity of fine English plate of the seventeenth and eighteenth centuries. I have only alluded to one or two examples, for fear of widening too far the scope of this book. After all, the splendid pieces in the cathedrals of Christ Church, Dublin, and Kilkenny do not supplement our knowledge to the same extent as do the medieval English pieces scattered about the Continent.

It seems unlikely that any appreciable amount of English plate reached Scotland during the Middle Ages. After the succession of James VI to the English throne, a few London communion cups and flagons found their way to Scotland. They seem to have exerted little influence, since the plate of the Scottish Episcopalian period is very individual. If the influence of English church plate on Scottish was small, that of Scottish on English was non-existent.

In general I have accepted the locations of the plate which are given in the works quoted in the bibliography, unless I have discovered them to be incorrect. Changes of location have occurred mainly in the towns. A lot had already taken place in the City between the time of the publication of Edwin Freshfield's *Church Plate of the City of London* in 1894 and the outbreak of the Second World War. I understand that a good deal of redistribution has been done with regard to the plate of the blitzed churches, but I have been able to obtain no coherent account of what has happened. The same sort of thing has been taking place with the plate of the blitzed, disused, and demolished churches in nearly all the major towns of medieval England. It would not have been practicable to check the presence of every one of the many pieces which I have mentioned.

CHARLES OMAN

Putney
July, 1957

CONTENTS

PART III

SINCE THE REFORMATION

PART IV

THE CATHOLIC RECUSANTS

LIST OF PLATES

Where the photograph of an object from a church, college, museum, or private collection is reproduced without further acknowledgement, it is by courtesy of the owner concerned.

Frontispiece. THE RAMSEY ABBEY CENSER. Gilt. Second quarter of fourteenth century. H. $10\frac{3}{4}$ in. Victoria and Albert Museum (Crown copyright).

1. THE TREWHIDDLE CHALICE. Second half of ninth century. H. $5\frac{1}{2}$ in. GROUP I. British Museum.

2. CHALICE. Parcel-gilt. From the grave of Archbishop Walter (d. 1205). About 1160. H. $5\frac{5}{8}$ in. GROUP II. Canterbury Cathedral.

3. *a.* CHALICE. From the grave of Bishop Swinfield (d. 1316). 1180–1280. H. $4\frac{5}{8}$ in. GROUP III. Hereford Cathedral.
   b. CHALICE. Gilt. From the grave of Bishop Gravesend (d. 1279). 1180–1280. H. $4\frac{7}{8}$ in. GROUP III. Lincoln Cathedral.

4. THE DOLGELLEY CHALICE. Gilt. About 1250. H. $7\frac{1}{4}$ in. GROUP IV. National Museum of Wales, Cardiff.

5. CHALICE. Gilt. About 1250. H. $6\frac{3}{4}$ in. GROUP IV. Dragsmark, Sweden (*Antikvarisk-Topografiska Arkivet, Stockholm*).

6. CHALICE. Gilt. From the grave of an unidentified archbishop. About 1250. H. $5\frac{5}{8}$ in. GROUP IV. York Minster.

7. THE BØRSA CHALICE. Gilt. About 1250. H. $5\frac{1}{2}$ in. GROUP IV. Kunstindustrimuseum, Oslo.

8. *a.* CHALICE. Parcel-gilt. From the grave of Archbishop Melton (d. 1340). About 1320. H. $5\frac{1}{2}$ in. GROUP V. York Minster.
   b. CHALICE. Gilt. From a church in western Sweden. About 1320. H. $7\frac{3}{8}$ in. GROUP V. Statens Historiska Museum, Stockholm.

9. CHALICE. Parcel-gilt. About 1360. H. $4\frac{7}{8}$ in. GROUP VI. Victoria and Albert Museum, on loan from Hamstall Ridware, Staffs.

10. CHALICE. Gilt. About 1370. H. $5\frac{1}{2}$ in. GROUP VI. Aston-by-Sutton, Chesh.

11. CHALICE. About 1410. H. $5\frac{5}{8}$ in. GROUP VI. Goathland, Yorks.

12. *a.* CHALICE. Gilt. Maker's mark, *grasshopper*. Hall-mark for 1479. H. 6 in. GROUP VII. Nettlecombe, Som.
    b. CHALICE. Gilt. Second half of fifteenth century H. $4\frac{5}{8}$. in. GROUP VII. Ampleforth Abbey, Yorks.

13. *a.* CHALICE. About 1500. H. $6\frac{7}{8}$ in. GROUP VII. Stadarhraun, Iceland.
    b. CHALICE (one of a pair). Gilt. Maker's mark, *MW in monogram*. Hall-mark for 1498. H. 6 in. GROUP VII. Brasenose College, Oxford.

30. *a.* PATEN. Gilt, with enamelled print. Maker's mark, *grasshopper*. Hall-mark for 1479. Diam. 4⅞ in. Nettlecombe, Som.

b. THE BEDINGFIELD PATEN. Gilt, with enamelled print. Maker's mark, *fish*. Hall-mark for 1518. Diam. 5½ in.

c. Print on back of last (full size). Victoria and Albert Museum (Crown copyright).

31. *a.* PATEN. Gilt. Maker's mark, *Vernicle*. Hall-mark for 1527. Diam. 6¼ in. Trinity College, Oxford.

b. PATEN. Gilt. Maker's mark, *sceptre*. Hall-mark for 1527. Diam. 6 in. Royal Scottish Museum, Edinburgh.

32. ICONOGRAPHY—CHALICES. Details on the foot of the gold chalice of Bishop Foxe at Corpus Christi College, Oxford (cf. Pl. 18). Saints Mary Magdalene, Jerome, Margaret, and Augustine.

33. ICONOGRAPHY—CHALICES. *The Crucified Christ*. Details of the feet of the chalices at (*a*) Old Hutton, Westmorland, and (*b*) Bacton, Hereford. Both about 1500.

34. ICONOGRAPHY—PATENS

a. *Agnus Dei*. About 1450. Chewton Mendip, Som.

b. *Lamb of the Apocalypse*. Hall-mark for 1521. Milwich, Staffs.

c. *Agnus Dei*. Hall-mark for 1537. National Museum, Melbourne, Australia.

d. *Cross*. About 1450. Pentrobin, Flint.

35. ICONOGRAPHY—PATENS. *The Vernicle*

a. About 1500. Hanworth, Norfolk.

b. Hall-mark for 1514. Heworth, Durham.

c. About 1450. Beeston Regis, Norfolk.

d. About 1480. Saham Tony, Norfolk.

e. Hall-mark for 1527. Victoria and Albert Museum.

f. Hall-mark for 1528. Morval, Cornwall.

36. ICONOGRAPHY—PATENS

a. *Vernicle*. Hall-mark for 1507. Corpus Christi College, Oxford.

b. *Christ of the Doom*. About 1500. R.C. church, Claughton-on-Brock, Lancs.

c. *The Saviour*. 1480–1500. Earl's Colne, Essex.

d. *St. Margaret*. 1480–1500. Felbrigg, Norfolk.

37. CRUETS

a. Gilt. Rhenish, about 1400. H. about 6 in. Aachen Münster.

b. Parcel-gilt. About 1480. H. 3¼ in. Mrs. G. E. P. How.

c. Parcel-gilt. About 1525. H. 6⅛ in. St. Peter Port, Guernsey.

38. PORTABLE ALTAR. Red porphyry, mounted in silver, parcel-gilt. First quarter of eleventh century. L. 10⅓ in. Musée de Cluny, Paris.

39. HANGING RELIQUARY CROSS. Wood plated with gold, with cloisonné enamel mounts; the figure of ivory. About 1000. H. 7½ in. Victoria and Albert Museum (Crown copyright).

40. PAXES

a. Gilt. About 1480. H. 4⅝ in. Lee Collection, Hart House, University of Toronto.

b. Parcel-gilt. About 1520. H. 5⅝ in. New College, Oxford.

41. *a.* FOOT AND STEM OF A STANDING PYX. Gilt. Maker's mark, *HI crossed.* Hall-mark for 1507. H. 5 in. London Museum, on loan from St. Martin, Ludgate.
b. CHRISMATORY. Crystal and silver-gilt. About 1520. H. 2¾ in. British Museum.

42. THE SWINBURNE PYX. Gilt, formerly enriched with enamel. About 1310. Diam. 2¼ in. Victoria and Albert Museum (Crown copyright)
a. Inside of bottom.
b. General view.
c. Outside of bottom.

43. THE SWINBURNE PYX
a. and *d.* Two illustrations from a manuscript in the Cambridge University Library (MS. Dd. 417).
b. Outside of cover.
c. Inside of cover.

44. BASIN FOR ABLUTIONS (one of a pair). Gilt, with enamelled medallion. Maker's mark, *horseshoe.* Hall-mark for 1493. Diam. 16¾ in. Corpus Christi College, Oxford.

45. THE RAMSEY ABBEY INCENSE-BOAT. Parcel-gilt. Last quarter of fourteenth century. L. 11¼ in. Victoria and Albert Museum (Crown copyright).

46. RELIQUARY OF ST. CUTHBERT'S ALTAR. Gilt. Eighth and tenth centuries. L. 5¼ in. Durham Cathedral.

47. RELIQUARY OF ST. THOMAS OF CANTERBURY. Parcel-gilt, with nielloed plaques. About 1180. W. 2¾ in. Metropolitan Museum of Art, New York.

48. SALT-CELLAR. Gilt. 1494–1501. H. 11¾ in. Corpus Christi College, Oxford.

49. COMMUNION CUP AND PATEN. Maker's mark, *RD in monogram.* Hall-mark for 1551. H. 7¾ in. Beddington, Surrey.

50. COMMUNION CUP WITH PATEN-COVER. Gilt. Maker's mark, *W.* Hall-mark for 1549. H. 7½ in. (*Inset,* enamelled medallion on knob or foot of paten-cover.) Victoria and Albert Museum, on loan from St. Mary Aldermary.

51. *a.* COMMUNION CUP. Gilt. Maker's mark, *covered cup.* Hall-mark for 1548. H. 9¼ in. St. Lawrence Jewry.
b. COMMUNION CUP. Gilt. Maker's mark, *RD in monogram.* Hall-mark for 1549. H. 9½ in. St. Peter-upon-Cornhill.

52. *a.* COMMUNION CUP WITH PATEN-COVER. Gilt. Maker's mark, *bird's head erased.* Hall-mark for 1551. H. (without cover) 7⅛ in. St. Michael, Southampton.
b. COMMUNION CUP. Maker's mark, *bird.* Hall-mark for 1552. H. 8¼ in. Owslebury, Hants.

53. *a.* COMMUNION CUP. Maker's mark, *daisy.* Hall-mark for 1552. H. 8 in. Battle, Sussex.
b. COMMUNION CUP. Maker's mark, *RM.* Hall-mark for 1553. H. 6¾ in. Great Houghton, Northants.

54. COMMUNION CUP WITH PATEN-COVER. Gilt. Hall-mark for 1558. H. 9 in. St. Michael-le-Belfrey, York.

67. COMMUNION CUP WITH PATEN-COVER. Maker's mark, *IW.* Dated 1576. H. 7½ in. Bodmin, Cornwall.

68. *a.* COMMUNION CUP WITH PATEN-COVER. Mark of John Jones of Exeter. About 1574. H. 7¾ in. Victoria and Albert Museum (Crown copyright).
b. COMMUNION CUP. Mark of John Jones of Exeter. About 1574. H. 7 in. Veryan, Cornwall.

69. *a.* COMMUNION CUP WITH PATEN-COVER. Mark of Lawrence Stratford of Dorchester. Dated 1574. H. 6½ in. Church Knowle, Dorset (Crown copyright, by permission of H.M. Stationery Office).
b. COMMUNION CUP WITH PATEN-COVER. Maker's mark, *OOOO.* About 1574. H. 9¾ in. St. Mary, Swansea.

70. *a.* COMMUNION CUP WITH PATEN-COVER. Maker's mark, *TS conjoined.* Hall-mark for 1580. H. 9½ in. St. Mary, Stockport, Chesh.
b. COMMUNION CUP WITH PATEN-COVER. Maker's mark, *RB in monogram.* Hall-mark for 1597. H. 9½ in. St. Mary, Reading.

71. *a.* COMMUNION CUP WITH PATEN-COVER. Maker's mark, *JS interlaced.* Hall-mark for 1581. H. 7 in. Worshipful Company of Goldsmiths.
b. COMMUNION CUP. Maker's mark, *RW.* Hall-mark for 1589. H. 4¾ in. Wendens Ambo, Essex.

72. *a.* COMMUNION CUP. Maker's mark, *TS above eagle.* Hall-mark for 1599. H. 7 in. Brightwell, Berks.
b. COMMUNION CUP. Dated 1594. H. 5¼ in. St. Clement, Jersey.

73. TWO COMMUNION BOWLS
a. About 1600. Diam. 7 in. St. Brelade, Jersey.
b. Dated 1627. Diam. 7 in. St. Brelade, Jersey.

74. CHALICE WITH PATEN-COVER. Maker's mark, *RS above rose.* Hall-mark for 1610. H. 9 in. Paten-cover 2½ in. Beddgelert, Caern.

75. CHALICE. Maker's mark, *AB above anulet.* Hall-mark for 1619. H. 6¼ in. St. Werburgh, Bristol.

76. *a.* CHALICE WITH COVER. Gilt. Maker's mark, *TE in monogram.* Hall-mark for 1622. H. 9¾ in. Victoria and Albert Museum, on loan from St. Mary Aldermary.
b. CHALICE WITH PATEN. Gilt. Maker's mark, *HB in monogram.* Hall-mark for 1626. H. 9¾ in. St. Mary Woolnoth.

77. *a.* CHALICE. Gilt. Maker's mark, *RC.* Hall-mark for 1629. H. 8¾ in. Victoria and Albert Museum, on loan from Holy Trinity, Kensington Gore.
b. CHALICE WITH PATEN-COVER. Maker's mark, *WS with bow.* Hall-mark for 1635. H. 10 in. St. Botolph, Aldgate.

78. THE ARUNDEL CHALICE. Gilt. Dated 1636. H. 9 in. Canterbury Cathedral.

79. CHALICE. Maker's mark, *TB in monogram.* Hall-mark for 1646. H. 10 in. Victoria and Albert Museum, on loan from North Ockendon, Essex.

80. CHALICE WITH PATEN-COVER. Gilt. Maker's mark, *FS in monogram.* About 1615. H. 11 in. St. John's College, Oxford.

92. *a.* CHALICE. Gilt (from a set of four). Maker's mark, *RL with fleur-de-lis*. Hall-mark for 1683. H. 10⅝ in. St. James, Piccadilly.
b. CHALICE WITH COVER. Gilt. Maker's mark, *IH crowned*. Hall-mark for 1695. H. 8¾ in. Wapping.

93. *a.* CHALICE, PATEN, AND STRAINER-SPOON. Gilt. Maker's mark, *RL with fleur-de-lis*. Hall-mark for 1688. H. 10⅝ in. Royal Hospital, Chelsea.
b. CHALICE WITH COVER. Maker's mark, *three storks*. Hall-mark for 1692. H. 10 in. Swanage, Dorset (Crown copyright, by permission of H.M. Stationery Office).

94. *a.* CHALICE. Mark of Wm. Denny & John Bache. Hall-mark for 1697. H. 12⅝ in. Victoria and Albert Museum, on loan from St. Mary Abbots, Kensington.
b. CHALICE WITH COVER. Gilt. Mark of John Chartier. Hall-mark for 1699. H. 10¼ in. Christ Church Cathedral, Oxford.

95. *a.* CHALICE. Gilt. Mark of Paul de Lamerie. Hall-mark for 1720. H. 9 in. Victoria and Albert Museum, on loan from Patshull, Staffs.
b. CHALICE. Gilt. Mark of Thomas Parr. Hall-mark for 1703. H. 7¼ in. St. Nicholas Cole Abbey.
c. CHALICE WITH PATEN-COVER. Gilt. Mark of Benjamin West (design by Paul de Lamerie). Hall-mark for 1747. H. 9¾ in. Melbury Osmund, Dorset (Crown copyright, from *Royal Commission on Historical Monuments, West Dorset*).

96. *a.* CHALICE AND PATEN. Mark of Wm. Cripps. Hall-mark for 1756. H. 9⅞ in. Stoke Climsland, Cornwall.
b. CHALICE AND PATEN. Gilt. Mark of Thomas Heming. Hall-mark for 1766. H. 9 in. St. Marylebone (from the Portland Chapel).

97. *a.* CHALICE. Gilt (one of a pair). Mark of F. Butty and N. Dumee. Hall-mark for 1766. H. 9 in. Durham Cathedral.
b. CHALICE. Mark of F. Butty and N. Dumee. Hall-mark for 1772. H. 11 in. Binley, Warw.

98. *a.* CHALICE. Gilt (one of four). Mark of Paul Storr. Hall-mark for 1821. H. 9½ in. St. Pancras.
b. CHALICE. (one of a pair). Mark of J. E. Terry & Co. Hall-mark for 1821. H. 6⅛ in. Falmouth, Cornwall.

99. *a.* CHALICE (one of a pair). Mark of B. Preston. Hall-mark for 1827. H. 9½ in. St. Giles-in-the-Fields.
b. CHALICE (one of a pair). Mark of John Bridge. Hall-mark for 1830. H. 10⅞ in. York Minster.

100. *a.* CHALICE AND PATEN-COVER for the communion of the sick. Dated 1734. H. 3½ in. St. Edward, Cambridge (Crown copyright, by permission of H.M. Stationery Office).
b. CHALICE WITH COVER for the communion of the sick. Gilt. Mark of Samuel Wood. Hall-mark for 1743. H. 8¼ in. Victoria and Albert Museum, on loan from St. Margaret Pattens.

101. *a.* PATEN. Gilt. Maker's mark, *AT in monogram*. Hall-mark for 1608. Diam. 5⅝ in. Victoria and Albert Museum, on loan from St. Michael Paternoster Royal.

b. PATEN. Maker's mark, *DG with anchor.* Hall-mark for 1629. H. 3¾ in. St. Michael Bassishaw.

102. *a.* PATEN. Gilt. Maker's mark, *WS with bow.* Hall-mark for 1633. 8¾ in. sq. All Hallows Barking.
b. PATEN. Gilt. Maker's mark, *TF between two stars.* Hall-mark for 1617. H. 5½ in. St. Olave, Hart Street.

103. *a.* PATEN. Gilt. Maker's mark, *IB below a stag.* Hall-mark for 1683. Diam. 6¼ in. Withcote, Leics.
b. PATEN. Gilt. Maker's mark, *escallop.* Hall-mark for 1629. Diam. 7½ in. Kingham, Oxon.

104. *a.* COVERED PATEN. Gilt. Maker's mark, *Tb in monogram above bird.* Hall-mark for 1638. H. 11 in. Kenilworth, Warw.
b. COVERED PATEN. Gilt. Maker's mark, *hound sejant.* Dated 1653. H. 8½ in. Fulham Palace.

105. *a.* COVERED PATEN. Gilt. Maker's mark, *CS with arrow.* Hall-mark for 1663. H. 7⅞ in. Bidford-on-Avon, Warw.
b. COVERED PATEN. Gilt. Mark of John Plummer. York hall-mark for 1675. H. 9½ in. Ripon Cathedral.

106. PATEN. Gilt. Mark of F. Butty and N. Dumee. Hall-mark for 1766. Diam. 7⅜ in. Durham Cathedral.

107. *a.* FLAGON. Gilt. Maker's mark, *IP.* Hall-mark for 1572. H. 12½ in. Wells Cathedral.
b. FLAGON. Parcel-gilt (one of a pair). Maker's mark, *RH in monogram.* Hall-mark for 1577. H. 13½ in. Cirencester, Glos.

108. *a.* FLAGON. Maker's mark, *SO.* Hall-mark for 1608. H. 13 in. St. Michael Paternoster Royal, from All Hallows the Great (lent to the Victoria and Albert Museum).
b. FLAGON. Gilt. Maker's mark, *AB above an anulet.* Hall-mark for 1619. H. 12⅞ in. Victoria and Albert Museum, on loan from St. Mary Abbots, Kensington.

109. *a.* FLAGON. Maker's mark, *EL over fleur-de-lis.* Hall-mark for 1619. H. 13 in. Severn Stoke, Worcs.
b. FLAGON. Gilt. Maker's mark, *RC above mullet.* Hall-mark for 1618. H. 10½ in. St. Andrew by the Wardrobe, from St. Anne, Blackfriars.

110. FLAGON. Gilt. Maker's mark, *AB.* Hall-mark for 1619. H. 12⅝ in. St. Werburgh, Bristol.

111. *a.* FLAGON. Gilt (one of a pair). Maker's mark, *hound sejant.* Hall-mark for 1654. H. 10 in. Victoria and Albert Museum, on loan from the National Trust. From Staunton Harold, Leics.
b. FLAGON. Gilt (one of a pair). Maker's mark, *PG with rose.* Hall-mark for 1636. H. 11½ in. St. Anne and St. Agnes, from St. John Zachary.

112. *a.* FLAGON. Gilt (one of a pair). Made by M. Houser (?) 1660–1. H. 13 in. Auckland Castle, Durham.
b. FLAGON. Gilt (one of a pair). Mark of Charles Shelley. Hall-mark for 1664. H. 20 in. Buckingham Palace, from Whitehall Palace. Reproduced by gracious permission of Her Majesty the Queen (Crown copyright).

140. *a.* CANDLESTICK. Gilt. Maker's mark, *HW above escallop.* About 1655. H. 17¼ in. Lambeth Palace.

b. CANDLESTICK. Gilt. Maker's mark, *hound sejant.* Hall-mark for 1653. H. 22¾ in. Victoria and Albert Museum, on loan from the National Trust. From Staunton Harold, Leics.

c. CANDLESTICK. Gilt. Maker's mark, *hound sejant.* Hall-mark for 1661. H. 16½ in. Gloucester Cathedral.

141. *a.* CANDLESTICK. Gilt. Maker's mark, *WM with mullet.* Hall-mark for 1663. H. 26 in. Salisbury Cathedral.

b. CANDLESTICK. Gilt. Maker's mark, *FL with bird.* 1660. H. 28½ in. St. George's Chapel, Windsor.

c. CANDLESTICK. Gilt. Maker's mark, *IB above crescent.* Hall-mark for 1676. H. 24 in. Ingestre, Staffs.

142. CANDLESTICK. Gilt. Maker's mark, *IB above crescent.* Hall-mark for 1675. H. 13⅞ in. Harthill, Yorks.

143. CANDLESTICK. Gilt. Maker's mark, *RL with fleur-de-lis.* Hall-mark for 1688. H. 39 in. Royal Hospital, Chelsea.

144. *a.* CANDLESTICK. Gilt. Mark of Anthony Nelme. Hall-mark for 1694. H. 42 in. St. George's Chapel, Windsor.

b. CANDLESTICK. Mark of Gabriel Sleath. Hall-mark for 1712. H. 21¾ in. Bristol Cathedral.

c. CANDLESTICK. Gilt. Mark of Paul de Lamerie. Hall-mark for 1738. H. 23½ in. Queen's College, Oxford.

145. *a.* CANDLESTICK. Maker's mark, *SW in Gothic script.* Hall-mark for 1759. H. 26 in. Trinity College, Oxford.

b. CANDLESTICK. Gilt. Maker's mark, *IV.* Hall-mark for 1777. H. 30 in. Christ Church Cathedral, Dublin.

c. CANDLESTICK. Gilt. Mark of F. Butty and N. Dumee. Hall-mark for 1766. H. 24 in. Durham Cathedral.

146. *a.* BAPTISMAL BOWL. Mark of R. Gurney and T. Cook. Hall-mark for 1730. H. 4⅝ in. St. Paul, Deptford.

b. BAPTISMAL BOWL. Mark of D. and R. Hennell. Hall-mark for 1766. H. 6 in. St. Mary, Reading.

147. BAPTISMAL EWER. Maker's mark, *spearhead between IH.* Dated 1729. H. 7 in. St. Andrew, Guernsey.

148. STRAINER SPOONS. *a.* Gilt. Dated 1613. L. 7¾ in. St. Peter-per-Mountergate, Norwich.

b. Maker's mark, *WM crowned.* Hall-mark for 1685. L. 5¾ in. Bristol Cathedral.

c. Maker's mark, *IW crowned above star.* Hall-mark for 1693. L. 8 in. St. Dunstan, Stepney.

149. STRAINER SPOONS. *a.* Gilt. Dated 1717. L. 7¾ in. Wapping.

b. Mark of Ralph Good of Bristol about 1730. L. 7¾ in. Formerly at the Temple Church, Bristol.

150. BREAD KNIFE WITH BOX. Gilt. Mark of James Shruder. Hall-mark for 1753. L. (box) 10¾ in. Melbury Sampford, Dorset (Crown copyright, by permission of H.M. Stationery Office).

151. BREAD KNIFE AND SHEATH. Gilt. Dated 1755. Stinsford, Dorset (Crown copyright, by permission of H.M. Stationery Office).

152. RECUSANT CHALICE AND PATEN. Early seventeenth century. H. 5¾ in. GROUP CR I. R.C. church, Creswell, Staffs.

153. TWO RECUSANT CHALICES. Early seventeenth century. GROUP CR I.
a H. 6½ in. Lord Kenyon.
b. H. 4⅜ in. Oscott College, Birmingham.

154. *a*. RECUSANT CHALICE. About 1630. H. 7 in. GROUP CR 2. Bradoc (C.E.), Cornwall.
b. ANGLICAN CHALICE WITH PATEN-COVER. Maker's mark, *WR below bow*. Hall mark for 1633. H. 9½ in. Llanafon (C.W.), Cardigan.

155. TWO RECUSANT CHALICES. GROUP CR 2.
a. Maker's mark, *WR below bow*. Hall-mark for 1633. H. 6½ in. National Museum, Dublin.
b. About 1630. H. 7 in. Ampleforth Abbey, Yorks.

156. TWO RECUSANT CHALICES. Gilt. About 1630–40. GROUP CR 2.
a. H. 7⅝ in. Danby Hall, Middleham, Yorks.
b. H. 7¼ in. Danby Hall, Middleham, Yorks.

157. RECUSANT CHALICE. Gilt. About 1630–40. H. 8½ in. GROUP CR 2. Ashow (C.E.), Warw.

158. RECUSANT CHALICE. Gilt. Maker's mark, *RM above rosette*. Hall-mark for 1637. H. 7½ in. GROUP CR 3. St. Ignatius, South Tottenham.

159. RECUSANT CHALICE AND PATEN. Gilt. Maker's mark, *RM above rosette*. Hall-mark for 1638. H. 9½ in. GROUP CR 3. Wardour Castle, Wilts.

160. RECUSANT CHALICE. Maker's mark, *RM above rosette*. Hall-mark for 1639. H. 8 in. GROUP CR 3. Solihull (C.E.), Warw.

161. TWO RECUSANT CHALICES. GROUP CR 3.
a. Maker's mark, *RM above rosette*. About 1638. H. 7 in. Stonyhurst College.
b. Maker's mark, *WT below two anulets*. Hall-mark for 1639. H. 7¼ in. St. Mary-on-the-Quay, Bristol.

162. TWO RECUSANT CHALICES. Parcel-gilt. 1650–70. GROUP CR 3.
a. H. 5 in. Sawston Hall, Cambridge.
b. H. 6½ in. Stonyhurst College.

163. TWO RECUSANT CHALICES. GROUP CR 3.
a. Parcel-gilt. 1650–70. H. 8 in. R.C. church, Clitheroe, Lancs.
b. Maker's mark, *WB in pointed-topped shield*. About 1690. H. 6½ in. Oscott College, Birmingham.

164. RECUSANT CHALICE. Gilt. Mark of Benjamin Pyne. Hall-mark for 1704. H. 9½ in. GROUP CR 4. Lulworth Castle, Dorset (Crown copyright, by permission of H.M. Stationery Office).

165. TWO RECUSANT CHALICES. GROUP CR 4.
a. Mark of Frederick Kandler. Hall-mark for 1739 (bowl remade about 1810). H. 8½ in. R.C. church, Worcester.
b. Mark of Wm. Pitts and Jos. Preedy. Hall-mark for 1791. H. 10½ in. Stonyhurst College.

ACKNOWLEDGEMENTS

THE first debt of gratitude which I must acknowledge is to the Pilgrim Trust, whose generous contribution towards the cost of producing this book has made its publication possible. Secondly I must record my thanks to the Prime Warden and Wardens of the Worshipful Company of Goldsmiths, who allowed me access to the minute books of the company, which contain much material which has remained unused until now. In addition to the individuals already mentioned in the Preface, I should like to record my thanks to the following, who have allowed me the benefit of their time and knowledge: Mr. Charles Brocklehurst, Mr. A. J. Collins, Mr. Arthur Grimwade, the Rev. Peter Hawker, Mrs. G. E. P. How, and Dr. N. M. Penzer. Dr. F. C. Eeles, of the Central Council for the Care of Churches, has not survived to see this work to which he gave much help and encouragement in its early stages. Since his death I have received similar help and advice from his former assistant, Dr. Judith Scott.

To the following, who kindly allowed me access to plate which is their property (sometimes also providing photographs of it), I must express my gratitude. First of these is Her Majesty the Queen, by whose gracious permission I was allowed to examine the plate of all the chapels royal, active or defunct, which is on the charge of the Lord Chamberlain's Department. Next to Capt. R. F. Eyre Hudleston, R.N., of Sawston Hall, Cambridge, Lord Kenyon, Lord Leigh of Stoneleigh, Lieut.-Col. H. Levin of Corby Castle, Cumberland, His Grace the Duke of Norfolk, Lord Rossmore, Richard Scrope, Esq., of Danby Hall, Middleham, the Earl of Stamford, H. Hornyold-Strickland, Esq., of Sizergh Castle, Westmorland, Capt. S. Temple of Broughton Hall, Skipton, Lieut.-Col. J. L. B. Leicester Warren of Tabley Hall, Cheshire, and J. W. Weld, Esq., of Lulworth Castle, Dorset.

It is hardly necessary to add that I have received the greatest help from the clergy, who have not only made accessible to me the plate in their charge but have often gone to much trouble in arranging for it to be photographed. I must thank them also for much hospitality and for transport.

To the following institutions I am indebted for the use of their facilities. Firstly I must express my thanks to my colleagues at the Victoria and Albert Museum, and then to the Controller of H.M. Stationary Office, the Royal Commission on Historical Monuments (England and Wales), the British Museum; the City Museum and Art Gallery, Birmingham; the National Museum of Wales, Cardiff; the National Museum, Dublin; the Mortimer Museum, Hull; the Museum and Art Gallery, Leicester; the Usher Art Gallery, Lincoln; the

Museum and Art Gallery, Northampton; the Castle Museum, Norwich; the Ashmolean Museum, Oxford; and the Royal Institution of Cornwall, Truro.

I am indebted for help of the same sort to the following institutions abroad: the Instituto Amatller de Arte Hispanico, Barcelona; the National Museum, Melbourne; the Metropolitan Museum, New York; the Kunstindustrimuseum, Oslo; the Musée de Cluny, Paris; and the Statens Historiska Museum, Stockholm.

From the following I have also received much help, particularly in the provision of photographs: Ampleforth Abbey; Mrs. Moir Carnegie of Blackheath; Mademoiselle Elizabeth Dhanens of Ghent; the Rev. Stefan Eggertson of Thingeyri, Iceland; Sidney G. Faire, Esq., of Bidford-on-Avon; D. B. Hague, Esq., of Aberystwyth; the Rev. H. Jacques of Portesham, Dorset; the late Lord Lee of Fareham; James Nelson, Esq., of Birmingham; Senhor A. Cardoso Pinto of Lisbon; Raymond Richards, Esq., of Gawsworth, Cheshire; Messrs. Sotheby & Co.; Messrs. Spottiswoode, Dixon, & Harting; and Stonyhurst College.

PART I

THE MIDDLE AGES

I

THE CHURCH AND THE GOLDSMITHS

1. *To* 1300

SO much has been written about the benefits, spiritual and temporal, conferred upon England by St. Augustine and his missionaries that it might easily be assumed that they set to work in a cultural vacuum. To what extent this assumption may be justified with regard to the other arts does not concern us, but it cannot be too strongly emphasized that the English had been accomplished goldsmiths long before the arrival of the missionaries. If this fact is kept in mind it will be easier to understand the relationship between the Church and the goldsmiths during the remainder of the medieval period.

For the last hundred years nearly all of those who have written about English goldsmiths' work have assumed that most of the treasures with which the churches were enriched down to the thirteenth century were made by goldsmith monks. For this entirely erroneous picture the Abbé Texier[1] must bear much of the blame, since only those who were prepared to check his references discovered that he misinterpreted his texts in a most reckless manner.[2] Well-attested Anglo-Saxon clerical goldsmiths are rare indeed. The most authentic is probably the otherwise forgotten anchorite St. Billfrith, who lived in the first half of the eighth century and who made a gem-encrusted cover for a book of the Gospels, mentioned in the story of the wanderings of the body of St. Cuthbert.[3]

The claims of most of the bishops and abbots who have been described as goldsmiths too often depend on a misinterpretation of the word *fecit*, and fail if it be accepted that this is better translated as 'had made' than as 'made'. Even in the cases of St. Dunstan and of St. Æthelwold, who have been described as goldsmiths quite unambiguously, it is necessary to be very guarded. The nearly contemporary lives of both saints make no claim that they possessed any skill of this sort. The first references to the matter occur only in lives written after the Conquest. Manny,[4] Abbot of Evesham (1044–54), and Spearhavoc,

[1] *Dictionnaire d'orfévrerie*, 1857.

[2] The strictures of R. E. Swartwout (*The Monastic Craftsman*, 1932) are entirely deserved.

[3] Simeon of Durham, Rolls Series, 1882, i. 68. The cover was still in existence in the seventeenth century when Selden saw it in the Cotton Collection (*Acta Sanctorum*, 1 Mart. 450).

[4] It would seem, however, that Abbot Thomas de Marleberge (d. 1236) had some fairly definite basis for his stories about his predecessor (Evesham Chronicle, Rolls Series, 1863, 86). Originally a monk of Bury, he is described by the twelfth-century chronicler as *aurificis arte peritissimum.* On the

Abbot of Abingdon, a contemporary, are both credited with a knowledge of the goldsmith's art, but only upon the authority of writers of a much later date.

If the idea must be rejected that most church plate made before the Conquest was the work of goldsmith monks, there is little enough that can be asserted confidently about the lay goldsmiths of this period, as has been remarked recently by Mr. Ronald Jessup,[1] and he is also doubtless right in concluding that these elusive artists ranked fairly high in the social scale. They probably profited greatly by the conversion of England, which provided them with an entirely new class of patron, since it is unlikely that they had been much employed in furnishing the previous pagan temples. The abandonment of the pagan practice of burying a chieftain with all his treasures was also favourable to them, since every important funeral no longer involved the withdrawal from circulation of a certain amount of gold or silver. The presentation to churches of costly vessels did not really mean that just so much precious metal was permanently immobilized. Our ancestors paid little respect to ancient plate (unless it could be considered as a relic) and no medieval abbot felt any pangs of remorse about melting down old plate when he had set his heart on some new work. Thus the same precious metal might, over a long period, serve an abbey in several capacities, providing successive generations of goldsmiths with the wherewithal to show their skill. Similarly, gold and silver returned to circulation when used to pay off the debts of an abbey or to satisfy the cupidity of a king. Even the Viking invasions profited the goldsmiths in the long run, since the conversion to Christianity of the northern kingdoms opened up a whole new area to English artists.

The immediate effect of the Norman Conquest, like that of the Danes, was detrimental to the interests of the goldsmiths, but, again, it was not long before it transpired that the intruded bishops and abbots regarded the provision of rich new vessels as the proper conclusion to the reconstruction of their churches. It should be emphasized that the Church was by far the most important patron of the goldsmiths down to the end of the thirteenth century. The king was the only important secular patron until the barons began to develop civilized tastes in the thirteenth century.

We know nothing about the makers of church treasures during the forty

translation of Robert of Jumièges to Canterbury, he was nominated as his successor in the see of London in 1050. The archbishop, however, refused to consecrate him and eventually he made off to the Continent with the ready money belonging to the see and the materials for making a crown, which had been entrusted to him by the king (Abingdon Chronicle, Rolls Series, 1896, i. 463; ii. 281). Edward the Confessor does not seem to have been lucky in his choice of goldsmiths, for William of Malmesbury records that he entrusted one of his lay goldsmiths with an arm of St. Ouen, confiscated with Queen Emma's goods in 1043. The goldsmith stole it and gave it to Malmesbury Abbey where his brother was a monk (*De Gestis Pontificum*, Rolls Series, 1870, 419–20).

[1] *Anglo-Saxon Jewellery*, 1951, 38–39.

years after the Conquest, but we get illuminating glimpses of some of the goldsmiths who worked for the great abbeys during the twelfth and thirteenth centuries. We are best informed with regards progress at St. Albans and Ely, so that if the goldsmithing activities of these two houses is retold in some detail it will be possible to form some idea as to how things were managed in other rich Benedictine abbeys.

The greatness of St. Albans[1] dates from the election of the first Norman abbot, Paul of Caen (1077–97), who succeeded an abbot of mixed Danish and German blood who had been elected in 1064 and had managed to maintain himself uneasily for eleven years after the Conquest. Abbot Paul is mainly remembered as the rebuilder of the abbey church, but he is also mentioned as the donor of a sanctuary lamp, richly mounted book-covers, and of altar and processional candlesticks.[2] At this point a digression may be permitted to explain how monastic purchases of plate were financed. During the twelfth century it became usual for monasteries to allow their abbots a fixed income in order to escape the danger of having all the income of the house seized by the king during a vacancy. Besides the abbot's personal savings, the purchase of plate might be financed from the savings from the annual income assigned to the sacrist for the performance of his duties, which included the maintenance of the church plate. The savings of an abbot might build up a considerable fund, but it is unlikely that a sacrist's economies would do much more than pay for an occasional chalice. It is often difficult to visualize exactly how the funds for a really important commission were provided. The shrine of a saint would attract alms from the laity. Otherwise the abbot could always weed out and sell the old-fashioned plate in the sacristy or raid the savings of the other abbey officials. Borrowing from the Jews usually led to trouble later on.

Nothing is known about Abbot Paul's goldsmiths nor of those employed by Abbot Richard (1097–1119) to make two shrines which he presented.[3] In 1124 Abbot Geoffrey (1119–46) started work on the long-projected shrine of St. Alban. This he entrusted to one of his monks, Anketyl, and to a young layman named Salomon of Ely.[4] Anketyl had spent seven years in Denmark; he had gone to execute an order for the king who, however, had persuaded him to stay on as royal goldsmith and warden of the mint. Coming back on leave to England, he was so attracted by life at St. Albans that he applied for permission to become a monk. His is, in fact, an example of the type of career which has been used by the unwary to bolster up the legend of the monastic

[1] I dealt with this subject at length in 'The Goldsmiths of St. Albans Abbey in the twelfth and thirteenth centuries' in the *Trans. of the St. Albans and Herts. Arch. Soc.*, 1932, 215–36.

[2] The principal authority for the goldsmiths at St. Albans is the *Vitae Abbatum* of Matthew Paris, which is printed in Thomas Walsingham's *Gesta Abbatum monasterii Sancti Albani* in the Rolls Series, 1867. The immediate reference is to i. 58–59.

[3] Ibid. i. 69.

[4] Ibid. i. 83–84, 87.

workshops. There is reason to believe that quite a number of the authentic goldsmith monks learnt their art as laymen. Late admissions were mutually beneficial. The lay goldsmith of the twelfth and thirteenth centuries was generally a business man and often, like Anketyl, held a job which demanded administrative as well as technical ability. Such an individual could be an invaluable addition to a monastery. The monastic life was in high repute, and a goldsmith who was unmarried might well be disposed to exchange the uncertainties of a career in the world for the security of the cloister when old age began to loom on the horizon. Even if the abbot could not promise him a long-time job like the making of a shrine, he could count upon preserving his skill by doing running repairs on the abbey plate and so relieving the sacrist.

We have no information about the goldsmiths who worked for Abbot Robert de Gorham (1151–67), although we hear of a number of pieces made at this time. On the other hand, we have the names of two master goldsmiths employed by his successor Abbot Simon (1167–83), but as they are not credited with making all of the pieces which are mentioned, it is clear that there must have been at least a third. Master Baldwin was the maker, amongst other things, of a gold chalice 'than which we have seen none more noble in the realm of England' and of a vessel of gold set with gems to carry the Eucharist when suspended above the high altar. It pleased Henry II so much when he saw it that he sent a 'cup' to hold the wafer within it.[1] It seems likely that Baldwin was also in the king's service.[2] Abbot Simon's other known goldsmith was Master John of St. Albans who was employed on making the precious outer cover for the shrine of the Protomartyr, which he began in about 1170 and completed within a few years.[3] It is mentioned that he spent some time in the service of the king of Denmark, but we are not told at what period of his career. He was presumably the John of St. Albans, the king's goldsmith, who received a payment from the sheriff of Kent in 1192–3 and John the goldsmith who received a payment of £4. 11*s*. 4*d*. annually or 3*d*. a day from the sheriff of London and Middlesex from 1169–70[4] until 1213.[5] He was known personally to the chronicler Matthew Paris, whose memories of St. Albans went back a few years before his own profession as monk in 1217. Master John had two sons, one of whom bore the same name but who is never described as a goldsmith when mentioned in the Pipe Rolls. His brother Nicholas followed in his father's footsteps by training as a goldsmith and seeking his fortune in Denmark, where he served Waldemar II (1202–41) for thirty years as an officer of the mint. He

[1] T. Walsingham, op. cit. 190–1. The admiration freely expressed by Matthew Paris for the work of Master Baldwin is a tribute to his own critical powers. Baldwin must have worked in the late Romanesque style, which was quite *demodé* in the time when Matthew Paris was writing.

[2] Pipe Roll Soc. xxix, 1908, 123; xxxiv, 1913, 152; xxxvi. 124.

[3] T. Walsingham, op. cit. i. 189.

[4] Pipe Roll Soc. xv, 1892, 14.

[5] P.R.O. Pipe Roll, E. 372, 61.

was back in England in 1237 when he is found serving Henry III in the same capacity. He was a secular priest so that the king was able to reward him with church preferment. He was on friendly terms with the abbey of St. Albans, but there is no record of his ever having done any work for it. His greatest opportunity of showing his skill as a goldsmith came when the king entrusted him with the making of three images for the shrine of St. Thomas of Canterbury in 1243.[1] He died ten years later.

Abbot Simon's successor Abbot Warin (1183–95) ordered the shrine of St. Amphibalus, but nothing is recorded of the goldsmith. The abbacy of John de Cella (1195–1214) was made notable by the admission into the abbey of Walter of Colchester, who was attracted to St. Albans by Brother Ralph Gubiun, who came of an Essex family. He was not only a goldsmith but also a sculptor and painter. He was appointed sacrist in about 1215 and died in 1248. For his own abbey he made the frontal for the high altar and two book-covers.[2] He appeared prominently at the elevation of the shrine of St. Thomas of Canterbury on 7 July 1220, since he and Master Elias of Dereham had been responsible for the design.[3] Walter of Colchester had a brother Simon who is described as a painter and whose son Richard became a monk. Matthew Paris describes him as a painter though a note in the *Additamenta*[4] shows that, assisted by a certain goldsmith, he was responsible for the making of the cresting of a shrine.

We know nothing for certain about the goldsmithing activities of Matthew Paris. We do not know whether he was born early enough to learn the elements of the craft from Master John, but he must obviously have come under the influence of Master Walter, though it would be only natural if the latter used his nephew Brother Richard as his principal assistant. Matthew's lively interest in goldsmiths' work is amply attested by his writings, but it is difficult to believe that had he been responsible for some major work no mention should have been made of it. For the greater part of his monastic career there were two other goldsmith monks at St. Albans. With Matthew's death in 1259 our information about goldsmiths' work for St. Albans becomes meagre. By the second half of the thirteenth century the great period of the goldsmiths was drawing to its close and the later acquisitions of which we hear are fewer and usually of lesser importance.

Having sketched the conditions obtaining at the great Hertfordshire abbey, we may compare the results with what has been discovered about the only

[1] *Calendar of the Liberate Rolls*, 1240–5, 196.

[2] T. Walsingham, op. cit. i. 232.

[3] The phrases used do not actually claim that he had any actual hand in the making (M. Paris, *Historia Anglorum*, Rolls Series, 1866, ii. 242; M. Paris, *Chronica Majora*, Rolls Series, 1857, iii. 59). Master Elias of Dereham, with whom he is mentioned as co-operating, was a former royal clerk who ended up as a canon of Salisbury, where he supervised the building of the new cathedral. He does not appear to have had any technical qualifications (A. Hamilton Thompson, 'Master Elias of Dereham and the King's Works', in *Arch. Journal*, xcviii, 1941, 1–35).

[4] M. Paris, *Chronica Majora*, vi. 202.

other abbey about which we have much information. Nearly fifty years have elapsed since F. R. Chapman discovered the existence of hereditary goldsmiths who served the cathedral priory of Ely for at least a century and a half.[1] The story starts with Prior Salomon who granted a rent charge on a neighbouring estate and an annual payment from the sacristy to Salomon the goldsmith. To this was coupled a royal confirmation of the grant which must be dated between 1166 and 1175. In due course Salomon was succeeded by his son Jordan, who in the course of the first quarter of the thirteenth century made over the emoluments as abbey goldsmith to his nephew Salomon, son of his brother Stephan. Salomon II was succeeded by his son Alan who had two sons, Salomon and Alan, who are both described as goldsmiths. The three sons of Salomon III all became distinguished ecclesiastics and F. R. Chapman supposed that the succession to the family business passed to Adam of Walsingham, whom he supposed to have been a son-in-law of Alan II. Adam of Walsingham was the father of Alan of Walsingham who became sacrist and later prior, who is known to have been trained as a goldsmith. Nothing is recorded of later hereditary goldsmiths, so that it may be supposed that the arrangement lapsed in the early years of the fourteenth century.

F. R. Chapman was aware that Salomon I was the assistant of Anketyl in the making of the shrine for St. Alban, but he had not discovered that he was a royal goldsmith who received a retaining fee of 60*s.* payable from the mill at Cambridge annually from 1157 to 1175,[2] a fact which explains why it was necessary for the king to confirm the appointment of an abbey official. The post of goldsmith to a large Benedictine house can never have been a whole-time job, so that happy was the abbot who could entice a good goldsmith to enter the community: someone who could execute new work and also carry out repairs as soon as the damage was done. The alternative was to seek some experienced goldsmith who could not only do the new work but would pay the abbey regular visits to execute repairs and alterations. F. R. Chapman smelt nepotism in the coincidence that both prior and goldsmith bore the name of Salomon. This was perhaps not entirely fair to the former. An abbot of St. Albans had all the resources of the goldsmiths' shops in Cheapside within a day's journey. A prior of Ely might well think that he was not paying an excessive price for securing that the needs of his inconveniently placed church should receive regular attention. As far as we know the arrangement worked out well and the two parties seem to have remained on friendly terms.

Both St. Albans and Ely were major monasteries of ancient foundation. In the century after the Conquest there sprang up a host of new foundations, some of which were destined to prosper and others to stagnate or wither. All

[1] F. R. Chapman, *Sacrist Rolls of Ely*, 1907, i. 151.

[2] Hunter, *Great Rolls of the Pipe*, 1844, 14; Pipe Roll Soc. xxv, 1906, 70.

of these must have found work for goldsmiths, though we seldom have precise information about either their furnishing or the goldsmiths employed. Cumulatively, monastic patronage must have meant much to Cheapside at this period.

The monasteries and monastic cathedrals were not the only important customers for church plate in the two centuries after the Conquest. Of the character of the patronage of the secular cathedrals we have much less information. No one seems ever to have suggested that secular canons dabbled in goldsmithing, so that it will pass without fear of contradiction that the canons of St. Paul's in London and of St. Peter's in York would give their commissions to some of the goldsmiths who worked within a few hundred yards of each cathedral. These two churches were, of course, particularly lucky as there would always have been a competent goldsmith at hand. Probably the practice of employing a special cathedral goldsmith is of quite an early date, though the sacrist rolls of York only provide the names of the individuals who served the minster in this capacity from the fifteenth century. Other cathedrals were not so fortunate in having local talent always available. Doubtless there was always someone in Lincoln or Salisbury who could take a dent out of a chalice or solder a pinnacle on to a censer, but the evidence seems to suggest that important orders for new work usually went to a Londoner.

The character of the patronage extended by secular cathedrals differed in important respects from that provided by monastic establishments. In the latter the wealth of the house and the funds derived from the gifts of the faithful were concentrated in the hands of the abbot or cathedral prior, who decided the manner of their disposal. This favoured the incepton of really important long-time undertakings of types, like altar-frontals, not likely to appeal to the generosity of the faithful as did the shrines of saints. On the other hand, they could expect little from the benefactions of individual monks.[1]

By contrast the less autocratic secular cathedrals profited much from the benefactions of rich deans and canons. Since such personages had usually made their way in the service of the king or of a bishop, their taste can be assumed to have been generally fairly sophisticated, so that we may feel sure that they would not have been content with the inferior work of some local goldsmith. The class of gifts provided by such benefactors is well illustrated in the thirteenth-century inventories of St. Paul's, where it will be found that many of the most valuable possessions had been given by members of the chapter.[2]

[1] Monks did occasionally produce gifts. Matthew Paris passed on to St. Albans the gifts which he had received from foreign sovereigns when on missions overseas (B.M. Nero D. VII, 51). John Savage, sub-cellarer at St. Albans in the middle of the fourteenth century, gave two reliquaries (J. Amundesham, *Annales*, Rolls Series, 1870, ii. 334–5).

[2] For instance, Dean Alan de Burnham (d. 1216) and Prebendary Robert Chaplain had each provided a gold chalice and a pair of silver cruets. Other prebendaries had given a wide range of objects (*Archaeologia*, l, 1887, 464–74; Dugdale, *St. Paul's Cathedral*, 1818, 310–14).

Amongst the benefactors of both regular and secular cathedrals was the bishop. Perhaps the secular cathedrals profited most, though not all bishops were as generous as was Osmond (1078–99) to Sarum.[1] Relations between the bishop and cathedral priory tended to be less cordial, but even if the bishop refrained from generous actions during his lifetime, custom often allowed to the cathedral certain pickings from his estate.[2]

Having considered the patronage of the major regular and secular establishments, we may turn to the parish churches. Even in the thirteenth century their furnishing remained simple—how simple will be shown in the next chapter. We should probably be right in guessing that nearly every item encountered in an inventory was the gift or bequest of a parishioner or else of the rector, who was only too likely not to be the parish priest. However, it is obvious that the parish and its parson must be allowed to have exercised some sort of patronage, since there were circumstances which necessitated the parish coming into direct relations with the goldsmith.[3] Every piece sooner or later requires repair, and if such repairs are neglected it has ultimately to be replaced. When the time came for the chalice to be refashioned it was doubtless the priest who decided the pattern for the new one. The patronage exerted by or on behalf of the parish churches in the twelfth and thirteenth centuries was cumulatively very important. Rich donors may have given handsome pieces, but when the responsibility was left with the priest we may feel sure that his first concern would be to get something which would be passed by the archdeacon as sufficient. This adjective would seem to describe the Ashprington, Devon, and Berwick St. James, Wilts., chalices, which are the only pieces of parochial church plate which have survived from this period. We cannot tell where either of these were made, but it is likely that the provincial goldsmiths got more of this class of work than of the more lucrative orders.

A considerable proportion of the plate of any cathedral, regular or secular, or of any other church was composed of gifts from the laity. It seems fair to suppose that down to the end of the twelfth century the wishes of the head of the recipient church would be closely followed in selecting the craftsman and the type of piece desired. A Norman baron had little domestic plate and so had no need to keep himself informed as to the merits of contemporary goldsmiths. His Plantagenet descendants cannot be assumed to have been equally ignorant, and a gift from a thirteenth-century earl is likely to have shown

[1] *C.P. Wilts.* 233–4.

[2] Thus Durham Priory appears to have got the bishop's chapel (J. Raine, *Brief Account of the Episcopal Castle or Palace of Auckland*, 1852, 14.

[3] By the rulings of Archbishop Walter Gray (1216–55) for the province of York, and of Archbishop Robert Winchelsey (1293–1313) for that of Canterbury, the church plate became a responsibility of the parishioners (E. Peacock, *English Church Furniture*, 1866, 175–9). Until the churchwardens began to function efficiently the dissatisfaction of the archdeacon must have been vented mainly on the parson.

something of his taste (as cultivated by his chaplain), and was probably made by the goldsmith who repaired and fashioned his considerable domestic plate. Not all benevolent laymen were, however, capable of intelligent artistic patronage, and if it were a case of a squire presenting a chalice to his parish church, there would be little guidance obtainable from the priest. In such circumstances the donor probably trusted to his own instincts to select the best chalice for the price when next he visited London. There was more than an aesthetic problem involved for, as we shall see anon, the hall-marking laws owe their origin to the need for protecting the customer from the wiles of the dishonest goldsmith who worked in metal below the accepted standard.

2. 1300 *to* 1548

The character of the church patronage of the goldsmiths altered in several ways during the two and a half centuries which preceded the Reformation. Firstly, it should be noted that the craft of the goldsmith was no longer esteemed so highly as it had been during the early Middle Ages. As a consequence the goldsmiths no longer received so large a share of the funds available for adorning churches as heretofore. The control of the funds was, moreover, rather differently distributed. It is notorious that monasticism was in decline in the later Middle Ages and that many houses were in financial difficulties. Our information is fullest with regard to the monastic cathedrals, and judging from them, major works were seldom commissioned, although there were some exceptions, such as the reconstruction of the high altar of Canterbury Cathedral carried out by Prior Chillendon (1390–1411). It would be quite wrong, however, to suppose that the monastic cathedrals and great abbeys had entirely ceased to be important customers of the goldsmiths, though this was the case with most of the lesser priories. The sacrists' and feretrars' rolls of Durham,[1] for instance, bear witness to a flow of work for the goldsmiths, but the orders do not usually sound very rich and they were mostly executed with scrap metal. These minor orders reflect a change which had been altering the appearance of the monastic and the secular cathedrals. In early days the plate of a cathedral or abbey was all nominally for the use of the high altar. By the thirteenth century the minor chapels were well advanced in the process of accumulating their own plate. All was not gold that glittered upon the chapel altars, but the plate of the endowed chantries was usually richer, since it was often provided by the founder and represented the furnishing of his private chapel.

Pari passu with the decline of the lesser monasteries there grew up numerous collegiate churches to bridge the gap previously existing between the secular

[1] *Durham Account Rolls*, ii, Surtees Soc. 1898, 400–10.

cathedral and the parish church. Another development of this period was the university college. These varied greatly. Some colleges, like King's College, Cambridge, were most lavishly furnished, others had no chapel or used one in a neighbouring parish church.

When we reach these last it becomes quite impossible to generalize. At the close of the Middle Ages there were still very poorly furnished churches, rural and urban. At the other end of the scale were a number of very richly furnished town churches which contrasted very much more with their more modest neighbours than they had in 1300. Catering for the same classes as the parish churches were the religious guilds. The majority of these had little or no plate, but scattered over England there was a limited number of rich guilds whose requirements must have produced quite a considerable amount of work for the goldsmiths.

Down to the thirteenth century the direction of taste in church plate was in the hands of a small number of high ecclesiastics, and church work formed by far the most important part of the goldsmith's trade. In the latter Middle Ages his time would be spent largely in executing orders of medium or minor importance for collegiate or parish churches in which the laity were now mainly interested. Though it would be wrong to suggest that the laity ever suggested new forms for religious plate, it is clear that in this period they usually took an intelligent interest in the work for which they paid. They were no longer unfamiliar with plate, for the amount in domestic use was annually increasing. Some time towards the close of the fifteenth century the manufacture of secular plate became more important for the goldsmiths than that of religious.

The introduction and gradual elaboration of the laws regarding hall-marking may be regarded as a symptom of the gradual change of which we have been speaking. The casual customer was becoming of more and more importance and the respectable members of the trade saw that it was in their interests to protect him from falling into the clutches of their less scrupulous brethren. It is necessary to go into the subject of the hall-marking of medieval church plate in some detail, as the matter has been much neglected.

From time immemorial the standard for plate had been the same as that for the coinage. In the year 1300 the first hall-marking law was passed, which ordered that the wardens of the London goldsmiths should mark with a leopard's head all plate before it left the hands of the maker.[1] This was followed in 1363 by a further command that goldsmiths should stamp their work with a personal mark before taking it to be assayed and marked officially.[2] So far the marking of church and of domestic plate had been governed by the same regulations, but in 1370 the *Ordinances of the Goldsmiths* forbade the gilding of any work of

[1] 28 Edward I, stat. 3, c. 20.
[2] 37 Edward III, c. 7.

copper or latten, or the setting of real stones therein, except for church work.[1] In 1403 the gilding or silvering of copper or latten except for church work was forbidden by statute.[2] Gilt or silvered pieces were to have a bare patch under the foot, so that no one should have any doubt as to the material of which they were made. Copper-gilt chalices were expressly forbidden.[3]

In the year 1423 a statute laid the obligation of assaying and marking the work of the local goldsmiths upon the civic authorities of York, Newcastle, Lincoln, Norwich, Bristol, Salisbury, and Coventry.[4] In the case of York this merely reinforced a regulation contained in the ordinances of the goldsmiths of that city, which had been passed in 1410.[5] Only one example of the York mark is known, however, before the ordinances were revised again in 1561, and it is likely that the first attempt at marking was not of long duration.

All these laws and ordinances were passed with the very best intentions and might have afforded a real protection to the less sophisticated members of the clergy and laity when faced with the purchase of a piece of church plate. In actual fact the regulations regarding marking would appear to have been almost completely ignored until a tightening-up occurred in the second half of the fifteenth century—probably at the time of the grant of a new charter to the Goldsmiths' Company in 1462.[6] In the year 1478 the Goldsmiths replaced the leopard's-head mark by one showing the head crowned, and at the same time introduced an extra mark to show the date by means of a letter which was to be changed annually on St. Dunstan's day (19 May).[7]

The earliest example of a fully hall-marked piece of church plate is the chalice and paten at Nettlecombe, Som. (Pl. 12). From now until the Reformation an appreciable proportion of the surviving church plate is hall-marked—that is to say, rather less than half of the chalices and about a third of the patens. According to modern standards so low a proportion of marked pieces would be regarded as a reflection upon the diligence of the wardens of the Goldsmiths' Company, but it is clear that they were by now making a serious attempt to fulfil their legal obligations. The records of the company mention cases of goldsmiths who were called to account for having delivered unmarked pieces

[1] W. Prideaux, *Memorials of the Goldsmiths' Company*, 1896, i. 9.

[2] 5 Henry IV, c. 3.

[3] This did not entirely stop their manufacture. There is at the Victoria and Albert Museum a nicely finished copper-gilt chalice (945–1904) of mid-fifteenth-century date, dug up near the Tower in 1887. Copper chalices appear occasionally in the Edward VI inventories, e.g. Wimborne Minster and St. Martin, Wareham (*C.P. Dorset*, 80, 168).

[4] 2 Henry VI, c. 20.

[5] *York Memorandum Book*, Surtees Soc., 1912, i. 74–75.

[6] For the use of the mark showing the leopard's head with the annual letter on the tongue, see G. E. P. and J. P. How, *English and Scottish Silver Spoons and Pre-Elizabethan Hall-marks*, iii, 1957, VI, section 2.

[7] Thus the hall-marking year 1478 ran from 19 May 1478 until 18 May 1479. I wish to emphasize this point since some pieces made during the Reformation period have to be very carefully dated.

of church plate.[1] Since there is little evidence to suggest that the authorized provincial centres made any prolonged effort to mark plate, a conscientious provincial goldsmith would have had no alternative but to send his work to Goldsmiths' Hall—an expensive course involving delay in delivery. In actual fact they probably seldom followed this course, but this is not demonstrable.[2]

[1] For the case of a goldsmith who sold to the Abbot of Kenilworth an image and other pieces which had not been marked see Prideaux (op. cit. i. 27).

[2] It must be understood that the strictness wherewith the hall-marking laws have been administered has varied from age to age. Some of the variations derive from ambiguities in the wording of the statutes, others to administrative interpretations of them. Medieval plate is usually either fully marked or not marked at all. Some assay-wardens appear to have considered that a chalice and paten was a single item and satisfied their consciences by marking the former and leaving the latter untouched. Another anomaly probably arose from the fact that the 1363 statute, which laid down that every goldsmith should mark his work, stipulated he should stamp it *after* it had been passed by the officers entrusted with assaying it. Since such officers never came into existence in the smaller towns, this seems to have led some goldsmiths into adopting an attitude of 'no officer, no maker's mark'. When the wardens of the Goldsmiths' Company toured the provinces at the time of the conversion of chalices into communion cups in the days of Elizabeth I (see 141), they came across in small towns some goldsmiths who had marks and others who had not got them. They took steps to get the former registered, but the minute books make no reference to pressure upon the others to obtain them.

In London, of course, there was never any difficulty in getting work assayed at Goldsmiths' Hall, but there was an ambiguity about the phrase 'put for sale'. It was perhaps argued that a direct sale of a piece made to order did not require to be hall-marked. There are numerous examples of pieces, both religious and secular, which bear the mark of some London goldsmith who worked between the middle of the sixteenth and the first quarter of the eighteenth centuries. The original purchaser would seem not to have bothered that a piece which might possibly be 'sold' legally without hall-marks could not properly be 'offered for sale' at some later date.

In the following pages we shall come across a number of other ways in which the intention, if not the letter, of the hall-marking laws were circumvented, but it must also be realized that there were always plenty of goldsmiths who did not avail themselves of these loopholes.

II

THE PLATE OF THE CHURCHES

IN the last chapter we discussed the Church as the patron of the goldsmiths and attempted to show how this patronage was exercised in successive periods. Our present aim is to give some sort of idea of the character of the plate to be found in the different sorts of establishment as each developed.

Though we have numerous references to the benefactions made to cathedrals and monasteries by Anglo-Saxon kings, nobles, and bishops, there appears to be no complete inventory dating from before the Conquest.

We are happy in possessing two late eleventh-century inventories of the abbey of Ely.[1] The first of these belongs to the year 1079 and was made after the death of Abbot Theodwin. Unfortunately it does not provide a picture of the possessions of a typical first-class abbey of the day, as it was taken only a few years after the monks had had to sacrifice much of their plate in order to pay the fine of a thousand marks for their part in the rising under Hereward. It is, therefore, not a very long or complicated list, but consists merely of twenty-three chalices (four without patens), nineteen large crosses and eight small, twelve richly bound books and the covers for two more, and nine phylacteries.[2] The second inventory was taken in 1093, after the death of Abbot Simon. Though the chronicler rather suggests that the abbot had been somewhat imposed upon after he had become a chronic invalid, it would seem that he had, in fact, done rather well. There was certainly much more than he had taken over fourteen years earlier. The number of chalices had risen from twenty-three to twenty-six and one is of gold. There are now three chalice-reeds. The number of crosses has risen to twenty-seven. The number of richly bound books is now fourteen, as the two empty covers are now filled. The number of phylacteries is eight instead of nine, but there are twelve shrines, large or small, and six silver-covered images (three showing signs of pilfering by thieves). There are three richly mounted portable altars, two retables, and four altar-frontals adorned with gold and silver, a pair of gilt candlesticks, three cruets (one gilt), and a ewer and basin for ablutions.

Series of inventories relating to the same church are most rare, and we are not able to trace in the same detail the furnishing of the church after it became a cathedral in 1109. In the Ely inventories we get a complete list of the plate, but as time went on the administration of the treasures of a large church tended to

[1] *Liber Eliensis*, ed. D. J. Stewart, 1848, 249 and 282.

[2] A variety of small reliquary which could be worn round the neck during processions.

become more complicated. Each church was free to make its own arrangements, but ordinarily the plate for use at the high altar was kept distinct from that assigned to the lesser ones, which might include specially endowed chantries. The shrines and reliquaries formed a third group. The first two categories were the responsibility of the sacrist in monastic foundations and of the treasurer in secular ones. The third might be under a feretrar if they were sufficiently numerous and important. Only too often the inventories of the three categories were not taken simultaneously, so that we do not get a complete picture of the possessions of the church.[1] The sacrist rolls[2] of Durham and the *Rites*[3] combine to give us the impression that the sacrist of this rich and usually well-run Benedictine house probably had a fair idea of the plate for which he was responsible though, unfortunately, we are unable to check this by any complete inventory. We are told, however, that the plate for the high altar consisted of a fairly simple service for everyday use and a richer one for festivals. The plate for each of the lesser altars was kept in the aumbry in the chapel where it was used. It was part of the duty of the sacrist to lock it up after use and to see that the key was available for the celebrant next morning. In Lanfranc's *Constitutions*[4] it is laid down that the sacrist should wash the chalices and the cruets on Wednesdays and Saturdays and more often if necessary. How far the sacrists and treasurers were able to work out a routine for cleaning the rest of the plate is difficult to decide. According to the *Rites of Durham*[5] two of the bell-ringers were charged with the duty of cleaning the five pairs of censers and the other ornaments of the high altar. We do not know whether the feretrar had anyone to rub over the reliquaries or whether it was customary to leave them unattended, relying on the partial immunity from tarnishing given by gilding. To clean a shrine properly was a job for a goldsmith and not one for an ordinary abbey servant. Clearly there were gaps in the routine of cleaning, since one of the most treasured belongings was the Black Rood of Scotland captured at the battle of Neville's Cross, which owed its name to being 'all smoked black over'![6] Considering the rapid changes of temperature to which the plate must have been exposed in unheated medieval churches, it is likely that a considerable amount of tarnishing must have been considered inevitable.

In default of a really full monastic inventory of the twelfth or thirteenth centuries, an analysis[7] of the 1315 inventory of Christ Church, Canterbury,

[1] Thus one of the best monastic inventories is that taken at Westminster Abbey in 1538 (*London and Middlesex Arch. Soc. Trans.* iv, 1873, 317–56. Though it lists the plate for the high altar and lesser altars in great detail, there is nothing about the reliquaries as the feretrar's inventory is missing.

[2] *Durham Account Rolls*, ii, Surtees Soc. 1899, 372–479.

[3] *The Rites of Durham*, Surtees Soc. 1902.

[4] *The Constitutions of Lanfranc*, ed. D. Knowles, 1951, 83–84.

[5] p. 22.

[6] Ibid. 19.

[7] It should be emphasized that this analysis and the following ones can only be considered as approxi-

will give an impression of the furnishing of a first-class Benedictine cathedral at the height of the Middle Ages.

CANTERBURY CATHEDRAL, 1315[1]

HIGH ALTAR

Chalices: Gold 5, Silver-gilt 4, Silver 1. *Cruets* (pairs): Crystal 2, Silver-gilt 4, Mixed (1 gilt, 1 plain) 1, Silver 4. *Ampullae*: Silver-gilt 2. *Candlesticks* (pairs): Silver-gilt 2, Parcel-gilt 2. *Candlesticks, Processional* (pairs): Silver-gilt 1. *Censers*: Silver-gilt 9. *Incense-boats*: Silver-gilt 1, Silver 3. *Basins for ablutions* (pairs): Silver 5. *Crosses, Altar*: Gold 2. *Crosses, Processional*:[2] Silver-gilt 4. '*Cups*': Gold 3, Silver-gilt 1. *Pyxes*: Silver-gilt 3. *Books of the Gospels, &c.*: Gold 7, Silver-gilt 7, Silver 3.

RELIQUARIES

Shrines (materials not specified): 10. *Heads*: Silver-gilt 3. *Arms*: Silver-gilt 9, Parcel-gilt 2. *Crosses*: Silver-gilt 7. '*Phylacteries*': Silver-gilt 4. *Tables* (frames filled with relics): Silver-gilt 4.

LESSER ALTARS

Chalices: Silver-gilt 23, Silver 4. *Censers*: Silver 2.

The first thing which will be noted is that there was little plate to spare for the altars of the lesser chapels. Even in the sixteenth century a minor altar would have usually only a cross of copper-gilt, cruets of pewter, and pax and candlesticks of brass. Nothing is said of any frontal or retable for the high altar, but the rearrangement and adornment of the east end of the choir was undertaken at the end of the century by Prior Chillendon, and will be described later on. Legg and Hope were, unfortunately, unable to publish any later complete inventory compiled before the dissolution of the monastery, but the documents which they provide suggest that otherwise no very material additions were made except in the furnishing of a few more chantry chapels.

The following analysis will give some idea of the treasures of another great Benedictine cathedral a little before its dissolution. It cannot be regarded as complete, however, as it is known that the penultimate prior had been selling off on the quiet. The general balance of the inventory seems to suggest that most of the plate was still in its place. At St. Swithun's, Winchester, it would

mately correct. Puzzling items appear in nearly every long inventory, and it is only too likely that some of these have slipped into wrong categories. Very unusual items are often left out so as to avoid making the tables unduly complicated.

[1] J. W. Legg and W. H. St. John Hope, *Inventories of Christ Church, Canterbury*, 1902, 69–73, 78–93.

[2] As is explained later on, most processional crosses were provided with a foot so that they could be used on an altar.

appear to have been the practice to pool the plate for the high and the lesser altars, only the Lady Chapel having an establishment of its own.

WINCHESTER CATHEDRAL, about September 1538[1]

Chalices: Gold 3, Silver-gilt 12. Lady Chapel: Silver-gilt 3. *Cruets* (pairs): Silver 6. *Candlesticks* (pairs): Gold 1, Silver 1 (also single one for St. Swithun's shrine). *Censers*: Silver-gilt 7. *Incense-boats*: Silver-gilt 1, Silver 1. *Basins* (pairs): Silver-gilt 3. *Ewers*: Silver-gilt 1, Silver 1. *Crosses* (not separable into categories): Gold 6, Silver-gilt 10, Silver 1. *Pyxes*: Gold 1, Crystal and silver-gilt 9. *Paxes*: Gold 1, Silver-gilt 4. *Books of the Gospels*: Gold 1, Silver-gilt 8. *Sacring-bells*: Gold 1, Silver-gilt 4. Lady Chapel: Silver-gilt 1, Silver 1. *Altar frontal*: Gold 1. *Retable*: Silver-gilt 1. Lady Chapel: Silver-gilt 1.

Reliquaries

Shrine of St. Swithun: Silver-gilt. *Other shrines*: Gold 1, Silver-gilt or Silver 21. *Arms*: Gold 1. *Foot*: Gold 1.

The odd candlestick before the shrine of St. Swithun may be the large one with seven branches given by Cnut, to which we shall have to return later on. The absence of any sort of monstrance for the Corpus Christi procession is paralleled at Canterbury, where there is no reference to anything of the species before the 1563 inventory. As it is described as 'a Monstraũt of latten to carry the sacrement in uppon Festyvall Dayes' it may have been added only in the reign of Mary.

The furnishing of a second-class regular cathedral like Worcester was a rather simpler version of what we have noted at Canterbury and Winchester. Though we have only an inventory of the Dissolution period, when some of the plate had perhaps already been made away with, the list of objects declared is very impressive, e.g. two gold chalices and nineteen of silver-gilt. The most spectacular item was, however, an image of Our Lady of the Assumption made of silver-gilt and weighing 204¼ ounces.[2]

The cathedral priory of Worcester was probably rather better supplied with plate than most of the second-class abbeys, but most of these last would appear to have been quite well furnished down to the time when their abbots began to be troubled by rumours of dissolution. On the other hand, there were many minor monasteries, mostly founded in the twelfth century, which had long since ceased to be valuable customers for the goldsmiths and had degenerated into the category of being useful sources for scrap metal.

Of course, nunneries tended to be more poorly furnished than monasteries, but to illustrate how meagrely some of these were equipped towards the close of the Middle Ages, we may look at a précis of the treasures of the

[1] J. Strype, *Memorials of Thomas Cranmer*, 1812, ii. 709–12.

[2] *Brit. Arch. Assoc. Journal*, N.S., xxxviii, 1932, 158–82.

two Benedictine nunneries of Easebourne,[1] Sussex, and Langley,[2] Leics., in 1451 and 1485 respectively.

EASEBOURNE

Chalices: Silver 2. *Cruets* (pairs): Silver 2. *Cross, Processional*: Silver 1.

LANGLEY

Chalices: Silver 2. *Cross, Processional*: Silver-gilt 1. *Crosses, Reliquary*: Silver-gilt 1, Silver 1. *Reliquary*: Silver-gilt 1, Silver 1.

When, therefore, the inventory taken at the dissolution of a minor priory shows very little plate, it is not entirely safe to assume that a good deal more had been sold in anticipation of seizure.[3]

The houses of the mendicant orders, as might be expected, were generally poor in plate. A minor friary at the time of the Dissolution appears usually to have had no more than a small silver chalice.[4] An establishment in a considerable town might have one or two chalices, a censer and incense-boat, a cross, and even a pair of candlesticks. The plate of the Black Friars at Oxford was quite exceptionally rich and included a gold chalice with a paten set with stones weighing 36½ ounces.[5] In London the Grey Friars were very well furnished. At the Dissolution their plate more than outweighed that of the three other orders combined.[6]

On the whole we are better informed about the furnishing of the secular than of the regular cathedrals, though there are wide gaps in our knowledge—we have no inventory for any of the Welsh cathedrals. We have good single inventories of Lincoln[7] (1536), Lichfield[8] (1345), and York[9] (*c.* 1510), two apiece for Exeter (1327 and 1506) and Salisbury[10] (1222 and 1536), and three for St. Paul's (1245, 1295, and 1402). We shall examine only the

[1] *Sussex Arch. Soc. Collns.* ix, 1857, 10–12.

[2] *Leicestershire Arch. Soc. Proc.* iv, 1878, 119–22.

[3] There are some revealing inventories of poverty-stricken East Anglian priories in *Proc. of Suffolk Institute of Archaeology*, 1894, 85–113.

[4] e.g. Black Friars at Ilchester (*Reliquary*, xxv, 1884, 78) or Newcastle-under-Lyme (ibid. xvii, 1876, 133). When the friaries were dissolved, the Bishop of Dover reported 'I have chales bothe of tynne and coper, plate in some places I find none" (T. Wright—*Letters relating to the Suppression of the Monasteries,* Camden Soc., 1843, 212).

[5] Ibid. xxiii, 1882, 215.

[6] Grey Friars, gilt plate 1,520 oz., parcel-gilt 600 oz., silver 700 oz.

Black Friars	,,	400 oz.,	,,	400 oz.,	,,	332 oz.
White Friars	,,	114 oz.,	,,	100 oz.,	,,	244 oz.
Austin Friars	,,	200 oz.,	,,	176 oz.,		

(*Account of the Monastic Treasures confiscated at the Dissolution*, Abbotsford Club, 1836, 19.)

[7] *Archaeologia*, liii, 1892, 7–36.

[8] *Journal of the Derbyshire Arch. Soc.* iv, 1882, 107–38.

[9] *Fabric Rolls of York Minster*, Surtees Soc., 1858, 212–35.

[10] *Registrum S. Osmundi, Episcopi*, Rolls Series, 1884, i. 127 and 138.

St. Paul's[1] and the Exeter[2] inventories, which can be taken as examples of a first-class and of a second-class cathedral.

ST. PAUL'S

HIGH ALTAR

1245. *Chalices*: Gold 5, Silver-gilt 9, Parcel-gilt 1, 'Greek' 1. *Cruets* (pairs): Mixed (1 gilt, 1 plain) 3, Silver 3. *Ampullae* (sets of three): Silver 1. *Chrismatories*: Silver 2. *Candlesticks* (pairs): Silver 3. *Censers*: Silver-gilt 2. *Incense-boats*: Parcel-gilt 2. *Basins* (pairs): Parcel-gilt 3, Silver 3. *Crosses, Altar*: Silver-gilt 1, Parcel-gilt 1. *Crosses, Processional*: Parcel-gilt 1, Silver 2. 3. *Pyxes*: Silver-gilt 3. *Hand-warmer*: Parcel-gilt 1. *Holy-water Bucket*: Silver 1, 'Greek' 1. *Reliquaries*: *Shrines* (miscellaneous), 11.

1295. *Chalices*: Gold 5 (all 1245), Silver-gilt 6 (2, 1245), 'Greek' 1. *Cruets* (pairs): Silver-gilt 1, Mixed 1 (1, 1245), Silver 1 (1, 1245). *Ampullae* (sets of three): Silver 1 (1, 1245). *Chrismatory*: Silver 1 (1245). *Candlesticks* (pairs): Silver 2 (1245). *Censers*: Silver-gilt 11. *Incense-boats*: Parcel-gilt 1. *Basins* (pairs): Parcel-gilt 1 (1245), Silver 2. *Crosses, Altar*: Silver-gilt 3 (1, 1245). Parcel-gilt 1. *Crosses, Processional*: Parcel-gilt 1 (1245), Silver 3 (1, 1245). *Pyxes*: Silver-gilt 2 (1, 1245). *Books of the Gospels*: Parcel-gilt 11. *Hand-warmers*: Parcel-gilt 2 (1, 1245). *Holy-water Buckets*: Silver 2. *Reliquaries*: *Shrines* (miscellaneous), 14 (7, 1245.)

1402. *Chalices*: Gold 3 (1, 1245), Silver-gilt 3 (11, 245). *Cruets* (pairs): Silver-gilt 2, Mixed 2, Parcel-gilt 1, Silver 1. *Sconce or Lantern*: Parcel-gilt 1. *Censers*: Silver-gilt 8. *Incense-boat*: Parcel-gilt 1. *Basins* (pairs): Silver-gilt 1, Parcel-gilt 2½, Silver 1½. *Crosses*: Altar: Silver-gilt 4.[3] *Crosses, Processional*: Silver 11.[3] *Cross, Monstrance*: Crystal 1. *Pyxso*.[4] *Hand-warmer*: Parcel-gilt 1. *Holy-water Bucket*: Silver 1. *Image*: Silver 1.

Only the 1295 inventory includes the lesser altars. There were nineteen of these, of which two had two chalices because they housed an endowed chantry. The rest had a single chalice (except that of St. Thomas of Canterbury, for which none is mentioned). Of the nineteen chalices twelve were parcel-gilt and seven were gilt. The material of the chalice belonging to the chapel of St. Andrew is not mentioned. It was probably of pewter.

Before proceeding to discuss these we may look at the analyses of the two Exeter inventories.

[1] The 1245 and 1402 inventories are in *Archaeologia*, l, 1887, 464–518; the 1295 is in Dugdale, *St. Paul's Cathedral*, 1818, 310–30.

[2] G. Oliver, *Lives of the Bishops of Exeter*, 1861, 310–11, 320–66.

[3] From an undated list of relics. It is not clear whether these were altar or processional crosses (Dugdale, op cit. 331).

[4] Makers of inventories were rather prone to forget the pyx, which was out of sight above the high altar and evidently tended to be out of mind also. There were two silver-gilt pyxes at the time of the making of the Edward VI inventory in 1552.

EXETER CATHEDRAL

HIGH ALTAR

1327. *Chalices*: Gold 2, Silver-gilt 10, Silver 1. *Cruets* (pairs): Silver-gilt 1, Silver 2½. *Ampullae*: Silver 1. *Candlesticks* (pairs): Parcel-gilt 1, Silver 1. *Censers*: Silver-gilt 4, Parcel-gilt 2. *Incense-boats*: Silver 2. *Basins* (pairs): Silver 1. *Crosses, Altar*: Silver-gilt 2, Silver 4. '*Cups*': Silver-gilt 1, Parcel-gilt 1. *Books of the Gospels*: Silver 7. *Holy-water Bucket*: Silver 1. *Reliquaries* (miscellaneous): 6.

1506. *Chalices*: Gold 1, Silver-gilt 11 (1 Grandison gift), Parcel-gilt 1. *Cruets* (pairs): Gold 1, Silver-gilt 3½. *Ampullae*: Silver-gilt 2 (Grandison gift), Parcel-gilt 1 (Grandison gift). *Candlesticks* (pairs): Silver-gilt 1, Parcel-gilt 1, Silver 1 (Grandison gift). *Sconce or Lantern*: Silver 1. *Censers*: Silver-gilt 5 (3, 1327?), Silver 2. *Incense-boat*: Parcel-gilt 1. *Basins* (pairs): Silver-gilt 1, Parcel-gilt 1, Silver 1. *Crosses, Altar*: Silver-gilt 3 (2 Grandison gift). *Crosses, Processional*: Silver-gilt 3. *Cross, Monstrance*: Silver-gilt 1. *Pyxes*: Gold 1, Silver-gilt 3. '*Cup*': Silver-gilt 1. *Books of the Gospels*: Silver-gilt 4 (1 Grandison gift), Silver 1. *Holy-water Bucket*: Silver 1. *Images*: Silver-gilt 3 (2 Grandison gift). *Retable*: Silver-gilt 1 (Grandison gift). *Sanctuary Lamps*: Silver 2. *Sacring-bell*: Silver 1. *Reliquaries* (miscellaneous) 1.

Only the 1506 inventory covers the lesser altars. Of these the Lady Chapel alone was richly equipped. It had, of silver-gilt, three chalices, a pair of cruets, a pair of candlesticks, a censer with incense-boat, a pair of basins, a book of the Gospels, and four reliquaries. There were besides eleven other altars, including those belonging to memorial chantries and the chapel of the Holy Ghost in the cloister. Of these, two possessed two chalices of silver-gilt or silver, the remainder had one apiece, except the chapel of St. John which had no silver at all. Five altars had cruets of silver-gilt or silver, and two had a silver-gilt pax.

In composing these analyses I have tried to trace the individual items through the successive inventories. Though I must have missed some identifications, it is quite clear that the expectation of survival of any piece of medieval church plate was quite poor. The two churches selected remained financially sound throughout the period, so that they would have felt no special urge to get rid of old plate to clear off debts. Thus in the half-century between the first two St. Paul's inventories a lot of plate had been refashioned. Two chalices are the only items which can be traced through all three inventories. Very much the same story is told by the Exeter inventories, where three censers are the only items in use in 1327 which were still there in 1506. The date of the first inventory was, however, of great significance in the history of the cathedral, for in this year John de Grandison became Bishop of Exeter. It will be noted that a number of the benefactions of this munificent bishop (who died in 1369) still survived in 1506. It is evident that the authorities of a large medieval church no more respected the ancient plate committed to their charge than they did its architecture. The Romanesque plate was apt to be condemned to the melting-pot at the same time that the Norman choir was reconstructed in a more fashionable style.

A second point to be noted is that in these large and financially sound churches the quantity of plate allocated to the high altar does not seem to have increased or diminished markedly between the thirteenth and the sixteenth centuries. Types of plate which had become obsolete were roughly balanced by fresh varieties evolved in response to changes in ritual. It was probably in the furnishing of the lesser altars that improvement was most marked. However, the minimum plate for a lesser altar was meagre enough even in the sixteenth century. *The Fabric Rolls of York Minster* provides us with a fairly complete picture of the furnishing of the lesser altars of that great church and confirms that the equipment of those at Exeter was quite average.

The collegiate churches bridge the gap between the cathedrals and the parish churches. Though the idea of colleges of secular canons was regarded after the Conquest with disfavour by some bishops, who endeavoured to hand them over to regular canons, a number of important establishments survived including Beverley, Ripon, and Southwell, of which the first was certainly well provided with plate, though no inventory seems to have survived. The later Middle Ages saw a revival of the collegiate idea, some of the foundations being for canons and others for chantry priests. There were rich and poor examples of both sorts, nor was there any significant difference in the type of plate which they tended to attract.

The chapel of St. George in Windsor Castle was made collegiate in 1348, and an inventory of 1383 shows that it was already rich. By the time that the 1534 inventory was compiled it would appear to have been by far the richest collegiate church in the country, thanks to the patronage of successive sovereigns and of the Companions of the Order of the Garter.

SAINT GEORGE'S CHAPEL, WINDSOR, 1534[1]

Chalices: Gold 1 (with spoon), Silver-gilt 12 (3 with spoons), Parcel-gilt 7. *Cruets* (pairs): Silver-gilt 4, Parcel-gilt 4. *Chrismatory*: Silver-gilt 1, Parcel-gilt 1. *Candlesticks* (pairs): Silver-gilt 4, Parcel-gilt 2. *Sconce*: Parcel-gilt 1. *Censers*: Silver-gilt 4, Parcel-gilt 2, Silver 1. *Incense-boats*: Silver-gilt 1, Silver 1. *Basins* (pairs): Silver-gilt 2, Parcel-gilt 1. *Ewer*: Silver-gilt 1. *Crosses, Altar*: Gold 1, Silver-gilt 5. *Crosses, Processional*: Silver-gilt 2, Parcel-gilt 1. *Pyxes*: Gold 1, Silver-gilt 2. *Pyx, Standing*: Gold 1. *Monstrance*: Silver-gilt 3. *Paxes*: Gold 1, Silver-gilt 4, Parcel-gilt 1. *Holy-water Bucket*: Parcel-gilt 1. *Hand-warmer*: Silver 1. *Images*: Silver-gilt 4, Silver 1. *Sacring-bell*: Parcel-gilt 1. '*Box for Singing Bread*': Silver 1. *Reliquaries of all sorts*: Gold 1, Silver-gilt 25, Parcel-gilt 2, Silver 5.

Though we miss a few items which might have been expected (e.g. books of

[1] Maurice F. Bond, *Inventories of St. George's Chapel, Windsor*, 1947, 165–80.

the Gospels and sanctuary lamps) St. George's was really inordinately rich. To give an idea of a more average example of a well-endowed college we may look at the inventory of the Yorkist foundation at Fotheringhay, Northants, taken in 1546.[1]

FOTHERINGHAY COLLEGE

Chalices: Silver-gilt 5, Parcel-gilt 4. *Cruets* (pairs): Silver-gilt 1, Silver 1. *Candlesticks* (pairs): Silver-gilt 2, Parcel-gilt 4. '*Sconces or Lanterns*': Parcel-gilt 2. *Censers*: Silver-gilt 3, Parcel-gilt 4. *Incense-boats*: Parcel-gilt 2. *Basins* (pairs): Silver-gilt 1, Parcel-gilt 1. *Cross, Altar*: Silver-gilt 1. *Cross, Processional*: Silver-gilt 1. *Pyxes*: Silver 2. *Holy-water Bucket*: Silver 1. *Sacring-bell*: Silver-gilt 1. *Reliquaries*: Silver-gilt 4. *Lectern for altar*: Parcel-gilt 1.

This weighed 1,442 ounces—a very respectable amount. Poor colleges, like poor monasteries, made shift with very little. Though Cobham College, Kent, had been established for over a hundred years when the 1479 inventory was compiled, it boasted only three silver chalices, one silver-gilt 'cup' for the Sacrament, and a silver-gilt pax. Everything else was of base metal.[2]

A similar disparity existed in the distribution of plate amongst the university colleges. Thanks to the generosity of Henry VI, King's College, Cambridge, surpassed all the others.[3]

KING'S COLLEGE, CAMBRIDGE, 1452

Chalices: Gold 2, Silver-gilt 12. *Cruets* (pairs): Silver-gilt and crystal 1, Parcel-gilt 3. *Ampullae*: Silver-gilt 3. *Chrismatories*: Silver-gilt 2. *Candlesticks* (pairs): Silver-gilt 3. *Censers*: Silver-gilt 2, Parcel-gilt 1. *Incense-boats*: Silver-gilt 1, Parcel-gilt 1. *Basins* (pairs): Silver-gilt 4, Parcel-gilt 2, Silver 1. *Crosses, Altar*: Gold 4 (two with relics), Silver-gilt 1. *Crosses, Processional*: Silver-gilt 4. *Monstrance*: Gold 1. *Paxes*: Silver-gilt 2, Silver 1. *Book of the Gospels*: Silver-gilt 1. *Holy-water Buckets*: Silver-gilt 1, Parcel-gilt 1. '*Box for Singing Bread*': Silver 1. *Reliquaries* (miscellaneous): 7.

The richest college at Oxford was All Souls, another fifteenth-century foundation. Unfortunately the inventory is so full of ambiguities that it is impossible to produce a précis of it.[4]

The colleges founded towards the end of the Middle Ages to cater for the educational needs of novices from monasteries would appear to have been generally poorly provided with chapel plate. Canterbury College, Oxford, which was maintained by the cathedral priory of Christ Church, Canterbury, was in its palmier days rather well furnished.[5] Durham College, Oxford, had

1 *Arch. Journal*, lxi, 1904, 261.

2 J. Thorpe, *Registrum Roffense*, 1769, 23.

3 *Ecclesiologist*, xviii, 1860, 4–7.

4 J. Gutch, *Collectanea Curiosa*, 1781, 239–61.

5 W. A. Pantin, *Canterbury College, Oxford*, 1947, 1, 9–10, 28, 50–51, 53–56, 75–76.

in 1456 five silver-gilt chalices, a pair of silver cruets, and a cross.[1] Colleges maintained in common by several monasteries were probably poorly supplied with plate.

It seems probable that the ordinary urban or rural church possessed no plate before the Norman Conquest. During the twelfth century English bishops, like their contemporaries abroad, were inciting their clergy to obtain silver chalices. A story related by Giraldus Cambrensis suggests that the latter were, rather understandably, unresponsive since they did not believe that the silver chalices, if bought, would adorn their churches for very long. The anecdote concerns Henry de Blois, brother of King Stephen, who settled down in his old age to be a model bishop of Winchester. It tells[2] that:

> When he heard that the priests throughout his diocese, after many warnings and instructions about having silver chalices, were celebrating in pewter ones far and wide, he called them all together as if to ask for an aid (for he had given King Henry a short time before, 500 marks for the Toulouse expedition (1159)). He told them that he was seeking an aid for himself from their silver chalices to compensate or make good in part the losses incurred on behalf of their churches in respect of their dues.[3] This was very readily agreed to by all and when the chalices had been collected on the appointed day, at least one from each church and from some very rich churches several were brought in, he consecrated and blessed them all and gave them back saying 'Those things which you were unwilling to give to God and his services, you were ready to give to me a lowly monk and most miserable sinner; now let these chalices by a wiser counsel be given to God and be used in His service for ever!'

The bishop was undoubtedly as much interested in setting an example to his colleagues as to his own clergy, as it was obvious that silver chalices would never multiply as long as they remained subject to episcopal depredations. It is quite likely that his gesture did have some effect, as we do not hear more of this particular abuse. However, the struggle to secure that every church should have a silver chalice was to be a long one. At a council held at York in 1195, Hubert Walter, Archbishop of Canterbury, ordered that within a year every church should have a silver chalice, buying it out of its funds if necessary.[4] Bishops continued to emphasize the need for silver chalices down to the end of the thirteenth century, but by that time the battle was really won, though base-metal chalices were to be found in out-of-the-way churches down to the reign of Edward VI.

Early in the thirteenth century the bishops were beginning to suggest that a

[1] Oxford Hist. Soc. *Collectanea*, iii, 1896, 36, 43, 51.

[2] Giraldus Cambrensis, *Opera*, Rolls Series, 1877, vii. 47–48.

[3] The assessment of the bishops for this tallage had been very inequitable, so that the clergy would readily understand that the bishop had a grievance about it (Sir James Ramsey, *History of the Revenue of the Kings of England*, 1925, i. 71–72).

[4] Wilkins, *Concilia*, 1737, i. 502.

silver chalice was not enough. As to the next requirement, they did not speak with one voice. Richard Marsh, Bishop of Durham (1217–26), suggested that the parish priest should have a 'vessel of silver or of pewter set aside especially for this purpose, that he may always take it to the sick; that out of it he may give the sick man the water in which he has washed his hands after receiving the Eucharist'. The idea that the vessel for the ablutions should be of silver definitely did not catch on, although reference to the project was made at Bishop Quivil's Exeter synod.[1]

The other object which bishops in the thirteenth century were apt to suggest should be of silver was a pyx. Thus in the 1229 constitutions of William de Blois, Bishop of Worcester, repeated in those of 1240 by his successor Walter de Cantelupe,[2] it is ordered that churches should have two pyxes, 'one of silver, ivory, Limoges work, or other suitable material, in which the host may be reserved under the safe-keeping of a key,[3] the other decent and clean in which the wafers may rest'. The pyx of silver or 'other suitable material' also remained a pious aspiration and was not usual by the time of the Reformation. When, in 1368, William de Swyneflete compiled his inventory of his archdeaconry of Norwich, only twenty-nine of the 358 churches had silver pyxes.[4] Henry VII, who as a boy had lived in the diocese of St. David's, must have got a better idea of what a really poorly furnished church was like than any of his more expensively brought-up predecessors since the Conquest, felt the ignoble housing of the Sacrament as a matter of reproach. Accordingly in his will[5] he declares that because he

> had seen in divers and many Churches of our Realme, the Holy Sacrament of Altar kept in full simple and inhonest pixes of copper and timber, we have appointed and commanded the Treasurer of our Chamber and the Master of our Jewel House, to cause to be made forthwith pixes of silver and gilt in a great number, for the keeping of the Holy Sacrament of the Altar after the fashion of a pixe that we have caused to be delivered to them, every of the same pixes to be of the value of four pounds, garnished with our arms and red roses and portcullises crowned, of which pixes we will that . . . every house of the four orders of Freres, and likewise every parish Church within our Realm not having a pixe . . . have of our gift . . . one of the said pixes, as soon and speedily as goodly may be done.

I have found no evidence that this good resolution produced any result.

For the most part the growth of parish church plate was the product of the

[1] Ibid. i. 580; ii. 139.

[2] Ibid. i. 623, 666.

[3] The usual fastenings for pyxes were either a hasp with pin or else a bayonet-joint. A pull-off lid would be dangerous, as the pyx was usually suspended over the altar in English churches and priests must have dropped them occasionally.

[4] Norfolk Record Soc. xix, 1947; xx, 1948.

[5] Sir H. Nicholas, *Testamenta Vetusta*, 1826, 33.

spontaneous acts of generosity of the laity and not the result of episcopal and archidiaconal urging. If we are right in assuming that all the churches started from scratch in the eleventh century, it was probably not very long before some disparity arose in their furnishing. For convenience we will class them as 'poor rural' and 'rich rural', 'poor urban' and 'rich urban'. It will be realized that the plate of a really poor rural church did not alter after the acquisition of a silver chalice, except that in the course of time the latter would need to be refashioned. Churches just above the poverty line were more likely to have a second silver chalice than a silver pyx.

Thirteenth-century inventories of country churches are rare, but an interesting little group are a memorial of visitations of prebendal churches made by William de Wando, Dean of Salisbury, taken in the years 1220 and 1224.[1] The eleven churches are in Wiltshire or in the eastern part of Berkshire. Only two of them fall into the category of rich churches. Heytesbury, which must already have become a small town, had three silver chalices and two crosses plated with silver. Sonning, where the bishops of Salisbury had inherited a residence from their predecessors of Ramsbury, had two silver chalices, a parcel-gilt pyx, and a book of the Gospels with a silver-plated cover. A visitation of the churches belonging to St. Paul's, carried out by Dean Ralph de Baldock in the autumn of 1297, provides interesting evidence about a chance collection of parishes in Essex, Hertfordshire, and Middlesex. None of the twenty-two churches can be classed as anything but poor. Four Essex churches could show two silver chalices. Two others produced silver-mounted ivory pyxes and one a silver pyx. The rest could only produce a silver chalice, except one church which only had one of pewter. The dean was rather keen that the churches should have both a silver and a pewter chalice and generally made a note when one of the latter was wanting.[2]

An invaluable picture of the furnishing of rural churches in the reign of Edward III is provided by the inventory of his archdeaconry taken in 1368 by William de Swyneflete, Archdeacon of Norwich.[3] Ignoring his account of the churches of Norwich, Lynn, and Thetford, we will concentrate on the part of the inventory which concerns rural parishes and minor towns. The deaneries of Blofield, Breccles, Briselee, Flegg, Holt, Ingworth, Lynn, Sparham, Taverham, Tofts, and Walsingham were of unequal size and importance. Except in the deanery of Breccles, amongst the fifteen parishes of which only three had a second chalice of silver, between a third and a half of the churches in each deanery had more than the minimum single silver chalice. Though among

[1] *Register of St. Osmund*, Rolls Series, 1884, i. 276, 279–83, 295, 312–13.

[2] *Visitations of the Churches belonging to St. Paul's Cathedral*, Camden Soc. 2nd ser. lv, 1895.

[3] *Inventory of Church Goods temp. Edward III*, ed. Dom Aelred Watkins, Norfolk Record Soc. xix, 1947; xx, 1948.

these the possession of a second silver chalice was quite common, it is rare for any other sort of plate to be mentioned (e.g. cross, cruets, or pyx), and churches which could be described as well furnished are very rare indeed. Only four need be mentioned. Of these the one with the widest range of plate was that in the small town of Aylsham, which had two chalices, a pair of cruets, a processional cross, a chrismatory, and a holy-water bucket. Cley had five chalices, a pyx, a 'cup' for the Sacrament, and a censer. Stewkey had three chalices, a pyx, and a cross, Folesham four chalices and a censer. We do not get the impression that amongst the plate listed were many pieces of more than average artistic importance. Gold plate was usually better finished, so that the gold chalices at Little Ellingham and at West Walton were probably good, though small. Doubtless the 'solemn silver chalice' at Aylsham and the 'enamelled and silver-gilt chalice of great weight' at Folesham were both important. Of the pyxes the best was probably one 'in the form of a box, gilt and enamelled' at Walsham St. Lawrence. We can be less sure about the one at Beston, which was 'gilt with a crucifix and Mary and John on the top', as it was a gift from the parishioners, who are unlikely to have insisted upon a piece of unusual quality. On the other hand, a chalice and a pair of cruets given to Helgheton by Sir Robert Knollys, may have been fine, since he had done well out of the wars and could afford the best.[1]

For a contrast to these East Anglian inventories we may now turn to Dean Chaundler's visitation in 1405 of the peculiars of the cathedral of Salisbury. This covers a number of churches in Berkshire, Wiltshire, and Dorset and includes all those visited by Dean Wando. The only church which can be described as reasonably well furnished was the one which was tacked on to the west end of the Benedictine abbey of Sherborne. It had seven chalices (but two were unfit for use), one silver-gilt and one silver pyx, and a silver-gilt censer. Elsewhere there was hardly a church which had any plate except chalices. Only two had silver pyxes, one a pax, and Lyme Regis a reliquary cross. More than half the churches had only one silver chalice and only a quarter had two.[2]

The churches belonging to St. Paul's were again visited in 1458 and we can compare the reports on the Essex churches with those of 1297.[3] Walton-le-Soken had now three chalices, as had also Tillingham. One more church had now a second chalice and there was also a single silver pyx. Otherwise we need

[1] Perhaps these pieces may really fall outside the scope of this book, as the leader of 'The White Company' may well have looted them from some French church.

[2] MS. in Diocesan Registry, Salisbury, Extracts in *C.P. Dorset*, 147–8.

[3] Dean Say also visited the Hertfordshire and Middlesex churches, but he allowed himself to get distracted from the condition of the church possessions by the task of recording the immoralities of the parishioners. Mention of the plate is omitted from more than half of the entries. *Visitations of the Churches belonging to St. Paul's Cathedral*, Camden Soc. 2nd ser. lv, 1895.

only note that the pewter chalices had all disappeared. Clearly it is wrong to assume that parish churches went on steadily accumulating plate throughout the Middle Ages.

The general picture which we have drawn of the plate of rural churches down to the middle of the fifteenth century will serve as a background to that which we obtain from the inventories prepared in 1552 for the purpose of spoliation. These inventories survive for a large part of England and a great many have been printed. Whereas inventories compiled at the time of an archdeacon's visitation or for the benefit of future churchwardens may be accepted as complete, it will be readily understood that there was an only too human tendency to omit items from the Edwardian inventories. Having given this warning, it is necessary to add that the amount of discretion which must be used in handling these documents differs from county to county.

In order to get some idea of the plate of two counties which fall below the average in wealth, we look at statistics for Buckinghamshire[1] and Cumberland.[2] There survive returns for 122 parishes, mainly in the southern part of the former county. Ignoring the churches of towns like Amersham, Chesham, and Wycombe, we find that twelve other churches reported three chalices, and forty-one two. Seven churches acknowledged pyxes and Dorney a monstrance (reliquary?). Altogether, there were only three pairs of cruets and one odd one, two paxes, three crosses, seven censers, and two chrismatories.

Turning to Cumberland, we have reports on 113 churches of which three report having four chalices, sixteen have more than one, eighty-three have a single chalice, and ten have either a pewter one or none at all. Brampton alone acknowledged a silver pyx.

Though the churchwardens of neither county have much to say about sales of plate, thefts, &c., we are inclined to accept the general picture which they present, whilst realizing that a certain scaling down has taken place. The temptation to falsify returns was much greater in areas where there was more to hide, and we shall not attempt to provide statistics with regard to them.

If there was at the close of the Middle Ages rather less plate in the rural churches than is generally supposed, there was certainly a lot in the town churches. Here again it is necessary to proceed with caution. A visitation of twenty churches in the City of London, under the patronage of the Dean and Chapter of St. Paul's, was carried out in about 1250.[3] It reveals that with the exception of St. John, Knight Rider Street, which owned a silver-plated cross, none possessed more than a silver chalice. Two churches, St. John Walbrook and St. Michael le Quern, had only ones of pewter. Though it has been suggested that this general poverty may reflect the much-publicized

[1] *Edwardian Inventories for Buckinghamshire*, ed. F. C. Eeles, *Alcuin Club Collns.* 1908.

[2] *C.P. Carlisle*, 314–15.

[3] *Archaeologia*, lv, 1897, 291–9.

exactions of a recent papal legate, it seems clear that we can only date the build-up of the wealth of the City churches from the fourteenth century. The three following analyses will give some idea of the possessions of typical City churches towards the close of the Middle Ages.

ST. CHRISTOPHER-LE-STOCKS, 1488[1]

Chalices: Silver-gilt 2, Silver 3. *Cruets* (pairs): Parcel-gilt 2. *Candlesticks* (pairs): Silver 1. *Censers*: Parcel-gilt 2. *Incense-boat*: Parcel-gilt 1. *Cross, Altar*: Silver-gilt 1. *Cross, Processional*: Silver-gilt 1. '*Cup*': Silver-gilt 1. *Monstrance*: Silver-gilt 1. *Pax*: Silver-gilt 1. *Reliquaries*: Silver-gilt 3, Silver 1.

ST. PETER-UPON-CORNHILL, 1546[2]

Chalices: Silver-gilt 4, Parcel-gilt 3. *Cruets* (pairs): Silver-gilt 1. *Chrismatories*: Parcel-gilt 1. *Candlesticks* (pair): Parcel-gilt 1. *Censers*: Silver-gilt 2, Parcel-gilt, 1. *Incense-boat*: Parcel-gilt 1. *Basins* (pairs): Parcel-gilt 2. *Cross, Altar*: Silver-gilt 1. *Cross, Processional*: Parcel-gilt 1. *Pyx*: Silver-gilt 1. *Monstrance*: Silver-gilt 1. *Paxes*: Silver-gilt 1, Parcel-gilt 1. *Book of the Gospels*: Silver-gilt 1.

ST. NICHOLAS COLE ABBEY, 1552[3]

Chalices: Silver-gilt 2. *Chrismatory*: Silver-gilt 1. *Candlesticks* (pairs): Silver-gilt 1. *Censers*: Parcel-gilt 2. *Incense-boat*: Parcel-gilt 1. *Cross, Altar*: Silver-gilt 1. *Cross, Processional*: Silver-gilt 1. *Pyx*: Silver-gilt 1. *Monstrance*: Silver 1.

The first of the above tables shows the possessions of a good second-class church at a time when the future was still clear. The second represents a first-class church just before the wave of spoliation set in. The last illustrates the possessions of a third-class church at the time of the spoliation. The parson would appear to have had conscientious objections to making away with the church goods and his return professes to be complete. It reads convincingly.

The fashionable church of a large provincial town might have as much late as any one in London. We are fortunate in possessing three inventories tor St. Peter Mancroft, Norwich, ranging from 1368 to the first quarter of the sixteenth century. The 1552 inventory has not been found.

ST. PETER MANCROFT, NORWICH, 1368[4]

Chalices: Silver-gilt 1, Silver 1. *Basins* (pairs): Silver 1. *Cross, Processional*: Silver 1. '*Cups*': Silver-gilt 2.

1 Ibid. xlv, 1880, 111–12.

2 H. B. Walters, *London Churches before the Reformation*, 1939, 576–7.

3 Ibid. 534.

4 Norfolk Record Soc. xix, 1947, 1–3, 18.

c. 1400. *Chalices*: Silver 8. *Cruets* (pairs): Silver 1. *Candlesticks* (pairs): Silver 1. *Censer*: Silver-gilt 1. *Incense-boat*: Silver-gilt 1. *Basins* (pairs): Silver 1. *Cross, Processional*: Silver 1. '*Cups*': Silver-gilt 2, Silver 1.

c. 1525.[1] *Chalices*: Silver-gilt 6, Parcel-gilt 8. *Cruets* (pairs): Silver-gilt 2. *Chrismatory*: Parcel-gilt 1. *Candlesticks* (pairs): Silver 1. *Censers*: Silver-gilt 1, Parcel-gilt 1, Silver 1. *Incense-boats*: Parcel-gilt 2. *Basins* (pairs): Silver-gilt 2, Silver 1. *Ewer*: Silver-gilt 1. *Crosses, Altar*: Silver-gilt 2. *Cross, Processional*: Silver 1. *Pyx*: Silver-mounted ostrich egg. *Pyxes, standing*: Silver-gilt 1, Parcel-gilt 1. *Monstrance*: Silver-gilt 1, Parcel-gilt 1. *Paxes*: Silver-gilt 4. *Holy-water Bucket*: Parcel-gilt 1. *Reliquaries*: Silver-gilt 3.

We may conclude this chapter with two more tables chosen to illustrate the possessions of prosperous churches in country towns.

HADLEIGH, SUFFOLK, 1480[2]

Chalices: Silver-gilt 9, Silver 2. *Cruets* (pairs): Silver 2. *Chrismatories*: Silver 2. *Candlesticks* (pairs): Silver 1. *Censers*: Silver-gilt 1, Parcel-gilt 1, Silver 1. *Incense-boats*: Silver-gilt 1, Silver 1. *Basins* (pairs): Silver 1. *Crosses, Processional*: Silver-gilt 1, Silver 2. *Pyxes*: Silver 2. *Pax*: Silver-gilt 1.

HIGH WYCOMBE, 1519[3]

Chalices: Silver-gilt 3, Silver 2 (defective). *Cruets* (pairs): Silver 1. *Chrismatory*: Silver-gilt 1. *Candlesticks* (pairs): Silver 1. *Censers*: Parcel-gilt 3. *Incense-boats*: Parcel-gilt 3. *Basins* (pairs): Silver 1. *Crosses, Altar*: Silver-gilt 2. *Pyxes*: Silver-gilt 3.

[1] *Norfolk Archaeology*, xiv, 1901, 206–13.
[2] *Proc. of the Suffolk Institute of Archaeology*, iii, 1863, 253–6.
[3] *Edwardian Inventories for Bucks.* 138–9.

III

THE PLATE OF PRIVATE CHAPELS

HAVING studied the plate accumulated by the various types of religious establishments, it is now necessary to discuss the much smaller, yet very important, subject of the plate made for private ownership.

At all periods the king was by far the largest lay owner of religious plate. Though we may assume that costly altar vessels bore witness to the piety of the early English kings, we do not possess any detailed information about the furnishing of the Chapel Royal before the fourteenth century. It would seem likely that in earlier times the plate was rich rather than plentiful. A cursory inventory dated 4 May 1324 lists seven chalices, four pairs of cruets, a pair of candlesticks, two censers with one incense-boat, three sacring-bells, a holy-water bucket, and a 'cup' for the Sacrament decorated with the story of Our Lady. All the above were of silver-gilt, parcel-gilt, or silver. The only gold item was a cross having a foot of silver-gilt. Altogether it is not a very impressive list, but it is probably incomplete.[1]

The next important inventory was taken on 20 November 1399, when the plate which had belonged to Richard II was being checked over for his successor.[2] Though very much more detailed, it is also obviously incomplete—there is no mention of a pyx or 'cup'. There was now a gold service including two chalices, a pair of cruets, a pax, and a sacring-bell. There were similar objects in silver-gilt and the only items which catch the eye are three images (one of amber) and a magnificent reliquary altar-cross to which further reference will be made later on.

On 13 March 1462 the royal plate was checked over by William Porte, Treasurer of the King's Chamber. Again we are conscious of omissions, since no mention is made of King Richard's altar-cross which certainly survived into the reign of Henry VIII. There is nothing to suggest that the amount of chapel plate had greatly increased under the pious Henry VI, but there had been some interesting and important additions. There were now two silver-gilt monstrances besides a lectern or book-rest for use on the altar—a rare item to which it will be necessary to return. More interesting are four gold images, three of which represented St. George and the fourth St. Michael.

The suspicion of incompleteness is gone when the 1521 inventory of the

[1] F. Palgrave, *Antient Kalendars and Inventories of the Exchequer*, 1836, iii. 123–4.

[2] Ibid. 313–58.

plate of Henry VIII is examined. Some idea of it can be obtained from the following analysis:

CHAPEL ROYAL, 14 April 1521[1]
(with additions to 13 December 1522)

Chalices: Gold 1, Silver-gilt 17. *Cruets* (pairs): Gold 2, Silver-gilt 6. *Candlesticks* (pairs): Silver-gilt 13. *Censers*: Silver-gilt 9, Parcel-gilt 2, Silver 1. *Incense-boats*: Silver-gilt 4, Parcel-gilt 1. *Basins*: Not distinguishable from secular ones. *Crosses, Altar*: Gold 5, Silver-gilt 8. *Crosses, Processional*: Silver-gilt 10. *Pyx*: Silver-gilt 1. *Monstrances*: Silver-gilt 5. *Paxes*: Gold 1, Silver-gilt 8. *Holy-water Buckets*: Gold 2, Silver-gilt 9, Parcel-gilt 2. *Images*: Gold 3, Silver-gilt 49. '*Tabernacles*': Gold 3. *Reliquaries*: Gold 3, Silver-gilt 3, Parcel-gilt 1. *Sacring-bells*: Silver-gilt 2, Silver 2. '*Box for Singing Bread*': Silver-gilt 2. *Lectern*: Silver-gilt 1. *Font*: Silver-gilt 1.

Although certain items bearing the initials H and E must have been ordered by his father, it is pretty clear that the vast increase must have been due to purchases by Henry VIII to which there are numerous references in the *Calendar of Letters and Papers*. It is characteristic of him that he should have squandered thus the wealth which his father destined to benefit the poorer churches of his kingdom.

Two further inventories exist of the plate of Henry VIII. Of that compiled in 1532 we shall say nothing, but proceed to consider the final results of the king's operations as shown in the inventory completed after his death and dated 20 January 1550. A careful examination discloses that though numerous minor changes had taken place, the additions had not done much more than replace what had been scrapped. The financial stringency which had led him to seize the treasures of the abbeys had not, however, compelled him to make any inroad into the possessions of his own chapel. On the other hand, as is noted elsewhere, the amount of abbey plate which he had reserved for his own use was insignificant. His love of images, which he seems to have inherited from his father, must have shocked his more Protestant associates, and is shown by the fact that there were now nine of gold and sixty-eight of silver-gilt. The number of chalices had doubled, but there was still only one of gold.

The making of the 1550[2] inventory was the prelude to an extensive inroad on the chapel plate. A very intricate calculation would be required in order to discover how much Mary actually did inherit from her brother. The only notable addition with which she can be credited is the second royal font.[3] The

[1] *Assoc. Architectural Societies Reports*, xvii, 1884, 156–229. The original manuscript is at present missing.

[2] The 1452 inventory is P.R.O. Exchequer, T. of R. Misc. Bk. 85; the 1550 inventory survives in two manuscripts, B.M. Add. 46348 and Soc. of Antiquaries 126. For an appraisal of the Tudor inventories of plate see A. J. Collins, *Inventory of the Jewels and Plate of Queen Elizabeth I*, 1955, 231–43.

[3] See p. 250. On the other hand, an inventory of what Mary left behind has survived: National Library of Scotland, MS. 2825.

end of the old medieval plate will be related when the furnishing of the Chapel Royal of Elizabeth I is discussed.

Although the maintenance of a private chapel by a layman was quite usual at an early date, it is unlikely that their furnishing was very splendid. From the thirteenth century we seem to be able to trace an improvement, though there would always remain a notable difference between the chapel plate of a rich nobleman and that of a well-to-do squire. Even at the end of the fourteenth century the chapel plate of Thomas of Woodstock, Duke of Gloucester, remained simple, although he was a generous donor of plate. The inventory of his goods taken after his death in 1397[1] discloses only a chalice and a holy-water bucket of silver-gilt and a pair of cruets and a censer with incense-boat of silver. The chapel of Thomas, Earl of Warwick (d. 1400), was furnished on much the same scale, but included an altar cross enamelled with scenes from the Passion.[2]

During the fifteenth century baronial chapels tended to become very much richer. The plate which the Duchess of Suffolk had at Wingfield Castle, Suffolk, in 1467[3] was more complete than that of the two noblemen who have just been mentioned, and was clearly of good quality. She had:

ALICE, DUCHESS OF SUFFOLK, 1467

Chalice: Silver 1. *Cruets* (pairs): Silver 1. *Altar Cross*: Silver 1. *Basins* (pair): Silver 1. *Candlesticks* (pair): Silver 1. *Pyx*: Gold 1. *Pax*: Gold 1. *Holy-water Bucket*: Silver 1.

The plate at Wingfield included no unexpected items such as appear in some other inventories of the period, which rather suggest that some people liked their private chapel to look like a collegiate church. For instance, Sir William Bruges, Garter King of Arms, who died in 1447, had not only considerably more plate than the duchess, but also an elaborate feretory for the Corpus Christi procession.[4]

Sir John Fastolfe (d. 1459), who had done so well out of the French war, had probably as rich a chapel as any subject in his day. It comprised:

SIR JOHN FASTOLFE, 1459[5]

Chalices: Silver-gilt 2, Silver 1. *Cruets* (pairs): Silver-gilt 3. *Candlesticks* (pairs): Parcel-gilt 4. *Censer*: Silver-gilt 1. *Incense-boats*: Parcel-gilt 1, Silver 1. *Basins* (pairs): Silver-gilt 1. *Cross, Altar*: Silver-gilt 1. *Cross, Processional*: Silver-gilt 1. *Pyx*: Parcel-gilt 1. *Pax*: Silver 1. *Holy-water Bucket*: Silver 1. *Sacring-bell*: Silver 1. *Images*: Silver 2. '*Box for Singing Bread*': Silver 1. *Alms Dish*: Silver 1. *Ewer*: Silver-gilt 1.

The total weight of the above was about 1,000 ounces .

1 *Arch. Journal*, liv, 1897, 275–310.

2 H. Nicholas, *Testamenta Vetusta*, 1826, 154.

3 *R. Commission on Historical Manuscripts, 8th Report*, 628–9.

4 *Testamenta Vetusta*, 267–8.

5 J. R. Gairdner, *Paston Letters*, 1900, i. 467–75; *Archaeologia*, xxi, 1827, 243–51.

The most extensive inventory of all, however, is that of the plate amassed by John de Vere, 13th Earl of Oxford (d. 1513), in the happy evening of his life after his adventurous career during the latter part of the Wars of the Roses.

JOHN DE VERE, 1513[1]

Chalices: 5. *Cruets* (pairs): 4. *Candlesticks* (pairs): 3. *Censers*: 4. *Incense-boats*: 2. *Basin*: Silver-gilt 1. *Cross, Altar*: 1. *Cross, Processional*: 1. *Pyx*: 1. *Monstrance* 1. *Pax*: 1. *Holy-water Bucket*: 1. *Sacring-bell*: 1. *Images and Reliquaries*: 22. *Alms Dish*: 1.

Nearly everything was of silver-gilt and the whole weighed about 2,500 ounces. The earl, it will be observed, was particularly fond of silver statuary, and the inclusion of a number of reliquaries (not always in the form of images) was unusual in a private chapel.

Chapel plate was a matter of necessity for a bishop. As time went on less attention was paid to considerations of portability. The plate of Thomas Hatfield, Bishop of Durham (d. 1381),[2] consisted of a chalice, a 'cup', a pair of candlesticks, all of silver-gilt, and a pair of basins and a holy-water bucket of silver. All these pieces were, judging from the descriptions, both full size and of artistic importance. The 'cup' is mentioned as being enamelled on the outside. The range of objects bequeathed in the wills of bishops is often much larger, and gold chalices occur fairly frequently. Of the quality of a bishop's chapel plate we are fortunately able to judge from the remains of that of Bishop Foxe at Corpus Christi College, Oxford, which include his gold chalice[3] and paten and basins[4] and salt,[5] of silver-gilt.

We have, unfortunately, no inventory of Wolsey's chapel plate although we have a lot of his accounts with his goldsmith.[6] In quantity it far exceeded that of any bishop or noble, and its character is best described as a reduced edition of the plate of the Chapel Royal. It was perhaps for this reason that his master retained so little of it after it came into his possession.

[1] *Archaeologia*, lxvi, 1914, 328–38.

[2] *Wills and Inventories of the Northern Counties*, Surtees Soc. 1835, 37.

[3] See p. 45. [4] See p. 87. [5] See p. 101.

[6] J. Gutch, *Collectanea Curiosa*, 1781, 283–344.

IV

SECURITY IN MEDIEVAL TIMES

LITTLE attention has been paid to the problem of the security of church plate during the Middle Ages. As will have been gathered, the problem was not generally an acute one in the case of rural churches where the plate was ordinarily neither very great in quantity nor very valuable. Thefts did occur, but sources like Archdeacon Swynflete's visitation in Norfolk in 1368 do not lead us to think that they gave much cause for alarm.

Rich town churches faced much more of a problem, but we get the impression that their precautions were, on the whole, adequate. All this ended in the reign of Edward VI. The Edwardian inventories of parish churches, both urban and rural, are full of records of thefts. Many of these were doubtless collusive—the churchwardens could have named the culprits had they chosen. It seems fair to suppose, however, that a great many were also genuine. The churchwardens may well have relaxed their vigilance when it became clear that their plate was doomed anyhow, not caring whether it went to His Grace or to some 'valiant rogue'.

During the later Middle Ages collegiate churches, monasteries, and cathedrals enjoyed such a reputation for security that the laity were quite glad to avail themselves of facilities for storing their valuables within the precincts. Thus it will be found that Sir John Fastolfe (d. 1459) stored his surplus country plate at the abbey of St. Benet at Holme and his town plate at Bermondsey Abbey.[1] John de Vere, 13th Earl of Oxford, at the time of his death in 1513, had deposits of plate at three religious establishments in the neighbourhood of his country residence at Castle Hedingham.[2]

The religious, however, did not rely solely upon the prestige of a well-run establishment or the sacredness of their precincts to secure their treasures. A modern visitor would find himself very cramped if he were to enter an important cathedral which had been left exactly as it was at the beginning of the sixteenth century. The 'restorers' of the nineteenth century tended to have a blind spot for medieval wrought ironwork, and removed many screens, &c., which were not merely decorative but which had once served quite a practical purpose. Thus the grille across the monument of Humphrey, Duke of Gloucester, once acted as the last line of defence for the shrine of St. Alban, whilst that above the tomb of Eleanor of Castille helped to protect that of Edward the Confessor.

1 *Paston Letters*, ed. J. Gairdner, 1900, i. 467–75.

2 *Archaeologia*, lxv, 1915, 320–48.

The public, however, did not enjoy ready access to the eastern parts of a large abbey or of a regular cathedral. Similarly, we do not get the impression that there was much left lying about without the protection of good oak doors and wrought ironwork. It was part of the duty of the sacrist to lock up the chalices, &c., in the aumbries each morning after mass had been said. At Durham, about which we are particularly well informed, the only way of access from the nave to the east end was by a wrought-iron gate which was opened only for festivals and for processions. It was surmounted by a trellised screen reaching almost to the vault and was finished off with good 8-inch spikes.[1] Access from the south aisle to the transepts and choir was entirely blocked, partly by an iron screen and partly by Bishop Neville's chapel, behind the altar of which was a watching-chamber where a bell-ringer slept.[2] There were two bell-ringers sleeping in a room above the door to the vestry[3] (a danger spot) and another two bell-ringers in a room at the west end of the north aisle[4] (conveniently placed for keeping an eye on the sanctuary-takers, who slept behind an iron grille at the end of the south aisle).

The security arrangements for an important secular cathedral were not very different. At Lincoln the three bell-ringers guarded the minster by night and were allowed thirteen or fourteen candles a week in winter and seven in summer. They were supposed to patrol the church twice during the night, but the one who held the office of watchman was on duty all night and had to tell the hours on his flute. Besides the bell-ringers, there were three special guardians for the shrine of St. Hugh, two of which were expected to be on duty all night.[5]

Thieves usually broke into churches through one of the windows, but those who robbed Waltham in the time of Edward the Confessor mined under the foundations. This was probably quite easy to do, since Harold had not yet rebuilt the church in stone. They came to grief, however, whilst trying to dispose of their loot to a prominent London goldsmith named Theodoric, who happened to have made one of the pieces. The church had no difficulty in recovering its goods, so that it would seem that the Confessor was less grasping about felons' goods than some of his successors.[6]

During Whitsun 1103 the abbey of Peterborough was the victim of an audacious attempt by a gang of Germans, Flemings, and French who used ladders to enter the church through the window above the altar of St. Philip

[1] *Rites*, 37.
[2] Ibid. 40.
[3] Ibid. 22.
[4] Ibid. 41.
[5] The use of the flute was, of course, to reassure the dean that the fire-watch was on the alert for fire was an even greater danger than robbery. For the Lincoln security arrangements (Katherine Edwards, *The English Secular Cathedrals in the Middle Ages*, 1949, 230).
[6] One thief who pleaded clergy was burnt in the face with the church key (*The Foundation of Waltham Abbey*, ed. W. Stubbs, 1861, 33–34).

and St. James. One of the accomplices stood with a drawn sword over the sacrist, lest he should give the alarm. Meanwhile the others made off with a gold cross set with gems, two large chalices with patens, and a pair of candlesticks. The chronicler Hugh Candidus, who was later prior, comments ruefully that it was little consolation that the malefactors were caught as the king kept all the booty.[1]

In the year 1364 the Midlands were startled by a series of burglaries of which religious houses were mainly the victims, Thornton Abbey lost some reliquaries, Merevale an image of Our Lord, and Monks Kirby one of Our Lady. Leicester Abbey was saved by the vigilance of the sacrist, who disturbed the thieves whilst entering the church through a window. Most sensational, however, was the loss of the head of St. Hugh from Lincoln Minster. The relic was left lying in a field whence it was soon recovered. The reliquary was carried off for sale in London. The thieves gave themselves away on their return to Lincoln and were tried and hanged.[2] The reliquary was recovered as the Crown laid no claim to it.[3]

Of course there were occasions when the security arrangements broke down completely. During the 1327 riots at Bury, the townsmen got all over the abbey and its precincts. They made off not only with the refectory plate but with a number of valuable pieces from the church. Even the gold 'cup' was taken and the Sacrament was left lying on the altar.[4] This abbey fared badly also during the Peasants' Revolt of 1381. After the prior had been murdered, the monks were glad to give as pledges to the rioters a cross and a chalice of gold, and other valuables worth more than £100.[5] These were extreme cases; ordinarily the abbots parried the threat to their property by temporizing and by promising concessions which could afterwards be revoked. They usually succeeded.

[1] Sparke, *Historia Anglicana Scriptores Varii*, 1723, 64–65.

[2] *Chronicon Henrici Knighton*, Rolls Series, 1895, ii. 120.

[3] Rymer, *Foedera*, iv. 433. We have no record that Ramsey Abbey was robbed by this gang, but the Ramsey Abbey censer and incense-boat (now at the Victoria and Albert Museum) are clearly the proceeds of a robbery of about this date. They were found in 1850 by a man named Coles whilst searching for eels, during the draining of Whittlesea Mere, Hunts. Their connexion with Ramsey is established by the fact that the rebus of the abbey appears on the incense-boat. For further discussion of these pieces see pp. 89, 91.

[4] *Memorials of St. Edmund's Abbey*, Rolls Series, 1894, ii. 322.

[5] *Chronicon Anglie*, Rolls Series, 1874, 304.

V

MASS PLATE

A. CHALICES[1]

IN view of the fact that the number of gold and silver chalices in use in Anglo-Saxon times was never very great, we are fortunate in possessing even a single example, albeit one of scant artistic importance. This was discovered in 1777 at Trewhiddle, near St. Austell, Cornwall, forming part of a hoard which contained a silver scourge and a number of silver mounts, elaborately decorated but of uncertain use. Some coins suggested that the hoard had been deposited about 875, when Cornwall was being threatened by the Vikings.[2]

Group 1

The Trewhiddle chalice[3] (Pl. 1) stands $5\frac{1}{2}$ inches high and is entirely undecorated. Technically a competent piece of work, but like most of the foreign chalices of its age it is poorly proportioned.[4] It must be classed as a travelling chalice made for the purpose of providing ecclesiastics with the wherewithal for saying mass when on their journeys.

The larger chalices used in Western Europe up to the twelfth century were usually equipped with two handles.[5] It seems likely that the more important chalices made in this country had handles, but we know so little about those in use in Anglo-Saxon and Norman times that this cannot be regarded as certain. The only literary evidence for the use of this type is provided in a late fourteenth-century inventory of Westminster.[6] The chroniclers have also recorded little which will help us to visualize the chalices of this period. Often, in fact, they had never seen the chalices which they felt bound to mention since these had already been destroyed. When they do provide a description they tend to catch on to the form of decoration and not on to the shape.

[1] For a complete list of known examples see Appendix I.

[2] The best discussion of the hoard is by Reginald Smith in *Proc. of the Soc. of Antiquaries*, 2nd ser. xx, 1904, 47–55.

[3] Fr. Josef Braun, S.J., who was prejudiced against all early chalices which do not have handles, dismissed the Trewhiddle one as a secular cup on the grounds that it was found along with a considerable sum of money. He seems to have failed to realize that the hoard was probably just the proceeds of a robbery. It contained also a silver scourge as well as broken up jewellery (Braun, *Christliche Altargerät*, 1932, 72).

[4] Braun, op. cit., pl. i.

[5] And many of the smaller also; cf. ibid., pl. xi.

[6] *Archaeologia*, lii, 1890, 231–2.

After about 1300 there would seem to have been a regular sequence of chalice forms, but since it is impossible to interpret with confidence the descriptions of lost pieces it seems best to proceed directly to the next extant example.

Group 2

In the year 1890 the authorities of Canterbury Cathedral decided to open the tomb of an archbishop in order to identify the individual whose remains were contained therein. The investigation was highly successful, as besides settling that the grave was that of Archbishop Hubert Walter (1193–1205), a silver chalice[1] and paten and fragments of a silver-mounted pastoral staff were discovered. The chalice (Pl. 2) is parcel-gilt and is in very good condition. The wide bowl has a pronounced lip and is engraved with a sort of intersecting arcade. It is distinguished from the chalices of succeeding types by having no stem but only a 'knot'[2] formed of twelve vertical gadroons between two bands of beading. The round foot is embossed with twelve flattened lobes which are

[1] Until the end of the Middle Ages it was a general practice to bury a priest with a chalice and paten or with the semblance of one. The chalice was usually placed on one side of the body in an upright position, as it might have some wine in it. A clear reference to the filling of the chalice occurs in *The Book of John of Schalby, Canon of Lincoln, 1294–1333, concerning the Bishops of Lincoln and their acts*, trans. by J. H. Sawley, D.D., 1949, 10, or Giraldus Cambrensis, *Opera*, Rolls Series, vii. 202, where in the account of the translation of the body of Bishop William of Blois (d. 1206), it is commented that after a lapse of a hundred years 'his body was found to be unimpaired, and the wine in the chalice with which he was buried, was fresh and pure, so it seemed'. The material of which the chalice and paten were made depended on the circumstances of the deceased. Thus a monk of Durham at the time of the Dissolution had a chalice of wax, but the prior got 'a little challice of silver, other metell or wax, w[ch] was laid upon his brest w[th]in his coffine' (*Rites*, 52–53). I know of no directions by a testator regarding the chalice with which he was to be buried, so that it may be inferred that the matter was left to those arranging the funeral to select one which could be spared. It is not safe, therefore, to infer that the chalice was new when buried, though some certainly were, whilst their present fragile condition may sometimes be due to their not having been sound when placed in the coffin. The silver chalice found in the grave of Archbishop Absalon (d. 1201), at Sorø, Denmark, was recovered in good condition, but only a fragment of the pewter paten remained. This appears to be the only recorded instance of a chalice and paten of different materials. The Sorø chalice is claimed as English in Appendix I both because it is indistinguishable from examples of English provenance and because the monastery had been ruled by three English abbots for the thirty-seven years previous to the archbishop's burial.

There is no doubt that the silver chalices found in coffins had been made for use. The earlier pewter chalices were also made for use, but after the period when they had been ousted by ones of silver their manufacture was continued for funerary purposes. Their stylistic development seems to have been arrested, so that fourteenth-century examples are very obviously decadent reproductions of an earlier pattern. There are some references in the thirteenth and fourteenth centuries to craftsmen called 'calicers' who presumably specialized in making chalices. In 1349 the will was proved of Nicholas Caleyser, 'peautrer' (*Calendar of Wills proved and enrolled by the Court of the Husting*, 1889, i. 596), and since the use of pewter chalices was frowned upon by this time it seems likely that the 'calicers' made funerary chalices.

[2] In the Middle Ages the ornamental boss in the middle of the stem of a chalice was the KNOT (*nodus*). The word KNOP was applied to a type of ornament on the foot of a fifteenth-century chalice.

engraved with scrollwork and foliage. The character of the ornament shows that the chalice must be dated not much later than the middle of the twelfth century.[1] Though neither well-proportioned nor finely finished, the Canterbury chalice is of extreme interest as the sole survivor of its period.

From this point we shall not be further troubled by groups represented by single specimens. At the time when public interest in church plate began to be awakened there were only two thirteenth-century chalices still in use in English churches.[2] This number can now be brought up to about eighteen by chalices derived from other sources. They may be divided into two groups which would appear to have been contemporary with each other.

Group 3

The first of these is characterized by the use of a broad, shallow bowl with a pronounced lip. The stems, which are sometimes decorated with fluting or other simple forms of decoration, are either jointed on to the foot (Pl. 3*a*) or else the latter are socketed on to them (Pl. 3*b*). The knots are generally rounded, but some are polygonal or lobed. The feet are plain and round. The chalices of this group represent the basic design in use for a hundred years from 1180.

Group 4

Before the discovery of Archbishop Walter's chalice there was a tendency to assume that thirteenth-century chalices progressed from simplicity to elaboration. It is now clear that there was no question of progress but merely of price range. The bowls and stems of the chalices of this group are identical with those of the last, and their individuality consists in their more elaborately decorated knot and feet. In only one case is the knot plain, the others being either lobed, writhen, or decorated with chevron ornament. The feet are embossed with radiating plain or cusped lobes or else with pointed leaves. Of the half-dozen chalices in this group, four are outstanding. These are the chalice from Dolgelley[3] in the National Museum of Wales (Pl. 4), the chalice from Børsa in the Kunstindustrimuseum, Oslo (Pl. 7), which is closely related to one found in the grave of an archbishop of York (Pl. 6). The fourth is the chalice still remaining at Dragsmark (Pl. 5) in southern Sweden.[4] All except the York

[1] This is the date suggested by Sir William St. John Hope (*Monumenta Vetusta*, vii, 1890, 9). Fr. Braun (op. cit. 87) assumed that it was new when buried in 1205.

[2] Ashprington, Devon, and Berwick St. James, Wilts. The latter is now at the British Museum.

[3] This chalice and its paten were discovered in 1890 either within a dry-stone wall or concealed beneath a rock by the roadside. Underneath the foot is neatly engraved NICOL'VS ME FECIT DE HERFORDIE. Nothing is known of such an individual. The earliest published accounts of the find are by W. Cripps (*Arch. Journal*, xlix, 1892, 83) and by W. Boore (*Proc. of the Soc. of Antiquaries*, 2nd ser. xiv. 104).

[4] Both Børsa and Dragsmark lay within the kingdom of Norway in the thirteenth century. Dr. Thor Kielland (*Norsk Guldsmedskunst i Middelalderen*, 1927, 130–6, 502–3) calls both chalices English, but also remarks that two English goldsmiths (Walter of Croxton and Edward of Westminster) were

example are equally notable for the fine quality of the engraved foliage on their feet as for their good proportions. There is no means of dating any of them exactly, but together they afford us a glimpse of first-class English goldsmiths' work in the middle of the reign of Henry III.

Towards the close of the thirteenth century there was a tendency in some countries abroad for the wide, rounded chalice bowls to be replaced by deeper ones with straighter sides. We do not know how soon this change affected England, as the number of known fourteenth-century chalices is very small.

Group 5

The next example to be noted is the chalice discovered in the tomb of Archbishop William de Melton (d. 1340) in York Minster (Pl. 8*a*). It has a bowl of the new form, an eight-lobed knot recalling those used on the simpler thirteenth-century chalices, and a plain round foot engraved with a crucifix. It is likely that the chalice was made a score of years before the archbishop's death. Differing only in having a cast and applied crucifix on the foot is a chalice (Pl. 8*b*) in the Statens Historiska Museum, Stockholm, which came from an unrecorded church in western Sweden.[1]

All the chalices so far described have round feet. From the beginning of the fourteenth century there was a tendency to adopt other shapes in most of the countries of Western Europe. It is usually accepted that the reason behind this change was that it had become customary to lay the chalice on its side on the paten at the ablutions on the conclusion of mass.[2] Round-footed chalices have a tendency to roll if laid on their sides, so that there was an obvious advantage in adopting forms which avoided this form of inconvenience. No official encouragement was given to obtain chalices of a new pattern, so that

working in Norway in the second quarter of the thirteenth century, quite apart from Matthew Paris, who went on a diplomatic mission in 1248 to King Haakon, founder of the abbey of Dragsmark. It is therefore possible that both chalices were made in Norway by English goldsmiths.

Chalices at Tingvall, Nordmør, and Tonjum, Sogne Fjord, both have later bowls. The former is very like the Børsa chalice, but Dr. Kielland is of the opinion that it is a Norwegian copy. The Tonjum chalice is much more obviously derivative. The chalice at Arendal, Jarlsberg, still retains some thirteenth-century features connecting it with the above, but has been grievously treated.

[1] English influence is also evident in the medieval parts of the chalices at Alingsås, Bälinge and Humla, all three in western Sweden. They have recently been made known by Aron Andersson in *Silberne Abendmahlsgeräte in Schweden aus dem XIV Jahrhunderts,* 1956, pl. 101–4. A chalice and paten, considerably corroded by burial, which appeared in the London market in 1914, I am inclined to regard as a Scandinavian adaptation of an English type. It is now in the Lee Collection, Hart House, University of Toronto (W. W. Watts, *Catalogue of Silversmiths' work . . . Lee Collection*, 1936, pl. 1).

No details are recorded of a chalice, now missing, found in about 1770 in a fourteenth-century tomb at Bushbury church, Staffs. (S. Shaw, *History of Staffordshire*, 1801, ii. 178).

[2] Thus in an early fourteenth-century Sarum missal in the library of the University of Bologna occurs the instruction: 'Hic involvet calicem super patenam' (J. Wickham Legg, *The Sarum Missal*, 1916, 222 n.).

round-footed chalices were still being made for important churches in the third quarter of the fourteenth century.[1] They were still being used up to the Reformation.

Group 6

The designs favoured in England for a hundred and fifty years are all variations on the theme of a hexagon with incurved sides. The earliest literary evidence which we have for the use of a chalice of this type occurs in a will of 1378.[2] The earlier examples are not only few but very difficult to date. None of them can be said definitely to antedate the Ramsey Abbey incense-boat (Pl. 45) which also shows this type of foot and which may be placed about 1360. The Hamstall Ridware chalice (Pl. 9) is probably the earliest surviving example of the new type. It has a writhen knot similar to the one used a hundred years earlier on the Børsa chalice (Pl. 7), but the stem is hardly more than two grooved rings. Unlike most other English medieval chalices it is not soldered up, and can be taken to pieces. The form is excellent but the finish is a little slapdash.

Attention was only directed to the Aston-by-Sutton chalice (Pl. 10) after the small Cheshire church to which it belongs got damaged in the Second World War. The foot is flatter than that of the last chalice and is engraved with the Crucifixion and a coat-of-arms.[3] The hexagonal stem merges into the knot in which the form of the foot is reproduced. No chalice with a comparable stem and knot has so been recorded either in England or abroad. The workmanship is good and the general appearance of the chalice suggests that it was made for a private chapel of some importance.

The third chalice, which completes this group, belongs to Goathland church, near Whitby (Pl. 11). The foot is engraved with the Sacred Monogram and is quite distinct from the well-developed stem, which carries a plain hexagonal knot. It seems likely that it represents a stock pattern of the early years of the fifteenth century.[4]

[1] Thus in the dissolution inventory of Westminster Abbey is a reference to four chalices with round feet. These had been given by Abbot Litlington (1362–86) whose initials were on the patens (*Trans. of the London and Middlesex Arch. Soc.*, iv, 1873, 321).

[2] Sir John Foxley bequeathed a gilt chalice 'cum pede de forma molette sex punctorum'. *Arch. Journal*, xv, 1858, 268.

[3] So far the arms (on a cross, five lions rampant), have remained unidentified. In an inventory of 1789 the two pieces are described as 'French plate'. I am not inclined to attribute much importance to this (*Trans. of the Hist. Soc. of Lancashire and Cheshire*, cii, 1950, 129).

[4] It has unfortunately been necessary to use an old photograph of this chalice, which was sent away to be 'restored' in 1908 and came back with a new bowl and knot, neither of which were strictly in accordance with the original ones. A chalice at the Statens Historiska Museum, Stockholm (Ugglas, *Kirkligt guld- och silversmede*, 1933, no. 4), formerly belonging to the church of Askersund on Lake Wettern, shows that English influence was still active in Norway. It closely resembles the Goathland chalice, but amongst the saints engraved on the foot are St. Olaf and St. Halvard, patron saint of Oslo.

Group 7

An appreciable interval probably separates the chalice just described from the earliest of the next group. The characteristics of this last are a deeper and less conical bowl, tending to become hemispherical; a hexagonal stem carrying a six-lobed knot with bosses variously decorated, between which are traceried compartments, usually pierced; whilst the foot is again hexagonal, with in-curved sides. The bosses on the knot are variously decorated, some with angel heads and others with leopard heads or quatrefoil flowers stamped out from dies, or else with the Sacred Monogram. One panel of the foot is usually engraved with a crucifix with a background of foliage, but a cast and applied crucifix or crucifixion group also appear. Of the fourteen examples which are at present known only three bear hall-marks. These are either for the year 1479 or 1498. Of the examples illustrated the one of 1479 at Nettlecombe, Som. (Pl. 12*a*), probably illustrates the best quality likely to be found in a small village church. The Ampleforth Abbey (Pl. 12*b*) chalice would seem to belong to the same social stratum but to be of provincial manufacture. The one belonging to the Roman Catholic church at West Grinstead, Sussex (Pl. 14*a*), is of more humble workmanship, but is important as being one of the rare medieval travelling chalices made in three pieces which screw together. The similar chalice at St. Patrick's College, Maynooth, which is similarly constructed, has unfortunately got a modern bowl.[1] The idea of the screw-up chalice was destined to become very popular with the Recusants after the Reformation. The form of the bowl of the chalice at Stadarhraun, Iceland (Pl. 13*a*), suggests that it is a few years later than the two examples at Brasenose College, Oxford (Pl. 13*b*), which have the 1498 hall-mark.

Group 8

Around about the year 1490 it began to be customary to embellish the points of the hexagonal foot with a cast ornament. The contemporary name for these appears to have been 'knops'.[2] About a quarter of the surviving examples have crescent-shaped knops, two-thirds have, or have had, some sort of conventionalized leaf—for the knops tended to get broken off, and when this happened it was less trouble to shear off the survivors than to solder on the fragments.

[1] The fact that these chalices unscrew is the proof that they are travelling chalices. Their smallness is no proof, as the Edwardian inventories disclose many instances of chalices weighing only 3 or 4 ounces. Even rich abbeys might have small chalices, e.g. 'unus parvus calix argenteus deauratus, pro Communione Juvenum'—presumably for the boy bishop (J. Amundesham, *Annales Monasterii Sancti Albani*, Rolls Series, 1871, ii. 326). The smallest extant chalice and paten appear to be those in the possession of Colonel E. J. Pyke. The chalice (Pl. XIV*b*) is 4½ inches high and weighs 4 ounces. The paten is 3 inches in diameter and weighs 1 ounce. The chalice does not take to pieces.

[2] In the 1557 inventory of Lincoln Minster is a chalice 'lackinge ij Knoppys on the foote' (*Archaeologia*, liii, 1892, 71); at St. Margaret Pattens in 1526 is one 'in the fote of it iij half mones otherwise called Knappys' (*Arch. Journal*, xlii, 1885, 326).

Of the score of chalices composing the group only three are hall-marked, and these range between 1494 and 1507. The chalice belonging to Coombe Keynes church, Dorset (Pl. 15*a*), shows the design in its greatest simplicity, whilst the one belonging to the Roman Catholic church at Hornby, Lancs. (Pl. 15*b*), which comes from the parish church of Caton, near Lancaster, is a rather more ambitious version. The foot is engraved with the Crucifixion instead of the more common Crucifix, whilst round the bowl is an appropriate inscription which will be discussed a little later on. The Leominster (Pl. 16) and Calcena (Pl. 17) chalices are strikingly similar and are amongst the most beautiful examples of English late-medieval goldsmith's work. The Leominster chalice has lost all its knops and both have lost the enamelled plaque of the Crucifix or Crucifixion which was originally framed in one panel of the foot. At Leominster it has been replaced with one with IHC, matching up with the IHC and XPC on the others. At Calcena the replacing panel bears the coat-of-arms of an ecclesiastic who was perhaps responsible for bringing the chalice from England to an obscure township on the slopes of the Sierra de Moncayo. This is, however, merely a guess, since the charges are obliterated.

Group 9

The attractive but unpractical chalice with a foot with six incurved sides with fragile knops appears to have been superseded soon after 1500 by one with a sexfoil foot. On some examples the six sides continue to slope upwards towards the stem, but more commonly the top of the foot is domed. The stem and knot show the same variations as in the last group, but the bowl tends to be more square than heretofore. For the first time the hall-marked examples outnumber the unhall-marked, the latest bearing the date-letter for 1537. The fifteen examples are unusually representative and range from the gold chalice from the chapel of the wealthy Bishop Foxe (Pl. 18), which is one of the very finest examples of English medieval goldsmith's work, down to pieces intended for poor rural parish churches. Although it is of gold the chalice at Corpus Christi College, Oxford, is one of the simplest in its form. Richness is added by the touching up of the facets of the knot with crimson and green enamel and by decorating the foot with figures of saints beneath canopies (Pl. 32) besides the usual Crucifix.

The Bedingfield chalice (Pl. 19), hall-marked 1518, may be regarded as a simpler version of the last, the general proportions of which are followed closely. It is, in fact, an excellent example of the sort of chalice which we may imagine was being turned out for a private chapel or a country church which enjoyed the good will of the lord of the manor.[1] Socially it ranks in this group in the same position as the Nettlecombe one in the last.

[1] When this chalice and paten were first sold at Christie's by Sir Henry Bedingfield, Bart. (28 June 1905,

The two remaining chalices in this group which have been chosen for illustration show the later form of foot having the domed top. The one belonging to Lord Hatherton (Pl. 20)[1] cannot be far distant in date from the one at Westminster Cathedral (Pl. 21), which bears the hall-mark for 1529. The bowl of the former shows the squarer form which was preferred by some goldsmiths of this period and which had already appeared on some of the latest chalices of the last group. Both show inscriptions round the bowl and foot, whilst Lord Hatherton's has a traceried arcade round the junction of the stem and the foot more elaborate than those on the Calcena and Leominster chalices.

Group 10

The last three chalices to be mentioned are really more elaborate versions of those just discussed, in which the simple sexfoil foot has been abandoned in favour of a wavy one. This new type appears to have been evolved only a few years before the period of spoliation set in. The earliest belongs to Wylye church, Wilts. (Pl. 22), and bears the hall-mark for 1525 with, as maker's mark, a *sceptre*. A stem beautifully pierced with tracery is the distinctive feature of the other two, which are identical except for the details of their knots and the engraved decoration. One, which was bought in 1953 for the Royal Scottish Museum, Edinburgh (Pl. 23), bears the hall-mark for 1527 and the same maker's mark as appears on both the Wylye and the Westminster Cathedral chalices—the knot on the latter is decorated with human masks from the same dies. The chalice which was given to Trinity College, Oxford, by its founder Sir Thomas Pope in 1556 bears the hall-mark for 1527 and a *Vernicle* as the maker's mark.[2]

It is often assumed that a medieval chalice was entirely the work of a single craftsman, or at least of one workshop, as is often the case with one ordered from a modern artist craftsman. This would appear not to have been the case in the later Middle Ages. The dies for the little heads round the knot would be made by a specialist who supplied the trade. The engraving seems usually to

lot 47), it was stated that they had long been in the possession of the family at Oxburgh Hall, Norfolk. On the foot of the chalice, thrice repeated, are the initials E H tied by a knot and engraved in a style suggesting a date about 1600. This may commemorate Elizabeth Howard, daughter of Lord William Howard of Naworth, who married Sir Henry Bedingfield and who was probably dead by 1607 (*Country Life*, ciii, 1948, 1077).

[1] Found in 1750 with nearly £10,000 worth of gold coins when the old hall at Pillaton, Staffs., was being demolished. No accurate account exists of the coins, but since it is stated to have included guineas it cannot have been hidden for longer than ninety years (*Proc. of the Soc. of Antiquaries*, 2nd ser. x, 1885, 260).

[2] H. C. Moffatt wisely rejected the story that this chalice had belonged to St. Alban's Abbey, for which there is no supporting evidence. Pope was deeply involved in the task of suppressing the abbeys, so that there is no improbability in its having been monastic loot from somewhere (*Old Oxford Plate*, 1906, 155).

have been handed out, but this point can be better demonstrated when we deal with the patens. There can be little doubt that the chalices and patens at the Edinburgh Museum and Trinity College, Oxford, are engraved by the same hand, although they bear different maker's marks. Similarly we can trace the same design being used by engravers of varying degrees of competence. Thus the sensitive rendering of the crucified Christ against a background of foliage which is found upon the foot of the chalice at Old Hutton, Westmorland (Pl. 33*a*), is used again on the one belonging to Combe Keynes, Dorset (Pl. 33*b*), and copied by less skilled artists on those at Bacton, Hereford, and Nettlecombe, Som. (Pl. 12). Altogether it has to be admitted that the quality of the engraving is quite uneven and that there are many instances where it is manifestly below the standard of the goldsmith's work which it is intended to embellish.

B. PATENS

Only two basic designs for patens were used during the Middle Ages. In one the central part is sunk into a single depression, either circular as in a dish, or multifoil. In the other there is a second depression, the first being circular and the second multifoil. The form of a medieval paten affords no certain clue as to its date. The style of the decoration, the subject depicted, and such aids as may be afforded by historical associations or hall-marks are the only means by which we can hope to arrive at a chronological arrangement. There has been a tendency to attempt to date much too closely patens which have lost their chalices. The dangers to be encountered will be explained when the iconographical section is reached.

The earliest surviving paten (Pl. 24*a*) is that which was found in the tomb of Archbishop Hubert Walter at Canterbury, which has already been dated as being early in the second half of the twelfth century. It belongs to the single-depression type, but the double depression is represented by a crudely decorated example found in the grave of a bishop at Chichester which cannot be much younger.

Three magnificent double-depression patens survive from the middle of the reign of Henry III. The one belongs to the little church of Wyke (Pl. 24*b*) on the outskirts of Winchester, and has the spandrels round the octofoil depression engraved with foliage which has not fully lost its Romanesque character. The device of the Agnus Dei is on a third depression, which is an unusual feature.

The second of these patens (Pl. 25*a*) was found in the grave of Bishop Walter de Cantelupe (d. 1266) at Worcester Cathedral in 1861. It has a quatrefoil depression with the spandrels engraved with foliage and has an elaborate cross behind the Manus Dei in the centre.

The third is the paten (Pl. 25*b*) which was discovered along with the Dolgelley chalice, which is indubitably the finest of all the earlier examples. Two of the spandrels are filled with engraved foliage and the remainder with the symbols of the Evangelists.

Compared with these three the paten (Pl. 26*b*) belonging to the Dragsmark chalice and that (Pl. 26*a*) found in the grave of Bishop Gravesend (d. 1279) must appear pedestrian. The former is certainly disappointing when seen alongside its chalice, but the latter is interesting as being the only paten having a depression in the form of a square in a quatrefoil.

The few fourteenth-century patens which have so far come to light are undistinguished both as regards design and workmanship. The one (Pl. 27*a*) belonging to the Hamstall Ridware chalice presents no unusual features but may be regarded as representative.

There are about 120 patens which must have been made between 1400 and the Reformation. It is doubtful whether any of them belong to the first half of the fifteenth century. Nearly all belong to the two main types having either a single or a double depression. The latter nearly always have a sexfoil depression with the spandrels engraved with a conventionalized rayed leaf. A very few have the central device, ordinarily engraved, replaced by one decorated with translucent enamel inserted from the back, through a hole. In four the inserted plaque is decorated on both back and front.[1] Inscriptions on the rim, rare in earlier periods, now appear not infrequently.

Such then are the standard forms of medieval patens, from which deviations are rare. Lest it should be thought that everything is known about the work of this period, we have as a warning the very exceptional paten at Walmer, Kent (Pl. 29*b*), in which the central device of an engraved Sacred Monogram appears in the middle of an embossed Tudor rose.

C. ICONOGRAPHY

1. *Chalices*

It has already been noted that the surviving fourteenth-century chalices have a *crucifix*, either engraved or else cast and applied, to decorate the foot.

[1] Nettlecombe, Som. (Pl. 30*a*), Bedingfield in the Victoria and Albert Museum (Pl. 30*b*, *c*), and Kirk Hamerton, Yorks., all have the Vernicle on the front and the Sacred Monogram on the back. The Oscott College example (Pl. 29) has the Trinity on the front and the Sacred Monogram on the back.

Literary evidence for the decoration of both sides of the plaque is scanty. A chalice given by Henry VI to King's College, Cambridge, described in the 1452 inventory, had the Trinity on the front and the royal arms on the back (*Ecclesiologist*, xviii. 5). Wolsey also had a paten with the Trinity on the front and his arms on the back (Gutch, *Collectanea Curiosa*, 1781, ii. 310).

It would appear to be likely that the engraving of both sides of the centre of medieval patens goes back considerably farther than the extant silver examples suggest. There is a curious copper-gilt paten at Bredhurst, Kent, apparently dating from the thirteenth century, which has the Manus Dei engraved on the front and the Sacred Monogram on the back (*Archaeologia Cantiana*, xxviii, 1909, 301).

The purpose evidently to give the chalice a definite front.[1] This practice would seem to date from the latter part of the thirteenth century since a chalice presented to St. Paul's, by Eleanor of Castile (d. 1290), is stated as being so decorated.[2] When chalices ceased to have round feet one side was always reserved to carry some symbol which was either engraved, cast and applied, or enamelled on a plaque which was visible through a window cut in the foot. The *Crucifix* was by far the commonest subject, but the *Crucifixion*, including the *Virgin and St. John*, also appeared frequently. One or other, indeed, is found on 95 per cent. of surviving late medieval chalices.

Naturally this did not exhaust the repertoire of the medieval artists. The *Man of Sorrows* seated on a rock is found on the chalice of 1525 at Highworth, Wilts., but the subject does not seem to have been common.[3] The *Figure of Pity* is also known to have been used, as is proved by the 1506 inventory of Exeter Cathedral.[4] Unusual subjects sometimes had some special reason. Thus the chantry of the Name of Jesus in York Minster had a chalice with 'JHC in ye foytt'.[5] Similarly St. Peter and St. Paul appeared on either side of the Saviour on two chalices recorded in the same Exeter inventory.[6] They are the patron saints of the cathedral. It was inevitable that the *Virgin and Child* should be used in this position and a special justification can be found sometimes for its appearance also.[7] St. Edward appeared on a chalice belonging to the chantry of Henry V which adjoined the shrine of the Confessor in Westminster Abbey.[8] It seems to have been unusual for a non-biblical saint to appear in this position.

The feet of some chalices were decorated with a second subject in addition to the *Crucifix* or *Crucifixion*. This arrangement was quite rare and no examples are at present known.[9] Chalices engraved with more than two subjects are

[1] A roughly scored cross on the foot of the thirteenth-century chalice from Berwick St. James performed the same function.

[2] Dugdale, *St. Paul's*, 1818, 313.

[3] A variant in the Chapel of the Martyrdom at Canterbury Cathedral showed the Christ seated in the sepulchre (Legg and Hope, 304).

[4] Oliver, 322.

[5] *Fabric Rolls of York Minster*, Surtees Soc. 1859, 304. The chalices at Goathland, Yorks., and Ebbesbourne Wake, Wilts., both have the *Sacred Monogram* on the foot, but in neither case is there any connexion with the dedication of the church.

[6] Oliver, 322 and 362; but there is no obvious reason for the subject appearing at Christ Church, Canterbury (Legg and Hope, 182).

[7] e.g. on the example in the fifteenth century of Winchester College which is dedicated to Our Lady (*Arch. Journal*, ix, 1858, 235), but there is no special reason for its use on a chalice belonging to the chapel of St. James and St. Catherine in York Minster (*Fabric Rolls*, 287).

[8] *Trans. of the London and Middlesex Arch. Soc.* iv, 1873, 352.

[9] A chalice in the 1536 inventory of Salisbury had the *Annunciation* as the second subject (*C.P. Wilts.* 238), and it appeared also on one presented by William of Wykeham, Bishop of Winchester, to Lincoln Minster, where, however, it accompanied the *Resurrection* instead of a *Crucifix* (*Archaeologia*, liii, 1892, 13, 44). An Exeter Cathedral chalice had as its second subject *St. Peter* vested as pope (Oliver, 322).

also rare and descriptions in inventories seldom describe carefully the subjects illustrated.[1] The gold chalice of 1507 at Corpus Christi College, Oxford, is the only known example having each panel of the foot filled with a subject. It may be supposed that Bishop Foxe had some special devotion for the persons represented, since the choice is not very obviously coherent. The subjects are, in addition to the *Crucifixion*, the *Virgin and Child*, *St. Mary Magdalene*, *St. Jerome*, *St. Margaret*, and *St. Augustine*. The character of the drawing and particularly the traceried canopies (Pl. 32) strongly suggest that the artist had some German woodcut or engraving to copy from.

2. *Patens*

The custom of decorating the paten with a devotional subject antedated that of placing one on the foot of the chalice by at least a century. The range of subjects used upon patens was not quite so restricted as on chalices, and some of them enjoyed greater popularity at some periods than at others.

Both surviving examples and inventories agree in showing that the most popular subjects in the thirteenth century were the *Manus Dei* and the *Agnus Dei*.[3] The first of these shows the right hand of the Almighty in the act of blessing, with some sort of sleeve over the wrist and often emerging from clouds. Ordinarily the *Manus Dei* (alias *Dextera Dei*), was shown upside down, since the Almighty was assumed to be seated in the skies and the hand, fingers downwards, and is so represented in many medieval pictures of the Crucifixion. At an early stage this convention must have been forgotten by engravers of patens, since the inscription surrounding the subject on the thirteenth-century paten found in the grave of Bishop Swinfield (d. 1316) in Hereford Cathedral, shows that the hand was already supposed to be seen erect.[4] The paten (Pl. 25*a*) found in the grave of Bishop William de Cantelupe (d. 1266) at Worcester Cathedral shows the hand against an elaborate cross, a feature which is repeated on several later examples.[5] The cross may have helped to have obscured the identity of the subject, since in the 1510 inventory of York Minster the treasurer, Robert de Langton, refers to a paten with the Saviour's hand.[6] The *Manus Dei* was still being used on patens at the end of the Middle Ages, though

[1] An exception is a chalice bequeathed in 1426 by Thomas Beaufort, Duke of Exeter, which had censing angels round the foot (*Archbishop Chichele's Register*, ii. 358).

[2] It was quite unusual for both chalice and paten to be engraved with the same subject, but in the chapel of St. John of Beverley in York Minster both pieces bore the *Sacred Monogram* (*Fabric Rolls of York Minster*, Surtees Soc. 1859, 289), and at Winchester College a *Crucifix* (*Arch. Journal*, x, 1858, 238).

[3] In the 1245 inventory of St. Paul's there were seven patens with the *Manus Dei*, and two each with the *Agnus Dei*, *Majesty*, and *Trinity* (*Archaeologia*, l, 1887, 464 et seq.).

[4] Compare also the hand on the Dragsmark paten (Pl. 26*b*).

[5] Ampleforth I; Beighton, Norf.; Preston, Rutl.; Weston-on-Trent, Staffs.; York Minster.

[6] 'Manu Salvatoris in patena in modum benedictionis et benedicendo' (*Fabric Rolls of York Minster*, 216).

a deceptive archaism in the drawing has misled some writers into dating certain examples too early.[1]

The *Agnus Dei*, a subject directly suggested by the service of the mass, appears on the earliest and on the latest medieval patens. Thus we get the subject treated competently on the paten from the grave of Archbishop Hubert Walter (Pl. 24*a*), and crudely upon the earliest of the Chichester patens, both of which belong to the second half of the twelfth century. From the following century we have only a good conventionalized rendering on the Wyke paten (Pl. 24*b*). No examples survive from the fourteenth century, but both the Chewton Mendip, Som. (Pl. 34*a*), and the Merton, Norfolk, patens are probably engraved from designs originating from that period.[2] Four other fifteenth-century examples require no special comment, but the sixteenth century is represented by the unmarked paten (Pl. 34*c*) which accompanies the 1537 chalice in the National Gallery, Melbourne. This is also decorated with a rendering of a much earlier date. All the above represent, with varying degrees of skill, a standing lamb supporting a banner. The 1521 paten at Milwich, Staffs. (Pl. 34*b*), introduces a fresh variety—the *Lamb of the Apocalypse*, seated on the Book with Seven Seals. Unfortunately the engraver was unable to do justice to the design.

The *Sacred Monogram* would seem to have been introduced in the second half of the fourteenth century. It was a particularly appropriate subject since it was commonly stamped on the wafers, as is shown on many monumental brasses. It was in common use during the remainder of the Middle Ages and no iconographical peculiarities need be noted. Except when the owner's arms were preferred, the *Sacred Monogram* seems to have the usual device on the underside of the paten when there was one.

The cult of the *Vernicle*, the impression of the face of Our Lord left in the napkin on which He wiped it on the way to Calvary, became very popular all over Europe after the Black Death. The subject was in use on patens in England by 1386, since Westminster Abbey once had one which bore the initials of Abbot Litlington, who died in that year.[3] The majority of late medieval patens are engraved with the *Vernicle*, but no great strictness or uniformity was maintained in the manner in which it was represented. Few examples

[1] The drawing of both the Castle Bromwich and Foxley patens retains a fourteenth-century flavour, but I have come to the conclusion that this is due to the use of old designs. The drawing on the Ampleforth I paten (Pl. 37*b*) might suggest an earlier date than the second half of the fifteenth century which is given by the chalice.

[2] Both have the triple rayed leaf engraved in the spandrels, which is a late feature. The Rev. C. R. Manning (*Norfolk Archaeology*, xii, 1895, 5) commented on the earlier character of the rendering of the lamb on the Merton paten, but other authors have dated the Chewton Mendip paten as '*c.* 1500', although the drawing and lettering of the inscription would suggest *c.* 1300.

[3] *Archaeologia*, lii, 1890, 232.

show an agonized face and the Crown of Thorns.[1] Most show an impassive head wearing a halo, which by a stretch of imagination can be held to conform with the legend. Quite commonly, however, we encounter a representation of a head and shoulders covered by a mantle held by a clasp, such as is to be seen on the superb paten of 1507 at Corpus Christi College, Oxford[2] (Pl. 36*a*). There is little contemporary evidence that the change was noted.[3]

Unfortunately this was not the only form of laxity which was prevalent. Though it would be possible to enumerate several distinct versions of each of these three basic types, it is clear that the number of original designs in use in London in the late fifteenth and early sixteenth centuries was quite limited, so that we are able to trace their use by the same artist or by separate artists over considerable periods. Thus the version used on the enamelled medallion on the Nettlecombe paten of 1479 (Pl. 30*a*) reappears on the Bedingfield paten of 1518 (Pl. 30*b*) at the Victoria and Albert Museum. In this case it seems likely that the artist was the same, though the goldsmiths were different. On the other hand, the fine and dignified head on the undated paten at Hanworth, Norfolk (Pl. 35*a*), is clearly inspired by the same design used by a much less skilful engraver for the paten of 1514 at Heworth, Durham (Pl. 35*b*). The same contrast is observable between the skill of the engraver of the paten at Beeston Regis, Norfolk (Pl. 35*c*), and the indifferent version on the one at Saham Tony (Pl. 35*d*) in the same county. As examples of the work of a thoroughly bad engraver working simultaneously for two different goldsmiths may be instanced the 1527 Eyrarbakki paten (Pl. 35*e*) at the Victoria and Albert Museum and the 1528 paten at Morval, Cornwall (Pl. 35*f*).

It should be emphasized that both the general public and the goldsmiths were much too tolerant towards the incompetent engravers. It is not surprising to find that the engraver selected to decorate Bishop Foxe's gold paten should have risen to the occasion, but time and again we come across engravers whose lack of skill marred first-class pieces of goldsmith's work. To this category belonged the individual who failed to interpret adequately the excellent decoration which had been selected for the chalices and patens at Trinity College, Oxford (Pl. 31*a*), and the Royal Scottish Museum, Edinburgh (Pl. 31*b*).

Having dealt with the four commonest designs for patens we must proceed to deal with as many more which would seem to have been somewhat less popular. Of these the most numerous are those with a cross similar to that

[1] Melksham Forest, Wilts.; Oulton, Norf.; St. Edmund, Salisbury.

[2] It is curious that Bishop Foxe chose the *Vernicle* instead of the *Pelican* (symbol of Christ in the Eucharist), which he used as his coat-of-arms. Henry VIII had a paten decorated with a pelican (B.M. Add. MS. 46348, f. 40^{v}).

[3] In the 1540 inventory of Canterbury Cathedral there are two references to 'Saint Johns heade in the patent' (Legg and Hope, 182). Had someone noted that there was no cross on the halo of the *Vernicle*? I have noted no example of a truncated head such as would be correct for the Baptist.

customarily placed on the nimbus behind the head of Christ. All the surviving examples date from the last hundred years before the Reformation, but they may well have come in earlier. The example at Pentrobin, Flint. (Pl. 34*d*) is the finest.

Two subjects with which time has dealt unkindly are the *Majesty* and the *Trinity*. The paten (Pl. 25*b*) belonging to the Dolgelley chalice is now the only known example of the former of these. There were, for instance, two in the 1245 inventory of St. Paul's, and others occur in inventories down to the end of the Middle Ages, although it is seldom possible to establish the date of their manufacture.[1]

The *Trinity* was also represented on two patens listed in the 1245 inventory of St. Paul's, but the only known examples belong to the end of the Middle Ages. The examples at Cliffe-at-Hoo (Pl. 29*a*) and Oscott College (Pl. 28) are particularly interesting. In both the subject is shown on an enamelled plaque inserted in the bottom, but the rendering is not identical. The two patens are, however, closely linked, as the surrounding engraving is clearly derived from the same designs. The hand which engraved the subject on the paten at the Royal Scottish Museum (Pl. 31*b*) is by comparison much inferior to these.

Fate appears to have been especially unkind to patens bearing representations of Christ seated on a rainbow at the Last Judgement. The only surviving examples are those at the Roman Catholic church at Claughton-on-Brock, Lancs. (Pl. 36*b*), and at St. Magnus the Martyr in the City. Both belong to the late phase of medieval art. The *Christ of the Doom* appears to have been quite a popular subject, as three examples are listed in the fifteenth-century inventory of Winchester College[2] and as many in the dissolution inventory of Westminster Abbey.[3]

The only other standard subject which is still found is Christ as *Saviour*, standing and blessing with his right hand and holding an orb in his left. The only surviving example is one of about 1500 at Earl's Colne,[4] Essex (Pl. 36*c*). A paten with a demi-figure of the *Saviour* is mentioned in the 1295 inventory of St. Paul's, but there is nothing much to suggest that it was of frequent use.[5]

[1] For instance, two are mentioned in conjunction with chalices bearing the arms of England amongst the plate of Innocent VII (H. Hoberg, *Die Inventare des Päpstlichen Schatzes in Avignon*, 1944, 278).

[2] *Arch. Journal*, x, 1858, 238.

[3] *London and Middlesex Arch. Soc. Trans.* iv, 1873, 321.

[4] When I inspected this paten I noted an uncertainty about the draughtsmanship which suggested that the engraver was copying a design which he did not quite understand. I appealed to Mr. Christopher White of the Print Room of the British Museum, who in due course reported that the engraving on the paten closely resembled a woodcut in the 1479 and 1481 editions of the *Fasciculus Temporum* published by Jan Veldener of Utrecht. There were differences, however, the cuts showing Our Lord standing on the globe and not holding it. In this respect the paten was closer to the 1474 edition printed by Arnold Thur at Cologne, which is in other respects less close. The conclusion would seem to be that the paten was copied from a cut in an edition which has not yet been identified.

[5] Dugdale, *St. Paul's*, 1820, 313.

Other stock subjects are encountered in records but no examples of them are known.[1]

All the subjects so far discussed were particularly suitable for mass vessels. Representations of saints appear to have been used much more commonly on patens than on chalices. Usually the saint was the patron of the church or chapel. This, for instance, is the explanation of the appearance of St. Margaret upon the very beautiful paten at Felbrigg, Norfolk (Pl. 36*d*). Similarly, St. Stephen appears on a paten once at St. Stephen Colman[2] and St. Thomas upon a paten at Canterbury Cathedral.[3] The latter saint also appears upon a paten at Winchester College. Since there is no obvious justification for his presence, it must probably be explained by the personal devotion of some donor. The *Coronation of the Virgin* appeared upon a paten given by Bishop William of Wykeham to Lincoln Minster.[4] The bishop may fairly be claimed as having a special devotion to Our Lady since he dedicated his two colleges to her. A bishop engraved on the paten found in the grave of Bishop Grosseteste (d. 1253), probably represents one of the saints connected with Lincoln Minster. It carries no emblem.

Patens seem seldom to have been left unengraved. One of the patens recovered from the graves of thirteenth-century archbishops of York is unengraved and so is one from that of a bishop of the same period at St. Davids. The paten found in the grave of a fourteenth-century priest at Bushbury, Staffs., is also unengraved. There survive several more single depression unengraved patens which have been claimed as medieval. One such accompanies the chalice at Highworth, Wilts. It seems incredible, however, that so meagre a paten should have been made for so ornate a piece, and it is more likely to have been a replacement of the seventeenth century.[5]

D. INSCRIPTIONS AND HERALDRY

The inscriptions for chalices and for patens will be treated together. Inscriptions were in Latin—French and English appear hardly to have been used.[6]

[1] e.g. *Twelve Apostles* at King's College, Cambridge (*Ecclesiologist*, xxi, 1860, 5); the *Last Supper* at Lincoln Minster (*Archaeologia*, lii, 1892, 13). When the paten accompanying the second York Minster chalice was removed from the tomb, it had an applied plaque engraved with the *Holy Dove* (Drake, *Eboracum*, 1736, 486). It was already lost by the time that Poole and Hugall's *York Cathedral* was published in 1850.

[2] *Archaeologia*, l, 1887, 34.

[3] Legg and Hope, 133.

[4] *Archaeologia*, liii, 1892, 13, 44.

[5] The same is probably true of the patens at West Grinstead, Sussex; Knook, Wilts.; and Syston, Leics. A plain, single-depression paten very like these accompanies the seventeenth-century Recusant chalice in the parish church at Wrexham.

[6] They were sometimes used for mottoes, e.g.: *Item a chaleis all gilt my lordes woorde* EN DIEU EST TOUT *written in the fote*, in the inventory of John de Vere, 13th Earl of Oxford (*Archaeologia*, lxvi, 1914, 331).

They may be grouped as follows:

1. Possessory.
2. Dedicatory and donative.
3. Appropriate.

In contrast to post-Reformation plate, the use of possessory inscriptions appears to have been rare. On the other hand, those entitled to bear arms used them freely to record ownership or donorship. On chalices heraldry was used both on the knot and on the foot. On patens it appears usually to have been confined to the underside. The Aston-by-Sutton chalice is now the sole witness to this once common practice.

Dedicatory and donative inscriptions might consist merely of the donor's name, such as that of **John Capull** on either side of the Crucifix on the foot of the chalice at Bacton, Hereford, or 'Memoriale domini Willelmi Wikham' on a scroll round the rim of the paten accompanying the chalice which that celebrated bishop gave to Lincoln Minster.[1] A prayer for the donors are inscribed upon the chalice belonging to West Drayton, Middlesex,[2] and the paten at Pilton, Som.[3]

That the vessels used for the most sacred church ceremonies should bear suitable inscriptions will be readily understood. In actual fact no English chalice made before the fifteenth century includes an inscription in its decoration. It would be rash, however, to assume that the earlier chalices were always uninscribed, since the practice was quite common abroad. Even in the later Middle Ages only quite a small proportion of the chalices bore inscriptions. They were placed either round the bowl or round the foot. There was also, of course, sometimes IHS or IHESVS on the bosses of the knot.

Whereas doubt remains regarding the early use of inscriptions on chalices, their use on patens in the twelfth century is attested by the very interesting ones on the paten found in the tomb of Archbishop Walter (d. 1205). Paten inscriptions might either occupy the rim or surround the central subject. Their subject-matter might be derived from Holy Writ, church services, or religious literature. The Canterbury paten (pl. 24*a*) has around the Holy Lamb ✠ AGNVS DĪ QVI TOLL' PECCATA MVNDI MISERERE NOB', taken from the mass. Around the rim is: ✠ ARA CRVCIS TVMVLIQ CALIX LAPIDISQ: PATENA: SINDONIS OFICIVM CANDIDA BISSVS hABET :[4] derived from the *De mysterio Missae* of Hildebert of Lavardin, Bishop of Le Mans. The choice must have been made by someone who was well acquainted with contemporary literature and who may even have known the author.[5]

[1] Ibid. liii, 1892, 13.

[2] **Orate p aiabȝ Johis porpyll et Johanne uxor ei'.**

[3] **orate pro bono statu d. j. dier uicarius hius loci.**

[4] 'The altar has the office of the Cross, and the Chalice of the Tomb, and the Paten of the Stone, and the white Corporal of the Shroud.'

[5] Migne, *P.L.* clxxi, 1854, *De mysterio Missae*, col. 1194. Hildebert died early in 1135 and the

From the scanty evidence available it would seem that in the twelfth and thirteenth centuries the clergy took a considerable interest in the matter of inscriptions. Though some of these are not much more than captions,[1] the ✠ CVNTA CREO : VVIRTVTE REGO : PIETATE REFORMO on the Wyke paten (Pl. 24*b*), or 'FIT CARO PER VERBUM DE PANE MANENS CARO VERBUM' on a paten once at Westminster Abbey,[2] do not read as if they came straight out of a goldsmith's copybook. In contrast the inscriptions of the later Middle Ages show little sign of individual selection and were probably considered by the goldsmith as being merely part of the design. The mass continued to contribute the 'AGNUS DEI' &c., and the words of consecration 'HIC EST ENIM CALIX NOVI TESTAMENTI'[3] and 'ACCIPITE EX HOC OMNES, HOC EST ENIM CORPUS MEUM QUOD PRO VOBIS TRADETUR',[4] which were used on chalices and patens respectively, though not very frequently. The inscription **Vere pceptio Corporis et Sanguinis dñi jesu xpe** on the 1529 chalice at Westminster Cathedral appears to be a paraphrase of a prayer used at the reception of the Sacrament.[5]

Compline contributed two inscriptions:

'BENEDICAMUS PATREM ET FILIUM CUM SPIRITU SANCTO'[6]

and

'LAUDEMUS ET SUPEREXALTEMUS IN SECULA'.[7]

From litanies came:

'PATER DE CELIS MISERERE NOBIS',[8]
'SANCTA TRINITAS, UNUS DEUS, MISERERE NOBIS',[9]

Canterbury chalice and paten must be a quarter of a century later in date. It is interesting to note, however, that Hildebert spent some time in England as an unwilling guest of William Rufus, whom he had offended. His sojourn was not entirely unprofitable, as when he was released he was able to present to Le Mans Cathedral a pair of silver dishes and vestments acquired in England. He is recorded to have made a specific tribute to the skill of English craftsmen (op. cit. *Ven. Hildeberti Cenoman. Episc. Gesta*, col. 92). Whereas Hildebert knew England and corresponded with a number of prominent Englishmen, his works were read extensively all over Western Europe. The quotation under discussion is also found on a Rhenish champlevé enamel portable altar which belonged to the church of S. Maria in Kapitol, Cologne (O. von Falke and H. Frauberger, *Deutsche Schmelzarbeiten des Mittelalters*, 1904, 30–31, pls. xxxi–i). The altar is probably a few years earlier than the Canterbury paten.

[1] e.g. 'DEXTRA DEI' round the *Manus Dei* on the Hereford Cathedral paten or the words of benediction round the Dolgelly one.

[2] Given by 'Prior Robert'. There were two of this name in the first part of the thirteenth century (*Archaeologia*, lii, 1890, 232).

[3] Will and inventory of John de Vere, 13th Earl of Oxford (*Archaeologia*, lxvi, 1914, 313, 337).

[4] Happisburgh, Norf.

[5] 'Perceptio corporis et sanguinis domini nostri Ihesu Christi proficiat mihi misero ad vitam eternam' (J. Wickham Legg, *Sarum Missal*, 1916, 227–8).

[6] Patens at Cliffe-at-Hoo (Pl. 29*a*), Oscott College (Pl. 28), and Royal Scottish Museum (Pl. 31*b*). Chalice mentioned in inventory of Winchester College (*Arch. Journal*, x, 1858, 238).

[7] Inventory of John de Vere, *ut supra* 331.

[8] Lord Hatherton's chalice (Pl. 20).

[9] Lord Hatherton's paten.

'JESU CHRISTE FILI DEI VIVI MISERERE NOBIS',[1]
'CRUX CHRISTI SALVA NOS, CRUX CHRISTI PROTEGE NOS'.[2]

It was, however, the Psalter which provided what we know from inventories to have been by far the most popular inscription for chalices: 'CALICEM SALUTARIS ACCIPIAM ET NOMEN DOMINI INVOCABO'[3] (Ps. cxvi. 13). This is still to be found on four chalices and, as a further illustration of the carelessness of medieval engravers, on one paten.[4] Other borrowings from the Psalter could not claim the same appropriateness, e.g.:

'DOMINE NE IN FURORE TUO ARGUAS ME, NEQUE IN IRA CORRIPIAS ME', (Ps. vi, xxxvii [xxxviii]),[5]
'IN DOMINO CONFIDO' (Ps. xix),[6]
'BENEDICAM DOMINUM IN OMNI TEMPORE' (Ps. xxxiii [xxxiv]),[7]
'MISERERE MEI DEUS SECUNDAM MAGNAM MISERICORDIAM TUAM' (Ps. l [li]),[8]
'SALVUM ME FAC IN NOMINE TUO' (Ps. liv).[9]

The marked preference for the first lines of psalms might suggest a somewhat superficial acquaintance with the Psalter, but is perhaps to be explained by regarding the quotations as having been derived from Breviary responses.

New Testament inscriptions were drawn entirely from the Gospels, and I have found no trace of the use of 'CALIX BENEDICTIONIS', &c. (1 Cor. x. 16) which was to be used so extensively in the seventeenth and eighteenth centuries. The texts actually used were:

'BEATI QUI AUDIUNT VERBUM DEI ET CUSTODIUNT ILLUD' (Luke xi. 28),[10]
'BENEDICTUS DOMINUS DEUS ISRAEL QUIA' (Luke ii. 68),[11]
'BENEDICTUS QUI VENIT IN NOMINE DOMINE (Matthew xxi. 9).[12]

Again it will be noticed that the thoughtless engraver has spoilt the appearance of the quotation from the *Benedictus* by including a word too many.

A hymn doxology prescribed in the Sarum Breviary for use between Ascension and Whitsun was inscribed on a chalice in the chapel of St. Michael in Canterbury Cathedral.[13]

1 Chalice, Highworth, Wilts.

2 Chalice, Westminster Cathedral II.

3 Chalices, Leominster (Pl. 16), Trinity College, Oxford, Wylye (Pl. 22), Royal Scottish Museum (Pl. 23).

4 Royal Scottish Museum.

5 Chalice in will of John Ganvill, Canon of Wells, 1407 (*Somerset Medieval Wills*, ii. 307).

6 Chalice, Wylye.

7 Chalice, Calcena, Spain (Pl. 17); paten belonging to chapel of St. Catherine in Canterbury Cathedral in 1506 (Legg and Hope, 358).

8 Paten, Bierton, Bucks.

9 Paten, Claughton-on-Brock R.C. church, Lancs.

10 Chalice, Highworth, Wilts.

11 Paten, Dronfield, Derby.

12 Paten bequeathed by Archbishop Rotherham (*Testamenta Eboracensia*, Surtees Soc. iv. 149).

13 Legg and Hope, 149.

Lord Hatherton's chalice has the inscription **Sancta maria ora pro nobis** and the paten at Kirk Malew, I.O.M., has an invocation of St. Loup, to whom the church is dedicated. Invocations of saints appear to have been used much more sparingly than might be expected.

The last category to be mentioned may be described as religious mottoes, e.g.:

'IHC EST AMOR MEUS',[1]
'SPES MEA IN DEO EST',[2]
'DNS PROTECTOR VITE MEE'.[3]

Such mottoes were very popular towards the end of the Middle Ages and are also to be found on many rings and brooches.

It must not be thought that the subject of the inscriptions on chalices and patens has been treated exhaustively in the preceding paragraphs. The aim has been rather to quote characteristic examples and to explain their selection. Lastly, it should be emphasized that as a consequence of the excessive dependence on copybooks, the engravers came to concentrate solely on giving a pleasing result. Judging from surviving examples, it would seem that one-third of the inscribed plate exposed for sale by the goldsmiths in Cheapside exhibited some form of illiteracy due to miscopying—a wrong letter, and not merely a misplaced stop.[4] Special inscriptions seem usually to have come through fairly well and the rendering of the obscure quotation from Hildebert is correct if undistinguished. The best lettering amongst the early pieces is upon the Dolgelley paten (Pl. 25*b*), whilst amongst the later ones that on the Cliffe-at-Hoo paten (Pl. 29*a*) is outstanding. Carelessness was usually confined to the miscopying of inscriptions, for the engravers seldom really failed to transmit the beauty of the lettering which they found in their copybooks. They were, in fact, much more successful with alphabets than figure subjects.

E. CHALICE SPOONS

The spoons which are found associated with chalices in certain English medieval inventories are by use unrelated to either those employed in the Eucharist by the oriental churches or to those intended for removing impurities from the communion wine in post-Reformation times. Their purpose was, in

[1] Chalice in will of Canon Ganvill *ut supra.*

[2] Chalice in will of John Barnyngham, treasurer of York, 1457 (*Testamenta Eboracensia*, ii. 189).

[3] Paten in inventory of Winchester College (*Arch. Journal*, 1858, x. 238).

[4] The type of carelessness of which complaint is made is exemplified by the inscriptions on the chalice at Trinity College, Oxford. With singular lack of imagination the engraver inscribed the same text twice on the chalice and again on the paten, although it was quite inappropriate for the latter. He observed no uniformity in the spelling. His rendering of the inscriptions on the chalice and paten at the Royal Scottish Museum is also faulty.

fact, to ladle out the few drops of water which was by custom added to the wine in the chalice.[1]

Their period of popularity was the thirteenth and early part of the fourteenth centuries, but examples were still to be found at the time when the inventories of the Reformation period were being compiled. They are mentioned generally amongst the plate of important churches, but many of these appear to have managed without them. In most cases they are mentioned in connexion with a particular chalice and paten, though occasionally they are grouped together.[2] They were not unknown in parish churches, but the only evidence that they were widely used in any area is provided by the inventory of church goods made in 1368 by William de Swyneflete, Archdeacon of Norwich.[3] Spoons are mentioned in connexion with thirty-six churches, some of them having as many as three.[4] They were generally of silver, but were occasionally of silver-gilt. In one instance a spoon is mentioned in conjunction with a pewter chalice. The evidence regarding the Norwich archdeaconry is so at variance with that for other parts of the country that it would seem that some past bishop must have taken special measures to encourage the use of chalice spoons.

Descriptions of the spoons are extremely rare. One accompanying a very rich gem-set gold chalice mentioned in the 1384 inventory of St. George's Chapel, Windsor, was made of the same metal and had a large pearl at the end.[5] Another mentioned in the 1552 inventory of St. Paul's was of silver-gilt with a crystal at the end.[6] This had probably been made before the middle of the fourteenth century, since the accompanying chalice had a round foot. Though the above details tend to suggest that the spoons were rather ornate, they are not sufficiently explicit to enable us to identify any surviving examples.[7]

[1] 'Cocliare argenteum pro aqua ponenda in calicem', as one example is described in the 1501 inventory in M. F. Bond, *Inventories of St. George's Chapel, Windsor*, 1947, 151.

[2] As in the 1222 inventory of Salisbury Cathedral (*Registrum Sancti Osmundi Episcopi*, Rolls Series, 1884, 127.

[3] *An Inventory of Church Goods temp. Edward III*, ed. Dom Aelred Watkin, Norfolk Record Soc. xix, 1947; xx, 1948, lxxxi.

[4] St. Michael Coslany, Norwich; and St. Lawrence, South Walsham, ibid. 5 and 37.

[5] Bond *ut supra* 170.

[6] *Ecclesiologist*, xviii, 1856, 198. In the 1536 inventory of Salisbury Cathedral 'two gilded spoons' are mentioned in conjunction with a chalice given by Gilbert Keymer, who became dean in 1449 (*C.P. Wilts*. 238). This is very late for the provision of spoons, and why there should have been two is not obvious.

[7] When dealing with the twelfth–thirteenth-century spoons discovered at Pevensey Castle, Taunton Castle, and the nunnery at Iona, Commander and Mrs. G. E. P. How wrote: 'one cannot exclude the possibility that these beautifully fashioned and highly decorated spoons were made solely for ceremonial or religious purposes' (*English and Scottish Silver Spoons, Medieval to Late Stuart*, i, 1952, 22–23). Though they seem on the whole to reject the idea, its acceptance would explain away the present difficulty that these spoons appear to be entirely unrelated to the later English medieval spoons. Moreover, they resemble in all essentials, except the form of their bowls, the Anointing Spoon in the Regalia.

The characteristics of this group are a stem made in two or three sections of which the lowest is

F. OBLATION SPOONS AND PATENS

Besides spoons and patens used in connexion with the chalices in the manner already described, special ones were occasionally used in late medieval times[1] for the oblation of the hosts at the altar. The examples noted belonged to Benedictine establishments.[2] The patens would appear to have been rather larger and heavier versions of those used with chalices. The spoons appear to have weighed much the same as the contemporary ones. Whether they formed a distinctive type is difficult to decide for want of information. The spoon belonging to Worcester Cathedral Priory, which was set with stones, would seem to have been unlike any English medieval spoon which has so far come to light.

G. CRUETS

The vessels to hold the wine and the water for the mass were generally of much the same shape as those for the Holy Oils and are sometimes included under the same heading in inventories. It is not, therefore, always easy to see to which category items really belonged. Cruets for the mass should appear in pairs, ampullae for the Oils in threes, but numbers are always liable to be upset by casualties.

It was, of course, necessary to distinguish the contents of the two cruets. This was done either by inscription, colour, or decoration. The first method was usually preferred, so that one cruet would be marked 'A' (*aqua*) and the other 'V' (*vinum*). Distinction by colour was effected either by making silver-mounted crystal cruets, which appear quite often in late-medieval inventories, or else by gilding one cruet and leaving the other plain. Thus there are three odd pairs mentioned in the 1245 inventory of St. Paul's.[3] Another way was to

round and the upper round or twisted, and each has a monster's head at the junction of the stem with the rather pointed bowl.

The case against these being chalice spoons would seem to rest on two points: (1) Although the spoons are rather elaborately decorated, none shows a religious motif. (2) Their rather shallow bowls would not be very suitable for ladling water.

[1] But there is a rather obscure reference to 'vasculum unum in modum patenae, in quo hostiae deferuntur in refectorio pro Communione Sancta' given by Abbot Faritius (1100–35). Abingdon Chronicle, Rolls Series, ii, 1858, 151.

[2] 'ij Patentes for oblacyons, of sylver and gylt, with Jhs crowned in the myddes of either of the patentes xij unces.

An Oblacyon Spone, flat of sylver parcell gylt, with Jhus gravyn in the myddes, wanting the knop at the end, j unce qrt.'

Dissolution inventory of Westminster Abbey (*London and Middlesex Arch. Soc. Trans.* iv, 1873, 322).

'Item a patten parcel gylt to make oblation, weying 6 oz. 1½ qrs.

Item a silver spone for oblation with three stones in hym, weying 1 oz. 1 qr.'

Dissolution inventory of Worcester Cathedral Priory (*British Arch. Assoc. Journal*, N.S. xxxviii, 1932, 171).

[3] *Archaeologia*, l, 1887, 460.

provide only one of the cruets with a gilt stopper.[1] Distinction by ornament could be made in many ways. Another pair of cruets in the St. Paul's inventory already mentioned had a vine scroll round the middle of one of the vessels. In the early sixteenth century inventory of York Minster[2] is mentioned a pair of cruets, one of which was engraved with St. Peter and the other with St. Paul. A more peculiar way of distinguishing the contents is recorded in inventories of the plate of Henry VI and of Edward IV, where there is reference to a pair of gold cruets, one of which had on the top a great pearl and a little bell.[3]

We know much less about the form of the cruets than about their decoration. In the will of Thomas Beauchamp, Earl of Warwick (d. 1400), is mentioned a pair of cruets of silver and gilt, in the shape of angels.[4] Freak designs like this appear to have been quite rare. Two English silver cruets have survived. Both are parcel-gilt and they probably represent two of the common designs in use towards the close of the Middle Ages. The first of these (Pl. 37*b*), which is now the property of Mrs. G. E. P. How, is without spout or handle, and is shaped like a small measure on a low foot. The contents is indicated by the letter 𝔄 engraved on a medallion on the lid, which had originally an enamelled ground. It is not marked, but it has always been dated in the second half of the fifteenth century.[5]

In contrast to the above, the cruet now belonging to the church of St. Peter Port, Guernsey (Pl. 37*c*), has both spout and handle. There can be little doubt that spouted cruets were quite common, although it is only occasionally that we can recognize them in inventories.[6] Despite its elegant appearance, the Guernsey cruet illustrates the inattention to detail characteristic of only too much late-medieval English silver. Thus the inscription round the belly reads: ❁ SANCTE ❁ PAVLE ❁ (spout) ❁ PORA ❁ NOBIS, and the superfluous 'P' has been only partially obliterated. Similarly the junction of the handle and the body is masked by a demi-figure of St. James between two cockle-shells. Unfortunately the figure is upside down. The lid is engraved with a letter A. It is unhall-marked, but Sir William St. John Hope's dating of about 1525 seems correct.[7]

1 e.g. the example in the 1376 inventory of Corpus Christi College, Cambridge (*Cambridge Antiquarian Soc.* xvii, 1911, 111).

2 *Fabric Rolls of York Minster*, Surtees, Soc. 1858, 212.

3 Palgrave, ii. 171, 243.

4 H. Nicholas, *Testamenta Vetusta*, 1826, 154. There is a pair of fourteenth-century angel cruets in the treasury at Aachen. The wings serve as handles (Pl. 37*a*).

5 It made its appearance in a pawnbroker's shop in Rochester (*Proc. of the Soc. of Antiquaries*, 2nd ser. 1885, xi. 244).

6 e.g. 'my best ij Cruett͛ with spowt͛ like dragons' and 'ij Cruett͛ wt Ravonsbilles' belonging to John de Vere, Earl of Oxford (*Archaeologia*, lxvi, 1914, 314, 338).

7 Said to have been dug up in St. Saviour's parish and already known in 1831. Presented to the church of St. Peter Port by the Rev. Hubert Stevens-Guille in 1895.

It so happens that both the cruets which have come down to us are lidded. Cruets with pull-off covers appear to have been quite common, since there are frequent references to missing covers.

Cruets were normally quite small, but those used at principal feasts in cathedrals are sometimes described as large. Those used at Durham Cathedral held a quart apiece.[1]

In the 1506 inventory of Exeter is mentioned a round, covered jug of silver for fetching wine for masses. Such vessels were normally made of pewter.[2]

H. EUCHARISTIC REEDS

Although the eucharistic reed is still used by the Pope when he solemnly pontificates, it enjoyed its period of popularity over seven hundred years ago. When Adam of Usk was in Rome at Easter 1405 he noted that Innocent VII 'sucked and drew in the blood from the chalice, facing the people, through a long reed of gold, decorated in the middle with the arms of the king of Aragon'.[3] Clearly the custom appeared strange to the observant Welshman, but all the same there were still eucharistic reeds to be found in English treasuries up to the Reformation.

The earliest reference to the reed occurs in the record of the gifts of St. Ethelwold (d. 984) to Peterborough Abbey, which included four silver chalices, four silver patens, and a pipe.[4] Bishop Leofric (1050–72) is recorded to have given to his new cathedral at Exeter 'five silver chalices and four corporals and one silver pipe'.[5] Amongst the plate which Ely Abbey had to sacrifice in order to placate the Conqueror for the help afforded to Hereward the Wake there is mentioned *fistulas*, but there were still three parcel-gilt *calami* when the 1079 inventory was taken.[6] When the chroniclers[7] record the plate distributed to the 'more worthy churches' by William Rufus as executor for his father, there is mention of reeds. Clearly they were still in ordinary use, but reference to them in later times is extremely scarce. Two are mentioned in association with a Greek chalice in the 1295 inventory of St. Paul's,[8] but thereafter the only unequivocal reference which Professor Tancred Borenius[9]

[1] *Rites*, 9.

[2] Oliver, 324.

[3] Adam of Usk, *Chronicon*, 1904, 98, 274.

[4] 'iiij silurene calices, iiij patenen y sylurenen pipe' (*Liber Niger* of Peterborough, Soc. of Antiquaries, MS. lx. 39^{v}).

[5] Kemble, *Codex Diplomaticus*, 1846, iv. 275.

[6] *Liber Eliensis*, 1848, 246, 282.

[7] Roger of Hoveden, *Chronica*, Rolls Series, 1868, i. 140. Florence of Worcester, *Chronicon*, 1848, ii. 21. The same phrase in both places.

[8] Dugdale, *St. Paul's*, 1820, 313.

[9] 'The Eucharistic Reed or Calamus' (*Archaeologia*, lxxx, 1930, 99–116). I am not satisfied that the 'two pipes of silver' in the 1570–1 inventory of Crosthwaite church, Cumberland, were necessarily eucharistic reeds.

was able to produce was one concerning the church of St. John, Beverley, where in 1552 there was a 'loker for the sacriment, with ij pypes of everye, one with little silver'.[1]

I. PORTABLE ALTARS

Already in Anglo-Saxon times it was strictly enjoined that no priest should say mass without a hallowed altar.[2] The use of small, flat pieces of consecrated material which could be laid upon an unconsecrated altar or table was a convenience as long as there was a scarcity of places supplied with permanent altars. In early times the altar might merely be a piece of wood, but it is likely that such were already considered old-fashioned before the Conquest and certainly Symeon of Durham, writing early in the twelfth century, was puzzled when one composed of two pieces of wood joined with silver nails was found in the grave of St. Acca, Bishop of Hexham (d. 740).[3]

The portable altar of late Saxon times might be a much more sophisticated affair as may be seen from the example in the Musée de Cluny (Pl. 38), which was acquired in 1886 from the Stein collection. It consists of a slab of red porphyry, 10⅓ in. by 5½ in., framed in silver. The silver border is engraved with figure subjects in which the draperies are gilt. The edge bears an inscription in niello, whilst the back is of oak with silver corner-pieces and a silver quatrefoil in the middle. At the upper end is engraved a Crucifix between the bull of St. Luke and the eagle of St. John. At the bottom is the Agnus Dei between the angel of St. Matthew and the lion of St. Mark. On the sides are figures of the Virgin and St. John, each above an angel—evidently Raphael and Gabriel, whose names occur in the marginal inscription.[4] This piece was first claimed as English on the strength of the resemblance of the drawing to that in the Newminster Register[5] by the late H. P. Mitchell,[6] but still further confirmation can be obtained from the illustrations in the psalter, now in the Vatican Library,[7] which was written for the abbey of Bury St. Edmunds shortly before the Conquest.

[1] *Inventories of the Church Goods for the Counties of York, Durham, and Northumberland*, Surtees Soc. 1907, 65.

[2] 'We enjoin, that no priest, on any account, ever celebrate mass except on a hallowed altar', 31st Canon enacted under King Edgar (959–75); and also, 'If a priest, without a hallowed altar celebrate Mass, let him pay xij ore', no. 14 in Laws of the Northumbrian priests (Wilkins, *Concilia*, i. 219 and 227).

[3] *Symeon of Durham*, Rolls Series, 1882, ii. 33.

[4] ✠ DISCIPVLVS PLORAT RAPHAEL QVEMSEMPADORAT : —— NITRIX · MERET · GABRIEL CVISES ADHERET · —N GEMIT HIC LV —— PRORE——

The inscription on the fourth side is illegible.

[5] B.M. Cotton, Titus, D. xxii.

[6] *Burlington Magazine*, xlii, 1923, 63–71.

[7] Vatican, Regin. Lat. 12. For illustrations see Professor Francis Wormald, *English Drawings in the*

No other examples of English silver-mounted portable altars have come to light, but everything seems to suggest that they were in general use in important churches down to the end of the eleventh century. Thus the abbey of Ely, which had recently had to dispose of many of its treasures, had no silver-mounted portable altars when the 1079 inventory was taken, but had acquired three by the time that the next one was taken in 1093.[1]

By the beginning of the twelfth century the need for portable altars was becoming less urgent since the provision of consecrated stationary altars was becoming more general. Portable altars were doubtless being consecrated down to the close of the Middle Ages, but these were probably mostly of the unmounted sort suitable for ecclesiastics who travelled.[2] The rich examples which still appear in late medieval inventories appear to have been ancient possessions.

A number of the portable altars of which we hear were valued also as relics. Thus Henry de Blois, Bishop of Winchester, mounted up in gold, silver, and precious stones 'the sapphire of Glastonbury', which had a legendary connexion with St. David.[3] Similarly, St. Alban's Abbey possessed one of jasper which St. Augustine, apostle of the English, was reputed to have used. It was round and mounted in silver-gilt, with a ring so that it could be hung up. We are happy to have a picture of it and its donor in the abbey's book of benefactors.[4] Round altars were certainly exceptional, most examples being square or oblong. Some are mentioned as being mounted on four feet,[5] but these were probably exceptional, as also were those which contained relics.[6]

Amongst the treasures belonging to his father which William Rufus distributed amongst English abbeys was the portable altar which he gave to Battle. This was quite a different type of object from those which have been described, as is clear from the following description of it: 'a bier in the form of an altar (in which were many relics, on which mass was wont to be said when on expeditions), which amongst other things of divers sorts he had obtained

tenth and eleventh centuries, 1952, pls. 26–28. I am grateful to the author for his confirmation of the above opinion and for studying the lettering of the marginal inscription.

[1] *Liber Eliensis*, 1848, 249, 282.

[2] Dr. Rock seems to imply that the cheaper portable altars were always framed up in wood. This appears quite doubtful, as many references describe the stone but say nothing at all about any mounting (*The Church of our Fathers*, 1849, ii. 247). Rich portable altars were sometimes kept in cases (*Durham Account Rolls*, Surtees Soc. 1898, 433).

[3] William of Malmesbury, *De antiquitate Glastoniensis ecclesiae*, in T. Hearne's *Adam de Domerham*, 1727, i. 40–42; ii. 317.

[4] B. M. Cotton, Nero, D. vii, f. 101v. It is also described in the inventory of the time of Henry IV (J. Amundesham, *Annales*, Rolls Series, 1870, ii. 333–4).

[5] *Fabric Rolls of York Minster*, Surtees Soc. 1858, 233.

[6] One mentioned in the 1295 inventory of St. Paul's enclosed relics of saints Andrew, Blaise, Dennis, and Philip, as well as a piece of St. Andrew's cross (Dugdale, *St. Paul's*, 1818, 338).

from his royal predecessors with the acquisition of the kingdom, and which had hitherto been preserved in the royal treasury.'[1]

From the above it is clear that Edward the Confessor had owned an altar similar to the one on which Harold is shown making his oath in the Bayeux Tapestry. This last is shown with handles like those on a bier, but appears to have been decorated mainly with hangings. The Confessor's was evidently richer since it was kept in the treasury.

[1] *Historia fundationis monasterii de Bello*, 1846, 37.

VI

ALTAR PLATE

A. BOOKS OF THE GOSPELS, ETC.[1]

BOOKS of the Gospels and Epistles for use at the altar, with covers or cases of gold and silver, were already in general use in the cathedrals and greater abbeys of Anglo-Saxon England. They were probably as numerous then as at any subsequent time,[2] for they never became part of the normal furnishing of second-class abbeys or colleges. They were practically unknown in private chapels or in parish churches.[3]

The earliest decorated book-cover or case of which we have record is that made by St. Bilfrith in the first part of the eighth century for the Gospels which accompanied the body of St. Cuthbert on its peregrinations.

No decorated book-covers of the Anglo-Saxon period have come down to us,[4] but the 1506 inventory of Exeter Cathedral includes what is probably the best description of one. It may be translated as follows:

> A silver-gilt textus with the Crucifix, Mary and John, with the Four Evangelists in the four corners, with a vase below the foot of the Crucifix; with this inscription in Roman letters '*this textus was decorated at the common expence of Leofric and his court*'.[5]

No late-medieval book-covers covered with gold or silver appear to have survived, but it is clear from inventories that they did not greatly differ from

[1] The contents of these volumes was not uniform, but that does not concern us. In inventories they are regarded as part of the furnishing of the high altar, though in the 1506 one of Exeter there is one attributed to the Lady Chapel (Oliver, 352).

[2] It is now generally conceded that the Anglo-Saxon period of art lasted until about 1100. The following will demonstrate how numerous these richly bound volumes were at the end of the eleventh century. Abbot Godfrey of Jumièges made away with twelve when he had to pay the Malmesbury contribution towards the purchase of Normandy from Duke Robert (William of Malmesbury, *De Gestis Pontificum*, Rolls Series, 11870, 432). Fourteen are listed in the 1079 and 1093 inventories of Ely (*Liber Eliensis*, 249–82), ten were given to the cathedral of Sarum by Bishop Osmund (d. 1079) (*C.P. Wilts.* 233).

[3] Sonning, Berks., had one in 1220. There had long been an episcopal residence in the village, so it was probably a benefaction from some former bishop. See p. 26.

[4] Recently Dr. Hanns Swarzenski (*Monuments of Romanesque Art*, 1954, 26, 48, pl. 64), following upon an article by M. C. Ross (*Art Bulletin*, 1940, xxii. 83 et seq.), has claimed as Anglo-Saxon, *c.* 1050, the cover of the Weingarten Gospels in the Morgan Library (MS. 708). Though the book itself indubitably belonged to Judith wife of Tostig, Earl of Northumbria, d. 1066, I am quite unconvinced of the English origin of the cover and would be prepared rather to consider that it had been added at Weingarten.

[5] Oliver, 323. Leofric translated the see of Crediton to Exeter in 1050 and died in 1072.

those in use abroad. We can recognize two varieties, the richer having both back and front adorned, the poorer having the front only decorated. Since the subjects found on the under covers of the richer volumes were very much the same as those mentioned on the fronts of the poorer, we may suspect that economical sacrists and treasurers sometimes split a rich cover into two in order to adorn two volumes.

The principal design was shown on a depressed panel in the centre of the cover and was protected by a wide ornamental framing. The latter in its turn was often protected by bosses at the four corners, which helped to take the weight of the volume when open. The reverse covers seem to have been generally similar, though the artists probably avoided the use of high relief. Beyond this point it is necessary to proceed warily, since the inventories are sparing of technical details though liberal in giving information about materials and iconography.

The 1245 inventory of St. Paul's makes no mention of richly bound books, but the one of 1295 is perhaps the most valuable document which we have regarding those in use in post-Conquest times.[1] Eleven volumes are listed, but only five of them had both back and front decorated in silver. None were decorated with gold nor with precious stones.

The first on the list was unusual in that the front cover was of plain silver embossed with the Crucifix and lateral figures, whereas the back was of silver-gilt engraved with the Majesty surrounded by the Four Evangelists. Next come three volumes given by Henry of Northampton, prebendary in 1181–92. The first was of silver parcel-gilt and was embossed with the Crucifixion group and 'with prelates' on the front, whilst the back was of plain silver engraved and nielloed with the Majesty. It is interesting to note that three other volumes had covers decorated with niello.

In the 1315 inventory[2] of Canterbury Cathedral there are mentioned seventeen book-covers decorated with precious metal besides two with copper-gilt. Though none of them had decorated backs, they sound much richer than those at St. Paul's. Seven were wholly or partly covered with gold, two being set with gems and one of these having figures of ivory. All but two of the silver-covered volumes were gilt, and several are mentioned as being set with gems or with ivory carvings. Unfortunately, with the exception of a volume with a gem-set silver-gilt cover which had been given by Edmund Earl of Cornwall (d. 1310), and the psalter of St. Thomas, which had a gem-set silver-gilt cover framing an ivory Majesty, there is no indication as to the date of any of these.

Though there are several other inventories providing fairly good descriptions of book-covers, they omit so much that is essential that we can only extract iconographical information from them.

[1] Dugdale, *St. Paul's*, 1818, 313.

[2] Legg and Hope, 78–79.

Iconography

Five-sixths of the book-covers listed in inventories from the thirteenth to the sixteenth century have as their principal decorative theme one or other of two subjects. When there was an ornamental back-cover, both subjects are represented. These were the *Crucifixion* (rarely without the attendant figures) and the *Majesty* (sometimes described as the *Doom*). Since the seated Christ on the rainbow was usually depicted within a *mandorla*, there was room for the symbols of the Evangelists in the corners. The *Holy Dove* and the *Agnus Dei* were also sometimes worked into the composition.

Subjects other than these appear quite rarely. The *Trinity* appears twice in the 1388 inventory of Westminster Abbey[1] (once in the space above the *Crucifixion*) and again in the 1552 inventory of St. Paul's.[2] In 1295 the same cathedral owned a cover with the *Ascension* in niello, and in the 1331 inventory of Canterbury Cathedral the *Annunciation* appears thrice. It also appeared with the *Presentation in the Temple* and the *Nativity*, presumably one above the other. The *Virgin and Child* were depicted on a cover mentioned in the 1222 inventory of Salisbury Cathedral,[3] whilst the *Assumption* was shown on a cover recorded in the 1388 inventory of Westminster Abbey.

B. CANDLESTICKS

Before the Reformation only a pair of candlesticks were ordinarily placed on the altar in English churches. As has been shown, the use of silver candlesticks was not very common, but there must have been many dozen scattered up and down England when the spoliation started. It would be easy to quote statistics of numbers and weights, but the compilers of inventories were very sparing of descriptive details.

In the 1245 inventory of St. Paul's occurs[4] the following:

Two old portable candlesticks of silver, with pierced feet chased with dragons.

Two candlesticks which were the property of R. de Storteford [chancellor in 1184] of pierced work, made with men riding upon lions.

Both pairs represent designs well known in bronze, but so far none of these have been attributed to England.[5] So far no silver examples of 'dragon' or 'Samson on the lion' candlesticks have come to light.

It is safe to assume that most of the silver candlesticks mentioned in inventories consisted merely of a moulded stem with some sort of knot, a round or polygonal grease-pan with pricket, and a base to match.

[1] *Archaeologia*, lii, 1890, 235.

[2] Walters, 77.

[3] *Registrum Sancti Osmundi*, Rolls Series, 1884, i. 127.

[4] *Archaeologia*, l, 1887, 468.

[5] Examples of both varieties of candlesticks in bronze are in the Victoria and Albert Museum. For a discussion of both types see O. von Falke and E. Meyer, *Bronzegeräte des Mittelalterse*, 1935.

When the period of spoliation began there were a few very elaborate altar candlesticks in use, the richest being a pair given to Lincoln Minster by John of Gaunt (d. 1399). They were of gold, weighing 450 ounces, and described as having 'a great knot with divers buttresses like to the fabric of a church or monastery . . . and at the top of the said candlesticks is a castellated and buttressed bowl with a spike for affixing the candle'.[1]

The next richest set turn up in the 1536 inventory of Salisbury Cathedral,[2] and the entry reads:

> Eight great and fair Candlesticks of Gold, they stand on bases pierced through like windows, and curiously ornate with dyvers workings and chasings in each of them, weighing 642 ounces.

There is no indication as to how they were disposed on or about the altar, but they must have been acquired since the making of the 1222 inventory, in which they do not appear.

On the 27th of December 1447 Cardinal Beaufort presented to the chantry of his father John of Gaunt, in St. Paul's, a pair of silver-gilt images of angels holding candlesticks, standing on square bases adorned with the arms of the donor.[3]

It would be easy to quote other examples of rich candlesticks of fancy designs, but enough has been said on the subject. It may have been noted that the dragon candlesticks in the St. Paul's inventory are described as being portable. Silver candlesticks for processional use occur infrequently in the inventories, and it is clear that the smaller varieties of altar candlesticks did duty at processions when it was deemed necessary to have candles at all.

C. CROSSES

If we begin with the largest type of cross and work down to the smallest, attention must first be focused upon those Benedictine cathedrals and abbeys which rose to prominence before the Conquest. In the inventory of the cathedral priory of St. Swithun at Winchester, taken at the time of its dissolution by Henry VIII, there is a heading, *Things that be abroad in the church.* Amongst these are:

> Item, Above that Altar a great Cros, and an Image of plate of gold garnished with stones. . . . Item, in the body of the Church a great Cross, and an Image of Christ

[1] *Archaeologia*, liii, 1892, 9 and 19. They disappeared before the 1548 inventory was compiled.

[2] *C.P. Wilts.* 239.

[3] *Archaeologia*, l, 1887, 520. Angel candlesticks are mentioned in inventories of Clare College, Cambridge (*R. Commission on Historical Manuscripts, 2nd Report*, 1873, 111), Fotheringhay College (*Arch. Journal*, lxi, 1904, 261), and Westminster Abbey (*London and Middlesex Arch. Soc. Trans.* iv, 1873, 317).

and Mary and John, being of plate silver and partly gilt. . . . Item, A cross of plate of silver and gilt with an Image over the Iron dore. And the two Images of Mary and John are but Copper gilt.[1]

The second of these was probably the cross with images which Archbishop Stigand had had made from the proceeds of the gifts of Queen Emma, and which is recorded with admiration in the *Annales de Wintonia*.[2]

Winchester may have been exceptional in preserving, until the reign of Henry VIII, three of these large crosses, but the species was certainly represented elsewhere. In the dissolution inventory of Canterbury Cathedral Priory is mentioned 'the grete Rode cov'ed wth Sylver',[3] and we know that the neighbouring abbey of St. Augustine had also once possessed, as a gift from Archbishop Stigand, 'a great cross covered on all sides with silver', which stood on the pulpitum.[4] It is unlikely that many of these large crosses were made after the Conquest and some were doubtless stripped and destroyed during the ensuing disturbances.[5] Up to the Reformation, however, there stood at the end of the south choir aisle of Durham Cathedral 'the Black Rood of Scotland'[6] which had been captured at the battle of Neville's Cross in 1346, and which King David insisted on taking out of Holyrood Abbey before starting on his disastrous expedition. Since the abbey had only been founded in 1128, the 'Black Rood' was probably amongst the latest of its sort.

When the thirteenth-century English bishops began to list the ornaments which they considered to be necessary for parish churches, they mentioned two crosses, one for processions and the other for the office of the dead. We need not bother further about the latter, which never provided work for goldsmiths. Bishop Quivil, at his Exeter synod of 1287, stipulated for 'two crosses; one fixed and the other portable'.[7] If this was the first attempt at ordering that there should be a cross upon the altar, that is all that need be said about it. The other bishops, who had only stipulated for a processional cross, knew that if their injunctions were effective each church could at least use the head of its processional cross upon the altar. Bishop Quivil's approach to the problem was proved wrong. If we look at the lists of church ornaments in the *Registers of*

[1] J. Strype, *Memorials of Thomas Cranmer*, 1812, ii. 709. The space which had been occupied by the first of these is clearly visible in a photograph of the great screen after the removal of the seventeenth-century reredos. See G. W. Kitchen, *The Great Screen of Winchester Cathedral*, 1892, 15.

[2] *Annales Monastici*, Rolls Series, 1865, ii. 25 and 30.

[3] Legg and Hope, 192.

[4] Twysden, *Historiae Angliae Scriptores Decem*, 1652, cols. 1785–6.

[5] Thus, during the Danish invasion of 1069 Hereward encouraged a party of the invaders to occupy Peterborough Abbey, which was on the point of receiving a new Norman abbot. The Danes tried to carry off the rood, but finding it too large contented themselves with the gold and jewelled crown and the *suppedaneum* (Chronicle of Hugh Candidus in J. Sparke, *Historiae Anglicanae Scriptores Varii*, 1723, 49).

[6] *Rites*, 18.

[7] Wilkins, *Concilia*, ii. 139.

Walter de Stapledon[1] we shall note that the churches of Devon were still deficient in altar crosses a hundred years later. Most of the churches were, doubtless, actually using the head of their processional cross upon the altar.

Perhaps we have rather digressed, since neither Bishop Quivil nor his more level-headed colleagues would have dared to suggest that parish churches should have silver processional or altar crosses. Already in 1220 the church of Heytesbury,[2] Wilts., had two crosses covered with silver and one of copper, but down to the reign of Edward VI silver crosses were only to be found in wealthy parish churches.

Only the smallest oratory crosses were made of solid silver. All the larger crosses had a core of wood sheathed with silver, which was often engraved, embossed, or chased. The crucifix and the other figures in whole or in half relief might be either cast or else raised. The cross slotted into the stem, and just above the knot there might be two further sockets into which fitted branches carrying figures of the Virgin and St. John. Beneath the knop was a large socket which could fit either on to a staff for use processionally or else on to a base to stand on the altar. Not all of these features were invariable. Some crosses did not have the side figures and, since many crosses are mentioned without special reference to either staff or foot, it is likely that these were to some extent pooled.[3]

With the help of wills and inventories we may now attempt to recapture something of the appearance of a few medieval crosses. Reliable information is much more abundant with regard to those belonging to cathedrals, abbeys, colleges, and private chapels. The descriptions of crosses in parish church inventories and in churchwardens' accounts tend to be meagre, since the compilers were seldom faced with the embarrassment of having to produce an account which would distinguish one cross from another. Similarly, their crosses were not so elaborate that an intricate description was necessary in order to draw attention to deficiencies.

We may begin with the description in a fifteenth-century inventory of Lincoln Minster of a cross which must have been associated with Richard, Earl of Cornwall, before he laid claim to the Empire in 1257. It may be translated:

> Item a cross of crystal with a crucifix of silver-gilt and a socket having a knop of silver-gilt with the arms of England, France, and Cornwall on divers shields and with divers stones set in it. It has four joints, back and front, and on the back the Lamb

[1] Ed. F. C. Hingeston-Randolph, 1892, *passim*.

[2] *Register of St. Osmund*, Rolls Series, 1884, i. 295.

[3] This seems certainly to have been the case of the cross-staves at Canterbury and Westminster Abbey, as appears from the dissolution inventories of both (Legg and Hope, 182, and *London and Middlesex Arch. Soc. Trans.* iv, 1874, 320).

in silver-gilt and with divers stones of different colours and with the Four Evangelists at the four ends. The gift of Master Roger de Morval, Weight 47 oz.[1]

As far as we can gather from the three descriptions of this cross, it was intended entirely for processional use. Crystal crosses appear to have been rather popular for use in the Easter ceremonies[2] though this is not specifically stated in the present case.

It seems rather surprising that a private chapel should have required a processional cross, but in her will Lady Margaret Beaufort bequeathed to Christ's College, Cambridge, 'On [*sic*] crucifix, silver and gilt, with Mary and John, full gilt and enamyled to beare in processions . . . a hole garnyssh for a crosse staff, gilt and enamyled to beyre the said crucifix in procession'.[3]

Towards the close of the Middle Ages there existed in England a small group of very rich altar crosses which far surpassed any of the processional crosses or processional/altar crosses. The richest of all was one which had been commissioned by Richard II and which can be traced through the inventories[4] down to 1550. It was of gold set with all sorts of precious stones and decked out with the king's badge of the white hart. The descriptions, however, are not quite so good as are those of the silver-gilt cross given by his cousin, Cardinal Beaufort, to the chantry of John of Gaunt in St. Paul's in 1447. It may be rendered as follows:

A cross of silver-gilt of outstanding beauty and fine workmanship, with images of the Crucified, Mary and John, and of the Four Evangelists at the four corners. A figure of the Majesty is in the middle behind the Crucifix. Leaves spread out freely from the side of the cross and from under the brackets for Mary and John. The said cross stands on a very beautiful base decorated with branches and vine-leaves and splended enamels and rests on four lions. The said base has a stem in the middle of the form of a tower with pinnacles, windows and turrets. In the middle of the front is an image of St. Paul and in the corresponding position behind, one of St. Peter. The cross and base together weigh nineteen marks and seventeen ounces troy and are twenty-six inches high.[5]

Another account of the base discloses that it had sixteen towers, great and small, round the outer enceinte and seventeen round the inner.

Roods, processional and altar crosses formed the principal varieties that were decorated in the precious metals. Cross-monstrances will be described later on (p. 82).

[1] *Archaeologia*, liii, 1892, 8.

[2] Rock, *The Church of our Fathers*, ed. Hunt and Frere, 1904, 290–1.

[3] C. H. Cooper, *Memoirs of Margaret, Countess of Derby and Richmond*, 1874, 130.

[4] First mentioned in Palgrave, ii. 118, but the best description is in the 1521 inventory of the royal plate (*Assoc. Architectural Soc. Reports*, xvii, 1884, 163).

[5] *Archaeologia*, l, 1887, 519–20.

In the later Middle Ages both the processional and the altar cross might be used as a receptacle for relics. In the earlier centuries there existed a type of reliquary cross which was really a species of *filacterium*. It was quite small and had neither base nor socket, but was suspended from a loop at the top.

A fair claim for inclusion in this class can be made for a small cross in the Victoria and Albert Museum.[1] It consists of a core of fine-grained wood plated with gold. On the front (Pl. 39*a*) is an ivory Crucifix which is surrounded with filigree scrolls. At the four angles are roundels depicting the symbols of the Evangelists and at the top is a *titulus*, all of which are in cloisonné enamel. The covering of the back (Pl. 39*b*) is lightly embossed with roundels with the symbols of the Evangelists and with the Agnus Dei in the middle. A very lightly incised marginal inscription, which is partly illegible and partly missing, gives a list of relics. The cross was the subject of a study by H. P. Mitchell,[2] whose conclusion that the ivory figure was made in England *c.* 1000 has been generally accepted. With regard to the goldsmith's work he hesitated between an English or a German origin, finally coming down rather on the side of the latter on the ground that the enamels were similar to those also representing the symbols of the Evangelists on the cover of the 'Perikope of Henry', a manuscript formerly belonging to Bamberg Cathedral and now in the Staatsbibliothek, Munich.[3] The resemblance of the enamels, as far as the colours are concerned, is undeniable, but proves little. The Perikope is also decorated with pieces from divers sources, including a group of Byzantine cloisonné enamels, so that it cannot be claimed as being any more homogeneous than the cross, which can therefore be fairly claimed as having been put together in England in about the year 1000. The importance of this addition to the brief list of examples of late Anglo-Saxon goldsmiths' work should not be exaggerated. The distinction of the piece is confined to the ivory carving and the enamels (the source from which these last came must be regarded as quite uncertain). The quality of the filigree decoration and of the embossed work is poor, and neither provides any decisive evidence of the place of manufacture. Mitchell was equally unable to make any useful deductions from the list of relics.

D. FRONTALS AND RETABLES

It is unfortunate that in medieval times the name 'table' (*tabula*) was used both for what we now call an altar-frontal and also for the retable above and behind the altar.

[1] No. 7943–1862. Acquired at the sale of the Soltikoff Collection.

[2] *Burlington Magazine*, xlvii, 1925, 324–30.

[3] No. Clm. 4452. The latest discussion of the cover is in W. Messerer, *Der Bamberger Domschatz*, Munich, 1952.

Many English churches of the first rank possessed 'tables' decorated with gold and silver already in Anglo-Saxon times and although we come across references to the destruction of examples during the succeeding centuries, there were still quite a number to send up to the royal treasury when Henry VIII started on his campaign of church robbery. The demand for altar-frontals seems to have been at its height during the hundred and fifty years after the Conquest. We know that the abbey of Ely supplied itself with three between 1079 and 1093.[1] Most important cathedrals and abbeys contented themselves with one. Abbot Geoffrey supplied St. Albans with 'a table skilfully made of gold and silver and set with choice gems', but had the mortification of having to condemn it to the melting-pot in 1142 in order to prevent the abbey being burnt down when the abbey knights got involved in a skirmish with some of Stephen's supporters who were trying to arrest Geoffrey de Mandeville.[2] Perhaps this sad story discouraged Abbot John de Cella (1195–1214) from replacing it with one of comparable value, since he contented himself by ordering 'a great table, partly of wood and partly of metal, most skilfully made'.[3]

The ambiguity as between frontal and retable only becomes acute after the twelfth century, since the latter was a comparatively late development. Thus at Bury St. Edmunds the silver frontal was made in the time of Abbot Ording (1148–56), whilst the silver-gilt retable followed only in the first years of the thirteenth century.[4]

Triptych retables were already in use by the middle of the fourteenth century, as in the 1506 inventory of Exeter Cathedral the one presented by Bishop Grandison (1328–64), is described as follows:

> A folding silver table with the Crucifix, Mary and John in the middle and with Twelve Apostles and with other figures below, the gift of John de Grandison, as is evident from the back. The crest lacks nine flowers.[5]

The adornment of the high altar of Canterbury Cathedral was one of the achievements of Prior Chillendon (1390–1411). It may well have been one of the richest in England, but the descriptions of it are most obscure. However, we know that Archbishop Courtenay (1381–96) contributed figures of the Apostles and one of the Trinity, all of silver-gilt and costing £340.[6]

[1] *Liber Eliensis*, 1848, 249 and 282.

[2] T. Walsingham, *Gesta Abbatum*, Rolls Series, 1867, i. 93–94.

[3] Ibid. 232. Metal in this context would mean copper-gilt. Altar-frontals of this material were certainly not common in this country, and it is interesting to reflect that St. Albans had special contacts with Denmark at this period (see pp. 5–6), when the manufacture of copper-gilt frontals was in full swing there (Poul Nørlund, *Gyldne Altre*, 1926). Thus Master John of St. Albans, who worked on the shrine of St. Alban, could have seen the earlier of the copper-gilt frontals in Jutland whilst working for Waldemar I (1157–82).

[4] *Memorials of St. Edmund's Abbey*, Rolls Series, 1894, ii. 290 and 292.

[5] Oliver, 322.

[6] Legg and Hope, 101 and 107–9.

The retable at St. George's Chapel, Windsor, took the form of a diptych. One leaf had an inscription on the outside and the Crucifixion inside. The other had a plain wooden outside and relics inside.[1]

E. LECTERNS

Silver-mounted book-rests for use on the altar were very rare. An example is mentioned in the dissolution inventory of the college at Fotheringhay, Northants., but it only reveals that it was parcel-gilt and weighed 49 ounces.[2]

Another appears first in 1439[3] amongst the furnishing of the Chapel Royal, and is described as:

> Furst a lectrō̃ of silver ov' gilt wᵗ a fote in the maner of a tabernacle standing upon iiij fete.

This is amplified in the 1521[4] inventory of the royal plate, where it reappears as:

> A Deske of tymber plated with silver and gilte. A Goodely worke wayng to gidders with the said tymber clxxx oz.

F. PAXES

In the days of the primitive church the members of the congregation gave each other at mass the kiss of peace. As time went on the custom was modified so that men only kissed men, whilst women kissed women. The first evidence for the use of an object which could be handed round and kissed instead is found in England, and since the *osculatorium* is mentioned without comment as an object which every parish church should possess both in the constitutions of Walter Grey, Archbishop of York, in 1250,[5] and the statutes of John Peckham, Archbishop of Canterbury, in 1280,[6] it is clear that the use of some sort of pax was already in general use in England in the second half of the thirteenth century, though foreign references only begin in the early years of the fourteenth.

What also appears clear is that the pax[7] started at parish level and worked its way upwards until it reached the great abbeys and cathedrals. As a consequence of this we only begin to hear of silver paxes in the second half of the fourteenth

[1] M. F. Bond, *Inventories of St. George's Chapel, Windsor*, 1947, 56.

[2] *Arch. Journal*, lxi, 1904, 261.

[3] Palgrave, iii. 378, also ii. 250.

[4] *Assoc. Architectural Soc. Reports*, xvii, 1884, 211.

[5] D. Wilkins, *Concilia Magnae Britanniae et Hiberniae*, 1737, i. 698.

[6] Ibid. ii. 49. In Bishop Quivil's synod at Exeter in 1287 the object is called an *asser ad pacem* (ibid. 139).

[7] The pax or pax-brede got its name from the words *pax vobiscum* which the giver said as he passed the object to the recipient.

century. It would seem that they already took the form of a small, upright, oblong panel, sometimes with an arched top, framing some sort of religious subject and furnished with a handle on the back. Though by the beginning of the fifteenth century every important abbey and cathedral had one or more silver paxes, they are frequently found allocated to one of the minor altars. This would seem to suggest that they mostly derived from private chapels and had not been made for places in which they are recorded. In the list of plate, mainly given by Bishop William of Wykeham, belonging to Winchester College, no fewer than seven silver paxes are listed, but most of the richest paxes are mentioned amongst the contents of the chapels of the laity, who were often not content with a single example.

About four-fifths of the paxes of which we have any details were decorated with a Crucifix or the Crucifixion, so that it is no strange coincidence that both the two known examples show the latter. The other subjects used are mostly derived from the common stock of late medieval objects of devotion—the Trinity,[1] the Virgin and Child,[2] the Vernicle, St. Peter and St. Paul,[2] and St. Christopher.[3] Less usual are two mentioned in the 1521 inventory of the royal plate, one of silver-gilt being decorated with St. Jerome,[4] whilst the other is described as follows:

> Item a paxe of golde of the Baptym of Criste garnisshed wt x Rubyes and xxiiij garnisshing pearlis and a Saphure Sett in the Toppe.

In the general way we learn little from these records except the material, subject depicted, and the weight. In one Vernicle paxes belonging to John de Vere, the subject was executed in mother-of-pearl.[5] Enamel is frequently mentioned; in some cases it was used for the central subject and at others for decorating the frame.

Surviving English base-metal paxes belong to several different types, but the two surviving silver examples are alike in essentials. Both consist of an upright oblong frame with a cast cresting and depressed centre enclosing a representation of the Crucifixion. In the example formerly in the possession of Lord Lee of Fareham the figures are engraved (Pl. 40*a*), but in the one belonging to New College, Oxford, they are cast and applied (Pl. 40*b*). The former must date from about 1480 and is of inferior craftsmanship. Though the engraver has come to grief over the figures of Mary and John, his Christ possesses great dignity and must have been copied from a really good design. The engraver of the New College pax, which must be dated about 1520, was, on the other hand,

[1] Westminster Abbey (*London and Middlesex Arch. Soc. Trans.* iv, 1873, 319).

[2] Winchester College (*Arch. Journal*, x, 1853, 237–8).

[3] Owen ap Meredith (Palgrave, ii. 173).

[4] *Assoc. Architectural Soc. Reports*, xvii, 1884, 165).

[5] John de Vere (*Archaeologia*, lxv, 1914, 335).

thoroughly competent and was able to make the most of the fanciful design on the frame. The cast figures of the Crucifixion are clearly from stock patterns which, though good enough in their way, could have been made very much finer with some careful chasing.

G. VESSELS FOR THE SACRAMENT

Any attempt to describe the vessels used in connexion with the Reservation of the Sacrament is made difficult by the fact that during the later Middle Ages the sacramental usages were changing rapidly, whilst the greatest lack of concision prevailed with reference to the names used for the various utensils employed.

It is hardly necessary to mention that the Reservation of the Sacrament was the universal practice in the churches of England down to the Reformation. It was the character of the devotions used in connexion with the Reserved Sacrament which were evolving and giving occasion for the introduction of new types of sacramental plate. The pieces now to be considered may be divided into two categories:

(*a*) Those used in connexion with the actual Reservation.
(*b*) Those used in connexion with sacramental devotions, including exposition.

It is virtually impossible to form any opinion as to the manner of Reservation in use up to the Norman Conquest, or the types of vessels employed. By the twelfth century the Sacrament was usually preserved in a vessel hung over the altar by a rope passing over a pulley, so that it could be lowered at will. This remained the normal practice for the remainder of the Middle Ages, but it should be noted that the vessel was not normally visible, since it was concealed by a canopy. This last might be attached to a silver crown.

A number of different names were used for the vessel containing the Sacrament, the most usual being pyx (*pixis*) or cup (*cuppa*). The various names denote difference of form rather than of function, the pyx being merely a little box, whilst the cup resembled the covered cups in secular use. Ordinarily the host was placed directly inside the pyx or cup, but sometimes there was an inner case (*capsula*) for it. Thus Godfrey of Croyland, Abbot of Peterborough (1299–1321), presented 'a silver-gilt cup with three chains and a silver circlet and within it a silver-gilt case for the Corpus Christi'.[1] On the other hand, references to chains and crowns and circlets are relatively uncommon, so that it may be inferred that normally the pyx or cup was merely placed in some sort of box attached to the rope.

[1] Walter of Whytlesey, *Coenobii Burgi Historia* in Sparke, *Historiae Anglicanae Scriptores Varii*, 1723, ii. 170.

Certainly the only surviving English pyxes, silver or base metal, are without any means of attachment, and this is true also of many foreign examples.[1] Since there was a danger of the pyx opening and of the host dropping out if lowered carelessly, the episcopal injunctions[2] sometimes stipulate for an adequate fastening for the pyx, and visitation articles make frequent allusion to the same point.[3]

It is difficult to visualize the standard patterns for silver pyxes and cups, since at present only one of the former is known and there is no agreed example of the latter.[4]

The Swinburne pyx (Pls. 42, 43) is a cylindrical box with a flat cover secured by a bayonet joint, and was originally decorated with translucent enamel. The side is engraved with an arcade, but the subjects which once filled the arches have been obliterated. The cover and bottom are both formed of two plaques framed back to back. The top of the cover shows the Virgin and Child, whilst inside is the Nativity. Inside the bottom is the head of Christ and outside the Agnus Dei. The pyx can be dated about 1310, since two of the designs are derived from the same source as the illustrations in two English manuscripts of about that date.[5] In its original condition it must have been an extremely beautiful little object, and even in its present state it is a reminder of the high quality attained by English goldsmiths' work in the early years of the fourteenth century.

For the rest we have to fall back upon literary sources which are seldom

[1] But abroad there were other ways of disposing of the pyx.

[2] Constitutions of William de Blois, Bishop of Worcester 1229 (Wilkins, *Concilia*, i. 623); Bishop Quivil's synod at Exeter, 1287 (ibid. ii. 139).

[3] e.g. the visitation of the prebendal churches of the cathedral of Sarum in 1220 (*Registrum Sancti Osmundi*, Rolls Series, 1884, 276–313) and the Visitation of some Devon churches in 1301 (F. C. Hingeston-Randolph, *Register of Walter de Stapledon, Bishop of Exeter*, 1892, *passim*). Probably the sort of unseemly incident was not uncommon which occurred on Candlemas Day, 1140, when Stephen was attending mass and the rope holding the pyx broke and the host dropped on to the altar, as the fastening of the pyx was also defective. The story got into a number of chronicles (e.g. Ralph Diceto, *Opera*, Rolls Series, 1876, i. 253); as Stephen was captured shortly after at the battle of Lincoln, the mishap was regarded as an omen.

[4] Recently Dr. Hanns Swarzenski (*Monuments of Romanesque Art*, 1954, 77, pl. 198, figs. 457–9) has claimed as English, *c.* 1175, the well-known bottom of a 'cup' from the Dune hoard in the National Museum, Stockholm, and the one formerly in the Basilewsky Collection, Leningrad, and now in the Metropolitan Museum, New York. Both are of nielloed silver decorated with monsters, or men and monsters, amidst scrolled foliage. Indubitably this was a popular artistic theme in England, but it was used also elsewhere, and I am not entirely convinced of the error of the traditional attribution to southern France.

[5] The illustrations are in Cambridge University Library, MS. Dd. 417 (Pl. 43 *a, d*), and Corpus Christi College, Cambridge, MS. 53. I discussed the whole history of the pyx in an article in the *Burlington Magazine*, xcii, 1950, 337–41, written at the time that it was acquired for the Victoria and Albert Museum. A further note was published by A. L. Raimes in *Proc. Soc. Antiquaries of Newcastle-upon-Tyne*, 5th ser. i, 1951, 66–68, dealing with the history of the ownership of the piece.

very explicit. An item added to the 1410 inventory of St. George's Chapel, Windsor, suggests that pyxes of this pattern were still being manufactured a hundred years later. It is described as a 'pyx of silver-gilt enamelled on the top with the image of the Vernicle and in the bottom both within and without with the Agnus Dei'. The pyx had probably not been made very long before it reached St. George's, since in 1410 the cult of the Vernicle was comparatively new in England.[1]

A silver-gilt pyx decorated with the Twelve Apostles and with the royal arms upon the bottom was amongst the plate with which Henry VI endowed King's College, Cambridge.[2] As is mentioned elsewhere, the pyxes to be made under the will of Henry VII were to have been of silver-gilt 'garnished with our arms, and red roses and portcullises crowned'.[3]

The form and material of pyxes was not entirely unaffected by the growth of the cult of the Corpus Christi, to which we shall have to return anon. The standing pyx, equipped with a foot, which appears rather to have supplanted the 'cup' at the end of the Middle Ages, was, of course, much more impressive when used processionally. Moreover, the desire to see the host was another factor of increasing importance. This was sometimes met by the use of crystal pyxes. Thus, in the dissolution inventory of Winchester Cathedral Priory are mentioned 'nine pixes of Christal, partly garnished with silver and gilt'.[4] A standing pyx with a crystal body was virtually a monstrance, as, for instance, one which appears in the 1536 inventory of Lincoln Minster,[5] which is described as:

> a rownd pyx of Cristall havyng a fote of sylver and gylte w^t^ one Image of ow^r^ lady yn the topp havyng a place for the sacrament for the rogacian days weyng xxi unces j quarter & dim.

No standing pyx has survived in its entirety, but when the churchwardens of St. Martin Ludgate decided to get a communion cup in the reign of Elizabeth I, they did so by fitting a new bowl on to the foot and stem of a standing pyx (Pl. 41*a*) with the hall-mark for 1507. Around the top of the lobed hexagonal foot is a band of tracery which masks the junction with the stem, as on some sixteenth-century chalices. The knot has its top and bottom spirally gadrooned and has round its middle a ribbon which is broken into sections by an ornament resembling coiled rope. It is possible to imagine several forms of upper part. All that is known, however, is that part of it must have been of

[1] M. F. Ford, *Inventories of St. George's Chapel, Windsor*, 1947, 116.

[2] *Ecclesiologist*, xviii, 1860, 5.

[3] H. Nicholas, *Testamenta Vetusta*, 1826, 33.

[4] Strype, *Memorials of Thomas Cranmer*, 1812, ii. 711.

[5] *Archaeologia*, liii, 1892, 18.

crystal, as the object is described in the will as 'oon pixe or monstre' (monstrance).[1]

The vessels already mentioned have all been of what we may suppose to have been normal designs. It is now necessary to say something of the exceptional ones. The idea of making a pyx in the form of a dove was well-known all over Europe in the twelfth and thirteenth centuries, but the only silver examples which are recorded in this country hung above the high altars of Battle Abbey[2] and Salisbury Cathedral.[3] Prior Chillendon (1390–1411) provided for Canterbury Cathedral[4] 'an image of the blessed Virgin with four angels of silver-gilt and in the hand of the Virgin a cup of pure gold with gems, for placing the Corpus Christi in, able to be pulled up or let down at will'. In 1545 King Henry VIII's College, Oxford, had 'a pixe of thymage of God, gilte, weing 33 ounces'. It had doubtless been inherited from the Augustinian house of St. Frideswide.[5]

It is now necessary to consider the vessels made in connexion with the carrying of the unexposed Sacrament in procession. The simplest sort of procession was, of course, that of the visitation of the sick. Special vessels seem seldom to have been detailed for this purpose, though St. Benet's,[6] Cambridge, possessed in 1396 'a cup gilte outside with a gilt cover given by Dame Alice Chaumberleyn for this use that the Corpus Christi may be carried to sick parishioners'. More ordinarily the object is described as a little box,[7] so that it is probable that it was not unlike those used nowadays, which are like old-fashioned 'hunter' watches.

[1] Under the foot is pounced the following inscription:

praye | for the | salle of | ſtewyn | pekoc | & marg | et hys | wyff wy | che ga | ve thys [i]n · the · w | uſſheppe | of the | ſacrement.

The piece is no less interesting for the sidelight which it throws on the ethics of the Reformation period. It was bequeathed to the church under the will of Sir Stephen Pecocke, dated 17 January 1535. It was then twenty-eight years old, and since City knights did not commonly run elaborately furnished chapels, it may be guessed that the testator had picked it up second-hand. It may well have come from one of the religious houses in East Anglia dissolved by Wolsey—the Pecockes, like the Cardinal, came from that area. Lady Pecocke must have begged it back from the churchwardens when the threat of spoliation threatened the parish churches in the reign of Edward VI, for in the 1552 inventory it was noted:

> M[d] that there Remayneth in thandes of the executours of the late lady Pecock these parcelles hereafter mencyoned. . . . Item a pyx of sylver all gylt weyinge ix ounces & a halffe.

Doubtless the executors held on to it until Mary came to the throne (*Proc. Soc. Antiquaries*, 2nd ser. xvii, 1899, 330–2).

[2] *Chronicon monasterii de Bello*, 1846, 138.

[3] *Registrum Sancti Osmundi*, ii. 129.

[4] Legg and Hope, 107–8. A similar piece in St. Stephen's Chapel, Westminster, included also a representation of the Trinity (*London and Middlesex Arch. Soc. Trans.* iv, 1873, 373).

[5] *Cartulary of the Monastery of St. Frideswide*, Oxford Hist. Soc. ii, 1896, 383.

[6] *Cambridge Antiquarian Soc.* xvii, 1911, 12.

[7] 'a lytell box of sylver to bere the sacrament in when the pryst dothe vyset', as it is described in the Edwardian inventory of All Hallows in Grimley parish, Worcs. (*Assoc. Architectural Soc.* xi, 1871, 322).

Down to the reign of Henry VIII the ordinary parish had only got some sort of pyx or 'cup' such as has already been described, for carrying the Sacrament in procession, but by that date cathedrals, abbeys, and even important parish churches had often something which might be classed as a monstrance. Before there arose any question of carrying the Sacrament exposed, the abbey of St. Albans had been provided with a sort of portable shrine of which Matthew Paris has left us a tolerably intelligible description:[1]

Abbot Simon (1166–89) presented to God and the church of the holy martyr Alban, for its eternal honour and adornment, a marvellous vessel fashioned in the form of a casket . . . the lid, indeed, is gabled in the form of a shrine, and on either side it is decorated with roundels in relief in which are shown with cast figures the story of the Lord's Passion, whilst the whole, including the base and the supports are covered with good solid plates.

The abbot's intention was that this shrine should be carried in procession on the shoulders of two of the brethren on Palm Sunday. Whilst he was obviously anxious to encourage sacramental devotions, it is clear that it would not have seemed proper to him to order a shrine in which the Sacrament could be seen by the faithful.[2]

The Feast of the Corpus Christi originated in the Liège district in the middle of the thirteenth century and was extended to the whole Western church by Urban IV in 1264. The accident that this pope died within a month of issuing the bull resulted in the affair getting shelved for half a century until further action was taken by Clement V in 1311 and John XXII in 1317. It is not surprising, therefore, that in England references to pieces which may fairly be called monstrances only become frequent after 1350. There was never any standard design for them, though we can distinguish several varieties.

Cross monstrances appear to have been a recognized type in the second half of the fourteenth century. Exeter Cathedral came to possess two of them, the earlier being a benefaction of Bishop John de Grandison (1328–69). It was of silver-gilt and stood upon a big foot, gilt and enamelled, resting on four lions. The cross was supported by two angels and had a Crucifix and figures of Mary and John at the top, and in the middle a glass behind which the Corpus could be placed. The other was a gift from John Holland, Earl of Huntingdon (1387–99), the unsavoury half-brother of Richard II, and differed from the first only in details.[3] It may be noted that in both examples the base formed an

[1] T. Walsingham, *Gesta Abbatum*, Rolls Series, 1867, i. 191–2.

[2] This sentiment lasted long. Thus in the very elaborate 'solempnitie of array for the fest of Corpus Christi' bequeathed in 1449 by William Bruges, Garter King of Arms, to St. George's, Stamford, the Sacrament was placed in a little silver box inside a 'cup' of the same material. H. Nicholas, *Testamenta Vetusta*, 1826, 367–8.

[3] Oliver, 321.

essential part of the whole, so that they must have been carried in procession on some sort of bier. On the other hand, a crystal cross mentioned in the 1402 inventory of St. Paul's was equipped with both a staff and a base.[1]

Reliquary monstrances date from the same period.[2] Two are mentioned in the 1384 inventory of St. George's Chapel, Windsor. The first showed two angels supporting a crystal bier inside which was placed the Corpus. It was surmounted by an enamelled cross. In front was a small kneeling angel holding a crystal vase for relics. The other was a gift from Thomas of Woodstock, the troublesome uncle of Richard II, and was a tabernacle with a crystal for the Corpus. It also contained two fingers of St. George.[3]

Large architectural compositions appear at about the same date. Abbot Thomas de la Mare (1349–96) equipped St. Albans with 'a silver-gilt tower . . . in which the Corpus Christi is carried about, and can clearly be seen by the people. It has in the lower part of the same tower, in silver-gilt, a Resurrection of Christ, with two angels and four soldiers guarding the sepulchre.'[4]

This required four bearers, so that it was clearly much larger than Abbot Simon's shrine, which is never afterwards mentioned.

Image monstrances were a development of the idea of the image reliquary. The image was inevitably that of the Christ of the Resurrection and they were designed especially for use on Easter Day. The example which belonged to Lincoln Cathedral[5] is described as follows:

> an Image of our Saviour, silver and guilt, standing uppon 6 lions, void in the brest for ye Sacrament for Easter day, haveing a berall before, and a Diademe behind wth a Crosse in hand weighing xxxi unces.

The weight shows that this was not a large piece and, indeed, a similar example mentioned in a sixteenth-century inventory of St. Peter Mancroft, Norwich, weighed 53½ ounces.[6]

Though, as has already been said, most parish churches owned no sort of monstrance before the Reformation, a few had more than one. Thus in 1466 the church of St. Stephen, Coleman Street, had no less than three.[7] One was a Risen Christ. The other two are described as 'a monstrance of sylv^{r} for the

[1] *Archaeologia*, l, 1887, 514.

[2] There is a good account of early continental reliquary-monstrances in an article by Michel Andrieu in *Analecta Bollandiana*, lxviii, 1950, 397–418.

[3] M. F. Bond, *Inventories of St. George's Chapel, Windsor*, 1947, 54 and 56. Thomas of Woodstock also gave a monstrance to Westminster Abbey (*Archaeologia*, lii, 1889, 226).

[4] J. Amundesham, *Annales*, Rolls Series, 1870, ii. 334; T. Walsingham, op. cit. iii. 383.

[5] *Archaeologia*, liii, 1895, 45.

[6] In a note upon the celebrated 'Rheims Reliquary' Dr. Joan Evans recently drew attention to the fact that it closely resembles the Resurrection monstrances recorded in English inventories. Her further suggestion that it might, indeed, be English appears to me rather less probable. I am inclined to attribute it to Flanders (*Antiquaries Journal*, xxxv, 1955, 52–54).

[7] *Archaeologia*, l, 1887, 34.

sacrament w^{t} the hande of our lady', whilst the other was 'j mone of sylv to ber the sac^{t}'. This last serves as a reminder that quite humble examples existed in addition to the masterpieces of goldsmiths' work with which we have been mainly concerned.

H. PYXES FOR UNCONSECRATED HOSTS

References to silver 'Boxes for Singing Bread' are relatively rare. This is probably to be explained partly by the use of boxes of inferior materials for storing the unconsecrated hosts and partly to the use of any ordinary pyx which was not being used for its primary purpose.

Descriptions of these boxes are even rarer. One mentioned in the 1550 inventory of the royal plate was of silver-gilt chased with the initials H and K, roses, portcullises, and fleurs-de-lis.[1] It must clearly have dated from the period when Henry was united to Catherine of Aragon, but it is curious that it appears to have borne no indication of its religious use. Another, in an early sixteenth-century inventory of York Minster, bore the inscription *Elige de optimis*.[2]

[1] B.M. Add. MS. 46348, f. 43^{r}.

[2] *Fabric Rolls of York Minster*, Surtees Soc. 1858, 221.

VII

MISCELLANEA

A. AMPULLAE AND CHRISMATORIES

IT has been remarked elsewhere that it is frequently difficult to distinguish in medieval inventories between ampullae used for the holy oils and the cruets used for the wine and water for mass. Silver ampullae were only found amongst the furnishing of important churches, and no examples are at present known. As in the case of cruets, the contents of the vessels was sometimes distinguished by the colour of the latter. Thus in the 1315 inventory of Canterbury Cathedral[1] there are mentioned two sets of three ampullae, each including one that was gilt. Descriptions are most uninformative and we can do little more than assume that they were shaped like measures. Some probably had a slot in the lid for a spoon, but the latter are not at all frequently specified. By way of example we may quote a description from a fifteenth-century inventory of Lincoln Minster:[2]

In primis A Ampull playn w^t^ a foote, silver and gylte and a cover chased parcellgylte w^t^ broken gemelles [hinges] and a spone w^t^ an Akorn, ordeyned for crem [chrism].

Item one other Ampull sylver w^t^ a cover chased w^t^ a spone w^t^ an Akorn ordeyned for Oleum Sanctum.

Item A nother Ampull w^t^ broken gymelles w^t^ a cover chased and a spone havyng an Akorn of the end, ordeyned for Oleum Infirmorum.

In the 1506 inventory of Exeter Cathedral we get a description of what must have been an exceptionally beautiful set of fourteenth-century date. It consisted of two gilt and of one parcel-gilt vessels. One of the gilt vessels was decorated with figures of a pope, a king, and a bishop, the other with trees and leaves, whilst the third had grapes and vine-leaves.[3]

In the 1245 inventory of St. Paul's[4] are mentioned two poor portable ampullae for oil with chains, but examples specified as portable are rare. Though we need not imagine that any of the pieces mentioned were large, they were all larger than was dictated by necessity, and this consideration was not negligible in view of the fact that the *oleum infirmorum* was not used at all in church.

1 Legg and Hope, 73.

2 *Archaeologia*, liii, 1892, 23.

3 Oliver, 325. The first cruet was clearly intended for chrism. As I failed to recognize the appropriateness of the decoration of the other two, I referred the problem to Dom Aelred Watkin, O.S.B. He suggested that the vessel decorated with trees was for the Oil of the Sick, as the blessing of the oil makes mention of palm-trees. The third would have to be the Oil of the Catechumens and the vine-leaves and grapes an allusion to John xv. 4–5.

4 *Archaeologia*, 1887, 467.

The chrismatory, a case fitted with three small oil flasks, was a concession to utility which had probably originated in bishops' chapels; two had reached St. Paul's by 1245. One of these had belonged to Bishop Gilbert Foliot (1163–7) and had a wooden foundation covered with sheets of silver embossed with figures. In the later Middle Ages cathedrals and abbeys continued to own ampullae, though there was often a chrismatory as well. By the fourteenth century parish churches were beginning to own silver chrismatories. They were not common, and Archdeacon Swyneflete found only six in the 358 Norfolk churches which he visited in 1368.[1]

When the inventories of the churches of the City of London were compiled in the reign of Edward VI, nearly half of them admitted to owning or having owned a chrismatory of silver. Many were quite substantial pieces weighing from 17 to 27 ounces, and only four weighed less than 10 ounces. The example belonging to St. Peter upon Cornhill was parcel-gilt, weighed 29 ounces, and was decorated with the Four Evangelists.[2] Descriptive details are rare, and we are told nothing about the example at St. Magnus,[3] which was unusually heavy and weighed 88¾ ounces. In rural England silver chrismatories remained rare, but examples are listed in the Edwardian inventories of almost every county except for the very poorest, like Cumberland.

Two standard forms of chrismatory can be distinguished. One of these consisted of an oblong box with a four-sloped lid and looked like a miniature shrine. Inside, the flasks fitted into three holes in a plate. A plate of this sort has survived at New College, Oxford. Descriptions give the impression that the chrismatories belonging to this class were usually fairly simple. On the other hand, in the 1536 inventory of Lincoln Minster is an account of a most elaborate one with sixteen images and plenty of buttresses and pinnacles.[4]

The alternative design had the three flasks arranged in a trefoil. This could be carried out with less silver, but this does not imply that there was anything necessarily mean about them. One at St. Peter Mancroft, Norwich, at the beginning of the sixteenth century, weighed 24 ounces and had the flasks arranged on a triangular base supported by three angels.[5]

The only surviving chrismatory (Pl. 41*b*) belongs to the type with only two flasks which has since become common. It is made from an oblong block of rock crystal with truncated corners. The cover and base are of silver-gilt. The former is surmounted by a knob from which radiate eight panels engraved with H and K bound by a knot, the spaces between being filled with flowers. The records of the British Museum cannot throw any light on the history of this charming little relic of Henry VIII and his first wife beyond the middle of last century.

[1] *Norfolk Record Soc.* xix, 1948, lxxxxiii.
[2] Walters, 577.
[3] Ibid. 345.
[4] *Archaeologia*, liii, 1892, 23.
[5] *Norfolk Archaeology*, xiv, 1901, 210.

B. BASINS AND ALMS DISHES

Basins for the ablutions were commonly made in pairs, the water being poured from one over the celebrant's hands into the other. Less commonly a ewer and basin were used.[1] Several sets of basins were to be found in major cathedrals and abbeys at the close of the Middle Ages, and single sets in well-furnished collegiate[2] and parish churches.[3] York Minster still treasured in the reign of Edward VI a pair of little gold basins, weighing 21 ounces each, which had been bequeathed by Archbishop Gifford[4] (d. 1269). No other cathedral appears to have had gold basins.

The almost total loss of examples of these basins is all the more regrettable because they appear to have been made to order and to have had much care lavished upon them. It is likely that change affected the ornament but not the form of these basins in the four and a half centuries in which they were in use, as those mentioned in inventories seem to have had much the same proportions as those of the only pair which have survived.

The basins, presumably from his own chapel, which were bequeathed by Bishop Foxe to Corpus Christi College, Oxford, are both 16¾ inches in diameter and have a plain rim surrounding a central depression, in the middle of which is a medallion with the arms of Foxe impaling those of the see of Winchester. This is encircled by twenty-four wavy rays on a punched ground. One dish bears the hall-mark for 1493, which shows that the medallion must be a replacement, since Foxe was then only Bishop of Bath and Wells. The second basin (Pl. 44) bears the 1514 hall-mark and differs in that it has a lion's-head spout on the underside which drained the water through a trefoil hole in the well of the basin. Ewer-basins of this sort are only occasionally specified in inventories, so that it is likely that they were unusual. The ewers which are also occasionally mentioned presumably went through a course of development from the Romanesque to the late Gothic period, but it is now quite impossible to trace it.

The basins were often engraved or embossed with pairs of religious subjects, e.g. the Virgin and Child matching the Majesty[5] or the Trinity,[6] representations of patron saints,[7] or benefactors.[8] Very often the principal decoration was the arms of the donor in the middle, and this raises the question whether such basins had not been intended originally for meal-time ablutions. The same question arises with regard to basins with decoration of no religious significance, such as the pair mentioned in the 1245 inventory of St. Paul's, decorated with

[1] The earliest reference to a ewer and basin is in the 1093 inventory of Ely (*Liber Eliensis*, 1848, 282).

[2] e.g. Fotheringhay, 1546 (*Arch. Journal*, lxi, 1904, 261).

[3] e.g. St. Peter Mancroft, Norwich (*Norfolk Archaeology*, xiv, 1901, 206–13).

[4] *Fabric Rolls of York Minster*, Surtees Soc. 1858, 216, 307.

[5] J. Amundesham, *Annales*, Rolls Series, 1870, 325.

[6] *Archaeologia*, lii, 1890, 236.

[7] Ibid. l, 1887, 469.

[8] Oliver, 310.

'dragons and lions intertwined'[1] and another in the 1295 inventory 'with embossed work in the bottom with lions biting stags'.[2] Still more strange were the pair given to St. Albans by Dom John Blount, decorated 'with wild men in the bottom'.[3] Though all these pieces sound as if they had been intended originally for someone's dining-hall, we must recognize that medieval ideas about appropriate and inappropriate decoration were quite different from our own.[4]

It was only after the Reformation that a silver alms dish became part of the furnishing of a well-equipped church. In the fifteenth century they occur frequently with the plate of rich private chapels, but the descriptions are colourless. In the will of Bishop William of Wykeham[5] (d. 1404) he bequeathed to Archbishop Arundel an alms dish, newly made, in the form of a ship. Though descriptions of similar objects occur elsewhere,[6] it is by no means clear whether they are properly to be regarded as chapel plate.

C. CENSERS

We possess remarkably little information about the censers made in the precious metals during the Romanesque period. Illustrations and surviving bronze examples suggest that they were generally spherical, the upper half being pierced and the lower standing on a ring base. The purely spherical type appears to have already begun to be modified by the addition of a small turret on the top of the cover before the arrival of the Gothic period. Representations of censing angels in sculpture and paintings give us a fair idea of thirteenth-century censers of silver—for we can not imagine that the artists would have conceived that angels would use anything cheaper!

Most Gothic silver censers both in England and abroad had covers of a more or less architectural form. They were not infrequently like perfect little buildings, but they were not all made to one pattern, since the source of inspiration was not always the same. Thus the covers of the censers swung by the sculptured angels in the triforium of Westminster Abbey take the form of a little cruciform church with steep roofs and a central tower capped by a spire.[7] The chains pass through three uncapped turrets. These date from the reconstruction by Henry III in the middle of the thirteenth century, but the same form appears in the Angel Choir at Lincoln, which is some twenty years later. It would not be hard to extend the list.

[1] *Archaeologia*, lii, 1890, 236.

[2] Dugdale, *St. Paul's*, 1818, 312.

[3] J. Amundesham, *Annals*, Rolls Series, 1870, 325.

[4] For instance, in the Victoria and Albert Museum there is a standing pyx, made at Cordova at the end of the fifteenth century, decorated with wild men fighting monsters.

[5] R. Lowth, *Life of William of Wykeham*, 1759, App. xxxviii.

[6] e.g. Palgrave, ii. 144; iii. 324–5.

[7] In the 1552 inventory of St. Paul's is listed 'on little Sensoure all silv^r^ & gilte the cov^r^ in the forme of an olde Chirche' (Walters, 75).

We are indeed fortunate that the only surviving English medieval silver censer is a work of primary importance, in fact the finest fourteenth-century example in Europe. The Ramsey Censer (frontispiece) owes its name to the fact that the accompanying incense-boat (which will be described shortly) was demonstrably made for the great Benedictine abbey in Huntingdonshire. The bowl is unornamented and the base is only decorated with a band of pierced quatrefoils, but the cover takes the form of a miniature chapter-house with finely traceried windows, giving a date in the second quarter of the fourteenth century. It is all of cast work and weighs 48 ounces.[1]

It is usually very difficult to visualize the appearance of censers of which we have mention, even when the maker of the inventory has attempted some sort of description. Censers decorated with 'lions' heads' or 'leopards' heads' are mentioned fairly frequently from the middle of the fourteenth century. The description of one belonging to St. Peter Mancroft, Norwich, in 1368 states that it had 'six leopards' heads to vomit the smoke'.[2] The number of heads on these censers ranged from three to eight, but it would not be safe to assume that they were always functional and not purely decorative. One in the 1552 inventory of St. Paul's is recorded as having 'iij libardes heddes on the cover with vj wyndowes & pynacles'.[3] This suggests just a variant of the chapter-house censer with leopards' heads used, perhaps, to mask the passage of the chains through the cover.

It is hard to piece together very much more about the forms and decoration of late-medieval censers and only too often we are left guessing. What, for instance, was the censer like which is mentioned in the 1315 inventory of Canterbury Cathedral as decorated with salamander's feathers?[4]

Before leaving the subject of hand-censers, it is perhaps as well to emphasize that we are extremely fortunate to retain one example made for the high altar of a first-class Benedictine abbey and that it was stolen and secreted at such an early stage in its career. We must not imagine that all the censers which we encounter in inventories were either so finely finished or of such solid construction. Still less may it be assumed that they were normally in good condition. However much we may admire these miniature essays in Gothic architecture, it must be admitted that they were not extremely well designed to perform their function. There were too many pinnacles to be knocked off and traceried windows into which the incense could cake. Sometimes we hear of enamel decoration (by this date almost certainly translucent enamel) which would

1 The 'principall sensers' belonging to the high altar of Canterbury Cathedral each weighed 50 ounces, but the 'Comon Senser' together with two incense-boats only came to 80 ounces (Legg and Hope, 182). An unimportant censer might weigh about 25 ounces. Important censers, like the Ramsey one, were probably mostly cast; unimportant ones might be largely embossed, but, being of lighter fabric, might be almost as big.

2 *Norfolk Record Soc.* xix, 1947, 1.

3 Walters, 75.

4 Legg and Hope, 72.

splinter at the first serious knock. Moreover, the medieval thurifer evidently went about his business with the same zest as the sculptured angels in the triforium, but with much less skill. The repair of the censers is an annual item in the sacrist rolls of every large church, and it is clear that the carelessness of the thurifers was an unending cause of damage to their charges.[1]

Canon Rock drew attention to the use in Anglo-Saxon times of large censers suspended from the church roof. He may have been rash in assuming that they were often made in the precious metals, as his only evidence is a monk's essay in Latin verse. He was probably wrong in supposing that they were in common use.[2]

Information about hanging censers in the later Middle Ages is extremely scanty. The best-attested examples are those used at St. Paul's. In the 1552 inventory occurs the following entry:

> A greate large Sensoure all silver with manye windowes & battilmentes used to Sense withall in the penticoste weeke in the bodie of the chirche of pawles at procession tyme clviij unc. iij quarters.[3]

This cannot have been very old, as the example mentioned in the 1402 inventory was of silver-gilt and weighed 146 ounces.[4] This was evidently still a novelty, for the maker of the inventory adds with pride: 'Archbishop Thomas [Arundel] would gladly have given eighty marks of sterlings for it.' In 1295 there had been two pairs of great silver-gilt censers.[5] The larger pair weighed 110 ounces each, whilst the lesser weighed about 73 ounces and were decorated 'with engraved and embossed work, with churches and towers, and with sixteen little bells hung on'. Neither of these pairs are identical with the pair of plain silver ones which had featured in the 1245 inventory. These had been decorated with angels in relief and had weighed 100 ounces and 92 ounces respectively.[6]

The rapid turnover in censers will not surprise anyone who has seen in action 'Botafumeiro', the giant censer at Compostella. This censer is suspended from the vault of the crossing and is gradually worked up, until it swings in a wide arc, by six well-drilled young men with ropes and pulleys. It is obvious that censers not carefully sited or inexpertly handled would soon get shattered against the fabric of the church.

A pair of great censers, weighing 266 ounces together, appear in the dissolution inventory of Westminster Abbey,[7] and there were doubtless other examples,

[1] For instance, every one of the seven censers belonging to the collegiate church of the Holy Trinity, Arundel, was defective at the time of the taking of the 1517 inventory (*Archaeologia*, lxi, 1908, 87–88).

[2] *Church of our Fathers*, 1849, i. 207.

[3] Walters, 75.

[4] *Archaeologia*, l, 1887, 203.

[5] Dugdale, *St. Paul's*, 1818, 311. Georgian tea-urns range about the same weights.

[6] *Archaeologia*, l, 1887, 467.

[7] *London and Middlesex Arch. Soc. Trans.* iv, 1874, 315–16.

but makers of inventories were all too ready to catalogue a *magnum* or a *maximum turribulum*, which may refer to a particularly heavy hand-censer and not to one hung from the vault.

INCENSE-BOATS

Nearly all the names applied to the vessel from which the censer was replenished imply that it was boat-shaped. Beyond this we know remarkably little about them, and only one example has as yet been identified. This is of silver parcel-gilt and was discovered, together with the censer which has just been described, when Whittlesea Mere, Hunts., was drained in 1850. The vessel (Pl. 45) has the fine lines of a well-built craft. The hinged lid and the closed half of the cover are both decorated with a rose, engraved and gilt, and end in a finial of the fore-part of a ram. This is clearly the rebus for Ramsey—a ram emerging from the waves—which is known to have been used by this great abbey. The spreading foot with six incurved sides resembles those of the chalices of the last quarter of the fourteenth century. The incense-boat is, therefore, perhaps fifty years younger than the censer.

Inventory descriptions of incense-boats are, with few exceptions, very uninformative. One which had been presented by Abbot Islip (1500–30) to Westminster Abbey[1] is described as:

> A Shyp for incense of sylver parcell-gylt withe the armes of the monasterye and *Eslyp* graven on the lydds and with a lytell dog of sylver for the haspe of the same.

A boat mentioned in the 1388 inventory of the abbey was mounted on four wheels.[2] As far as we can interpret the evidence, the boats continued generally to have both ends alike. An example in the 1452 inventory of King's College, Cambridge, is, however, described as having a forecastle and a sterne castle.[3]

Besides incense-boats there are rare references to incense-dishes and bowls.[4] In one instance there is mention of a spoon attached by a chain.[5]

A spoon necessarily accompanied the boat or dish. It was always included in the weight of the latter, so that we get no indication as to whether it was generally smaller or of the same size as the contemporary secular spoon. The forms of the terminals on the handles are either of sorts with which we are still familiar on extant secular spoons, or can easily be imagined.[6]

D. FANS

Whilst there is plenty of evidence for the use in England of fans to keep flies away from the eucharistic elements, the subject need only be treated summarily,

[1] Ibid. 322. [2] *Archaeologia*, lii, 1890, 227. [3] *Ecclesiologist*, xviii, 1860, 5.

[4] St. Paul's, 1245 (*Archaeologia*, l, 1887, 467), and Canterbury, 1315 (Legg and Hope, 72).

[5] St. Paul's, 1295 (Dugdale, *St. Paul's*, 1818, 312).

[6] One mentioned in the 1506 inventory of Exeter Cathedral had a St. Michael finial (Oliver, 324).

since they seem seldom to have been made in the precious metals. Though there still survive a number of quite ornate silver *flabella* of continental origin, I have been unable to add to the single reference quoted by Dr. Rock a century ago. This occurs in the 1222 inventory of Salisbury Cathedral where is mention of 'a fan of silver given to the church by the lord bishop—broken'.[1]

Fans with the handle alone of silver are no less rarely mentioned. An enamelled silver-gilt one, having a figure of a bishop at the end of the handle, was presented to York Minster by John Newton, who was treasurer at the beginning of the fifteenth century.[2]

E. FONTS

In view of the antipathy towards the use of baptismal basins felt by English bishops from the time of Archbishop Parker, it is not a little surprising to find that this type of vessel was not entirely a product of the more advanced form of Protestantism.

The royal font is first mentioned in connexion with the baptism of Prince Arthur in Winchester Cathedral in 1486. According to one authority:[3] 'There was made a highe stoke [block] for a fonte with grecis [steps] round abowght, and the fonte was of sylvar, browght from Cawnterbury.' Another writer[4] contributes the information: 'Over the Font, of a good Height, a rich Canape, with a great gilte Bolle celid and fringed, without Curteyns.'

The cover for the font was a later addition, as appears from the detailed description in the 1521 royal inventory:[5]

Item Received of the Queenis grace for a founte callid in her indenture A wyder [voider] or a disshe chasid w^{t} bestis, men and fowlis di. gilte (parcel-gilt) w^{t}oute a cover waiyng in the said indenture clxxiiij oz. di. to the whiche founte oon William hollande hath made a Couer gilte chase w^{t} men bestis and foulis waiyng c oz. di. and wayeth now to gidders in all cclxxv oz.

There is a reference to 'the riche Font of Canterbury' in an account of the christening of Princess Margaret in Westminster Abbey in 1489, and doubtless it was used later on for the children of Henry VIII.[6] It is last heard of in the 1550 inventory,[7] and it is not known how it came to be scrapped.

[1] Rock, *The Church of our Fathers*, 1853, i. 100, 197–201.

[2] *Fabric Rolls of York Minster*, Surtees Soc. 1859, 223.

[3] *Three Chronicles of the 15th century*, Camden Soc. N.S. 1880, 105.

[4] *Johannis Lelandi Collectanea*, ed. T. Hearne, 1774, iv. 204. In the same volume (180) is Lady Margaret's record of the proper ceremonial for the christening of royal infants.

[5] *Assoc. Architectural Soc. Records*, xvii, 1884, 181.

[6] *Johannis Lelandi*, op. cit. iv. 253. The font is mentioned in the account of the christening of Edward VI at Hampton Court (ibid. ii. 671).

[7] B.M. Add. MS. 46348, f. 32 b.

When Mary I believed that she was pregnant she ordered another silver font, which will be described later on (p. 250).

F. HAND-WARMERS

Spherical hand-warmers, filled with hot charcoal and intended to warm the celebrant's hands in cold weather, were in use down to the Reformation. Silver examples were comparatively uncommon and detailed descriptions are usually lacking. Amongst the few cases in which the decoration is detailed is one bequeathed to St. Paul's by Bishop Fulke Bassett (1242–59) which was of silver parcel-gilt and was engraved with figures symbolizing the months.[1] Another example, which occurs in the 1536 inventory of Lincoln Minster, is described as 'a Calefactory sylver and gylte w^{t} leves graven weyng ix unces and dim'.[2]

G. HOLY-WATER BUCKETS

The use of silver holy-water buckets appears to have been fairly common in cathedrals and first-class abbeys after the thirteenth century. By the end of the Middle Ages they were to be found in the private chapels of the rich. No examples are known to exist and informative descriptions are rare, but these prove that they were sometimes of considerable artistic importance.

At St. Paul's in 1295 was one described as 'a vessel of silver for Holy Water, with embossed work with images and interlaced vine-sprays, and the handle is [formed] of two dragons'.[3]

Images are again mentioned in the decoration of an example belonging to the collegiate church at Arundel in 1517. This was 'a greate holy water bokett of Silver with Bisshoppes in tabernacles about'.[4]

The unfortunate Duke of Buckingham, who was beheaded in 1521, owned a bucket elaborately ornamented with the heraldic devices of his family.[5] This did not prevent it from being incorporated amongst the plate of his royal murderer. The latter had already ten others, two of gold and eight of silver, some being decorated with Tudor badges. The description of one,[6] which had evidently been inherited from Henry VII, proves that the latter was not invariably parsimonious:

a hollywater stocke of golde garnisshed w^{t} v small diamondys, xiij small Rubyes oon coorse Emeroude, xix pearlis H and E crowned w^{t} a stryncle [sprinkler] and a small chayne of golde waiying xxv oz. q^{rt}.

[1] *Archaeologia*, l, 1887, 468.
[2] Ibid. liii, 1892, 21.
[3] Dugdale *St. Paul's*, 1818, seqq.
[4] *Archaeologia*, lxi, 1908, 88.
[5] 'A holy water stocke w^{t} a strenkell white w^{t} carte naves, swannys, stafford knottis, wydowes mantelles and antelopes' (*Assoc. Architectural Soc. Reports*, xvii, 1884, 181).
[6] Ibid. 164 and 181.

H. IMAGES

There would seem to have been a considerable vogue in Anglo-Saxon and Norman times for furnishing cathedrals and abbey churches with silver images. Abbot Brithnod (971–81) furnished Ely with four statues of St. Etheldreda and her companions, covered with silver, gold, and gems. They stood in pairs on either side of the altar, over which was probably placed a seated Virgin and Child which some other benefactor had contributed. All were stripped by the Normans who captured the abbey from Hereward the Wake. Their oaken cores still remained in the middle of the twelfth century.[1] Similarly, amongst the shortcomings of Walter, Abbot of Ramsey, was that in 1143, when civil war was raging, he alienated, without consulting the convent, the statues of the Majesty, St. Benedict, St. John the Evangelist, and St. Ives.[2]

Silver-plated images are sometimes mentioned in inventories of the thirteenth century or later, but it is probable that they were survivors from earlier periods. The images of the later Middle Ages were usually raised from silver sheet, so that weights are usually given for them in inventories. Neither type of image was particularly common in late medieval churches. On the other hand, they seem to have been rather popular in private chapels. The 1521 inventory of the royal plate describes elaborate gold figures of St. George and of St. Christopher, both studded with gems, and also a head of Becket. In silver-gilt the king had also a rich collection which represented his own religious preferences and those of his forebears and of his illustrious victims.[3] His venerable and pious subject John de Vere[4] owned representations of the Trinity, the Virgin and Child, two others of the Virgin (one matching a St. John and standing below the cross on the altar), nine Apostles, and saints Anne, Barbara, John Baptist,

[1] *Liber Eliensis*, 1848, 114–15, 249, 282.

[2] *Ramsay Abbey Cartulary*, Rolls Series, ii. 2734.

[3] The subjects represented were as follows: the Majesty, the Virgin and Child (7), St. Anne, St. John Baptist (5), St. Mary Magdalene (3), eight apostles (two each of Peter and Bartholomew), saints Barbara (3), Catherine (2), Dorothy (3), Francis, George (2), Margaret (6).

We can only be sure that saints Philip and Bartholomew were the king's own choice, as they were 'bowght of John mondye Anno Quinto'. A large number probably reflect the taste of Henry VII and of the Lady Margaret, for it seems safe to assume that some at least of the six representations of her patron saint had belonged to her. She is known to have bequeathed to Christ's College, Cambridge, four images (C. H. Cooper, *Memoir of Margaret Countess of Richmond and Derby*, 1874, 130). The Trinity had belonged to the unfortunate Duke of Buckingham (*Assoc. Architectural Soc. Reports*, xvii, 1884, 164–5, 176–180).

Wolsey also appears to have acquired a lot of silver statuary. Between 1526 and 1528 his goldsmith Robert Amadas received from him, in part payment for new work, figures of Our Lady, saints Anthony, Barbara, Catherine, Dorothy, Eustace, Francis, George, Henry of Windsor, John the Baptist, John the Evangelist, Margaret, Stephen, and Ursula. For the new college at Ipswich Amadas provided seven images of standard saints. It is interesting to note that the cardinal's images ran from 20 to 30 ounces, whereas the king's were from 30 to 200 ounces (J. Gutch, *Collectanea Curiosa*, 1781, 1319–36).

[4] *Archaeologia*, lxvi, 1914, 31–48.

George, and Margaret. Though churches, large or small, do not seem to have gone out of their way to collect images, they were glad to receive them by gift or bequest. Thus, when the earl came to draft his will (1509) he left some of his statuary to specified churches. Amiens Cathedral was to get his best Virgin, as well as the Baptist; Woburn Abbey his St. Andrew; the Black Friars at Cambridge his St. Peter; the priory of Hatfield Broad Oak his St. James. Though the earl bequeathed his images to religious houses, similar pieces are mentioned occasionally in parish churches. Doubtless the Annunciation group mentioned in the Edwardian inventory of St. Michael Cornhill was due to the generosity of some City merchant.[1]

I. LANTERNS

In a number of late medieval inventories of cathedrals, abbeys, and collegiate churches there is listed a silver 'sconce' or lantern. These, of course, served the very practical use of enabling the clergy to find their way about the church for the winter and night services.

There does not seem to be any evidence that they were elaborately decorated. At the beginning of the sixteenth century York Minster owned two, one of which was square and parcel-gilt, whilst the other was round and of plain silver.[2]

J. PASCHAL CANDLESTICKS

The paschal candlestick which featured prominently in the service for Holy Saturday, when its large candle was consecrated and lit, was a prominent feature in cathedrals and large abbeys, but was, it would appear, seldom made of silver. Some of the most important were of gilt bronze and were Romanesque versions of the seven-branched candlestick which had once adorned the Temple in Jerusalem.

The example given by Cnut to Winchester Cathedral was described in the thirteenth century[3] as 'a silver candlestick with six branches of the sort which the most costly which we see nowadays is of bronze'.

The paschal candlestick was not necessarily seven-branched, as is shown by the description of a Gothic example mentioned in the 1536 inventory of Salisbury Cathedral,[4] as follows:

> A Candlestick, silver and gilt, with dyvers images, it stands on great feet with four towers, with a pike of silver on either of them.

[1] Walters, 493.

[2] *Fabric Rolls of York Minster*, Surtees Soc. 1859, 217.

[3] *Annales de Wintonia* in *Annales Monastici*, Rolls Series, 1865, ii. 16. I have discussed English seven-branched candlesticks in an article in *Apollo*, lvi, 1952, 53–55.

[4] *C.P. Wilts.* 239.

K. RELIQUARIES

The use of relics as an aid to devotion was well established by the time of the conversion of the English and reached its peak in the thirteenth and fourteenth centuries. By the beginning of the sixteenth century it was clear to thinking persons like Erasmus that the whole idea had been overdone.[1]

We, however, are concerned with reliquaries and not with relics. First of all it is well to be clear about their incidence. The cathedrals, the great abbeys, and the major collegiate churches were generally well stocked with them. Lesser collegiate churches, university colleges,[2] and priories often had none. Parish churches seldom had any[3] and the chapels of the nobility were in much the same case.[4] On the other hand, the religious guilds sometimes had them.[5]

The simplest form of reliquary with which we have to deal is one in which the metal mounting is directly applied to the relic itself. This type is illustrated by the celebrated portable altar which was found in 1827 in the tomb of St. Cuthbert in Durham Cathedral. The altar was merely a rectangular square of oak, 5¼ in. by 4¾ in., incised with the usual five crosses and bearing an inscription which indicated that it was dedicated in honour of St. Peter. The silver mountings which render it eligible to be considered as a reliquary were only added after the altar had become a devotional object. They consisted of thin, embossed sheets of silver of the same size as the altar, bound with rather thicker strips bent over its edge. When recovered, both altar and mounting were in a very bad state, and much ingenuity has been expended in recovering what remains of its decoration. The mountings have long since had to be taken off the original piece of wood and attached to a new piece of the same size in what appears to be the original order.

The altar has a considerable literature of its own, beginning with the account

[1] The decline in the popularity of the cult of relics is well illustrated by a table, drawn up by Canon Venables, of the takings in the offertory boxes belonging to the shrine of St. Hugh and that of his head at Lincoln Minster. It will be found that although the annual takings in the reign of Edward III seldom fell short of £30, they declined steadily through the fifteenth century and in the last year for which a figure is given, 1532, had sunk to £6. 4*s*. 5*d*. (*Assoc. Architectural Soc. Reports*, xxi, 1941, 144–6).

[2] All Souls College, Oxford, appears to have had a couple of figure reliquaries and another of architectural form (J. Gutch, *Collectanea Curiosa*, 1781, ii. 260). The most important reliquaries at Cambridge were at King's College where there was a head of St. Ursula weighing 19 lb. 6 oz. and a 'monstrance-reliquary' with a foot set with precious stones. The remaining relics appear to have been mainly contained in jewels (*Ecclesiologist*, 1865, xviii. 5–7).

[3] St. Peter Mancroft, Norwich, which was one of the richest parish churches in the kingdom, listed 'ij pixes of silv^r^ & all gilte w^t^ div'se and many relikke' given by Alderman Ballis (d. 1506) (*Norfolk Archaeology*, xiv, 1901, 212).

[4] The laity went in for jewellery containing relics. John de Vere, Earl of Oxford, was an exception, as he had several reliquaries including three relic-bearing angels (*Archaeologia*, lxvi. 335).

[5] The Guild of the Corpus Christi at Boston had in 1534 five small reliquaries of which the heaviest weighed 10 ounces (E. Peacock, *English Church Furniture*, 1866, 190–1).

by Canon Raine,[1] who saw it before it was disturbed, but these have now been superseded by that of Mr. C. A. Raleigh Radford, F.S.A., who kindly allowed me to see it in the proof.[2] The front is shown to have been embossed with a representation of a seated St. Peter and the inscription SCS PETROS APOSTOLOS. So little remains of it that no photograph is of much use.

The reverse is slightly better preserved (Pl. 47). Ornamental foliage is distinguishable in three of the corners, and towards the centre is the remains of an inscribed ring.[3] The general style of the work suggests an eighth-century date, but it is tempting to advance the time to 698, when the saint's remains are known to have been translated; but, as an alternative, it is suggested by Mr. Radford that if the work was done a little later it may have been done by the goldsmith anchorite St. Billfrith, who adorned the Lindisfarne Gospels.

Occupying the middle of the reverse is a roundel showing an equal-armed cross decorated with a delicate interlace, whilst between the arms is conventional foliage. This is obviously a later addition dating from the end of the ninth or the beginning of the tenth century.

In pre-Conquest times the types of reliquary to which reference is made most frequently are *feretra* and *filacteria* (very variously spelt. Anyone familiar with medieval inventories will have discovered that it is very difficult to decide the exact meaning of the various names applied to reliquaries and, indeed, it seems likely that the same name was used differently as time went on).

The essence of the *feretrum* was, however, that it should be suitable for carrying in procession. It was, in fact, an oblong chest with a gabled roof of one sort or another. It seems likely that Anglo-Saxon *feretra* were relatively small,[4] but after the Conquest those of the most popular saints grew so much larger that they required four bearers.[5] From this it should not be inferred that the *feretra* of less favoured saints grew likewise. They seem to have remained fairly small and were kept over the altars in side-chapels or else relegated to the reliquary cupboards.[6]

[1] J. Raine, *St. Cuthbert with an account of the opening of his tomb*, 1828, 199–201.

[2] *The Relics of St. Cuthbert*, 1956, where a full bibliography is given and also a drawing of the suggested restoration.

[3] Mr. Radford suggests [OM]NIA [HA]EC ERAN[T SCI PETR]I, implying that it and the other relics belonged to the church of St. Peter at Lindisfarne.

[4] Thus the original *feretrum* of St. Alban, which was sent to Ely for safety at the time of the Norman Conquest, was afterwards stored in a case for old corporals (T. Walsingham, *Gesta Abbatum*, Rolls Series, 1867, i. 36).

[5] Two monks could manage the shrine of St. Alban but four were usually employed (ibid. i. 190). Some of the other shrines appear to have been so heavy that they were left behind when the convent went in procession. Thus at Durham it was St. Bede's which was ordinarily used and not St. Cuthbert's (*Rites*, 105).

[6] At Canterbury in 1315 the shrines of St. Alphege and St. Dunstan flanked the high altar, behind which was that of St. Blaise (apparently broadside-on to that of St. Thomas). Those of St. Odo and St. Wilfred were in the Chapel of the Holy Trinity, whilst those of St. Anselm and St. Ælfric were in

The *feretrum* or shrine of the principal saint came to be placed behind the high altar. It was not ordinarily visible, since it was protected by a wooden cover which was raised or lowered by means of a rope passing over a pulley-wheel fixed in the vaulting. The cover of the shrine of St. Alban was richly decorated with silver, but this was quite unusual. During the twelfth and thirteenth centuries the cathedrals and abbeys of England competed with one another in the adornment of the shrines of their saints. Though no scruples were felt about tinkering with the masterpieces of past artists, few new *feretra* were commissioned after 1300. The *feretrum* of St. Erkenwald, which was made for St. Paul's in the earlier years of Edward III, seems to have been the last of the first-class shrines and the only one executed in the late Gothic style. It is possible from descriptions and other sources to recover some idea of a certain number of these lost masterpieces, but space cannot be found here to discuss their involved histories in the necessary detail.[1]

It is not obvious why one of the popular types of medieval reliquary should have gone by the name *filacterium*, which is merely a latinization of the Greek word for an amulet. It is not possible to generalize very much about their

side chapels. The shrine of St. Salvius was on a beam beyond the high altar, whilst that of St. Owen was in the great reliquary cupboard. *Feretra* in such numbers were rare in the later Middle Ages (Legg and Hope, 79–80).

[1] The following is the position with regard to seven of the principal English shrines:

(*a*) *Canterbury*. There is a considerable literature on the subject of the shrine of Becket and it is represented twice in the stained glass in the Chapel of the Holy Trinity (B. Rackham, *Ancient Glass of Canterbury Cathedral*, 1947, pl. XII and fig. 49*d*). A drawing in B.M. Cotton, Tiberius, E. VIII, 269, shows the shrine with its wooden cover on and is reproduced in Stanley's *Memorials* and elsewhere.

(*b*) *Durham*. There is a plausible early twelfth-century drawing of the shrine of St. Cuthbert in a manuscript of Bede's life of the saint at University College, Oxford, MS. CLXV, f. 163.

(*c*) *London*. In Dugdale's *St. Paul's* there is an engraving by Hollar after an old drawing, showing one end of the shrine of St. Erkenwald. The original, stated to be in the chapter library, is now missing.

(*d*) *St. Albans*. There are two drawings of the shrine of St. Alban which I discussed in *Burlington Magazine*, lxii, 1933, 237–41, when I showed that the one in 'The Life of St. Alban' at Trinity College, Dublin (MS. E.I. 40, f. 61a) was to be preferred to that in 'The Lives of the Offas' in the British Museum (Cotton, Nero, D. I, fo. 22).

(*e*) *Bury*. The dozen representations of the shrine of St. Edmund in Lydgate's metrical 'Life of St. Edmund and St Fremund' (B.M. Harl. 2278) are entirely incompatible with one another.

(*f*) *Westminster*. It has long been realized that the drawings in 'La estoire de saint Aedward le Rei' (Cambridge, Univ. Lib. Ee. 3. 59, ff. 55 and 65) agree well with the descriptions which we have. W. Burges (G. Scott, *Gleanings from Westminster Abbey*, 1863, 132–7) accepted a date about 1245 for the manuscript which led to the conclusion that the artist had had access to the designs for the shrine, which was by no means ready at that date. Though M. R. James accepted this dating in the Roxburghe Club edition of the manuscript (1920, 12 and 18), it seems likely that W. R. Lethaby (*Westminster Abbey and the King's Craftsmen*, 1906, 295) was right in suggesting that it should be dated about the time of the translation of the remains of the Confessor into the shrine in 1269.

(*g*) *York*. There are three representations of the shrine of St. William in the window dedicated to him in the Minster. Two of them agree but are incompatible with the third (F. Harrison, *Painted Glass of York*, 1927, opp. 104 and 106).

appearance. At Bury[1] *filacteria* hung from the beam above the high altar in the twelfth century and nine of the twenty-six given by St. Osmund to his cathedral at Old Sarum[2] are specified as having silver chains. *Filacteria* were not necessarily hanging reliquaries, since some of those mentioned in the Canterbury inventory[3] of 1315 had bases, whilst others are described in the 1536 inventories of Lincoln and Salisbury[4] as having 'iiij fete lyke to a byrd'.

The large *feretra* usually contained the greater part of the remains of a saint, though few saints' bodies survived the Middle Ages absolutely intact. Many a valued relic, however, consisted of only an important part of the body of a saint. If the relic had artistic possibilities, the reliquary might take a form which would indicate the contents to illiterate devotees. It is likely that reliquaries in the form of heads, arms, fingers, feet, &c., had already come into use before the Conquest; they were certainly in use by the end of the eleventh century and maintained their vogue down to the Reformation.

Canterbury Cathedral possessed what was reputed to be the richest head reliquary in England, the 'Corona of St. Thomas', i.e. the top of his head, which had been struck off at his assassination. The 1315 inventory shows that it owned also three other heads of silver-gilt and eleven arms.[5]

An important relic without artistic possibilities might be combined with an image of the saint, but was more often contained in one or other of the non-allusive types of reliquary.

The commonest type of reliquary was of box form, and of these an example survives in the Metropolitan Museum of New York (Pl. 47). It is of silver parcel-gilt and is decorated with figure subjects in niello. The front depicts the head and shoulders of Becket and those of his three murderers, one of whom is striking him with his sword—to make everything clear there is the inscription S. TOMAS OCCIDIT; above, on the lid, an anguished angel raises his hand in benediction. The back panel shows the burial of the saint with ✠ SANGUIS E. S. TOM. A letter E above one of the figures supporting the corpse may designate the faithful monk Edward Grim. Above, on the lid, an angel receives the soul of the saint. The end panels of the box show half-figures of angels, whilst the corresponding panels of the lid are filled with foliage. The drawing suggests a date not much after the death of Becket in 1170.[6]

[1] *Memorials of St. Edmund's Abbey*, Rolls Series, 1894, i. 307.

[2] *C.P. Wilts.*, 233–4.

[3] Legg and Hope, 83.

[4] *Archaeologia*, liii, 1892, 15; *C.P. Wilts.*, 239.

[5] Legg and Hope, 80–81.

[6] The reliquary was presented by J. Pierpont Morgan and it had previously been in the Germeau Collection. A full description by Joseph Breck is in the *Bulletin of the Metropolitan Museum*, xiii, 1918, 220–4. Its claim to be considered as English rests largely on the resemblance of the drawing to that on a series of champlevé plaques depicting scenes mainly from the lives of saints Peter and Paul which were claimed as English by H. P. Mitchell (*Burlington Magazine*, xlix, 1926, 161). Though this claim has been disputed (ibid. liii, 1928, 276), no more convincing attribution has been produced.

Little shrines, even when decorated with a representation of the saint whose relic was within, did not entirely satisfy the curiosity of the devout. The demand that the actual relic should be visible became ever more insistent. As a consequence it was, whenever possible, enclosed in a crystal container. It is clear that there were countless varieties of these, and it is probable that most of them could be described as miniature architectural fantasies. Amongst these was one variety known as a 'monster' or 'monstrance', which usually refers to a vessel for exhibiting a relic when encountered in medieval inventories.[1] Another form of reliquary which enabled the relic to be clearly visible consisted of the figure of an angel holding a crystal case.[2]

Every church which went in for relics on a large scale was faced with the problem of exploiting a large number of minor relics, which generally included a proportion of souvenirs of pilgrimages to the Holy Land. Many of these were inserted in the reliquary crosses which are mentioned elsewhere (p. 74). At Canterbury there were in 1315 three silver-gilt triptychs, each enclosing about a dozen relics. One was studded with gems, whilst the doors of the other two were decorated with the Annunciation.[3]

Reliquaries are, after all, only repositories for relics, and the suspicion is often aroused that some of the pieces mentioned in inventories had been made for other purposes. Silver-mounted 'ampullae' and 'pyxides', of any material, filled with relics occur in many inventories. It is easy to imagine that when a handsome crystal ampulla had developed a leak which made it unsuitable for holding oil, it might be turned over for use as a reliquary. Surplus or defective pyxes may have been treated in the same way.[4] It is only occasionally, however, that we can be sure that the two Latin words are being used in their liturgical and not in their primary sense of flask or box.

Pieces of secular origin were also used for storing relics, but these fall outside the scope of this work.[5]

L. SACRING-BELLS

St. Æthelwold (d. 984) gave to Abingdon Abbey 'a certain wheel full of bells, which is called gold, because of the gilt plating, which he ordered to be revolved

[1] Thus, in an early sixteenth-century inventory of York Minster is a *monstrum* with bones of St. Peter (*Fabric Rolls*, 222). At Worcester at the time of the Dissolution was a *monstrans* with the brains of St. Thomas of Canterbury (*British Arch. Assoc. Journal*, xxxviii, 1932, 168).

[2] M. F. Bond, *Inventories of St. George's Chapel, Windsor*, 1948, 52; or at Lincoln, *Archaeologia*, liii, 1892, 4.

[3] Legg and Hope, 86.

[4] Thus, in the 1536 inventories of both Lincoln and Salisbury the sacramental and reliquary pyxes are grouped together.

[5] There was a horn stuffed with relics at Canterbury in 1315 (Legg and Hope, 93), and two at Exeter in 1327 (Oliver, 311). There are still horns used as reliquaries in the treasury of Maestricht cathedral.

at certain festivals for the purpose of exciting greater devotion'.[1] Presumably the wheel was made of wood and was covered with silver-gilt. There is no reason to think that such pieces were common, though the same benefactor gave to Peterborough Abbey two silver bells evidently of an ordinary sort.[2]

Little bells for ringing at the moment of consecration were widely used during the later Middle Ages. We know that they were made both of silver and silver-gilt and that their clappers were sometimes of silver and at others of iron. No information regarding their decoration appears to be available.

M. SALT-CELLARS

The symbolic use of salt is common to many religions and, considering the rather striking reference to it in the Sermon on the Mount, it is perhaps surprising that it does not feature more prominently in Catholic ritual. As it is, salt plays a part in christening and the hallowing of water.

Ecclesiastical salt-cellars appear quite rarely in medieval inventories. Since references to ones of base metal are no more common, it may be inferred that in practice a secular salt-cellar was borrowed whenever an ecclesiastical one was not available. This was done even on state occasions, for an account[3] of the christening of Prince Arthur in 1486 records that 'the sergeaunte of the pantry was redy with a ryche salte and my Lord of Essex bere ye same salte by fore my lorde prince to the churche'.

In some inventories the vessel is described as 'for blessing salt'[4] and in others as a 'salte Saler for holy water',[5] but it is probable that there is not much in this distinction.

The descriptions are not always very helpful. The one acquired for Durham[6] in 1408 is, however, mentioned as being in the form of a scallop and cost 17*s.* 4*d.* On the other hand, they might be of considerable artistic importance, such as one mentioned in the 1384 inventory of St. George's Chapel, Windsor, which was 'a noble silver-gilt salt with precious stones, of which the base and the cover are of jasper, from the cover of which is missing one stone.[7]

There is nothing in the description of this salt to suggest that it differed fundamentally from contemporary secular examples. If this be granted, it must seriously be considered whether the Founder's Salt of Corpus Christi College, Oxford, was not intended primarily for church use. It is of hour-glass form

[1] *Abingdon Chronicle*, Rolls Series, 1896, i. 345.

[2] *Liber Niger of Peterborough*, Soc. of Antiquaries, MS. LX, f. 39v.

[3] *Three Chronicles of the fifteenth century*, Camden Soc. N.S. 1880, 104.

[4] St. Paul's, 1245, 'ad sal benedicendum' (*Archaeologia*, l, 1887, 469).

[5] Canterbury, 1540 (Legg and Hope, 182).

[6] *Durham Account Rolls*, Surtees Soc. 1898, 402.

[7] M. F. Ford, *Inventories of St. George's Chapel, Windsor*, 1947, 52.

(Pl. 48), the body being decorated with openwork panels decorated with hounds, hares, stags, and a pelican. The knot has six sides, each of which is pierced with the Coronation of the Virgin against a green enamelled ground. The cover is in the same style, but has a representation of the Annunciation, whilst the finial is formed of three pelicans hung with pearls. The approximate date is provided by the letters 'R d' which appear on the base of the salt and on its cover and show that it was made whilst Richard Foxe was Bishop of Durham (1494–1501). The presence of the religious subjects makes plausible the claim that this is a religious salt, although it must be granted that there are also a number of secular mazers with enamelled medallions of religious subjects, so that the question cannot be claimed as settled.

N. SANCTUARY LAMPS

Only important cathedrals and abbeys had silver sanctuary lamps, though they may not have been quite so uncommon as might appear from the inventories, since the compilers of these documents tended to have a blind spot with regard to objects in constant use in the sanctuary.

The lamps at Durham are described as follows:

> Before the high altar . . . were 3 marveilous faire siluer basins hung in chaines of siluer, one of them did hang in the south side of the quire above the stepps that go upp to the high alter, the second on the north side opposite to the first, the third in the midst betweene them both and iust before the high alter, theise 3 siluer basins had lattin basons within them havinge pricks for serges or gilt wax candles to stand on, the lattin basons beinge to receiue the drops of the 3 candles wch did burne con-. tinually both day and night, in token that the house was alwayes watchinge to god.[1]

The fifteenth-century Book of Benefactors of St. Albans contains an illustration of the silver-gilt lamp given by Abbot Paul (1077–93).[2] It shows a very simple bowl, without decoration. I know of no description of any elaborately decorated English medieval lamp.

[1] *Rites*, 14. It is possible that these were the lamps which had been presented by Bishop Pudsey, d. 1195, though these are described as having been set with crystals (*Historiae Dunelmensis Scriptores Tres*, Surtees Soc. 1839, 11).

[2] B.M. Cotton, Nero D. VII, f. 13^v^.

PART II

CHURCH PLATE AND KING

I

THE KING AS DONOR

THAT the conversion of England was effected with such comparative ease was the consequence of the benevolent attitude of most of the early English kings. Though there was a period of ebb and flow in the fortunes of the Church, the missionaries were soon in a position to think about organizing themselves on a permanent basis. The first needs of the new Church were places for worship and estates to provide the wherewithal for those who served them. We know much more about the churches founded by the early English kings than about the plate which must often have accompanied the gift.

How far can we trust the elaborate account of the rich chapel at Glastonbury fitted out by King Ine (d. 726) of which William of Malmesbury gives such a circumstantial account, complete with the amounts of gold and silver?[1] In only too many of the post-Conquest accounts of the benefactions of the early English kings it transpires that the objects had perished either during the Danish invasions or after the Norman Conquest.

There need be no doubt that the later kings were very generous in their gifts of plate, as many are recorded by chroniclers who could still see them but who, alas! made too little effort to describe them adequately. Nearly all the kings between the Conquest and the Reformation can be classed as donors of plate to English churches. Of the activities of the Conqueror with regard to English church plate we shall have to speak in the next chapter, and all that we need say about William Rufus in this context is that he did fulfil his father's bequests to the abbey of Battle and elsewhere. Henry I and Stephen each founded an abbey and almost certainly would have included some plate amongst the 'Ornamenta' with which they endowed them.[2] Richard I is, in fact, the only king who is unlikely ever to have made a gift of plate to an English church, if we discount the boy-king Edward V. The anti-clerical Henry II and John both qualify as benefactors. Though doubtless the former was spurred into benefactions by the need to expiate the murder of Becket, he could be quite a spontaneous giver. We have already mentioned how he undertook to provide a gold 'cup' to be

[1] *Historia de rebus Glastoniensibus* in T. Hearne, *Adam of Domerham*, 1727, ii. 55. The same chronicler is equally circumstantial about the shrine of St. Aldhelm which King Ethelwulf (d. 859) gave to Malmesbury. He describes it as having cast figures on the front and embossed scenes of miracles on the back (*De Gestis Pontificum*, Rolls Series, 1870, 389–90).

[2] We may assume that the hand of St. James, which reached Reading shortly before the king's death, would have arrived suitably embellished (*Annales Monastici*, Rolls Series, iv. 318).

used in conjunction with a beautiful vessel which Abbot Simon had just had made for St. Albans.[1] In 1399 the abbey of Beaulieu, Hants, still boasted a gold shrine made out of a crown of its founder John.[2] The fantastic amounts expended by Henry III upon the shrine of St. Edward at Westminster by no means exhausted his benevolence. Canterbury Cathedral received from him a large gold chalice set with gems,[3] St. Paul's a large silver-gilt cup for the Sacrament.[4] Henry was genuinely pious and generous to profusion, but we must bear in mind another aspect of his gifts. There can be no doubt that the recipients valued them highly, since they were lasting tokens of royal benevolence and carried great prestige. However, they usually accompanied or ensued upon a state visit which inevitably involved an abbey in great trouble and expense. When at the end of a visit no gift had been promised, the monks were unfeignedly disappointed.[5]

Most medieval kings had one or more churches in which they were specially interested and of which they were, perhaps, also the founder. We have already seen on what a magnificent scale Henry VI fitted out King's College, Cambridge,[6] and we may be certain that he would have provided fittingly also for Eton. Much more interesting, however, than the conventional piety of 'the Royal Saint' was the clause in the will of Henry VII whereby he bequeathed a silver-gilt pyx, to the value of £4, to every church in his kingdom which did not already possess one in a precious metal.[7] The wording of the passage shows that he had thought out the project in detail, and although he left the fulfilment of his wishes to his heir, he was perfectly aware he would leave the latter a quite unprecedented accumulation of wealth, so that there would be no valid excuse for neglecting to fulfil his wishes. Evidently something of the simple piety of the Lady Margaret had been inherited by her son, who generally appeared so cold and hard-bitten. Unfortunately his son, whose brand of religion was untinctured by simplicity, did not inherit this trait. Though Henry VIII appears to have made no attempt to carry out his father's bequest, he can rank as a donor. In 1534 St. George's Chapel, Windsor, boasted the possession of a gold pyx, weighing 24½ ounces, which he had given.[8] Henry does not appear to have taken a personal interest in sorting out plate for Cardinal's College, Oxford,

[1] T. Walsingham, *Gesta Abbatum*, Rolls Series, 1867, 190. A crude drawing of the king with his gift appears in the fifteenth-century book of benefactors, B.M. Nero. D. 7, f. 5v.

[2] *Arch. Journal*, lxxxiii, 1929, 87.

[3] Legg and Hope, 69.

[4] *Archaeologia*, l, 1887, 468.

[5] For example, when John offered at Bury a roll of costly material borrowed by his servants from the sacrist on the previous night, or when Richard II took his bride for a cheap tour of the East Anglian abbeys in 1383. His aim was 'non offerre sed auferre', as Walsingham remarked!

[6] See p. 23.

[7] Sir H. Nicholas, *Testamenta Vetusta*, 1826, 33.

[8] M. F. Bond, *Inventories of St. George's Chapel*, 1947, 166. Henry also presented a monstrance to Notre Dame de Halle, near Brussels. It is probably of local workmanship but the foot (on which the hall-mark should have been) is now wanting.

when he became its 'founder', whilst his decision to found a college at Cambridge was made so late in life (1546) that plate for Trinity Chapel never became a pressing matter.

The tradition of bountiful royal gifts was broken at the Reformation. I have found no trace of gifts made by or on behalf of Edward VI. On the 12th of February 1556 Mary I presented to the Friars Observant of Greenwich 'oone pixe, parcell guilt' which weighed 6 ounces. Though doubtless the recipients were vowed to poverty, we can hardly believe that their feelings would have been outraged by a richer gift! I have traced no other gifts of church plate made by her.[1]

It is less surprising that no gifts can be traced to Elizabeth I or to James I. It seems fair to suppose that Charles I might have been more bountiful if he had not lived in constant want of money. In 1634 he appropriated to the use of York Minster a fine of £1,000 due to the Court of High Commission, and part of the money was spent on a handsome service of plate.[2] Though he was intimately connected with the provision of the large service of plate for St. George's Chapel, Windsor, he appears to have been almost completely successful in passing on the financial responsibility for the project to the Companions of the Order of the Garter. The only expense which fell upon himself was in respect of 'two silver-gilt Potts chast wth histories wh. were given by us unto our Dear Sonne Prince Charles for his offering at his instalation the 20th of may last 1638'.[3]

No benefactions of church plate appear to have been made by Charles II or James II. Gifts of plate were made by or on behalf of later sovereigns, but they fall outside the scope of this book since they benefited churches outside this country. Thus Mary II presented chalices to several Church of Ireland churches in the diocese of Ossory,[4] and Anne a service of plate to Holy Trinity, New York, in 1709[5] and another to 'Her Indian Chappel of the Onandawgus' in 1711.[6] These three benefactions can be fairly described as personal gifts, since both queens were good churchwomen. On the other hand, the services of plate distributed to the churches of Boston and elsewhere in the name of George II must be regarded not as an act of generosity on the part of the sovereign but as

[1] Similarly, the pastoral staff presented to Cardinal Pole was made out of church plate stolen in the time of her brother (J. Nichols, *Manners and Expences*, 1797, 26 and 28). The future founder of the Escorial must have found her difficult to understand!

[2] *Fabric Rolls of York Minster*, Surtees Soc. 1858, 322.

[3] Bodleian MS. Ashmole, IIII, f. 81. I am indebted to Mr. C. H. Josten for this reference.

[4] *Journal of the R. Soc. of Antiquaries of Ireland*, lxxxi, 1951, 29. A chalice for a church at Breaghmore Wheeler, which was never built, is now at Brasenose College, Oxford (*Brasenose Quatercentenary Monographs*, i. 117).

[5] E. Alfred Jones, *Old Silver of American Churches*, 1913, 333, pl. ciii.

[6] Ibid. 2, pl. iii.

the result of joint action by the Bishop of London and the Council for Trade and Plantations with a view to fostering loyalty to Church and king in the colonies.

Here, however, we have been digressing, and it only remains to conclude this chapter by pointing out that no English church appears to have received a gift of plate direct from the sovereign between 1660 and 1830.

II

THE KING AS SPOILER

THE plate belonging to the Anglo-Saxon Church was concentrated mainly in the possession of the monasteries. It suffered much from the depredations of the Vikings, but little from royal exactions.

The Norman Conquest changed all this. Churches, indeed, got looted in times of civil war, but the area subject to plunder by foreign invaders was restricted to the towns and villages on the south coast and to the counties adjoining the Scottish border. On the other hand, the churches' wealth in the precious metals became subject to three types of royal exaction. These may be distinguished as follows:

1. Collusive levies.
2. Direct levies.
3. Indirect levies.

The collusive levy made its appearance in the months following the Battle of Hastings, but does not seem to have been much used between the time of the Conqueror and that of Henry VIII. The collusive levy was an arbitrary extortion of plate to which a church submitted through fear and was, in fact, blackmail. Since the projected Norman invasion had received the prior approval of Pope Alexander II, the wealthy English abbeys found themselves friendless and faced with complete disaster after the victory of the invaders. It is not, therefore, surprising that they should have chosen to sacrifice part of their treasures with a view to preserving the remainder. They poured rich gifts at the feet of the Conqueror, with the result that a few months later he was able to make lavish distributions of plate to every church in northern and western France in which he took an interest. As William of Poitiers put it, 'the gifts which he bestowed on the smallest monastery were such as a metropolitan basilica would not have despised'.[1] A little later he adds, 'some princes are wrongly bountiful with holy things, using them as a means to increase their fame in the world, whilst increasing their guilt before God. They spoil churches and with the very loot enrich others. King William built up a true reputation for himself, entirely by fair means, giving things which were truly his, being intent on an eternal reward and not upon a glory which perishes.'[2]

Queen Matilda would seem to have been less squeamish than her husband,

[1] Migne, *P.L.* cxlix. 1259.

[2] Ibid. 1267.

since, as she was not satisfied with the voluntary levy from Abingdon Abbey, she sent back for more.[1]

The Conqueror also made use of both the other types of levy. Abbeys which had taken an active part in resisting the invaders were severely punished. Thus the New Minster at Winchester lost, apart from estates, the great cross presented by Cnut, since some of the monks had been on the battlefield at Hastings,[2] whilst Ely was fined 700 marks (later raised to 1,000) for aiding Hereward's defence of the Isle.[3] The direct levy on plate, such as was suffered by the former abbey, was destined to remain comparatively rare, but the indirect levy, whereby the monastery was obliged to pay in cash, was to become a routine affair. It left to the abbot the onus of selecting the treasures to be consigned to the melting-pot and, since the church vessels were recognized as a reserve of capital to be used in an emergency, it caused less ill-feeling. None the less it behoved the king to exercise a little delicacy about an indirect levy, and not to behave as did William Rufus when faced with the raising of a large sum to enable him to mortgage Normandy from his brother in 1096. The bishops and abbots were so outraged by the amount demanded of them that they flocked to court to warn him that if they tried to raise the money from their tenants there would be widespread distress. The king's unsympathetic reply was, 'Have you not shrines adorned with gold and silver, full of dead men's bones?' They took this hint![4]

The most celebrated instance of the direct levy prior to the sixteenth century was the churches' contribution towards the ransom of Richard I. It was ordered by the king in a letter to Queen Eleanor and the Justiciar, dated from Haguenau on the 19th of April 1193.[5] The Justiciar interpreted the instruction as a levy on all gold or silver chalices, and it would appear that the rich churches were expected to pay more besides. It was intimated that those churches which wished to redeem their chalices might do so by paying the equivalent of rather less than the weight of the silver.[6] The Abbot of St. Albans ransomed those of his house and the Bishop of Norwich put up half the value of those in his diocese.[7] The levy must have been very unpopular as many parish churches can only recently have got a silver chalice, and it is clear that many were not ran-

[1] *Abingdon Chronicle*, Rolls Series, 1896, i. 485 and 491.

[2] They were so fortunate as to get it back later on (*Hyde Abbey Chronicle*, Rolls Series, 1866, xxxviii and xlv).

[3] *Liber Eliensis*, 1848, 246–7.

[4] William of Malmesbury, *Gesta Regum Anglorum*, Rolls Series, 1889, ii. 371–2. The same author reveals that the Abbot of Malmesbury stripped twelve book-covers, eight crosses, and eight shrines (*De Gestis Pontificum*, Rolls Series, 1870, 432).

[5] Hoveden, *Chronica*, Rolls Series, 1869, ii. 209.

[6] William of Newburgh, *Historia*, Eng. Hist. Soc. 1856, i. 400.

[7] Matthew Paris, *Chronica Majora*, 1872, ii. 398. It was very generous of Bishop John of Oxford, since Norwich was not a rich see. None the less it should be realized that the smaller churches of Norfolk and Suffolk would probably not yet have got silver chalices.

somed. Abbot Samson of Bury dared the Justiciar to lay hands on the shrine of St. Edmund, but had to sacrifice other treasures.[1] Though the York Minster might be able to ransom the gold reliquary cross given by the late archbishop,[2] the indifferently endowed cathedral priory of Rochester had to condemn the silver frontal of the high altar.[3] Gervase of Canterbury[4] is particularly loud in his wails, but then Christ Church, Canterbury, probably fared particularly ill as Hubert Walter, the newly appointed archbishop, was also one of the commissioners for collecting the levy. Though full restitution was promised in the king's original letter, there is little likelihood that anyone was deceived. When, six years later, a well-aimed arrow laid low the king outside the castle of Chaluz, the bitterness at the spoliation of the chalices revived and was reflected by verses which circulated round the abbeys.[5]

No further direct levy on church plate in general was attempted until the reign of Henry VIII, but in the year 1338 Edward III is found pledging some of the plate of seven of the most important abbeys, in order to raise funds for the prosecution of the war in Scotland and for coastal defence.[6] Whether the interested abbeys redeemed the pledges is unknown.

During the later Middle Ages any grant voted by convocation must have been liable to occasion the destruction of plate belonging to the less well-to-do religious houses, but we cannot detect any concerted effort by the Crown to take toll of the plate of the churches by means of any of the forms of levy which have been mentioned.

The long period of immunity from the onslaughts of rapacious kings which the plate of the English churches enjoyed during the latter part of the Middle Ages has tended to make the spoliation which began under Henry VIII appear unique. In actual fact techniques of robbery used by the Tudors fit easily into

[1] *Memorials of St. Edmund's Abbey*, Rolls Series, 1890, i. 71. The abbot slyly subscribed the gold chalice given by the queen mother in memory of Henry II. Queen Eleanor redeemed it but exacted a written promise from the abbot that he would never part with it again! (ibid. 251).

[2] *Fabric Rolls of York Minster*, Surtees Soc. 1858, 152.

[3] J. Thorpe, *Registrum Roffense*, 1769, 119–20.

[4] Rolls Series, 1879, i. 519.

[5]
Christe, tui calicis praedo fit praeda Calucis,
Aere brevi dejicis qui tulit aera crucis.
Hic Ricarde, jaces, sed mors si cederet armis,
Victa timore tui cederet arma tuis.

Chronica de Melsa, Rolls Series, 1866, i. 336. A slightly different version was noted at Waverley (*Annales Monastici*, 1865, ii. 251).

[6] The abbeys were Bardney, Croyland, Osney, Ramsey, Reading, Thorney, and Thornton. St. Augustine's, Canterbury, preferred to pay down 50 marks (Rymer, *Foedera*, 1821, ii, pt. 2, 1039–40). No direct levy appears to have been attempted at the time of the seizures of the alien priories in the fourteenth and fifteenth centuries. When the alien priory problem was finally settled, the priories which disappeared may be supposed to have been virtually without plate. The more prosperous ones became denizened.

the classification given at the head of this chapter. Whereas the Norman, Angevin, and early Plantagenet kings pruned the plate of the English churches, the Tudors went far towards eliminating it.

It has long been realized that when Clement VII issued bulls in 1524 and 1528 to allow Wolsey to dissolve a number of religious houses in order to provide an endowment for his colleges at Oxford and Ipswich, he cleared the way for the large-scale dissolutions of a few years later. Wolsey's dissolutions differed from those of his pupil Cromwell in two important respects. They resulted merely in the transfer of assets from one religious body to another, as had been done a century earlier with those of the alien priories. Secondly, although Wolsey was not scrupulous about money matters, there seems to be no evidence to suggest that he embezzled any of the plate of the dissolved houses. The accounts of his goldsmith shows that the plate of the dissolved Augustinian priory of St. Frideswide, Oxford, was merely refurbished and slightly augmented before being returned to the college which was to occupy its site. The plate allocated to the Ipswich college would seem to have come out of the cardinal's own stock for, although some of it was 'newe dreste uppe and amendyd', it was of too rich a character to have been derived from the dissolved religious houses.[1]

When in 1534 the Act of Supremacy recognized Henry VIII as 'the only supreme head in earth of the Church of England', his indispensable minister Cromwell was ready to use to the utmost the unprecedented opportunity of laying hands on the wealth of the churches. Since we are not concerned with the justification for the spoliation, but only with the fate of the plate, we can proceed directly to the passing of the first acts which started the process.

The Act dissolving the monasteries having an income of less than £200 p.a. was passed on the 4th of April 1536, and commissioners were appointed to carry out the actual work of inventorying, selling off, or bringing to London the goods. The commissioners were composed of local men with only a stiffening of Londoners, so that their attitude was much more sympathetic than that of Cromwell's visitors.

At the meeting of Convocation Bishop Latimer had been asked to preach two sermons[2] and picked on the parable of the Unjust Steward for his text. Though he had much to say about 'Purgatory pick-purse' and about the abuse of images, no allusion was made to the temptation to falsify accounts or misappropriate goods. At this period the even more advanced bishops not infrequently failed to foresee developments only a few weeks ahead.

Only three weeks after the passing of the Act of Suppression, Archbishop Lee is found writing from Cawood to Cromwell that 'certayne monasteries beeinge nie to Yorcke' were rumoured to be selling off their goods and that he 'had warned the maiour of Yorke, and other of his brodren therof, and speciallie the

[1] J. Gutch, *Collectanea Curiosa*, 1781, ii. 283–4.

[2] *Sermons*, Parker Soc. 1844, 33–57.

maister of the mynte,[1] upon their peril and daunger that theye receive no goodes of anye suche monasterie'.[2]

The disposals of plate before the arrival of the commissioners fall into two categories:

1. Illegitimate and illegal.
2. Legitimate but not strictly legal.

The occupants of the lesser monasteries were given the choice between continuance in religion in one of the larger houses or of accepting a rectory or vicarage. Those who chose the former course would know that the house to which they would be transferred would be richly, over-richly, endowed with plate and would not welcome anything smuggled out of a suppressed monastery. On the other hand, the prior who preferred a country living to a return to a life in the ranks of a large monastery would be more likely to arrange for a hamper of refectory plate to be stowed out of sight when the commissioners arrived, rather than a chalice which might occasion gossip in his future parish. It is likely, in fact, that when monastic plate was embezzled it was sold for scrap.

At an early date it became known that the £200 p.a. minimum was not to be applied rigidly and that permission to continue might be obtained through the payment of a fine to the treasurer of the Court of Augmentations. No less than forty-seven houses did compound in this way; thus Dale Abbey, Derbys., paid £166. 13*s*. 4*d*. and St. Thomas, near Stafford, £133. 6*s*. 8*d*.[3] Such sums could, of course, only be paid out of capital and were in the nature of an indirect levy upon the monastery plate. It is not surprising, therefore, that when the royal forbearance which had been bought so dearly came to an end within two years, it was found that such houses had very little plate left. The sale or pledging of plate in times of emergency was, of course, an old monastic practice, and it was only illegal because the Act of 1536 had invalidated all sales of monastic goods after the 1st of March 1535.[4] In the case of the two houses which have been mentioned, when the commissioners for the suppression arrived in 1538 they found at Dale only three chalices, the plating of a processional cross, and eleven spoons, all the rest having been sold. At St. Thomas they found two chalices and a list of plate pledged to local gentry.[5] The commissioners appear to have understood that the king could not both eat his cake and have it. Furthermore,

[1] Lee's position was embarrassing, as the archbishops of Canterbury and York and the Bishop of Durham still had their mints, from which they derived a profit. Cromwell cured this trouble by abolishing these ancient privileges.

[2] T. Wright, *Letters relating to the suppression of the monasteries*, Camden Soc. 1843, 123.

[3] *Archaeologia*, xliii, 1871, 201.

[4] Cautious abbots used to apply to Cromwell for permission to sell.

[5] *Archaeologia*, xliii, 1871, 213 and 223.

they were local men who probably knew quite a lot about these deals! It would seem to be safe to assume that most church plate sold outright went straight into the melting-pot. The gentry naturally preferred refectory plate as pledges, but they would sometimes take a censer or a cross. It is to be feared that such pieces did not long survive the hope of their redemption.

By alluding to the final suppression in 1538 of the smaller houses licensed to continue, we have got out of order. It is, however, only necessary to allude to the Lincolnshire rising and to the Pilgrimage of Grace, because Cromwell added to his armoury at this juncture the use of acts of attainder in the case of some of the monasteries still incorporated, against which he was able to frame some sort of case. The new technique was to be his final weapon against all troublesome abbots during the next few years. It was another form of the direct levy on plate.

Father Philip Hughes[1] has estimated that only two-fifteenths of the property of the monasteries had fallen into the king's hands in 1536, such was the inequality of the distribution of wealth as between the 'greater' and the 'lesser' houses. The elimination of the latter under the most favourable circumstances could hardly have solved his financial worries, but the expense of suppressing the two rebellions must have entirely upset Cromwell's estimates. The servants of tyrants are not allowed to make miscalculations, and by the beginning of 1538 he must have felt it necessary to adopt desperate remedies in order to save himself.

The suppression of the monasteries recently licensed to continue was, after all, well within the law, but Cromwell's other methods of raising money were barefaced transgressions which he was only able to cover up to a certain extent by subsequent legitimation. The denunciation of the abuse of relics was a popular plank in the platform of the Reformers and provided him with a useful cover for lucrative depredations. A campaign against the shrines of the great English saints concerned mainly the great Benedictine abbeys and cathedral priories, but could also be made to include those in secular cathedrals such as St. Erkenwald in St. Paul's, St. Hugh at Lincoln, St. Richard at Chichester, St. Thomas at Hereford, and St. William at York. Why should those secular cathedrals which had no shrine go free? The addition of 'superfluous plate' to the articles to be confiscated brought such places as Exeter and Wells into the net and enabled the commissioners to pack up anything which they fancied.[2]

[1] *History of the Reformation in England*, 1950, i. 322.

[2] That this was literally the case is shown by a letter dated 6 March 1539 from the sub-dean of Wells to Cromwell which shows that the commissioners arrived with a letter under the privy seal authorizing them to take 'so moche of the saide Jewelles and plate to the use of the seid sovereign lorde as by their discretion should be thought expedient' (*Letters and Papers*, xiv, pt. i, 1539, 178).

It must not be supposed that a church which had a shrine to loot escaped the levy on 'superfluous plate'. The two following extracts from letters from commissioners to Cromwell will make quite

Simultaneously with the drive for the shrines of the saints and for 'superfluous plate', a new campaign was developed. It was another form of the collusive levy, but whereas the Conqueror had been willing to accept 'free gifts' of plate from the abbeys, it was now intimated to the religious houses that they might go into voluntary liquidation, transferring all their assets to the king! Behind this suggestion was the veiled threat of the use of the Act of Attainder which, though actually seldom used, was a very effective weapon. An Act of Parliament[1] was passed in 1539, when the process was well advanced, to give some sort of legality to what had been going on for months.

The fact that the most celebrated of the abbeys had been partly despoiled, often as much as a year before they agreed to surrender, is often overlooked. The effort of carrying on after the removal of the shrine and of the 'superfluous plate' must have told rapidly upon the morale of the monks. It is, indeed, surprising that one of the three great Benedictine abbeys of which Cromwell made an example by hanging the abbot had been carrying on under these depressing conditions.[2] The last religious house which gave in, without any promise of refoundation as a secular cathedral, was Waltham Abbey, which surrendered on 23 March 1540.

Whilst the 'greater' abbeys were falling one by one, Cromwell had been

clear the manner in which his instructions were carried out. The first must date early in 1538 and is as follows:

> 'Pleasith your lordship to be advertysed, that wee have ben at saynt Edmondes Bury, where we found a riche shrine whiche was very cumbrous to deface. We have takyn in the said monastery in golde and sylver m[l]m[l]m[l]m[l]m[l] [5,000] markes, and above, over and besydes a well and riche crosse with emereddes, as also dyvers and sundry stones of great value, and yet we have left the churche, abbott and convent very well ffurnesshed with plate of sylver necessary to the same.'

On the 21st of September the commissioners reported from Winchester in the following words:

> 'Pleasith your lordship to be advertised, that this Saturdaye, in the mornynge, aboutes thre of the clok, we made an ende of the shryne here at Wynchestre. There was in it no pece of gold, ne oon ring or true stone, but al greate counterfaictes. Nevertheles we thinke the sylver alone thereof woll amounte nere to twoo thousande markes. We have also receyved into our possession the crosse of emeraudes, the crosse called Hierusalem, an other crosse of golde, 2 chalices of gold, with some sylver plate, parcel of the plate of the vestrye; but thold prior made the plate of the house so thynne, that we can diminish non of it and leave the prior anything furnished. We found the prior and all the convent very conformable; having assistentes with us, at the opening our charge, the mayre, with 8 or 9 of the best of his brethrenn, the bisshops chauncellour Mr doctor Craiforde with a good apparence of honest personages besides; who; with oon voyce, most hartely gave lawde and prayse to God and to the kinges majestes godly and most christian herin as canne be devised. We have also this mornyng, going to our beddes warde, vieuwed thaulter, whiche we purpose to bring with us. It woll be worth the taking doune, and nothing therof seen; but suche a pece of work it is, that we thinke we shal not rid it doing our best, befor Monday night or Tuesdaye morning'

(T. Wright, op. cit. 144 and 218–19).

[1] 31 Henry VIII, cap. 13. This Act included, besides monasteries, 'colleges, houses of friars, and other religious and ecclesiastical houses and places'.

[2] Glastonbury had been raided, but Reading and Colchester, neither of which had an important shrine, appear to have escaped.

putting through another operation which would nowadays be justified under the name of 'rationalization'. It would have been illogical for the friars to have survived after the monks had gone, so that he got rid of them by using the same form of blackmail. There was little money involved for, although at a place like Salisbury the Black Friars might yield plate to the weight of 303 ounces and the Grey Friars 278 ounces,[1] the smaller houses often produced only a single silver chalice. Frequently this had been pledged, and then the commissioners had to decide whether it would be profitable to redeem it. The friars, though poor, were not always simple, for Bishop Roland, who visited the Ludlow friaries, had brought in to him two chalices, one paten, a pair of cruets, and the foot of a monstrance which the brethren had hidden in an old hose in a ditch at the back of their house.[2] The prior of the Austin Friars at Northampton, 'a great dicer', was reported to have divided plate to the value of £30 amongst the brethren. At any rate, a spell in gaol only had the effect of getting him to disgorge 40*s*.[3]

As we have already seen, the idea of making away with the plate of the community had occurred to some of the heads of religious houses at a very early stage. William Thirsk, Abbot of Fountains, had not waited for the passing of the 1536 Act before starting to sell the abbey plate and jewels to a London goldsmith named Warren.[4] When Thomas Parry went as visitor to St. Swithun's Cathedral Priory, Winchester, in March 1539, he wrote that 'a stranger Bestyan' had been before him and had been buying jewels from the prior and four or five of the monks—'he hathe ben in diverse religious Houses throughout the Reallm for a like Purpose'—and suggested that Cromwell should question him.[5] The fear that the abbots would make away with all their valuables became so acute that Dr. Layton, whilst touring monasteries in East Anglia in January 1538, made a practice of calling the 'honest men' into the chapter house and telling them that 'babblers, alleging that the King would suppress them all, slandered their natural sovereign'.[6]

In the early days it was hardly possible for the head of a 'lesser' monastery which had been refused licence to continue to dispose of the plate without a qualm of conscience. When pressure began to be applied to the 'greater' monasteries the position was rather different. It was then clear that monasticism in England was doomed, not merely the priory of X, and that the only alternative

[1] *Letters and Papers*, xiii, pt. 2, 1538, 204. [2] It is not clear which order was involved (ibid., pt. i, 473).

[3] Ibid. xiii, pt. 2, 297. Elsewhere (276) he is stated to have got rid of £100 worth of plate within the last year.

[4] Wright, *Letters*, 100. Warren would seem to have handled quite a lot of monastic plate in one way or another. He bought the plate of Brewood and Lilleshall Priories when they were sold up (Dugdale, *Monasticon*, 1846, iv. 501; *Archaeologia*, xliii, 1871, 209).

[5] H. Ellis, *Original Letters*, 1846, 3rd. ser. iii. 233.

[6] It was strictly true, too! The king would get everything by other means! (*Letters and Papers*, xiii. pt. 1, 35).

to submission was to flee abroad with anything which could be taken. The number of religious who followed the latter course was small and it is unlikely that much plate escaped destruction through them.

Was any plate secreted with an intention of bringing it out again when better times returned? There is very little evidence of this, as is not really surprising.[1] Monastic fervour had sunk low before the process of spoliation began, and it is not surprising that most monks took a pessimistic view of the future of the religious life in England. It was obvious that any revival would only be partial, and that if this occurred the monasteries which could be revived without excessive trouble were the cathedral priories, now being refounded as secular establishments. It would seem that the new dean and canons, who were almost always ex-religious from somewhere or other, were allowed to take over the plate which had been left behind after the levy which had been made a few months before the dissolution of the priory. The cathedrals of the new foundation did not, in fact, start off too badly, and it is perhaps not unlikely that by juggling with the accounts they carried forward more than the amount of plate with which they were credited.[2]

The procedure for the collection and realization of monastic plate differed according to the circumstances. The commissioners went on tours covering all the houses in a particular area. Not all of these would have reached the final stage, so that, for instance, only the 'superfluous plate' of Glastonbury, Bruton, Hinton, Witham, Bath, and Keynsham was collected by the commissioners, who cleared the cupboards of the already surrendered Shaftesbury, Tarrant,

[1] Cardinal Gasquet was able to write a book on *The Last Abbot of Glastonbury* without as much as alluding to the mystery of what Abbot Whiting was trying to do with the abbey plate. When Cromwell's commissioners swooped on Glastonbury, they found in the treasury and vestry neither jewels, plate, nor ornaments sufficient for a poor parish church. They immediately arrested the two treasurers and two lay clerks of the vestry and started a diligent inquiry. This led to the recovery of plate, which had been hidden in walls, vaults, and other secret places, and of more which had been conveyed into the country. They succeeded in recovering 11,000 ounces of silver and a certain amount of gold. They were not satisfied that this was all, and even pestered the abbot about it on the day of his execution. He denied knowledge of anything more—and left them guessing (*Letters and Papers*. xiv, pt. 2, 1539, 70, 150, and 186).

Large-scale secretion like this could not have escaped notice, so that it is obvious that the abbot must have had some plan. The Abbot of Barlings had conveyed plate out of his abbey three or four weeks before the Lincolnshire rising, which was taken as an indication that he was privy to it (ibid. xii, pt. 2, 1537, 123). There is no suggestion, however, that there was ever to have been a Somersetshire rising. Merely to have secreted the plate about the abbey would have been futile, since it must have been known that the process of wrecking would begin as soon as the commissioners had sold everything off. Similarly, there is nothing to suggest that the plate which had been smuggled out of the abbey was to be evacuated overseas. Was the abbot merely intent on giving as much trouble as possible?

[2] It cannot be taken for certain that the cathedrals of the new foundation retained at the death of Henry VIII all the plate which they had taken over from the suppressed priory in 1540. Canterbury had certainly been subjected to further pilfering on behalf of the king (Legg and Hope, 195–7).

Bindon, Cerne, Sherborne, Abbotsbury, and Milton. The winding-up of an abbey was not a simple affair, for the most 'conformable' abbot was apt to have some undisclosed assets which it might be necessary to chase down and recover.

The large consignments of plate from the important houses were always sent up to London. At the other end of the scale the wretched chalices from the friaries in small country towns were also brought along because it was impossible to find a purchaser on the spot. In between these categories there would be the plate of medium-sized houses where, for one reason or another, the haul might be disappointing. This might be sold on the spot, as goldsmiths from London sometimes followed in the tracks of the commissioners. It is pretty clear that the commissioners took good care of their own interests when the monastic plate was being sorted through, and Cromwell also took his toll.[1]

Our principal source of information regarding the final disposal of the monastic plate is a roll, 57 feet in length, representing the accounts for the period from 26 April 1537 to 4 December 1545 of John Williams, Master of the King's Jewels.[2] Unfortunately the accounts are dated 14 December 1551, by which time Sir John (as he now was) had been away from the Jewel House for seven years, for he had accepted in 1544 the treasurership of the Court of Augmentations which had been created to deal with confiscated church property. During the period of active spoliation he was often on the road with the other representatives of the Court, who were engaged in collecting the booty. It is not, therefore, surprising that the document is vague about dates and often obscure.[3] However, the general picture is quite clear. The primary object of the spoliation was to procure ready money, and though under more favourable circumstances the art-loving king might have been tempted to withhold much of the loot for use in the Chapel Royal, it is evident that he held

[1] Thus on 21 July 1537 Thomas Thacker wrote to Cromwell, who was away from home, that there had arrived 'to your Lordship's use certain parcels of plate'. The objects were a silver-gilt cross, a pair of candlesticks, a censer and incense-boat, a pax, two salts, and some other pieces of refectory plate, mainly parcel-gilt. They weighed in all 221½ oz. (*Letters and Papers*, xii, pt. 2, 1537, 123). The lay members of the Court of Augmentations were mainly interested in church lands, the clerical in good benefices. Dr. Layton picked up the Deanery of York and put his past experience to good use. When he died in the Low Countries in 1544, it was discovered that he had pledged some of the Minster's jewels and plate. The chapter had hurriedly to redeem them (B.M. Harl. 6971, 261).

[2] *Account of the Monastic Treasures confiscated at the dissolution of the various houses in England*, ed. W. B. D. D. Turnbull, Edinburgh, 1836.

[3] Sir John was, to put a charitable interpretation on the facts, one of those unwise civil servants who allow government property to accumulate in their private houses. When his house was burnt down on Christmas Eve, 1541, 'divers juells and goodes of the Kinges and allso of his were embesylled and conveyed awaye' (*Wriothesley's Chronicle*, Camden Soc. 2nd ser. i. 133). Doubtless a lot of files from the office were left to feed the flames! Furthermore, he had to make his accounts balance since the Jewel House acted as a sort of emergency bank for the other departments. Consequently, mixed up with matters which were the proper concern of the Jewel House are returns for victualling the fleet, repairing the royal parks, &c.

his hand so that almost everything was dealt with quite ruthlessly at the Jewel House, where it was sorted through before being passed on to the Mint. A few items were retained, however, of which the most important was the triptych retable from Ely Cathedral.[1] This was evidently a very important piece, the inside being of gold set with precious stones and the outside of silver-gilt. It reappears in the inventory of 1550,[2] but is not heard of again. A temporary respite was also allowed to a dozen images of gold, including ones of the Almighty, Our Lady, and some kings and queens. These evidently derived from some shrine or retable where only their fronts were visible, since John Barnes, one of the royal goldsmiths, had to overhaul them and supply silver-gilt backs where necessary.[3] Some of these also appear in the 1550 inventory, but the portable altar known as the 'Great Sapphire of Glastonbury' and a pair of crystal candlesticks mounted in silver-gilt, which came from Bury, did not last so long.

Before leaving the subject of the fate of the monastic treasures, it is perhaps necessary to emphasize two points. Firstly, if it be granted that the pipe which sucked all the gold and silver up to London leaked at every joint, it must not be inferred that the final result was negligible as far as the Exchequer was concerned.[4] Secondly, it seems almost certain that little of what escaped the royal clutches was in any sense saved. Piety played little part in the preservation of monastic treasures from the royal commissioners. The religious made few and uncertain efforts to preserve any of their plate for a sacred use. The laity who got hold of monastic church plate were activated by the hope of profit. It would seem that practically none of the monastic church plate which was in use at the time of the Dissolution has survived to our time.[5]

[1] *Account, &c.* 42, 50–51. [2] Soc. of Antiquaries, MS. 129, f. 8b. [3] *Account, &c.* 71–73, 96.

[4] Cardinal Gasquet, who tackled Sir John Williams's figures, made a total of £85,000 (*Henry VIII and the English Monasteries*, 413 and 480).

[5] There are only three items for which I think a plausible claim can be made. The best authenticated is the chalice with its paten which is preserved as a gift from the founder at Trinity College, Oxford. Sir Thomas Pope, who was the first treasurer of the Court of Augmentations, would have had as many chances of waylaying abbey plate as any of his colleagues. The story that the chalice and paten came from St. Albans does not seem to be traceable beyond Shaw and Meyrick, *Specimens of Ancient Furniture*, 1836, 56. The third piece is the St. Martin Ludgate pyx (p. 81 n, *supra*).

The chalice and paten (Pl. 20), now the property of Lord Hatherton and on loan to the Birmingham Museum, was found in about 1750, with nearly £1,000 worth of gold coins, during the demolition of Pillaton Hall, Staffs. (*Proc. Soc. of Antiquaries*, 2nd ser. x, 1885, 260). Since the hoard is said to have included guineas, it must have been deposited after 1675. The Littletons of Pillaton do not seem ever to have been Recusants but they do appear to have been on friendly terms with the canons of St. Thomas, near Stafford. Two members of the family are stated in the Dissolution records to have accepted pledges of the abbey's plate (*Archaeologia*, xliii, 1873, 213). Sir Edward Littleton of Pillaton Hall was constable of Stafford Castle at the time and may well have helped his neighbours at St. Thomas by buying one of their chalices when they were pressed for money by reason of their composition for licence to continue (see above, 113). It is not clear why he should have clung to the chalice any more than did Sir Thomas Pope—he only became a founder in 1554.

For a short time after the surrender of the last of the monasteries King Henry was able to get along without making further inroads upon the treasures of the Church. The lack of confidence in the king's good intentions and the general lowering of the standards of morality with regard to church goods is illustrated by the seizure, by the corporation of Lynn, of the plate of the chapel of St. Nicholas at the beginning of 1543.[1] The next crisis did not actually develop until the summer of 1545, as a result of the wars with France and Scotland. About this time William Paget wrote to the Earl of Hertford to sound him on the proposal 'to borrow some of the plate of the churches'. The latter agreed to the suggestion 'for God's service which consisteth not in jewels, plate or ornaments of gold or silver, cannot thereby be anything diminished, and these things better employed for the weal and defence of the realm'.[2] The resulting measure was the 'Act for the Dissolution of Colleges, Free Chapels, Chantries, Hospitals, Fraternities, Brotherhoods, Guilds and Stipendiary Priests'.[3] Since these bodies were given personally to the king, the gift lapsed on his death on 28 January 1547, as by now it was realized that the spoliation of the churches could not be rushed if the full benefit was to be secured. The reprieve was, of course, only temporary, as the measure reappeared as 1 Edward VI, c. 14, with certain modifications which included the exemption of the colleges of Oxford and Cambridge, Eton and Winchester, and of the collegiate church of St. George's Chapel, Windsor.

Of the four categories doomed by the statutes of 1545 and 1547 only the collegiate churches possessed plate in important quantities. They were, however, relatively few, and their plate was dealt with, properly or improperly, in much the same manner as had been that of the monasteries.

The plate of the chantries would probably have been left undisturbed had it not been for the fact that their endowments were well worth seizing. Even the chantries in the cathedrals were, with notable exceptions, meagrely furnished. Those attached to well-to-do town or country churches usually possessed a

It is well known that vestments, alabaster carvings, and even brass lecterns were exported after the Dissolution of the monasteries. Plate was, however, in a different category, since it was readily convertible into money. A goldsmith who bought a piece, either on the quiet from the abbot or publicly from the commissioners, would have to pay something near its market value. Abbey plate would not, therefore, be a very profitable export, since the vendor could only hope to exploit the workmanship of the piece. The only sort of exporter who may have been in a position to make a good profit out of abbey plate were those who had not had to pay for it!

[1] In the records of the corporation of King's Lynn under the date 11 February 1543 is the entry: 'This day the Mayor and Aldermen and Common Council for certain reason and urgent consideration received of the guardians of the Chapel of St Nicholas these parcels of plate hereinafter . . . to the intent to put the same for sale, and the money thereof received to bestow and convert to the advancement of the commonwealth of the town' (E. M. Beloe, *Our Borough, Our Churches*, King's Lynn, 1894, 156–7). The list is quite a long one, so that there is no reason to doubt that the two chalices found by the Edwardian commissioners were all that had been left (*Norfolk Archaeology*, i, 1837, 80).

[2] *Letters and Papers*, xx, pt. 1, 1545, no. 1145, p. 563.

[3] 37 Henry VIII, c. 37.

silver chalice—often a very small one, but in the north of England two-thirds and in the south one-third of the chantries in rural churches reported no plate at all. In some chantry certificates it is expressly mentioned that the priest used the parish chalice; elsewhere he may have used a pewter one. Some few persons had seen the threat to the chantries from afar—the patron of a chantry in Holy Trinity, Goodramgate, York,[1] is recorded to have made off with a chalice as early as 1538–9. It seems likely that when the crisis actually arrived, quite a number of chalices disappeared quietly.[2]

The decision to suppress the colleges, chantries, &c., has been assailed from all sides by writers of different complexions ever since the middle of last century. From the point of view of the Exchequer the restriction of the levy to these particular institutions was disastrous. As has already been mentioned, the original intention had been to take some at least of the treasures of the parish churches. The chantries were to be found in so many places that it was impossible for the churchwardens and parochial clergy to overlook the threat to their own church plate. The rumour that the parish churches were to be robbed had fanned the flames of rebellion in Lincolnshire in 1536, when the lesser monasteries were being dissolved, but ten years later, when the threat was becoming actual, the mood of righteous indignation had evaporated.[3] As the winding-up of the chantries proceeded, ominous rumours about the safety of the goods of the parish churches began to reach the Council, and in 1547 the bishops were ordered to make inquiries about them. The matter was allowed to rest until 15 February 1549, when the Privy Council sent letters to commissioners in every county instructing them to compile inventories of church goods and to deposit these with the *custos rotulorum* of each shire. The commissioners were warned to forbid the sale or embezzlement of any church property.[4] From this date squeamish churchwardens began to consult the Council about projected sales of church plate,[5] but the majority boldly continued to exercise their customary rights, which had not yet been overridden by any Act of Parliament.[6]

[1] *Yorkshire Chantry Surveys*, Surtees Soc. 1894, i, 52.

[2] In May 1553 Lincoln Minster declared three chalices but in May 1557 they had seven. The difference was made up by two chalices from suppressed chantries and two which had fallen to the Minster by the bequest of Bishop Longland (d. 1547), and which his executors had delayed in handing over (*Archaeologia*, liii, 1892, 64, 71–72).

[3] We hear of a riot in Cornwall in December 1547, when a rumour went round that the parish churches were to be robbed. It was quietened by the local gentry before it became serious (*Acts of the Privy Council*, 1547–50, 535). When seizure was actually decreed three and a quarter years later, the West had just gone through the sanguinary rebellion which had been mainly occasioned by the introduction of the Prayer Book.

[4] *Calendar of State Papers Domestic*, 1547–80, 14.

[5] e.g. the Council wrote to the inhabitants of Sandwich on 14 August 1550 to say that the king was content to allow them their church plate so that the proceeds of its sale might be applied to the repair of their harbour (*Letters and Papers*, iii. 104).

[6] Dr. W. Page, who printed one of these commissions in the preface to *Inventories of Church Goods*

The next step was not taken by the Privy Council until 3 March 1551, when it is recorded that: 'This daie it was decreed that forasmuch as the Kinges Majestie had need presently of a masse of money, therfore commissioners shulde be addressed into all shires of England to take into the Kinges handes such church plate as remaigneth, to be emploied unto his Highnes use.'[1] Even after this decision had been reached progress was slow, as it was not until 29 January 1552 that the *custos rotulorum* of each shire was instructed to release the 1549 inventory to the commissioners.[2]

The nomination of the commissioners took place in the early summer and thereafter progress was fairly rapid. The instructions were to make fresh inventories and to demand an account of all objects which had been sold or lost since the 1549 inventory was made.[3] The inventories and reports compiled by the commissioners are of immense importance for the light which they throw upon the furnishing of English churches at the close of the Middle Ages. Here, however, we are concerned only with what they tell us about the actual fate of the plate belonging to the parish churches. The inventories for the City of London and for a large part of England have survived and are preserved in the Public Record Office. Many of them have been printed in the course of the last hundred years, probably enough to give a fair idea as to what happened in England itself—about Wales we have no information.

The returns for ninety-five out of one hundred and nine parish churches in the City of London have survived and are particularly instructive. As might be expected, the churchwardens understood much more clearly the financial than the religious issues. The moral issue was, however, kept in mind at St. Nicholas Cole Abbey, where no hanky-panky had taken place. Everything was reported to be in its place and the nearest approach to irregularity was that the churchwardens had sold the 'defaced' service books to Sir Thomas Sudlee, parson, who had not actually handed over the agreed sum of 13*s*. 4*d*.[4] Elsewhere the churchwardens appear to have been not so much anxious to avoid becoming parties to sacrilege as eager to find ways to counter the government's attempt to nationalize the capital belonging to the parish. They had recourse to two main devices. Both involved the sale of the whole[5] or part of the plate and ornaments and the use of the proceeds either for what they guessed would be allowable expendi-

for the counties of York, Durham and Northumberland (Surtees Soc. 1897) assumed (p. xiii) that the order not to alienate had some effect but that by that time a lot of the damage had been done.

[1] *Letters and Papers*, iii. 228.

[2] Ibid. 467. The 1549 inventories have mostly disappeared.

[3] The commissions have been frequently printed, e.g. by Dr. Page *ut supra*, 1–3; Daniel-Tyssen, *Inventories of Church Goods and Ornaments in Surrey*, 1869, 2–8; W. Money, *Parish Church Goods in Berkshire in 1552*, 1879, 20–28.

[4] Walters, 535.

[5] Seven churches (All Hallows the Great, St. Andrew Hubbard, St. Benet Fink, St. Benet Paul's Wharf, St. John Walbrook, St. Margaret Pattens, and St. Peter-le-Poer) had no longer any plate

ture or its investment in securities which they hoped would not be subject to seizure. Everywhere there is mention of bills for repairs. Some of these are for making good after the removal of the altar and the rood, but Protestantism could be made quite expensive if it were decided that the windows must be reglazed since 'Imagerye was contrarye to the Kinges proceedinges'.[1] Much was done in the way of structural repairs, a form of expenditure which was not likely to be challenged, as the general standard of maintenance of the City churches was poor.

A form of reinvestment favoured by ten parishes was the purchase of house property, but forty-nine had bought communion cups or else existing (secular) cups for use for communion. Twelve churches had two communion cups, two had three,[2] and one had two (secular) cups for the communion. There are two reasons for classing the communion cups as reinvestments instead of as necessary expenditure. There had been as yet no overt action to encourage the churches to acquire communion cups, but it could be regarded as certain that if a rigorous spoliation was decreed, the communion cups would probably be the only things left. Anyone who has handled any of the surviving Edwardian communion cups from the City will have been struck by their splendid solidity—in fact they weigh as much as two heavy medieval chalices. This is no accident, since only five out of the sixty-two City communion cups surviving or mentioned in the inventories weighed less than 20 ounces. The majority ranged between 30 and 45 ounces. They are not, in fact, an entirely reliable guide to the religious preferences of the churchwardens[3] but represent, their idea of a really safe investment. They guessed that if they left their capital in the form of chalices, the commissioners would leave behind only the lightest one for parish use.

If emphasis has been laid upon the plate which the king did not get, it should be realized that when the orders for seizure came, there was still a considerable amount of loot, although the quantity was nothing compared with what it

at all. How were the churchwardens to guess that the government would put back the clock to the standard of church furnishing of the days of Henry II, instead of to that of Henry I (when most churches had not had silver chalices)?

The instructions given to the commissioners were to inquire about alienations of church treasures since the beginning of the reign, but in actual fact the churchwardens had begun to sell out in about 1545, when the first Act for the dissolution of the chantries had been passed. In that year St. Mary Magdalen, Milk Street, sold 156 ounces (Churchwardens' accounts in Guildhall Library).

[1] St. Stephen Coleman (Walters, 603). [2] St. Mary Colechurch and St. Peter upon Cornhill.

[3] In fact some churchwardens hedged—fifteen churches had at the time that the reports were made both chalices and communion cups.

The idea of the communion cup as an investment spread into Surrey. Churches which in 1552–3 possessed communion cups which weighed 30 ounces or over, or where it is mentioned that the cup was made from two chalices, are Beddington (Pl. 49), Lambeth, Lingfield, Mitcham, Putney, and St. Saviour, Southwark. The remaining Surrey communion cups must have been made either from one chalice of good weight or from two light ones (Daniel-Tyssen, op. cit. *passim*).

would have been if it had been taken at the same time as that of the chantries. The report of each of the ninety-five churches tells an individual story, and even when corroborative evidence is available from the churchwardens' accounts it is not often easy to reconstruct exactly the policy adopted by each parish during those difficult years. On the whole the City churchwardens appear to have acted with considerable acumen and reasonable honesty.[1]

Before discussing what happened in the shires, it is necessary to say something about the composition and working of the commissions. The number of commissioners ranged from five to eight. The majority of them were local gentry, but there were always one or two peers or persons in close touch with the Privy Council in London. Large counties had more than one commission, whilst important towns were also dealt with separately. What we may call the London members of the commissions did not get involved in riding round; indeed, many of them were on several commissions, the Earl of Northampton on six. The Londoners were, however, usually possessed of some local knowledge of the county—perhaps they had picked up some abbey lands in it. Their function was to read the reports and to look after the king's interests. The greater part of the work was done by the gentry commissioners, who broke up into parties and ordered the churchwardens to meet them at convenient points. What an appalling job they had—something much worse than the conscientious objectors' tribunals or county agricultural committees of our own days! Every day whilst the task lasted they would find themselves listening to dreary tales which they would instinctively recognize as being half-truths or not true at all! Always told by the most respected people in the village!

The rural churchwardens had also taken advantage of the opportunity to repair their churches. Money derived from the sale of the plate and vestments had been used for the repair of bridges or for paying for a soldier for the king's war. The trouble began with the deficiencies for which no convincing explanation was proffered. Thefts of sacred vessels have occurred in every century, but the number reported by the churchwardens in 1552 is quite abnormal; moreover, they cannot be dissociated with the disappearance of vestments, candlesticks, and even bells. Doubtless the churchwardens, faced with the prospect of losing their belongings anyhow, had been less than usually cautious, but it is perfectly clear that the village Cromwells had been out in every county sequestrating church goods on their own account. It was comparatively rare for the churchwardens to venture any information as to the whereabouts of the missing goods. When they did so, it was probably because the delinquent was regarded as rather a poacher.[2] It is obvious that in many cases the churchwardens

[1] For instance, fifteen parishes admitted that they had a balance of over £25 (St. Mary-le-Bow, £120) derived from the sale of the plate and ornaments.

[2] Thus the churchwardens of five churches in the Rochford area made no bones about accusing Sir

must have known much more than they admitted. Sometimes, perhaps, the goods had been removed by someone who felt that he had some sort of title to them,[1] at others a removal may have appeared the best way of securing the preservation of the object for future use. However, it is perfectly evident that much of what had been removed had been embezzled, as this was made clear when efforts at recovery were made during the next reign.

Generally speaking, the returns for the southern counties are the more frank and revealing. It is much more difficult to assess those which have survived relating to the northern ones. The return for the East Riding, for instance, has very little to say about sales, thefts, and embezzlements, but it is incredible that at the close of the Middle Ages some of the huge churches along the Humber should be only able to produce a single chalice.[2]

On 16 January 1553 a fresh series of commissions were sent out to authorize the seizure of all plate except for one or two chalices for each cathedral, collegiate church, or the parish churches of large towns, and a single chalice for every small parish church.[3] The local commissioners were left with very little scope for the use of their discretion and were practically confined to making the decision as to whether a given church was entitled to keep a second chalice or, if not, whether it should keep the more or the less valuable one.

Many harsh words have been said about the local commissioners, who generally left behind a single chalice and that the worst! However, we must remember that they had to keep before their eyes the necessity of producing a total

William Stafford of having sent men to carry off bells from their churches (*Trans. Essex Arch. Soc.* iv, 1869, 201). More typical of the general attitude was the report of the commissioners for Hertfordshire who headed their return with a list of embezzlements. Everyone on the list was either dead or else no longer resident in the county. The churchwardens of Kelshall, when notifying the loss of a chalice, tried a real backhander: 'thei suspecte Mr Todde who was persone their, and now chappleyne to the kinges Majestie' (J. E. Cussens, *Inventory of Furnishings and Ornaments remaining in all the parish churches of Hertfordshire in the last year of Edward VI*, 1873, 18).

[1] In three cases in Herefordshire the churchwardens reported that the chalice used at the church or chapel was private property and had been removed by the owner. Since the chalice in each case was the only one, this did not much matter. However, it might have protected it if there was another levy later on! (*C.P. Herefordshire*, x).

[2] e.g. Hedon, Howden, Patrington, and South Cave, also St. Mary, Beverley. It seems better to attribute this dearth of chalices to concealment in 1552 rather than to looting by the royal army at the time of the Pilgrimage of Grace.

The returns for the West Riding have come down in such a fragmentary condition that it is impossible to pass a judgement upon them. Those for the North Riding and Durham have not survived, whilst the Northumberland ones leave out many parishes. The commissioners for Cumberland did their work very summarily. Whilst the returns give the impression of a poor neighbourhood, as might be expected, there is no reference to sales or embezzlements. Many of the churches, as is pointed out by the editor, were deficient in essential utensils (*Cumberland and Westmorland Arch. Soc. Trans.* viii, 1886, 192–204). The surviving Lancashire returns use a formula quite different from that used elsewhere and it is difficult to extract information from them (*Chetham Soc.* O.S. cvii, 1879, N.S. xlvii, 1902).

[3] See note 3 on p. 122 and *Calendar of the Patent Rolls, 1550–3*, 393–7.

which would satisfy the expectations of their hard-bitten colleagues in London. This would be difficult when a lean county was being plundered. When they left the better or a second chalice, they seem to have been influenced by unwonted probity on the part of the churchwardens. Thus a long list of plate belonging to Dartford church, Kent, bore witness to the integrity of the churchwardens, so the commissioners put in a special plea that the church should be allowed to convert a chalice weighing 9 ounces and a pyx weighing 15 ounces into two communion cups.[1] Similarly the Surrey commissioners found the contents of Putney church intact when they received the inventory in 1552. Was it at their suggestion that the churchwardens had 'ij chalices made into a cupp poiz. xxiv oz. di'. which the second lot of commissioners left them in 1553?[2]

It is characteristic of the ill luck of Mary that she should have to go down to history as the last sovereign to benefit by the stealing of church plate. The collection and dispatch to London of the confiscated plate was by no means over when Edward VI died on 6 July 1553. In the latter part of the year letters were sent to the commissioners for Dorset, Lancashire, Norfolk, Somerset, and the city of Salisbury, giving instructions for the return of seized church plate wherever possible. It appears to have been the practice to flatten the chalices at the collecting centre, but the patens were still fit to return. Amongst the Somerset stuff were nineteen chalices, evidently still in good condition, which it was ordered should be returned to nineteen of the biggest churches in the county. All the 'defaced' chalices were to be sent up to London as originally intended.[3]

Though it was largely lack of subject-matter which saved Elizabeth I from joining the list of robbers of church plate, some small credit must be allowed to her. At the time of her accession some cathedrals still possessed something more than the bare minimum of plate, whilst the university colleges, after their lucky escape at the end of the reign of her father, still possessed 'superstitious' plate. In both cases she left the matter to the attention of the ecclesiastical authorities, and made no attempt to make a profit which would certainly have eluded her.

We may here say good-bye to the subject of the spoliation of church plate by the Crown. It is characteristic of the higher moral attitude towards the property of the Church, which had developed since the death of Elizabeth I, that the Royalists made no attempt to impound church plate during the Civil War.[4] The Parliamentarians were not quite so scrupulous, but we shall consider their behaviour in a later chapter.

[1] *Archaeologia Cantiana*, viii, 1872, 141.

[2] Daniel-Tyssen, op. cit. 120 and 157.

[3] *Acts of the Privy Council*, iv. 355, 360–1, 371, 376.

[4] King Charles intervened personally to secure the execution of a soldier who had looted a chalice at Wing in 1645 (*Diary of Sir Henry Slingsby*, 1836, 161). Although *The History and Fate of Sacrilege* was not to be printed until 1698, many Royalists must have been familiar with Spelman's theories. His earlier *De non temerandis ecclesiis* must have been read during the Civil War, as it was being reprinted at Oxford at the time of the Royalist collapse in 1646.

PART III

SINCE THE REFORMATION

I

THE CHURCH AND THE GOLDSMITHS

1. 1548–1660

THOUGH the church historian may prefer to date the beginning of the Reformation from the passing of the Act of Supremacy in 1535, the decisive date for us is 1548 in which the first pieces of plate were made expressly for Protestant use.

Protestant church plate was called into existence by a combination of sentimental, utilitarian, and economic forces, the interaction of which it is extremely interesting to trace.

Most writers have accepted the advent of the communion cup as the inevitable consequence of the introduction of the new sacramental service. This was not so, as is proved by the survival of numerous medieval chalices (and the wrecks of medieval chalices) in the Protestant churches of Scandinavia and Germany. The Lutherans saw nothing unseemly in the continued use of mass chalices and, when occasion arose for ordering a new one, the design was generally of a traditional sort, though brought up to date in respect of its decoration.

The suggestion that the communion cup was the result of the need for a larger vessel because of the return to the custom of administering the sacrament both in bread and wine to the laity is only partly valid. The surviving Edwardian communion cups are generally of considerably greater capacity than ordinary medieval chalices, but this is not invariably the case, whilst the weights of some of those which we know of only from inventories would not have allowed them to be large. The proper reply to the embarrassment resulting from the large consumption of wine at the communion was the provision of special flagons. This fact was fully understood from the first, as will be shown presently.

It seems, therefore, that the introduction of the communion cup must be regarded as a conscious deviation in the direction of the advanced Protestantism as practised in Switzerland. The next curious point to be noted is that although there is no reason to doubt that Cranmer and the Privy Council approved the innovation, no action was taken to compel the use of the new type of vessel, such as was adopted in the reign of Elizabeth I. There is some evidence to suggest that some sort of official lead was given to encourage the use of communion cups within the City of London. The earliest surviving cup is that belonging to St. Lawrence Jewry (Pl. 52*a*) which bears the hall-mark for 1548 and must, therefore, have been made within a very short time of the authorization of communion in both kinds (1 May 1548) and that of the First Prayer Book (21 January 1549). There is little likelihood that the parish church of the Guildhall would have risked an innovation which had not been approved by the lord mayor. Henry Amcotts, Stockfishmonger, came into office at Michaelmas 1548. He received the customary knighthood and seems to have been on very good terms with the government. Besides the St. Lawrence Jewry cup of 1548, four more surviving examples were probably made for City churches during his year of office.[1] We cannot, of course, guess how many more of those others which are mentioned in the 1552 inventories but which have since disappeared were made thus early. At any rate, by the time that the despoiling commissioners came round nearly half of the City churches had either communion cups or else cups of secular origin for use at the communion. If the returns for these forty-nine churches are examined in detail, the impression arises that about a third of them had invested in communion cups because it seemed a wise thing to do, but this does not mean that they had entirely divested themselves of the sort of plate for which there would be no use in Protestant services. Some other returns reveal no definite bias, but eight seem to show a serious attempt to meet more fully the needs occasioned by the new Prayer Book. Thus St. Dionis Backchurch and St. Margaret, New Fish Street, had each got a communion flagon, and six churches had got a basin for collecting the alms.[2] The paten at St. Olave, Hart Street, was square and the weights of some of those in the other churches were heavy according to medieval standards. They were, therefore, presumably largish.[3]

Nearly half of the surviving Edward VI communion cups were made for churches in the City of London. It seems most unlikely that the ratio would be the same if we had a correct list of those in existence at the time of his death on 6 July 1553. Our information with regard to communion cups outside the City is derived from surviving examples, the 1552 inventories, and churchwardens' accounts. The records show that many parishes in the vicinity of London had them. St. Margaret, Westminster, had bought two gilt and two parcel-gilt cups from Robert Taylboyes in 1551 and may be considered to have gone over wholeheartedly to Protestantism. Our information about Surrey is good and shows that communion cups were to be found not only in the suburban fringe but in some of the small towns and even in rural churches.[4] Our infor-

[1] St. James Garlickhythe I, St. Mildred, Bread Street, St. Michael, Wood Street (now at St. Andrew, Greenwich), and St. Peter upon Cornhill. These all bear the 1549 hall-mark which would have been current for eighteen weeks of Amcott's mayorality.

[2] St. Botolph, Billingsgate, New Fish Street, St. Martin, Outwich, St. Michael, Cornhill, St. Peter upon Cornhill, and St. Stephen, Walbrook.

[3] The use of household bread was authorized by the Second Prayer Book in 1552.

[4] Beddington, Bermondsey (2), Carshalton, Caterham, Croydon (2), Kingston (2), Lambeth (2),

mation about Kent and Essex is less complete, but, as far as it goes, seems to show that the acquisition of silver communion cups had not gone so far. Three of the four Kentish churches recorded by the 1552 commissioners as having, or being about to acquire, cups are close to the part of Surrey (around the archi-episcopal residence at Croydon), where the new vessels are mentioned most commonly.[1] The two Essex churches to have silver communion cups were on the eastern fringe of London.[2] No other communion cups are mentioned in the commissioners' returns for the Home Counties. The distribution of the other Edwardian cups shows a strong bias towards the south of England, the most northerly being at Hunstanton, Norfolk. The rest are scattered, without any pattern, in the towns and villages of the southern counties, the most westerly example being at Totnes, Devon.[3]

The chalice and paten now in the Melbourne Gallery bear the hall-mark for 1537, the year after the suppression of the 'lesser' monasteries, and must have been amongst the very latest pieces of medieval church plate to be made. Since about that date no plate had been made for church account until the earliest communion cups were ordered in 1548. It is obvious that the change in the flow of the tide must have been welcome to the goldsmiths, but by the time of the king's death possibly a hundred and fifty pieces of all sorts had been made, spread over six years. There was no probability that the demand for Protestant plate would increase rapidly in the immediate future, for as soon as the confiscated parish plate had been garnered in the churchwardens were likely to be more careful of expenditure than of late.

The accession of Mary revolutionized the situation and left the goldsmiths with a baffling outlook before them. The queen's attempt to put the clock back brought no immediate flow of rich orders to Cheapside. When the episcopal injunctions began to circulate, one of the few items which most parishes could answer satisfactorily was that it possessed a silver chalice. This was the only object which it was now stipulated should be made of silver. There were some defaulters even so. Firstly, there were the churches which had recently invested in communion cups about which we shall have to speak anon, and secondly, the churches which had carried self-spoliation to the utmost limit during the last reign. Retribution came slowly, and when Nicholas Harpsfield made his visitation of his archdeaconry of Canterbury between 31 July and 30 September 1557 there were still thirteen churches requiring chalices and

Lingfield, Putney, Saunderstead, Southwark (2), Walton-on-the-Hill, and Wandsworth. We seem to see Cranmer's personal influence radiating from his residences at Lambeth and Croydon. On the other hand, Sir William Cecil's church at Wimbledon had not got a cup although, as a commissioner for Surrey, he might have been expected to have urged for one.

1 Crayford, Dartford (2), and Farnborough. The fourth was Wouldham.

2 Dagenham (2) and Walthamstow.

3 For the list see Appendix II.

twenty-two patens. Since the queen died just over a year later his Protestant successor had to deal with some of the defaulters, whilst he had gone to languish in the Fleet.[1]

How the churchwardens managed who found themselves with a communion cup but no chalice we can only guess in part. The surviving examples prove that some were hidden away, but we are left to speculate about the fate of many of the others: were they sold in order to provide funds for the new chalice, &c., or were they saved only to perish at a later date? Thus in 1552 St. Michael Cornhill had had two communion cups—were these sacrificed to pay for the deprotestantizing of the church?[2] It had been very advanced. If so, the churchwardens' accounts provide no record of it. Similarly, we get no indication of the ultimate fate, in the reign of Elizabeth I, of the silver chalice weighing 12½ ounces bought in 1554. There are similar tantalizing lacunae in the churchwardens' accounts of that other very advanced church, St. Margaret, Westminster, which still retains two of its Edwardian communion cups. The churchwardens started off by buying a silver-gilt chalice weighing 15 ounces, with a paten which was in a poor state, as its burnishing is charged separately. At the same time, or a little later, they supplied themselves with a pyx, censers, cross, and monstrance, all of base metal. When the churchwardens resumed quadrennial inventories in 1560 they entered up a little pyx of silver parcel-gilt. This must have come as a gift, since no payment was made for it.[3] We may note that both the St. Michael's and the St. Margaret's accounts give an 'all-in' price for the chalices and make no reference to 'fashion'. This suggests the requirements of both churches had been met with chalices which had disappeared from some other church during the previous reign.

If the goldsmiths did not make much money out of the advanced churches, they did not necessarily do much better out of the conservative ones. St. Mary at Hill had conformed as far as was necessary in the reign of Edward VI, without going so far as to buy a communion cup. Deprotestantizing was, consequently, not quite so troublesome as at St. Michael's where, for instance, the pews in the chancel had been arranged so that their backs faced the space for the altar. On the other hand, it had prided itself on the high standard of its music, and it was on the choir that any surplus funds were lavished during the reign of Mary. No

[1] Thus, Harpsfield instructed the inhabitants of Lyminge 'to provid a chalyce of silver . . . thissyd Allhallon' (*Archdeacon Harpsfield's Canterbury Visitations, 1556–8*, Catholic Record Soc. 1950, 58), but in 1561 the parish was still without a chalice. The churchwardens, however, told the new archdeacon that David Spicer had bequeathed the money for one. He had outlived the old queen by only six weeks, and his widow, who had remarried, had done nothing about the bequest. The archdeacon's intervention resulted in the provision of the present communion cup, which bears the 1561 hall-mark (*Archaeologia Cantiana*, xvi, 1886, 334).

[2] My reasons for concluding that the Edward VI cup now at this church has not always been there are given in Appendix II.

[3] Churchwardens' accounts in Westminster Public Library.

purchases of plate were made, but for the patronal festival, Lady Day, the churchwardens hired plate, presumably from a goldsmith.[1] It was not, of course, usual for the churchwardens to buy plate in excess of the archdeacon's requirements, but the hiring of plate suggests that gifts were not forthcoming. This would seem to have been a rather general experience. We do, indeed, come across mentions of gifts and bequests of plate during these four years, but they are not rich ones. The one important order which came through was for the splendid service of altar plate given by Cardinal Pole to Canterbury Cathedral. It will be realized that from the trade point of view the reign of Mary was a disappointment.[2]

When Elizabeth I ascended the throne on 17 November 1558, it was hardly open to doubt that she would favour some form of Protestantism, but the manner in which her course, when chosen, would affect Cheapside was anyone's guess. We are not concerned with how the queen felt her way during the winter of 1558–9, since the first landmark for us is the restoration of the cup to the laity by proclamation on 22 March, Wednesday in Holy Week. Since only eight weeks of the hall-marking year remained to run, it is really remarkable that we should still retain a communion cup marked during this short period. There is nothing, however, suggestive of haste or uncertainty about the cup belonging to St. Michael le Belfrey, York (Pl. 54), which is perhaps the finest in the Elizabethan series. Communion cups with the 1559 hall-mark are rare. Except for one at Lambourne, Essex, all the examples are to be found in or about London.[3] They may be accepted as evidence of advanced religious views amongst the congregations concerned except in the case of the chapel of St. Peter ad Vincula, which must have been ordered by someone who felt a special concern for the spiritual needs of the poor prisoners in the Tower! The pattern of the manufacture of communion cups during the 1560 hall-marking year is very much the same, so that it must have by now become evident that at the existing rate of progress it would be a very long time indeed before massing chalices would disappear from English churches.

Matthew Parker and Edmund Grindal were consecrated, respectively, to the sees of Canterbury and London in mid-December 1559, and some time must have elapsed before they could pay attention to the problem of the plate proper for English churches. The decision that every English church should get

[1] In 1556 they hired for 8*d.* a cross, a pair of candlesticks, and a censer. Next year they spent 1*s.* and got a couple of crosses (*The Medieval Records of a London City Church* (*St. Mary at Hill*), ed. H. Littlehales, Early English Text Soc. 1905, 407–10).

[2] The founders and the other workers in the base metals must have done much better. There can be little doubt that many of the copper-gilt crosses with crocketed sides, which are still found in country presbyteries, were made in response to the injunctions of Marian archdeacons.

[3] St. Botolph, Aldgate; St. Dunstan, Stepney; St. George, Southwark; St. Martin, Ludgate; St. Mary-le-Bow; St. Stephen Walbrook, and St. Vedast.

its chalice converted into a communion cup must be attributed mainly to these two, but chiefly to the archbishop. It is a little surprising that a change about

MAP OF THE ENGLISH DIOCESES TO ILLUSTRATE THE CAMPAIGN FOR THE REFASHIONING OF CHALICES IN THE REIGN OF ELIZABETH I

which many Protestants did not feel strongly should have been sponsored by Parker, who was in many ways so tolerant.[1] The conclusion that this conversion was a means and not an end appears to be almost inevitable. It was notorious that in the early years of this reign there were many clergy who were prepared not only to celebrate the communion at the parish church but also to say

[1] The Swiss reformers, who so freely gave their advice to the English bishops at this period, do not appear to have said anything about the supersession of massing chalices.

mass up at the manor for those who preferred the old service. The conversion of the parish chalice into a communion cup would help to curb the activities of these unreliable individuals.[1]

Parker must have made his views known at quite an early date, since already in 1560 the churchwardens of Elmsted are found presenting their vicar at a visitation by the archdeacon of Canterbury, because 'yn the tyme of the popyshe masse he to reverence that order did use to mynister in a challyce of sylver; Whereas, now in contempte of thys ministracion he useth a boole too unsemely to put mylke yn'.[2] It must have been about this time that the alteration of chalices into communion cups was put upon a compulsory basis. At first this was done only in the dioceses of Canterbury and London. It is possible that the instructions were given verbally by the archbishop and the bishop to their archdeacons, since no document has been found which throws any light upon the matter.[3] At any rate, during the hall-marking year 1562 a large number of communion cups were provided for these two dioceses. Of course, the success of the scheme was not complete. There were parishes which evaded the conversion for a few years and there were probably others which only lost their chalices in Stuart times. Odd communion cups belonging to this year are to be found in most of the other dioceses of the southern province, but their distribution suggests no concerted effort.

Though no general order for the conversion of chalices was ever made, there exist a number of instructions at diocesan level, and as a result of them it will be found that in most dioceses the Elizabethan communion cups were made within quite a short time of one another, varying from one to four years. The earliest document on the subject is Bishop Guest's injunction for the diocese of Rochester, issued in 1565, which reads as follows:

Item, that the chalice of every parish church be altered into a decent communion cup therewith to minister the Holy Communion, taking away no more thereof but only so much as shall pay for the altering of the same into a cup. And the said cup to be provided in every parish within my said diocese by or on this side of the feast of Saint Michael the Archangel next coming after the date thereof.[4]

We are unable now to estimate the success of this injunction, since there is no

[1] William (later Cardinal) Alleyn was in England in 1562–5. In a letter to Dr. Vandeville he wrote: 'Many priests said mass secretly and celebrated the heretical offices and supper in public' (*First and Second Diaries of the English College at Douay*, ed. T. F. Knox, 1878, xxiii).

[2] *Archaeologia Cantiana*, xvi, 1886, 337.

[3] One was included in a list of articles submitted to convocation in 1563, but not allowed (Strype, *Annals of the Reformation*, 1824, i, pt. 2, 564). It is possible that no general instruction was ever given, although it was certainly believed that one had been issued. Frere and Kennedy (iii. 193) quote a complaint by Prebendary Gardiner which would seem to imply an order, but the passage to which reference is made (Strype, *Life and Acts of Matthew Parker* 1821, iii, App. liv) seems to show the prebendary as a very bad witness!

[4] Frere and Kennedy, iii. 162.

large number of 1565 cups in the diocese of Rochester similar to the 1562 ones which still bear witness to Parker's and Grindal's efforts.

The basis outlined in Guest's injunction was the same as was recommended for all subsequent replacements of chalices. It emphasized that in obeying the order the churchwardens need not involve themselves in raising any money. The Edwardian cups had mostly been ordered at a time when money did not matter, since the parish plate was just about to be seized. The 1558 and 1559 cups were commissioned by confirmed Protestants who, although having to count the cost, were seriously concerned to see that the Holy Table was furnished in a seemly manner.[1] The later Elizabethan cups were made with a very careful eye as to expenditure. A large chalice could be made into quite a fair-sized communion cup with perhaps double the capacity. On the other hand some rural parishes possessed minute chalices, and unless the churchwardens were prepared to add metal the resulting cup would be of very small capacity indeed. Quite a number of such cups do exist.[2] Responsible churchwardens used their discretion in cases of difficulty and we can frequently trace signs of petty adjustments. Thus Thomas Turpyn, who made the communion cup for Leverton, Lincs., in 1570, added ¾ ounce of new metal and charged 2*s.* for it.[3] On the other hand, at Stratton, Cornwall, the churchwardens could only get £1. 17*s.* for their chalice in the same year. Rather than buy an inadequate communion cup of that value, they bought one at £3. 19*s.* from John Jones, the Exeter goldsmith. They economized by getting a 'sawcer to put the communion bred on' which cost 4*d.* It was not until 1576 that they went back to the goldsmith for a proper paten-cover costing 17*s.* 6*d.*[4] It would seem that Bishop Guest's formula fitted the circumstances of most English churches. At least one church made a profit out of the conversion of its chalice.[5]

The archbishop's decision with regard to the chalices was a godsend to the goldsmiths. Church patronage had been worth practically nothing for a generation and lay patronage had not been very much better. At the accession of

[1] The provident City churchwardens who had had a communion cup made out of two chalices in the reign of Edward VI and converted it back into a chalice in the time of Mary would still have been able to get a good communion cup again in 1559–60 without raising fresh money!

[2] The fact that some of these minute communion cups were made is the irrefutable proof that the conversion of the chalices was not the result of an effort to secure larger vessels because of the administration of the communion in both kinds to the laity. No injunction ever prescribed a minimum capacity for the new cups.

[3] *Archaeologia*, xli, 1867, 364.

[4] Ibid. xlvi, 1881, 229–30. It is not clear why the Stratton churchwardens could not get more for their chalice. They ought to have been exceptionally well off, since under Mary they had two chalices weighing 25 ounces (*Edwardian Inventories of Church Goods for Cornwall*, ed. L. Snell, 1956, 50).

[5] The churchwardens of Smarden, Kent, sent to John Sadler, goldsmith of Maidstone, a gilt chalice and paten weighing 23¾ ounces. He returned to them a communion cup plus 7*s.* 4*d.* (*Archaeologia Cantiana*, xvi, 1886, 335).

Elizabeth I the country was on the brink of an economic revival and the prospect of a vast number of bread-and-butter orders must have had a very heartening effect on the trade. The thirteenth-century bishops had bullied their parsons for a good many years before every church (or nearly every church) had a silver chalice, but the archbishop was now out for conversion in a hurry. Though there is no evidence that Parker discussed his plans beforehand with the wardens of the Goldsmiths' Company, it is clear that he had worked out a scheme of his own. To have ordered all the bishops to instruct their dioceses to convert their chalices simultaneously would have resulted in chaos.[1] The plan actually adopted was that one or two dioceses at a time were incited to replace their chalices. Churches elsewhere which did not wish to wait their turn were at liberty to make their own arrangements.

It would seem that the news that the diocese of Norwich was on the short list filtered out in the summer of 1564, and that the London Goldsmiths' Company warned their Norwich colleagues to set their house in order. Although the hall-marking of silver at Norwich had been authorized by the statute of 1423, nothing whatever seems to have been done about it. On 2 October 1564 the Norwich goldsmiths petitioned the mayor, sheriffs, and aldermen of the city to authorize the institution of a complete hall-marking scheme, complete with town mark, date-letter, and maker's mark.[2] The authority of the company of the Norwich goldsmiths did not extend beyond the suburbs of the city, so that the goldsmiths resident in Suffolk fell directly under the London Goldsmiths' Company. On the analogy of what was afterwards done elsewhere, it is likely that they were made to swear an oath to maintain good workmanship and to register their marking punches, if they had them. It was obviously not feasible to insist on their sending their work to London to be assayed, nor was it possible to impose any corporate responsibility upon them, since they were spread over at least four different towns.

The order for the conversion of the chalices was included in the articles for a visitation by the archbishop in 1567. The East Anglian goldsmiths were not found asleep, for we still have 234 communion cups bearing the Norwich date-letter for 1567. This output was achieved mainly by the efforts of six goldsmiths, but nine others appear to have made small contributions. The Suffolk goldsmiths looked after the needs of their county,[3] so that the services of the Londoners

[1] It is not unlikely that the attempt to replace at the same time all the chalices in the dioceses of Canterbury and London had raised supply difficulties. This may explain why Bishop Bentham's injunctions for Coventry and Lichfield, issued in the same year as Guest's, say nothing about converting chalices (Frere and Kennedy, iii. 165–70). He may have been advised to go slow.

[2] Jackson, *Goldsmiths*, 301–4.

[3] John Casley, in his 'An Ipswich worker of Elizabethan Church Plate' (*Suffolk Institute of Archaeology*, xii, 1905, and xiii, 1907, 103–5), gives a useful analysis of the marks used by the Suffolk goldsmiths, but was only able to attribute one of them (Jeffrey Gilbert of Ipswich). The Goldsmiths'

were hardly required at all. The operation seems to have been virtually completed (as far as such things ever were completed) by the close of the next Norwich hall-marking year.

By then the Londoners had been turned on to the diocese of Chichester. Very little local talent was discovered, so that most of the cups bear the London hall-mark for 1568. The conversion of the chalices in the dioceses of Winchester and Lincoln were spread over the hall-marking years 1568 and 1569. The former diocese would seem to have been provided almost entirely from London, but it is impossible to gauge the success of the campaign as the numbers of surviving Elizabethan cups is not large. Plenty of evidence exists to bear witness to the success of the drive in the unwieldy diocese of Lincoln. In the southern area the work was carried out by the Londoners. In Lincolnshire the work was shared between them and at least one considerable local goldsmith whose working-place was almost certainly the cathedral city. There are twenty-nine communion cups bearing the date 1569–70 (Pl. 65*b*) made by this goldsmith, whose principal mark consisted of ᛗ,[1] and another thirty-three which cannot be dated definitely. Some parishes on the western side of the county employed one or other of the two goldsmiths who appear to have been established in Leicestershire[2] and contributed considerably to the work of replacement in that county.

The next on the list were the two small dioceses of Ely and Peterborough. Work began before that on Lincoln was completed and continued into 1570. Amongst the goldsmiths who had helped in the refashioning of the chalices of the Norwich diocese in 1567 had been one who used as his mark *a flat fish on a dish*. He afterwards moved to Cambridge in anticipation of the conversion of the Ely chalices, so that his later work is without the Norwich hall-mark. He was, however, one of those individuals for whom hall-marking was invented, since when the wardens of the London Goldsmiths made their ride through East Anglia in 1569 their *Minute Book* notes: 'brake and defaced viij communion cuppes with iiij covers, all white, fond in the handes of Th. Buttell of Norwiche

Minute Book (which he did not use) supplies a few names of Suffolk goldsmiths, but it is difficult in most cases to decide whether the individuals named were more than petty repairers of jewellery. The wardens were in Suffolk both in the autumn of 1568 and that of 1569. They had a meeting of local goldsmiths at Bury on each occasion, but it seems likely that all those who attended were not inhabitants of the town. A goldsmith of the name of Stone had trouble over a communion cup on the first occasion, but we do not know where he lived. Erasmus Cooke of Bury was a person of some importance, for he kept an assistant, 'John Stalker, a Scottisman'. We are left rather in the dark regarding Thos. Clerke, G. More, and John Wyhers. At Harleston they found John Shrybbes and at Woodbridge Robert Dale. They found at Ipswich William Myles with a journeyman, Christopher Buttell. They do not refer to Jeffrey Gilbert.

[1] Perhaps John Morley of Lincoln (see p. 200, n. 2).

[2] Marks, *rose and leopard's head in shaped shield*. Another goldsmith, who marked his work with *an animal's head* between the incised letters N and G, probably filled in gaps in 1571 whilst he was working on the replacements in Nottinghamshire. Several other goldsmiths made minor contributions in Lincs. and Leics.

then workynge in Cambridge.'[1] Some two dozen Cambridgeshire churches retain communion cups (Pl. 60*a*) by Buttell, who was also the most considerable local man engaged on refashioning in the Peterborough diocese, which was otherwise almost entirely handled by London craftsmen. Although these two dioceses included several important Recusant centres, there is still plenty of evidence that the process of refashioning went according to plan.

Work began in the small diocese of Worcester about the time that it was finishing in Ely and Peterborough. There is now no evidence that any parish had voluntarily anticipated the order to convert, as the earliest communion cups merely bear the 1571 London hall-mark, for this was an area where little local talent was available.[2] Although there was little Protestant enthusiasm in this diocese as yet, a plentiful supply of communion cups bears witness to the thoroughness with which the instructions were carried out. This must be attributed to the ruthlessness of Bishop Sandys, who, however, was translated to London before the operation was completed.

The vacancy in the see of London had been occasioned by the translation of Edmund Grindal to York. The new archbishop began by ordering a visitation of the whole province, and stipulated in the injunctions for a 'Communion cup of silver, and a cover of silver, appointed also for the ministration of the Communion-bread'.[3] Grindal's previous conversion operation had gone off well because Protestantism had a strong hold on London. It could easily have been foretold that a similar success would be unlikely in the northern province, a large part of which had been devastated by a religious rebellion which had only recently been suppressed. Special efforts do not seem to have been taken to overcome the greater difficulties. The York goldsmiths, for instance, do not seem to have given the wholehearted co-operation obtained from those at Norwich.[4] As a result $\frac{2}{3}$ of the communion cups with the 1570 hall-mark in the county of York bear London marks. In the East Riding a small contribution was made by Peter Carlill of Hull. The relatively small number of Elizabethan communion cups to be found in Yorkshire suggests that many medieval chalices survived until a later date.

Local talent of a sort was more forthcoming in the southern part of the diocese. Judging from surviving examples, the work of replacement in Notting-

[1] Vol. KL, 11. It was doubtless because of this contretemps that Buttell submitted his cup for Little Harrowden, Northants, to be assayed at Goldsmiths' Hall and get the hall-mark for 1569.

[2] A goldsmith using a circular stamp showing a *rose* made a number of cups in this area and also in north Oxon. The mark appears to be identical with the one mentioned as having been used in Leics. (p. 138, n. 2 above), but the design differs. The Goldsmiths' *Minute Book* (KL, 86) mentions a Henry Shirley as working at Worcester in this year.

[3] Frere and Kennedy, iii. 275.

[4] The York goldsmiths had overhauled their hall-marking and had started to use date-letters in 1558. The reason for their abstention was certainly not inefficiency.

hamshire was fairly evenly divided between local and London goldsmiths. At least four local craftsmen can be traced.[1]

There is no evidence that the goldsmiths of Newcastle co-operated at all in the replacement drive. Even the two communion cups at All Saints, Newcastle, bear London hall-marks, as do all the others in the counties of Durham and Northumberland, with the exception of a single York example.[2] If co-operation was not forthcoming, effective resistance was equally absent. The number of surviving communion cups is not inconsiderable, remembering that the area was then lightly populated. The failure of the rebellion of the northern earls meant that the government's wishes could not be ignored.

The campaign for communion cups went rather well in the diocese of Carlisle. Inevitably the Londoners did most of the work, but there are five cups with the mark of the Carlisle goldsmith Edward Dalton.

It is not yet possible to form any opinion as to what happened in the notoriously Recusant diocese of Chester, since the plate of Cheshire has not yet been completely listed and whilst that of Lancashire has not been begun. It seems likely that it was an expected demand for communion cups which moved the Chester goldsmiths' guild to order, about this time,[3] that all plate should be stamped with a maker's mark. A local goldsmith whose mark was *an animal's head in a shaped shield* (Pl. 63), made cups for several churches in Chester and in the vicinity.

It is now time to return to the southern province, where the campaign had not yet touched the western dioceses. Work was begun on that of Bristol in 1570, but progress was unusually slow, for it was spread over four years. Two useful goldsmiths were found in Dorset, one at Dorchester and the other probably at Sherborne.[4] Though the replacement of the chalices in Dorset was long drawn out it appears to have been carried out quite thoroughly. Although this county formed part of the diocese of Bristol, the goldsmiths of that city took no part in the work nor do they seem to have shared in that of Bath and Wells. It is pos-

[1] One of these used a mark showing a *leopard's head in a shaped shield.* Another of them used a *leopard's head in a circle*, which is sometimes found associated with the Lincoln ꟽ mark. It would seem that these two marks awoke the interest of the wardens of the Goldsmiths' Company (who may have considered that these local workers were imitating the London mark), since it is recorded in their minutes under the date 11 July 1571, 'Agreed that a letter shalbe directed from this companie to my lord ye archebishop of Yorke to request him to suffer no communion cuppes to be used in any parish of his diocese but only such as be touched with the liberdes head crowned'.

[2] Elton, near Stockton.

[3] Undated, but the next item is dated 1573 (Jackson, *Goldsmiths*, 374).

[4] For the identification of Lawrence Stratford see *C.P. Wilts.* xiii. Mark, *circle filled with pellets.* This mark Jackson (*Goldsmiths*, 468) suggested might be that of Richard Orange. This is almost certainly wrong. In 1571 Orange was still apprenticed to Richard Asheborne who, like his rival William Troublefyld, is known to have used a mark (*Minute Book*, KL, f. 76). It seems fair to attribute the mark *A* (Jackson, *Goldsmiths*, 475) to Asheborne. It is found on the cups at Upcerne and Nether Compton, Dorset.

sible that the news that things were going slow in the west led to an appeal to the wardens of the London Goldsmiths' Company to make a tour in that region in July and August 1571. Their principal concern was with the observance of their own regulations regarding good workmanship, but the subject of the communion cups must have cropped up at every stage. At Mawdlyn Fair, outside Winchester, they took the oath of both the Winchester and the Southampton goldsmiths. They then proceeded on a tour of the West Country towns where goldsmiths were to be found, stopping only short of Cornwall. The Gloucester goldsmith was waiting with the four local men when the wardens reached Bristol. Their oaths were taken, but they showed no disposition to take advantage of their rights under the 1423 statute. It was a different story when the wardens reached Barnstaple, where the three goldsmiths with their two servants gave their oaths and were evidently warned to set their house in order in anticipation of the rush order which would shortly come their way. The Exeter goldsmiths, like those of Barnstaple, had no rights under the 1423 statute, but were also co-operative. There were nine of them and, as only one of them was ordered to send his marking-punch to be registered at Goldsmiths' Hall, it seems probable that the remainder were already known.[1] From Exeter the wardens wended their way home.[2] The fruits of their journey were to be very visible in the next few years.

It is likely that the wardens left behind a threat that if the Bristol goldsmiths failed to organize themselves effectively they would get none of the communion-plate business in the diocese of Bath and Wells. The process of replacement in this diocese was quite different from that in any other English one, for instead of being shared by a team of locals and Londoners it was carried out almost entirely by one London goldsmith, whose mark was *IP*.[3] He provided twenty-two cups in the hall-marking year 1572 and seventy-one in the following one. Other Londoners contributed small numbers and one Exeter goldsmith a dozen. The credit for dealing so effectively with this diocese, where Recusancy was widespread, must be divided between the Goldsmith's Company and Bishop Gilbert Berkeley.

The conversion of the chalices in the diocese of Exeter must have begun very shortly after the visit of the wardens of the Goldsmiths.[4] The process was lengthy because it was left almost entirely to local men. It was finished about the end of

[1] Their marks are mostly known to us, but from pieces probably of later date.

[2] Their route cannot be traced. They do not seem to have seen Lawrence Stratford, the Dorchester goldsmith. Besides the two Sherborne goldsmiths, George Barefote of Ilminster was ordered to send up his punch for registration.

[3] Jackson attributes this mark (*Goldsmiths*, 98) to John Pikeninge, but there appears to be no evidence to support this suggestion. See Appendix III for a summary of his output.

[4] Canon Chanter habitually refers to the early Exeter cups as being '1570–4', but in actual fact none appear to be dated before 1571.

1576. Nearly two-thirds of the work was done by John Jones of Exeter. Thomas Mathew and John Coton, both of Barnstaple, held the next two places. The other Exeter goldsmiths did not enter very seriously into the business, but five local workers can be distinguished in Cornwall.[1] There is rather more evidence of the intervention of the Londoners in the latter county than in Devon. The large number of Elizabethan cups which have survived demonstrate that the campaign was a success in this diocese.

Whilst the churches of Dorset and Somerset were being supplied with cups in 1571, the turn came for the small diocese of Hereford. This was, of course, an area which had to be supplied from London, though a few unmarked pieces are probably local work. Elizabethan cups are now rare in this diocese and, since it was noted for Recusancy, it seems likely that many chalices escaped for the time being.

The earliest Elizabethan communion cup in Wales bears the hall-mark for 1561,[2] but it was not until twelve years later that Parker directed his attention to any of the Welsh dioceses. If the country was distant and difficult, the archbishop possessed one invaluable asset in that his bishops were Welsh and knew their dioceses. The first to be taken in hand was also the most difficult, the large and remote one of St. Davids. Wales has always produced goldsmiths, but seldom a decent livelihood for them. Welsh goldsmiths have usually found it best to sell their skill in England. It seems likely that Bishop Davies sought out a Welsh goldsmith whom he tempted back to his native land by the promise of full employment for at least a few years. The only probable site for his workshop is Carmarthen, which was, moreover, situated conveniently close to the bishop's residence at Abergwili. The three earliest cups marked with OOOO are engraved with the date 1573. The dated cups mostly belong to 1574 (Pl. 69*b*), but a large number of cups which have lost their covers, whereon the date was customarily engraved. At any rate there still survive seventy-three cups from this workshop, distributed over the archdeaconries of Cardigan, Carmarthen,[3] and Pembroke, but there are none in the fourth archdeaconry of Brecon. No compulsion would seem to have been used to employ the bishop's protégé, for there are a sprinkling of London cups and even strays from Barnstaple and Exeter. The latest dated cup with the OOOO mark belongs to 1587, but the process of replacement was practically completed in the years 1573–6.

Bangor seems to have been dealt with in the years 1574–5, but it is less easy to estimate the success of the drive since the number of extant Elizabethan cups is small. One-third of the cups came from London, the remainder were the work of two local goldsmiths.[4]

[1] *Journal of R. Institution of Cornwall*, xx, 1920, 536–9.

[2] Llanfrwog, Angl.

[3] This included the deanery of Gower.

[4] E. Alfred Jones (*C.P. Bangor*, xxii–xxiii) suggested that the goldsmiths whose marks were

The turn of Llandaff came in 1576. The number of surviving cups shows that the work was done thoroughly. London goldsmiths provided most of the cups, but there are a few unmarked ones with blundered English inscriptions which suggest Welsh workmanship. Again there is no sign of intervention by Bristol goldsmiths.

The diocese of Gloucester was also on this year's programme. The task was easier as a number of churchwardens had already replaced their chalices. The work went mainly to the Londoners, but several local men joined in it. Judging from the location of their works, they would seem to have resided at Gloucester, Tewkesbury, and Winchcombe.[1]

Oxford, which had been left without a bishop throughout this period, had been on the list for 1575. Here also a lot of churches already had cups. Most of the work was done by the Londoners, since Oxford seems to have had no responsible goldsmith at this time. Some churches in the vicinity of Banbury have cups probably provided from Worcester.

The large diocese of Salisbury was left until the years 1576–7. Quite a number of the Berkshire churches already had cups, but very few Wiltshire ones had moved at all. When the orders came they were carried out fairly drastically, although this was an area where Recusancy was rife. It can be no accident that three adjacent parishes in the Wylye valley stuck to their chalices.[2] The Berkshire cups, as might be expected, came from London. Most of the Wiltshire ones did also, but there are nineteen unmarked cups which would appear to have been made locally. They have not been examined sufficiently carefully to decide whether more than one maker was involved. Their distribution seems to indicate that at least some were made in Salisbury.

Two more dioceses have yet to be mentioned. No sort of inventory exists of that of St. Asaph, so that it would be unwise to suggest what may be discovered there. The only parts of the Tudor diocese of Coventry and Lichfield which have been listed are the archdeaconries of Shrewsbury and Stafford. These now contain few Elizabethan cups and the dates of manufacture are fairly widely spaced. A clearer view might be obtained if the old archdeaconry of Derby were inventoried. It is even possible that further investigation may prove that there was no formal date for conversion in this diocese. The situation had changed radically since Parker initiated his campaign in 1562. The archbishop himself had succumbed in 1575 and had been replaced by the inept Grindal. In the early days pressure from a high level had been required to get churchwardens to convert their chalices, but by the middle of the seventies the idea of getting a communion cup no longer appeared strange. The danger that established clergy might use the parish chalice for saying mass on the quiet must have practically

respectively *IL* and *bird's head erased* were probably domiciled in Chester. Nothing has since turned up to confirm this suggestion. [1] *C.P. Glos.* xv–xvii. [2] Berwick St. James, Codford St. Mary, and Wylye.

gone. Though the decision of Pius V regarding the impropriety of attending the services of the established church took some time to become effective, there inevitably came a time when an established priest had to realize that he could not carry on with both services. When this stage was reached the *raison d'être* of the Elizabethan communion cup had gone. Another thirty years were to elapse before a reaction began against it.[1]

To realize what the introduction of the communion cup meant to the goldsmiths, it is only necessary to mention that we still retain some two thousand examples made before the year 1578. It is impossible to guess how many have perished during the last three hundred and fifty years. The work was pretty evenly divided between the London and the provincial workers. No other London goldsmith approached the output of *IP*, but about a dozen went into the business on a large scale. The refashioning meant much more to the provincial workers. The fillip given to the goldsmiths of Norwich, Exeter, and Barnstaple was reflected in the excellent work which continued to be produced in these towns until the Civil War. Well-made communion cups acted as advertisements of the skill of local goldsmiths in every town and village. There was now more money for plate in Norfolk, thanks to the disturbances in the Low Countries. In the west the minor followers of Drake and Hawkins might well prefer to spend their savings in Exeter or Barnstaple instead of going to London. Likewise, the centres which did not co-operate did not easily make up the lost ground.[2] For the small local goldsmiths the years of refashioning chalices were just a happy interlude. When all was over they reverted to making spoons and doing repairs.

Church patronage was worth very much less to the goldsmiths during the last twenty years of the reign. To judge from the number of surviving examples, the annual output of communion cups became quite small, since it was now mainly a matter of filling in gaps.

An inevitable consequence of the administration to large congregations of communion in wine was that the communion cup had frequently to be replenished. This involved the presence of a flagon or flagons to contain the re-

[1] The Elizabethan communion cup failed to penetrate into two areas. Little is known as to how the Reformation got introduced into the Isle of Man. It would seem that the English authorities decided that the island could be safely ignored.

The Channel Islands had been transferred to the diocese of Winchester from that of Coutances by an arrangement between Henry VII and the pope. There is little sign that the pre-Reformation bishops of Winchester paid much attention to this new acquisition. Because of their strategic position it was important to preserve the islands for Protestantism. Since it was impossible, as in the Isle of Man, to find native preachers to inculcate Anglicanism, the Privy Council allowed the islands to be organized on a Presbyterian basis by Huguenots from Normandy.

[2] The evidence seems to suggest that the Chester goldsmiths were ready to co-operate, but that their natural customers in Lancashire and Flint showed no eagerness to order communion cups, and preferred to squander their money on Recusancy fines instead of adding to the family plate!

serve wine. Silver flagons were not unknown in Edwardian times, but although they were to be found occasionally in parish churches in the reign of Elizabeth I, it was only latterly that the bishops began to allude to the need for them. At first it was only suggested that pewter ones should be provided, but Archbishop Whitgift's articles for the deanery of Shoreham,[1] which were issued in 1597, inquire after 'two comely pots of silver or pewter to fetch wine to serve the Lord's table, reserved and kept clean to that use only, being no tavern pots'. Though it was most unlikely that any of the churches in this unimportant Kentish deanery would possess even a single silver flagon, the inclusion of such a clause in standard visitation articles was not completely unrealistic.

By the end of the century Anglicanism had found more and abler exponents than it had had heretofore. Though some of them were restrained from accepting the higher church posts because of the simoniacal deals which remained the rule under the old queen, they were ready enough to be promoted under the cleaner rule of James I.

The greatest single influence on the development of English church plate during the seventeenth century was Lancelot Andrewes, who at the time of the queen's death was dean of Westminster, having for reasons of conscience refused two bishoprics. As master of Pembroke Hall, Cambridge, he had proved a good administrator as well as a first-class scholar. As vicar of St. Giles, Cripplegate, he had shown that he could cope with a difficult City parish, whilst his preaching had won him a post as a royal chaplain. Like Hooker, he had got right away from the negative attitude of the Protestantism of the last generation. He was extremely interested in ritual and in attempting to enrich the services of the English Church, felt no scruple about borrowing ideas direct from the Early Christians or else from the Greek Church. He viewed with an open mind the practices of the medieval Western Church and felt free to adopt those which he considered desirable.

Andrewes was already a person of importance at the time of the accession of James I, and thereafter his promotion was rapid. In 1605 he became Bishop of Chichester, but in 1609 was translated to Ely. In 1619 he was promoted to Winchester, where he remained until his death in 1626.

It was inevitable that in his efforts to enrich ritual he should become a patron of all the crafts which could contribute to the embellishment of churches, but it is clear that he had a particular love of goldsmiths' work.[2] Though there is now only one piece of plate directly associated with him which has survived,[3]

[1] Frere and Kennedy, iii. 286.

[2] Thus, in his will he bequeathed to Pembroke Hall facsimiles of some of the oldest pieces of the college plate, being afraid that the originals might go astray and their memory be lost (Andrewes, *Minor Works*, xxi and ci). The originals remain but the replicas were probably amongst the Cambridge college plate which was smuggled out to the Royalist exchequer at the beginning of the Civil War.

[3] The chalice made for St. Mary Extra, Southampton; see *C.P. Hants*, 309–11, with illustrations.

there is no lack of plate made in accordance with his views. With Andrewes we get right away from the problem of minimum requirements. Austere in his private life, he spent lavishly on his private chapel when he became a bishop. He was a confirmed ritualistic experimenter. Some of his ideas were impractical and remained unimitated, but others profoundly affected the development of English church plate.

Amongst his innovations was the idea of a service of communion plate. This idea was not unknown in the Middle Ages, but was not a common one. It had fallen into disuse since then.[1] Services of plate began to appear in the middle of the reign of James I, when the influence of Andrewes was at its height. They were not of uniform size nor did they contain exactly the same items, but a theme seems to run through them. It is possible, indeed, to trace his influence on the form and decoration of pieces for fully fifty years after his death. It may be deduced from the choice of designs made by his admirers that he was not entirely averse to contemporary forms and decoration, but his most interesting contribution was his preference for late medieval art. Of his Gothic communion plate and his choice of iconographic motifs we shall have to treat later on.

The influence of Andrewes was based upon his personality and not upon his authority. The articles for his two visitations of the diocese of Winchester are not particularly exacting in their stipulations about plate.[2] At no stage of his career do we hear of quarrels about the furnishing of the communion table, and it would seem that he got what he wanted gradually and by general consent.[3]

In the past it has been usual to attribute the great increase in the output of church plate during the first half of the seventeenth century to the influence of Laud. There can be no doubt that the authority of the archbishop raised the standard of the furnishing of the cathedrals, but in the case of the parish churches, where inspiration and not the heavy hand was needed, he had merely to build upon foundations laid by Andrewes. Whereas much is known about the latter's taste in plate, it is very difficult to discover anything about Laud's preferences.

It is only necessary to turn to a chronological list of the plate of any county or diocese to see how important church work was for the goldsmiths between the middle of the reign of James I and the outbreak of the Civil War. To a great extent this was the result of the rise of the High Church—of Andrewes rather than of Laud, for there were High Churchmen like the Earl of Arundel who

[1] Thus in 1572 the chapter of Wells decided to convert their mass plate into communion plate. The job was entrusted to the goldsmith *IP*, who produced a flagon and two communion cups. The medieval plate had included two chalices of different weights. Instead of making a pair of cups, he made two of different weights and slightly different design.

[2] *Minor Works*, 114 and 128.

[3] 'This I dare affirm that wheresoever he was a parson, a dean, or bishop, he never troubled parish, college or diocese with pressing other ceremonies upon them than such which he found used before his coming thither' (Thos. Fuller, *Church History*, 1868 edn., bk. xi, iii. 391).

disliked the archbishop but approved well-furnished churches. Though the plate in the Gothic style is manifestly of High Church origin, it would be wrong to give all the credit to that section of the Church. There can be little doubt that many of the fine and massive pieces made at this period were contributed by those who disapproved of unseemly services but preferred to see the Holy Table in the middle of the chancel or of the nave, rather than against the east end of the church.

The majority of the gifts of plate contributed by the laity came in singly, but there were some notable benefactors on a large scale. Amongst these may be classed the financier and diplomatist, Sir Paul Pindar. His first benefaction consisted of three flagons and two alms basins, all of silver-gilt, and valued at £113. 14*s*., given in 1633 to his parish church of St. Botolph, Bishopsgate.[1] This was followed in the next year by a communion cup and a pair of flagons for the church of his native place, Wellingborough.[2] In 1639 he made a similar gift to Peterborough Cathedral.[3]

The generosity of Lady Dudley[4] was much greater but was spread over a longer period. She presented services of plate to churches upon her estates and to others in which she took an interest. Poverty was not amongst the hardships which she endured, but it was natural that the scope of her generosity was not manifested until her family of daughters were off her hands. Before she died in 1668 she had presented services of plate, usually consisting of a chalice, covered paten, and a flagon, all of silver-gilt, to eleven churches.[5] She patronized a

[1] B. Malcolm, *Londinium Redivivum*, 1807, i. 328. All sold in 1828 (*C.P. City*, 28).

[2] *C.P. Northants*, 306–7.

[3] Ibid. 232.

[4] Alice, daughter of Sir Thomas Leigh of Stoneleigh Abbey, Warw., married in 1596 Robert, son of Robert Dudley, Earl of Leicester, by Douglas, daughter of Lord Howard of Effingham. At the time of his marriage the legal status of young Dudley was uncertain, but he at once set about establishing that his father and mother had been secretly married in 1573. Unfortunately it had suited both of his parents to disavow the marriage, and his suit was opposed by Lettice, his father's widow. By 1605 he realized that no favourable verdict would ever be obtained and, stung by frustration, he obtained permission to travel abroad. He set off, leaving his wife and family but taking his young cousin, Elizabeth Southwell. At Lyons he went through a form of marriage with her and she afterwards bore him a large family.

His relations with the English government became embittered when he began to call himself Earl of Warwick. He settled down in Florence, where he wrote a book on naval architecture and drained the marshes around Leghorn. The Emperor Ferdinand II created him Duke of Northumberland in 1620. He died in 1649.

[5]

Ladbroke	Warw.,	1623	Acton	Middx.,	1639
Monks Kirby	,,	,,	Bidford-on-Avon	Warw.,	1663
Ashow	,,	1638	Pattishall	Northants,	,,
Kenilworth	,,	,,	St. Peter, St. Albans		*c*. 1663
Leek Wootton	,,	,,	St. Giles-in-the-Fields		?
Stoneleigh	,,	?			

The Stoneleigh and St. Giles sets have disappeared.

number of goldsmiths, some of whom used Gothic and others contemporary designs. All her gifts are fine and seem to reveal a person of a discriminating taste. In 1645, the fatal year for the Royalist cause, Charles I found time to reward her virtuous life by creating her Duchess Dudley.

Less appears to be known about her daughter Lady Frances Kniveton and of the circumstances which prompted her to give in 1640, to a number of churches on her husband's estates in Derbyshire,[1] a silver-gilt chalice with paten-cover and a flagon. The chalices came from one goldsmith and the flagons from another. Both were excellent craftsmen, but it is curious to note that neither was patronized by her mother.

The Civil War brought a temporary intermission in the manufacture of church plate, but this did last through the Commonwealth. The really important orders came from the owners of private chapels, for there was a fortunate minority of Anglicans who managed not to be ruined by the collapse of the Royalist cause. A small amount of plate was made also for the parish churches.[2] That little was made is not surprising. Few parish churches were looted during the war and their furnishing was not so meagre as it had been fifty years earlier. Naturally the plate called into existence by those who had inherited the artistic tradition of the Low Church at a time when money was scarce is mostly 'austere' in the sinister sense of the word.

2. 1660–1830

When King Charles entered London on 29 May 1660 twelve Presbyterian ministers marched in the triumphal procession. When he arrived at St. Paul's he was met by the whole assembly of the City ministers and received from their hands a richly bound Bible. Farther along a less conspicuous presentation was made—a Bible bound up with a Book of Common Prayer—the donors being Anglican clergy whose livings had been sequestrated.

That the Presbyterians were in possession was a result of a process by which Monk undid Cromwell's work. The fact that the tactical advantage was with the Presbyterians at this juncture greatly complicated the outlook and even had its influence on the history of church plate. It is not necessary to follow the

[1] The following survive: Bradley, Kirk Langley, Kniveton, Mugginton, and Osmaston-by-Ashbourne.

[2] One of the most important gifts belonging to this period was that of Thomas Riche, merchant, to St. John Baptist, Gloucester. On 13 February 1659 he presented 'for the use of the Sacrament of the Lord's Supper viz. five cases with Eight peices of plate, two large Gilt flagons, two Great Gilt Cupes with Covers, one Gilt Bason for the Collection, one Gilt Plate for the Breade' (*C.P. Glos.* 98). Another important benefaction is recorded upon a pair of flagons with 1658 hall-mark once belonging to the demolished church of St. Benet Fink. The inscription states 'George Holman, Esqre gave £1000 to the parish of St Bennett Finck for the ornaments of ye church whereof the flaggons are part for the use of the communicants' (*C.P. City*, 93).

administrative measures whereby they were edged out during the autumn of 1660, but it was only when the results of the election to the new Parliament were known in the spring of 1661 that it became clear that a full restoration of the Laudian régime was in prospect.

Since the Cavalier Parliament met on the 8th of May, seven weeks only remained of the hall-marking year 1660.[1] In view of the religious uncertainties of this first year and the fact that some of the best goldsmiths were busy preparing the new Regalia, it is not surprising that the output of church plate was not very great. Three important commissions may be noted. Dean Earle was determined that Westminster Abbey should be re-equipped at the earliest possible date and an austere service of nine pieces was ready at the end of January 1661. The other two orders were not emergency replacements and are of much greater artistic merit. It is not known who paid for the handsome set of altar plate for Gloucester Cathedral. It was made by the unidentified goldsmith whose mark was *a hound sejant* who had made much plate for the Royalist private chapels during the Commonwealth. The order was still being completed during the summer of 1661, since the candlesticks (Pl. 140*c*) bear the 1661 mark.[2] The energetic Dr. John Fell, newly appointed dean, was doubtless responsible for the set of plate for Christ Church Cathedral, Oxford. Though of uniform design, it was made by three different goldsmiths and its production also ran into the 1661 hall-marking year.

The re-equipping of the cathedrals was spread over several years. Though nearly all were short of plate at the Restoration, some had suffered very much worse than others in the way of general delapidation. Lichfield had withstood a siege and Durham had been wrecked by Scottish prisoners confined therein after the battle of Dunbar. In most cases the provision of new communion plate had to rank with a host of other essentials to be made good. As a result of this, the plate acquired at this time displays a simplicity due to the lack of money to pay for 'fashion' at a higher rate.

The more urgent requirements of the cathedrals had mostly been provided by the time that London was devastated by the Great Fire. Not much plate of any sort was lost in the actual conflagration, and the urge to raise money for the rebuilding by melting down their treasures affected the citizens and the livery companies more than the churchwardens, whose position was to a certain extent cushioned by the prospect of drawing funds from the Coal Duty. The effect of the Great Fire on the plate of the churches was, however, profound. Everyone agreed that the opportunity should be taken to reduce the excessive number of

[1] The return of the king in 1660 gravely upset the routine at Goldsmiths' Hall. The date letter ℭ was only introduced on Friday 13 July 1660, and was allowed to run on until Thursday, 27 June 1661.

[2] The alms dish also bears the 1661 mark but was made by another goldsmith.

churches, but the parishioners of every threatened church were unanimous that theirs should not be sacrificed. Eventually it was decided that thirty-five churches should not be rebuilt, with the result that thirty-three churches served two parishes and St. Mary-le-Bow three. Though in some cases the decision not to rebuild had clearly been made on grounds of public utility, there was a general feeling that many churches had been doomed because of the successful lobbying by rival churchwardens. As a result of the bitter taste about the whole affair, the reduction of City church plate for the purpose of providing rebuilding funds was rather less than might have been expected. There still survive many pieces which once belonged to churches which disappeared in 1666. Church life in the City remained seriously disrupted for the greater part of the reign of Charles II; though the rebuilding of churches began in 1670, half had not been started six years later, and it was only towards the close of the century that the new pattern became clear. The new churches were not too austerely furnished and it was, therefore, fitting that there should be plenty of altar plate. The effect of the merging of the parishes was to accentuate the tendency towards duplication. Thus Christchurch with St. Leonard Foster found itself with five communion cups, whilst several others had four, which could not have all been used simultaneously since the space within the altar rails limited the number of ministering clergy. Most churches now had silver flagons, but the alms basin which formed the centre-piece of a well-furnished altar remained rare in the City, and many churches had not yet got them by the date at which we close. There can be no doubt that the Great Fire dealt a blow to the development of church plate in the City from which it did not recover.

The falling off in the number of benefactions to the City churches[1] cannot be taken as a measure of the decline in the religious zeal of the wealthier citizens. It was partly due to their tendency to spend their money to the best purpose. The Fire had accentuated the tendency to live outside the City and many of them felt that some once-rural church within a three-mile radius had a better claim upon their generosity than the church in whose parish their City office stood. The benefactors to the suburban churches were not, however, only City merchants, their wives, and widows. Many of the aristocracy preferred to live near rather than in London. By contrast, the donors of plate to the churches east of the City appear to have been local people who probably derived their wealth from shipping.

If the furnishing of the suburban churches over the period 1660–1830 provided quite a lot of work for the goldsmiths, the really rich orders were for the

[1] The most considerable City benefactor was Eleanor James. She gave a large service of plate (including some foreign secular pieces) to St. Benet, Paul's Wharf, in 1712 (*C.P. City*, 24). It included the only silver candlesticks recorded in a City church after the Reformation. These last were, however, melted down with much of the rest of the plate in 1843. At the same time a pair of flagons were passed on to St. Mary-le-Strand (*C.P. County*, 55–56). For more about this eccentric lady see p. 240.

churches of Westminster and the area immediately northwards. Both the old parish churches and the new ones founded during the period did well, as will be demonstrated in the next chapter. The plate of the new church might be given by a single benefactor or it might be bought by subscription.[1]

Turning to the country at large, we may note that the bishops made no attempt to lengthen the list of plate which a parish church might be expected to possess. Visitations, of course, always revealed some churches deficient in plate, but it would be unjust to the memory of the archdeacons of this period to suggest that they did not make serious efforts to keep negligent incumbents and churchwardens up to the mark. The period was one of growing national prosperity and the churches got a reasonable share of the increasing wealth.

Gifts usually came in singly. Few churches now lacked a silver communion cup, but many incumbents were now glad to have one rather larger than the one bought in the days of Elizabeth I. The least costly gift was a strainer spoon for removing the impurities from the wine. The use of sliced bread rendered rather inconvenient the Elizabethan paten-covers designed for wafers. This favoured the acquisition of larger patens shaped like salvers. These varied in size, but a 7-inch paten might weigh only 7 ounces and would not be expensive. This was not the case of the other two items most commonly added at this time. The smallest standard size for communion flagons was the 12 inch, which weighed over 40 ounces. Alms basins also varied in size and were inevitably costly. Nearly every county can show a complete set of plate given at this period, but with the exception of Duchess Dudley, whose later gifts belong to the reign of Charles II, the only donor on a large scale was Mrs. Strangways Horner, who fitted out on a very liberal scale five churches in Dorset and Somerset.[2]

[1] The splendid service at St. James, Piccadilly, was given at its consecration on 13 July 1683 by Sir Richard Geere. That of St. George, Bloomsbury, was a gift of Wriothesley, Duke of Bedford, in 1731. That of new St. Pancras came from the Duke of York in 1821. On the other hand, the plate of St. John the Evangelist, Westminster, was a gift from the first churchwardens, whilst that of St. George, Holborn, was bought by subscription in 1706.

[2] It would be difficult to imagine two more different personalities than Duchess Dudley and Mrs. Strangways Horner. The former was a misused wife whose meekness and piety won her a terrestrial coronet instead of qualifying her for a celestial one. Susannah Strangways belonged to quite a different type and her story has been told, thinly disguised, by Thomas Hardy (*The First Countess of Wessex* in *A Group of Noble Dames*), and by her descendant the Earl of Ilchester (*Henry Fox, First Lord Holland*, 1920, 32–33, 44–47). She was born in 1689 and married in 1713 Thomas Horner, of Mells, Som. Their only child was born in 1723. From the first she ruled the roost, but her husband strongly objected when in 1736 she proposed to marry their daughter, aged thirteen, to a neighbour, Stephen Fox of Redlynch, aged thirty-six. On this she took the daughter to London and arranged a clandestine marriage. Though her husband did not attempt to get the marriage annulled, he was mortally estranged from his wife and died within a few years. Hardy ascribes to compunction his widow's generosity to all sorts of charitable causes in her later years. This would appear to be partly literary licence, since her first gift of church plate was given in the year of the clandestine marriage. However, her gifts of plate certainly increased after her husband's death and included the parish church of his birthplace as well as those on the Strangways estates. For a list of her gifts see p. 171.

So little of the plate made between 1660 and 1830 is actually used nowadays that it is easy to underestimate the importance of church work to the goldsmiths. During the Commonwealth the provision of plate for Anglican private chapels was practically the monopoly of one goldsmith, but this ended in 1660. Thereafter, any enterprising goldsmith was ready to book an order for church or chapel plate, and not infrequently the satisfied customer would come back for domestic plate for his own use.[1]

Though the first effect of the Restoration on church plate appeared to be a return to the position of twenty years earlier, in fact a revolution was taking place. Ever since the reign of Edward VI the development of church and secular plate had run parallel. The common forms of communion cups were in shape and decoration closely akin to secular drinking cups. The alms basins were little different from those used for washing in the dining hall. The two standard forms of communion flagons were identical with those which decked the dressers in large houses. The change in domestic arrangements in the time of Charles II put an end to this. On the dining-table glasses replaced silver cups, whilst the spreading use of forks gradually eliminated the silver basins. Similarly the abandonment of the great hall in favour of the dining-room dealt a death-blow to the appurtenances of the dresser.

The tendency for religious and secular plate to develop on different lines was also the result of another event which gravely upset the London goldsmiths at the close of the seventeenth century. As a result of the Revocation of the Edict of Nantes in 1685 a considerable number of Huguenot goldsmiths established themselves in London, and it was not long before the English goldsmiths found that they were losing customers. Their attempts to fight back were only in part successful. They saw many lucrative orders for domestic plate go to the foreigners, but on the whole they managed to retain the custom of the Church of England.[2]

Every writer on English domestic plate has emphasized that the Huguenots formed the most progressive element in the London goldsmiths' trade at the beginning of the eighteenth century. Since the Huguenots made little church plate, it is not surprising that a falling off in respect of inventive power is noticeable. This might have been mitigated had there been a prelate like Andrewes to

[1] Thus Isaac Liger received the order for the earlier pieces of the Dunham Massey chapel plate when he had only been working on his own for three years. He gave such satisfaction that he continued to supply plate to the 2nd Earl of Warrington for over thirty years. Likewise Paul de Lamerie had only been on his own for five years when he received an order for church plate for her old family church, Milton Clevedon, Som., from Susannah, wife of Thomas Strangways, of Melbury, Dorset. Not only did he continue to supply plate for Melbury; ten years later he was recommended to a niece, Mrs. Judith Ayliffe, for a set of plate for Foxley church, Wilts. When Mrs. Strangways Horner started to scatter church plate around, it was natural that she should give the orders to her mother's goldsmith.

[2] The only goldsmith of Huguenot extraction to make an appreciable amount of church plate was Paul de Lamerie. He was, however, born in Holland and learnt his trade in England.

set the goldsmiths working on fresh lines. Though Archbishop Sheldon and Bishop Cosin had provided a healthy influence in the early years after the Restoration, death had removed them in 1677 and 1672 respectively. Their influence survived particularly at the Jewel Office, which procured splendid plate for the Chapels Royal until the close of the century. The plate made for Dublin Castle Chapel in the reign of William III was the last artistically important order from the Jewel Office for quite a long time. The cessation of these royal orders was all the more regrettable because many of those about the court had been wont to buy plate for their parish churches from the royal goldsmiths.

During the reign of Charles II a considerable amount of the church plate shows decoration characteristic of the period. The cathedrals, however, had mostly been refurnished in a hurry on the cheap, with unornamented plate. Unfortunately the uninspired plate of the cathedrals came to be regarded as the proper models for the parish churches, and the deadly force of tradition is very evident on eighteenth-century church plate. When the various species come to be examined, emphasis will be laid on the pieces displaying originality, but it should be realized that these are the exceptions. Each goldsmith, indeed, had his sheets of designs for church plate, but they seldom differed much from those of his rivals. Thus Paul de Lamerie only once changed his designs for communion plate, although his secular plate provides a fascinating study of artistic virtuosity and unending change. It will be realized, therefore, that it is considerably more difficult to date at a glance eighteenth-century church plate than the secular plate of that period. Individuality begins to be more visible in the later years of George III, and both Paul Storr and John Bridge, who directed the artistic side of the great Regency firm of Rundell, Bridge & Rundell, took trouble to produce original designs for communion plate, although such work formed a very small part of their business.

II

THE PLATE OF THE CHURCHES

1. 1553–1660

THE process of church spoliation during the reign of Edward VI can only be regarded as the continuation of that begun by his father, and the condition of the churches at the time of the accession of Mary has been made clear.

There are fewer categories of ecclesiastical establishment to be considered in this chapter than in the corresponding chapter of the first part of this work. The religious orders can be ignored, since we have no inventories of the few houses restored by Mary. There are now only secular cathedrals, to which may be added, for convenience, the few remaining collegiate churches. Beyond these there are only the chapels of the university colleges and the parish churches to be considered.

A similar simplification has taken place in the contents of the inventories. Even though account has to be taken of some of the surviving medieval ornaments, the list has shrunk to about a third of its former length.

At the time of the accession of Mary, it would seem that a cathedral could not be counted upon to possess more than a few chalices—there is no record of any having acquired a communion cup. It was possible for the queen to bring back the old services, but the ornaments of gold and silver, given by the faithful over the centuries, were gone beyond recall. In effecting replacements deans and chapters thought only in terms of copper-gilt and brass, so that even at the close of the reign little of the old splendour had been regained. Thus the 1557 inventory of Lincoln mentions only seven chalices and one pair of cruets.[1] Canterbury, thanks to the generosity of Cardinal Pole, had done considerably better. An inventory taken in 1563 shows that he had given:

> a payre of candelstickes of sylver and gilte waying ccxxvij ounc.
> Item a greate cross of sylver and gilte waying cxliij ounc. j quarter.
> Item one senser wth a shipp and a spone of sylver parcell gylte waying cvj ounc.
>
> . . . . .
>
> Item a holy water pott wth sprynkell of sylver parcell gilte waying lxi ounc.
> Item a crismatory of sylver gilte waying x ounc.[2]

Without these the cathedral would have had from its old stock, including objects brought out of concealment, five chalices, a pair of cruets, a cross, and a pair

[1] *Archaeologia*, liii, 1892, 71–72.

[2] Legg and Hope, 230–1.

of censers. Nothing is said about a pyx, so that it may be presumed that the one used was of copper-gilt. Certainly the canons of Windsor were content with one which cost 3*s.* 4*d.*[1]

After the accession of Elizabeth I some years elapsed before attention was focused upon the 'superstitious' plate of the cathedrals. The 1563 visitation inventory of Canterbury has survived in the form of four drafts. Between the compilation of the first and that of the final one, two of the chalices had been converted into a communion cup, but the other three, the cruets, cross, and the censers, are listed without comment. All the Pole gifts are described as defaced. It was not until 1567 that the unused plate was sent up to London to be sold. The proceeds would seem to have bought more communion plate since the 1583 inventory credits the cathedral with

> One silver-gilt communion cup and cover,
> Two silver parcel-gilt basins,
> Two silver-gilt flagons.[2]

There was no rigid formula for the plate of an Elizabethan cathedral, but in fact there was very little variation. Thus Wells still preserves the two silver-gilt communion cups and covers and the flagon, all acquired in 1572.[3]

The interval between the accession of James I and the outbreak of the Civil War saw a general improvement in the furnishing of the cathedrals. The Elizabethan higher clergy had not been generous donors of church plate, but the flagon given by Dean Suckling to Norwich in 1614 illustrates the beginning of a change in this respect.

The translation of Laud to the see of Canterbury in 1633 affected the plate of the cathedrals in several ways. His decision that the communion table should stand permanently in the position formerly occupied by the high altar carried with it the corollary that the manner in which it was arrayed mattered very much more. The addition which appeared most shocking to conservatives like William Prynne was the pair of handsome candlesticks.[4] Though no cathedral now retains any candlesticks made before the reign of Charles II, it is pretty clear that they were in general use in the 1630's. The more fortunate cathedrals were now aiming at a balanced effect on the altar, with the utensils in pairs and a large alms basin standing upright in the middle. This was already the rule at

[1] M. F. Bond, *Inventories of St. George's Chapel*, 1947, 220.

[2] Legg and Hope, 240. The fate of the cardinal's plate is obscure, but it may have provided the funds for a nice little collection of secular plate which appears as being in the possession of the chapter without any explanation.

[3] It is curious that the old plate should have remained so long at Wells, since Dean Tanner was reputed to be an advanced Protestant. It was not until Dean Weston took over that the refashioning was arranged.

[4] At his trial Laud was charged with responsibility for the provision of candlesticks for the cathedrals of Canterbury, Chichester, Durham, Gloucester, Hereford, Winchester, and Worcester (*Canterburie's Doome*, 1646, 479).

Canterbury in 1634, where the inventory discloses that there had been added a large basin, a pair of candlesticks, and a second communion cup to match the one mentioned in 1584.[1] York had done very much better thanks to the generosity of Charles I, who in 1634 had utilized part of a large fine due to the Court of High Commission to provide a very handsome service of plate for the Minster.[2] There were therefore really two services, as follows:

OLD SERVICE	ROYAL GIFT
2 Communion cups with paten-covers, silver-gilt.	2 Chalices, silver-gilt.
3 Bowls for communion bread, silver.	3 Patens, silver-gilt.
1 Alms basin, silver-gilt.	2 Flagons, silver-gilt.
	1 Alms basin, silver-gilt.
	2 Candlesticks, silver-gilt.
	Bible and Book of Common Prayer with covers mounted in silver-gilt.

We may now turn to the collegiate churches. It is unfortunate that little is known at present with regard to the plate of Westminster Abbey at this period. It is likely that Dean Williams saw to it that his church kept abreast of the cathedrals, since he liked good plate as much as he hated Laud.

By contrast, we are very well informed about the furnishing of St. George's Chapel, Windsor. At the accession of Mary the chapel was meagrely furnished, since it had been raided by commissioners sent by the Privy Council in 1552, on news that the canons were embezzling the plate. Two chalices and three patens were all the silver items bought during the reign of Mary. The chapel did poorly during the reign of Elizabeth I, since in 1600 it had only a communion cup and cover, a small flagon, and an alms basin.[3] St. George's shared in the Jacobean revival, and if it lost the Elizabethan communion cup and the flagon, they were more than replaced by '2 fayre gilt Chalices wth Couers and crosse on the topps' and by '2 faire gilt potts with couers' which all survive. These had either been given by a local benefactor or bought by the dean and chapter. The idea that each new Companion of the Order of the Garter should subscribe £20 towards the plate of St. George's probably originated with the Prince of Wales, since nothing practical was done until he had succeeded as Charles I. At the first chapter after the king's accession, Laud deputized for the dying Lancelot Andrewes, Prelate of the Order, and tried to shame the Companions into paying up by offering a subscription equal to that which he was

[1] Legg and Hope, 216.

[2] The alms basin and the flagons belonging to the old service appear to have been sold. The distinction between communion cups in the old service and chalices in the royal gift probably indicates that the latter were of the new Gothic form (*Fabric Rolls of York Minster*, Surtees Soc. 1858, 316).

[3] Bond, op. cit. 236.

trying to collect. Although this offer was not an immediate success a considerable sum was eventually raised, and it now became a question as to how it should be used. Hitherto Charles had depended upon Laud, but when it came to ordering a handsome service of plate it seemed best to seek help elsewhere. This presented no difficulty, as the Earl Marshal was Thomas Howard, Earl of Arundel, who was linked to the king by his love of the arts. Arundel, who was the first Companion to pay his subscription, doubtless suggested the name of Christian van Vianen of Utrecht. He had passed through Utrecht when escorting the Princess Elizabeth to the Palatinate. In 1613 the best-known goldsmith in Holland was Adam van Vianen of Utrecht. When Arundel was next in Holland, in 1633, he would have heard that Adam was now dead, but that his son Christian was just as good a craftsman. At any rate, on St. George's Day 1634 the Chapter of the Order of the Garter authorized an imprest of £600 to Christian van Vianen, and by June 1637 he had completed nine pieces. By the outbreak of the Civil War the Garter Service comprised the following pieces, all of silver-gilt:

2 Chalices,
4 Patens,
2 Flagons,
2 Small Candlesticks,
2 Large Candlesticks,
2 Flower Pots,
Bible and Book of Common Prayer with decorated covers.

The whole weighed 2,807 oz. 12 dwt.[1] and must have been superb. Though

[1] Elias Ashmole (*Institution of the Order of the Garter*, 1672, 496) makes it weigh 3,580 oz. 7 dwt.

History is commonly less mindful of the crimes of the victors than of those of the vanquished, so that whilst the misdeeds against private property of Lord Goring's dragoons are remembered, those of the Parliament and their soldiery against the plate of the cathedrals is usually forgotten. For the most part both Cavaliers and Roundheads respected the plate of the parish churches. Unmindful of the traditional relationship between bishop and dean, the Roundheads regarded the cathedrals as hot-beds of episcopacy which might be plundered with profit and merit.

The plundering of the cathedrals and collegiate churches falls into two classes—plunder by more or less orderly requisition, and sheer looting. The robbery of St. Paul's and of Westminster Abbey fall into the first class. In the *House of Commons Journal*, under the date 17 April 1644, is the following entry:

> Resolved: That the Chest, or Silver Vessel, in Paul's, shall be sold for the best Advantage, & employed towards the providing of Necessaries for the Train of Artillery, by the Committee at Grocers' Hall.

Under the date 8 May 1644 is:

> Ordered, That the Plate lately found, that belongs unto the College of Westminster, now in the Possession of Sir Rob. Harley, be forthwith melted; & the Proceed of that Plate be disposed by the committee . . . for such Uses concerning the said Collegiate Church & such Servants, Workmen & others as they think fit.

The liability of the corporation of Norwich for the seizure of part of the cathedral plate was admitted at the Restoration and compensation was given in the form of a handsome alms basin (Blomefield, *Norfolk*, 1806, iv. 32). This appears to be the only instance of redress being obtained. Thus no com-its life was short, it is of great importance as the source of inspiration for pieces made at a later date.

The colleges of the universities had narrowly escaped dissolution at the close of the reign of Henry VIII. No direct attack was made upon them during the reign of Edward VI, but threatened foundations at this period showed a tendency to dispose of a part of their plate on the quiet. It may be supposed that the colleges would have had no difficulty in putting their hands upon everything necessary when the old services were restored under Mary. In the celebrated ornaments rubric in the Prayer Book of 1559 it was enjoined that 'the minister at the time of the communion, and at all other times in his ministration shall use such ornaments in church as were in use by authority of parliament in the second year of King Edward VI'.[1] The suggestion that they should actually use everything which was permitted offended the advanced Protestant clergy, who invented their own gloss on the rubric, viz. that the ornaments should remain until the queen should have time to arrange for their confiscation.[2] This plan did not appeal to the more level-headed Privy Councillors, who realized that whilst every church possessed its silver chalice, it was only in the university

pensation was ever obtained for the sale by the lord mayor of York of the candlesticks and three patens which he seized (*Fabric Rolls*, 333).

We probably do not know all the instances of the seizures by the municipal authorities, but the net result was that the only cathedrals which now retain an appreciable amount of plate dating from before the Civil War are Bangor, Exeter, Llandaff, Salisbury, and Wells.

Turning to the instances of pure looting, the first loss was that of the Christian van Vianen plate at St. George's Chapel. On 22 October 1642 Sir John Seyton seized Windsor Castle, and two days later one Captain Fogg broke open the treasury and made off with all of the Garter Service, leaving only the old one (Ashmole, op. cit. 496).

On Tuesday, 12 December 1642, Sir William Waller occupied Winchester, and two days later his troops broke into the cathedral and looted the plate (Bruno Ryves, *Mercurius Rusticus*, 1685, 151). On the 28th he occupied Chichester, and on the following day his troops broke into the cathedral and stole what plate they could find. Some more plate, which had been hidden behind the panelling in the chapter house, was later betrayed by one of the cathedral servants and occasioned another visit by the troopers. On this occasion Sir Arthur Haslerig was the responsible officer (ibid. 139, 142–3).

In mid-April 1643 Peterborough was occupied by Col. Hubbart's regiment of foot. The cathedral remained locked and there was no trouble until Col. Cromwell's regiment of horse arrived two days later. Next morning the troopers hacked their way into the cathedral and started plundering. Col. Hubbart intervened and succeeded in securing the return of most of the plate, but had to leave his colleague's troopers with the candlesticks (S. Gunton, *History of the Church of Peterborough*, 1686, 333–4).

The Royalists were responsible for turning the close of Lichfield into a fortress, but the cathedral plate was intact when they surrendered to the Parliamentarians. The latter were then besieged by Prince Rupert, to whom they surrendered on terms. When the garrison marched out on 21 April 1643 'the governor [Col. Russell] carried away the church plate and linen and whatsoever else was of value' (J. Britten, *History and Antiquities of Lichfield*, 1836, 30, quoting from Dugdale, *Short View of the Late Troubles in England*, 560).

[1] For an interpretation of this definition see Frere and Kennedy, iii. lx.

[2] See the letter of 30 April 1559 from Dr. Edmund Sandys to Matthew Parker (not yet archbishop) in *Parker Correspondence*, 1853, 65.

college chapels that articles like pyxes, paxes, cruets, censers, &c., of silver were to be found in any quantity. It was decided that the advanced party should have its way by indirect means. The queen would disinterest herself in any possible profit, whilst the question would be handled as a question of the suppression of superstition.

The bringing of the college chapels into line with the general policy regarding church plate was effected by several methods.

Though the outlook of the colleges was on the whole conservative, there was often a vociferous opposition which was ready to draw attention to attempts to conceal plate. Thus at King's College, Cambridge, it was declared that the provost, Dr. Baker, 'kepith still, to the great offence of the godly, and the infame of our college, a great heap of popish pelfe, as . . . candlesticks, crosses, pixes and paxes'; moreover, whereas by the statutes one of the fellows should have the key of the vestry, the Provost retained it in his own possession. The complaint was successful and the Provost was deposed.[1] There were colleges where it was possible to present a united front. The warden and fellows of All Souls College, Oxford, bought a communion cup in 1564 and hoped that this would pass as showing a proper readiness to fall in with the government's wishes. On 5 March 1566 Archbishop Parker, in his capacity as visitor, wrote to the warden to remind him that he had already been warned that 'for the avoiding of suspicion of superstition' he should melt down the old plate and keep the proceeds for the benefit of the college.[2] He was required to send an inventory, showing the form and fashion of the said plate. We cannot estimate the effect of this letter, but on 27 April 1567 the royal commissioners charged with the eradication of superstition were still bothering the college authorities, but this time they took the precaution of making it quite clear what might and what might not be preserved.[3]

The campaign against 'superstitious' plate seems to have been more successful at Cambridge than at Oxford, where four colleges still retain relics of their medieval plate.[4] The net result was, however, much the same, and it seems unlikely that in 1580 any college chapel would have shown upon the Holy Table anything of silver except the communion cup and cover. By 1600 it is likely that some would have had a silver flagon as well, but a more generous feeling followed the accession of the Stuarts, and its effects can be traced on the plate of colleges with a Low as well as those with a High tradition.

The two largest surviving services of this period are those given by Henry,

[1] J. Heywood and T. Wright, *Ancient Laws of King's College, Cambridge*, 1850, 215.

[2] J. Gutch, *Collectanea Curiosa*, 1781, 275.

[3] Ibid. 279. The commissioners connived at the recataloguing of the ablution ewers and basins as secular pieces. These have since disappeared. It is pretty clear that the device of recataloguing was used elsewhere.

[4] Brasenose, New College, Trinity and, above all, Corpus Christi.

6th Earl of Kent, to Sidney Sussex College, Cambridge, and that provided almost entirely out of the bequest of William Sandecraft, Master of Emmanuel.

The former bears the hall-mark for 1610 and comprises:

2 Communion cups with paten-covers,	2 Flagons,
2 Patens,	1 Alms basin.

The latter has the 1637 hall-mark and includes also a second alms basin.

There are reasons for supposing that these were not the most richly furnished chapels at the outbreak of the Civil War. Peterhouse was richly furnished by Matthew Wren and John Cosin in accordance with the ideas of Lancelot Andrewes. A bill from Cosin's goldsmith mentions a pair of candlesticks, a censer, and a flagon engraved with St. Peter. All these have gone, but there still survive a chalice and a flagon engraved with the Good Shepherd, acquired whilst Wren was master.

The plate of the Oxford chapels appears to have been built up with smaller benefactions, though Dorothy Wadham gave or bequeathed to her college a communion cup with paten-cover and two flagons (the latter of secular origin). St. John's is the best furnished with plate of this period, having a communion cup and two chalices and two pairs of flagons.

The plate of the chapels of both universities suffered as a result of the Civil War, but it is difficult at this distance to trace exactly how or when the losses occurred.[1]

In the last chapter it was emphasized that very few parish churches possessed at the end of the reign of Mary any silver ornaments other than a chalice and paten. The Elizabethan campaign for the conversion of chalices into communion cups has also been described and an estimate of its success given in the case of every diocese. It should not be too readily assumed that by the time that the conversion period drew to a close in the 1570's churches could be divided into two classes—those which had obeyed and now owned a communion cup with paten-cover, and those (an annually diminishing number) which still clung to their old chalice and paten. Two further classes must be mentioned.

If we refer back to Bishop Guest's injunctions, issued in 1565,[2] it will be noted that he orders that the chalice should be altered into a communion cup, but that nothing is said about the paten. There can be little doubt that it was intended that every communion cup should have a paten-cover, but, owing to the ambiguity in the injunction, most cups made before 1564 were sold without them,

[1] The only definite story which I have collected is the theft from the communion table of the plate of St. John's College, Cambridge, after an attempt to requisition it had failed owing to the intervention of Parliamentarian notabilities (Ryves, op. cit. 189). It is likely that other colleges besides Peterhouse lost candlesticks, although probably none other had a censer. It seems a fair guess that Pembroke, where Andrewes had been master, was robbed, since it had to be refurnished at the Restoration.

[2] See above, p. 135.

whilst the first direct mention of the covers appears in Bishop Parkhurst's 1569 injunctions for the diocese of Norwich.[1] Since the conversion of the chalices of this diocese had been made as a result of Archbishop Parker's metropolitical visitation of two years earlier,[2] the bishop was in effect asking the churchwardens to go to the further trouble of getting a paten-cover. The fact that this bishop's control over his diocese was not very good is probably the reason for the survival, mainly in north-eastern Norfolk, of thirty-six medieval patens, since the general indications are that Protestantism was firmly rooted in the area. Elsewhere early Elizabethan communion cups with covers made a few years later are not uncommon.

Churchwardens who were unwilling to exchange their chalices disobeyed the injunctions and, if their parish was small and obscure, their deviation might escape notice, at any rate for a time. In a paper on disorders in the Chichester diocese in the year 1569 it is remarked that many parishes retain their chalices 'hoping for the mass again although they had been ordered to turn them into a communion cup, keeping weight for weight, and not to burden the parish with the price of a new one'.[3] There were parishes all over the country where the acquisition of a communion cup did not involve the melting down of the chalice. There are still two churches which retain both a medieval chalice and an Elizabethan communion cup—Leominster, Hereford; and Nettlecombe, Som.[4] In both cases the communion cup was made by the prolific goldsmith *IP*, the former in 1576 and the latter three years earlier. The instinct to retain the chalice would appear not to have been uncommon and was presumably indicative of a desire for a return to the old service.[5] In the ordinary way the chalice would seem to have been reprieved for only a few years, perhaps until the appointment of new churchwardens.[6]

It is now time to say something of deviations in a Protestant direction. Down to the close of the reign of Elizabeth I there were more churches which could show two communion cups than ones which boasted a communion cup and a

[1] Frere and Kennedy, iii. 210.

[2] Ibid. 199.

[3] *Calendar of State Papers Domestic, 1547–80*, 357.

[4] It is curious to note that when the Rev. E. H. Bates and Prebendary Hancock described the Nettlecombe plate in *Proc. of the Somerset Arch. Soc.* xlv, 1899, 167–70, they were so overwhelmed by the earliest hall-marked chalice that they overlooked both the Elizabethan communion cup and the Charles II flagon.

[5] This would seem to be the obvious gloss, and would suggest that the papal directives which ordered the rigid separation of the Recusants were still not taken at their face value. It seems to have taken quite a long time to establish the idea that there was anything improper in the continued use of the old chalice. Thus the notoriously Protestant St. Margaret, Westminster, which had preserved two communion cups during the reign of Mary, did not sell its Marian chalice until 1570–2. The proceeds would seem to have been applied to the purchase of a third cup, which was bought between 1576–8 (*Churchwardens' Accounts*).

[6] e.g. Strood, Kent, bought its communion cup in 1565 and sold its chalice in 1574 (*Archaeologia Cantiana*, xvi, 1886, 335.

silver flagon. Churches having two communion cups were usually in small towns with a single parish, or in the main churches of large towns. The two cups when ordered simultaneously might form a pair, but this was not always the case.[1] Some churches added another cup a few years later, in which case it never matched.[2] From the practical point of view a flagon was of more use than a second communion cup, but it was, of course, also much more costly. Few churches could show a silver flagon before the queen's death. Those having a pair were very rare indeed.[3]

During the reign of Elizabeth I the parish churches received little by way of gifts, and sometimes, when more than the minimum is found, it is explained by some windfall.[4] Within a few years of the accession of the Stuarts, donors of plate had become plentiful and, since for practical reasons communion cups and flagons of considerable capacity were preferred, they did not escape cheaply. The process of endowing parish churches with plate went on without interruption until the outbreak of the Civil War. It was still, of course, the urban churches which did best, and some idea of their wealth can be gathered from the following reconstructed inventories of three provincial town churches in 1640.

KING'S LYNN, ST. MARGARET[5]

Communion cups with paten-covers: 2. *Patens*: 2. *Flagons*: 5. *Weight*: *c.* 390 ounces.

NEWCASTLE-UPON-TYNE, ALL SAINTS[6]

Communion cups with paten-covers: 4. *Patens*: 2. *Weight*: *c.* 100 ounces.

SALISBURY, ST. THOMAS[7]

Communion cups with paten-covers: 2. *Patens*: 2. *Flagons*: 2. *Weight*: *c.* 100 ounces.

There still survives plenty of evidence of the wealth accumulated by the churches of the City of London at this period, but, owing to the manner in which the plate of the churches not rebuilt after the Fire has been mixed up with that of the survivors, it is difficult to discover how much any one possessed at the date chosen above.

[1] e.g. All Saints, Newcastle, where both cups were bought in 1571, but one of them weighs 15 oz. 10 dwt. and the other 12 oz. 3 dwt.

[2] e.g. Beccles, 1567 and 1568; Thame, 1569 and 1570; Beverley Minster, 1570; and another undated.

[3] e.g. Cirencester, 1576, and St. Margaret, Westminster, 1583. There are other churches with two Elizabethan communion cups or flagons but the date of their acquisition is generally not fixed.

[4] e.g. in 1566 the commissioners for the suppression of superstition were informed by the churchwardens of Grantham that they had bought 'a silver pott parcell Gylt and an Ewer of sylver for the ministracion of the holye and most sacred supper of oure lorde Jhesus Crist called the holye comunyon' with the proceeds of the sale of two chalices and patens and of the copper-gilt shrine of St. Wulfram, the patron of the church (E. Peacock, *English Church Furniture*, 1866, 88).

[5] *Norfolk Archaeology*, xxiv, 1930, 19–23.

[6] *Proc. Soc. Antiquaries of Newcastle*, iii, 1887–8, 272–3.

[7] *C.P. Wilts.* 18–19.

The rural churches were also not forgotten, and by the outbreak of the Civil War there were many which could show more than the minimum required by the visitation articles. Of the seven churches which Lady (later Duchess) Dudley endowed with plate before war broke out, some were quite unimportant. To such, the gift of a fine chalice with paten-cover, a covered paten, and a flagon represented wealth such as they had never owned in the past. These were by no means the only parish churches which within a hundred years of the Edwardian pillage had more than made good their losses.

For reasons of expediency the spiritual welfare of the Channel Islands was handed over by the Privy Council of Elizabeth I to Huguenots from Normandy. An attempt by Bishop Horne to recover control for the see of Winchester came to nothing, and the Presbyterian régime got firmly rooted. Though no immediate steps were taken to end this anomaly after the accession of James I, the governors of both islands regarded critically their *colloques*. In 1609 Sir John Peyton, Governor of Jersey, imported an Anglican chaplain, but it was not until 1620 that internal dissensions amongst the Presbyterians provided an opening for the introduction of an Anglican dean of Jersey who at once set to work to turn the elders into churchwardens, &c. The Presbyterian régime had not been inimical to the accumulation of plate, though for economic reasons most parishes had probably made do with pewter.[1] The first form of communion vessel favoured in Jersey was a bowl. The church of St. Brelade has four (Pl. 73) and that of St. Mary, one. Already in 1594 the parish of St. Clement had a cup on a baluster stem (Pl. 72*b*). This became the standard form until 1660. Whereas the most populous English parish would not have had more than four cups for the communion, the churches of St. John and St. Owen had six and seven, respectively. The only place where plate showing the ordinary Anglican forms was well represented was the chapel of the governor.

The Guernsey presbytery managed their dissensions with greater decency, so that no opening was left for Anglican aggression before 1660. The island was, however, less prosperous than Jersey, so that the churches collected little plate. There is evidence that the church of St. Peter Port had four cups, and single examples seem to have existed in some of the other churches. There is no reason to suppose that the medieval chalice at St. Sampson ever went out of use.

The churches of the Isle of Man were even poorer and would appear to have been furnished almost exclusively with pewter down to 1660.

2. 1660–1830

When the cathedrals came to life again in 1660, some would appear to have

[1] Tradition in the Channel Islands says that the *seigneurs* used to bring their own silver cups down from their houses—a practice against which the bishops fought hard in England in the days of Elizabeth I.

been completely stripped of plate, most of them had suffered more or less severe losses, but one or two would seem to have escaped intact.[1]

The minimum replacement order was placed by the dean and chapter of Lichfield and consisted of a chalice, a paten on foot, and a pair of flagons. Cathedrals which were not so overwhelmed by structural repairs aimed rather higher, but their orders were not uniform and depended, of course, on how much survived from the time of Charles I.

The following table attempts to give an idea of the plate possessed by six typical cathedrals in 1665, when the urgent deficiencies had been made good:

CANTERBURY

NEW PLATE

Chalices with paten-covers: 2. *Standing patens*: 2. *Flagons*: 2. *Alms basin or altar dish*: 1. *Candlesticks*: 2.

OLD PLATE

Chalices: 1. *Alms basins*: 2.

CHESTER

NEW PLATE

Chalices with paten-covers: 2. *Standing patens*: 2. *Flagons*: 2. *Alms basin or altar dish*: 1. *Candlesticks*: 2.

GLOUCESTER

NEW PLATE

Chalices with paten-covers: 2. *Standing paten*: 1. *Flagons*: 2. *Alms basin or altar dish*: 1 *Candlesticks*, 1.

NORWICH

NEW PLATE

Standing paten: 1. *Alms basin or altar dish*: 1. *Candlesticks*: 2. *Bible with silver mounts*: 1.

OLD PLATE

Chalice: 1.* *Flagon*: 1.

OXFORD

NEW PLATE

Chalices with paten-covers: 2. *Flagons*: 2. *Alms basin or altar dish*: 1. *Candlesticks*: 2.

OLD PLATE

Paten: 1. *Bible and Prayer Book with silver mounts*: 1.

* A cup of secular origin.

[1] Wells appears to have escaped scot-free. The Bangor plate also escaped, although Caernarvonshire saw quite a lot of the Civil War.

SALISBURY

NEW PLATE

Standing patens: 2. *Candlesticks*: 2.

OLD PLATE

Chalices with paten-covers: 2. *Patens*: 3.

Though all the cathedrals listed above had made haste to get a pair of altar candlesticks, these were not regarded as essential. Had Dean Cosin returned to Peterborough at the Restoration, doubtless those stolen by Cromwell's troopers would have been replaced. In fact the only addition to the plate of this cathedral between 1660 and 1830 was an alms basin acquired to replace one stolen in 1672. There were a number of other cathedrals which managed without silver altar candlesticks.[1] On the other hand, both St. Paul's and York had two pairs. Between 1660 and 1714 many cathedrals received important gifts and bequests of plate, one of the richest being the service made during the Commonwealth for the chapel of Charles, Duke of Lennox, at Cobham Hall, which was bequeathed to Rochester in 1701 by Sir Joseph Williamson. In 1699 two large altar dishes and a pair of enormous flagons were presented to St. Paul's by Prebendary Smith, Archdeacon of Colchester. This benefaction seems to have completed the refurnishing of this cathedral which, unlike that of most of the others, was done regardless of expense.[2] St. Paul's then had:

2 Chalices with paten-covers,	5 Altar dishes,
2 Standing patens,	4 Candlesticks,
4 Flagons,	Bible and Prayer Book with silver mounts.

After the death of Anne the flow of gifts to the cathedrals almost dried up. The largest benefaction was the gift of a second service of plate to Bangor in 1778. The donor was Bishop Moore, afterwards Archbishop of Canterbury. During the eighteenth century three cathedrals had their plate refashioned, Durham in 1766–7, Hereford in 1772, and Winchester in 1792. Only the first of these was well done, and we shall have to recur to it in succeeding chapters.

In the year 1830, when we close, the treasuries of the cathedrals presented a somewhat sorry spectacle. Bangor alone, with its two massive services of plate, was probably richer than before the Reformation. At the other end of the scale was St. Paul's, where no effort had been made to make good the loss of the

[1] I have found no trace of silver candlesticks having been owned by Carlisle, Chichester, Lichfield, Wells, Winchester, nor any Welsh cathedral.

[2] There is no clue as to the exact date of manufacture, but the descriptions suggest that it was of the same class as was supplied to the chapels royal in the early years of Charles II.

whole plate stolen twenty years earlier. York was not in a much better case, as all the plate except the two pairs of candlesticks and the silver-mounted Bible and Book of Common Prayer had been destroyed when Jonathan Martin set fire to the choir in the previous year. Archbishop Vernon Harcourt, however, had stepped in at once with an offer to replace what had been lost. The resulting service was made in the Regency Gothic style by Rundell, Bridge & Rundell. Though it bears the 1830 hall-mark, it was only formally handed over in 1831.

The picture of the plate of the cathedrals in 1830 is one of unfulfilled promise. There was no reason why an Anglican cathedral, with its different organization of worship, should emulate either the quantity or the diversity of a medieval one. The ideals of Andrewes and of Laud had been that the cathedrals should aim at a higher standard of equipment than was in use in other churches. The notable advance made in the reign of Charles I had been undone during the Civil War. The tradition was not forgotten at the Restoration when the deans and chapters did their best to restore the standard of their services, having due regard to time and expense. The best available in 1660–5 was not really good enough a quarter of a century later. By this time the Church of England was entering upon the period of religious upheaval in the reigns of James II and William and Mary. The period of stagnation which overtook the plate of the cathedrals must be regarded as part of the price which the Church of England paid for the loss of the Non-Jurors.

Turning to the collegiate churches, it would seem that nothing at all remained at Westminster Abbey. The new dean, John Earle, and the chapter set about ordering an emergency set of plate. This was executed so expeditiously that it got into an inventory dated 30 January 1661.[1] It was simpler than the services then being made for Gloucester and Oxford both in its lack of applied ornament and the absence of candlesticks. It comprised:

2 Chalices with paten-covers, 2 Flagons,
2 Standing patens, 1 Altar dish.

Perhaps the dean and canons made at the same time a resolution to replace this makeshift service by a better one when circumstances permitted, as in 1671 the Dean of Durham, who had been a prebendary ten years earlier, contributed a pair of much more handsome chalices with paten-covers, the work of the same goldsmith who had made the first pair. It was not until 1684 that a pair of flagons in the same style, a very handsome embossed altar dish (Pl. 131*a*),[2] and two plain ones were added. The transformation was completed with the

[1] Jocelyn Perkins, *Westminster Abbey, its Worship and Ornaments*, Alcuin Club, 1952, iii. 214.

[2] The 1660 altar dish has disappeared.

gift of a pair of candlesticks in 1690. No further additions were made before 1830.

In 1660 the case of St. George's Chapel, Windsor, was very much better than that of the abbey. When the plate of the latter had been seized for the Parliamentary Treasury, it was probably believed that Captain Fogg had made a clean sweep at Windsor. Actually there still remained the plate which the chapel had owned before Charles I had embarked on his project of the Garter Plate. With this the services could have been carried on with decency, but the new dean was Bruno Ryves, who cared a lot about plate.[1] His first move was to go up to London to get the king to re-enact the regulations for a levy on the Companions for the acquisition of plate for St. George's. Whereas it had taken Charles I sixteen years' hard badgering to collect enough money to warrant placing orders for his plate, Dean Ryves was able to extract from the Companions a pair of chalices and two pairs of flagons bearing the hall-marks for 1661 and 1662.[2] One of the canons who had been chaplain to Princess Mary, sister of Charles I and mother of William III, obtained a promise from the princess of an altar dish and a pair of candlesticks,[3] whilst at the same time the Duchess of York gave two smaller altar dishes. With the exception of the first pair of flagons, which are of standard design, all the new plate was of the finest workmanship and was made by the goldsmiths who were employed by the Jewel Office. By the time that the 1667 inventory was compiled[4] the chapel was magnificently fitted out as follows:

NEW PLATE

2 Chalices with paten-covers,	4 Flagons,
1 Chalice,	3 Altar dishes,
1 Paten,	2 Candlesticks.

OLD PLATE

2 Chalices with covers,	1 Alms basin.
2 Flagons,	

Dean Ryves would appear to have been content with the result of his appeal, since no further additions were made before his death in 1677. He had, in fact, replaced all the stolen plate with the exception of the flower-pots, of which he may not have approved, the silver-mounted Bible and Book of Common Prayer, and the larger pair of candlesticks. A later dean secured the last item in 1694. The silver-mounted books were never obtained, but in other respects

[1] His accounts of the looting of Chichester and Winchester have been used on p. 158, n. 1.

[2] According to Ashmole (op. cit. 498) the subscriptions resistance of the Companions crumbled on the news that the Duke of York had promised £100.

[3] This turned out badly. The princess died and the dean and chapter had to pay the bill.

[4] Bond, op. cit. 247–8.

St. George's was quite exceptionally well furnished, both as regards quantity and quality. It is not, therefore, surprising that no additions were made in the eighteenth century.

At the universities the colleges which had lost their chapel plate during the Civil War set about replacing it in several ways.[1] At Pembroke College, Cambridge, the essentials were provided by a fine Gothic service comprising a chalice, two patens, a flagon, and an alms basin, which had probably been made for some private chapel during the Commonwealth. A pair of candlesticks followed in 1664 and another flagon and alms basin in 1669.

During the first half of the century the universities had been rent by religious dissensions, and the chapel plate had tended to reflect the views of the head of the college. The Restoration brought a total victory for the High Church, and for the future there was but one model for the plate of a college chapel, the attainment of which was only delayed by financial considerations. The ideal college chapel altar was for the future to imitate that of a cathedral. Actually only St. John's College, Cambridge, was given a complete service of plate. In 1728 the Earl of Exeter presented one consisting of two large and two small chalices with paten-covers, a pair of flagons, and an alms basin. The colleges played a waiting game, not unsuccessfully. Whereas the plate of the cathedrals stagnated during the eighteenth century, that of the college chapels grew steadily.[2] The series of altar candlesticks to be found at the universities is particularly important, since it includes varieties not to be found elsewhere. During the eighteenth century the standard maintained by the chapels in the universities must have had a considerable and a beneficial effect, both through the former undergraduates who later became patrons of livings, and through the fellows who become accustomed to seeing good plate on the altar before they married and retired to a college living.

The parish churches had got through the Civil War and the Commonwealth without many losses. For them the period 1660 to 1830 is one of pretty steady progress. Each year there were fewer churches having only a communion cup with paten-cover. Too little attention has been paid to archidiaconal visitations to permit of progress reports, but the following analysis of the results of those in the Rochester diocese in 1733–44[3] will give some idea of the state of affairs in a district which was neither particularly rich nor poor.

[1] At St. John's, Cambridge, some sort of emergency service must have been got. It was probably scrapped when the 1728 service was given. At Peterhouse no attempt was made to replace Cosin's elaborate service. A chalice with paten-cover and a flagon alone survived, and only an alms basin was acquired. Perhaps the fellows hoped that their former master, Bishop Cosin, would step in with a gift. He, however, seems to have thought that £300 subscribed towards the restoration of the chapel was quite enough.

[2] The period of stagnation for university chapel plate was between 1800 and 1830, during which no important piece was got at either Oxford or Cambridge.

[3] *Archaeologia Cantiana*, xvi, 1886, 359–61.

ROCHESTER DEANERY, 1733–41

34 Parishes. All have one chalice, three have two (Chatham; Gravesend; St. Nicholas, Rochester).

Twenty-one have patens (presumably not paten-covers) and Chatham uses two silver plates.

Ten have flagons, two have a pair (Chatham and St. Nicholas, Rochester).

Four have alms basins, one a baptismal basin (Chatham), one a straining spoon.

DARTFORD DEANERY, 1735–42

21 Parishes. All have one chalice, four have two (Dartford; Greenwich; Lewisham; Woolwich).

Fifteen have patens, one has two (Charlton).

Eleven have flagons, four have a second (Dartford; Greenwich; Lewisham; Woolwich).

There was one baptismal basin (Greenwich) and two straining spoons.

MALLING DEANERY, 1735–42

32 Parishes. All have silver chalices, three have two (Cowden; Mereworth; Westerham), one has three (West Malling).

Twenty have patens, two have two (Cowden; Westerham).

Six have flagons.

Seven have some sort of alms basin.

A picture of a larger area at the close of our period is obtainable from the returns for the visitation of the archdeaconry of Leicester in 1832.[1] On this occasion 232 churches were visited, and all but six had a chalice,[2] thirty-two possessed a second, one had a third (Newbold Verdon). Fifty-two churches had a flagon, eight of these had two. A large number of these had patens, but Archdeacon Bonney was not always very clear in his descriptions, so that since we cannot be sure whether a piece which has since disappeared was a paten or an alms basin, it seems best to leave them out of account. Taking the returns as a whole, we get the impression that there was probably in the parish churches of England in 1830 almost or quite as much plate as there had been in 1530. Many of the chalices in use were not those made out of the medieval ones in the reign of Elizabeth I, but larger and heavier ones. Any church which owned a chalice and a 12-inch flagon had the equivalent of four average medieval chalices and, as we have seen, not many churches possessed as much as that at the end of the Middle Ages.

We may now take a glance at the plate of a number of churches which did

[1] *C.P. Leics.* ii. 463–71.

[2] These six used chalices of pewter or of Sheffield plate, except Muston, which had a silver-mounted mazer. There were also two or three cases of churches with no plate at all. These were churches of villages which had virtually disappeared, and the plate of the neighbouring church with which it was run was borrowed when needed.

particularly well during this period. As examples of lucky rural churches, we cannot do better than list the plate of the churches in Dorset and Somerset, which received benefactions from Mrs. Strangways Horner. They are particularly interesting as reflecting the ideas of this remarkable lady on how a church should be furnished.[1]

		Paten					
	Chalice	*Large*	*Small*	*Flagon*	*Bread box*	*Knife*	*Weight*
1737 Stinsford . .	1	..	1	1	..	1 (1755)	51 oz. 6 dwt.
1747 Melbury Osmund .	1	..	2	1	..	1 (1755)	72 oz. 18 dwt.
1747 Melbury Sampford	1	1	..	1	1 (1753)	1	?
1748 Mells . . .	1	1	1	1	..	1 (1755)	?
1748 Abbotsbury . .	1	1	1	1	..	1 (1755)	79 oz. 2 dwt.

This table gives only Mrs. Strangways Horner's benefactions, and the apparent neglect of Melbury Sampford is due to the fact that this church already possessed two chalices and two patens given by earlier members of her family.

Turning to the provincial towns, we may note how the three churches inventoried in 1630 had fared by 1740.[2]

St. Margaret, Lynn, gained two alms basins in 1689, a pair of candlesticks in 1702, and a strainer spoon in 1708. The total weight had risen from *c.* 390 to *c.* 513 ounces.

All Saints, Newcastle, had meanwhile obtained a flagon in 1697 and an alms basin in 1713. This raised the total weight from *c.* 100 to *c.* 195 ounces.

At St. Thomas, Salisbury, there had been alterations as well as additions, with the result that there was now one more flagon and one more paten. In the process the weight had more than doubled, so that it now stood at 235 ounces.[3]

For really sensational returns it is necessary to go to Westminster, where the westward spread of London had rendered the few existing parishes quite unwieldy. Recourse was had to the building of chapels of ease, some of which developed into parish churches, whilst the remainder were eventually reabsorbed.

St. James, Piccadilly, was one of the new chapels which soon became

[1] She was evidently interested in the after-care of her gifts, since in the box which contains the Stinsford plate is a piece of paper with *Directions to keep the Gilt Plate clean, from the silversmith that made it* [Paul de Lamerie]. *Clean it now and then with only warm water and soap, with a Spunge, and wash it with clean water, and dry it very well with a soft Linnen Cloth, and keep it in a dry place for the damp will spoyle it.* Dean Smith, when presenting plate to Carlisle Cathedral in 1680, also left instructions about cleaning which emphasized that abrasives should not be used (*C.P. Carlisle*, 29). In the second part of the eighteenth century goldsmiths sold boxes of *crocus martis* for cleaning plate.

[2] See above, p. 163.

[3] It is sad to note that all the plate of this church was refashioned in 1867.

parochial. It started off at its consecration in 1683 with a splendid service of gilt plate comprising:

- 4 Chalices,
- 4 Patens,
- 3 Flagons,
- 1 Altar dish.

Within a few years there were added three chalices for the communion of the sick and a strainer spoon. This brought the weight to 590 ounces. No further additions were made between 1700 and 1750, at which date we may look at the plate of St. Martin-in-the-Fields, out of whose parish St. James's had been carved. The following would appear to be the plate given for use at St. Martin's, including the plate of the two chapels at ease:

- 6 Chalices with paten-covers,
- 3 Chalices with paten-covers (for the sick),
- 3 Standing patens,
- 7 Flagons,
- 3 Alms basins,
- 1 Baptismal ewer,
- 1 Strainer spoon,
- 1 Knife.

With the exception of one of the chalices for the sick, everything was gilt, and the total weight was 1,228 oz. 7 dwt.

Church plate in Jersey continued to develop on individualistic lines after the Restoration. English forms of chalice (made locally) competed with the old local variety with a baluster stem. A corollary to the local preference for large numbers of chalices was a relative rarity of flagons. There is a large one of peculiar shape at St. Owen, evidently made towards the end of the seventeenth century. Besides this there are two of 1766 at St. Helier, and three others of later date. Another local feature was the appearance of silver baptismal bowls to replace the pewter ones made necessary by the loss of the fonts during the Calvinistic period. According to English rural standards, the churches of Jersey were very well supplied with plate in 1830.

Guernsey, unlike Jersey, backed the Parliament in the Civil War, and Presbyterianism fell in the island in the same way as it did in England at the Restoration. In time the islanders became accustomed to their French version of the Book of Common Prayer and, since economic conditions were improving, the churches began to collect plate. The character of the plate acquired differs somewhat from that in Jersey. Though the churches seem to have aimed at possessing two chalices (which was a generous allowance according to English rural standards), they did not attempt to emulate the greater number customary in Jersey. A plain platter was favoured as a paten, since the paten-cover did not reach the island. The earliest flagon is at St. Saviour's and bears the London hall-mark for 1734, and by 1830 half the churches had them. The main peculiarity of Guernsey plate is the number of baptismal ewers, due mostly to the enthusiasm of one donor. The plate of a Guernsey church would not have appeared nearly so strange to a visitor from England in 1830 as would that of the sister isle. Though mostly of local make, it does not often differ from standard English forms.

In 1660 there was even less plate in the churches of the Isle of Man than there was in those of Guernsey. The island did not prosper as did the Channel Islands, whilst its ecclesiastical history included very stormy periods. The plate acquired by Manx churches was mainly both poor and scanty. Several churches acquired beakers as communion cups, a form seldom used in England. The finest plate to reach the island is at Kirk German. It would appear to be that which was used by Henry Bridgeman, Bishop of Sodor and Man from 1670 to 1682, whilst running an Anglican congregation during the Commonwealth.

III

THE PLATE OF PRIVATE CHAPELS

I. 1553–1660

IT is exasperating that we have not anything like the same amount of information about the furnishing of the Chapel Royal during the second half of the sixteenth century as we have for the first. It is clear that Mary must have inherited a certain amount of mass plate which had escaped melting in her brother's time. So far little has been found to suggest that Mary ordered much plate. The single exception was the font which she ordered when she believed herself to be pregnant and which will be described elsewhere. On 1 October 1560 nearly two years after the accession of Elizabeth I, Sir Thomas Stanley, Master of the Mint, signed for a large quantity of chapel plate which was sent in for melting.[1] This was not the end of the popish plate but only of that part which could be melted with most profit. The inventories of 1574 and 1596 still contain a considerable amount of old chapel plate, but it is possible to note a tendency to preserve articles mainly of crystal, mother-of-pearl, and other unprecious materials. There were, as well as these, some massive chalices, crosses, and candlesticks, but the typical survivors were exotic items like:

> Item oone Shippe of mother of pearle garnished with silver guilt and the Cover of like silver guilt being a hedde w[t] hornes, the eies being garnettes, poz. xxxvi oz.[2]

It is unfortunate that we have no clear guidance as to what items were actually in use, and it seems likely that the chapel plate in these two inventories was regarded really as a reserve. The only indubitably Protestant items are a Bible and a Book of Common Prayer with silver-gilt mounts.

Accounts of the queen's chapel emphasize that the communion table was placed altar-wise against the east end and that it carried candlesticks and the cross which so much provoked the Puritans.[3] We have no notice of communion cups, but had the queen stuck to chalices her critics would certainly have recorded the lapse. A pair of flagons may also be assumed. For reasons which will be explained, there is a likelihood that these were derived from her father's stock of secular plate.[4] A pair of alms dishes are perhaps more probable than a single one as long as the crucifix maintained its place.

We have a good account of the queen's chapel when decked out for a special

[1] P.R.O., *Pipe Roll Declared Account*, 1953.

[2] Collins, 312.

[3] Cf. pp. 246–7.

[4] Cf. p. 222.

occasion.[1] In the late summer of 1565 she received a visit from Christopher II, Margrave of Baden, and his wife Cecily, daughter of Eric XIV of Sweden. The margravine, who almost immediately gave birth to a son, took Elizabeth by storm. The Master of the Jewel House was ordered to prepare a royal christening. This presented a problem, since the latest precedent dated from the reign of Henry VIII and a lot had happened since then. The result of the Master's deliberations was what we should describe as sheer Hollywood, with something to offend both the advanced Protestants and the conservatives. The communion table was loaded with plate, and besides the crucifix the Puritans would note four pairs of candlesticks. In front stood three incense-boats garnished with silver-gilt, whilst above, on a shelf, were twenty-one candlesticks of gold or silver-gilt. The more conservative onlookers would, similarly, dislike seeing the crucifix peering out from amongst a host of pieces of secular plate of the most incongruous sorts, such as an agate bird set with stones and pearls and 'a Shipe or Arke garnished with stones'. Ten chandeliers of silver-gilt, suspended from the roof, illuminated the rest of the chapel.[2]

It is likely that the appearance of the communion table on ordinary occasions remained during the reigns of James I and Charles I very much the same as we have suggested for that of Elizabeth I. Doubtless, when Bishop Andrewes became dean in 1619, greater care was taken in the ordering of the services, but there is no indication of his attempting to introduce any of the innovations practised in his own chapel. If we can only conjecture the altar plate in use in early Stuart times, we have no information with regard to the individual pieces. We have no knowledge of any additions made by Charles I, who took such a lively interest in the embellishment of St. George's Chapel, Windsor.

The part played by private chapels in English religious life in post-Reformation times is generally underestimated. It is apt to be assumed that the chapel was no more than a customary appendage to a large house and that the services were performed by a harmless drudge who also made himself useful as secretary and librarian. The real fact was that everything depended on the character of the master of the house, and when we look at the surviving examples of seventeenth- and eighteenth-century chapel plate we have often to ask ourselves the question whether it was originally commissioned by very religious or very ostentatious men. In many cases they certainly fell into the former category.

One of the symptoms of the religious revival of the early seventeenth century

[1] J. Leland, *Collectanea*, ed. T. Hearne, 1774, ii. 691–2.

[2] We long for one of Bishop Jewel's wailing letters to his friends in Switzerland, but he had been called in to hallow the water and may have felt that it was best not to mention the whole affair.

The luck of the Badens broke at this point. Londoners got sick of the margrave, and he was actually arrested by the mayor of Rochester, because of his outrageous behaviour, as he made his way to the coast. The margravine lingered a little longer but left behind her £1,500 of debts, mainly to jewellers.

was the increasing importance of the plate in the private chapels. Little of this remains *in situ*, since chapel plate tended to drift into parish churches, just as it had done in the Middle Ages. During the Commonwealth, Anglicans found themselves suffering from some of the disabilities long endured by the Catholic Recusants. Just as the deprivation of the use of parish churches had led the latter to establish chapels in their houses, so now Anglicans did the same. Just as Recusant chapel plate seldom went to Goldsmiths' Hall, so a considerable proportion of the plate made for Anglican chapels during the Commonwealth is without a hall-mark. The reason for this caution was that many of the Anglican customers liked plate in the Gothic tradition founded by Lancelot Andrewes, which to Puritans was particularly objectionable as a reminder of the vanquished episcopacy.

The most notable example of this is the plate of the Shirleys of Staunton Harold, Leics. Sir Henry Shirley, Bart., had died in 1633 leaving two sons who had been brought up as enthusiastic Anglicans, although the family had a Recusant tradition. The elder brother, Charles, was a Royalist and had to pay for it before his early death in 1646. Robert, the younger, was born in 1629 and was prevented from getting mixed up in the Civil War by his tender years and by his guardian the Earl of Essex. The latter, however, died within a few months of his succession to the baronetcy of his ward, who immediately gave free expression to his Royalist and Anglican enthusiasms. He decided to build and furnish in a handsome manner a chapel which would act as a church for the neighbourhood whilst Anglicanism was banned. He appears to have started by picking up a chalice and cover in the Gothic style (Pl. 83*a*), made in 1640 by the goldsmith *RB*.[1] He then ordered another chalice to match it, a pair of covered patens, a pair of flagons, a pair of candlesticks, and an alms basin. All of these were made by one of the most notable goldsmiths of the century, who can only be identified by his mark of *a hound sejant*.[2] To his religious he added political activities which were quite enough to warrant his committal to the Tower, where he died in 1656.[3]

Thomas Chicheley, of Wimpole, Cambs., was born in 1681 and served as high sheriff in 1637, and member of Parliament for his county in 1640. He was ejected when he joined the king on the outbreak of war and was heavily fined

[1] Jackson, *Goldsmiths*, 116; it has usually been assumed that the 1640 chalice had been bought by the elder brother, but this seems unlikely, since there does not seem to have been a chapel at that date.

The late Lord Ferrers presented the chapel and all its contents to the National Trust, which has deposited the plate at the Victoria and Albert Museum.

[2] Ibid. 123.

[3] Sir Robert's religious activities were probably guided by Dr. Gilbert Sheldon, with whom he ran a fund for distressed Royalists and whom he appointed his executor. It seems likely that Sheldon was responsible for a similar set of plate by the same goldsmith, consisting of a chalice, covered paten, and two flagons, now at Fulham Palace, which was his home whilst Bishop of London, 1660–3.

on the collapse of the Royalist cause. His Anglicanism was no less fervent than that of Sir Robert Shirley, but he was maturer and more discreet. He commissioned from the same goldsmith a chalice, a flagon,[1] and an alms basin (Pl. 125), none of which are hall-marked. On the Restoration he returned to Parliament and resumed a not undistinguished career. Having no further need to maintain a private chapel, he presented his plate to the parish church, twenty years before his death.

Charles Stuart, Duke of Lennox and Richmond, born in 1639, was much too young to take part in the Civil War, and spent the succeeding years living in considerable state at Cobham Hall, Kent. His chapel was furnished by the same goldsmith with two chalices, two covered patens, two flagons, two candlesticks, and an alms basin, all with the 1653 hall-mark. The choice can hardly be taken as representing the duke's religious convictions, and if he favoured 'Church and King' it was merely because he was a cousin of the exiled monarch. The plate got left behind when Cobham changed hands and was bequeathed to Rochester Cathedral in 1701 by the next occupant, Sir Joseph Williamson.

These three instances give some idea of how the Anglican resistance movement operated during the Commonwealth. Most Royalists were not left in such easy financial circumstances and could not afford to order whole services of plate. There remain, however, a number of chalices, now mainly in parish churches, which serve as memorials to those who kept the Anglican tradition alive during this decade.

Whilst it is easy to list the minimum amount of plate which would have been found in the chapel of a medieval bishop, it is impossible to be certain that their immediately post-Reformation successors had more than a communion cup with paten-cover.[2] Yet we may feel sure that the cultured Archbishop Parker, whose domestic plate still adorns two Cambridge colleges, would have had more than this, and that it would have been of the best quality.

The only episcopal chapel plate which we know intimately is that which belonged to Bishop Andrewes, thanks to the misguided industry of William Prynne who, when allowed the run of Archbishop Laud's papers in order to frame his accusation, came across a number of documents relating to a richly furnished chapel which he mistook for that of his victim.[3] These included a plan

[1] The second flagon is an inferior copy.

[2] Archbishop Grindal bequeathed to the church of his native place, St. Bees, his silver-gilt communion cup. It is still there (*C.P. Carlisle*, 162).

[3] 'At the reading of this paper I was a little troubled. I knew I was not then so rich as to have such plate, or furniture; and therefore I humbly desired sight of the paper. So soon as I saw it I found that there was nothing in it in my hand but the endorsement, which told the reader plainly that it was the model of reverend Bishop Andrews, his chapel. . . . And this copy was sent me by the household chaplain to that famous bishop' (Laud's *Works*, iv. 251).

of the chapel with a description of the furnishing and the relevant bills.[1] These documents are of great interest, but it must be remembered that Andrewes was a confirmed experimenter and that some of his ideas, such as the 'tun' for the sacramental wine, with its cradle, and the 'tricanale' for the water to be added to it, appear never to have been imitated. On the other hand, some of his other innovations were of great importance. The following is a list of the items:

Chalice and cover,
2 Patens,
Tun with cradle and funnel,
'Canister' for wafers,
Cruet with three spouts '(tricanale'),
Cruet with spout like a bird's bill,
Alms basin,
Ewer and basin (for ablutions),
2 Candlesticks,
Censer.

All the pieces were gilt, and those of especial interest will be discussed in the appropriate sections.

2. 1660–1830

At the Restoration the order for plate for the Chapel Royal was given the same priority as that awarded to the Regalia, since it was essential that the altar of Westminster Abbey should be worthily adorned on the day of the coronation, which was fixed for 23 April 1661. Whilst the bills for the Regalia were miraculously preserved when there was a holocaust of old records in 1830, those for the making of plate for the Chapel Royal appear to have perished. Similarly, no late seventeenth-century inventory of the royal plate has yet been discovered.

The reconstruction of the history of the plate of the various Chapels Royal during the years 1660–1700 has to be deduced mainly from the surviving pieces and is beset with difficulties. Amongst these is the fact that Sir Robert Vyner, Royal Goldsmith until his death in 1688, was not a craftsman but a goldsmith banker who dealt out the orders to whom he chose and habitually had several goldsmiths working for him simultaneously. These goldsmiths often sent their work to be marked at Goldsmiths' Hall, but a certain proportion was not sent and either bears the maker's mark only or, more rarely, no mark at all. When there is a maker's mark, it cannot always be regarded as a reliable clue to the real artist concerned. There were a number of craftsmen, mainly foreigners, who decorated plate which had been made in the rough by English goldsmiths, who saw it through Goldsmiths' Hall.

Royal arms and initials have to be regarded with caution, since the masters of the Jewel House were prone to order the removal of the insignia of the late

[1] The original plan, &c., is at the British Museum (Harley, 3795, f. 23). It was first reproduced in Prynne's *Canterburie's Doome*, 1646, 122, and has been frequently illustrated within the last century. The best-known version is in Andrewes's *Minor Works*, 1854, xcvii–xcix.

monarch in order to replace them by those of the new one. An altar dish with the initials of Anne, but the hall-mark for 1660, may be easily recognized, but some of the goldsmiths taken on at the Restoration were still working for the Jewel House at the end of the reign and did not greatly alter their style in the interval.

The plate made for the coronation of Charles II would appear to be the following:

Chalice and paten, gold, no hall-mark.[1]	2 Flagons, silver-gilt, 1660.[4]
Large altar dish, silver-gilt, 1660.[2]	2 Flagons, silver-gilt, 1660.[5]
2 Smaller altar dishes, silver-gilt, no marks.[3]	2 Candlesticks, silver-gilt, no marks.

In addition, there were made a pair of chalices with covers and patens for use in the chapel on ordinary occasions.

It is not clear when or why the 1660 set of plate drifted to the Chapel Royal, St. James's, since it would have been more natural to have allocated it to the more important one in Whitehall. The mystery is deepened by the fact that the plate actually used at Whitehall until the closure of the chapel in the nineteenth century would seem to have been intended for St. James's. The service in question closely resembles the one just mentioned, but bears the 1664 hall-mark. The pieces are engraved with a cipher of the letters *DL* beneath a coronet and/or the royal arms with/without a label and surmounted by a ducal coronet. It has been shown conclusively that the cipher *DL* was used by James II whilst Duke of York,[6] so that it would have been natural for the service to have remained at St. James's where he resided until he came to the throne.[7] It probably originally consisted of the following pieces, which are all of silver-gilt:

3 Chalices with paten-covers,[8]	2 Flagons,[10]
Large altar dish,[9]	2 Flagons,[11]
2 Smaller altar dishes,	2 Candlesticks.[12]

[1] Two maker's marks, *AS monogram* (Jackson, *Goldsmiths*, 124) and *TV above a bunch of grapes*.

[2] Embossed with the Last Supper, maker's mark illegible.

[3] Borders embossed with flowers and cherubs.

[4] Round-bellied, embossed with feathers, maker's mark *TB conjoined* (ibid. 127).

[5] Straight-sided, embossed with feathers, maker's mark *AM monogram* (ibid. 124).

[6] *Antiquaries Journal*, xv, 1935, 134–43.

[7] The service was already at Whitehall when the unfortunate goldsmith Charles Shelley was at length paid for it on 26 March 1686 (*Moneys received and paid for secret services of Charles II and James II*, Camden Soc. 1851, 154).

[8] Pl. 86. *S crowned*, maker's mark of Charles Shelley (Jackson, *Goldsmiths*, 135).

[9] Pl. 128. Embossed with Last Supper, maker's mark *HG* (ibid. 129).

[10] Pl. 112*b*. Round-bellied, embossed with feathers, maker's mark of C. Shelley.

[11] Straight-sided, maker's mark *WM* (ibid. 127).

[12] Maker's mark *a hound sejant*.

In 1667–8 the Chapel Royal, Hampton Court, was fitted out. The plate which was provided, and which mostly remains there, consisted of the following pieces, which are all of silver-gilt:

Chalice with paten-cover, 2 Flagons,
Alms basin.[1]

The above does not form a complete list of the orders for chapel plate in the reign of Charles II, since the Jewel House was able to furnish out of stock the chapel of Kensington Palace, which dates only from William III.[2] It was probably able to do the same for the German Lutherans, who had had a chapel in St. James's Palace since 1700,[3] and also for the former Roman Catholic chapel in Somerset House which was run as an Anglican chapel royal from 1711 to 1775.[4]

Despite the fact that much of the plate of the chapels royal is engraved with the arms and initials of William and Mary, the only important orders which we can trace are one for a second gold chalice for the coronation service and a quite simple set for the private chapel in Windsor Castle.

It is not surprising that few additions to the plate were made under the first two Georges, but in 1717 a splendid pair of candlesticks, 41 inches high, were provided for the chapel at Whitehall, probably because those which belonged to the Duke of York's service were deemed too small.

When George III was making alterations at Windsor Castle in 1779, a new service of plate was ordered for the private chapel. It was executed by the royal goldsmith, Thomas Heming, but the designs are much inferior to those which he had used fifteen years earlier for the Jewel Office's order for the plate now at Trinity Church, New York.

The last important Jewel Office order which need be mentioned is that for the Royal Pavilion, Brighton, and was entrusted to Rundell, Bridge & Rundell in 1821. It is rather surprising that the Gothic style should have been selected for such surroundings. It was never properly finished, but the chalices are copied from the gold ones belonging to the coronation service, whilst the candlesticks are not unintelligent essays in seventeenth-century Gothic. The project of

[1] Maker's mark *HS monogram*. The other two pieces by C. Shelley (paten-cover now wanting).

[2] Lionel and Philip Crichton, *Antique Plate of the Chapel Royal, Kensington Palace*, 1894. The chapel was closed in 1901 and the plate is now at St. James's or Buckingham Palace.

[3] The German chapel only moved into the Marlborough House chapel in 1781. It is pretty clear that it must have been issued with plate from the Jewel House at a much earlier date, since the pieces which it had at the time of its final closure had escaped the 1721 inventory of the royal plate.

[4] In the 1721 inventory of the royal plate, Somerset House chapel is credited with a 'large gilt Challice & Cover'. This, perhaps, a particularly large one in the Gothic style formerly in the possession of Lord Brownlow (*Country Life*, 21 October 1922, lxxiv) and now in a private collection. It is engraved with the arms of Queen Anne but has the 1672 hall-mark.

completing the service was kept alive, more designs prepared, but nothing actually done.[1]

So far we have dealt quantitatively with the refurnishing of the Chapels Royal. We may now pause to consider exactly how the results were reached. It may be assumed that King Charles did not interest himself beyond, perhaps, giving instructions that his chapels should not be fitted out too much on the cheap. The Lord Chamberlain, Edward Montagu, Earl of Manchester, a former Parliamentary general with a Presbyterianism background, would probably have been only too glad to pass the orders on to the Master of the Jewel House. Sir Gilbert Talbot had occupied minor diplomatic posts under Charles I and had no special qualifications for his present office. When he went to assume office he found neither a loyal, if elderly, staff[2] nor even the records.[3] On the credit side was only Sir Robert Vyner, his own nominee, who, although no goldsmith himself, could put his hand on anything or anyone who was wanted. Talbot's way of making up for his own ignorance of church plate would seem to have been to co-opt Dr. John Cosin as an unofficial adviser. The two had probably met in Paris during the Commonwealth. Cosin was at the moment in London occupying himself with such unprofitable tasks as disputing with the leaders of the Presbyterians, whilst waiting until the king should show his hand by nominating to the vacant bishoprics. That Cosin was in the know with regard to the 1660 orders of plate for the Chapel Royal is proved by the fact

[1] B. Ferry in his biography (*Recollections of A. Welby Pugin*, 1861, 51–52) states that when the young Pugin was engaged in copying old master drawings at the British Museum, he was accosted by a member of the firm of Rundell, Bridge & Rundell, who was so struck by his work that he offered him a job as a designer. He did not stay long with the firm but 'much beautiful plate was executed from Pugin's designs'. At the Victoria and Albert Museum are a set of five coloured drawings (E. 751–5–1925) showing an alms basin with the cipher of George IV, a chalice, a flagon, a pair of patens, and a candlestick. All are in the most elaborate Gothic style and signed *A Pugin jun. Invent. et fecit 1827.* At this date Pugin was only fifteen years old, so that his ideas would not have been taken too seriously by the royal goldsmiths. Though none of the designs were used for the Royal Pavilion, the design for the flagon appears to have been watered down for the flagons supplied to York Minster a few years later; see Pl. 122*b*.

[2] He only found one 'peevish old man', who behaved so insolently that he was summarily dismissed (Sir George Younghusband, *The Jewel House*, 1921, 242).

[3] The late Master of the Jewel House, Sir Henry Mildmay, had been appointed as long ago as 1617. He had been a *collaborateur* and was at present in prison. He had not erred so far as to endanger his neck, but, in due course, received a sentence of imprisonment for life coupled with such ingenious indignities as his judges considered appropriate. His plan to escape these last was to hold out to his successor the hope of recovering the Jewel Office records. He played his cards well, and there is no record that on the anniversary of the condemnation of Charles I he was ever actually dragged on a hurdle from the Tower to Tyburn, passed through the gallows, and dragged back again. Though Talbot appears to have been able to persuade him to co-operate in providing material for a vindication of the rights of the Master of the Jewel House against the Lord Chamberlain (ibid. 232–49), he was still applying for a warrant to search for Mildmay's papers on 4 June 1663 (*State Papers Domestic, 1663–4*, 163), within a year of the latter's death. By this date all the decisions about the replacement of the plate of the Chapel Royal had been made.

that on his nomination to the see of Durham he placed an order for his chapel at Auckland, which included a chalice (Pl. 84*a*) which is a slightly simplified version of the two at St. James's (Pl. 85), and an altar dish which is almost an exact replica of the one in the same place.[1] The form of the co-operation was probably that Cosin censored the designs of the craftsmen found by Vyner. Cosin's taste cannot be traced in every piece. Some belonged to standard patterns, whilst the flagons embossed with feathers (Pl. 112*b*) probably recall ones which had belonged to the former Chapel Royal. Vyner had probably traced some of the craftsmen who had repaired the plate in the time of Charles I.

Though many of the private chapels started during the Commonwealth closed after the Restoration, the large, and frequently also the medium-sized country houses often included one down to the end of our period. The plate of the chapel of a medium-sized house like Powderham Castle, Devon, which was equipped in the reign of George I, consisted of a chalice with paten-cover, a standing paten, a flagon, and an alms basin. The plate of the chapel at Welbeck Abbey consists of a chalice, standing paten, and a pair of flagons bought by Henry, 2nd Duke of Newcastle, in 1677, supplemented by a pair of standing patens in 1723, and an alms basin in 1758. None of the pieces are of exceptional merit, for the chapels of large houses aped the cathedrals, and these, as we have seen, had seldom improved upon the plate bought just after the Restoration.

The possession of altar-candlesticks was exceptional, although, doubtless, there was often a pair from the dining-room which would do on the few occasions in the year when the plate was in use. A very splendid pair of baroque candlesticks emerged at Christie's[2] from the chapel of the Duke of Manchester, whose ancestor, the first duke, had retained them with the plate issued to him as ambassador in the time of William III.[3]

The most interesting and complete set of eighteenth-century chapel plate

[1] That Cosin was brought in by Talbot and not by Vyner is shown by the fact that when he was in a difficulty about estimating a fair price for a piece of plate, he preferred to invoke the aid of Alderman Backwell, who was Vyner's principal rival (cf. p. 186, n. 1).

[2] 16 March 1949, lot 48.

[3] During the sixteenth century it became usual for an ambassador to draw plate from the Jewel Office with which to support the dignity of his master whilst abroad. It was rigorously exacted from him on his return. Owing to the religious fragmentation of Europe, it probably soon became necessary for at least a communion cup to be included, though it seems unlikely that ambassadors took much chapel plate before the Restoration. The Revolution of 1688 altered the whole position with regard to official plate, since those who had been appointed by James II refused to surrender their plate to the usurper. Since the new government did not feel strong enough to compel the return, it was faced in due course by the refusal of its own ex-ambassadors to be treated worse than their Jacobite predecessors. As a consequence of this ambassadorial plate became a perquisite and remained so until after the Napoleonic wars. A new start was then made and the principal embassies were equipped with chapel plate which is handed on from ambassador to ambassador.

There is some reason for supposing that colonial governors, who were also entitled to official plate, got into the habit of handing over their chapel plate to their successors at an earlier date. The plate of the governors' chapels, which was lost with the American colonies, is mostly of George II date.

is in the possession of the Earl of Stamford at Dunham Massey Hall, Cheshire, and was bought by his ancestor George Booth, 2nd Earl of Warrington. It marked a revolution in the religious allegiance of the family, as the earl's grandfather had fought on the winning side in the Civil War and had only redeemed his reputation by engaging in an abortive attempt to restore the king after Cromwell's death. The tradition at Dunham Massey had been Presbyterian and the chaplain a minister ejected under the Act of Uniformity. The second earl inherited his estate whilst still a minor, but at an early date became a strict Anglican and started setting his chapel to rights. His first order for plate was given in 1706 and consisted of a chalice, paten, flagon, and altar dish, all made by the young Isaac Liger, who had emerged from his apprenticeship two years earlier and was in need of noble patrons. All the pieces are notable for their fine proportions, but the finest is the altar dish which is engraved after Annibale Caracci and will be fully described later on (Pl. 133). In 1716 Liger supplied a plate for the communion bread and a pair of tripod candlesticks. The chapel at Dunham Massey and its contents form a unique monument of the best tradition of country house Anglicanism in the eighteenth century.

The episcopal residences had suffered terribly during the Civil War and Commonwealth, and no Restoration bishop would have expected to find any plate left in the chapel, if the latter had not been demolished.

The episcopal chapels still contain some plate which may be regarded as memorials to the occupants of the sees in the early years after the Restoration. Thus at Lambeth there is still a chalice with paten-cover and a flagon, hall-marked or datable to 1635, which were probably acquired by Archbishop Juxon when Bishop of London. The discovery that Lambeth contained the necessary plate probably induced Bishop Sheldon to leave behind at Fulham the plate which he had used whilst organizing Anglican resistance during the Commonwealth.[1]

The plate at Auckland is a memorial to a character of a different sort. Dr. John Cosin, Dean of Peterborough, had served as chaplain during the Commonwealth to the Anglican community in Paris which worshipped incongruously and insecurely under the protection of Queen Henrietta Maria. Whilst trying to protect his flock from the inroads of the Roman wolf, he had himself been conquered by the splendours of Paris under Louis XIV in which he could take so small a share. When appointed to the rich see of Durham, he saw an end to his life of frustration. He was not dismayed by the fact that his cathedral, diocese, and palace were in a deplorable condition. The last, after having been plundered by the Parliamentary Commissioners, had been sold to Sir Arthur Haslerig for £6,102. 8*s.* 11½*d.*, who had been busy modernizing it with the aid of gunpowder. In the course of his alterations the medieval chapel had dis-

[1] See above, p. 177, n. 5.

appeared, but the great hall survived, and this Cosin determined to convert into the largest episcopal chapel in England. It is necessary to remember its size when considering the plate which he ordered for it. Whilst elsewhere bishops and deans were busy with emergency measures, Cosin went ahead reorganizing Auckland on a permanent basis. He did not believe that it was impossible to get first-class work in a hurry. It was now that an acquaintance with Sir Gilbert Talbot, Master of the Jewel House, would have been so useful, since he was able to deal direct with a first-class goldsmith of the name of Houser without having to approach him through Sir Robert Vyner.

Cosin had not returned empty handed from Paris, as he brought a chalice and a paten given in memory of one of his congregation and bearing the Paris mark for 1651. One chalice was not enough for Auckland, however, so another was made, though not an exact match. Cosin's original order would seem to have been:

Chalice and cover, and cover for the French chalice,
2 Patens, 2 Candlesticks,
2 Flagons, 1 Altar dish.

The patens and the cover of the French chalice, all simple jobs, were executed by two goldsmiths who marked their work, but only the former pieces bear the 1660 hall-mark. The flagons (Pl. 112*b*) and candlesticks are entirely unmarked, whilst the dish bears the 1659 hall-mark with the maker's mark *FL above a bird* (Pl. 127). Since it is incredible that Houser should have risked making this elaborate piece before the king's return, it is probable that he followed the not very economical method of chasing up an existing piece. At any rate, Cosin appears to have suspected that the goldsmith made his pieces unnecessarily solid because he was paid by weight, as his steward mentions in a letter in which instructions were being given for the silver-mounted Bible and Book of Common Prayer which complete the service.[1]

Cosin, with his knowledge of the world and his efficient staff, managed to get a large and ornate service of finely efficient plate for his chapel at Auckland considerably before most of the deans, who went through the normal channels and bought fully hall-marked plate, had got their austere sets for their cathedrals.

[1] Letter dated 27 November 1662, from Mr. Arden (steward) at Auckland, to Mr. Miles Stapylton (secretary) in London:

> My Lord commands me to tell you what we paid Mr Houser for the Chappell plate he made for my Lord, which was nine shillings an ounce for the gilt plate, which is a great price; but he may well deserve it if he makes the booke covers indifferent thinne; for if he makes them thick and massie he may aford them better for 5*s*. an ounce than he canne for 10*s*.; and if you do not looke well to him he will make them as heavie as he canne, that, being paid by the ounce, he may advance the price. Mr. Alderman Blackwell [sic] is a good judge of what it is worth an ounce. You may show it to him for his opinion, and to any other goldsmith of your acquaintance before you pay all he demands. He is a good man but deere. (*Proc. Soc. Antiquaries of Newcastle*, v, 1891, 195.)

Cosin was exceptional in another way. Having secured one of the best jobs in the Church of England, he settled down to make the see of Durham his life-work, abandoning all dreams of Lambeth and Bishopthorpe. His deed presenting his magnificent service of plate to his successors at Auckland was drafted on 11 July 1667, nearly five years before his death.[1] Most late seventeenth- and eighteenth-century bishops kept a tight hold on their plate—it would have been foolish to leave behind at Hartlebury that which might be useful at Farnham. When death overtook them, it was as likely as not that their chapel plate would be bequeathed not to some ill-furnished church in their diocese but to one with which they had family connexions.[2] Though the episcopal chapels usually ended by getting some plate of their own, they often had to wait some time for it. Thus Bishopthorpe has plate bequeathed by Thomas Lamplugh, fourth archbishop after the Restoration.

In conclusion, it should be emphasized that an ordinary set of episcopal chapel plate resembled Cosin's neither in quantity nor quality. It normally consisted merely of a chalice, standing paten, flagon, and alms basin. I have found no record of silver candlesticks except at Auckland.

[1] *Cosin Correspondence*, ii, Surtees Soc. 1879, 169.

[2] e.g. Peter Gunning, Bishop of Ely (1675–84), bequeathed his plate to Dalham, Suff., and Simon Patrick, Bishop of Ely (1689–1707), to Hoo, Kent.

IV

SECURITY IN POST-REFORMATION TIMES

FOR sixty years after the accession of Elizabeth I the security of the church plate ceased to be one of the constant sources of anxiety for incumbents, churchwardens, and treasurers of cathedrals. Few parish churches owned more than a single communion cup with paten-cover, and, as we have seen elsewhere, the cathedrals were not much more richly furnished.

With the beginning of the seventeenth century the security problem began to come to the front again as a result of the numerous gifts of plate. Probably the custom of storing the church plate at the manor-house or the parsonage was already well established. From the strict security point of view there was a great deal to be said in favour of the practice of leaving the plate at the manor, since it seemed to secure that it would receive the same amount of care as the domestic plate of the family. That so much old plate has come down to our times is a proof how successful this method of dealing with the problem was under favourable circumstances. Amongst the objections to it was, however, that the sacred use of the plate tended to be forgotten when once it had left the church. The inscription 'For the sole use of the Communion Table', not infrequently found on flagons, is a reminder that the church plate was liable to be used to help out the family plate on occasions. In extenuation it should be remembered that the borrowing was often both ways and that the family plate also helped out the church plate. A very real objection to storage at the manor-house was that a change of butlers might leave in doubt the true ownership of a cup or dish which was not properly inscribed.

The same sort of objection obtained, and obtains, with regard to the custom of allowing one of the churchwardens to store unused church plate. The house of a churchwarden never possessed that sort of permanence which once was associated with the manor-house, and there can be no doubt that much church plate has been lost through being sold up with personal belongings after a death.

Not all church plate was kept in the relative safety of the manor-house or the parsonage. Much was kept in cupboards or chests in the church. Throughout the period with which we are dealing, tales of churches cleared of the plate recur. No really adequate steel safe was yet on the market. Some incumbents reacted curiously to the security problem. The churchwardens' accounts of North Bradley, Wilts., show that the church once possessed a silver chalice, but now there are only a chalice, paten, and flagon of Sheffield plate, all dated 1818. The living was held from 1778 to 1827 by Archdeacon Daubenay, who when he believed himself to be dying, made the following testamentary provision: 'Let the Communion vessels be plated. I have always condemned those who have placed unnecessary temptations in the path of their fellow mortals, and I am anxious that the last act of my life should hold out to others no inducement to sin.'[1]

When in Caroline times the preservation of the mounting quantity of plate began to be a cause of anxiety for deans and treasurers, it was found that most medieval cathedrals contained excellent vaulted vestries with narrow windows guarded with iron bars. These proved adequate against ordinary risks and there is only one[2] record of the burglary of a cathedral before the Civil War—we are not concerned here with the looting by the Parliamentary soldiery during the struggle. It does not seem to have been possible to build up a good security tradition in the cathedrals during the reign of Charles II, when several robberies are recorded. Thus in 1672 Peterborough lost the alms basin which Colonel Hubbart had rescued from Cromwell's troopers, and two verges as well.[3] At Christmas in the same year three nondescript individuals tried to sell to Henry Mangy, goldsmith of York, silver scrap which he recognized to be of church origin. Disbelieving the story that it came from a papist chapel, he had them arrested. It later transpired that the fragments represented all that remained of the candlesticks and alms basin of Chester Cathedral.[4] On 5 February 1676 York Minster was robbed, but it is not clear what was lost. An attempt to bring the theft home to certain local people nine years later led to an acquittal.[5]

Sometime in the course of the years 1791–2 Winchester Cathedral was robbed. The records allude to the payment in November, 1792, of a 'Bow St. Office Bill' for the recovery of the plate, but as it was all refashioned in the following year, it would seem that it was received back in a very bad condition. The whole affair was very well hushed up and did not get into the local papers.[6]

On Sunday, 14 July 1805, it was discovered that all the plate had been stolen from the vestry of Lincoln Minster. The robbers had picked five locks, four of which had been afterwards reshot. It afterwards transpired that the impending burglary had been spoken of by one of the inmates of the local jail some time before it took place. No one was ever brought to justice and nothing was ever

[1] *C.P. Wilts.* 124.

[2] I am indebted to Mrs. Carpenter Turner for pointing out an allusion to the theft of a chalice and paten in the 1633 inventory of Winchester Cathedral.

[3] S. Gunton, *History of the Church of Peterborough*, 1686, 339.

[4] *Depositions from York Castle*, Surtees Soc. 1861, 190.

[5] Ibid. 281–2.

[6] I am indebted again to Mrs. Carpenter Turner for the above information and also for drawing my attention to the fact that 'some plate' was returned to the cathedral in 1660–1 by a Mr. John Dassh. It does not seem possible to decide exactly what was recovered.

recovered. The cathedral made do with a set of Sheffield plate until the next dean provided a silver-gilt set made by John Bridge in 1824.[1]

The possession of excellent storage accommodation in a vestry difficult of access could be nullified by bad security routine. The plate of St. Paul's, weighing 1,761 ounces, was duly stored in a vestry accessible only by unlocking eight doors, one of iron. On Sunday, 23 December 1810, the sacrist went to fetch the plate and found to his surprise that the iron door was double-locked. This was unusual, since he did not hold the second key. When the key had been fetched and all the other doors unlocked, it was found that every piece of plate had gone! The thieves had used no force and had locked the doors as they left. The theft must have taken place quite recently, since the plate had been used on the previous Thursday. Nothing was recovered nor was the crime brought home to anyone. The loss could not have been due to the carelessness of the sacrist alone, since he did not hold all the necessary keys. It seems more likely that some unauthorized person had had access to the treasurer's set. This may well have been the explanation, as the Rev. William Bell had been appointed as long ago as 1766, and must have been long past performing the few duties expected of a canon of that cathedral at that date. He would appear to have received the news of the loss with greater equanimity than Archdeacon Daubenay, for he survived another six years—he was, of course, irremovable.[2]

The possession of a good medieval vestry did not save much of the plate of York Minster, when Jonathan Martin set the choir alight in 1829. Unfortunately it had been customary to store much of it in a cupboard under the archbishop's throne. Everything which was there was lost.[3]

[1] I am indebted to the Rev. Peter Hawker for tracing this story through the Lincoln diocesan archives.

[2] *Gentleman's Magazine*, lxxx, 1810, 655.

[3] Ely lost some of its plate a few years after the date at which this study closes, but in the last hundred years the plate of the cathedrals has generally been looked after with much greater care.

V

COMMUNION PLATE

A. CHALICES[1] AND PATEN-COVERS

THE study of church plate in England was taken up at a period when anything which was medieval was considered to be in good taste and anything of later date was regarded as admirable only in so far as it approximated to what had been used in the supposed Golden Age. Since the communion cups of the Reformation period had been specially designed so as not to look like medieval chalices, they were regarded somewhat dubiously. The large number of Elizabethan communion cups presented another obstacle, since some of the earlier writers expressed opinions which were certainly based on too little study.[2] By contrast the comments of Sir Charles Jackson[3] were eminently sound when he simply stated that the communion cups made in the reigns of Edward VI and Elizabeth I do not follow any special design but are modelled upon the plainest types of domestic cups.

If pieces of secular origin be excluded, only eighteen Edward VI communion cups are at present known.[4] Half of these have London provenances and all were made there. As has already been pointed out, many churchwardens in and around London preferred to convert their plate into communion cups rather than see it seized by the king. Under such circumstances there was no urgent call for economy, and most examples weigh between 20 and 40 ounces, three-quarters of them being gilt. Not all the surviving cups had been made before the arrival of the despoiling commissioners, but these latter usually acted indulgently when the churchwardens pleaded to be allowed a conversion. The

[1] In this work I have maintained the distinction between the terms 'chalice' and 'communion cup' only when dealing with the actual Reformation period, when the two terms really did carry different meanings. The distinction is of no importance in later times and both terms are applied to the same object in the 1662 revision of the Book of Common Prayer.

[2] Wilfred Cripps, usually an acute observer, was so ill advised as to found his description of Edwardian and Elizabethan communion cups on some remarks by Octavius Morgan in an article in *Archaeologia* (xliii, 1869, 414). Morgan had not seen nearly enough examples and had become obsessed with the idea that they were of uniform design and decoration. When it came to analysing this design, he had to qualify his remarks to such an extent that doubts should have been raised as to the correctness of his approach. Similarly, he grossly over-simplified the facts regarding the decoration: 'the ornaments on all these chalices and paten-covers, as they may be called, is invariably the same; it consists simply of an engraved band round the body of the cup and on the top of the cover, formed by two narrow fillets, which interlace or cross each other with a particular curvature, in every instance the same, the space between them being occupied by a scroll of foliage, and this ornament is marked by a total absence of letters, monograms, emblems or figures of any kind.'

[3] *History*, 1911, i. 387.

[4] For a list of Edwardian communion cups see Appendix II.

formula for conversion was almost always two chalices for one communion cup; only a few provincial churchwardens were content with one cup made from a single chalice.

Though there was nothing resembling a prescribed pattern for Edwardian communion cups, as a matter of fact seven examples are virtually identical. They have a bell-shaped bowl, spool-shaped stem with a moulded rib round the waist, and a bold ogee-moulded base. The communion cup of 1551 belonging to Beddington church, Surrey (Pl. 49), is typical and illustrates also what appears to have been the usual paten. This was a plain dish which could be used as a cover, like its medieval predecessor.

The goldsmiths who used the above design did not feel tied to it, as is shown by the fact that two of them used alternatives.

Four other cups form a rather less coherent group. Of these by far the most important is the one, hall-marked 1549, which belongs to St. Mary Aldermary, but which was probably made for the Chapel Royal (Pl. 50). It has a wide, bell-shaped bowl, a narrow neck connecting it with a frilled collar below which is a spreading stem of ogee section and wide base. The cover if reversed forms a paten standing on a short trumpet-shaped foot, on the flat base of which are the arms of Edward VI in champlevé enamel, surrounded by THE · BODY · OF · OVR · LORDE · IESVS · CHRISTE · WHICHE · WAS GEVEN · FOR YOV · P[re]SERVE · Y[our] SOVLE · VNTO. This is the first appearance of the paten-cover which was to become such a feature of Anglican church plate during the next century and a half.

The remaining six cups are all unique. The earliest is that of 1548 belonging to St. Lawrence Jewry (Pl. 51*a*) which closely resembles, except in the form of the bowl, the example made in the following year for St. Peter-upon-Cornhill (Pl. 51*b*). The ornament round the base of both of them are cast from the same repeating die, although they were made by different goldsmiths. The cup belonging to Owslebury church (Pl. 52*b*),[1] near Winchester, was made in 1552, and is a rendering of a less magnificent design borrowed from domestic use.

The interest of the last three cups which have to be mentioned lies not in the beauty of their designs but in the fact that they have been made from the silver of a single medieval chalice. A conversion on this basis offered no economic attraction, so that it must be presumed that they were made for churchwardens purely actuated by Protestant fervour. Though the chalices from which these cups were made were bigger than many which were in use, their silver content did not leave the goldsmith very much scope. The response of the craftsmen to this challenge was to avoid expensive cast work by having greater recourse to

[1] Inscribed ✠ THE COMMVNION CVP OF OWSYLBVRY. Although lighter (17 oz. 18 dwt.) than the cups already mentioned, it seems best to group it with them. It was probably made from two medium-sized chalices such as were often found in country churches.

raising. The results are very instructive. The earliest of the three bears the 1551 hall-mark and belongs to St. Michael's church, Southampton (Pl. 52*a*). It takes the form of a standing beaker. The proportions of the paten-cover are wrong, and it has been loaded at a later date to make it less top-heavy when used as a paten.

The example at Battle (Pl. 53*a*), Sussex, has a bowl like a truncated beaker mounted upon a spool-shaped stem and a moulded foot.[1] It bears the 1552 hallmark. The lower portion of the cup at Great Houghton (Pl. 53*b*), near Northampton, is not unlike that of the Battle one, but the bowl is a beaker with two bands of engraving. It bears the 1553 hall-mark, so that it must have been delivered before the king's death on 6 July.

Since no chalices made in the reign of Mary have been identified, we may proceed directly to consider the communion cups made after the accession of Elizabeth I on 17 November 1558.

It is physically impossible to discuss the communion cups made in this reign in the same detail as for those made under Edward VI. As against less than a score made under the latter, there are still something in the region of two thousand Elizabethan cups, divided fairly evenly between those made in London and those made in the provinces. It is obvious that we can do no more than look at a few selected examples.

It has long been realized that although English opinion was much divided in religious matters at the time of the accession of Elizabeth I, there was a number of determined Protestants who knew exactly what they wanted. One of these must have been the donor of the communion cup with paten-cover belonging to the church of St. Michael-le-Belfrey, York (Pl. 54). There is nothing suggestive of hurry about its workmanship and its design is carefully considered,[2] so that it may be guessed that the order was placed in anticipation of the restoration of the cup to the laity during Holy Week, 1559. It must have been completed before the date-letter was changed on 19 May. It is unfortunate that the identity of the goldsmith is hidden by a quite illegible maker's mark. The St. Michael's cup is both typical and very abnormal. The proportions are the same as those of an army of communion cups which were to be made during the next thirty years, whilst the engraved arabesques arranged in panels were to become equally familiar. On the other hand, the elaborately decorated foot and stem are cast and unlike that of any other Elizabethan example. The weight of 18 ounces is also very much above the average.

[1] When described in the *Sussex Arch. Coll.* lv, 1912, 183, J. E. Couchman mistook the ornamental bosses on the moulding round the stem for representations of the Vernicle. Actually they show a lion's head with the tongue out! The same model was used in 1554 on a secular cup, later used as a communion cup, at St. Werburgh, Bristol (*C.P. Bristol*, frontispiece).

[2] e.g. the knob of the paten-cover is engraved with a bell.

Communion cups with the 1559 hall-mark are, with one exception, to be found in or around London. They are fine solid pieces and were evidently bought for parishes with a strong Protestant feeling. The cup of silver parcel-gilt belonging to St. Botolph Aldgate (Pl. 55) was made by the goldsmith who had provided the Owslebury cup seven years earlier. The proportions are much the same but the effect is made much richer by the use of the finely lettered sacramental inscription on the band round the bowl[1] and by an elaborately decorated stem and base.

Other goldsmiths also harked back to the designs used in the reign of Edward VI. The Victoria and Albert Museum has a cup (Pl. 56*a*) with the mark of Robert Taylboyes, but with no hall-mark. The proportions are much the same as those of the two cups which he had made for St. Margaret, Westminster, in 1551, but in view of the fact that he was allowed only a third of the metal used on the previous occasion, he modified the form of the stem and base and worked the silver more economically. It was probably made between 1560 and 1562[2] and intended to be used with a paten of dish form.

The year 1559 was made memorable by the appearance of what was to become the most popular form of Elizabethan communion cup, of which the St. Michael-le-Belfrey one may be regarded as an expensive prototype. It has a beaker-shaped bowl, spool-shaped stem usually with a moulding round the middle, and a stepped and moulded base. With it went a slightly domed cover with a flat knob which would serve as a foot when being used as a paten. It has sometimes been stated that this form of Elizabethan communion cup, with its paten-cover, was adapted from German drinking-cups known through engraved designs.[3] It is pretty clear, however, that it was evolved in this country, since it is really no more than the combination of the form of the Edwardian Great Houghton cup with the paten-cover at St. Michael, Southampton.

In the normal way a design wins its way into favour because of its attractiveness and, after it has been copied time and again, it becomes hackneyed and ceases to please. The Elizabethan standing beaker communion cup did not quite follow this progress. The 1559–60 cups of this pattern found in or around London tend to be ungainly.[4] Although a reasonable amount of silver was allocated for their manufacture, the goldsmith was evidently expected to do too

[1] ✠ AND · HE · TOKE · THE · CVP · AND · THANKED · AND · GAVE · IT · TO · THEM, SAYING · DRINKE · OF · IT · EVERI · ONE · FOR · TIS · MI · BLOVD · OF · THE · NEW · TESTAMENT, THAT · SHALL · BE · SHED · FOR · MANY · FOR · THE · REMISSION · OF · SINNES. The weight is 31 oz. 10 dwt.

[2] The 1559 cup by Taylboyes at Lambourne, Essex, has a slightly different form of base, but the 1563 example at Romford is exactly similar (*C.P. Essex*, pl. v).

[3] W. W. Watts, *Catalogue of Chalices and other Communion Vessels in the Victoria and Albert Museum*, 1922, 36.

[4] e.g. St. Mary-le-Bow; St. Stephen, Walbrook; St. Vedast, 1559; and St. Ethelburga and Christ Church, 1560. The last is by the good goldsmith who had made the St. Botolph, Aldgate, cup in the previous year, but it is no better than the others.

much with it. After a few years' practice they came to understand the possibilities of the design better, and the results are examples of cheap goldsmithing at its best.

We have already told how the drive was made for the conversion of the 'massing chalices' into communion cups, but we have now to see exactly how the orders were carried out. In the early years there existed some doubt in the minds of the churchwardens as to whether it was intended that the medieval paten should go the same way as the chalice. As a consequence of this there is a large number of communion cups which now possess a paten-cover of a few years later in date, often with the mark of a different goldsmith. From the hall-marking year 1564 onwards, paten-covers were normally supplied with communion cups.

We may look at two of the early communion cups made in 1562 complete with paten-covers. They illustrate well the range of effects possible with this design. Both the cup at Ashby-de-la-Zouche (Pl. 57*a*)[1] and the one at Beeford (Pl. 57*b*), E. Riding, bear the London hall-mark though the latter was the work of Peter Carlill of Hull.[2] It is interesting to note that the latter had already got on to the idea of the paten-cover two years before it came into general use. The cup belonging to St. Michael, Oxford (Pl. 56*b*), illustrates a very original treatment of the concept of the standing beaker. It belongs to a group of four examples all made by this goldsmith in 1564.[3] The idea did not find favour, although the cups are quite nicely finished and should not have been expensive, since they weigh only about 10 ounces.

Next we may turn to the cups produced for the diocese of Norwich in the years 1565–6. The London goldsmiths played an unimportant part in this area, but the cup at Reedham (Pl. 58*a*), Norfolk, is a first-class example of the work of one of the most prolific makers of cups in the decade 1567–76.[4] That the job should have gone to a Londoner is probably due to the fact that it was a gift from a wealthy squire.

The assumption that a better cup could be obtained in London than in Norwich was not, in fact, warranted. The communion cups made by the best Norwich goldsmiths are amongst the finest in the kingdom. They evolved their own design, which has a bell-shaped bowl supported on a spool-shaped

[1] The maker's mark is *GK in a heart* and not *SR in a heart* as shown in *C.P. Leics.* and Jackson, *Goldsmiths*. It is a good solid piece weighing 20 ounces.

[2] Of Carlill's cups, with his Hull mark, only two are exactly datable (Wootton, Lincs., 1568; Ludford, Lincs., 1571). I am inclined to think that most of his work was done at the time of the general conversion of chalices in Lincs. and Yorks., where it is to be found.

[3] St. Stephen, St. Albans; Chobham, Surrey; Elsenham, Essex. The last has been altered.

[4] Mark, *a bull's head erased* (Jackson, *Goldsmiths*, 100). Jackson's representation of the mark on this cup (on the same page), is hopeless. The arms engraved on the cup are those of Henry Berney, whose monument is in the church.

stem on a foot with an ogee moulding. The paten-covers are generally of the London type, but owing to the ambiguity in the wording of the instructions for refashioning the chalices, many are a few years later than their cups.

The best of the Norwich goldsmiths was certainly the owner of the *orb with cross* mark.[1] Both a typical and an exceptional example of his work are illustrated. The cup belonging to St. Martin at Palace, Norwich (Pl. 58*b*), bears the Norwich hall-mark for 1567 and is a beautifully executed example of one version of the standard local design. Around the upper part of the body and on the knob of the cover is the inscription, THE GYFT OF LADY CALTHROP, and her arms.[2]

The cup at St. Andrew, Norwich (Pl. 59*a*), was made in the same year, but is exceptional both in its form and decoration. The band of openwork acanthus leaves which masks the junction of the stem and bowl is a feature borrowed from Germany. The rich chasing on the foot is also unparalleled on any other communion cup.[3]

The cup belonging to St. Lawrence, Norwich (Pl. 59*b*), bears the Norwich hall-mark for 1565 and as maker's mark *a slipped trefoil*.[4] It illustrates another version of the Norwich design, but the form of the finial on the cover should specially be noted. It was probably cast from the model for a spoon knob, and is a feature to be found not only on Norwich pieces but also on those made by the local goldsmiths working on the borders of Norfolk and Suffolk.

The next Norwich goldsmith to be mentioned was never more than com-

[1] An interesting problem is connected with the ownership of this mark, which is found, with three forms of escutcheon, on over eighty communion cups dating from 1565 to 1570.

The mark is found on the 'Ransom Cup' belonging to the city of Norwich. The history of this piece is as follows. On 21 September 1574 Peter Peterson, goldsmith, was excused from serving as sheriff, &c., in return for promising to provide a silver-gilt cup weighing 15 ounces together with £40 in money. The resulting cup actually weighs 31 oz. 2 dwt., but bears the inscription, THE MOST HEREOF IS DVNE BY PETER PETERSON. It has been assumed that as Peterson was by far the wealthiest goldsmith at Norwich at the time, he was also the maker of the cup to which he contributed. This cannot be taken for certain. I have noted eight pieces of post-Reformation church plate given by goldsmiths before 1660 and in no case could the donor have been the owner of the maker's mark. It would seem that the goldsmith donor tended to use his knowledge of the trade to pass the order on to the firm which specialized in the particular line.

The position is further complicated by an entry in the churchwardens' accounts of St. Margaret, Norwich, where under the date 1567 is *p^d^ to Peter Peterson ye goldsmyth for making ye comunyon cuppe—and for making ye cover*. The cup exists and has as the maker's mark *a sun*. It would be easy to dismiss this by assuming that Peterson handed out the job to a friend, but there are reasons for supposing that he did use a badge of a sun. In his will there are references to pieces of plate and to a garnish of pewter marked with a sun.

Sir Charles Jackson (*Goldsmiths*, 307–9), who discusses the problem in detail, arrived at what appears to be the one inadmissible conclusion—that Peterson used both marks.

[2] The cup must be a replacement, since the donor had died in 1550 (*Norfolk Archaeology*, x, 1884, 94).

[3] On the knob of the cover is, in four lines, THIS CVP ꝑ | TAYNYNG T. | O S. ANDRES | ꝑRISHE 1568.

[4] Above the engraved band is ✠ SAINCTE · LAVRANCE · ANNO · DOMINI · 1568. There are forty-eight cups by this maker, of which thirty-nine bear the 1567 mark.

petent and sometimes less than honest. Thomas Buttell, whose mark was *a flat fish*, made forty-two cups with the Norwich mark for 1567. He was still resident in Norwich when the wardens of the London Goldsmiths' Company visited the city in the summer of 1568, but seems to have moved to Cambridge soon afterwards in order to help in the refashioning of the chalices of the dioceses of Ely and Peterborough. From the time of his removal his work ceases to bear the Norwich mark, but a number of his pieces are dated 1569 and 1570. In the summer of 1569, as has already been mentioned, the wardens of the London Goldsmiths pounced upon him and broke and defaced eight of his communion cups. Probably as a result of this incident, the cup which he made for Little Harrowden, Northants., bears the full London hall-mark for 1569. The grounds of complaint against Buttell are not stated, but it had probably got around that his silver was not always up to standard. It was probably with a view to quietening rumours that he was robbing churches by returning cups of baser metal than that of the chalices of which they professed to be made that he had recourse sometimes to a device used also by some other local goldsmiths. Inside the paten-cover of the cup which he made for Westley Waterless (Pl. 60*a*), Cambs., the Vernicle engraved on the original medieval paten is clearly visible (Pl. 60*b*)—a convincing demonstration that the new piece was not of worse metal than its predecessor.[1]

Another curious instance of transformation without the complete destruction of the medieval design is provided by the communion cup in the form of a covered beaker belonging to Fitz church (Pl. 60 *c*, *d*), near Shrewsbury. Inside the bottom of the beaker is engraved in black letter the Sacred Monogram, above which is scored roughly the date of the conversion—1565. The diameter of the engraved medallion, 2¼ inches, is too large for the centre of a paten. It seems more likely that the original piece was a pyx.[2]

It has already been pointed out that when ordering the conversion of the chalices into communion cups, the bishops gilded the pill by pointing out that

[1] He had already had recourse to this device whilst he was at Norwich, since the paten-cover of the cup which he made for Heigham in 1567 shows the remains of the Sacred Monogram on the medieval paten. It is obvious that in both these instances the communion cup and paten-cover had been made out of the chalice and paten belonging to these particular churches. This was probably often the case when the churchwardens dealt with a small local goldsmith. On the other hand, if they went to a larger goldsmith and brought in a chalice and paten of normal weight, they could effect an exchange for a communion cup of the appropriate weight, made out of the chalice brought in by some previous customer. Cups made at Norwich commonly bear inscriptions such as '✠ THIS CVP IS FOR THE TOWNE OF' followed by the name of the parish. There are several instances, e.g. Barnham Broom (*Norfolk Archaeology*, xviii. 24) and Wickhampton (ibid. xx. 271), where the name was never filled in as the customer would not wait.

[2] No marks, weight 5½ ounces. Around the lip, BLESSED IS HE THAT COMET IN THE NAME OF THE LORDE OSANNA. The paten-cover is of the usual type but of rather lighter build. Either the goldsmith found himself short of silver, or else it is not contemporary.

the parishioners need not be put to any expense. In most cases the medieval chalice could be made into a decent communion cup without much difficulty. Trouble arose in the case of very small country churches, where the chalice might be minute. Thus the chalice of Chessington, Surrey, weighed only 4¾ ounces,[1] so that, since the churchwardens refrained from adding any silver, the resulting communion cup (Pl. 61*a*) weighs only 2 oz. 13 dwt. and stands 3¾ inches high.

The idea that the cost of the communion cup should be exactly covered by the chalice which was brought in was sometimes adhered to with quite unnecessary rigidity. On 19 November 1572 the chapter of Wells Cathedral decreed[2] 'that the plate that beforetime were used to superstition shal be defaced, and of the great challaice shalbe made a fayer Communion cuppe with as much convenient speede as may be before the ffeaste of Easter, and of the lesser challaice another by the time before limite'. The problem of the shortage of silver did not arise, the chalices were both good big ones. It might have been thought that since the order for the conversion of the two chalices was given simultaneously, the opportunity would have been taken of getting a pair of communion cups. This did not happen. The larger chalice became a communion cup 9¾ inches high (Pl. 61*b*), whilst the lesser became one 9 inches high. Their designs and decoration do not match exactly.

It so happens that both the Chessington and the Wells communion cups were made by the same goldsmith. The owner of the mark *IP*[3] entered whole-heartedly into the business of making communion cups, and at least 168 examples from his workshop still survive. Not unnaturally he entrusted the making of the cup for the impoverished Surrey church to a rather less skilful craftsman than those for the cathedral. Seen side by side they afford an instructive contrast as well as regards workmanship as for size.

A cup from an unknown church, which was formerly in the Swaythling Collection, is typical of the ordinary work executed by this goldsmith (Pl. 61*c*).

It is clear that the town of Cirencester was one of the places where Protestantism caught on firmly. In 1570 the churchwardens decided to get a pair of communion cups which was six years before the majority of the churches in the diocese of Gloucester converted their chalices. This was no ordinary case of conversion, however, since one of the cups weighs 53 oz. 15 dwt. and the other 52 oz. 17 dwt. The job went to Robert Taylboyes but he would seem to have been rather hampered by the desire of the churchwardens to have cups of the largest capacity. They do, in fact, hold 2½ pints each, but the proportions of bowl

[1] J. R. Daniel-Tyssen, *Inventories of the Goods in the Churches of Surrey*, 1869, 171.

[2] *Trans. Somerset Arch. Soc.* xliii. 1897, 211.

[3] Jackson, *Goldsmiths*, 98. There would appear to be no evidence to support the attribution of this mark to John Pikenynge.

and stem are not entirely happy (Pl. 62*a*). The use of simple 'hit-and-miss' engraving on such expensive pieces is also somewhat disappointing.

Taylboyes is not known to have produced any cups for the diocese of Worcester, but it is possible that the Cirencester cups had been seen and admired by a provincial goldsmith, whose mark was *a rose*, who made a group of communion cups in Worcestershire and in north Oxfordshire. They are characterized by the use of a stem with a frill round it and by decoration of 'hit-and-miss' ornament in panels. The example at Barcheston, Warw. (Pl. 62*b*), shows his standard design admirably.[1]

Local circumstances did not favour the production of a large number of communion cups at Chester, but there is a small group in the city and county evidently made by a local goldsmith whose mark was *an animal's head*.[2] The cups are not particularly notable, but it is interesting to note that for two of them patens of the dish form were supplied, instead of the fashionable paten-covers. One of these is at Great Budworth, Cheshire (Pl. 63*a*). The cup at St. Mary-without-the-Walls, Chester (Pl. 63*b*) has the ordinary paten-cover.

Patens of dish form were produced both in London and in the provinces throughout the reign of Elizabeth I. Few of them show any serious attempt at decoration, but the most important exception is one (Pl. 64) which accompanies a communion cup of rather exceptional design at Wombourn, Staffs. In the centre of the paten is engraved a Tudor rose surrounded by rays, whilst the rim is decorated with a flowing floral scroll. So far no other examples of the work of this local goldsmith, whose mark was an incised HB, has been noted.

The Midland goldsmiths whose work has been mentioned were all thoroughly competent. This was not the case with all of them. Amongst the less successful workers may be instanced one who supplied a group of eleven cups which are to be found in the area where the counties of Leicester, Lincoln, and Nottingham meet.[3] The blame cannot be laid entirely at the door of the goldsmith, since it is clear that he suffered from a chronic shortage of silver. The sturdy little cup and cover at Walton-le-Wolds, Leics. (Pl. 65*a*), weighs only $5\frac{1}{2}$ ounces.[4]

[1] I am indebted to Mrs. G. E. P. How for drawing my attention to the curious fact that this cup and cover would seem to have been made out of four medieval patens. The engraving of one paten is visible underneath the foot, but in one place or another there are the remains of four fifteenth-century London leopard's-head hall-marks. If, as seems probable, these cups emanate from Worcester, they may have been the work of Henry Sherley, whom the Goldsmiths' Company's *Minute Book* (l. 238) shows to have been resident there between 1563 and 1575.

[2] In the eleventh (posthumous) edition of Cripps (p. 132) this mark is attributed to a William Mutton who is stated to have died in 1596. Mr. Charles Brocklehurst informs me that he has failed to find the authority for this.

[3] Breedon, Goadby, Walton-le-Wolds, Wyfordby, in Leics.; Long Bennington, Lincs.; Broughton St. Matthew, Kneveton, Maplebeck, West Markham, and Syerston, Notts. Also Christie's, 24.xi.1919, lot 59.

[4] The knob of the foot of the paten-cover has been mended with a groat of Mary.

Three marks appear on these cups, the letters *N* and *G* separated by an escutcheon charged with what Archdeacon Trollope described, imaginatively, as a 'maiden's head couped'.[1]

Whilst the lot of some provincial goldsmiths was to attract the least remunerative orders, most of them managed to get both thick and thin. Amongst these we may place the goldsmith ᛗ, whose sixty-odd marked pieces seem to centre on Lincoln.[2] As a typical example of his work is illustrated the one belonging to the church of Mumby, Lincs. (Pl. 65*b*). Besides the mark above mentioned, the cup at Auborne, near Grantham, has one resembling *a seven-petalled flower*, whilst at Sutton-on-Trent it appears with *an ape's head* (?)[3] in a circular stamp.

As has already been mentioned, the York goldsmiths made no attempt to retain in their own hands the business of converting the chalices in their own area. Without going so far as to refuse the work—we have communion cups by eight York goldsmiths—their total output was very small. To judge from the surviving examples, Robert Beckwith, who has thirteen cups still to his credit, did by far the largest trade. This is about one-third of the output of the goldsmith at Lincoln, and only just more than Peter Carlill of Hull. Beckwith's cups belong to two patterns, neither of which are individual. The greater number have rather bell-shaped bowls, the remainder have the familiar ones of beaker form.

Much less competent was Edward Dalton of Carlisle, to whom are attributed a group of cups stamped with a rose and with an *ED monogram*.[4] They are of particularly crude construction, the base of the bell-shaped bowl being made separately from the upper part, which has been soldered on to it.

Since it is impossible to attempt more than a dipping audit of the work of the provincial goldsmiths, we shall now turn to some of the south-western centres.

When the wardens of the Goldsmiths visited Barnstaple in July 1571 they made mention of four local workers.[5]

Of these Thomas Mathew, John Coton, and Peter Quick became makers of

[1] *C.P. Leics.* xi; Jackson, *Goldsmiths*, 475.

[2] Col. Mansel Simpson (*Arch. Journal*, lxvii, 1910, 217) made a thorough search of the freemen's lists, the wills in the probate court, and the municipal registers in order to identify this maker. However, John Morley of Lincoln is mentioned as paying a fine in 1573 in the Goldsmiths' *Minute Book* (l. 159) and may prove to be the man.

[3] This mark is found alone on cups at Bassingham, Cammeringham, Glentham, and Heighington, Lincs.; Kirklington, Notts.; Princeton University Museum; Repton, Derby.; and on a paten-cover at Farnsfield, Notts.

[4] Bolton, Ireby, Cumbd.; Cliburn and Long Marton, Westd. Chancellor Ferguson also attributes to this maker the unmarked cups at Hayton and Lazonby, Cumbd. (*C.P. Carlisle*, 53–54, 232, 294). For the identification of Dalton see Jackson, *Goldsmiths*, 494.

[5] *Minute Book*, l. 75. Prebendary Chanter finds record of two further Barnstaple goldsmiths, but they do not seem to have made church plate (*Trans. Devon. Assoc.* xlix. 163–89.

communion cups. There are twenty-three examples of the work of the first of these, scattered over North Devon and Cornwall, with a straggler in Glamorgan.[1] Of these only three are dated, two with 1576[2] and one with 1608.[3] He was a good careful worker, but his capacity is best shown not in a communion cup but in a little standing salt at the Victoria and Albert Museum.

The cups made by John Coton can be told at a glance, because of his preference for bands of hit-and-miss engraving round the bowl and a stem formed like a double spool. His cup at Morwenstow, Cornwall (Pl. 66), is typical of the nine examples which have survived in the same area for which Mathew worked.

Peter Quick was still working for Thomas Mathew in 1571, but the communion cup at Loxhore, Devon, bears his mark.

The wardens of the Goldsmiths seem never to have penetrated into Cornwall, nor does it seem possible to trace any Cornish goldsmith from their Minute Books. Canon Mills,[4] however, was able to distinguish the work of five local goldsmiths with a combined output of some thirty cups. Only two of these marked their work, one with *WL in a circle* and the other with an incised *IW*. Both were capable craftsmen and worked, respectively, at St. Ives and Bodmin. The finest example of the latter's work is at Bodmin (Pl. 67).[5]

When the wardens of the Goldsmiths' Company were in the West Country in 1571 they took bonds for true workmanship from nine Exeter goldsmiths, whilst a tenth is mentioned incidentally.[6] Six of these, and another who was then still an apprentice, are known to have made communion cups. Of these John Jones alone matters, since his workshop produced more communion cups than any other goldsmith except the Londoner *IP*. About 130 examples of his work survive, mainly in Devon, Cornwall, and Somerset. Of these eighty-two were produced in the years 1571–4, before the introduction of the Exeter date-letter, eleven in 1575, and twenty-six in 1576. By that time the work of replacement had mostly been done, so that his output in later years was insignificant. He maintained an excellent standard of workmanship, and it was doubtless he who devised the cup with a vertical lip (Pl. 68*a*) by which it is possible to recognize

1 Nicholaston.

2 Bishop's Tawton and Braunton, Devon.

3 Barnstaple.

4 Canon R. W. Mills put all that he could discover about the Cornish goldsmiths into his 'West Country Goldsmiths' (*Trans. of the Royal Institution of Cornwall*, xx, 1920, 535–49).

5 Canon Mills, followed by Mr. Arthur Grimwade (*Exhibition of Silver Treasures from English Churches*, 1955, no. 12), regarded this piece as an early sixteenth-century secular cup which had been decorated and furnished with a cover by *IW*. I maintain that he was responsible for all of it. His signature appears on both cup and cover.

6 Richard Bullyn, Philip Driver, Henry Hardwyke*, Richard Holland* (Hilliard ?), John Jones*, William Nicholls*, John Northe*, Stephen More*, and Richard Osborne*. Those marked * made communion cups. John Avery*, who later made cups, was still employed by Nicholls. No reference is made to C. Easton*, who cannot be traced before 1576. John Eydes* appears only in 1583.

Exeter cups at a glance. It is, of course, a mistake to suppose that any of the major makers of communion cups never deviated from their stock pattern. At Veryan, Cornwall, there is a cup by Jones which has a bell-shaped bowl, with a rounded knot and trumpet-shaped foot (Pl. 68*b*).

Immediately to the east of the country served by the Exeter goldsmiths lay the territory in which two Dorset craftsmen were active. William Troublefylde of Sherborne would seem to have been the owner of the mark showing *a circle filled with pellets*, and produced quite good cups for churches over the Somerset and Wiltshire border, as well as in North Dorset.[1] The southern part of the latter county was served by Lawrence Stratford of Dorchester, a capable craftsman but without much individuality, whose work is well exemplified by the cup which he made for Church Knowle, Dorset (Pl. 69*a*).

Since the goldsmiths who operated in south-eastern England all worked on a very small scale, we may now proceed to deal with the one remaining important provincial goldsmith. For reasons which have already been explained, it seems likely that the Welsh goldsmith whose mark showed OOOO probably lived at Carmarthen. In the number of his surviving works he ranks third amongst the Elizabethan makers of church plate. From the technical point of view his work is satisfactory, but he was not good at getting the right proportions. With two exceptions, all of his cups are engraved round the middle with the name of the church. Thus the example illustrated (Pl. 69*b*) has ✠ POCVLVM ⋆ ECLESIE ⋆ DE ⋆ SWANSEY. For the cathedral of St. David's he provided a chalice with a paten of dish form, but ordinarily he made paten-covers.

By about the year 1578 the campaign for converting chalices was over and the production of communion cups became spasmodic. The late Elizabethan communion cup by no means always followed one of the established designs, though these continued to be made—the examples at St. Mary, Stockport (Pl. 70*a*), made in 1580, and at St. Mary, Reading (Pl. 70*b*), made in 1598, are still in the old tradition, which was to be reproduced with varying degrees of accuracy for many a long year. A marked modification of the standard design is illustrated by a cup made in 1581, belonging to the Goldsmiths' Company (Pl. 71*a*). Other craftsmen diverged even more markedly. In 1568 the churchwardens of Wendens Ambo, Essex, got their chalice and paten converted into a communion cup with paten-cover, but at the visitation at Saffron Waldon on 23 April 1588 it was noted that 'There wanteth a Com^{n} Cuppe'. Three months later the churchwardens certified that they had provided 'a comely Comm^{n} Cuppe'.[2] This is a very fair description of this beautiful little piece (Pl. 71*b*), which is used in conjunction with the paten-cover of 1568. Because of the mistaken idea that the designs of Elizabethan communion cups were entirely

[1] See above, p. 140, n. 4.
[2] *C.P. Essex*, 266.

standardized, cups of this sort have been regarded as being of secular origin. There is little evidence to support this.[1]

That the churchwardens at the end of the reign of Elizabeth I were more prone to select original designs is symptomatic that the new régime was now firmly established. Another example of the use of an abnormal design, this time one which was used widely for secular purposes, is afforded by a cup of 1599 bought for Brightwell church, Berks. (Pl. 72*a*).[2] That cups of this sort were being used in English churches makes their appearance in the churches of Calvinist Jersey appear less anomalous. The example of 1594 at St. Clement (Pl. 72*b*) is one of the earliest of these.[3]

On the other hand, the use of wide bowls for communion is quite un-English.[4] The parish of St. Brelade possesses four of these, acquired between the last years of Elizabeth I and the first of Charles I. Two of these are illustrated (Pl. 73). The parish of St. Mary has another two. It should, of course, be recollected that at the time in question the congregation would be quite accustomed to drinking out of bowls of this sort, so that they would not have been unpractical as they would be now. Their use was not, however, a success, for none appear to have been made after 1627, though no concerted effort was ever made to eliminate them.

With the death of Elizabeth I, and of her régime which was stifling good and bad developments indifferently, a new age began for church plate. The period of cut-price communion cups was over, since when a new piece was wanted it was now possible to find a donor to provide it.

The parish of Beddgelert, under Snowdon, was so fortunate as to contain the birthplace of Sir John Williams, goldsmith to James I. He was not a craftsman himself, but he knew where to go for good work. The Beddgelert chalice (Pl. 74) was made in 1610 by a goldsmith whose mark shows the letters *RS*. It is a well-designed piece with a useful knot formed of cast ornament. Its unusual feature, however, is the engraving of the three Marys on the bowl.[5] On the knob of the paten-cover is engraved the arms of the donor.

Belonging to the church of St. Werburgh, Bristol, is another unique chalice

[1] Other cups of the same form by the goldsmith *RW* (Jackson, *Goldsmiths*, 104) are at Grimston, Leics., 1581, and Hale, Hants, 1589. A pair of 1573 by another London goldsmith is at St. Austell, Cornwall. The only example of this type, which probably was originally in secular use, is the one with the York mark for 1598 at Dagenham, Essex.

[2] Inscribed round the lip: THE COMMUNION CWP [*sic*] OF THE PARISH OF BRITWELL GATHERED AND MADE BY THE PAYNS OF JOHN GOODAY WILLIAM PERREY AND JOHN LEIRPIN JUNE 12 1600. The Sacred Monogram was engraved on the bowl in 1841.

[3] Inscribed: CETE COUPE APARTIENT A LA PAROISSE DE S[t] CLEMENT 1594. No marks.

[4] A number of English churches possess mazers, but these were probably seldom used for communion.

[5] Left to right: *M. Cleophae, M. Virgo, M. Salome.* On the foot: *Donum Iohannis Williams aurificis regis, 1610.*

(Pl. 75). It is in the style of the standing bowls so popular in the second half of the sixteenth century, but bears the hall-mark for 1619. Inside the bowl is engraved a representation of St. Peter, whilst on the outside of the lip is a long dedicatory inscription.[1]

We may now turn to some chalices of less unusual form. The maker of the 1622 chalice at St. Mary, Aldermary[2] (Pl. 76*a*) was evidently intent upon improving upon the popular Elizabethan design and has completed it with a stepped cover.

On the other hand, the chalice of 1626 at St. Mary Woolnoth (Pl. 76*b*) is a throwback to Edwardian times. It is significant of the increased prestige of the Church that a design which had originally been chosen because of its extravagant use of silver was now accepted on its own merits. Edwardian Revival chalices form a distinct variety as they are not to be found only in churches which need a pair for an original one. We may note at this point that paten-covers dating from the second quarter of the seventeenth century onwards are sometimes made to fit with the foot inside the bowl of the chalice, instead of serving as a knob as heretofore.

The chalice belonging to St. Botolph Aldgate (Pl. 77*b*), made in 1635, is of Elizabethan inspiration, but is of special interest because of the engraved decoration on the bowl and paten. On each is a representation of the Sacrifice of Isaac surrounded by VIDET DEVS ET PROVIDEBIT SIBI VICTIMAM; above is the Sacred Monogram; and below the initials of the church and the name of the donor.

The chalice of 1629 now belonging to Holy Trinity, Kensington Gore, closely resembles the last, but is particularly interesting because it was a gift from Laud, when Bishop of London, to the Trinity Chapel, Knightsbridge, on the day of its consecration.[3] The chalice which he presented to Manningtree, Essex, is equally Elizabethan in inspiration, but is engraved with his arms.[4] These two pieces make it very difficult to believe that Laud had any very pronounced views as to forms most appropriate for church plate.

The very opposite was the case of Thomas Howard, Earl of Arundel, with whom we have found him associated in the provision of the plate for St. George's Chapel. In 1636 the earl was sent by Charles I on an embassy to the Emperor Ferdinand II and, when passing through Canterbury, presented to the cathedral a chalice of a highly individual design, but unfortunately unmarked (Pl. 78). The knot is decorated with the heads of a lion, a horse, and a talbot. The first two animals were the supporters of his own arms and the third those of his wife. On the shaped foot decorated with husk ornament, the horse of the

[1] See p. 230.

[2] *ET monogram* (Jackson, *Goldsmiths*, 115). This piece originally belonged either to St. Antholin or to St. John Walbrook.

[3] Inscribed: SANCTAE ET INDIVIDVAE TRINITATI and *The guift of the Right Reverent Father in God William Lord Bishop of London.*

[4] *C.P. Essex*, 236, pl. xvi.

Arundels is shown standing beside the seated talbot of his wife's family, with, below, the inscription CONCORDIA CVM CANDORE. It would be tempting to consider this very exceptional piece as the work of some foreign goldsmith if there were any comparable piece abroad.[1]

The large chalice (Pl. 79) belonging to North Ockendon church, Essex, illustrates the Edwardian design in a very much simplified form. It bears the hall-mark for 1646, but was made as the result of a bequest which had accrued three years earlier. The delay cannot be regarded as surprising, since the Civil War was at its height.[2]

It is now necessary to return to the early years of the century in order to trace from the beginning one of the most interesting developments in post-Reformation church plate. The responsibility for the seventeenth-century Gothic Revival church plate[3] has in the past been attributed to Laud, but we have already remarked on the difficulty in assigning any particular fashion to him. Laudian it can fairly be called, since the style was certainly propagated by the archbishop's followers, but the original initiative probably derived from Lancelot Andrewes. The strongest reason is iconographic, and will be given in the appropriate section. The earliest datable example was made for the church of St. Mary Extra, Southampton,[4] out of the money collected on the day of its consecration by Andrewes in 1620. It bears the maker's mark only, *RB above a mullet*, and is almost identical with the one made by the same goldsmith twenty years later, which was acquired for the chapel at Staunton Harold (Pl. 73*a*).

Probably a few years earlier than the Southampton chalice is one at St. John's College, Oxford (Pl. 80), which bears only the maker's mark *SF in monogram*. The design, modelled on those of the medieval Group VIII, is in all essentials the same as that used for the chalice already described. It retains, however, its paten-cover, whilst the bowl is engraved with the Good Shepherd, a feature which we shall see links it directly with Bishop Andrewes. The early date attributed to this chalice might suggest that it was acquired whilst Laud was president of the college. If this were so, it must be regarded as just another instance of his tendency to exploit the ideas of Andrewes.[5]

1 Inscribed VOTIVVM · HVNC · CALICEM · DEO · OPT · MAX · HVMILLIME · OBTVLIT · ALTARIQVE · HVIVS · ECCLESIAE · CATHEDRALIS · SACRANDVM · RELIQVIT · THOMAS · HOWARD · SERENISS · MAG · BRIT ·REGIS · AD · CAESAREM · LEGATVS · HAC · TRANSIENS · 7 APRILIS · 1636. Another curious feature about this chalice is the emphasis on his wife, Lady Alethea Talbot, who was a Recusant. It would be tempting to consider it as having been made for use in her chapel, but it is a little large for a Recusant chalice. It is 9 inches high, the bowl being 4½ inches in diameter and 3 inches deep.

2 Arms of Poyntz within a wreath. Inscribed: *Ex dono Rici Poyntz Ar. in usum Sacrament Coen Dom 1643 North Ockendon in Essex.*

3 For a list of Anglican Gothic Revival chalices see Appendix IV.

4 *C.P. Hants*, 309.

5 The gist of the argument against Laud having been responsible for the Gothic Revival is that it would put him in the position of having been an influence on Andrewes. No one has ever suggested that this was the case.

By the sixteen-thirties the Gothic Revival chalice was well established. During this decade eight goldsmiths, including one who was probably a provincial, were turning them out. They are all variants of the medieval Groups VII and VIII, except for three examples made by a goldsmith whose mark was *WR below a bow*, who tried to sell to Anglicans modified versions of a type of chalice which he was selling to the Recusants (Pl. 154*b*). His work will be discussed further when the plate of the Recusants is reached. We may mention here, however, that out of twenty-six makers of Anglican Gothic Revival chalices, only two can be recognized as makers of Recusant chalices.[1]

Two other undated chalices made about this time have interesting associations. The example at Peterhouse, Cambridge, is linked up with the building of the college chapel and must have been ordered either under Matthew Wren, who was Master from 1626 to 1634 (later Bishop of Ely), or else by his successor John Cosin (later Bishop of Durham).[2] Similarly, an example now at Lambeth Palace is probably a relic of Bishop Juxon, who was consecrated bishop of London in 1633.

Of the seven chalices remaining from the year 1638, four were made by a goldsmith, whose mark was *Tb above a bird*, for the churches on Lady Dudley's Warwickshire estates. A fifth, which she gave to Acton, Middlesex, followed in 1639. All of them match the example at Kenilworth (Pl. 81) and are characterized by their rich engraved decoration and by having the sides of their feet straight, instead of incurved as on the other examples illustrated. This last peculiarity is repeated on the five chalices made for her daughter, Lady Kniveton, for the churches on her late husband's estates in Derbyshire. These all follow the pattern used at Mugginton (Pl. 82*a*), and are simpler versions of the Warwickshire group, but were made by a goldsmith whose mark was *RP below a fleur-de-lis*.

The second Gothic Revival chalice at St. John's College, Oxford (Pl. 82*b*), was made in 1641 by a goldsmith whose mark was *FT in monogram*. It must have been amongst the last made before the outbreak of the Civil War, during which probably a number were destroyed. The Parliamentary soldiery were particularly prone to loot the cathedrals, which had received considerable additions to their plate in recent years.

We now reach the group of chalices made for use in Anglican private chapels after the use of the Book of Common Prayer had been banned in parish churches. With the exception of a pair of chalices without any marks at Trinity

[1] The goldsmiths who can be recognized as having made plate for the Recusants do not appear to have abstained from making Anglican plate, but used designs not so intimately connected with the High Church.

[2] It was probably got by Wren, as it is not mentioned in the bill for chapel plate supplied to Cosin in 1638 by Richard Blackwell: *Cosin Correspondence* i, Surtees Soc. 1869, 223–4.

College, Cambridge, and a rather coarsely made example at Pendomer, Somerset, all are the work of a very fine goldsmith whose mark was *a hound sejant*. This goldsmith's earliest recorded piece of church plate is a communion cup in the Elizabethan tradition, made in 1639 for Winslow, Bucks. A pair of cups made in 1653, probably for some private chapel, are similar.[1] In this year, however, he began to make chalices in the Gothic style. There are a pair of fully marked examples, made for the chapel of the Duke of Lennox at Cobham Hall and now at Rochester Cathedral, a single dated but not hall-marked example (Pl. 83*b*), perhaps made for Dr. Sheldon, at Fulham Palace, and one forming part of the service of plate made for Sir Robert Shirley's chapel at Staunton Harold. This last provides a clue, since it is exactly copied from the one already mentioned, made in 1640 by the goldsmith *RB*, who still retained designs dating from Bishop Andrewes's days.[2] It seems safe to assume that the other unhall-marked chalices by this goldsmith were made during the years 1653–60.[3] No others have the orb and cross upon the top of the paten-cover,[4] but otherwise they do not vary much. The *hound sejant* goldsmith who served the Royalists so well during the Commonwealth does not appear to have profited much by the Restoration.[5]

The triumph of the High Church party at the Restoration added greatly to the prestige of the Gothic Revival designs. This was partly brought about because of their being chosen for the Chapel Royal, for it will be found that several of the chalices in country churches were made for royal officials by the Jewel House goldsmiths.

Hitherto the designers of chalices in the Gothic style had, with one exception, sought inspiration from medieval chalices of Groups VII and VIII. From 1660 onwards the adherence to the original forms becomes much less close and in some cases we might not recognize the children if we did not know the parents. The tendency towards a greater freedom of interpretation is already noticeable in the designs obtained by Sir Robert Vyner for the chalices wanted for equipping the Chapel Royal in the early months after the Restoration. The form of the gold chalice[6] prepared for the coronation of Charles II is adequately reproduced in a silver replica made in the reign of George IV (Pl. 99*a*). The bowl, except for the cut-card work underneath, is passably Gothic, but the stem

1 Christie's, 10 June 1943, lot 245.

2 As will be shown when the subject of iconography is treated, he did not merely reproduce the design of the Southampton chalice of 1620, but decorated it with subjects dear to Andrewes but not used on that piece. The only notable differences between the two chalices are that the Staunton Harold example is gilt and 10 inches high, whereas the Southampton one is plain and 7½ inches high.

3 e.g. the example at Hawkden, Suffolk, accompanies a flagon with the 1659 hall-mark.

4 The orb and cross unscrew.

5 His latest work appears to be a porringer with the 1666 hall-mark, at Wadham College, Oxford.

6 H. D. R. Sitwell, *The Crown Jewels*, 1953, pl. xii. This chalice and its paten have two makers' marks (see Appendix IV).

is utterly unmedieval, though the knot still carries traces of the bosses which were on its sixteenth-century original. The foot owes something, but not much, to the chalices of Group IX. Anyone who has had experience with judging goldsmiths' designs will have encountered exasperating cases where the finished product does not come up to expectations. It is possible that it was always regarded as a failure, since with the exception of the replica made on the occasion of the coronation of William and Mary, the design was left alone until the eighteen-twenties.

The pair of silver-gilt chalices made about the same time for the ordinary needs of the Chapel Royal have even less true medieval feeling about them, but are much more successful (Pl. 85). There is nothing Gothic about the decafoil base nor the baluster stem. It will be noted that whereas the chalices at St. James's Palace are equipped with covers in the form of embossed dishes (quite distinct from the patens), the simpler version of the same design made for Bishop Cosin's chapel at Auckland has a domed cover (Pl. 84*a*).

The pair of chalices presented in 1661 to St. George's Chapel, Windsor, represent a much more serious attempt at being medieval (Pl. 84*b*). The cut-card work underneath the bowls reveals the true date, but the stem, knot, and base are plausible.

The chalice (Pl. 87*a*), 'made out of the purest gold of Guinea', which was presented in 1662 by Thomas Davies to the church of Welshpool, Montgomery, is a very well thought out adaptation of the medieval Group IX by a goldsmith who would appear to be otherwise unknown.[1]

A chalice at St. George's Chapel, Windsor[2] (Pl. 84*c*), which is without a hallmark but which is listed in the 1667 inventory, appears Gothic without having any really medieval detail. The baluster stem is decorated with three cherubs, whilst the octofoil foot is engraved with a cross patonce. The form of the stem links it with some Recusant chalices which though unmarked can be safely attributed to the goldsmith whose mark, *AM monogram*, appears on the present one.

[1] E. A. Jones (*Y Cymmroder*, xliv, 1935, 2) failed to read the maker's mark, which is, however, *GW below two anulets in a shaped shield.* He gives the lengthy Latin inscription. There is an extraordinary resemblance between this chalice and one made in 1667 by Michel Pohl the elder for the Maria kyrka at Stockholm (Pl. 87*b*). It is not easy to explain this as English influence, since Gothic designs had been in more or less constant use in Sweden since the Reformation, whereas in England they were a conscious revival.

[2] It was the gift of Lady Mary Heveningham. Her husband had been one of the Regicides, though he had had just enough sense not to sign the death warrant. During the Commonwealth he had speculated in church lands and only awoke to the possibility of the Restoration at a very late date. He then decided not to flee the country but to trust to the influence of his wife's Royalist relations. The Careys do not seem to have liked William Heveningham and, after they had secured that his sentence of death should be commuted to one of life imprisonment, concentrated on seeing that his wife should not suffer too severe financial losses. Colonel Heveningham remained a prisoner in Windsor Castle from 1660 until his death in 1678. The chalice was probably a thank-offering on the commutation of his death sentence.

Charles Shelley, whose mark was *S crowned*, was amongst the finest goldsmiths of the reign of Charles II. The three chalices which he made for the Duke of York are superbly conceived and executed (Pl. 86). The foot is an accurate rendering of that of the medieval Group VIII, but with cherubs as 'knops', but the stem is a baluster such as was used in contemporary loving-cups. The bell-shaped bowl is engraved both with the arms of the duke and his *DL* cipher.

Shelley's other Gothic chalices, the latest of which bears the 1683 hall-mark, have mostly got feet derived from Group VII and plainly moulded hexagonal knots, but the one made in about 1675 for Sir Stephen Fox's presentation service for Redlynch (Pl. 88*a*), Som., is copied from Group IX.

Another prominent goldsmith who made chalices in the Gothic style had as his mark *IB above a crescent*. His first Gothic piece appears to have been a flagon which he made in 1669 for Pembroke College, Cambridge, to match one made during the Commonwealth by the *hound sejant* goldsmith. His chalices all belong to the years 1671–80. They all imitate the medieval Group VII but have hexagonal stems with plain moulded knots, and have cut-card work under their bowls. The chalice forming part of the service of plate presented by Walter Chetwynd to celebrate the completion of the rebuilding by Wren of Ingestre church (Pl. 88*b*), Staffs., is hall-marked 1676 and is typical of his work.

A popular form of decoration for drinking-vessels, both religious and secular, used in the second half of the seventeenth century in most of the countries of northern Europe consisted in encasing the bowl in a pierced openwork sheath. The earliest examples of the use of this attractive but quite unmedieval form of decoration on chalices in this country are two examples bearing the cipher of the Duke of York and preserved at Buckingham Palace and St. James's.[1] The outer casing on these is engraved and pierced with flowers in the Dutch style, but two further examples of the use of this form of decoration, at Ashby-de-la-Zouch and Lichfield Cathedral, show the more usual variety of the technique in which the sheathing is embossed and pierced. They are both probably by the same maker, though his mark is only visible on the former (Pl. 89*b*), which bears the 1676 hall-mark. They differ considerably in detail: the Lichfield chalice has a hexagonal foot, whilst that of the one at Ashby is octagonal (Pl. 89*a*). Both have little cherubs set upright on the angles.[2]

During the reign of Charles II thirteen goldsmiths can be traced as making chalices of a more or less Gothic character. Most of the production belongs to the years 1660–70, during which the Jewel House was re-equipping the Chapels Royal, but there was no suggestion at the time of the king's death that the taste for Gothic was at the point of extinction. This was, however, the case, for no

[1] *Antiquaries Journal*, xiv, 1934, pl. xxxvii.

[2] The Lichfield chalice was given in 1670 by Theophilus, 7th Earl of Huntingdon. The one at Ashby was a gift from his wife.

Gothic Revival chalices were made during the reign of James II. Thereafter, a second gold chalice was thought necessary for the coronation of William and Mary, when much of the regalia was duplicated. Fifteen years later a last example was made for Hampton church, Middlesex.

The fates were unfavourable to the Gothic Revival chalice. The design was affected by the High Church party and it was this section of the Church of England which suffered most severely at the Revolution. The numerically insignificant Non-Jurors included a large proportion of individuals who had already reached posts of importance. Their loss sapped the vitality of the cathedral chapters and, as has already been shown, the emergency cathedral plate acquired in the years 1660–5 was now ripe for replacement. Had the Church of England been allowed to develop peacefully during the last years of the seventeenth century, it is likely that there would have been many more Gothic Revival chalices.

It should be emphasized that the preference for Gothic forms was affected by only a section of the High Church party, especially that part which came in contact with the Chapel Royal. Those who ordered plate in this style did so because they admired the traditional forms. There is no hint that they attached great significance to the matter. Both the High Churchman and the Recusant would have scouted the nineteenth-century misconception that Gothic was the only truly Christian form of art.

Some High Churchmen did not like Gothic chalices. The individual who placed the order for the Gloucester Cathedral plate at so early a date that it was able to get the 1660 hall-mark employed the *hound sejant* goldsmith, the leading maker of Gothic chalices, but chose a simple goblet on a baluster stem (Pl. 90*a*). Duchess Dudley, when she resumed her benefactions after the Restoration, abandoned her preference for Gothic-style chalices in favour of designs evolved from the Elizabethan communion cup. Two of these, at Bidford-on-Avon (Pl. 90*b*), Warw., and Pattishall, Northants, are identical, and were made by the same goldsmith in 1663. They have bowls richly embossed with flowers and, in front, the Sacred Monogram flanked by two angels.[1]

Immediately after the Restoration a lot of replacement orders were given by customers who were mainly interested in an early delivery. A bad tradition was started, particularly by the cathedrals, but as an example of the worst efforts of the Charles II goldsmiths is illustrated a chalice made in 1664 for St. Augustine, in the City (Pl. 91*a*). Customers who preferred simple forms, but really cared about the results, fared very much better. The chalice of 1674 at Oriel College, Oxford (Pl. 91*b*), is well proportioned and carefully executed. The only applied ornament is the donor's arms on the back and the Virgin and Child (patron of St. Mary Hall) on the front.

An interesting contrast is provided by the chalice (Pl. 92*a*), forming part of

[1] Her third chalice of this period, at St. Peter, St. Albans, is of a similar form but by a different maker.

the lavish gift of plate to the church of St. James, Piccadilly, on its consecration in 1683, and the more austere version (Pl. 93*a*) thought appropriate when the Royal Hospital, Chelsea, was furnished out five years later. Both are the work of a goldsmith, whose mark showed *RL above a fleur-de-lis*, who was one of the leading makers of church plate at this time.[1]

An effective contrast to these pieces is provided by the chalice provided in 1695 for Wapping (Pl. 92*b*) which is decorated only with the engraved figure of the patron, St. John the Evangelist, and reproducing very much the same design as was used for St. Mary Aldermary (Pl. 76*a*) over seventy years earlier.

The forms of seventeenth-century Anglican chalices (except those in the Gothic style) were much affected by the changes in fashion in the form of contemporary secular drinking-cups. In general it was the forms and proportions of the smaller cups which was borrowed, but during the reigns of William and Mary and of William III there is a recognizable tendency to model chalices on guild cups. This is very apparent in the case of the large chalice of 1692 at Swanage, Dorset (Pl. 93*b*), which is one of the rare pieces of church plate to be decorated with the fluting and gadrooning so popular on contemporary secular pieces.[2] A simpler form of guild cup is imitated in the handsome chalice made in 1697 for St. Mary Abbots, Kensington (Pl. 94*a*).[3] The inspiration of the guild cup was a passing phase, since just at this time the baluster-stem cup was being ousted by a two-handled, bell-shaped bowl which was quite unsuitable for church use.

At the end of the seventeenth century the chalice was beginning to be a line of its own. The smaller form of secular drinking-cups had given way to glasses, whilst the guild cups were developing in a manner which provided no useful experience for a designer of chalices. Unless the goldsmith was prepared to fob off on his customer an old design—a course which only too many adopted—the question of the form required much more serious thought than heretofore.

In 1698 the Huguenot John Chartier entered his mark at Goldsmiths' Hall and in the following year executed the superb covered chalice at Christ Church Cathedral, Oxford (Pl. 94*b*). The Huguenots did not get many orders for Anglican plate, and this design does not appear to have been re-used. The chalice forms during what, judging purely from the secular pieces, is one of the most glorious periods of English silver, are distinctly disappointing. A fresh design was not always much better than a repeat of a Caroline one, as may be seen from

[1] Jackson, *Goldsmiths*, 140. This goldsmith also provided the plate for Farley church, Wilts., which was another of Wren's buildings. The suggestion that he was a protégé of the architect is rather strengthened by the fact that Sir Stephen Fox, who put up the money, had previously employed Charles Shelley, who was a Jewel House goldsmith.

[2] Inscribed: *Given by Mrs Elizabeth Toope, wife of Abraham Story, Citizen and Mason of London, 1693.*

[3] Engraved with the arms of Christina Verney, wife of the Hon. John Verney, heir to the 3rd Lord Willoughby de Broke.

the stock pattern used by Thomas Parr, of which an example belongs to St. Nicholas Cole Abbey (Pl. 95*b*).[1]

Paul de Lamerie, whose name is connected with the most finely executed secular silver in the Rococo style, designed chalices which, if much better than some produced in his day, are unworthy of an artist of his reputation. His first chalices were made in 1717, five years after he had entered his mark. The pair which he made for the chapel of the Prince of Wales in Hanover[2] are plain standing beakers with paten-covers, in the Elizabethan tradition. The chalice which he made in the same year, as a gift from Mrs. Strangways to the church of Milton Clevedon, near Shepton Mallet, has, however, a cover with a knob, which would appear to be the only occasion on which he did not provide a paten-cover.

After 1717 Lamerie appears to have stuck to a design which was evolved in his own workshop. This is exemplified by the chalices made for Patshull, Staffs., in 1720 (Pl. 95*a*) and made in 1747 for Melbury Osmund, Dorset[3] (Pl. 95*c*). Lamerie's chalices differ principally in the presence or absence of the moulding round the bowl and in slight variations in the curves of the stem. The rayed band round the bowl at Melbury Osmund is exceptional, but the cherubs alternating with the Sacred Monogram, which are engraved on the foot, appear fairly often.

Just as Lamerie's stock design got right away from the monotonous standing-beaker form, so did that of William Cripps, who is also noted as a maker of good Rococo domestic plate. The chalice which he made in 1756 for Stoke Climsland, Cornwall (Pl. 96*a*),[4] is a good safe piece of work. It is accompanied by a paten of dish form.

In 1765 Lady Mary Cavendish Harley, widow of the 2nd Duke of Portland, presented a set of plate to the Portland Chapel which she had founded. It was made by Thomas Heming, who cannot, however, really be credited with the design of the chalice (Pl. 96*b*). On the accession of George III he had been appointed royal goldsmith, and so got the task of providing the Jewel Office with chapel plate for the Plantations. In 1764 Heming supplied the chalices of identical design now at Trinity Church, New York, and Christ Church, Williamsburg, but the type had certainly been in general use since 1729[5] under the previous Jewel Office goldsmiths, Joseph Allen and Mordecai Fox. The paten supplied by Heming with chalices of this design was a plate on a low foot.

[1] It was admired, however, by the formidable Eleanor James (see p. 240), who ordered a repeat in 1711 for St. Benet, Paul's Wharf. It now belongs to St. Mary le Strand.

[2] Now amongst the plate of the Duke of Brunswick.

[3] Lamerie's workshop appears to have been full when the order for the service of plate for Melbury Osmund arrived. Only the flagon bears his mark—the chalice was handed out to Benjamin West and bears his mark. I treated more fully the subject of the church plate of Paul de Lamerie in *Apollo Miscellany*, 1949, 45–49.

[4] Engraved with the arms of Mrs. Elizabeth Prowse.

[5] e.g. St. Philip, Charleston, South Carolina.

The pair of chalices belonging to the service of plate made by Francis Butty and Nicholas Dumee in 1766 for Durham Cathedral (Pl. 97*a*) are perhaps the finest which were made in England in the eighteenth century and are alone in displaying freely Rococo ornament. They revert to the traditional forms and are beautifully proportioned—most continental chalices at this time suffered from having too small a bowl in proportion to the foot.

The Rococo style was in its last stage of development when the Durham service was made. The Neo-Classical style affected the design of chalices as little as had the Rococo, for the majority of the goldsmiths continued to make reproductions of the simpler and less well-proportioned Restoration types. For a good example of a chalice in the Adam style we have to turn again to the work of the firm of Butty & Dumee, who in 1772 made a service of plate for presentation by William, 4th Lord Craven, to Binley church, Warw. The chalice (Pl. 97*b*) retains exactly the same proportions as the Durham ones, but below the lip of the bowl is a band of laurel from which depend swags. The lower part of the bowl, the baluster stem, and the foot are all fluted. As is the case with much of the domestic Adam silver, there is little archaeological accuracy in either form or decoration, but this did not necessarily prevent the results from being highly satisfactory.

In the early years of the nineteenth century little interest was taken in developing fresh forms for chalices, but during the reign of George IV there was considerable activity. In 1821 the Duke of York presented a service of plate, including four chalices,[1] to the new church of St. Pancras. He entrusted the work to Paul Storr, who had been until the previous year in charge of the workshop of the royal goldsmiths Rundell, Bridge & Rundell. Though an immense amount of plate had been made under his supervision, it does not seem to have included much church work, so that the St. Pancras job came as a challenge. Storr had won his laurels working in the classical style, and the highly archaeological character of Inwood's design for the church added a further argument in favour of designing the chalices as classical vases (Pl. 98*a*). The cast and chased ornament is beautifully executed, but the pieces are too heavy in every sense. It might have been better had he contented himself with an engraved Crown of Thorns and Sacred Monogram. The last feature reappears on the chalices which he made in 1826 for the two Oxfordshire churches of Churchill and Sarsden, which have deep bell-shaped bowls on baluster stems and round feet.[2] Though Storr's workshop produced fewer chalices than Lamerie's, he also failed to produce a really good design.

In the year in which the Duke of York placed his order the king decided on

[1] Two were melted down in 1853 and converted into four smaller chalices.

[2] The baluster stems show a curious half-developed knot; see N. M. Penzer, *Paul Storr, the last of the Goldsmiths*, 1955, pl. lxx.

a set of Gothic plate for the chapel in the Royal Pavilion, Brighton. The idea presented difficulties to the royal goldsmiths, who had made their reputation with work in the classical style. They decided against an original design and copied the gold chalice which had been made for the coronation of Charles II. The two silver-gilt chalices, now at Buckingham Palace, bear the mark of Philip Rundell, but whether they really came from the firm's own workshop is uncertain, since the same design was used in 1827 for a pair of chalices for St. Giles-in-the-Fields, which bear the mark of B. Preston[1] (Pl. 99*a*). The manner in which the completion of the Royal Pavilion service hung round the neck of the firm of Rundell, Bridge & Rundell has been told elsewhere. This was not, however, their only effort in designing Gothic church plate. In 1830 Archbishop Harcourt placed an order for a complete service for York Minster, and the chalices (Pl. 99*b*) are again in the Caroline Gothic style but are not replicas. Though they reproduce the cut-card decoration under the bowl and have cut-card labels on the foot, this last is six-sided and not sexfoil, whilst the stem has a well-formed knot instead of a baluster.

The demand for Gothic chalices in the reign of George IV remained small. On the other hand, there was rather more activity in producing new chalice designs than there had been for some time past. From the modern utilitarian point of view the chalices of this period are much too large, but that is merely because church needs have changed. It was in their forms that the late-Georgian chalices were most unlucky. About the most unsuitable of the designs then current was the chalice in the form of a goblet with a thistle-shaped bowl. A pair made by J. E. Terry & Co. and bearing the 1821 hall-mark are at Falmouth church (Pl. 98*b*).

CHALICES FOR THE COMMUNION OF THE SICK

Deep obscurity surrounds the subject of how exactly the needs of sick would-be communicants were met during the century after the Reformation.[2] Though celebrations at the bedside were undoubtedly lawful, I have only discovered one instance of the setting aside for this purpose of a special chalice before the Restoration.[3]

In Elizabethan times, as we have seen, few churches had more than one communion cup, but in early Stuart times, when church plate was easy to come by, it might have been expected that small chalices would have been called into existence to meet this need. It would seem fair to infer that bedside celebrations were not frequent, and that when they took place ordinary chalices were used.[4]

[1] They are also stamped OSBORN, LONDON.

[2] The various forms for the communion of the sick are dealt with in an article by W. P. M. Kennedy in *The Law and Custom of Reservation, 1547–1661*, 1929.

[3] At Battle, Sussex, is a chalice inscribed *Given to the Deanery of Battle for the uſe of private Communi-*

Chalices specially made for the communion of the sick appear in the reign of Charles II.[1] Though many urban churches acquired them in the period between 1660 and 1830, others depended on one which was the private property of the incumbent. In the century after the Restoration a set of plate for the communion of the sick consisted of either a miniature chalice with paten-cover or else of a miniature chalice with a cover and a miniature 'salver' paten. In both cases it was usual to follow a current design for a chalice of the ordinary size, but some display a certain amount of originality. Thus the chalice with paten-cover belonging to St. Edward, Cambridge (Pl. 100*a*), consists of a bowl resting directly on the foot and without any stem. It is dated 1734, but the makers' mark is illegible. The chalice with cover belonging to St. Margaret Pattens (Pl. 100*b*), on the other hand, shows the very successful use by Samuel Wood in 1743 of a design for full-size chalices which had made its appearance some twenty years earlier.

At the close of the eighteenth century the communion set came to include a miniature flagon, also a reduction of a standard design, and sometimes a silver-capped glass flask for wine. It appears to have been assumed that bread would be available anywhere. The communion sets of the early nineteenth century are often extremely well designed and executed.

B. PATENS OTHER THAN PATEN-COVERS

It would seem that the form of paten most commonly used in conjunction with Edwardian communion cups was shaped like a dish and differed little from the simplest form used in medieval times. It was intended to be used as a cover, just as its medieval predecessor had been. The paten which accompanies the communion cup at Beddington, Surrey (Pl. 49), is typical of this design.

As has already been shown, the idea of a paten-cover with a flat knob which would serve as a foot when reversed was evolved during the reign of Edward VI and is represented by the examples belonging to St. Mary Aldermary (Pl. 50) and St. Michael, Southampton (Pl. 52*a*).

During the first years of Elizabeth I, patens of dish form with a single depression continued to be made for use with the communion cups of the type with the bell-shaped bowl such as had been popular in Edwardian times. This type was never entirely abandoned before the end of the reign of James I. It was made both by London and by provincial goldsmiths, and a nicely engraved example at Wombourn, Staffs. (Pl. 64), has been illustrated. Much rarer were

cants. The flowery cursive lettering suggests a date in the first half of the seventeenth century, but the piece itself is an ordinary Elizabethan communion cup, weighing with its paten-cover 8 ounces. It has the London hall-mark for 1568.

[1] The very well-found church of St. James, Piccadilly, had a chalice for the communion of the sick from the day of its consecration in 1683. Two more were added before the century was out.

patens of disk form, without any central depression, of which there are examples at St. Margaret, Westminster, and at Yarnscombe, Devon.[1]

The paten-cover was certainly a very convenient form and was able to be used with all the standard forms of communion cup evolved both in London and the provinces. It should be emphasized that it was conceived for use with the wafer bread, the use of which was prescribed by the royal injunctions of 1559.[2] When the Puritans began to use household bread, the small paten-cover which was admirable for piled wafers was found less satisfactory.

A nice theological controversy was bound up in the matter, but we need not enter into it. Archbishop Parker would seem to have felt that he had so many forms of indiscipline to correct that it was profitable to concentrate only upon the more important.[3] The battle of wafer bread versus household bread was never fought out; the use of the latter gradually ousted the former. The idea of encouraging churches to buy patens which were not covers appears to be implicit in Bishop Cooper's injunctions for the diocese of Lincoln, issued in 1574.[4] The normal reaction, however, was merely to enlarge the size of the paten-cover, and the foot was often made to fit inside the bowl of the cup instead of serving as a handle as heretofore. The need for a large paten-cover was generally admitted and was emphasized even in the 1625 visitation articles for the diocese of Winchester issued by Bishop Andrewes,[5] who used wafer bread in his own chapel.

The idea of a paten which was not intended to serve as a cover for a communion cup hardly spread beyond the bounds of the City during the reign of Elizabeth I. The surviving examples take the form of a flat dish on a trumpet-shaped foot, and it may be assumed that their form was evolved from the paten-cover. They are quite plain and of little artistic importance.[6] During the reigns of James I and Charles I the popularity of this form of paten grew, and at the same time its resemblance to the Elizabethan paten-cover decreased. The

[1] *Trans. of the Devon Assoc.* xlviii, 1916, 190.

[2] Frere and Kennedy, iii. 28.

[3] Parker to Burghley, 1575: 'Does your Lordship think that I care either for cap, tippet, surplice or wafer-bread, or any such?' (*Zurich Letters*, i. 248; *Parker Correspondence*, 478).

[4] 'Whether you have . . . two handsome communion cups and a decent paten of silver to minister the Lord's bread' (Frere and Kennedy, iii. 371). The idea appears implicit in most of the later Elizabethan articles, including those of Archbishop Whitgift for the deanery of Shoreham in 1597 (ibid. 286).

[5] 'A large cover of silver' (*Minor Works*, 128). Nothing is said about the size of the paten-cover in the 1619 article (ibid. 114).

[6] The London examples are:

1560, Allhallows, Lombard Street.
1575, St. Michael Paternoster Royal (from Allhallows the Great).
1593, St. Margaret, Lothbury (from St. Olave, Old Jewry).
1597, Allhallows, Lombard Street.

The only example outside London appears to be one of *c.* 1590 at Bramley, Surrey.

example of 1629 belonging to St. Michael Bassishaw (Pl. 101*b*) has a well-developed stem and moulded base. It has still got a depression in the dish, but otherwise it has completed the evolution into the 'salver' design which was destined to come into general use in the reign of Charles II and thereafter to remain the most popular type until the end of our period. These later 'salver' patens are so plentiful and so like their secular contemporaries that it does not seem necessary to illustrate an example.[1]

There were a number of different types of paten current in the first half of the seventeenth century. An example now belonging to St. Michael Paternoster Royal and given to Allhallows the Great in 1608 is merely a flat dish, 5½ inches in diameter, with a vertical rim (Pl. 101*a*).

An example of 1617, belonging to St. Olave, Hart Street (Pl. 102*b*), has, however, a hexagonal dish mounted upon a baluster stem and base similar to those used for the smaller varieties of secular drinking-cups.

A unique paten of 1633 belonging to All Hallows Barking (Pl. 102*a*) takes the form of a square trencher, 8⅞ inches wide, on four ball feet.[2] It is curious to note that in the 1552 inventory of the neighbouring St. Olave, Hart Street, is mentioned 'a square patten'.[3] It has since disappeared.

By the reign of Charles I, as an alternative to the 'salver' paten, there was a definite drift towards the use of a bowl. This was even specified in Bishop Richard Montague's visitation articles issued in 1635 for the diocese of Chichester, where it is asked: 'Have you a plate or patten, faire and deepe, of the same material [silver] for the bread?'[4]

The type of vessel envisaged was probably such as the bowl on a low foot with the 1629 hall-mark at Kingham, Oxon (Pl. 103*b*).[5] Examples of this design persisted until the close of the century. Thus at Withcote, Leics., is an example of 1683 which is a very shallow bowl on a trumpet foot (Pl. 103*a*).

With the benefactions of Alice (later Duchess) Dudley appears the covered paten. This consisted of a standing bowl with a cover which, if reversed, could also serve as a paten. The earliest examples are her gifts to Ladbrooke and Monks Kirby, Warw., which both bear the same maker's mark.[6] These do not greatly differ from those in her next benefactions to the churches of Ashow, Kenilworth (Pl. 104*a*), and Leek Wootton, Warw., all of 1638, and Acton, Middx., of

[1] It does not seem to have been noted previously that the domestic salver of the reign of Charles II was evolved from a type of paten. The smaller secular salvers are indistinguishable from those made for use as patens in the second half of the seventeenth century. In the eighteenth century the secular salver was replaced by various forms of waiters on feet. The salver paten still remained popular until the end of our period.

[2] Though it shows knife scratches, like only too many old patens, there is no particular reason for supposing that it was reserved for cutting up the bread and not for serving it also.

[3] Walters, 540.

[4] W. Prynne, *Canterburie's Doom*, 1646.

[5] Inscribed: *This was bought* ANNO DMI *1629 George Morecroft being Parson and Anthony Bromesgroue and Henry Huckin Churchwardens.*

[6] *WC with an arrow* (Jackson, *Goldsmiths*, 115).

1639. Both bowl and cover are richly embossed with cherubs and fruit. On the flat knob of the cover is engraved the Sacred Monogram and in the centre of the bowl the Instruments of the Passion. The stem and foot of the latter is modelled on that of the contemporary standing cup. It is curious to note that Lady Dudley's covered patens[1] were made by the same goldsmith[2] who was making her Gothic-style chalices, although they are covered entirely with Mannerist ornament.

The idea of the covered paten in the Gothic style was developed by the *hound sejant* goldsmith who in the years 1653–4 made five of identical design and differing only in their applied decoration.[3] Each has a hexagonal foot with incurved sides and cherub 'knops' at the angles. The bowl rests on the lower part of a knot, and inside is engraved the Sacred Monogram with rays. The cover resembles the paten-cover of a communion cup, but the foot is surmounted by an orb and cross which can be unscrewed (Pl. 104*a*).[4]

The covered paten had quite a long history after the Restoration, although the type never became common. The earliest were a pair forming part of the emergency service of plate made in 1660 for Westminster Abbey. Of these only the covers remain. Another pair survive from Duchess Dudley's benefaction to Bidford-on-Avon, Warw. (Pl. 105*a*) and Pattishall, Northants. They bear the 1663 hall-mark. The foot of each is embossed with acanthus ornament and the inside of the bowl with the Sacred Monogram surrounded by tulips and daffodils. The cover takes the form of a deep bowl, similarly decorated. The flat knob is unengraved.

Next comes an example presented to Durham Cathedral by Bishop Cosin. It is not hall-marked, but is included in the list of benefactions compiled in 1668.[5] It consists of a standing dish with scolloped edge, whilst the cover is a bulbous dome richly embossed with flowers and surmounted by an orb and cross.[6]

Another original design is shown in a pair made by John Plummer of York for Ripon Minster (Pl. 105*b*) in 1675. It consists of a dish engraved with a representation of the church and standing upon a low foot. The cover, as at Durham, is purely ornamental and not a second paten. It takes the form of a

[1] There can be no doubt that the usual name for this vessel was a *paten*. Those given by Duchess Dudley were sometimes described as *bread boules* (*Birmingham Archeological Soc. Trans.* lviii, 1934, 63–64). The name *ciborium* had hardly entered into the Anglican vocabulary, though I have met it used in reference to an ordinary salver paten in 1702 (*C.P. Leics.* i. 6–7).

[2] *Tb over two stars and a bird* (Jackson, *Goldsmiths*, 121).

[3] Fulham Palace, dated 1653; a pair each made for Cobham Hall and Staunton Harold are hall-marked 1654. For iconography and inscriptions see pp. 227 and 232.

[4] The only post-Restoration covered paten of Gothic design belongs to a set of plate once the property of Lord Brownlow and now in a private collection in the Cotswolds. The maker's mark is *IB over a crescent* (Jackson, *Goldsmiths*, 130). It has not got the orb and cross on the cover.

[5] *Cosin Correspondence*, ii, Surtees Soc. 1870, 172.

[6] *Hierurgia Anglicana*, pt. 2, 1903 edn., pl. x.

canopy engraved with the Agnus Dei, surmounted by an orb and cross and supported on three claw-and-ball feet.

The Durham and Ripon covered patens failed to found a new tradition. The later examples are all undecorated versions of the type chosen by Duchess Dudley for her later gifts. The two last are at Ealing, Middx.,[1] and St. James, Bristol,[2] and bear the hall-marks for 1717 and 1760, respectively.

The salver paten was widely used from the end of the seventeenth century onwards and did not differ in form from those made for secular use.

The eighteenth century produced no new design, but increasing recourse was made to patens resembling dinner plates. These had made their appearance before the middle of the seventeenth century. Their form followed that of the contemporary dinner plates and, indeed, many examples had been in secular use before being presented to a church. Two mid-eighteenth-century patens of this type are illustrated. The one of 1756 at Stoke Climsland, Cornwall (Pl. 96*a*), has a gadrooned rim and a coat-of-arms in the centre and could not be recognized as a church piece if it were not associated with a chalice. The other (Pl. 106) belongs to the superb set of plate made by Butty & Dumee in 1766 for Durham Cathedral. The inscription, PANIS QUEM FRANGIMUS COMMUNIO CORPORIS CHRISTI EST, leaves no doubt as to its use. What is less easy to explain is the presence in the centre of the arms of the see of Durham accollé with those of Bishop Cosin, since this good prelate had been dead for almost a century.

C. FLAGONS[3]

When the commissioners of Edward VI visited the churches of the City they discovered two which had acquired silver flagons for the communion wine. These were St. Dionis Backchurch, which had 'j sylver pot cleane gylt ffor the communion tabyll' and weighed 42½ ounces,[4] and St. Margaret, New Fish Street, which owned 'a sylver quart pott'.[5] Both of these were probably got rid of during the reign of Mary.

A silver flagon is heard of at Grantham in 1566,[6] but the earliest survivor is the one made for Wells Cathedral in 1572 by the goldsmith *IP*, who at that

[1] *C.P. Middlesex*, 10.

[2] *C.P. Bristol*, fig. 70.

[3] I have referred throughout to the vessels for the communion wine as 'flagons'. In Elizabethan times they were known as 'pots', the name 'flagon' being reserved for a stoppered bottle with or without a chain handle (Collins, 33–36). During the reign of James I some uncertainty began to be felt with regard to the proper name for the vessel with which we are concerned. In Bishop Andrewes's 1619 articles for the diocese of Winchester he refers to 'a fair standing pot or stoop of silver', but in his 1625 articles it has become 'a flagon of silver' (*Minor Works*, 114 and 128). In the 1630 inventory of the plate of All Saints, Newcastle-upon-Tyne, are mentioned 'ffoure flagon Potts' (*Proc. Soc. Antiquaries of Newcastle*, iii, 1887, 272–3). The new meaning of the word 'flagon' appears only to have won general acceptance about the time of the outbreak of the Civil War.

[4] Walters, 237.

[5] Ibid. 361.

[6] See above, p. 163, n. 4.

time was supplying most of the communion cups for the diocese. The body is pear-shaped, and round the neck is a band of engraving similar to that found round the bowls of the communion cups. The stem and base are inspired from the same source. The lid is similar to those of the silver-mounted earthenware drinking-jugs which were so popular at the time.

Next in date come the pair of flagons with the 1577 hall-mark provided for the very Protestant church of Cirencester (Pl. 107*b*). These have more bulbous bodies and long, cylindrical necks. Each weighs about 66 ounces, which indicates that the churchwardens had plenty of money available. Virtually the only applied decoration is a fanciful representation of the town engraved on the lid of each (Pl. 124*a*). Another pair of flagons, with the hall-mark for 1583, belong to St. Margaret, Westminster, which was another church with a long-standing Protestant tradition. These are perhaps the only flagons of the bulbous-body design, which date from the reign of Elizabeth I and which were undoubtedly made for sacramental use. The history of all types of communion flagon down to the close of the seventeenth century is much complicated by the fact that the same designs were used both for religious and for secular purposes. Many of the examples now in churches originally adorned the dressers in large houses.[1]

The flagon with the bulbous body was destined to compete in one form or another right down to the nineteenth century with the flagon with a cylindrical body. Amongst the earliest and finest of the church flagons of this type are the pair of 1598 at Corpus Christi College, Oxford. Each is adorned on its front with a cast representation of the arms of the founder.[2]

The cylindrical flagons of the early years of the seventeenth century are perhaps the most attractive which were ever produced. They do not vary much in design, the most notable differences being often in the form of the finial on the lid. The example formerly belonging to Allhallows the Great (Pl. 108*a*) and made in 1608 combines an effect of richness with extreme simplicity.[3] The flagon at Severn Stoke (Pl. 109*a*), near Worcester, is more austerely simple, the only applied decoration being a delightful little representation of the Good Shepherd in contemporary costume, which is engraved thrice round the drum.[4] The flagon made in the same year for St. Mary

[1] I am inclined to include in this category the splendid pair of flagons, made in 1588, at Minster, Cornwall, and those of 1592 at Rendcombe, Glos. Had they been made for church use, it is at least probable that so important a gift would have been recorded by an inscription. Though some flagons spent quite a short time in secular use, quite a number were given to churches in the reign of Charles II. The dresser loaded with plate had gone out of fashion, so that the flagons were no longer wanted at home.

[2] Moffatt, pl. lxiv.

[3] Now the property of St. Michael Paternoster Royal. The front is delicately pounced with a coat-of-arms surrounded by THE GVIFT OF THOMAS KADDY. Below is *This Pott belongeth to the Parish Church of Allhallowes in Thamstreet London 1608.*

[4] Inscribed: *Thomas Chapleyne et Joan his wife.*

Abbots, Kensington (Pl. 108*b*), is richly decorated with flowers and dolphins, so that those not familiar with seventeenth-century church plate might suspect that it was made for secular use. There is, however, no particular reason for doubting that this example went straight to the church. It is quite clear that decoration of this class did not appear incongruous to donors, as Lady (later Duchess) Dudley picked on flagons so ornamented for all her early benefactions.[1]

Whereas collectors of domestic silver have learnt to eschew tankards with spouts, since the latter have usually been added in Victorian times, the cylindrical communion flagon with a spout is found quite often in the reigns of James I and Charles I. The church of St. Margaret, Lynn, has a series of five, ranging from 1614 to 1639. An example of 1618, formerly belonging to St. Anne, Blackfriars (Pl. 111*b*),[2] will serve to illustrate this design, which, however, never ousted the spoutless pattern.[3]

The commonest type of flagon throughout the seventeenth century was one with a cylindrical body with no applied decoration other than engraving, and a rounded lid without any knob or finial. An example of 1636, originally the property of St. John Zachery (Pl. 111*a*), illustrates this variety, which is found scattered all over England. The particular distinction of the present example, and of its pair, lies in the verses inscribed round their skirted bases.[4]

In the hands of a first-class goldsmith the plain cylindrical flagon could achieve real distinction. The *hound sejant* goldsmith was one of these, and his standard design is illustrated by one of the flagons which he made for the private chapel of Sir Robert Shirley, Bart., at Staunton Harold (Pl. 111*a*). The treatment of the handle, which has a row of tapering pellets down its back and a nicely chased cherub on the butt, is very characteristic. It is curious that this goldsmith, who made a speciality of chalices and covered patens in the Gothic style, should only once have attempted a Gothic flagon. At Pembroke College, Cambridge,[5] is a flagon with a pear-shaped body, short spout, flat lid, and a scroll handle. Its foot is hexagonal with incurved sides and cherub 'knops' similar to those on his Gothic chalices. The companion to it was made in

[1] Ladbroke, 1623; Ashow, Kenilworth, Leek Wootton, Warw., 1638; Acton, Middx. 1639.

[2] Now belonging to St. Andrew by the Wardrobe.

[3] Reference may be made at this point to an extremely interesting jug-shaped flagon belonging to St. Werburgh, Bristol (Pl. 110). It bears the same quaint inscription (p. 230) as appears on the very unusual chalice (Pl. 75) which was also made in 1619 and presented to the same church. Four other churches possess flagons of this form (Holy Trinity, Hull, 1606; Tong, Salop., 1606; Monken Hadley, Middx., 1609; and St. Martin with All Saints, Oxford, 1610). The Bristol example would appear to be the only one which was made for religious use. All the others seem to have spent a few years in domestic use.

[4] Now belonging to St. Anne and St. Agnes. For the inscription see p. 233.

[5] For an illustration see Jones, *Cambridge*, pl. xxv. Though in the photograph they look like medieval cruets, it should be remembered that they are 10 inches high.

1669 by another goldsmith who also earned a reputation for his Gothic work.[1]

The pair of flagons (Pl. 112*a*) made by M. Houser for Bishop Cosin's chapel at Auckland are unlike any others in the country but similar to those which were being made at the time in Lutheran Germany and Scandinavia. They are richly embossed with ornament derived from fish forms in a style which is German rather than Dutch, and which serves to frame a representation of a scriptural scene on either side.

The flagons made for the coronation of Charles II which are now at St. James's, those presented to St. George's Chapel by the Companions of the Order of the Garter in 1662, and those made in 1664 for the Duke of York (Pl. 112*b*), are all from the same design, although the last is by a different hand. The choice of flagons decorated all over with feathers was perhaps due to a memory that there had been such in the destroyed plate of the Chapel Royal of Charles I. As far back as 1521 the inventory of the royal plate[2] had included 'two greate gilte pottis chased w^t^ fethers', and it seems likely that when in the reign of Elizabeth I a demand arose for flagons for the Chapel Royal, these existing flagons were assigned to it. The only important difference between these three pairs of flagons is that the oval cartouche on the front of the first two is engraved with the Good Shepherd, whilst on the third pair there is the arms of the Duke of York, whose *DL* cipher appears also on the lid.

The flagons given after the Restoration by the aged Duchess Dudley show that her taste had progressed with the times. The flagons at Pateshull, Northants[3] (1663), and Bidford-on-Avon, Warw. (1664), are identical. As can be seen from the illustration of the latter (Pl. 113*b*), they are of the familiar cylindrical form but are embossed all over with flowers except for a cartouche with the Sacred Monogram, which is flanked by two angels. A pair of flagons at Christ Church Cathedral, Oxford (Pl. 113*a*), which belong to the service of plate made in 1660–1, is also richly embossed with large flowers, but it is curious that the decoration includes no religious symbol whatever.

Jug-shaped flagons of a much more pleasing outline than those provided for Auckland were produced by several of the best goldsmiths active in the reign of Charles II. The goldsmith, whose mark was *ID in monogram*, who made in 1672 the flagon for Easton Mauduit, Northants (Pl. 114), is not well known, but was evidently an artist of great ability. On the other hand the goldsmith, whose mark was *RL above a fleur-de-lis*,[4] who made the three flagons (Pl. 115) and all of the rest of the plate for St. James, Piccadilly, in 1683, was perhaps the best maker of church plate at a very good period. The simpler flagons which

[1] *IB above a crescent* (Jackson, *Goldsmiths*, 130).

[2] *Assoc. Architectural Soc. Reports*, xvii, 1884, 190.

[3] *C.P. Northants*, 226.

[4] Jackson, *Goldsmiths*, 140.

he made four years later for the Royal Hospital, Chelsea, are no less successful. The flagon belonging to the set of plate of 1692 at Swanage, Dorset (Pl. 116), shows another essay with the same form. The virtually unknown goldsmith whose mark showed *three storks*[1] chose to decorate it with alternate fluting and gadrooning, such as was popular on domestic plate but very rare on religious.

The plain cylindrical flagon remained the most popular type throughout the eighteenth century and was used practically exclusively during the first quarter. The church of St. Margaret Pattens possesses a pair (Pl. 117*a*) made by Timothy Ley and bearing the hall-marks for 1709 and 1710. They are beautifully proportioned, but are free of ornament except for the Sacred Monogram and the donor's arms which are engraved on the front.[2]

The celebrated Paul de Lamerie entered his mark at Goldsmiths' Hall on 5 February 1712, but his earliest known flagon was made in 1717 for Milton Clevedon, near Shepton Mallet. It follows the design which he used with only slight variations for the next twelve years and which is here illustrated by the one made in 1727 for West Drayton, Middx.[3] (Pl. 117*b*).

During the first half of the eighteenth century some fresh forms of bulbous flagons made their appearance. The pair at St. Nicholas Cole Abbey (Pl. 118*a*) retain much of the form of their Elizabethan predecessors, but the one (Pl. 118*b*) made in 1730 by Gabriel Sleath for presentation by the Duke of Bedford to the new church of St. George, Bloomsbury, is, however, more happily proportioned. In 1730 Paul de Lamerie made a set of plate for the church of St. John, Eltham, Kent, which included the earliest example[4] of his second flagon design which was repeated with only slight variations in almost all his later orders. The flagon given by Mrs. Strangways Horner in 1747 to Melbury Osmund, Dorset, is fairly typical (Pl. 119*a*). It will be seen that he seems to have tried merging the cylindrical and the bulbous types. On the front is engraved the Sacred Monogram, whilst three cherubs are engraved over the mouldings of the foot. These last appear on most of the other examples but, although carefully executed, are rather ineffective. A flagon made in 1740 by Gabriel Sleath for St. Mary, Woolwich (Pl. 119*b*) affords an interesting contrast to Lamerie's design and a good understanding of the value of well-finished cast details on a large and solid piece, even though its form is simple.

An entirely fresh approach is shown in the flagon given by Mrs. Elizabeth Prowse to Stoke Climsland, Cornwall (Pl. 120*a*), in 1756. The maker, William Cripps, has produced a very beautiful ewer with a double scroll handle.

A firm, apparently of French extraction, Francis Butty & Nicholas Dumee,

[1] Ibid. 147.

[2] Also *The Gift of Sir George Thorold, Kt. Bt. and Alderman of the City of London, 1710.*

[3] Inscribed: *The Gift of Rupert Billingsley Esq. & Mary his wife to the Parish Church of West Drayton in Middlx.*

[4] Moir Carnegie, *Church Plate of the Hundred of Blackheath*, 1939, pl. xiv.

achieved a real success with the flagons (Pl. 120*b*) which they made in 1766 as part of the service for Durham Cathedral. They are splendid examples of late Rococo art, and we need not grudge praise to the designer because he has put to good account his experience gained in designing coffee-pots.

On the whole the Adam style did not affect church plate very profoundly, but the piece which the goldsmiths found most susceptible to classicizing was the flagon. These were changed into finely proportioned ewers and, once more, we note the result of experience gained in the making of domestic plate. The example illustrated (Pl. 121*a*) was made in 1791 by Edward Fennell as a gift from William Harris of Kenegye to Madron church in Cornwall.

It was unfortunate that the first opportunity of producing an important service of church plate came to Paul Storr in 1821 after he had separated from the firm of Rundell, Bridge & Rundell, whose second partner, John Bridge, was always brimful of ideas. The flagons (Pl. 121*b*) which form part of the service given by the Duke of York to the new church of St. Pancras are meticulously decorated with classical ornament, but the form is poor.

At the time of the accession of George IV, John Bridge was sixty-five years of age, but was still receptive of new ideas. The firm had never done much church work, although its trade card advertised '*Dressing* and *Church Plate* in *Sets*', so that when their royal master ordered a service of chapel plate for the Royal Pavilion, Brighton, fresh thinking had to be done—all the more so because the Gothic style was stipulated. Though the chalices and candlesticks were completed fairly promptly, the form of the flagons was still undecided in 1827, when the young Augustus Welby Pugin was called in. The ageing goldsmith may well have boggled at the boy's design (Pl. 122*a*), and nothing was completed before the king's death. By that date Archbishop Harcourt's order for plate for York Minster had come along. We may still see some trace of Pugin in the finials of the lids of the York flagons (Pl. 112*b*), but the rest is in a much more restrained form of Gothic—and more practical, since there is not an ornamental knot at the point where the handle would be gripped!

D. ICONOGRAPHY AND INSCRIPTIONS ON CHALICES, PATENS, AND FLAGONS

Whereas in Part I it was quite convenient to deal with the iconography and inscriptions on chalices apart from those on patens, it is more practical to treat them as a single subject when dealing with post-Reformation times. Furthermore, communion flagons have to be added to the group. The justification for this is the fact that it was the practice to consecrate the wine in the flagon before it was poured out. As a consequence of this practice, any subject or inscription which was appropriate for a chalice was equally so for a flagon.

The overlapping between chalice and paten subjects is not so obvious, but they were not kept rigidly apart.

ICONOGRAPHY

Compared with the wealth of iconography displayed on medieval plate, that on post-Reformation pieces must appear meagre, but it is not without interest.

None of the church plate produced during the reigns of Edward VI and Elizabeth I appears to have been decorated with any religious subject unless we include the *Sacred Monogram*, which has been used uninterruptedly. On Anglican plate this was usually represented by the letters IHS with a cross above and three nails below. On Recusant plate there was a tendency latterly to add a heart below the nails. The heart also appears on some Anglican examples, and it would seem that no rigid rule was observed. At any rate, Benjamin Rhodes made use of both designs on the Anglican plate which he engraved for the customers of Sir Richard Hoare at the close of the seventeenth century (Pl. 124*d*).[1]

Anglican post-Reformation iconography really begins from the days of Lancelot Andrewes. The engraving of religious subjects on chalices, patens, and flagons remained a High Church characteristic, and the custom died away almost completely after the Revolution.

Subjects were derived from the New Testament. The only exception appears to be the *Sacrifice of Isaac* which is engraved on a chalice and paten of 1635 belonging to St. Botolph, Aldgate (Pl. 77*a*).

Considering the repugnance felt against the representation of the *Crucifix*, it is a little surprising that it appears at all on the plate under consideration. It occurs, however, on a chalice of 1607 presented to Melbury Sampford church, Dorset, by Grace, wife of John Strangways, and again on a chalice made by the same goldsmith[2] in 1611, belonging to Weston St. Mary, Lincs. It appears on both chalice and paten (Pl. 123*d*), with the 1638 hall-mark, at Kingerby, Lincs. The Restoration period provides no example, but there are three dating from the first thirty years of the eighteenth century.[3] Thereafter the subject disappears.

The *Crucifix* accompanied by the *Instruments of the Passion* appears inside the covered patens given in 1638 to Ashow, Kenilworth, and Leek Wootton churches in Warwickshire by that stalwart Anglican, Lady (later Duchess) Dudley. The choice is remarkable since the subject was much affected by the Recusants.

[1] His account book covering the years 1693 to 1698 is at Hoare's Bank, by whose courtesy I have been allowed to illustrate a sample of his work.

[2] *T over W* (Jackson, *Goldsmiths*, 100).

[3] Thornton-in-Lonsdale, Yorks., 1703; Rose Ash, Devon, 1716; and Henley, Suffolk, 1728. The last is the *Crucifixion* and is obviously copied from some tail-piece in a prayer book.

The other New Testament subjects which appear are the *Flight into Egypt* and the *Temptation* on a chalice of 1684 at Ealing, the *Last Supper* on a chalice of 1625 at Steynton, Pembs., and on a paten of 1728 at Henley, Suffolk. The chalice for this last is engraved with the *Flagellation*.

The most interesting subject added during the first half of the seventeenth century was the *Good Shepherd*. A subject often found in Early Christian art, it had been curiously neglected during the Middle Ages. Its reappearance in England is not matched abroad, so that it may be regarded as an especially Anglican type. The first reference to the use of the subject on a piece of plate occurs in the account of the chapel of Bishop Andrewes, where there is mentioned a 'Chalice having on the outside of the bowl Christ with the lost sheep on his shoulders'.[1] We may reasonably suppose that the bishop had used this subject because he knew the passage in Tertullian,[2] which showed that the early Christians used chalices decorated with the *Good Shepherd*. It would be too strong to say that Andrewes rediscovered the *Good Shepherd*, since several London printers were using an attractive little cut of the subject on the title-pages of religious books published in the latter years of Elizabeth I. Andrewes, however, certainly attached great importance to the subject, to which he alluded for the first time in a sermon delivered before the queen at Greenwich in 1590.[3] A much fuller dissertation occurs in a draft for a sermon prepared, but never delivered, at Easter, 1625.[4]

The *Good Shepherd* appears on four pieces made during the bishop's lifetime. The earliest exactly dated representation is on a flagon of 1619 at Severn Stoke, Worcs. (Pl. 123*a*), where the figure is thrice shown in contemporary dress on the drum of a flagon. This may be a few years later than the older chalice at St. John's College, Oxford (Pl. 80), which bears no hall-mark, but is probably some years earlier than the chalice and flagon at Peterhouse, Cambridge. On the Oxford and Cambridge, and on all the later renderings of the subject, the figure is dressed in 'New Testament costume'.

Between the death of Andrewes and the outbreak of the Civil War the subject appears upon a paten accompanying a chalice made by John Plummer and bearing the York hall-mark for 1637, at Bransdale, West Riding, and on the 1640 chalice (Pl. 123*b*) at Staunton Harold, Leics. During the Commonwealth it appears on a flagon of 1653 at Kirk German, I.O.M., and on much

[1] *Minor Works*, 1854, xcvii.

[2] 'Cui ille si forte patrocinabitur pastor, quam in calice depingis' (that shepherd will play the patron whom you depict on your chalice), *De Pudicitia*, x. Laud was able to produce the quotation at his trial (W. Prynne, *Canterburie's Doome*, 1646, 464–5).

[3] *Works*, ii, 1841, 29.

[4] 'You may see Him in the parable, coming with His lost sheep on His shoulders. That one sheep is the image of us all. So careful He was, as He laid him on His own neck, to be sure; which is the true portraiture or representation of his ἀναγωγή (ibid. iii. 89–90).

of the plate made by the *hound sejant* goldsmith for the private chapels of his Anglican Royalist clients. At Wimpole, Cambs., it appears on the alms bowl (Pl. 125) as well as on the chalice (Pl. 123*c*) made for Sir Thomas Chicheley.

In the early years after the Restoration the subject maintained its popularity. It appears on the fronts of the flagons made in 1662 for St. George's Chapel, Windsor, and on the lids of those made for the Duke of York in 1664 and now at Buckingham Palace. In the later years of the reign the *Good Shepherd* fell into disuse. Its last appearances are on chalices at Clipsham, Rutl., and Durston, Som., dated 1691 and 1695 respectively.

Found in association with the *Good Shepherd* on the plate in Bishop Andrewes's chapel was the star seen at the Nativity. This was another subject which had not been fully exploited during the Middle Ages. On the paten-cover of the chalice was engraved the *Wise Men's Star*. Andrewes clearly attached great importance to the star, to which he refers repeatedly in his Christmas sermons from 1611 onwards. Some of the sermons are almost entirely devoted to it, but by far the most striking passage occurs in the one preached before James I in 1620. It was, he says, 'not only *Stella gentium* but *Stella magorum*, the great men's, the wise men's Star', and 'in the old Ritual of the Church we find on the cover of the canister, wherein was the Sacrament of his body, there was a star engraven to show that now the star leads us thither to His body there'.[1] The star is found engraved on the inside of the covers of the patens of 1653 at Fulham Palace (Pl. 124*c*) and Staunton Harold.[2] The sets to which these belong are also linked by showing another rare subject, the *Crown of Thorns*.[3] This last subject recurs intermittently, a late example being upon the chalices made by Paul Storr in 1821 for St. Pancras (Pl. 93*a*).

The *pelican*, so frequently used as typifying Christ in the Middle Ages, makes a solitary appearance on a chalice of 1633 at Haverfordwest, Pembs., whilst the *Agnus Dei* appears on the paten-cover of the Gothic-style chalice at Lambeth Palace and on the paten-covers of 1676 (Pl. 105*b*) at Ripon Minster. In both of these cases there are grounds for supposing that it appears heraldically,[4] but there seems to be no reason to think that this is the case with the paten-cover of a chalice at St. Mary's Chapel, Castleton, I.O.M.

The range of saints depicted on post-Reformation plate is limited but

[1] *Works*, i, 1841, 247.

[2] Both of these, it has been suggested (p. 207), were made under the direction of Gilbert Sheldon. It does not appear on the similar pieces made at the same time for the Duke of Lennox and now at Rochester Cathedral.

[3] At Fulham on the chalice and at Staunton Harold on the flagons.

[4] It has already been suggested that the Lambeth chalice was made for Archbishop Juxon (p. 206), who may have originally destined it for St. John's College, Oxford, of which he had been president. T. M. Fallow (*C.P. Yorks* ii. 193) remarks that the *Agnus Dei* had been used as a device of the minster before the Reformation.

eccentric. The presence of the *Three Marys* upon the 1610 chalice at Beddgelert, Caern. (Pl. 74), has never been explained, and there is no obvious reason for the presence of St. Peter inside the bowl of the 1619 chalice belonging to St. Werburgh, Bristol (Pl. 75), nor of St. John the Evangelist on the covered paten given by Lady Dudley to Ladbroke, Warw., in 1623.

The medieval practice of engraving upon the sacred vessels a representation of the patron saint continued, but with an altered significance. Whilst representations of saints at large are extremely rare, those of patron saints are not uncommon. Churches still continued to be known by the name of their patron saints, and the appearance of the latter upon the plate merely recorded ownership. Whereas representations of the Virgin were rigorously banned, there appeared no reason why she should not appear upon a pair of patens of 1671 at Southwell Minster, nor upon the chalice of 1674 made for St. Mary Hall, Oxford (Pl. 91*b*). Similarly, St. Michael appears on a chalice of 1726 at St. Michael's Church, Basingstoke, and upon a flagon of 1731 at St. Michael, Coslany, Norwich. It seems unnecessary to labour the point further.[1]

If it was lawful to represent the patron saint upon a piece of plate, the use of his or her emblem was also free of offence. Thus the lily-pot of the Virgin appears on two chalices of 1633 at Southwell Minster, a dove upon two patens of much the same date at St. Columb Major, Cornwall. Most examples in this category come from urban churches, and we need only note the escallop added in the seventeenth century to the bowl of the 1549 communion cup at St. James, Garlickhithe, and the saltire cross over a shaft (arrow) on a paten of 1715 at St. Andrew, Undershaft.[2] One of the most curious extensions of this idea is the coat-of-arms of St. Edmund surmounted by a helm with crest (the wolf holding his head) which are to be found on a set of plate given in 1661 to the church of St. Mary, Bury St. Edmunds.

Cathedral chapters, colleges, and other corporate bodies continued to place their arms upon the altar plate. So, of course, did donors. During the Middle Ages the most convenient place on a chalice for engraving a coat-of-arms was upon the wide-spreading foot. In post-Reformation times the bowl of the chalice or the flat knob of the paten-cover were found more satisfactory.

The Elizabethan flagons at Cirencester are not unique in being engraved

[1] In the bill for plate supplied to Cosin for Peterhouse in 1638 there is a charge for engraving St. Peter upon a flagon (*Cosin Correspondence*, i, Surtees Soc. 1878, 224). This flagon has disappeared, although the earlier one showing the *Good Shepherd* has survived. This rather suggests that there may have been some selective looting during the Civil War, and that the representation of the saint, who was especially associated with popery, justified the disappearance of the flagon.

[2] The parish badge did not necessarily include any allusion to the patron saint. Thus a bell appears on the 1558 paten-cover of St. Michael-le-Belfrey, York, and a bow on the flagon of 1630 belonging to St. Mary-le-Bow. The sheep on the 1674 chalice at Eastchurch in Sheppey is not the *Agnus Dei*, but is allusive to the name of the Isle, as is made clear from the inscription (*Archaeologia Cantiana*, xxvi, 1904, 190).

with a representation of the town to which they belong (Pl. 124*a*). On the two patens of 1675 at Ripon Minster (Pl. 105*b*) are views of the church showing it with its three spires. A view of the east end of the church of St. Peter Port was engraved on a flagon which was sent to the melting-pot in 1845.[1]

INSCRIPTIONS

There is an extraordinary lack of spontaneity about most of the inscriptions on late-medieval church plate. Except when a gift had to be recorded, the inscription appears to have been selected by the goldsmith from a limited stock, whilst the customer seems to have taken very little interest in the matter and did not make a fuss about mistakes.

We find a greater intimacy in the inscriptions on post-Reformation chalices, patens, and flagons. Most plate is without any, so that when there is one, it is the result of someone's order.

It might have been expected that some plate would bear Hebrew inscriptions, seeing that in the centuries following the Reformation a smattering of that language was quite a common accomplishment amongst the learned. Actually, no piece bears anything more recondite than the name of Jehovah.

Greek appears only about a dozen times, beginning in about 1640, and is almost always in the form of New Testament quotations. English and Latin were used throughout, both for original inscriptions and for quotations. The earliest Welsh inscriptions record the gifts of chalices to Llanaelhaiarn, Caern., in 1638, and to Cwm, Flint., in 1647, but the use of the language remained very rare until after 1800.

The inscriptions on post-Reformation plate may be classified as follows:

1. Possessory.
2. Dedicatory and donative.
3. Quotations.
4. Miscellaneous.

Unfortunately there has never been any general regulation ordering that plate should be inscribed with the name of the parish to which it belongs. Such inscriptions can always be taken out, but as most migrations of plate are symptomatic of great slackness it is likely that some at least of the clergy who have taken the chalice from parish *A* on to their next benefice, parish *B*, would not have bothered to remove such an inscription. The lack of such inscriptions have also led to the loss of a considerable amount of plate which had been stored up at the manor or at the house of a churchwarden.

Possessory inscriptions appear to have been encouraged when the medieval chalices of the diocese of Norwich were being converted into communion cups

[1] Photographs from rubbings are, however, preserved in the Lukis Collection in the Priault Library at St. Peter Port.

in the years 1566–7. Norwich communion cups usually have a band round the bowl engraved with some such inscription as ✠ THIS CUP IS FOR THE TOWNE OF ——, OR THIS FOR THE TOEN. The name would be filled in above or below the band if the purchaser were prepared to wait—sometimes they were unwilling, so that the name is missing.

Possessory inscriptions elsewhere are quite often in Latin, particularly in Wales, where the use of English tended to result in obscurity. In Wales, also, there are instances of the inscription not being completed by the name of the parish.[1]

We may pass from these useful but uninspiring inscriptions to the dedicatory and the donative. I have only discovered one inscription recording an actual consecration. This occurs on a pair of flagons belonging to St. Alphege, Greenwich, which are engraved *Sacrum fecit Johannes Roffensis, Ex dono Mariae Squibb, Martij 24, A° 1671.*

Numerous simple and appropriate dedicatory phrases were used—for instance:

In honorem Sanctiss^i Redemptoris mei Jesu Christi (Flagons, 1638, St. Cuthbert, Wells).
Deo et Sacris (Chalice, 1653, Fulham Palace).
Deo Conservatori sacrum (Flagon, 1717, Great Whelnetham, Suffolk).[2]

Most donative inscriptions require no comment. When, however, the personal element was allowed to obtrude the result might be deplorable, as, for instance, in the inscription on a flagon at Stanford-in-the-Vale, Berks., which reads:

This Flaggon is dedicated to the Use of the Altar in the Parish Church of Stanford-in-the-Vale for ever by Joseph Cox Esqr and Kathe. Sophia his Wife as a humble testimony of their Unfeigned thanks to Almighty God for the Recovery of their three children Thomas, Sophia and Charlotte from the smallpox by Inoculation, Ano 1752.

In contrast to this pompous effusion is the simple bathos of *The Poor Widow Gapper's mite* (Chalice, 1629, New Windsor, Berks.), or halting rhymes such as:

The willing donor doth this gift intayle,
To the Great God and little Peryvale.
(Paten, 1625, since destroyed, Perivale, Middx.).

Or, worse:

Walter Jessett which did in Barton live,
Unto this Church did this Flagon give.
(Flagon, 1683, Kintbury, Berks.).

[1] Penaly, Pembs., and Spittal, Pembs.

[2] The following somewhat more quaint inscription appears on the chalice (Pl. 75) and flagon (Pl. 110) at St. Werburgh, Bristol, both dated 1619: *I cannot build unto thee A Temple with Sallomon wherefore I Humble Offer unto thee and Dedicatt to thy Service this vessell Beseeching thee to Receve into the number of thy elect whosoever shall receive out of that great mistery of thine Redempcion and that for Christe sake. Amen.*

It has already been remarked that our late-medieval ancestors found in the Sarum Missal all the texts which they engraved upon their chalices and patens. It was only natural that the reformed Church, which laid so much stress upon biblical study, should have blossomed forth into a much wider range of quotations. These are found in English, Greek, and Latin. As the engraving of texts did not become general until the reign of James I, the Authorized Version appears almost exclusively. With regard to the Latin, the predominant version is that of Beza, which appeared during the reign of Mary—just in time to be seen by the Protestant exiles who had taken refuge in Germany and Switzerland. Beza's version was a conservative one and cannot always be distinguished from the Vulgate. We can, however, find positive traces of the latter on the very early Elizabethan communion cup at Gawsworth, Cheshire, which has a text from John vi. 63, and on another at St. Matthew, Ipswich, which has one from Luke xxii. 19. Thereafter the Vulgate crops up only occasionally, the most extensive use of it being upon the lost set of plate made for St. Paul's after the Restoration.

With the beginning of the seventeenth century it became quite usual to give references with the quotations. This practice became absurd when carried to extremes, as on a chalice of 1638 at Prestbury, Glos., which is engraved:

Luc. 22. 20.	Ps. 116. 13.	1 Cor. 10. 21.	1 Cor. 10. 16.
Calix Testamenti	Calix Salutaris	Calix Domini	Calix Benedictionis.

Just as George Herbert wrote poems shaped as 'Easter Wings', so Lewis Southcomb, rector of Rose Ash, Devon, from 1675 to 1733, got his texts engraved in the form of a cross upon the chalice, paten, and flagon which he presented to his church.[1]

Besides actual quotations from the Bible, many adaptations were also used. Thus John vi. 51 appears as *Christ is the Livinge Breade which came down from Heaven* on the pairs of patens of 1622 and 1633 presented by two members of the Harryson family to St. Mary, Reading, and to All Hallows, Honey Lane.[2]

It will be frequently found that the quotation on the paten is part of the same text which is used on the chalice. Another peculiarity, arising out of the practice of consecrating the wine in the flagon, was that the latter was given a quotation suitable for a chalice. Thus at Bury, Lancs., a flagon is inscribed *Poculum benedictionis cui benedicimus* etc. (1 Cor. x. 16).

Only two of the quotations regularly used in the Middle Ages reappeared at all often after the Reformation. These were Ps. cxvi. 13 (Vulg. cxv), *I will take the cup of salvation* etc., and the other 1 Cor. x. 16, *The cup of Blessing* etc. . . .

[1] Southcomb's generosity to Rose Ash and to Creacombe churches were due to his remorse for not having joined the Non-Jurors. For his story see an article by Major W. H. Wilkin in *Trans. Devon Assoc.* lvii, 1925, 289–305. For his benefactions, ibid. xlii, 1910, 51, 61–62.

[2] Now united to St. Mary-le-Bow.

The bread which we break etc. The earliest appearance of the first of these is on a communion cup of 1567 from St. Olave, Old Jewry, now at St. Margaret, Lothbury.[1] The second part of the second quotation appears for the first time on the Edward VI paten belonging to Christ Church, Bristol.[2] The list of texts considered appropriate for chalices, patens, and flagons in post-Reformation times is quite considerable, but no attempt will be made to list them.[3]

We may now turn to the final category of miscellaneous inscriptions. Of the small groups which compose it, the ejaculations are amongst the more numerous and arrive earliest. These are of two sorts—those provided ready made by the goldsmith, and those added at the request of the customer. In the former category falls ALL HONOR AND GLORY BE VNTO GOD (variously modified), which is to be found on a number of Elizabethan communion cups in Norfolk.[4] Spontaneous ejaculations appear in the reign of James I. They are often in Latin, such as POSSIDET ME IVRE on a chalice of 1609 at Cadoxton-juxta-Neath, Glam., or CHRISTI SANGVIS MEI SALVS on one of 1611 at Andover, Hants. Amongst the quotations on the Staunton Harold plate appears, on the covered paten, MY LOVE IS CRVCIFIED.

Doctrinal inscriptions are quite rare. To this class belong *Non Sacrum non Sacris, He that eateth and drinketh unworthily, eateth and drinketh his own damnation. 1 Cor. xi. 11*, which appears on a chalice of 1626 at Attleborough, Norfolk. Since the administration of the communion to the laity in both bread and wine was one of the few things on which all sixteenth-century Protestants had agreed, it is curious to find a reference to this former dispute on some eighteenth-century plate. On the chalice and flagon of 1737 at Welford, Berks., is inscribed *Tam Laicis quam Clericis*, and on the paten, *Nemini sine Poculo*. Similarly, on a pair of chalices of 1738 at St. Giles, Norwich, is *Calix Laicis non est Denegandu.* A heartfelt protest against the controversies of the time is uttered on a late seventeenth-century paten at Harford, Devon, with the quaint rhyme:

Let sacraments and prayer be more in fashon,
We need not doubt or feare of tolloration.

[1] Many of the chalices which were converted into communion cups in the reign of Elizabeth I must have borne inscriptions. There does not appear to be any other instance of the transfer of the inscription to the new piece. It reads: *Donum Johīs Belgrave quondam vicarii hujus ecclie̅ Sci Olavi ī veteri Judaismo cū hiis sētēciis insertis benedicta sit Scā Trinitas atq. individua Unitas.* On the cover is *Calicem salutaris accipiam et nomen Domini invocabo.*

[2] *C.P. Bristol*, fig. 31.

[3] Only one quotation from a pagan source adorns a post-Reformation chalice. During the Middle Ages Cicero was included amongst the wise men of antiquity, and his statue fills a niche at Chartres Cathedral. On a chalice at Harlaxton, Lincs., are the inscriptions: *Presented by George de Ligne Gregory to the most sacred uses of Established Church at Harlaxton, 1815*, and *Henry Dodwell, B.D. Rector Spartam quam nactus es orna cicero.* Actually Cicero (*Letters to Atticus*, iv. 6) quoted without translating a passage from the *Telephus* of Euripides. The Latin version seems to be adapted from Erasmus.

[4] Great Cressingham, Southey, Stradsett, and North Wootton. A Midland goldsmith preferred GOD SAVE THE QVENE, which appears on paten-covers at Ilmington, Worcs., 1571, and Swepston, Leics., 1577.

There are quite a number of verses of this standard in which the thought has far outstripped the poetic powers of the composer. It is very curious that whilst the Church of England was particularly rich in religious poets in the seventeenth century, none of them appears to have turned his hand to supplying verses for church plate. Christopher Harvey wrote feelingly in *The Synagogue* upon the subject of 'Communion Plate', and so filled a gap left by his master, George Herbert in *The Temple*, but attempted no inscriptions.

There was only one serious attempt to write a poem suitable for engraving upon a piece of church plate. I have found no clue as to its author, but it is inscribed upon a pair of flagons (Pl. 111*a*), presented in 1636 by Mary Clarkson and Francis Draxe to St. John Zachery, which have descended to St. Anne and St. Agnes. On the flagon presented by the former is:

This potts for holy wine, This wine's pure blood,
This blood true life, This life containes all good.
Not potts, but Soules are fitt to hould such wine
Such blood, such life, such good. O Christ take mine.

On the flagon given by Francis Draxe is:

My Saviour by an art Divine
Conveighes his blood to me in wine.
Faith spies the secrett and reveales
As much to love, love closely steales
My heart into this pott when graven this stood
This for thy wine, sweet Lord, This for thy blood.

The first of these verses appears again on a flagon given in 1709 by Mrs. Mary Crossley to Friern Barnet church, Middlesex.

If England was rich in religious poets, she also owned many specialists in Latin epigrammatic verse. These also contributed nothing to the adornment of church plate. An inscription upon a chalice given in 1638 by Edmund Alston, rector, to Newton-by-Sudbury, Suffolk, may be of medieval origin. It reads:

Hauriat hinc populus vitam de Sanguine Sacro,
Inflicto aeternus quam fudit vulnere Cristus.

It reappears on a chalice of 1693 at Winterslow, Wilts.

It is strange that whereas the great religious poets Crashaw, Donne, and Herbert seem to have contributed no verses for the engraving upon church plate, Ben Jonson should have entered the field. The fact that he did so appears to have been overlooked, since when Christopher Markham catalogued the chapel plate at Burghley House,[1] Stamford, he failed to note that the poem engraved on the underneath of the paten is an abbreviation of one which appears

[1] *C.P. Northants*, 58.

in the folio edition of Jonson entitled *An Epigram on William Lord Burleigh Lord High Treasurer of England, presented upon a plate of gold to his son, Robert, Earl of Salisbury, when he was also Treasurer*. The paten is a shallow silver-gilt dish, 6¾ inches in diameter, and bears the 1609 hall-mark.[1] The inscription is very lightly engraved and runs round and round on the underside. It reads as follows:

If thou wouldst knowe the Vertues of Mankinde,
Reade heere in one what thou in all canst finde.
And goe no farther, lett this cirkle be
Thy Vnivers though his Epitome.
Cecill the graue, the wiſe, the greate, the goode;
What is there more that can ennoble blood.
The Orphants piller the true subiectes shield,
The poore man's ſtoore howſe, the iust ſervants feilde.
The only faithfull watchman of this Realme,
That in all tempeſtes neuer quit the helme.
Whoſe worthy sonne beſides his oune highe graces
Inheritts all his vertues, all his places.
—To the memorye of W Lo: Burleigh,
late high Treasurer of Englande.

It does not seem necessary to criticize the poem on the grounds either of suitability or veracity, about which there can hardly be two opinions. It may well be asked, however, whether there was ever any 'plate of gold'? It would seem to be most unlikely. The printed poem inserts ten extra lines after the ninth of the engraved version. A plate of gold large enough to take the whole poem in legible characters would have been beyond the means of the poet. To have employed an engraver who specialized in minute engraving would have defeated the donor's aim by diverting the admiration of the recipient away from the poem to the virtuosity of the craftsman.

[1] Maker's mark *SO in quatrefoil.*

VI

ALTAR PLATE

A. ALMS BASINS, ALTAR DISHES, ETC.

IN the reign of Edward VI, when the citizens of London were anxiously awaiting the pillaging of their churches, it occurred to the churchwardens of six parishes[1] that they might be able to preserve some of their capital by investing in a silver basin to collect the alms. They followed out the idea with varying degrees of confidence. The basin of St. Peter upon Cornhill weighed only 15 ounces,[2] that of St. Peter, Billingsgate, 17 ounces,[3] but that of St. Michael, Cornhill, ran to 40¼ ounces,[4] whilst the churchwardens of St. Martin Outwich, got 'a faire Bason of Silver parcell gilte weying xlii ounces' from a goldsmith named Jasper Fisher.[5] Though these basins probably escaped the pillage by the king's commissioners, they were probably sacrificed a little later in order to provide funds for the refurnishing of the churches under Mary. At any rate, none of them appear to have survived.

The reappearance of silver alms basins in the reign of James I may be regarded as further evidence of the increased prestige of the national Church. Examples are, however, rare, since most churchwardens regarded a second chalice or a communion flagon as more desirable. From the artistic point of view they are not very interesting. Thus the basin of 1619 belonging to St. Stephen Walbrook is rather larger than usual, being 16 inches in diameter. Its decoration is, however, confined to a raised boss in the centre which is enamelled with the initials of the church, *SS* linked together.

A small basin of the same year, in the chapel at Longleat, is more important. It has a flat rim engraved with *He that giveth to the poore lendeth to the Lord; and the Lord will recompence him that which he hath given*, whilst in the centre is set a cast medallion depicting Our Lord washing the feet of the apostles.[6]

With the replacement of the communion table at the east end of the chancel, the alms basin began to acquire a new function. In the plan of the chapel of Bishop Andrewes the 'bason for oblations' is shown,[7] probably propped against a cushion, in the middle of the altar, between the candlesticks. It occupied, therefore, the place of the altar cross of medieval times. Andrewes

[1] Listed on p. 130, n. 2. [2] Walters, 573. [3] Ibid. 213.

[4] Ibid. 500. [5] Ibid. 386, 398.

[6] Diameter, 11¾ inches. Maker's mark, *DB above a crescent*. The same medallion appears in the centre of the dish of 1617 presented by the 7th Duke of Norfolk to the city of Norwich. It was made by a different goldsmith. [7] B.M. Harley, 3795, f. 23.

does not seem fully to have realized the artistic possibilities of this arrangement for we know nothing specific about the decoration of the basin, which weighed only 30 ounces[1] and cannot have been much larger than the one at Longleat.

It was, perhaps, the Earl of Arundel who first exploited to the full the artistic possibilities of the new position. Amongst the plate supplied by Christian van Vianen to St. George's Chapel, Windsor, in 1637, were a great basin weighing 210 ounces and two lesser weighing together 251 oz. 15 dwt. We are told 'these three Basons contained the whole History of Christ in chased work'.[2] In later times such pieces would have been called altar dishes, since they served a purely decorative purpose.

By the outbreak of the Civil War most of the cathedrals probably possessed a substantial alms basin to occupy the centre of the altar. We know of no elaborately decorated examples, so that it is likely that they mostly carried no more than the Sacred Monogram.

The alms basins supplied by the *hound sejant* goldsmith for the Anglican private chapels set up during the Commonwealth were sometimes so decorated,[3] but the one acquired by Sir Thomas Chicheley for his private chapel at Wimpole, Cambs. (Pl. 125), illustrates the versatility of this craftsman. It is oval with a lobed border, whilst the raised centre is engraved with the Good Shepherd. The same goldsmith also introduced another extremely simple but effective design showing a cross in the bottom of the basin. This appears amongst the set of undated Gothic plate at Pembroke College, Cambridge,[4] and was later imitated by the goldsmith who made the basin presented to Norwich Cathedral (Pl. 126) in 1665.[5]

Nearly all the alms basins (or altar dishes) of primary importance were made between 1660 and 1700. The earliest group of these consists of the examples at St. James's Palace, Auckland Castle, and Buckingham Palace (from Whitehall). As is made clear by the correspondence relating to the second of these (p. 186, n. 1 above) the craftsman who really did the work was named M. Houser, whose method would seem to have been to decorate basins made in the rough by other goldsmiths, who saw to their hall-marking. In the process of chasing up the marks tended to get obliterated—the maker's mark on the first of the above is illegible; those on the Auckland and Buckingham Palace basins are not the same.[6] Though the Last Supper forms the central theme on all three, it is

[1] W. Prynne, *Canterburie's Doome*, 1646, 124; Andrewes, *Minor Works*, 1854, xcviii.

[2] E. Ashmole, *Institution of the Order of the Garter*, 1672, 493.

[3] Rochester Cathedral (from Cobham Hall), 1653; Staunton Harold, 1654; also Buckingham Palace (from Whitehall), 1664.

[4] Jones, *Cambridge*, pl. xxv.

[5] The same design was used on a paten, 9 inches in diameter, made for St. Cuthbert, York, by a local goldsmith in 1673.

[6] *FL with a bird* (?) and *HG*, respectively. It should also be noted that the former is only 21 inches in diameter, whereas the latter is 37 inches.

represented differently on each occasion. The fish forms which frame the subsidiary subjects round the rim are identical, but the Auckland dish has only one subject in common with the two in London. The two sets of subjects are as follows:

AUCKLAND (Pl. 127)	BUCKINGHAM PALACE (Pl. 128) AND ST. JAMES'S PALACE
Flight into Egypt.	Christ washing the feet of the apostles.
Temptation.	Christ and the disciples on the road to Emmaus.
Agony in the garden.	Christ showing himself to the apostles after the Resurrection.[1]
Christ and the disciples on the road to Emmaus.	Pentecost.

The large basin and the two smaller ones at St. George's Chapel, Windsor, would seem to have been decorated by Houser, although they are not directly linked either by design or ornament.[2] The large one is embossed with Christ washing Peter's feet (Pl. 129), whilst the rim is decorated with panels of fruit alternating with cherubs. The two smaller ones show Christ and the Little Child and the Last Supper (quite a different version from those on the large dishes), and are framed within rims of similar design.

Reverting to the subject of the adornment of the altar, it may be noted that the large dishes at St. James's and Buckingham Palace were accompanied by a pair of smaller ones. Those at the former chapel are decorated with flowers and cherubs, whilst those at the latter carry the Sacred Monogram. St. George's was not unique in having three basins with figure subjects, since the same arrangement obtained at St. Paul's, where there were available five large basins, three of which may have dated from the reign of Charles II, whilst the others were given by Archdeacon Smith in 1699.[3] The former group comprised one basin with the Last Supper, another with an angel carrying a scroll inscribed with the Greek version of the offertory sentence from Hebrews xiii. The third was engraved with the Sacred Monogram.

The archdeacon's basins were decorated with the Last Supper and the Widow's Mite and were accompanied by appropriate inscriptions from the Vulgate.[4]

The alms dishes attributed to Houser just miss being first class, and are unquestionably surpassed by the superb example presented to St. James,

[1] This subject has been wrongly described as Christ sending out the apostles.

[2] On the other hand, I am inclined to exclude from this group the basin embossed with the Last Supper, bearing the hall-mark for 1668 and the maker's mark *IB*, which was given to King's College, Cambridge, by Dr. Thomas Page (Jones, *Cambridge*, lxv). Though the ornament is derived from much the same source, the workmanship seems different.

[3] J. P. Malcolm, *Londinium Redivivum*, 1807, iii. 145.

[4] On the former Luke xxii. 16 and John xvi. 16, and on the latter the two offertory sentences, 2 Cor. ix. 6 and viii. 12.

Piccadilly (Pl. 130) in 1683. Once more the central subject is the Last Supper, the rim being decorated with cherubs and fruit separating little panels depicting the Annunciation, Nativity, Crucifixion, and Resurrection. Like the rest of the plate of the church, it bears the maker's mark *RL above a fleur-de-lis*, on whose artistic skill comment has already been made.

The only other surviving seventeenth-century basins with figure subjects were made by Francis Garthorne in 1691. The one belonging to the chapel of St. Peter ad Vincula[1] shows the Supper at Emmaus and is much superior to the other at St. Margaret, Westminster, which has the Last Supper.

The period 1660–1700 also saw the production of a considerable range of finely embossed and chased basins. The central motif for the massive example made in 1684 for Westminster Abbey (Pl. 131*a*) is the arms of the founder, Edward the Confessor, which to modern taste appear less incongruous than those of the donor, which were freely used in this conspicuous position, as in the case of the basin engraved with the arms of Robert, Earl of Ailesbury, made in the following year for St. Bartholomew the Less (Pl. 131*b*). The basin made in 1694 from the alms collected at the consecration of the chapel at Trinity College, Oxford (Pl. 132*a*), is equally fine, but has the Sacred Monogram as the central subject. None of these three bears the mark of a noted goldsmith.

The use of an engraved subject on an alms basin could only be artistically effective if it were to be used in a relatively small building. Only two attempts at this type of decoration appear to have been made during the eighteenth century. Both are of great distinction. In 1706 Isaac Liger received from the 2nd Earl of Warrington the commission for an alms dish for the chapel at Dunham Massey (Pl. 133). It is superbly engraved with the Deposition from the Cross. At the bottom is inscribed *Ann. Car. jnv. S. G. sculp*. The treatment of the subject is certainly in the style of Annibale Carracci, although the original design has not been located. The engraver was clearly Simon Gribelin, a native of Blois, who came to England in about 1680 and who published *A Book of Ornaments useful to all Artists* six years before he decorated the present piece.[2]

The other engraved dish belongs to St. Lawrence Jewry (Pl. 134*b*). It bears the hall-mark for 1750 and the mark of John Payne. There is no clue as to the actual engraver of the Last Supper.

On the whole, eighteenth-century alms basins are disappointing.[3] The

[1] H. D. R. Sitwell, *The Crown Jewels*, 1953, pl. xxii. Another basin made by the same artist and showing the same subject was formerly in the chapel at Dublin Castle and is now at Christ Church Cathedral.

[2] 'He executed a great number of small plates on gold, silver and copper; chiefly for books, but was fittest to engrave patterns for goldsmiths work' according to Horace Walpole (*Catalogue of Engravers in England*, 1763, 107–8). For a fuller account see my article in *Apollo Magazine*, June 1957.

[3] Embossed figure subjects were out of fashion in the eighteenth century. There is, however, at King's Nympton, Devon, a basin with the Last Supper, bearing the mark of Magdalene Feline and the

example made by Francis Garthorne for Stoke Newington in 1710 is extremely effective (Pl. 132*b*) and it is a pity that other goldsmiths did not have recourse to the use of embossed rays to emphasize the engraved Sacred Monogram which they used so freely.[1] In contrast to it is the basin made by Thomas Heming in 1765 for the Portland Chapel (now demolished) at the expense of its foundress Lady Mary Cavendish Harley, widow of the 2nd Duke of Portland. The oval form must, even in that age, have suggested a meat dish, and if a sense of decency restricted the size of the representation of the donor's arms, it also rendered them artistically ineffective (Pl. 135). The same criticism can be levelled against another type of subject, the patron saint, which was occasionally used, as on the basin of 1710 belonging to St. Paul's church, Shadwell (Pl. 134*a*).

Few of the alms basins produced in the early nineteenth century are of much artistic interest. The one which forms part of the altar service made by Paul Storr in 1821 as a gift from the Duke of York to the new church of St. Pancras (Pl. 136) shows impeccable workmanship, but the wealth of correctly rendered classical ornament can only be justified by recalling the peculiarly archaeological character of Henry Inwood's design for the church itself.

Alms basins were, of course, of all sizes, and merged into collecting plates. These last were modelled on contemporary dinner plates and, indeed, many had once served as such. Out of these was developed the collecting plate with a handle. A pair of these, made by John Babbage of Exeter in 1743, are at St. Ives, Cornwall (Pl. 137*b*), and are fairly typical.

Various devices were tried out in order that the exact extent of the generosity of each member of the congregation should not become public knowledge. At the chapel at Tabley Hall, Cheshire (Pl. 137*a*), is a charming little money-box, 3⅝ inches high, made by a goldsmith whose mark was *TC above a fish*, and bearing what appears to be the London hall-mark for 1677.

An equally original idea was developed at St. Aubin's, Jersey, which had two tankard-shaped collecting-boxes (Pl. 137*c*) made by a local goldsmith in 1750.

At Milford, Hants, there is a tray 4¾ inches by 2¼ inches, with a detachable cover over two-thirds of its length, so that the coin should slide out of sight. To judge from the engraving of the names of the subscribers, it would seem to have been made at the end of the seventeenth century.[2] A collecting-box on

hall-mark for 1756. The rendering would be classed as crude if it were not made grotesque by the inclusion in the scene of representations of the chalice, paten, and flagon which also formed part of the benefaction (*Trans. of the Devon Assoc.* xliii, 1910, 60).

[1] The banality of the church plate issuing from the workshop of Paul de Lamerie is illustrated by the basin belonging to the set of plate presented to Eltham, Kent, by Stephen Ram in 1730. In the engraved centre is the Sacred Monogram. The same motif is repeated thrice, alternating with cherubs, round the rim (Moir Carnegie, *Church Plate of the Hundred of Blackheath*, 1939, 36).

[2] The only mark is that of a local goldsmith, *NLV in monogram*.

the same lines, but shaped more like a slipper, is at St. Mary, Burnham Westgate, Norfolk. It was made by John Deacon & Co. and bears the 1770 hall-mark.

Those who liked an appropriate quotation on their alms basin seldom strayed beyond the offertory sentences.[1] The trouble was to know where to stop. On a dish of 1688 at St. Peter, Thanet, and on another of 1701 at St. Oswald, Durham, are inscribed no fewer than five offertory sentences.

Donative inscriptions are usually simple and in good taste, but some donors could not resist recording their gratitude in a manner which appears strange two and a half centuries later. Thus on the basin at Aston Somerville, Glos., is inscribed: *I John Parry gave this to God who preserved my life under the Colick and the feaver and my eight children under the smallpox 1683*. Similarly, on another belonging to St. Benet, Paul's Wharf, is another of 1712 with: *This is dedicated to the Great God of Abraham, Isaac, and Jacob, the Father of Our Lord Jesus Christ who has redeemed my soul and reserved my body. His name be glorified for ever by me Eleonor James*. There is much too much about Eleonor James on the plate of this church and on that of St. Mary le Strand.[2] She must have been a very tiresome parishioner!

B. BIBLES AND BOOKS OF COMMON PRAYER

The richly bound books of the Gospels and Epistles placed on the high altars of large medieval churches were replaced at the Reformation by a Bible and a Book of Common Prayer. Amongst the plate of Elizabeth I in 1574[3] were:

Item the Couering of a Bible of siluer and guilt faire wrought poiz ciiij^{xx}iiij.
Item the Couering of another booke of Commone praier in Englishe of the like siluer guilt likewise wrought iiij^{xx}xviij oz. quarter.

There are no references to the presence of such volumes in the accounts of the chapel of Bishop Andrewes nor in those of Little Gidding, but they appear to have formed part of Laud's scheme of altar arrangement. Included in the service of plate acquired in 1634 for York Minster at the expense of Charles I were a Bible (Pl. 138*a*) and a Prayer Book, both with crimson velvet covers decorated with silver mounts showing the royal arms and those of the minster.

Four years later Henry King, Archdeacon of Colchester and later Bishop of Chichester, presented to Christ Church Cathedral, Oxford (Pl. 138*b*), another pair of velvet-covered volumes with silver-gilt mounts showing in the corner-

[1] I have only noted two outsiders: ΠΑΝΤ ΕΥΣΧΗΜΟΝΩΣ [και κατα ταξιν] ΓΙΝΕΣΘΩ (1 Cor. xiv. 40) on a dish of 1751 belonging to St. George, Tombland, Norwich, and *Alms deliver from death* (Tobit iv. 10) on one of 1790 at Greystoke, Cumberland.

[2] Freshfield, City, 24, and Freshfield, County, 56.

[3] Collins, 152.

pieces very delicately engraved flowers and in the middle his arms and those of the church.[1]

Amongst the plate made in the same year for St. George's Chapel, Windsor, by Christian van Vianen, were:

> Two Covers for Books both weighing 233 Ounces; the one for a Bible contained the Histories of Moses and the Tables, David and the Ark on the one side, and on the other Christ's preaching on the Mount, the sending of the Holy Ghost, and St. Paul falling from his horse. The other Cover was for the Common Prayer; having an Angel of Incense on the one side and the King Healing the Evil, the manner of our Preaching and Christening on the other.[2]

The book-covers made by M. Houser for Bishop Cosin still remain at Auckland Castle and are the most elaborate of those produced after the Restoration. They are bound in red velvet and have in the middle the arms of the bishop and in the corner-pieces cherubs surrounded on the Bible by: OCVLI · DOMINI · SVPER · IVSTOS · ET · AVRES · EIVS · IN · PRECES · EORVM, and on the back DEVS · NOVISSIME · LOCVTVS · EST · NOBIS · PER · FILIVM. The Prayer Book is similarly decorated but has as the inscription on the front, HABENT · MOYSEN · ET · PROPHETAS · AVDIANT · ILLOS, and on the back, FIANT · PRECES · ET · SVPPLICATIONES · PRO · OMNIBVS.[3]

The thieves who robbed St. Paul's in 1810 got away with the covers of the two altar books. The Bible was embossed on the front with Moses and Aaron between the columns of a temple, and Jacob's Dream. On the back was Elijah being fed by the ravens. The Prayer Book 'was adorned with angels, a glory and pillars'.[4]

There are two Books of Common Prayer but no Bible at Norwich Cathedral. They are bound in red velvet and in the middle have a plaque engraved with the arms of the cathedral priory (Pl. 139*a*). The corner-pieces are engraved with cherubs. They cannot be dated exactly, but are described in an inventory of 1668.[5]

At Canterbury Cathedral there is a Bible (Pl. 139*b*) but no Book of Common Prayer. The covers are each formed of a silver-gilt plaque engraved in the centre with the arms of the cathedral and with cherubs in the corners. At the top is engraved *Verbum Dni manet in a ternum. 1. Pet. 1. 25* and on the back *Omnis scriptura divinitus inspirata, 2 Tim. III, 16*. It was a gift from Dean Turner (1660–72) and appears first in an inventory of 1689.[6]

[1] Inscribed on the clasps: *Henricus King Archidiaconus Colcestriae Huius Ecclesiae Canonicus 1638 Humillimedevovit Deo et Sacrosanctae Mensae.*

[2] E. Ashmole, *Institution of the Order of the Garter*, 1672, 496.

[3] *Proc. Soc. Antiquaries of Newcastle-upon-Tyne*, v, 1891–2, 194–5.

[4] The St. Paul's volumes carried the same texts, differently abbreviated, as were used on the Auckland ones (Malcolm, *Londinium Redivivum*, 1807, iii. 144.

[5] *Norfolk Archaeology*, x, 1888, 68–69.

[6] Legg and Hope, 278.

Though the custom of placing on the altar finely bound Bibles and Books of Common Prayer persisted in many cathedrals down to the date at which this book closes,[1] those made after 1700 appear invariably to have been examples of the art of the binder and not of that of the goldsmith.

C. CANDLESTICKS

It seems unlikely that it would ever have been necessary to order new altar candlesticks for the Chapel Royal during the reign of Elizabeth I. If the Henrician or Marian candlesticks were ever replaced by ones of more modern workmanship before all the royal plate was destroyed after the Civil War, it would have been a change dictated by taste and not by necessity.

The reappearance of silver candlesticks upon the communion tables of cathedrals and college chapels was a result of the movement initiated by Andrewes and promoted by Laud.[2] No altar candlesticks made before the Civil War have survived and the descriptions of those which have perished are not sufficiently precise to enable us to visualize them. An engraving of the high altar of Peterborough Cathedral, however, shows the candlesticks afterwards carried off by Cromwell's troopers.[3] They are trumpet-shaped and have a wide grease-pan. They are, in fact, enlarged silver versions of a popular form of brass domestic candlestick. It will be found that a considerable number of altar candlesticks made after the Civil War are also merely adaptations of popular domestic designs, and in selecting those to be discussed here preference has been given to those of more specifically ecclesiastical design.

The earliest surviving altar candlesticks are those made by the *hound sejant* goldsmith in 1653 for the chapel of the young Duke of Lennox at Cobham Hall, and now the property of Rochester Cathedral. They are identical with those which he made in the following year for the chapel of Sir Robert Shirley, Bart., at Staunton Harold (Pl. 140*b*). It will be noted that they have nicely chased and engraved baluster stems and tripod bases adorned with cherubs. They are, in fact, typically Baroque and would not have looked out of place on the altar of any cathedral in France or Flanders. It is difficult to explain why seventeenth-century Anglicans were ready to accept contemporary continental designs for altar candlesticks whilst markedly avoiding the forms of chalices used across the Channel. Similarly, they saw no incongruity in completing a set of altar plate made in the Gothic style with a pair of candlesticks of contemporary design.[4]

[1] G. W. O. Addleshaw and F. Etchell, *Architectural setting of Anglican worship*, 1948, 171–2.

[2] The only parish church which would appear to have had silver altar candlesticks before the Civil War was that most exceptional one of Little Gidding (Alan Maycock, *Chronicles of Little Gidding*, 1954, 45, 53–55).

[3] S. Gunton, *History of the Church of Peterborough*, 1686, 334.

[4] Similarly, the goldsmith *IB* (Jackson, *Goldsmiths*, 130), who provided the service of plate for

Another goldsmith, whose mark was *HW above an escallop*, probably made for some Anglican Recusant chapel during the Commonwealth the superb pair of candlesticks at Lambeth Palace Chapel (Pl. 140*a*) which recapture the feeling of late Gothic art most successfully.

In 1661 the *hound sejant* goldsmith completed the new service of plate for Gloucester Cathedral with a splendid pair of candlesticks with stems modelled on a Gothic column with six clustered shafts (Pl. 140*c*).

Not all of the attempts at producing altar candlesticks in the Gothic style were equally successful. A pair made in 1664 for Pembroke College, Cambridge, are extremely clumsy and seem to anticipate the worst type of nineteenth-century theatrical property.[1]

The output of silver altar candlesticks during the last forty years of the seventeenth century was not large but was marked by a wide range of designs which were almost always successful. The simplest of these consisted merely of a baluster stem set in a round base. There are a pair of these made for Norwich Cathedral in 1665, whilst a not dissimilar pair with an over-all honeycomb decoration were made two years earlier by James Beacham for Canterbury Cathedral.[2]

The pair of candlesticks made late in 1660 for presentation by Princess Mary of Orange to St. George's Chapel, Windsor (Pl. 141*b*), have baluster stems richly decorated with acanthus ornament, whilst the round ogee bases, each resting upon three lions, are embossed with Old Testament scenes.[3]

In 1663 Sir Robert Hyde, Lord Chief Justice of the Common Pleas, presented a pair of candlesticks to Salisbury Cathedral (Pl. 141*a*). It is probably wrong in this instance to attribute to Gothic influence the stems formed like banded clustered columns, since the design is really an enlarged version of a variety of domestic candlestick which was being made in the Low Countries at this date.

Another pair of candlesticks which may be regarded as having been inspired by the domestic candlesticks of the same region were given by Peregrine, 2nd Duke of Leeds, to Harthill church (Pl. 142), near Wakefield. They bear the 1675 hall-mark and were made by the goldsmith *IB above a crescent* who has already been noted as the maker of some of the best Gothic chalices made about this date. Another maker used a rather more austere version of the same design for the chapel of Trinity Hall, Cambridge, in the same year.

Ingestre, Staffs., in 1676, also combined a Gothic chalice with Baroque candlesticks (Pl. 141*c*). A similar pair of candlesticks by a different goldsmith were given to York Minster in 1676 by the future Archbishop Sancroft.

[1] Jones, *Cambridge*, pl. xxiv.

[2] *Archaeologia Cantiana*, xxvii, 1905, 271.

[3] One candlestick shows (1) Daniel in the lions' den, (2) A bearded prophet fleeing before a bear (? a free rendering of the story of Elisha and the mocking boys), (3) Elijah fed by ravens. The other has (1) Jonah and the whale, (2) David harping, (3) An aged man holding a large bone (? Ezekiel in the valley of dry bones).

Socket candlesticks formed like Corinthian columns are to be found at Chester Cathedral and were made in 1683.[1] A pair made in 1681, at Exeter Cathedral, stand on plinths and are much less satisfactory.[2] At St. Margaret, Lynn,[3] and at Harlow, Essex,[4] are rather successful candlesticks with baluster stems decorated with bands of gadrooning. Both pairs were made by John Barnard in 1704.

Throughout this period the Baroque pattern with the tripod base had no difficulty in holding its own. It is not possible to do justice to them here. They were commissioned only from the leading goldsmiths but, although their efforts were eminently successful, repeat orders hardly ever materialized. To treat them fairly would require the illustration of almost every pair.

The Baroque candlesticks made down to the middle of the reign of Charles II retain the stocky appearance of those made during the Commonwealth. Those made in the last twenty years of the century are generally more finely proportioned. Amongst the best are the pair bearing the cipher of James II in the chapel of Chelsea Hospital (Pl. 143). They were made in 1688 by the goldsmith *RL above a fleur-de-lis* who has already been discussed in connexion with the chalices which he made for the chapel.

The candlesticks at Chelsea are unusually restrained and refined, so that the pair of candlesticks bought by the dean and chapter for St. George's Chapel, Windsor (Pl. 144*a*), in about 1694 are in some ways more typical. They were made by Anthony Nelme, whose inventive powers fully equalled those of most of his Huguenot contemporaries. Round the bottom of the baluster stem are three little *putti*, each carrying the star of the Order of the Garter. Two of the sides of the base bear the badge of the order, whilst the third shows St. George in the armour of the Civil War period.

The last really important Baroque candlesticks of the 'Queen Anne period' are those which were made for the Chapel Royal, Whitehall, in 1717, by Benjamin Pyne. They are 41 inches high, with richly moulded baluster stems and tripod bases decorated with cherubs and ciphers. The type did not flourish under the Georges, but its extraordinary vitality is shown by two excellent pairs, made respectively in 1759 and 1763, for Trinity College, Oxford (Pl. 145*a*), and Emmanuel College, Cambridge.[5]

It is perhaps best to regard the candlesticks (Pl. 144*b*) presented on 3 August 1712 to Bristol Cathedral as the reaction of a 'modernist' Queen Anne goldsmith against the long predominance of the Baroque pattern. Gabriel Sleath clearly based his design upon the contemporary one for tea-kettle stands.

[1] T. S. Ball (*C.P. Chester*), who did not know the story of the robbery (see p. 188), misread the rubbed hall-mark as that for 1662.

[2] *Trans. Devon Assoc.* xliv. 1912, 74.

[3] *Norfolk Archaeology*, xxiv, 1930, 30.

[4] *C.P. Essex*, pl. xxiii.

[5] Jones, *Cambridge*, pl. cxiv.

Attached to each leg is an escutcheon, one of which is engraved with the arms of the cathedral, whilst the others show a ship in full sail. They were, in fact, a thank-offering from John Romsey, for a long time town clerk of Bristol, for the safe return of two privateers in which he was interested.[1] A similar pair of candlesticks was bought by the Earl of Warrington in 1716 for his chapel at Dunham Massey. The maker was Isaac Liger.

In 1738 Paul de Lamerie received what was probably his only commission for altar candlesticks. The pair at Queen's College, Oxford (Pl. 144*c*), represented a benefaction from Richard Dalton, a former upper commoner. The round bases are richly embossed with rococo scrolls, whilst the stems are formed of banded papyrus reeds, anticipating a type of domestic candlestick which came into use early in the reign of George III. Though the college authorities who drafted the inscription[2] described them as 'candelabra Magnifica exquisita opere consummata', they are hardly worthy of the most celebrated English goldsmith of the eighteenth century.

The candlesticks provided in 1766 by Francis Butty and Nicholas Dumee as part of their service of altar plate for Durham Cathedral are much more distinguished (Pl. 145*c*). They have to be classified as late Rococo because of the ornament on their bases, but their lines are regular and there is a suggestion that the designer was feeling his way towards the Adam style in which this firm was to produce some more good church plate, though they do not appear to have had another chance of making altar candlesticks. Few church candlesticks were, in fact, produced during the last quarter of the eighteenth century, and these can mostly be dismissed as outsize versions of types used on the dinner-table. For true altar candlesticks the triangular base was once more in fashion. The stem was usually adapted from some type of classical column. A good example is provided by a pair belonging to Christ Church Cathedral, Dublin (Pl. 145*b*), made by an unidentified goldsmith, whose mark was *IV*, and bearing the London hall-mark for 1777.

The only altar candlesticks of any importance made between 1800 and 1830 are two pairs commissioned from Rundell, Bridge & Rundell in 1821. One of these was intended to complete the plate for the private chapel at Windsor Castle. The stems are of baluster form and are richly decorated with acanthus ornament. The triangular bases are engraved with the Sacred Monogram on two of their sides and with the royal arms on the third.[3] According to the 1832 inventory of the royal plate they were 'modelled from the celebrated Amber Candelabra in the Jesuits' College at Rome'.

[1] The *Duke* and *Duchess* set sail on 1 August 1708 and returned home on 14 October 1711, having captured thirteen Spanish ships and sacked three townships. The voyage was also notable because Andrew Selkirk was brought back on one of the ships.

[2] For the full inscription see Moffatt, 45.

[3] E. Alfred Jones, *The Gold and Silver of Windsor Castle*, 1911, pl. c.

The other pair formed part of the service in the Gothic style intended for the chapel at the Royal Pavilion, Brighton. John Bridge, who provided the artistic direction for his firm, had probably never seen a genuine pair of Gothic altar candlesticks, but he managed to produce quite a plausible design, rather in the Caroline Gothic tradition but with a triangular base decorated with the Sacred Monogram and the royal arms.

The king's craving for Gothic art grew stronger every year, and it would appear that in 1827 he was envisaging replacing these candlesticks by another pair, for which the youthful A. W. Pugin prepared the design, which is preserved in the Print Room at the Victoria and Albert Museum.[1] It is a fantastic affair, loaded with the most complicated tracery. The shaft becomes so slender towards the top that it could only have supported a very thin candle.

The only candlesticks of interest iconographically are those made for St. George's Chapel in 1660, which have already been mentioned. The Old Testament subjects with which they are adorned appear to have no particular appropriateness, so that it can only be supposed that the goldsmith copied them from some sheets of printed designs.

None of the donative inscriptions are particularly interesting and very few of the candlesticks were engraved with texts. The 1660 pair at Gloucester Cathedral carry, respectively, LVMEN GENTIVM IESVS LVC. 2. 32 and VT LVMINARIA VOS. PHIL. 2. 15. On one of the lost pairs belonging to St. Paul's were three Vulgate inscriptions: IN LVMINE TVO VIDEBIMVS LVMEN (Ps. xxxv. 9; Auth. xxxvi. 9); DE TENEBRIS VOS VOCAVIT IN ADMIRABILE LVME SVVM (1 Pet. ii. 9); and SIC LVCEAT LVX CORAM HOMINIBVS (Matt. v. 16). Presumably all three texts were engraved round the triangular base of each candlestick.[2]

D. CROSSES

There would appear to be no evidence to show that a silver altar cross was made for Anglican use between the accession of Elizabeth I and the death of George IV.

The desire of Elizabeth I to retain a crucifix upon the altar of the Chapel Royal gave much offence to those of her bishops who had fled to Germany or Switzerland during the reign of her sister.

On 16 November 1559 John Jewell, not yet Bishop of Salisbury, wrote to Peter Martyr: 'That little silver cross of ill-omened origin, still maintains its place in the queen's chapel. Wretched me! This thing will soon be drawn into a precedent.'[3]

On 26 April 1564 Bishop Parkhurst wrote to Bullinger: 'I wrote you word that that cross wax candles and candlesticks had been removed from

[1] E. 755–1925.
[2] J. P. Malcolm, *Londinium Redivivum*, 1807, iii. 145.
[3] *Zurich Letters*, i, Parker Soc. 1842, 55.

the queen's chapel; but they were shortly after brought back again, to the great grief of the godly.'[1]

What was behind the removal and reinstatement of the cross does not appear to be known, but on a later occasion it was knocked down and trampled upon by 'a certain youth under the influence of great zeal for God', who may or may not have been Peach, the queen's fool, who is credited with a similar exploit.[2] Each time that it disappeared the more Calvinistic of the queen's entourage sighed with relief, and groaned when a little later they found that their hopes had been dashed. Archbishop Parker took quite a well-balanced view of the affair. When the cross reappeared again early in 1570 he wrote: 'I never knew of it, nor yet in good faith, I think it expedient it should be restored.'[3]

There had never been a clean sweep of the altar crosses in the reign of Edward VI, and in the 1574 inventory of Elizabeth's plate there were still three. The first of these is doubtless the one 'of ill-omened origin', since it would seem to have been acquired by Mary, whereas Mr. A. J. Collins has traced the other two to her father's time.[4] Reference is made to its being broken, as was also one of the other two. Since all three crosses would appear to have been in store at this time, it seems that the queen had given up the struggle. At any rate, two of the crosses were sent 'to be made into newe plate for her highnes service' at some date before 1583. The third cross met the same fate in 1600.

When Laud, at his trial, was charged with responsibility for the presence of a cross on the altar at the coronation of Charles I,[5] he replied that it formed part of the regalia. He thus exculpated himself and at the same time directed the attention of the court to his old enemy Archbishop Williams, who had been dean of Westminster at the time and responsible for the part of the regalia kept in the abbey. The publicity may have been responsible for the premature disappearance of the cross, which was not amongst the regalia confiscated in 1649.[6]

[1] Ibid. 129.

[2] P. Heylin, *History of the Reformation*, 1849 edn., 124; *Diary of the Rev. John Ward, A.M., Vicar of Stratford upon Avon, 1648–79*, 1839, 161.

[3] *Parker Correspondence*, Parker Soc. 1858, 379.

[4] Collins, 307.

[5] W. Prynne, *Canterburie's Doome*, 1646, 475.

[6] In 1606 it was described as 'a Crosse with a Crucifix set with precious stones' (L. G. Wickham Legg, *English Coronation Records*, 1901, 243, 272–6).

VII

MISCELLANEA

A. CENSERS

MUCH has been written on the use of incense in English churches since the Reformation. The matter before us is, however, the use of censers of silver, which is a very much more restricted subject.

The first document is the celebrated account of the chapel of Bishop Andrewes, to which repeated reference has been made.[1] In the accompanying plan is shown, standing in the middle of the choir, a square table bearing two objects which are described as 'a triquetrall Censer wherein ye Clarke putteth frankincense at ye reading of the first lesson' and 'the Navicula like ye keele of a boat w^t^ a half cover and a foot of which the frankincense is poured'.

The censer is further stated to have been gilt and weighed 84 oz. 14 dwt.[2] It stood upon a latten pan. As the incense-boat is not charged in the goldsmith's bill, it was presumably also of base metal—in fact there do not appear to be any references to Anglican post-Reformation silver incense-boats. It is not clear whether Andrewes retained his censer, since in the 'Coppie of the Forme used by the Lo: Bishop of Elye in consecrating the new church plate of the Cathedrall church of Worc'', the presenter brought forward a censer which a marginal note adds 'was my Lo: own'.[3]

The latest references to the use of a censer of silver appear to be those relating to the one provided by Cosin in 1638 for the chapel at Peterhouse. According to Prynne, 'in Peter-house there was likewise a carved crosse at the end of every seat, and on the Altar a pot, which they usually called the incence-pot'.[4] In the bill for the Peterhouse plate, Richard Blackwell charged up 'For a Sencor 36 oz. 4^wts^ at 8s. the ounce, is 14 l. 9 s. 6 d.'[5]

The preference shown by Andrewes for a static censer was probably due mainly to a desire not to appear to imitate popish customs. Had he been moved in this instance by the opinions of the Fathers he would have refrained from the use of incense. If the placing of the censer on a table in the middle of the choir could not fairly be used as a basis of a charge of popery, it was not a

[1] *Minor Works*, 1854, xcvii–xcix.

[2] The nearest approach to Andrewes's censer is perhaps a triangular perfume-burner, probably English, in the Hermitage Museum, Leningrad, but, as is pointed out by Mr. Paul Derwis (*Burlington Magazine*, lxix, 1936, 24), it must have been used with an aromatic candle and not with incense.

[3] *Minor Works*, 1854, 162.

[4] *Canterburie's Doome*, quoted in *Cosin Correspondence*, i, 1864, xxx.

[5] Ibid. 224.

solution to which recourse could often be made. On the other hand, if Prynne was accurate in stating that the censer at Peterhouse stood upon the altar, he might more fairly have charged Cosin with reviving a pagan than a popish practice.[1] It is interesting to note that when Cosin ordered his lavish service of plate for the chapel at Auckland, no silver censer was included.

B. FONTS, BAPTISMAL BASINS, AND EWERS

It would seem that the medieval royal font was sent to the melting-pot during the inroads on the royal plate at the beginning of the reign of Edward VI. At any rate, when Mary supposed that she was pregnant she ordered a new one, which is described in the 1574 inventory[2] as follows:

> Item oone Founte with a Couer having a guilt Crosse vpon the toppe chasid with Pomegranades the foote chasid with Antique faces likewise the Shainke and foote and with Rooses and pomegranades vpon the brym this scripture Maria Regina temporis filia veritas iiij[c] iiij[xx] viij oz.

If its use was restricted to more or less state occasions, it was probably used for the first time for the christening of the son of Christopher II, Margrave of Baden, on 30 September 1565.[3] Thereafter it is likely to have remained in store until the time came to baptize the younger children of James I. It was probably used last for the christening of the future James II in 1633.[4] It disappeared with the rest of the royal plate during the Civil War or the Commonwealth.

It is curious that there should have been such precipitation in the ordering of the next silver-gilt font. It bears the hall-mark for 1660 although Charles II remained unwed until 21 May 1662. It was presumably used for the baptisms of the children of his brother James, Duke of York, which were performed in the Chapel Royal, St. James's, until his accession to the throne.[5] It was last used for the children of George III. It is unnecessary to describe in detail this piece, which forms one of the most conspicuous exhibits amongst the Regalia in the Tower.[6] It is a pity, however, that so important a commission should have been entrusted to a goldsmith with such scanty powers of invention.

[1] e.g. Cuthbert F. Atchley, *History of the use of incense in divine worship*, Alcuin Club Collns. xiii, 1909, 90.

[2] Collins, 310.

[3] See above, p. 176. A subject (Elizabeth, daughter of Lord Cobham) had been baptized in the Chapel Royal a little earlier, but probably the royal font would not have been used (*Old Cheque Book of the Chapel Royal*, Camden Soc. 1872, 173).

[4] According to E. Sheppard (*Memorials of St. James's Palace*, 1894, ii. 28, 42) the younger children of Charles I were baptized privately.

[5] Ibid. 3–5.

[6] It has been frequently illustrated. The best recent view is pl. 28 in H. D. W. Sitwell, *The Crown Jewels*, 1953.

The pedestal so closely resembles the shaft of a civic mace that it would seem certain that he was engaged at the same time in helping to make good the devastations of the civic insignia which had taken place during the Commonwealth.[1] The cover, with its stepped dome surmounted by a representation of the Baptism in Jordan, is not happily conceived.

Whereas in Lutheran countries the baptismal basin is frequently the most decorative piece amongst the plate of a church, in England they are both rare and unornamented. The reason for this is not far to seek. In the Royal Order of 1560[2] it was laid down:

> Item, that the Font be not removed from the accustomed place; And that in parish churches the curates take not upon them to confer Baptism in basins but in the Font customably used.

On the whole this regulation was well observed, but silver baptismal basins are to be found in small numbers in all parts of the country and date mainly from the eighteenth century. They belong to two groups. The first hardly challenged the official regulation, since it consisted merely of a deep dish which fitted into the bowl of the font. An example of this type is to be found at Charlbury, Oxon, to the church of which it was given in 1716 by Henry Hyde, 2nd Earl of Rochester and 4th Earl of Clarendon. It is 15⅝ inches in diameter and plain except for an appropriate inscription.

The second form of baptismal basin was clearly made to serve instead of a font. The example belonging to St. Paul, Deptford (Pl. 146*a*), made by Richard Gurney and Thomas Cook in 1730, resembles a washing-basin. Others are like an oversize slop-bowl from a tea-set. A typical example of this form is at St. Mary, Reading (Pl. 146*b*), and bears the hall-mark for 1766 and what appears to be the mark of D. and R. Hennell.[3]

Whilst baptismal bowls in England are usually unpretentious, there is one remarkable exception. This is the gold bowl surrounded by figures of Faith, Hope, and Charity. It was made for the christening of William Henry, Marquis of Titchfield, in 1797 and is still at Welbeck Abbey. It was made by Paul Storr and is supposed to have been designed by Flaxman.[4] It is not one of their more successful efforts.

The royal and episcopal instructions regarding the use of fonts were not directed to the Channel Islands, so that when the churches of Jersey and Guernsey fell under episcopal control in the seventeenth century the fonts were gone and the use of baptismal bowls and ewers was well established. It is likely

[1] I have not noted a mace with *RF between five pellets* (Jackson, *Goldsmiths*, 127), but a large number of Charles II maces are unmarked.

[2] Frere and Kennedy, iii. 109.

[3] Inscribed: 'The Gift of Mrs Elizabeth Thorne for the Use of the Font of the Parish Church of St Mary in Reading, A.D. 1767.'

[4] Illustrated N. M. Penzer, *Paul Storr*, 1955, pl. xi.

that these were all of pewter. No serious attempt was made to break this tradition, and the silver ewers and basins still remaining in the islands belong to the post-Calvinistic period. Eight of the thirteen parishes in Jersey possess baptismal basins ranging in from one dated 1671 and of local manufacture at St. Peter, down to one made by Peter and William Bateman with the London hall-mark for 1806 at St. Ouen. They are mostly plain dishes with deep centres. The most important is that at St. Lawrence, which was made by a local goldsmith whose mark was *IG crowned* in 1748 and has a wavy gadrooned edge.

In contrast to Jersey, there are now no silver baptismal basins in Guernsey, but by 1830 six of the ten churches had ewers.[1] All had been provided in 1729 and were probably the work of one local goldsmith whose mark was *a spearhead between IH*. One, however, had already been refashioned, and two perished in the nineteenth century. With the exception of the ewer at St. Saviour's, all had been the gift of Elizabeth, widow of Philip Le Messurier of the parish of St. Peter-in-the-Wood. The example (Pl. 147) belonging to St. Andrew's is in every way typical of this group.[2] which is characterized by a better sense of form than of finish. The refashioned ewer at Forest church is also interesting. It is a little Adam-style ewer, 6 inches high, with a square base and with a round knob on the lid. It bears the London hall-mark for 1789 and the mark of Hester Bateman.[3]

C. STRAINER SPOONS, ETC.

Spoons for removing impurities from the communion wine made their appearance in the reign of James I. Their function, it should be noted, was quite different from that of the medieval chalice spoons which had been to ration out the drops of water to be added to the wine in the chalice.[4]

The spoon belonging to the church of St. Peter per Mountergate, Norwich (Pl. 148*a*), is perhaps the earliest surviving specimen. It resembles an ordinary domestic spoon of the period, except that it has a double knop—a crucifix which is cast in one piece with the common 'seal-top' finial. It is engraved *EW 1613*.[5] A considerable number of churches possess ordinary spoons belong-

[1] St. Andrew, Catel, Forest, St. Peter-in-the-Wood. The donor of the example at St. Peter Port is not recorded. Like the example belonging to the other church dedicated to that saint, it was melted down.

[2] Inscribed: 'Don d'Elizabeth le messurier ueuve du Sr Pierre le messurier de la paroisse de St Pierre du Bois pour la service du bapteme des peties [*sic*] enfant [*sic*] de la paroisse de St Andre, 1729.'

[3] Illustrated *C.P. Guernsey*, pt. i, pl. x.

[4] It is interesting to note that Bishop Andrewes, who followed the medieval custom of mixing water with the wine, does not seem to have had a spoon amongst his chapel plate.

[5] When published in *Norfolk Archaeology*, x, 1888, 106–7, it was suggested that the initials are those of Edward Warnes, rector of Lammas and Hautbois, born in the year in question and a benefactor to the church. If it is merely a christening spoon, it would not interest us.

ing to one or other of the patterns used during the first half of the seventeenth century and in some instances the bowl has been pierced with holes in order to serve better as a strainer. Spoons made specially for this use during the latter part of the seventeenth century did not always have perforated bowls, but are often rather larger and somewhat different in shape from those in ordinary domestic use. These characteristics are well illustrated by a spoon (Pl. 148*c*) bearing the 1692 hall-mark at St. Dunstan, Stepney.[1]

The revolution in the shape of domestic spoons which took place during the reign of Charles II is echoed by most church strainer spoons. An example (Pl. 148*b*) of 1685 at Bristol Cathedral differs from the contemporary household spoons only in the slightly pan-shaped form of its perforated bowl.

A much higher artistic standard is shown on a spoon of 1717 belonging to the blitzed church of St. John the Evangelist, Wapping (Pl. 149*a*). One side of the rounded bowl is pierced with arabesques, whilst the patron saint is engraved upon the lobed handle.[2]

A spoon with a rounded upturned end, which belonged to the blitzed Temple Church, Bristol (Pl. 149*b*), would seem to date from about 1730 and is one of the rare pieces which show Bristol marks.[3]

The strainer spoons of the latter part of the eighteenth century also usually follow the contemporary domestic patterns. A particularly attractive 'Old English' spoon belonging to Wanstead church has the bowl pierced with the Sacred Monogram. It is also unusual in being furnished with a tray.[4]

Strainer spoons sometimes broke away from the ordinary secular types. An example which was made as part of the 1687–8 service of plate at Chelsea Hospital has a round perforated bowl and a tubular handle resembling those of punch-ladles (Pl. 93*a*). This type of design did not really catch on.

Standard types of tea-strainer spoons and sugar-sifters are also found amongst the plate of churches, and were also used for straining the wine. They need not detain us any more than the wine-funnels. Although these last were in ordinary domestic use in the middle of the seventeenth century, those in the possession of churches are seldom earlier than the close of the following century.

D. KNIVES FOR COMMUNION BREAD

Although household bread had superseded wafers in most churches quite early in the seventeenth century, we have no clear evidence until much later

1 Stem inscribed with the name of Richard Hipkins, churchwarden in 1693, and others.

2 Inscribed: *In usum Eccles S^ti Johannis de Wappin, Johanne Russell, Rectore, Anno Salutis MDCCXVII.*

3 Cf. Jackson, *Goldsmiths*, 467. Maker's mark of Ralph Good.

4 They are not by the same maker. The spoon is by George Smith and William Fearn, whilst the tray is by Robert Hennell. Both have the 1790 hall-mark (*C.P. Essex*, pl. xxiii).

of the practice of keeping a special silver-hilted knife for cutting it up.[1] In the eighteenth century many town and some country churches acquired them. The knives themselves are seldom of any particular interest, since they belong merely to current domestic designs.

The church of Melbury Sampford, Dorset, possesses a silver-gilt box (Pl. 150) to hold the knife. It bears the hall-mark for 1751 and was made by James Shruder. On the bottom is engraved *The Gift of Mrs Strangways Horner to the Parish of Melbury.*[2] Two years later this formidable benefactress presented knives with handsome sheaths to the other churches in which she was interested —the example at Stinsford, near Dorchester, is illustrated (Pl. 151).

The chapel of the Royal Hospital, Greenwich, possesses a shovel-shaped spoon, 11½ inches long, for collecting the sliced-up bread. It was made by William Eley and William Fearn, and has the 1823 hall-mark. It is probably unique.[3]

[1] Prynne states that Cosin kept on the altar at Peterhouse a special consecrated knife but does not describe it (*Canterburie's Doome*, 1646, 74).

[2] Its full dimensions are: length 11¾ inches, width 3¼ inches, depth 1¼ inches, and it weighes 22 oz. 17 dwt. Nightingale (*C.P. Dorset*, 103) suggested that the box might have been intended for holding the cut-up bread.

[3] Moir Carnegie, *Church Plate of the Hundred of Blackheath*, 1939, 27, pl. x.

PART IV

THE CATHOLIC RECUSANTS

I

THE CATHOLIC RECUSANTS AND THE GOLDSMITHS

1. 1558–1688

THOUGH the government of Edward VI had effected a colossal reduction of the amount of church plate scattered up and down the country, attempts to give what survived a Reformist character had met with little success except in London and its environs. During the first fifteen years of Elizabeth I her bishops took up this task wherein their predecessors had failed, making a systematic drive to have all existing chalices converted into communion cups with a view to emphasizing the difference between those who accepted the Book of Common Prayer from those who adhered to the Missal. They were probably correct in assuming that none of the conforming clergy who were prepared to celebrate mass on the quiet would use a Protestant cup when so doing.

It has long been realized that as the division between conformist and nonconformist became more definite, the old manor-house chapels acquired an importance which they had never possessed in earlier times. Before considering the plate made for the Recusants, it is necessary to estimate what assets they had inherited from the past. It would be very easy to overestimate the wealth of the vestries of the manor-house chapels at the time of the accession of Elizabeth I. Half a century earlier there had been private chapels belonging to wealthy nobles, more richly furnished than any cathedral in Wales at that time. In 1558 this was a thing of the past. In recent times that portion of the major nobility which had affected the cause of religious conservatism had included few persons who could be described as truly spiritual. The exceptions, like the Courtenays and the Poles, had paid the price of their convictions, but had not fared much worse than the more worldly members of their party who had discovered too late that they could not play at the glittering game of high politics without temporal as well as spiritual loss.[1]

Plate had never tended to accumulate in the vestry of an ordinary manor-house chapel, since it was periodically drained off by benefactions to the high altar or the chantry chapels of the parish church or the local abbey. This probably meant, however, that the chalice and paten were not more than fifty years old and in sound condition at the time of the accession of Elizabeth I.

[1] Cf. David Mathew, *Catholicism in England*, 2nd edn., 1948, cap. 2.

If we peruse collections of mid-century wills and inventories, such as those published by the Surtees Society, which cover one of the areas where Recusancy was to become most pronounced, it becomes evident that in the modest private chapels in that area only the chalice and paten were invariably of silver, the candlesticks, censer, cross, pax, and pyx were of brass or copper-gilt, and the cruets of pewter. Many manor-houses had never had chapels. The piety of past generations had often located the parish church nearby and the squire had often been content to retain at most a chapel for family burials. Where this had been the case, the wherewithal for celebrating mass became a problem, when at length it became evident that the parish church and its equipment would not be available any longer. In some cases it ended in a parish chalice going up to the manor-house. Thus the chalices at Hornby and Leyland must have passed direct into the hands of local Recusants, since they are inscribed, respectively, *Restore me to layland in Lankeshire* and *Restore mee to Caton*. Though the authorities did their best to put an end to the use of parish plate for saying mass, during the long years when the chalices were streaming up to London for conversion into communion cups, it was probably not very difficult to obtain a second-hand one from some goldsmith in Cheapside. By one means or another the early Recusants seem to have had no difficulty about obtaining the minimum requirements for their services. Neither Father Weston[1] nor Father Gerard,[2] whose autobiographies cover the end of the reign of Elizabeth I and the beginning of James I, ever allude to any particular difficulty about securing sacred vessels even when in prison, and the former mentions that the chalice which he used in the Clink was of silver. When the pursuivants carried out a successful raid on a Recusant home, it would seem that they were just as likely to find two silver chalices as one.[3] It would almost seem that the royal authorities realized that the determined Recusant would always be able to find a chalice, since they are not listed amongst the 'vayne and superstitious things', the importation of which was prohibited by the statute of 1571.[4]

Though the average Recusant chapel in Elizabethan times was probably supplied with little plate, there were certainly exceptions. Father Gerard[5] gives a spirited account of the furnishing of the chapel maintained by Elizabeth Vaux at Great Harrowden, Northants. There were six massive silver candlesticks on the altar, which shows that she kept abreast of continental fashions, since two had been the usual number in pre-Reformation England. There were also two smaller candlesticks for use at the elevation. The cruets, sacring-

[1] *William Watson, the autobiography of an Elizabethan*, ed. Philip Caraman, 1955, 119–20.

[2] *John Gerard, the autobiography of an Elizabethan*, ed. Philip Caraman, 1951, 195.

[3] Cf. the account of the raid on the Bentley's house at Little Oakley, near Kettering, on 20 June 1595 (Godfrey Anstruther, *Vaux of Harrowden*, 1953, 254) or the list of the goods of Ambrose Rookwood, taken in 1605, which included also a sacring-bell and a pyx of silver (*9th Report of the Historical Manuscripts Commission*, i. 292–3).

[4] 13 Elizabeth I, c. 2 and 4.

[5] op. cit. 195.

bell, lamps, lavabo bowl, and censer were all of silver. There was a silver crucifix, but also a gilt one, a foot high, for use on principal feasts. It had a pelican at the top, on the right arm an eagle carrying on its back its young, and on the left a phoenix, and at the foot a hen gathering her young under her wings.[1]

Whence did she get all this? Some of it might have been picked up second-hand, but it would have been difficult to have assembled the whole collection in that way. It would have been impossible to bring it in openly from abroad except under some sort of diplomatic cover.[2] The unusual symbolism on the cross, which Gerard has described so minutely, does not recall any current continental design, but suggests, rather, a cryptic commentary on the times. On the whole it seems most likely that Elizabeth Vaux found an English goldsmith to carry out her behests.

Bad as the times often were, there appears to have been no insuperable difficulty in finding some goldsmith to make a piece of Recusant plate. That the goldsmiths who undertook such work were generally Recusants appears improbable. The same maker's marks are found on Recusant and on Anglican plate.[3] Similarly the Recusants do not appear to have been reduced to employing incompetent goldsmiths. The plate which we are about to describe is of varying artistic merit, but it is nearly always well made and often displays much simple beauty.

Though some important orders for chapel plate were given during the reign of Elizabeth, it would seem that the Recusants relied mainly on what had been left over from the Middle Ages. This source of supply could not be drawn upon for an indefinite period. The pursuivants in the course of their raids must have accounted for many chalices and, especially after the relaxation of persecution after the queen's death, there began to be a problem of supplying plate for those who had decided to give up going to church and to hear mass at home.

[1] All of this was captured when Harrowden was raided on Salisbury's orders in 1605. Gerard's description is very well supported by the catalogue of plate confiscated in 1612 in order to pay some of Lord Vaux's liabilities. The maker of the inventory was not out to make trouble and described everything as if it were domestic plate, e.g. 'one pair of cruets of silver for oil and vinegar, parcel-gilt, a plate of silver with the letters of *Jesus* in gilt, one silver bell to call servants'. Ultimately some of the plate which had not been forwarded to London was returned in 1613 (G. Anstruther, *Vaux of Harrowden*, 392, 406, 419).

[2] In actual fact there is little sign of the importation of foreign plate until the reign of Charles II. The collector Earl of Arundel (Anglican) picked up for his Recusant wife some of the chapel plate of a disgraced Venetian ambassador. Chances of this sort did not occur often and the earl probably pounced upon the stuff because he was an admirer of Italian art. (*Calendar of State Papers Venetian*, xvi, 1619–21, 82).

[3] An early instance of a goldsmith who made plate both for Anglicans and Recusants is Christopher Hunton of York, whose mark appears on a Recusant paten at Broughton Hall, Skipton, and on five Anglican communion cups, *c.* 1570, listed by Jackson (*Goldsmiths*, 285 n.).

Belonging to the first half of the seventeenth century are a number of chalices and patens which it is possible to form into groups, but which it is extremely difficult to distribute between the reigns of James I and Charles I. On the Continent the form and decoration of church plate had altered much since the middle of the sixteenth century. The plate of the Recusants was, however, as little affected by foreign fashions as was the Anglican, and even when it got free of the medieval tradition, remained highly individual. The increased production of plate reflects the improved conditions under which they were living and their success in disseminating their views. There is also a considerable likelihood that the visitation by Richard Smith, Bishop of Chalcedon, in the years 1625–7, showed a deficiency of plate and that some at least of these Caroline chalices were due to his attempt to bring in better order. So far there does not appear to have been printed any inventory of a well-furnished Recusant chapel of the second quarter of the seventeenth century. When one appears it will probably disclose that the range of articles made in silver was by no means confined to the chalices and pyxes which are all that have come down to us.

It has already been shown that during the Commonwealth a considerable amount of plate was made for the chapels of the Anglican Recusants. It is very much more difficult to estimate how much was done during these troubled years for the account of the Catholic Recusants. We may be certain, however, that they had nothing which would bear comparison with the plate of the chapels of Staunton Harold or Cobham Hall.

Owing to the intense conservatism of the goldsmiths who worked for the Recusants, it is still difficult to distinguish the plate made during the reign of Charles II from that which had been made in the days of his father. This is due to the fact that very few of the pieces of plate made for the Recusants during the period under discussion were hall-marked. Reference has been made elsewhere[1] to the law and practice with regard to marking silver in the Middle Ages, and it may be added that there was no legislation with regard to the marking of silver (ecclesiastical or secular) between the Reformation and the Revolution of 1688. Whereas most Anglican plate made after the reign of Elizabeth I is fully marked (i.e. both with the mark of the hall and of the goldsmith), even though it was made as a private order and not 'exposed for sale', Recusant plate hardly ever found its way to Goldsmiths' Hall. Hall-marked pieces belong to the years during which there was a lull in the war against Recusancy, particularly in the middle period of the reign of Charles I. Whereas the Anglican plate which was not sent to Goldsmiths' Hall, on the grounds that it was not to be 'offered for sale', is almost invariably stamped with the mark of the goldsmith who had made it, there are numerous Recusant

[1] See above, p. 14, n. 2.

pieces which are completely unmarked. The number of Recusant pieces bearing the maker's mark only greatly outnumbers those which were fully hall-marked. They would appear to belong to periods when it did not seem altogether too risky to acknowledge the patronage of the Recusants. The manner in which a piece is marked would appear to give some indication of the position with regard to persecution at the time at which it was made.

There appears to be nothing to suggest that the plate in the chapel of Henrietta Maria affected the development of Recusant plate. Similarly there appears to be no record of her ordering in England pieces to supplement what she had brought from France. Catherine of Braganza, who arrived in England with the equipment for a rich chapel, certainly supplemented it with purchases in this country. Her goldsmith, however, was a Fleming, John Cooquus, but there is little evidence that he picked up much of a Recusant clientéle. In 1679 he already claimed to be under the patronage of the Duke of York,[1] but his great opportunity did not come until after the latter had become king. In the years 1686–7 he provided plate for the king's chapel in Whitehall, a chapel in Windsor Castle, and the chapel in Dublin Castle.[2] None of this would seem to have survived long enough to give him any advertisement.[3]

2. 1688–1830

Whereas for the Anglicans the year 1660 marked the opening of a new period, for the Catholic Recusants the corresponding date is 1688. The Revolution dissipated finally the mirage of a return to power by political means which had distracted and deluded a minority of the Recusants ever since the reign of Elizabeth.

The period about to be discussed is often treated by church historians as one of retrogression. This view is not entirely correct. If the number of manor-houses supporting a Recusant chapel tended to decline, the more tolerant conditions allowed the urban congregations to organize themselves on a more permanent basis. The demand for silver chalices seems to have come mainly from the towns. The task of placing the order inevitably fell upon the priest, whose artistic susceptibilities seem usually not to have been sharpened during his years of training at one or other of the theological colleges overseas. To judge from results, a usual solution was to supply the goldsmith with a pewter chalice of North French or Flemish make to serve as a pattern.

Though some manor-house chapels closed down, the fervour of those who

[1] *Antiquaries Journal*, xiv, 1934, 285–6.

[2] *Moneys received and paid out for secret services 1679–1688*, Camden Soc. 1851, 144, 154, 160, and 179.

[3] Apparently James carried off to France the plate which had been used in his chapel at Holy Rood House (*Archaeologia*, xviii, 1817, 233).

supported those which continued to carry on did not necessarily diminish. The eighteenth-century squire was quite as capable of getting his goldsmith to turn out a good censer as had been his grandfather who had ordered the chalice in the days of Charles I. Things were now much easier and a Recusant squire had no difficulty in getting a first-class London goldsmith to execute his order. Rather naturally the custom of the Recusants went to the English goldsmiths and not to the Huguenots who dominated the market for secular plate from the end of the seventeenth century until the reign of George II. The most popular goldsmith for Recusant plate at the beginning of the eighteenth century was Benjamin Pyne, who was a thoroughly reliable craftsman. Later on the Kandlers got most of the orders, which they executed no less satisfactorily.

The task of dating pieces now becomes easy, since the goldsmith was no longer deterred by fear from taking his work to Goldsmiths' Hall to be marked. Though pieces without hall-marks are still to be encountered, they do not occur more frequently amongst Recusant than amongst ordinary domestic plate.

The disability under which English goldsmiths suffered when executing Recusant orders was practical and not legal. They were usually unfamiliar with the type of article which was required, so that each order tended to be an artistic adventure.[1] Few clients could produce a good continental piece to serve as a model, so that the goldsmith had usually to work out his own solution. The result of his long experience in making domestic plate is usually very visible.

Though the conditions under which the Recusants lived had much improved, they were still liable to be troubled, particularly at times when the government was frightened about the Jacobite peril. We are indebted to a deposition[2] made at Preston on 1 October 1716 by the Rev. Richard Hitchmough, formerly a Recusant secular priest and now an Anglican, for a detailed account of the plate of chapels in Lancashire and Staffordshire in which he had officiated. He had served as chaplain to Bishop George Witham, and perhaps it had been one of his duties to record the plate which was produced when his master toured the country. His memory appears to have been remarkably accurate as to quantities, though it may be suspected that the articles which he described as gold were really silver-gilt. At any rate, of the eleven chapels reported upon six had still only a silver chalice and paten.[3] At Southwith Hall, near Warring-

[1] Irish goldsmiths appear to have had no part in the provision of plate for chapels in England. Although this was the golden age of Irish domestic silver, this pre-eminence was bound up with the Protestant ascendency. The Irish goldsmiths were, in fact, mostly Protestants, and did not surpass their English contemporaries when making plate for Catholics.

[2] P.R.O. Forfeited Estates Papers, F.E.C. i, H. 28.

[3] Fazakerley Hall, More Hall, Garswood, Mosborough, Burchley, and Higbourth.

ton, seat of Mr. John Golden, there was 'One large silver chalice and paten finely carved, the chalice double gilt within with gold'. It had cost £35. Further, there were 'one small silver chalice used daily' and 'one ciborium of silver to preserve the consecrated Host, with a silver cover and a cross on the top thereof'. These had cost £3 and £5, respectively. Culchoth Hall, nearby, the home of Thomas Culchoth, Esq., had a silver-gilt chalice and paten and a pair of silver cruets on a tray. We now come to houses where a considerably higher standard obtained. At Mr. Gifford's house at Chillington, Staffs., was 'a large gold chalice and paten, six large silver Candlesticks, a large silver crucifix, a large silver Ciborium, double gilt within with Gold, with a Cover and Cross on the Top'. Next we come to Lord Molyneux's chapel at Croxteth Park, near Liverpool, the account of which is worth giving in full. It reads:

> One large silver chalice, double gilt within with gold; one large paten of pure gold; Two silver crucibles alias cruets, for wine and water; one silver plate upon which the said crucibles used to stand; six tall silver candlesticks; and a large silver crucifix; the whole solid silver and which the Lady Molyneux, wife to his present Lordship, told this deponent cost his Lordship £500 in London. All the above plate this deponent says he saw often in 1709 at which time he officiated there as chaplain to his Lordship.

Equally important is the account of the plate at St. Thomas, outside Stafford, the house of William Fowler but which was also used as his headquarters by Bishop Witham whilst he was in charge of the Midland District. There were:

> One large Massy silver chalice, one paten, one other silver chalice and paten double gilt with gold, Two large silver crucibles, one large silver plate for the said crucibles to stand upon; Two large silver Thuribles. Six large silver Candlesticks and a large silver Crucifix; one other large silver Crucifix carryed in procession on Maundy Thursday, and a large silver Ciborium double gilt with Gold.

It will be noted that a bishop *in partibus* at the beginning of the eighteenth century might have at his residence a better service of plate than any bishop of the Establishment, except the tenant of Auckland.[1]

Since the informer's intended victims steered a discreet course, his deposition appears to have been pigeon-holed and, indeed, a few of the pieces mentioned are still in existence. The days when pursuivants might descend on a house and carry its Recusant owner to prison were past. When we come to examine the individual items, it will be found that the wealthier gentry were steadily building up their stock of chapel plate during the eighteenth and early nineteenth centuries.

[1] It would be interesting to know whether any of the St. Thomas's plate still survives either in the Midlands or in the Northern District to which Bishop Witham was later translated.

Quite a lot of plate of excellent design and workmanship was made between 1800 and 1830, but when Europe was reopened to English travellers after the fall of Napoleon there developed an unfortunate custom of bringing back a piece of plate from Italy. Long-standing depression had lowered the standard of workmanship in that country, and Pugin was perfectly justified in decrying these importations.

II

MASS PLATE

A. CHALICES

IT has already been remarked that it would seem that the needs of the Recusants were met mainly, if not entirely, with medieval chalices during the reign of Elizabeth I. Though it does not seem possible at present to attribute any chalices to her lifetime, it seems almost certain that some were made, since the earliest examples with which we shall have to deal present a characteristic which would seem to have been developed during a period of acute persecution.

Chalices which could be unscrewed into three parts—bowl, stem with knot, and foot—had been well known in some countries during the Middle Ages. In England they had been rare, although the Hamstall Ridware chalice (Pl. 9) displays this feature. This device, which rendered chalices both more easy to conceal and to carry about, was used almost invariably on chalices made in England during the first three-quarters of the seventeenth century.

Whilst it is possible to fit the surviving seventeenth-century chalices into more or less satisfactory groups, it is much more difficult to date them accurately. It is obvious that several designs were being used at the same time. Though they will be described here as belonging to Group C.R. 1 or 2, such numbering must not be regarded as final.

Group C.R. 1

The chalices of the first of these groups retain the proportions and the size of their medieval predecessors. They are obviously the work of several goldsmiths, each of whom interpreted the old medieval design in his own way. Thus the example at the Catholic church at Creswell, Staffs. (Pl. 152) reproduces the sexfoil base of the medieval Group 9, but has a very pronounced domed centre engraved with a crucifix. The knot is very well proportioned and is set with six bosses separated by pierced Gothic tracery.

The chalice (Pl. 153*a*) belonging to Lord Kenyon, (of which there is a duplicate at the Catholic church at Lydiate, Lancs.) is a variant of the same design, but has an almost flat foot which is engraved with the Instruments of the Passion, a subject which was to become popular on Recusant chalices as a result of the contemporary absorption in meditations on this theme.

A third variety of this group is at present represented by four examples of which the one belonging to Oscott College is illustrated (Pl. 153*b*). The form of the foot closely resembles those of the two which have just been described, but the junction with the stem, which is round, is masked by a flat disc—a feature which will be noted on many other Recusant chalices belonging to other types. The last point to be noted is the decoration of the bowl with four wavy tongues of cut-card work. The Oscott chalice has no provenance, but the others are Heworth (C.E.) parish church in Durham, and the Catholic churches at Netherton,[1] near Liverpool, and Ugthorpe, near Whitby. The finish rather suggests a provincial origin which would probably mean at York.

Two further Lancashire chalices differ from these last only in lacking the cut-card decoration on the bowl. The chalice at Scarisbrick[2] is engraved *Pray for the soule of Isabel Daniel deceased the tenth of July 1623.*[3] This is about the only reliable indication which we have for dating the chalices of this group.

Group C.R. 2

The chalices of the next group differ from those of the last in that they are considerably taller and have deeper bowls. Their knots are of Gothic form but the junction of the hexagonal stem and the sexfoil base is always masked by the flat disc which was only occasionally used on the last group.

Perhaps the earliest surviving example of this type, if artistic criteria are applied, is the chalice belonging to the parish church (C.E.) at Bradoc, Cornwall (Pl. 154*a*). The bosses on the knot are engraved with three leaves conjoined, whilst the stepped base is decorated with bands of conventional ornament cast from a repeating die. This feature misled Canon Mills[4] into suggesting a Marian date for it, but this form of ornament was still being used on Anglican Gothic chalices made in the 1640's.

Though the maker of the Bradoc chalice did not mark his work, he was evidently in quite close touch with another goldsmith who sometimes stamped his own mark on his chalices, but also got them marked at Goldsmiths' Hall. His mark shows the letters *WR beneath a bow*.[5] The boldness of this goldsmith

[1] This chalice is incribed under the foot with *A* ✠ *S 1603*. It is difficult to believe that this can be the date of manufacture, although the use of cut-card decoration is more ancient than is generally allowed in the older textbooks. For conjectures regarding its history see Dom F. O. Blundell's *Old-time Lancashire Chalices* (*Trans. of the Historic Soc. of Lancs. and Cheshire*, lxxvi, 1924, 120).

[2] The other chalice is at the Catholic church at Bootle. The inscription upon it only records that it was presented in 1697 (ibid. 8–9, also xli, 1890, 205).

[3] Inscriptions of this sort are common on Irish plate but quite rare on that of the English Recusants. This is perhaps due to the survival of a parochial sense in Ireland. The plate of an English manor-house chapel was as much the property of the squire as was the loving cup and the great salt on his dinner-table.

[4] Typed manuscript *Record of the Church Plate in the Diocese of Truro*, in the library of Truro Cathedral.

[5] Jackson, *Goldsmiths*, 118, identified him as William Rainbow. The object above the initials might be a rainbow. At any rate, the goldsmith was probably the son of one who used a mark *WR above a bow* (ibid. 111) which is found on church plate from 1604 onwards.

is explained by two facts. As we have shown in an earlier chapter, the High Church party had, under the influence of Bishop Lancelot Andrewes, begun to commission communion plate reviving the old Gothic forms. There is no difficulty about distinguishing Anglican Gothic chalices made before 1630, since they all have bowls of larger capacity than was necessary for Recusant ones, whilst their feet copied the hexagonal ones of the medieval Group 8, whereas the Recusant chalices had sexfoil feet following the medieval Group 9. Since the Recusants were at this time enjoying a lull in persecution, this goldsmith thought it opportune to try to sell chalices of similar form to both denominations. The chalice belonging to the parish church (C.W.) at Llanafon, near Aberystwyth (Pl. 154*b*), is the most complete of his Anglican examples and bears the hall-mark for 1633.[1] Its design differs little from the Bradoc example except that it lacks the elaborate cast decoration round the base and is soldered up in one piece (as Anglican chalices normally were). It will be noted, also, that it is fitted with a paten-cover of the orthodox Anglican design. It is not known whether any objection was raised by the Anglicans to chalices of Recusant design, but this pattern definitely did not catch on with them. There are two Recusant chalices bearing the same hall-mark as the Llanafon example. One of these is at the Catholic church at Appleton, Lancs., whilst the other is in the National Museum, Dublin (Pl. 155*a*). They differ from each other in their engraved decoration (which would probably have been added after they had left Goldsmiths' Hall), and from the Llanafon example in the form of their bowls and in being able to be taken to pieces. The engraving on the stem and knot requires no comment, but that on the foot is important as it helps to link them up with other chalices which have no marks. On the Dublin chalice all the sections of the foot are outlined with a feather pattern, whilst one of them is engraved with a crucifix enclosed in a halo. The Appleton example, on the other hand, has the lobes of the foot outlined by a roped border and with a demi-fleur-de-lis on the ridges which separate the sections. The crucifix is engraved in exactly the same manner as on the former example. At least one other Recusant chalice bearing the mark of *WR* is known to exist,[2] but there are quite a number of unmarked examples which follow more or less closely

[1] A chalice of the same year at Launton, near Bicester, has an octofoil foot made on the same lines as the sexfoil. The plain round knot does not look original and the Rev. J. T. Evans (*C.P. Oxon*, pl. xvii, 97) considered that the paten-cover had been refashioned. The chalice at Marston Bigot, near Frome, is more puzzling. Its sexfoil foot bears the *WR* mark with the 1633 hall-mark. The stem and knot are also by him, but the bowl bears the 1636 hall-mark with the maker's mark *BF* (Jackson, *Goldsmiths*, 120). These marks also appear on a paten-cover of the ordinary Anglican type. The chalice does not unscrew, but this may not have been the case originally as it was heavily restored in about 1830. It is possible, therefore, that the Marston Bigot chalice is an example of the Anglicanization of a Recusant chalice, as it is difficult to explain otherwise the replacement of the original bowl within three years.

[2] *Burlington Magazine*, xxxiv, 1925, 231.

his design.[1] There are three at Ampleforth Abbey. One (Pl. 155*b*) which was formerly in the hands of the Collingridge family of Godington, Oxon, has the foot engraved with the same design as the Appleton chalice. The other two have no ornamental border and the Sacred Monogram in place of the Crucifix. One of them is engraved also with the Instruments of the Passion. Of the other chalices which resemble closely the known works of this goldsmith, reference may be made to two which were used by two of the victims of Oates. The chalice of the Blessed Thomas Kemble at Monmouth is engraved with the Sacred Monogram on its foot, whilst that of the Blessed Nicholas Postgate at Ugthorpe, near Whitby, has its foot engraved in exactly the same way as the Appleton and Collingridge examples.

It is unfortunate that the two most distinguished goldsmiths who made Recusant chalices in the Gothic style during the reign of Charles I did not mark their work.

Three chalices in the Yorkshire dales differ from those made by *WR* because of their squatter proportions which recall some of those included in Group C.R. 1. Two of them, not quite a pair, are at Danby-on-Yore, near Masham, whilst the third is at Broughton Hall, near Skipton. The bosses on the traceried knots are set with charming little cast cherubs suggestive of a date in the middle of the reign of Charles I. The two (Pl. 156*a*, *b*) belonging to the chapel maintained by the Scropes of Danby Hall have a simple crucifix engraved on the foot, but the one at Broughton has a background of Jerusalem, which must have been copied from some Flemish print. Unlike most Recusant chalices, these take into only two pieces—only the bowl unscrews.

The last chalices to be mentioned are also unmarked, but must date from about the same time. The example (Pl. 157) now belonging to the parish church (C.E.) at Ashow,[2] near Kenilworth, is also more squat than those made by *WR*, and has the lower part of its bowl engraved with alternate straight and wavy rays. The knot is untraceried and its bosses are engraved with cherubs. The sexfoil foot is engraved with a crucifix with a view of Jerusalem and with the Instruments of the Passion. At the Bar Convent, York, is a chalice which differs only in having the letters of I E S V S and a heart on the bosses of the knot, and in having an octofoil foot over which the same subjects are distributed slightly differently.[3]

[1] One of the most curious examples is at the parish church (C.W.) at Llechynfarwy, Anglesey. The foot is engraved exactly as on the Dublin chalice but the bowl is decorated with the arms of William Bold and an inscription recording its gift to the church in 1632. Since the chalice must have been made for a Recusant, it must be a little older than the date engraved on it. Perhaps Bold had inherited it from one of his Lancashire Recusant relatives? (*C.P. Bangor*, 13–14, pl. vi).

[2] It turned up about fifteen years ago amongst the plate of Lord Leigh at Stoneleigh Abbey. He subsequently presented it to the neighbouring church of Ashow.

[3] The appearance of this splendid chalice has been spoiled by the addition of the jewels of a pious Victorian lady.

Group C.R. 3

The chalices belonging to the next group retain no Gothic detail, though they are only one degree removed from those produced by *WR*, the typical but not the best artist of the previous one. The form of the bowl is identical, but the foot, with six or more lobes, is flatter. The characteristic feature is the baluster stem which is broken by a knot set with three cast cherubs. Several goldsmiths, some of whom marked their work, contributed to this group, which enjoyed a comparatively long period of favour.

The earliest chalice which it is possible to date belongs to St. Ignatius College, South Tottenham (Pl. 158). It bears the hall-mark for 1637 and the maker's mark *RM above a rosette*.[1] The eight-lobed foot is engraved with the Instruments of the Passion. At Wardour Castle chapel is an example made by the same maker in the following year, similarly decorated but having a ten-lobed foot (Pl. 159). An example acquired within recent years by the parish church (C.E.) of Solihull is similarly marked, but has a sexfoil foot engraved with a crucifix and with the same sort of ornamental border with demi-fleur-de-lis finials which have been noted on some of the examples of Group C.R. 2 (Pl. 160). A fresh variety is provided by an example at Stonyhurst College (Pl. 161*a*) which bears the maker's mark only. The eight-lobed foot has a domed centre, a form well known in France at this period.[2]

[1] Jackson, *Goldsmiths*, 120. The Anglican plate by this maker is of good quality but less remarkable. There are chalices at Keyham and Welby, Leics., of 1634; one of 1635 at Bethnal Green; and a flagon of the same year at St. Andrew Undershaft.

[2] It is interesting to note that this chalice reached Lancashire from Ireland, as a gift from the Bodkin family.

Although the Reformation began to affect Ireland at a later date than England, Irish goldsmiths were still making chalices with the six-pointed foot with incurved sides, similar to the English Group 8, as they had been since the end of the fifteenth century. The sexfoil foot (Group 10) which reached England from the Continent in about 1500, had not yet crossed the St. George's Channel when the Reformation froze the development of Irish church plate. Throughout the reigns of Elizabeth I and James I, the Irish Catholics were having chalices made on the lines of the old English Group 8, but with the foot rising steeply towards the junction with the stem.

Up to the reign of Charles I, the chalices of the Irish Catholics had little resembled those of their co-religionists in England, which had been developed out of the later Group 10 in the vogue when Henry VIII began his campaign of robbery. From the illustrations in J. J. Buckley's *Some Irish Altar Plate*, 1943, it becomes clear that the English Recusant developments began to affect Irish chalices in about 1640, when we begin to encounter chalices of the traditional Irish form but with a lobed foot. A more than usually elaborate one was presented by the celebrated Malachy O'Quaelly, Archbishop of Tuam, to the Franciscans of Rosserrilly (op. cit., pl. xxvii). The English origin of the lobed foot is placed beyond dispute if reference is made to two other chalices presented by the archbishop in the years 1641 and 1642 respectively. The one given to the Augustinians of Dunmore (ibid., pl. xxxi) is now at St. Mary's Abbey, Ballyhaunis; the other, which was given to the abbey of Ballinrobe (ibid., pl. xxxii), is now at Stonyhurst. In both cases the foot is engraved with a border with demi-fleur-de-lis finials such as has been noted on earlier English chalices. The conclusion would seem to be that one of the chalices made by *RM* must have reached the archbishop who, having been trained in Paris, would have realized how superior it was to the current Irish work. Both the Dunmore and Ballinrobe chalices

The goldsmith *RM*[1] did not have a monopoly of the production of Baroque chalices in the years just before the Civil War, as at least one other maker was using a very similar design. The chalice belonging to the Catholic church of St. Mary-at-Quay, Bristol (Pl. 161*b*), is very similar to those which have just been described but bears the maker's mark *WT*[2] with the 1639 hall-mark.

We must now turn to the work of a firm of goldsmiths which seems to have produced the greatest number of the Recusant chalices which have survived from the second half of the seventeenth century. They are readily identifiable by the use of a particular type of cherub on their knots. This is shown with the wings raised so as almost to meet above its head. Though it might seem rash to connect together this sub-group by means of a detail which was cast from a model probably obtained from a trade source, the general uniformity of the chalices which are attributed to it, seems to confirm that they do indeed come from the same workshop. The cherubs are found decorating round, oval, and pear-shaped knots which are combined with a baluster stem and a sexfoil foot with rather flat lobes are outlined with the familiar engraved border with demi-fleur-de-lis finials.

The three examples chosen for illustration show the different types of knot and come from Sawston Hall, near Cambridge (Pl. 162*a*), Stonyhurst College (Pl. 162*b*), and the Catholic church at Clitheroe, Lancs. (Pl. 163). It should be noted that the first of these is a miniature size, 5 inches high, and evidently intended for use by an itinerant priest.

Though the general appearance of these chalices might suggest a date soon after the middle of the seventeenth century, it seems likely that their production was, in fact, spread over quite a length of time. An example belonging to the parish church (C.E.) at Gosforth, Cumbd., is engraved with the date 1690.

The clue to the identity of the firm which produced these chalices is provided by the chalice (Pl. 84*b*) presented to St. George's Chapel, Windsor, by Lady Mary Heveningham, whose Regicide husband was a prisoner in the castle. The baluster stem is decorated with cherubs of the same form as appear upon the chalices of Group C.R. 3, and it is pretty clear that this Anglican piece came from the same workshop. It is not hall-marked, but bears as maker's mark the letters *AM in monogram*. This mark is first recorded on pieces with the hall-mark 1650.[3] Thereafter it appears regularly until 1667, but between 1668 and 1671 is found a crowned monogram[4] of the same letters. By 1676 a mark

are clearly Irish imitations and not the work of an English immigrant, as it will be noted that both show the steeply rising centre of the foot—a characteristic Irish feature. It is not necessary to pursue the matter further, but it may be noted that the influence of this type of English chalice is visible on Irish chalices made down to the end of the century, particularly on those of Galway origin.

[1] Unmarked chalices attributed to *RM* on stylistic grounds are at Beaumont College and at the Catholic church at Great Yarmouth.

[2] Jackson, *Goldsmiths*, 121 and 123. [3] Ibid. 124. [4] Ibid. 130.

resembling the original *AM in monogram*[1] appears and remained in use until the introduction of the Britannia Standard brought with it the compulsory use of a new set of maker's marks showing the first two letters of the surname of the goldsmith. Sir Charles Jackson attributed the *AM in monogram* to Andrew Moore, who entered the mark *MO in monogram* in 1697. This seems probable, but it is clear that the goldsmith of 1697 cannot have been the same individual who was at work in 1650. He might, however, have been a son who had the same initials.[2]

One other chalice is illustrated to show how another goldsmith interpreted this design in the latter years of the century. It will be observed that the chalice at Oscott College (Pl. 163*b*) is much more finely proportioned but has no applied decoration except the engraved crucifix on the foot. It is undated but bears an otherwise unrecorded goldsmith's mark, *WB in a pointed topped shield.*

Group C.R. 4

The Revolution of 1688 marked the beginning of a new period for the Catholic Recusants. It also saw the start of a new tradition in the designing of chalices. The chalices of Groups C.R. 1, 2, and 3 are entirely insular in form and decoration. Those of the period 1688–1830 have the same proportions as the chalices which were being made across the Channel, even though their decoration may be entirely English. This is well shown in the superb chalice at Lulworth Castle (Pl. 164) made by Benjamin Pyne in 1704. Unfortunately, as has already been explained, most of the orders for chalices came from customers whose taste was not sufficiently sophisticated to make them choose good designs. The chalice (Pl. 165*a*) made in 1739 by Frederick Kandler for the Catholic church at Worcester is pretty clearly a silver version of a continental one made in pewter. It is not at all what that very sophisticated artist would have turned out had he been given a free hand and a fair amount of money. The same limitations are apparent in the chalice (Pl. 165*b*) made in 1791 by William Pitts and Joseph Preedy.[3]

To emphasize the inferiority of the chalices turned out by most of the English goldsmiths in the second half of the eighteenth century it is only necessary to compare them with the excellent and simple design (Pl. 166*a*) used by the Jersey goldsmith, Jean Quenault, when commissioned in 1795 to make one for the use of the Norman and Breton priests who had fled from Revolutionary France.

[1] Ibid. 135.

[2] Besides the examples mentioned above, it seems possible to attribute to this workshop chalices at the following places: Beaumont College; Broughton Hall, Skipton; Downside Abbey; Dublin, National Museum; St. Dominic, Haverstock Hill; Goosnargh, Lancs.; Great Eccleston, Lancs.; Maynooth College; Mount St. Mary College, Sprinkhill, Sheffield; Stonyhurst College (2); Ushaw College, Durham.

[3] Another is at Lulworth Castle and one of 1792 at Winchester.

The revival of interest in Gothic art, which has left some trace on the Anglican plate of the reign of George IV, does not appear to have affected that of the Catholic Recusants. The period of decadence in chalice design would appear to have been ending about the date at which we close, killed not by a craving for medievalism but by more intelligent art patronage. A good example of this is afforded by a chalice made in 1830 by Robert Hennell for a chapel in Westminster (Pl. 166*b*). The form is a good eighteenth-century one of French or Flemish origin, whilst the bowl and foot are appropriately decorated with passion flowers—not the only piece of plate of this period to bear witness to the revived interest in symbolism.

B. PATENS

Although the Recusants retained many medieval patens of the type with the double depression, there is at present no evidence that the design was ever reproduced after the accession of Elizabeth I.

The medieval type having a single depression in the centre was used for the paten at Broughton Hall, Skipton, which was made in about 1570 by the York goldsmith Christopher Hunton. It appears intermittently during the seventeenth century and tends to be without any form of engraved decoration.

Nine-tenths of the patens made for the Recusants belong to a type which was unknown in medieval times. It may be described as a slightly hollowed disc. The curved underside is the one chosen for engraved decoration, when there is any, the top side being left plain.

Recusant patens show little variety in their iconography. The central motif is invariably *IHS* below *a cross fitchy* or *a cross passion*. Below there may be the three nails or, rather more commonly after the middle of the seventeenth century, three nails and the Sacred Heart. The whole may or may not be enclosed within a rayed border.

C. CRUETS

The earliest post-Reformation silver cruets of which we have mention are those belonging to the chapel of the Vaux family at Harrowden in 1605. We are told nothing of their form but that they were accompanied by a silver dish 'with the letters of Jesus in gilt'.

It is clear from the depositions of the Rev. Richard Hitchmough that at the beginning of the eighteenth century it was usual to provide a tray or dish for the cruets. At present the earliest known cruet-dish is rather earlier than any of the cruets which have been noted. It is a plain oval dish, $9\frac{1}{2}$ inches by $7\frac{1}{8}$ inches, stamped with the unrecorded maker's mark *TP in monogram*, and datable only by the style of the engraving of the coat-of-arms[1] on the rim,

[1] *On a chevron three mullets; impaling on a chevron three roses seeded.* Above is *an earl's coronet.*

which suggests that it may have been made in about 1670. It forms part of the furniture of the ancient chapel belonging to the Welds of Chideock, Dorset.

The earliest cruet (Pl. 168) turned up mysteriously amongst the plate of Lord Lonsdale. It is gilt and bears the mark of Charles Shelley with the hall-mark for 1682. The lid is surmounted by the usual V but the pear-shaped body is engraved with the cipher of William and Mary and the rare version of the royal arms used between the date of their accession and the adhesion of Scotland on 2 March 1689. Was it loot from the private chapel of James II? The problem is not made easier by the preservation in the same collection of a companion piece with the mark of George Garthorne and the hall-mark for 1693. It is also surmounted by a V but is engraved with the usual version of the arms of the joint sovereigns. Whilst the first of these is pretty certainly a mass cruet, the second would seem to be one made as a pair for it after it had been secularized.[1]

Most of the surviving eighteenth-century cruets have, unfortunately, become separated from their dishes. A pair which was given to York Minster a few years ago bears the hall-mark for 1707 and the mark of Benjamin Pyne (Pl. 169*a*). They do not compare favourably with most of the other work which he did for the Recusants.

A pair at Stonyhurst College (Pl. 169*b*) bears the mark of James Goodwin and the hall-mark for 1729. Seen without their pull-off lids they resemble the small milk-jugs which had recently been called into existence by the growth of the custom of drinking milk with tea.

In contrast to these extemporized pieces is the beautiful set at Lulworth Castle (Pl. 170) made by Frederick Kandler in 1776. They are, as might be expected by this date, little Adam-style ewers; the body of the one for the water is decorated with the representation of a fountain, whilst that for the wine shows a vine. The accompanying dish (which alone is marked) is engraved with the Sacred Monogram, and has a shaped and beaded rim.[2]

The firm of Rundell, Bridge & Rundell made comparatively little church plate, so that the cruets and dish made in 1820 for the chapel at Wardour Castle (Pl. 171) are especially interesting. The cruets are in fact modelled on the contemporary design for cream-jugs, their sacred use being only made evident by the engraved *V* and *A*.[3]

[1] The cruets probably fell into the hands of the Lowthers almost at once. Sir John Lowther, Bart., played quite an important part in the plot to depose James II, and William III rewarded him by making him Viscount Lonsdale and appointing him Vice-Chamberlain of the Household. This gave him the opportunity of acquiring some much more important pieces of the royal plate.

[2] The dish is inscribed: *Sacello de Brittwell Dono Dedit Maria Weld 1777.*

[3] These cruets were doubtless made to order, but some goldsmiths were not above taking cream-jugs out of stock. At Mount St. Mary's College, Sprinkhill, Sheffield, there are a pair of the familiar three-legged type having the 1761 hall-mark.

John Angel, another good Regency goldsmith, went to much greater trouble in designing the beautiful set of cruets with tray which are now at Westminster Cathedral (Pl. 172), though he did not, like Kandler, attempt an appropriate decorative motif for each cruet but used a vine scroll on all three pieces.

III

MISCELLANEA

A. BASIN FOR ABLUTIONS

THE only place where a silver lavabo bowl is recorded to have been used is the chapel of Elizabeth Vaux at Great Harrowden. It is listed both in Father Gerard's autobiography and in the 1612 inventory[1] which discloses that it was parcel-gilt but says nothing about its decoration. It is clear from these two authorities that there was only a single basin and neither a pair of them nor a ewer and basin, as there would have been in pre-Reformation days.

B. CANDLESTICKS

The fact that six massive silver candlesticks stood upon the altar of the chapel at Harrowden in the last years of Elizabeth I illustrates how early Counter-Reformation fashions began to be felt in England. Recusant chapels appear always to have had sets of six silver candlesticks, if they had ones of silver at all.

Whereas Anglican altar-candlesticks can be separated into several basic designs, Recusant ones appear all to belong to the Baroque design with triangular base and baluster stem.

The earliest set as yet identified (Pl. 173) consists of four candlesticks belonging to the year 1675, bearing the maker's mark *JC conjoined in script below a coronet*; and two bearing the maker's mark *IO* with the York hall-mark for 1684. They are extremely austere and are decorated only with cable mouldings. Four of the set are 12 inches high, whilst the remaining pair are only 11½ inches. Whether this variation is an intentional attempt at graduation or is accidental is not clear.[2]

The set of six 16½ inches-high candlesticks at Arundel Castle (Pl. 174*a*), bear the hall-mark for 1710 and a maker's mark which is probably that of Ambrose Stevenson. They are in the full Louis XIV style and have the Howard crest and the Sacred Monogram engraved on the sides of their triangular bases.

The set of candlesticks at Wardour Castle (Pl. 174*b*) are graduated, consisting of three pairs which are 12, 13, and 14 inches high, respectively.[3] They are in

[1] *John Gerard, the autobiography of an Elizabethan*, ed. P. Caraman, 1951, 195; G. Anstruther, *Vaux of Harrowden*, 1953, 404.

[2] Sotheby, 5 July 1956, lot 119.

[3] The 1612 Harrowden inventory refers to 'three pair of silver candlesticks', which may mean that they were graduated (G. Anstruther, *Vaux of Harrowden*, 1953, 404).

an austere, rather Flemish style, and bear the hall-mark for 1733 and the mark of Charles Kandler.

Though the surviving Recusant candlesticks are of good design and workmanship, they will not bear comparison with the contemporary Anglican ones. After all, the cost of six candlesticks must be more than that of a pair!

C. CENSERS

The sources from which early Elizabethan Recusants derived their chapel plate were unlikely to be able to produce silver censers. Similarly, there no longer existed the richly furnished chapels of the nobility, which sixty years earlier might have contained such objects. The position with regard to base-metal censers was very different. We should probably be correct in assuming that the censers used by the Recusants down to the middle of the seventeenth century were generally ones of brass or copper, derived from some parish church and obtained at scrap price.

Silver censers did not rank high on the list of the requirements for a well-furnished chapel. Only the richer ones ever had them, but, on the other hand, their owners were the sort of people to insist on good workmanship. The short list of surviving silver censers is notable for the almost invariably high quality of the workmanship and for the fact that there are almost as many designs as examples.

Though the rich chapel at Harrowden contained, as we know, a silver censer,[1] such pieces must have been very rare before the Restoration, since the earliest examples which I have encountered belong only to the beginning of the eighteenth century.

In the possession of Lord Rossmore is a little censer (Pl. 175) bearing the hall-mark for 1703 and the mark of Anthony Nelme, who was one of the best makers of Anglican plate at this date. It is beautifully proportioned, and the cover is delicately pierced with vases and arabesques such as this goldsmith used on his sugar-casters.[2]

The approach of Benjamin Pyne to the problem of designing a censer was almost the same. An example from his hand at Broughton Hall, near Skipton, bears the hall-mark for 1726, and differs only in that it resembles a sugar-caster rather more closely.

The censer at St. Dominic's Priory, Haverstock Hill (Pl. 176), bears the mark of Anne Tanqueray[3] and the hall-mark for 1732. It is of a much less extemporized design and is remarkable for the wealth of its iconography. The decoration on its hexagonal cover is divided into two tiers, the upper of which

[1] *John Gerard, the autobiography of an Elizabethan,* ed. P. Caraman, 1951, 195.

[2] It has been converted into a lamp, and the finial and chain for the cover are wanting.

[3] This is one of the few important pieces of Recusant plate attributable to a firm of Huguenot origin.

is pierced with Instruments of the Passion. The lower tier is pierced with the following subjects, each of which is repeated twice, as follows:

	Ω	
I H S	I O S	Spear, dice, purse
Nails	MRA	and Crown of Thorns.
	Birch.	

On the bowl is engraved a cartouche with a coat-of-arms on a lozenge.[1]

The censer at Corby Castle, Cumberland (Pl. 177), bears the hall-mark for 1742 and the mark of an unidentified goldsmith.[2] The bowl reflects the form of the mid-eighteenth-century casters but the shallow domed cover is more original. The piercing on the cover, which includes the Sacred Monogram, is clearly influenced by the patterns used on the cake-baskets of the period.

Although not much foreign plate was imported, the chapel at Wardour Castle provides an interesting instance of a censer in the late Rococo style, bearing the Paris hall-mark for 1778, for which a pair (Pl. 178) was made in 1786 by Charles Kandler.

The censers of the late eighteenth and early nineteenth centuries tend to be rather less satisfactory than those which have been described. An example of 1772 made by the unimportant goldsmith William Tuite, at Lulworth Castle (Pl. 179), has a cover with very indifferent piercing, resting on a bottom of sugar-bowl design. It may be added by way of conclusion that the piercing of the covers of these late censers is almost uniformly poor.

INCENSE-BOATS

English goldsmiths do not seem to have taken as much care over their designs for incense-boats as they did for censers. The former appear to be little better than reproductions in silver of contemporary designs used by the pewterers of northern France and Flanders.

The incense-boat of 1742 at Corby Castle (Pl. 180) is a much less inspired piece of work than its censer (Pl. 177) which was made by the same goldsmith in the same year.

D. CROSSES

The Marian archdeacons had done their best to see that every church should have its cross, but had not suggested that replacements should be of silver. Since the disposal of 'superstitious' scrap was not rigidly controlled, it was probably not very difficult for anyone bent on getting together the furniture

[1] *A fess embattled counter-embattled above a lion rampant impaling a saltire ermine.*

[2] *TK below a crowned fleur-de-lis.*

of a chapel in the early years of Elizabeth I to get hold of a cross of latten or copper-gilt. Some of these, which must have done duty all through the Penal period, are still to be found in the vestries of churches which have succeeded to the goods of some Recusant chapel.

The rich cross which Father Gerard saw in the chapel of Elizabeth Vaux has already been discussed.[1] There must have been very few chapels which could boast two crosses of silver as did that at Harrowden.

During the seventeenth and eighteenth centuries there grew up abroad quite a vogue for wooden crosses with finely finished gilt bronze or ivory Christs. It is likely, therefore, that a Recusant who wished for something better than an old medieval base-metal cross would set about securing one of these. However, by the beginning of the eighteenth century silver crosses cannot have been too uncommon, if we may judge from the fact that out of the eleven chapels covered by Hitchmough's deposition in 1716, three were furnished with them.[2] Furthermore, the house which was being used by Bishop Witham as his headquarters had a processional cross as well. It seems certain that some English silver crosses must survive in this country, but I have so far failed to identify one.

I am indebted to Senhor Cardoso Pinto for drawing my attention to a reliquary processional cross (Pls. 181–2) which he had discovered at the Palacio das Necessidades, Lisbon.[3] Its ends are adorned with cast fleurs-de-lis, whilst the limbs are round, as was necessitated by the fact that they served as a container for a relic of the pastoral staff of St. Thomas of Canterbury,[4] which is visible when a hinged cover is opened at the back. Around this opening is engraved:

CRVX
PASTORALIS
SANCTI THOMAE ARCHIEPISCOPI
CANTVARENSIS
A REGINA CATHARINA
IN AMPLIOREM
FORMAM REDVCTAM
ANNO 1664.

Below the inscription is the familiar cipher of two crossed Cs below a royal crown, which, of course, was equally appropriate for Catharine as for her husband. Below the cross is a silver ball knop which apparently replaces one

[1] p. 259. [2] Ibid.

[3] Described at length in *A Cruz Processional da Capela de D. Catarina de Bragança, Rainha de Inglaterra*, 1956.

[4] The relic was probably the one which was at Canterbury Cathedral before the Reformation (Legg and Hope, 71 and 197). St. Paul's, however, boasted a *potenta Beati Thomae Martyris* (*Archaeologia*, l, 1887, 470–1).

of crystal mentioned in early Portuguese records. The junction with the staff is masked by a band embossed with cherubs and with edging in the form of a coronet such as was used round the heads of the civic maces in the years following the Restoration. The staff itself is formed by a 'unicorn's horn'.[1] It has to be admitted that the cross is of greater historical than artistic interest. The tubular form of cross was a recognized pattern at this period and was particularly appropriate in the present instance because it suggested the shape of the relic which it contained. Foreign craftsman who have used this form have frequently failed to obtain artistically satisfactory results, so that it is understandable that an English goldsmith should have failed when set an entirely unfamiliar task.

E. FLOWER VASES

The set of four altar vases, $5\frac{1}{2}$ inches high, belonging to the chapel at Wardour Castle (Pl. 183), are probably the only surviving ones made either for Recusant or Anglican[2] use before the nineteenth century. Though the 1725 hall-mark is clearly stamped, the maker's mark is not legible on any of them.

F. HOLY-WATER BUCKETS

Though Hitchmough's depositions make no reference to silver holy-water buckets, it seems quite probable that some were made for the richer Recusant chapels during the reign of Charles II. At no period did they become common.

The most important example which has survived is one at Arundel Castle (Pl. 184). The hall-mark lacks the date-letter, but the maker's mark of Frederick Kandler is the one which he entered in 1735 and which was rendered obsolete by the statute of 1739. It is in the rich Louis XIV style which enjoyed a period of popularity between the disappearance of the Queen Anne and the arrival of the Rococo styles. The vase-shaped body is decorated with cherubs and floral swags, whilst the foot shows shells and scale ornament in alternative panels. The handle is clearly adapted from one for a tea-kettle, whilst the sprinkler is similarly modelled on a punch-ladle. Together they weigh just over 80 ounces.

At Lulworth Castle is a handsome example bearing the mark of Charles Kandler and the hall-mark for 1786. It is clearly inspired by one of the sugar-basin designs of the period, and is shaped like an egg-cup, having the lower part of the body decorated with gadrooning. Just below the beaded rim is, on

[1] The 'unicorn's horn' is likely to have been the one which Thomas Fuller tells us was presented by his friend Dr. Baldwin Hamey to the College of Physicians. By 1660 the belief in the medicinal properties of the 'unicorn's horn' was failing, so that the College thought it best to present the horn to the king since the royal collections had lost the celebrated horns which had been kept at the Tower and at Windsor Castle previous to the Civil War (T. Fuller, *Worthies*, 1811 edn., ii. 54).

[2] For the examples made in 1638 for St. George's Chapel, Windsor, see p. 158.

one side, the Sacred Monogram, which is matched on the other by the Weld arms.

The Lulworth bucket appears to have been seen and approved by the Arundells of Wardour, since they ordered, six years later, one which was virtually a replica except that it was still larger, being 12 inches high instead of 10 inches. It (Pl. 185) was made, however, by John Schofield. These were supplied with silver-handled brush sprinklers, instead of ball-ended ones.

So far no early nineteenth-century silver bucket has been noted.

G. HOLY-WATER STOUPS

There is nothing to suggest that silver stoups were ever anything but rare. The only known example (Pl. 186) is in the Ashmolean Museum, Oxford. It is a superb piece of work in the Louis XIV style, having the back plate embossed with the Baptism in Jordan contained within a richly chased frame. The stoup is decorated with the MARIA monogram and arabesques.

Whereas there is a certain *naïveté* about most eighteenth-century Recusant plate which was made by goldsmiths who had to extemporize their designs, it is clear that Joseph Barbitt, whose mark with the hall-mark appears on this piece, had either got a first-class French design before him or else he was French by origin.[1]

H. PAXES

In the reign of Mary a pax was still amongst the items which every church was expected to possess. No bishop or archdeacon would have been so unrealistic as to suggest that it should be of silver. A number of old Recusant families who maintained a chapel throughout the period under discussion managed to preserve a medieval brass pax.

It seems unlikely that any silver paxes were made in England after the Reformation.[2] On the Continent elaborate silver paxes were being made down to the end of the sixteenth century, but thereafter their use fell into disfavour, though they have never become obsolete. By the time when the English Recusants were beginning to furnish their chapels more richly the need for a pax had gone.

I. SACRING-BELLS

The kindly maker of the 1612 inventory who listed the Harrowden chapel plate as if it were composed entirely of pieces for domestic use, mentioned 'one

[1] Nothing appears to be known about him except that he had a shop in New Street, Covent Garden. The contemporary goldsmiths of the name of Barbot were of Huguenot origin.

[2] It is curious that there is no record of a pax belonging to the chapel at Great Harrowden.

silver bell to call servants'.[1] In this case the subterfuge was probably quite plausible, since the bells used in late seventeenth- and eighteenth-century chapels seem to have been of the same form as those which were sold with standishes. It has not seemed necessary to illustrate any example.

J. SANCTUARY LAMPS

No reference to any silver sanctuary lamp occurs in the accounts of the furnishing of Elizabeth Vaux's chapel at Harrowden and it may be considered doubtful whether they were to be found in Recusant chapels before the Restoration.

The earliest sanctuary lamp noted is in the chapel at Broughton Hall, near Skipton. It has a bulbous body with a band of pierced ovals round the neck. The body is decorated with pierced scrolls and fruit, interrupted by three cherubs to which are attached the chains for suspension. The hall-marks are not legible, but the general character of the piece suggests a date about 1670.

At Arundel Castle is a very fine and large gilt lamp (Pl. 187*a*) bearing the 1700 hall-mark and a maker's mark which appears to be *Si in a circle*. It is a good piece of raised work in the 'William and Mary' style but conforming fairly closely to the designs in vogue on the Continent at that date.

The Victoria and Albert Museum has a lamp (Pl. 188) which shows what a 'Queen Anne' rendering of this type of object might result in. Its fine, simple lines are clearly visible in the illustration, and it is only necessary to mention the row of applied leaves on the bulge at the bottom. It bears the mark of Charles Kandler entered on 29 November 1727, but has no hall-mark. Nothing is at present known of its provenance, though the inscription *The Gift of James Aveline who died ye 7th of Aprill 1726* should provide a clue.

A second lamp at Arundel Castle (Pl. 187*b*) is interesting in showing an Adam-style design. The goldsmith (who did not stamp his mark) appears to have had the idea that these pieces should be richly embossed. This form of decoration was rather out of fashion in 1789, and it is only possible to comment that the design is timid and the execution indifferent.

Though there is no reason to think that silver lamps were at all common, it is to be hoped that examples in the Rococo and in the Regency styles will come to light.

K. VESSELS FOR THE SACRAMENT

The earliest Recusant ciborium which has been noted is that at Danby Hall, Middleham, Yorks., where the Scropes maintained a chapel. It has a wide,

[1] G. Anstruther, *Vaux of Harrowden*, 1953, 404. This is not quite the earliest reference to a Recusant sacring-bell, since one is listed amongst the plate of Ambrose Rookwood, who was involved in the Powder Plot in 1605 (*9th Report of the Historical Manuscripts Commission*, i. 293).

flattish bowl which is supported on a baluster stem on a round foot. The cover is slightly domed and is surmounted by a cross. It is unmarked, but its general appearance suggests a date in the reign of Charles I. This design was not confined to England, but Recusant customers would have had little trouble in explaining their requirements to their goldsmiths, since the piece resembles a popular form of cup except that it is furnished with a cover.

An example at Sizergh Castle, Westmorland, is generally similar, but has a cross in cut-card work beneath the orb on the cover. It was probably made about the time of the Restoration but has been rather drastically restored. A similar example at Lulworth Castle is also unmarked.

A ciborium from an unknown source, which appeared recently in the sale room,[1] has a bowl of similar form to those which have just been described, but has cut-card work hung with little bells round its lower part (Pl. 189). The stem is cylindrical and the flat foot with an ogee moulding is also decorated with cut-card work, as is also the cover, which is surmounted with the usual orb.

In about 1700 appeared a type of ciborium which was destined to become the standard pattern for the rest of the century. The shallow bowl has a straighter side than had been customary heretofore, and stands on a baluster stem with a round foot. The slightly domed cover is surmounted by a cross with or without an orb. Benjamin Pyne, who was by far the most popular maker of Recusant plate at the beginning of the eighteenth century, made a number of these, of which the example of 1712 at the Victoria and Albert Museum is typical (Pl. 190). Stonyhurst College now possesses two examples of the year 1703, both of which are engraved with the arms of Sir Nicholas Shireburn, Bart., who held the Stonyhurst estate from 1690 to 1717. One of them is gilt and is quite unusually large, being 12½ inches high.[2]

Examples of the middle of the eighteenth century, such as the one made in 1748 at Beaumont College, differ hardly at all from Pyne's pattern, which has never really gone out of production.

The finest and the earliest post-Reformation pyx which has as yet come to light is at Westminster Cathedral (Pl. 191). It is of gold, and is a little flat round box with a hinged lid engraved on the outside with a Crucifix in front of a view of the Holy City, surrounded by rays and an egg-and-dart border. Inside the lid is the Sacred Monogram also surrounded by rays; whilst on the bottom is engraved the Agnus Dei within a border similar to that used on the lid. There is no hall-mark, but stamped inside is the maker's mark showing *a unicorn's head couped*. This mark has been found on a secular piece of 1612[3]—a date which would agree quite well with the style of the engraving on the pyx.

[1] Sotheby, lot 160, 17 November 1955.

[2] Pyne's ciboria are not exactly alike as the baluster stem is not always cast from the same candlestick model.

[3] Jackson, *Goldsmiths*, 112.

The earliest pyx in the little collection in the museum at Oscott College is of the same form as the one which has just been described. On the lid is engraved IHS with a cross above and the Sacred Heart and nails below. The border is formed by a delicately engraved floral scroll (Pl. 192*a*). On the bottom is engraved, rather more roughly, *IM 1649*. The character of the engraving on the lid suggests a date more in the middle of the reign of Charles I.

Another of the Oscott pyxes (Pl. 192*c*) would appear also to date from much about the same period. It is a little round box with a pull-off cover with knob. The cover is engraved with the usual IHS with nails, but instead of the usual plain cross is a Crucifix.

A pyx at Stonyhurst (Pl. 192*d*) is in the form of a little box with a pull-off cover engraved with the Agnus Dei. It probably dates from about the time of the Restoration.

Another Oscott pyx (Pl. 192*b*) would seem to date later in the century, judging from the rendering of the engraved Sacred Monogram. It will be noted that it belongs to the type with the hinged lid and suspensory loop.

The pyxes of the eighteenth and of the early nineteenth centuries are mostly variations of the two patterns which have been illustrated. They are seldom of much artistic value, since their decoration seldom consists of anything more than a small IHS within rays.

It has already been shown that few private chapels possessed a monstrance before the Reformation. The chapels run by the minor squirearchy during Elizabethan times would not have carried forward such an object from the Middle Ages. It is rather more surprising that the lavishly furnished chapel run by Elizabeth Vaux at Harrowden did not contain a monstrance, but, so far as is at present known, the use of such objects in Recusant chapels only began after the Restoration.

Sir Thomas Strickland of Sizergh Castle, Westmorland, had fought with distinction in the Civil War and served as a knight of the shire in the Cavalier Parliament. In 1669 he was appointed Keeper of the Privy Purse to Queen Catherine of Braganza, a post which would have given him ample opportunities of studying the chapel plate which she had brought from Portugal. The idea of a combined chalice and monstrance was evolved in Spain and Portugal towards the end of the sixteenth century. It became very popular in the Peninsula in the following century, but won no support elsewhere. In it the monstrance portion was made to clip on to the bowl of the chalice which thus became its base, as may be seen in an early seventeenth-century Portuguese example in the Victoria and Albert Museum (Pl. 193*a*). Sir Thomas would seem to have failed to convey to his goldsmith a correct idea of the piece which he wished him to copy, with disastrous results. The only way in which the piece can be assembled for use as a monstrance is with the *gloria* screwed on to the bottom of the stem of the chalice, so that the bowl has to serve as the base! (Pls. 193–4). There is no way of using the foot of the chalice. Had the *gloria* been made to fit on to the bowl of the chalice as intended, the result would have been a very handsome, if exotic, piece, since the goldsmith (who did not mark his work), was a good enough craftsman.

The next monstrance to be noted is in the National Museum, Dublin (Pl. 195). It is well made, but the proportions are not altogether happy—the cross is obviously too large. It bears the hall-mark for 1693, but the maker's mark is missing.[1]

An interesting mid-eighteenth-century monstrance is at Mount St. Mary's College, Sprinkhill, Sheffield (Pl. 196). In this case the *gloria* has been tastefully executed but the twisted baluster stem is unimaginative, whilst the base is too small. It bears the mark of John Payne and the hall-mark for 1756.

A monstrance at Stonyhurst (Pl. 197), made for Sir Thomas Weld, bears the hall-mark for 1808. In this case the stem and base are well proportioned but the upper part is far from satisfactory. So sound a goldsmith as Samuel Hennell should not have draped the little handkerchiefs round the rays of the *gloria*! Though crowns are frequently found surmounting foreign monstrances, the present one is much too large.

If it be admitted that during the period under discussion English goldsmiths never devised an entirely satisfactory form of monstrance, it should be remembered that the demand for such pieces was so small[2] that few of the artists can ever have had a chance of showing he had profited from past mistakes when designing a second one.

RELIQUARIES

Though the Recusants treasured many relics from the medieval churches and eagerly collected relics of their own martyrs, they appear to have made no serious attempt to get their treasures richly mounted up as their ancestors would have done. This was not due merely to lack of opportunity. Actually, as we shall see, the two most important reliquaries which have come down to us were made at a period when persecution was severe. There could have been no practical difficulty about getting a reliquary made in the eighteenth century, but in actual fact hardly any commissions reached the goldsmiths. None appear to have been important ones.

The two outstanding reliquaries already mentioned both enshrine pieces of the same relic. In his autobiography, Father Gerard relates that he was given by the daughter of Thomas Percy,[3] Earl of Northumberland, a thorn from the

[1] The hall-marks are on the rays of the *gloria*. The ray on which the maker's mark was originally has probably been renewed, or else it is missing.

[2] In this connexion it is interesting to recall that no monstrances are mentioned in Hitchmough's depositions.

[3] *John Gerard, the autobiography of an Elizabethan*, ed. Philip Caraman, 1951, 41.

Crown of Thorns, which he used to wear in a cross round his neck until the day of his execution at York in 1572. The relic was a gift from Mary, Queen of Scots, who had brought it with her when she returned to Scotland from France. Gerard merely records that his friend got this relic set in a gold case set with pearls. In actual fact the relic would appear to have been split and two reliquaries (Pls. 198–9) made, differing in design but both evidently the work of the same goldsmith and bearing underneath the same inscription.[1] This last gives the history of the relic as related above but reveals that it was mounted in gold at the expense of *IW*, who is clearly Jane Wiseman who was one of Gerard's most faithful friends.

The reliquary now at Stonyhurst (Pl. 198) has a diamond-shaped base decorated with the Instruments of the Passion in translucent enamel. The stem is a thin rod supported by three scroll buttresses, whilst the actual cylindrical container is held in place by four uprights, each of which takes the form of one of the Instruments of the Passion. The cap of the container is enamelled with the Crown of Thorns, and this subject is repeated vertically but with a crucifix in the middle.

The reliquary now at Sint-Michielskerk, Ghent (Pl. 199), has a round, spreading foot decorated with the Sacred Monogram, cherubs, and arabesques in translucent enamel, as is also the baluster stem. The relic is contained in a crystal cross which is framed by a representation of the Crown of Thorns. On the top is the Sacred Monogram with heart[2] and nails, all in openwork within a rayed frame.[3]

Just as Father Gerard was inaccurate in stating that there was only one reliquary of the Holy Thorn, so he also mentions three silver reliquaries which he handed over to the Superior, whereas there are actually four, all obviously by the same hand, preserved at Stonyhurst. They contain relics of saints Modwenna, Robert Sutton, Francis Xavier (with others), and Stephen, respectively. Though the engraving on their bases is somewhat similar to that on the

[1] ✠ *Haec spina de corona Do[min]i sancta fuit prima Mariae reg[inae] Scot[iae] Mart[yris] ab ea data Comiti Northumb[riae] Mart[yri] qui in morte misit illam Filiae Eliz[abeth]ae qui dedit Soc[ietati] hanc q[uam] I : Wis : ornavit auro*. The inscription on the Ghent reliquary is illustrated as fig. 37 in *Het Edelsmeedwerk op de testoonstelling Religieuse Kunst in Oostvlaanderen*, by Elizabeth Dhanens, Ghent, 1951.

[2] This is a very early instance of the inclusion of the heart in the *Sacred Monogram* motif (cf. p. 225).

[3] The history of the two reliquaries was told by Father John Morris in an article in *The Month* (xliv, 1882, 549–56). The authentication of the Ghent reliquary states that it was kept in the room of the Provincial of the Jesuits in London until 1666, when it was sent over to the Novitiate of the Jesuits at Watten in Flanders. At about the same time the Stonyhurst reliquary was sent to the Jesuit College at St. Omer. In 1762 both Jesuit communities were forced to remove into Belgium. On the suppression of the Jesuits in 1773, the reliquary from Watten fell into the hands of the Bishop of Ghent, who gave it to the church of St. Michael. The other got into the hands of a notary of Bruges, who in 1781 sold it to a travelling Englishman, Mr. Weld of Lulworth, who in 1803 presented it to Stonyhurst.

two gold reliquaries, the design and workmanship does not appear to be English. This is particularly noticeable in the figure of St. Stephen which surmounts the reliquary containing a fragment of his jaw-bone. This is quite unlike the sort of saintly image found on Elizabethan apostle spoons and suggests that a German or Flemish origin is more likely.

CONCLUSION

He doth not so adore the ancients as to despise the moderns. Grant them but dwarfs, yet stand they upon giants' shoulders, and may see the further. Sure as stout champions of truth follow in the rear as marched in the front. FULLER

IF in closing this study at the year 1830 I appear to fall short of 'The True Church Antiquary' as described by Thomas Fuller in *The Holy State*, it is not because I disagree with his sentiments. Ideally this book should have been brought down to the present day, but the practical difficulties in the face of such a course appeared too great. It might nowadays be possible to discuss dispassionately the ideals and achievements of the Victorian Gothic Revival with regard to church plate. It would, however, require very careful handling since there is no lack of examples, there is a copious literature, and many documents to digest. To deal with the subject adequately would require a substantial monograph; to have attempted it here would have upset the balance of this book. We shall, therefore, leave the history of English church plate at a time when Augustus Welby Pugin was only beginning to make himself known and when the future leaders of the Oxford Movement were still only of importance to themselves and to each other.

It follows naturally that if Victorian church plate be excluded the work of more recent times must be ignored. This is done without disparagement, since the present needs of churches may well be best satisfied by modern goldsmiths who may 'see the further', if they are prepared to mount upon giants' shoulders.

Something remains to be said about the present position of the ancient plate belonging to the churches in this country. Neither the Church of England, the Church of Wales, nor the authorities of the Roman Catholic Church have any grounds for complacency, but the disabilities under which they suffer are not always the same. All three bodies suffer from having a considerable number of priests who have no knowledge or appreciation of the works of art of which they are the temporary custodians. From this failing much harm has resulted. The sad story of the fourteenth-century Goathland chalice has already been told. Minor repairs had been neglected until they had developed into major ones, then the chalice was put into the hands of an incompetent goldsmith. The story of the thirteenth-century chalice at Ashprington was almost the same. The repairs were, however, not so drastically executed, and though the chalice was also electro-gilded it was done so economically that the gilt has now nearly worn away. It would be easy to extend the list of pieces damaged by neglect followed by injudicious repairs by following on with stories concerning less important pieces. It should not be inferred, however, that antique plate must be entirely withdrawn from use. What it is desired to emphasize is that it should be treated with proper care and respect.

In contrast to the plate which suffers from injudicious use is the vast quantity, mainly Anglican, which is lodged permanently in banks. It is a great pity that more incumbents do not make a point of getting out their plate and placing it on the altar at the great festivals. It is not necessary that it should be used. Good seventeenth- or eighteenth-century plate is fully as appropriate and more decorative than cheap brass flower-vases. It is good for the *amour propre* of a parish to be aware that its church is the possessor of beautiful things given by past parishioners.

The Victoria and Albert Museum has for some years had a loan collection arranged to illustrate the development of English church plate through the ages. The exhibits have been carefully picked and have, indeed, provided many of the illustrations for this book. The existence of this collection does not, however, provide the complete answer to the problem, since it is obvious that it would be neither feasible nor desirable greatly to extend it. It would seem well worth considering whether it might not be possible, by the foundation of diocesan museums such as exist in many continental countries, to bring into the light of day much of the plate which at present remains unused and unseen. Many of our ancient cathedrals could find space for one without great difficulty, whilst some must still have their medieval treasuries which could be brought up to date with regard to security without much trouble. Not only would such museums be likely to attract visitors but it might be possible to introduce the students of the theological colleges to the interest of church plate, so that they might more readily understand their responsibilities when, at a later stage, they find important pieces entrusted to their charge.

It is to be hoped that the type of incumbent who in time past used to sell the old church plate and buy new is now extinct, and that it is generally understood that no plate can be sold without a faculty from the chancellor of the diocese. On the other hand, quite a fresh danger is arising from the modern tendency of running parishes together under one priest. Not only is more and more plate getting immured in banks but there is the danger of the plate of parish *A* getting mixed up with that of parish *B*. No great harm may result if the parishes are situated in counties or dioceses where the plate has at some time been fully catalogued, but a lot of interesting local history may become obscured if it has not.

One-third of England and the Welsh diocese of St. Asaph have never been properly listed, so that in these areas the archdeacons have usually no exact idea as to what plate should be taken over by a new incumbent. Similarly, how is a priest, when taking over an adjoining parish on the death of an aged incumbent, discover that the latter once deposited a box of plate, perhaps in his own name, at one of the banks in one of the neighbouring market towns? It is quite likely that the churchwardens will have no knowledge of the matter, and there is a serious danger that if the task of cataloguing church plate is not resumed a lot of important pieces will simply get lost.

The compilation of a catalogue of the plate of a county or diocese need not lead to the publication of a volume, as was possible in former times. What is really important is that there should be available somewhere, either in the possession of the archdeacon or of the cathedral library, an exact list which can be checked over when there is a change of incumbent. Some archdeacons (e.g. St. Albans and Stafford) possess quite efficient card indexes, but perhaps the ideal arrangement is that which was adopted by Canon H. H. Mills, who compiled a catalogue of the plate of the diocese of Truro, taking a photograph of every piece, either individually or grouped. One typed copy is deposited in the cathedral library and the other is in the possession of the Royal Institution of Cornwall.

If, as seems inevitable nowadays, it is not intended to publish the catalogue in book form, a resumé should be printed in the transactions of the local archaeological society, the more important pieces being illustrated.

The cataloguing of the plate of a county or of a diocese must be an arduous undertaking, but it is not today as formidable as it was in the days of the gentlemen whose names are mentioned in the bibliography. When the Rev. E. H. Bates concluded in 1903 the cataloguing of the plate of Somerset, he recorded his gratitude to 'the inventor of the safety bicycle'. Nowadays cars are plentiful and every vicarage has a telephone.

It may be urged that it would not be possible to find the experts to compile the catalogues. This has not proved a bar in the past. It will be found that about half of the compilers have been clergy and half laymen. They have rarely been acknowledged experts at the time that they undertook the work —even E. Alfred Jones was an unknown quantity when he tackled the diocese of Bangor in 1906. Most of the compilers, having read up their subject as far as possible, have shown a capacity to learn from experience, and have been endowed with energy and enthusiasm. If a would-be compiler models his catalogue on that of one of the more able of his predecessors (the set-up of the Essex catalogue is excellent) he should be able to catalogue 80 per cent. of the plate without much trouble. He will have to think seriously over another 10 per cent., and for the remainder, which will probably include some foreign pieces, he may have to consult one of the national museums. Ideally, a catalogue should be the work of a single author, but this is not essential. The cataloguing of Essex was carried out by three clergymen in a very business-like manner. Half a dozen hands helped with Suffolk, but the co-operation of so many hands throws a lot of responsibility upon the editor who has to co-ordinate their work.

The position with regard to the Roman Catholic plate which is stored away in banks is much more delicate. The plate used in the old manor-house chapels during the Penal period was the property of the owner of the house. When eventually it became possible to found independent churches, most of the private chapels were closed and their plate was generally given to the new church. This course was by no means always adopted. Sometimes, after a lapse of time, the plate has found its way to one or other of the great religious foundations. The rest has drifted to the bottom of the plate chest, at home or in the bank, where it remains until everything is sold up, for the old Recusant homes, like the old Protestant ones, are being stripped ruthlessly. Since there is obviously not enough good old plate to serve the needs of all the modern churches, it would seem to be worth while for the ecclesiastical authorities to consider a campaign to round up these unused pieces. Unless this is done, it will all drift into the antique market; this almost inevitably results in secularization.

The plate which has come into the possession of the large ecclesiastical establishments is now being well looked after, but it is a great pity that in the past it has generally been nobody's job to catalogue accessions. As a result of this the provenances are now often unknown, and it is frequently impossible to decide which paten to allocate to a chalice. It is to be hoped that as more attention is focused on old Recusant plate, the heads of those institutions which possess valuable collections will attempt to interest in this subject those who are training to enter the priesthood. This would, in the course of time, improve the lot of the old plate scattered in churches all over England, and help to preserve it from injudicious repairs and unsightly electro-gilding.

It is important that a systematic attempt should be made to catalogue plate which once belonged to the old manor-house chapels and which has now descended to the churches founded about a hundred years ago. Thanks to the energy of the Rev. E. A. Clark, S.J., the Society of Jesus must have a good idea of what is contained in the churches which it serves. It is necessary, however, that the sacristies of all the churches ministered both by the regular and by the secular clergy should be investigated, lest this generation should be guilty of allowing to perish through heedlessness an important part of the national heritage. The task of cataloguing old Recusant plate is not so large as that which remains to be done for the Anglican churches. It is, however, rather more tricky, since the aid of hall-marks is less often available, but this book will have served a useful purpose if it enables future investigators to recognize the main varieties of the old Recusant plate which they may encounter.

BIBLIOGRAPHY

OF WORKS TO WHICH REFERENCE IS MADE BY ABBREVIATED TITLES IN THE FOOTNOTES AND CATALOGUE OF INVENTORIES OF EXTANT CHURCH PLATE, PRINTED OR UNPRINTED

GENERAL WORKS

Abbreviated title	
Cripps	Cripps, Wilfred Joseph: *Old English Plate*, 1st ed. 1878, 11th ed. 1926.
Jackson, *Goldsmiths*	Jackson, Sir Charles James: *English Goldsmiths and their Marks*, 2nd ed. 1921, reprinted 1949.
Jackson, *History*	Jackson, Sir Charles James: *An Illustrated History of English Plate*, 1911.
Watts	Watts, W. W.: *Old English Silver*, 1924.

COLLECTIONS OF DOCUMENTS, ETC.

Collins	Collins, A. Jefferies: *Jewels and Plate of Queen Elizabeth I, the 1574 inventory*, 1955.
Frere and Kennedy	Frere, W. H., and Kennedy, W. M.: *Visitation Articles and Injunctions of the Period of the Reformation*. Alcuin Club, 1910.
Legg and Hope	Legg, J. Wickham, and Hope, W. H. St. J.: *Inventories of Christchurch, Canterbury*, 1902.
Oliver	Oliver, H.: *Lives of the Bishops of Exeter*, 1861.
Palgrave	Palgrave, Sir F.: *Antient Kalendars and Inventories of the Exchequer*, 1836.
Rites	*The Rites of Durham, being a description or brief declaration of all the ancient monuments, rites, and customs belonging or being within the monastical church of Durham before the suppression.* Written 1593. Edited by Canon J. T. Fowler. Surtees Society, 1903.
Walters	Walters, H. B.: *London Churches at the Reformation*, 1939.

LOCAL INVENTORIES

ENGLAND

Bedfordshire

Nil.

Berkshire

C.P. Berks.	Walker, John W. and Margaret I.: *Church Plate of Berkshire*, 1927.
	Jones, E. Alfred: *Plate of St. George's Chapel, Windsor Castle*, 1939.

Buckinghamshire

Myres, J. L.: 'The Church Plate of Buckinghamshire', *Architectural and Antiquarian Society of Bucks. Records*, vii, 1896, 413 et seq.; viii, 1903, 10 et seq. (Covers deaneries of Claydon and Mursley only.)

Cambridgeshire

Atkinson, T. D., Foster, J. E., Macalister, R. A. S., and Raynes, W. L.: *Catalogue of Church Plate in the County of Cambridge*, 1893–*c.* 1900. This manuscript covers all but about half a dozen parishes, but is amateurish and unreliable. It is in the library of the Cambridge Antiquarian Society.

Jones, *Cambridge* — Jones, E. Alfred: *Old Plate of the Cambridge Colleges*, 1910. (College chapel plate).

Cheshire

C.P. Chester — Ball, T. S.: *Church Plate of the City of Chester*, 1907. (There is nothing for the county.)

Cornwall

Mills, Canon H. Holroyd: *Record of the Church Plate in the Diocese of Truro*, 1919. This typescript, which is accompanied by photographs showing every piece, is in the library of Truro Cathedral. The original manuscript is in the possession of the Royal Institution of Cornwall, Truro.

Mills, Canon H. Holroyd: 'Cornish Church Plate' in *Cornish Church Guide*, 1925, 235–40.

Cumberland

C.P. Carlisle — Ferguson, R. S., and nine others: *Old Church Plate in the Diocese of Carlisle*, 1882.

Ware, Mrs. H.: *A Supplement to the Old Plate of the Diocese of Carlisle*, 1908.

Derbyshire

Nil.

Devonshire

Chanter, Rev. J. F., and others: 'Church Plate in Devon' (arranged by deaneries) in *Transactions of the Devonshire Association*. Introduction, Deanery of Sherwell, xxxvii, 1905, 146–7; Barnstaple, xxxix, 1907, 110–30; South Molton, xlii, 1910, 91–111; Exeter, xliv, 1912, 86–125; Totnes, xlv, 1913, 93–116; Chulmleigh and Hartland, xlvii, 1915, 134–59; Holsworthy and Torrington, xlviii, 1916, 101–36; Ottery and Honiton, xlix, 1917, 109–58; Aylesbeare, l, 1918, 188–218; Cullumpton and Tiverton, li, 1919, 80–113; Cadbury and Kenn, lii, 1920, 80–121; Moreton, liii, 1921, 98–127; Okehampton, liv, 1922, 87–109; Woodleigh, lv, 1923, 64–82; Plympton and the Three Towns, lvi, 1924, 123–52; Ipplepen and Tavistock, lix, 1927, 87–125.

Dorset

C.P. Dorset — Nightingale, J. S.: *Church Plate in Dorset*, 1889.

Durham

Cripps, W. J.: 'The Church Plate of Northumberland and Durham', *Archaeologia Aeliana*, xvi, 1894, 249 et seq. Published in detail in gobbets to fill up white spaces in *Proceedings of the Society of Newcastle-upon-Tyne*, ii. 1885–v, 1892.

Essex

C.P. Essex Benton, Rev. G. Montagu, Galpin, Rev. Canon F. W., Pressey, Rev. W. J.: *Church Plate of the County of Essex*, 1926.

Freshfield, Edwin: *Church Plate in the parish churches of Essex*, i, 1899. Never proceeded beyond the deaneries of Barking, Chafford (Romford), and Chelmsford.

Gloucestershire

C.P. Glos. Evans, Rev. J. T.: *Church Plate of Gloucestershire*, 1906.

C.P. Bristol Cole, Rev. Thorold: *Church Plate of the City of Bristol*, i, 1932. Never completed.

Hampshire

C.P. Hants Braithwaite, Rev. P. R. P.: *Church Plate of Hampshire*, 1909.

Herefordshire

C.P. Hereford Stanhope, Ven. and Hon. Berkeley, and Moffatt, Harold C.: *Church Plate of the County of Hereford*, 1903.

Hertfordshire

Gardiner, Rev. E. R.: 'Notes on the Church Plate now existing in the Deaneries of Baldock and Hitchin', in *Transactions of the St. Albans and Hertfordshire Archaeological Society*, 1887, 9–40.

Carrington, John B., compiled a manuscript catalogue which is kept by the Archdeacon of St. Albans.

Huntingdonshire

Nil.

Kent

Robertson, Rev. Canon W. A. Scott: 'Church Plate in Kent', in *Archaeologia Cantiana*. Introduction, chronological list of pieces, and list of donors, xvi, 1886, 327–439. Detailed inventory by parishes, Acrise to Canterbury, xvii, 1887, 242–340. Never completed.

Woodruff, Rev. C. E.: Same title and place of publication. Arranged by deaneries, East Charing, Ospringe, and Westbere, xxv, 1902, 113–97; Dover, Sittingbourne, and Sutton, xxvi, 1904, 113–226; Canterbury, xxvii, 1905, 262–300.

Sandwich, and supplement to Canterbury Cathedral, xxviii, 1909, 115–55. Never completed.

Carnegie, Moir: *Church Plate in the Hundred of Blackheath*, 1939.

Lancashire

Ball, T. S.: 'Some Lancashire Church Plate', in *Lancashire and Cheshire Antiquarian Society Transactions*, xxix, 1911, 53–69; xxx, 1912, 130–52.

Blundell, Rev. F. O.: 'Old-time Lancashire Chalices', in *Historic Society of Lancashire and Cheshire Transactions*, New Series, xl, 1924, 118–28 (Recusant chalices).

Leicestershire

C.P. Leics. Trollope, Rev. A.: *An Inventory of the Church Plate of Leicestershire*, 1890.

Lincolnshire

Sympson, F. Mansel: 'Church Plate of the Diocese of Lincoln', in *Archaeological Journal*, lxvii, 1910, 213 et seq.; also in *Associated Architectural Societies Transactions*, xxx, 1909–10, 11 et seq. (General introduction).

Sympson, F. Mansel: same title. A detailed inventory by deaneries in *Lincolnshire Notes and Queries*, xv, 1918–19. Deaneries of Aveland, Beltisloe, Bolingbroke, Calceworth, Candleshoe, Lincoln, East Elloe, xv, 1918–19, 116–48, 178–212, 225–44; West Elloe, Graffoe, Grantham, East Holland, xvi, 1920–1, 81–118, 162–78, 208–22. (Remainder never published, but the notes for it are in the possession of the Lincolnshire Archives Committee, Exchequer Gate, Lincoln.)

London

C.P. City Freshfield, Edwin: *The Communion Plate of the Churches in the City of London*, 1894.

C.P. County Freshfield, Edwin: *The Communion Plate of the Parish Churches of the County of London*, 1895. (Covers old parish churches only and does not include the plate of the sometime chapels of ease which have since become parish churches or have been absorbed back into the mother church.)

Middlesex

C.P. Middlesex Freshfield, Edwin: *The Communion Plate of the Parish Churches in the County of Middlesex*, 1897.

Norfolk

Manning, Rev. C. R. M.: 'Medieval patens in Norfolk', in *Norfolk Archaeology*, xii, 1895, 85–99.

Manning, Rev. C. R. M.: 'Illustrations of Church Plate in Norfolk', in *Norfolk Archaeology*, xiii, 1898, 233–40.

Hopper, Rev. E. C., Manning, Rev. C. R., Radcliffe, Rev. H. S., and Walter, John H.: 'Church Plate in Norfolk' (arranged by deaneries), in *Norfolk Archaeology*. Deanery of Redenhall, ix, 1884, 68–113; Norwich, x, 1888, 66–116; Depwode, xv, 1904, 44–50; Breccles, Thetford, East Brooke, Humbleyard, and Taverham, xvi, 1907, 31–38, 153–68, 240–66; Rockland, South Ingworth, West Brooke, xvii,

1910, 165, 92, 263–76; Hingham Forehoe, Mitford, Lynn, xviii, 1914, 23–45, 261–82; Flegg, Sparham, xix, 1917, 185–96, 221–37; Walsingham, North Ingworth, and Blofield, xx, 1921, 22–30, 150–7, 257–72; Holt, Waxham, Repps, xxi, 1926, 37–51, 143–51, 310–30; Tunstead, Heacham, Burnham, and Elmham, xxii, 1926, 1-16, 260–91, 133–46; Brisley, Loddon, Thetford, Cranwich, Fincham, Rockland, and Walsingham, xxiii, 1929, 19–50, 221–40, 341–60; Lynn Borough, East and West Fincham, Lynn Marshland, and Wisbech, xxiv, 1930–4, 18–31, 262–90.

Northamptonshire

C.P. Northants. Markham, Christopher A.: *Church Plate of the County of Northampton*, 1894.

Northumberland

See Durham

Nottinghamshire

Some very rough notes were made by E. Alfred Jones in 1939. They now belong to the Thoroton Society.

Oxfordshire

C.P. Oxon. Evans, Rev. J. T.: *Church Plate of Oxfordshire*, 1928.

Moffatt, *Oxford* Moffatt, Harold Charles: *Old Oxford Plate*, 1906. (College chapel plate).

Rutland

C.P. Rutland Hope, R. C.: *An Inventory of the Church Plate in Rutland*, 1887 (also in *The Reliquary*, N.S. 1, 1887, 32–43.

Shropshire

The Archdeacon of Salop has a rough manuscript inventory of the plate of his archdeaconry. There is nothing similar for the archdeaconry of Ludlow.

Somerset

Bates, Rev. E. H., Hancock, Rev. F., Bush, T. S.: 'Church Plate of Somerset' (arranged by deaneries), in *Somerset Archaeological Society Transactions*, Bruton, Castle Cary, Merston, Milborne Port, and Shepton Mallet, xliii, 1897, 172–231; Frome and Martock, xliv, 1898, 160–87; Crewkerne, Ilchester, Ilminster, and Wiviliscombe, xlv, 1899, 126–78; Dunster, Taunton, and Wellington, xlvi, 1900, 149–87; Bridgwater, Pawlett, and Quantockshead, xlvii, 1901, 150–74; Axbridge, Burnham, and Glastonbury, xlviii, 1902, 79–101; Bath, Chew, Keynsham, Midsomer Norton, and Portishead, xlix, 1903, 88–172; additional notes, lix, 1913, 74–78.

Staffordshire

Jeavons, S. A.: *Church Plate in the Archdeaconry of Stafford*, 1957. Also in *Transactions of the Birmingham Archaeological Society*, lxxxiii, 1955.

Suffolk

Hopper, Rev. E. C., and six others: 'Church Plate in Suffolk' (arranged by deaneries), in *Suffolk Institute of Archaeology and Natural History*, Hoxne, Horningsheath, Thingoe, Hartismere, Wangford, and the Colneys, viii, 1894, 279–333; Clare, North and South Dunwich, Lavenham, Lothingland, Orford, South Elmham, Sudbury and Thedwastre, Bosmere, Carlford, Claydon, Ipswich, Loes, Samford, Hadleigh, Stow and Mildenhall, Blackburne, Thurlow, and Wilford, ix, 1897, 1–76, 145–230, 279–306.

Surrey

C.P. Surrey — Cooper, Rev. T. S.: *Church Plate of Surrey*, 1902 (arranged by deaneries). Also in *Collections of the Surrey Archaeological Society*, Farnham, Woking, x, 1891, 316–68; Dorking, Guildford, Leatherhead, Emly, and Croydon, xi, 1893, 39–105, 252–84; Kingston, Godstone, Beddington, xii, 1895, 52–92, 172–90; Kingston *cont.*, Reigate, and Barnes, xiii, 1897, 49–94, 166–76; Barnes *cont.*, Lambeth, Kennington, Newington, xiv, 1899, 72–81, 190–214; Southwark, xv, 1900, 137–58; Southwark *cont.*, xvi, 1901, 197–8.

Sussex

C.P. Sussex — Couchman, J. E.: *Sussex Church Plate*, 1912 (arranged by deaneries). Also in *Sussex Archaeological Collections*, Chichester, Arundel, Boxgrove, liii, 1910, 198–266; Midhurst, Petworth, Storrington, and Lewes, liv, 1911, 184–258; Brighton, Pevensey, Hastings, and Dallington, lv, 1912, 126–219.

Warwick

Arbuthnot, Ven. C.: *Church Plate of the Archdeaconry of Coventry*, 1921. (A meagre list, without descriptions or marks.)

Westmorland

See Cumberland.

Wiltshire

C.P. Wilts. — Nightingale, J. E.: *Church Plate of the County of Wilts.*, 1891.

Worcestershire

C.P. Worcs. — Lea, Ven. William: *Church Plate of the Archdeaconry of Worcester*, 1884. (Inadequate and without maker's marks.)

Yorkshire

C.P. Yorks.	Fallow, T. M., and McCall, H. B.: *Yorkshire Church Plate.* I. City of York, North and East Riding, 1912; II. West Riding, 1915.
	Sprittles, J.: *Survey of the Plate of Leeds Parish Church and its Ancient Chapelries,* 1951.

WALES

C.P. Bangor	Jones, E. Alfred: *Church Plate of the Diocese of Bangor,* 1906.
C.P. Brecon	Evans, Rev. J. T.: *Church Plate of Breconshire,* 1912.
C.P. Cardigan	Evans, Rev. J. T.: *Church Plate of Cardiganshire,* 1914.
C.P. Carmarthen	Evans, Rev. J. T.: *Church Plate of Carmarthenshire,* 1907. (With additions to *Church Plate of Pembrokeshire.*)
C.P. Gowerland	Evans, Rev. J. T.: *Church Plate of Gowerland,* 1921. (With an exhaustive summary of the church plate in the diocese of St. David's.)
C.P. Llandaff	Halliday, G. E.: *Llandaff Church Plate,* 1901.
C.P. Pembroke	Evans, Rev. J. T.: *Church Plate of Pembrokeshire,* 1905.
C.P. Radnor	Evans, Rev. J. T.: *Church Plate of Radnorshire,* 1910.
	(There is nothing for the diocese of St. Asaph.)

CHANNEL ISLANDS

Curtis, S. Carey: 'Church Plate of the Deanery of Guernsey', in *Transactions of the Guernsey Society of Natural Science* for 1913 and 1917.

Curtis, S. Carey: 'Church Plate of the Deanery of Jersey', in *Société Jersiaise, Bulletin,* xlii, 1917.

ISLE OF MAN

C.P. I.O.M.	Jones, E. Alfred: *Old Church Plate of the Isle of Man,* 1907.

APPENDIX I

LIST OF MEDIEVAL CHALICES AND PATENS

(References to Jackson's *Goldsmiths* are headed *J.G.*)

A. CHALICES

(Those marked with an asterisk have patens.)

GROUP I (*cf. p.* 39)

Bowl shaped like the lower half of an egg, slight knot, domed foot.

Ninth century

1. British Museum (from Trewhiddle, Cornwall). Pl. 1.

GROUP II (*cf. p.* 40)

Broad bowl with pronounced lip, no stem, knot with twelve vertical ribs between two bands of beading, round foot with twelve lobes.

c. 1160

2. Canterbury Cathedral* (from grave of Archbishop Walter, d. 1205). Pl. 2.

GROUP III (*cf. p.* 41)

Broad bowl with pronounced lip, knots of various forms, stems either jointed on to the round foot or with the latter socketed into them.

1180–1280

3. Ashprington, Devon.
4. British Museum (from Berwick St. James, Wilts. till 1879).
5. Chichester Cathedral* I (from grave of a bishop).
6. St. David's Cathedral* I.
7. St. David's Cathedral II.
8. Exeter Cathedral* (from grave of Bishop Bitton, d. 1307).
9. Hereford Cathedral* (from grave of Bishop Swinfield, d. 1316). Pl. 3*a*.
10. Lincoln Cathedral* (from grave of Bishop Grosseteste, d. 1253).
11. Lincoln Cathedral* (from grave of Bishop Gravesend, d. 1279). Pl. 3*b*.
12. Lincoln Cathedral* (from grave of Bishop Sutton, d. 1299).
13. Søro, Denmark (from grave of Archbishop Absalon, d. 1201).
14. York Minster* (from grave of an archbishop).

Details

KNOTS, rounded, 3–7, 9, 10, 12, 13; eight-sided, 14; eight-lobed, 8, 11.

STEMS, jointed on to foot, 4, 8–10, 12. Foot socketed into stem (usually not more than a ring above and below the knot). Stems, eight-sided, 3, 7; fluted, 14; the remainder are round. Foot wanting, 10.

GROUP IV (*cf. p.* 41)

Bowl broad with a pronounced lip, round foot embossed with lobes, sometimes engraved, socketed into stem, knots of various forms.

15. Cardiff, National Museum★ (Dolgelley find, 1890). Pl. 4.
16. Chichester Cathedral II★ (from grave of a bishop).
17. Dragsmark, Sweden.★ Pl. 5.
18. Oslo, Kunstindustrimuseum (from Børsa). Pl. 7.
19. Salisbury Cathedral (from grave of Bishop Longespée, d. 1297).
20. York Minster★ II (from grave of an archbishop). Pl. 6.

Details

KNOT, rounded, 16; eight-lobed, 19, 20; twelve-lobed, 15; writhen, 18; or decorated with chevron ornament, 17.

FOOT, round and embossed with a series of radiating lobes which are sometimes engraved. Lobes pointed, 19; rounded, 18; double and both cusped, 15 and 16; double and both rounded, 20; double, one rounded and one cusped, 17.

GROUP V (*cf. p.* 42)

Bowl deeper and of conical form, round stem, knot with eight lobes, round foot.

c. 1320

21. York Minster (from grave of Archbishop Melton, d. 1340). Pl. 8*a*.
22. Stockholm, Statens Historiska Museum (from South Sweden). Pl. 8*b*.

Details

Crucifix, engraved on foot, 21; cast and applied on foot, 22.

GROUP VI (*cf. p.* 43)

Bowl deep and conical, middle section various, foot hexagonal, with incurved sides.

Late fourteenth and early fifteenth centuries

23. Hamstall Ridware,★ Staffs. Pl. 9.
24. Aston-by-Sutton,★ Cheshire. Pl. 10.
25. Goathland, Yorks. Pl. 11.

Details

KNOT, writhen with ribbed ring above and below, 23; hexagonal with incurved sides decorated with a double row of quatrefoils, hexagonal stem, 24; rounded hexagonal, with hexagonal stem.

FOOT, plain, 23; engraved with Crucifixion and with a coat-of-arms (*on a cross five lions rampant*), 24; engraved with the Sacred Monogram, 25.

GROUP VII (*cf. p.* 44)

Bowl deeper and less conical, tending to become hemispherical; well-developed hexagonal stem; six-lobed knot with bosses variously decorated, between the lobes are traceried compartments usually pierced; foot hexagonal with incurved sides.

Second half of fifteenth century

Hall-marked

26. Nettlecombe,* Som. Pl. 12*a*. 1479. Maker's mark, *grasshopper* (*J.G.* 92, 'a jug')
27. Brasenose College, Oxford. Pl. 13*b*. 1498. Maker's mark *MW in monogram* (*J.G.* 92).
28. Brasenose College,* Oxford. Pl. 13*b* 1498. Maker's mark, *MW in monogram* (*J.G.* 92).

Without marks

29. Ampleforth Abbey I* (Selim Dean & Co., 1845, Bishop R. G. Willson, Dom E. H. and R. W. Willson, O.S.B.).
30. Ampleforth Abbey II. Pl. 12*b*. (Dom E. H. and R. W. Willson, O.S.B.).
31. Hinderwell, Yorks.
32. Manningford Abbas, Wilts.
33. Stadarhraun, Iceland. Pl. 13*a*.
34. Westminster Cathedral I.
35. Victoria and Albert Museum.
36. Heirs of the late Sir John Noble.

Travelling chalices

37. Maynooth, St. Patrick's College.
38. West Grinstead, Sussex, R.C. church. Pl. 14*a*.

Details

BOWL, original wanting, 34, 37.

KNOT, with bosses decorated with angel heads, 27, 28, 33, 35; leopard heads, 26; conventional floral motif stamped, 30, 31; engraved, 34, 37.

FOOT, original wanting, 32; engraved with Crucifix, 27–30, 35, 36; inset with enamelled Crucifix, 26; with cast and applied Crucifixion, 34.

GROUP VIII (*cf. p.* 44)

Differs from the preceding group only in having (or having had) leaf- or crescent-shaped 'knops' on the angles of the foot.

1490–1510

Hall-marked

39. Clifford Chambers,* Glos. 1494. Maker's mark, *eagle's head* (*J.G.* 92).
40. Chester Cathedral (Dean Darby, 1886, L. F. C. Darby till 1955). 1496. Maker's mark, *grasshopper* (*J.G.* 92, 'a jug').
41. West Drayton,* Middx. 1507. Maker's mark, *Vernicle* (*J.G.* 93 'a maidenhead').

Without marks

42. Arundel Castle,* Sussex.
43. Bacton,* Heref. Pl. 33*b*.

44. Beswick,* Yorks.
45. Blaston St. Giles, Leics.
46. Calcena, Zaragoza, Spain. Pl. 17.
47. Claughton-on-Brock,* Lancs., R.C. church.
48. Codford St. Mary, Wilts.
49. Combpyne, Devon (the knot is on a chalice at St. Peter, Warrington, Lancs.).
50. Coombe Keynes, Dorset. Pl. 15*a*.
51. Everingham, Yorks., R.C. church.
52. Hornby, Lancs., R.C. church (originally at Caton). Pl. 15*b*.
53. Leominster,* Heref. Pl. 16.
54. Little Faringdon, Oxon.
55. Llandudwen, Caernarvon.
56. Llanelian-yn-Rhos, Denbigh.
57. Mr. J. Lowsley-Williams (Mrs. Munday *c.* 1900).
58. Old Hutton, Westmorland. Pl. 33*a*.
59. Preston-on-Stour, Glos.
60. Col. E. J. Pyke.* Pl. 14*b*.

Details

BOWL, original wanting, 59; inscribed **Benedicam dñm in omni tempore**, 46; **Calicem salutaris accipiam et nomen dñi invocabo** (variously abbreviated) 52, 53.

KNOT, with bosses decorated with angel heads, 40, 43, 48, 50, 58, 59; *Vernicle*, 51, 58, 60; leopard heads, 54; IESVS, 39, 59; conventional floral motif, stamped, 44; engraved, 40–42, 45–47, 55–57.

FOOT inset with enamelled plaque of Crucifix, 47; Crucifixion, 52; engraved with **IHC**, **XPC**, 46–47, 53; **IHC**, 49. 'Knops' of crescent form, 39–40, 48, 59, 60; leaf-shaped, 42–45, 49–53, 55–58. The knops of the remainder are wanting.

GROUP IX (*cf. p.* 45)

Differs from the last two groups in the form of the foot, which is six-lobed. In some examples the form of the bowl is more square than heretofore.

Hall-marked

61. Corpus Christi College,* Oxford, Pls. 18, 32. 1507. Maker's mark, *fleur-de-lis* (*J.G.* 93).
62. Leyland, Lancs., R.C. church. 1517. Maker's mark, *two links* (*J.G.* 93).
63. Victoria and Albert Museum,* Pl. 19 (Bedingfield family until 1905, Swaythling Colln. until 1924, Duleep Singh Colln. until 1947). 1518. Maker's mark, *a fish* (*J.G.* 93).
64. Manx Museum, Douglas, I.O.M. (Jurby church until 1939). 1521. Maker's mark, *two links* (*J.G.* 93).
65. Highworth,* Wilts. 1523. Maker's mark, *a stirrup* (?)
66. Magdalen College,* Oxford ('a church in Hampshire' before 1903, Sir John Noble Colln. until 1936). 1527. Maker's mark illegible.
67. Victoria and Albert Museum* (Eyrarbakki, Iceland, until *c.* 1903). 1527. Maker's mark, *Tau cross* (*J.G.* 95).

68. Westminster Cathedral II. Pl. 21. 1529. Maker's mark, *sceptre* (*J.G.* 94).
69. Sturminster Marshall, Dorset. 1536. Maker's mark, *TW* (*J.G.* 95).
70. Melbourne, National Museum* (Sotheby, 19. iv. 1920). 1537. Maker's mark, *eagle on globe* (*J.G.* 95).
71. St. Sampson, Guernsey. Two illegible marks.

Without marks

72. Broughton Hall, Skipton, Yorks.
73. Ebbesbourne Wake, Wilts.
74. Lord Hatherton.* Pl. 20. (Pillaton Hall find, 1750).
75. Heirs of Sir Charles Jackson.

Details

BOWL inscribed: **Pater de celis miserere nobis**, 74, **Beati qui audiunt verbum dei ut custodint illud**, 65, **Vere pcepio corporis et sanguinis dni Jesu xpe**, 68.

KNOT decorated with angel heads, 62–65, 67, 72–73, 75; grotesque face, 68; conventional floral ornament, 70–71. No bosses, 66. Knot wanting, 69.

FOOT with domed centre, 62, 64–68, 73–75; engraved with Crucifix, 61–62, 63–64, 66–69, 75, also with Virgin and Child, SS. Augustine, Jerome, Margaret, Mary Magdalene, 61; with Man of Sorrows, 65; **IHC XPC**, 60; **IHC**, 70. Inscribed: **Sancta maria ora pro nobis**, 74; **Crux xpi salva nos Crux xpi protige nos**, 68.

GROUP X (*cf. p.* 46)

This group is similar to the last except for its characteristic feature, which is a foot with an outline of a wavy-sided hexagon.

Hall-marked

76. Wylye, Wilts. Pl. 22. 1525. Maker's mark, *sceptre* (*J.G.* 94).
77. Edinburgh, Royal Scottish Museum. Pl. 23. (Sotheby, 12.ii.1953). 1527. Maker's mark, *sceptre*.
78. Trinity College, Oxford. 1527. Maker's mark, *Vernicle* (*J.G.* 94 'a maid's head').

Details

BOWL inscribed: ✠ CALICEM SALVTARIS, &c., variously abbreviated, 76–78.

KNOT with angel heads, 76; grotesque heads, 77; embossed floral motif, 78.

FOOT engraved with a Crucifix, 76–78. Inscribed: CALICEM SALVTARIS ACCIPIAM, 78; ATHOREMVS TE XPE ET PEN, 77.

Note. The unmarked bowl and foot of a sixteenth-century chalice belonging to Trinity church, Jersey, are excluded on the grounds that they are probably of foreign origin.

B. PATENS

(Arranged according to iconography. Those marked with an asterisk accompany a chalice.)

Abbreviations indicating form:

I = Single depression.
II = Double depression.
(The arabic numeral denotes the number of lobes to the depression.)
p = Plain cusps.
e = Engraved cusps.

AGNUS DEI

1150–1175

1. Canterbury Cathedral.* Pl. 24*a* (from grave of Archbishop Walter, d. 1205).
2. Chichester Cathedral* I (from grave of a bishop).

Middle of thirteenth century

3. Wyke, Hants. Pl. 24*b*.

1450–1540

Hall-marked

4. Milwich, Staffs. Pl. 34*b*. 1521. Maker's mark, *a turret* (?)
5. Melbourne, National Museum.* Pl. 34*c*. 1537. Maker's mark, *eagle on globe* (*J.G.* 95).

Without marks

6. Chewton Mendip, Som. Pl. 34*a*.
7. Cold Ashton, Glos.
8. Hinderwell,* Yorks.
9. Kirkby Laythorpe, Lincs.
10. Merton, Norf.
11. Waterfall, Staffs.

Details

1. I. Rim inscribed: ✠ ARA CRUCIS TUMULIQ CALIX LAPIDISQ PATENA SINDONIS OFICIUM CANDIDA BISSUS HABET, round centre: AGNUS DI QUI TOLL' PECCATA MUNDI MISERERE NOB'.
2. II, 4, p. Round centre ✠ AGNUS DEI QUI TOLLIS PECATA MUNDI MISERERE NOBIS.
3. II, 8, e. Rim engraved: ✠ CUNTA CREO WIRTUTE REGO PIETATE REFORMO.
4. II, 6, e. Lamb of the Apocalypse, resting on book.
5. II, 6, e. } Round centre: ECCE AGNUS DEI IESUS.
6. II, 6, e. }
7. II, 6, e. 8. I. 9. II, 6, e. 10. II, 6, e. 11. II, 6, e.

MANUS DEI

1200–1300

12. Chichester Cathedral* II (from the grave of a bishop).
13. Dragsmark,* Sweden. Pl. 26*b*.
14. Exeter Cathedral* (from grave of Bishop Bitton, d. 1307).
15. Hereford Cathedral* (from grave of Bishop Swinfield, d. 1316).
16. Lincoln Cathedral* (from grave of Bishop Gravesend, d. 1279).
17. Lincoln Cathedral* (from grave of Bishop Sutton, d. 1299).
18. Salisbury Cathedral* (from grave of Bishop Longespée).
19. Worcester Cathedral (from grave of Bishop Cantelupe, d. 1266). Pl. 25*a*.

1300–50

20. Welford St. Mary, Northants.
21. York Minster* (from grave of Archbishop Melton, d. 1340).

1350–1400

22. Aston-by-Sutton,* Chesh.
23. Beighton, Norf.
23*a*. Hamstall Ridware,* Staffs. Pl. 27*a*.

1400–50

24. Foxley, Norf.

1450–1540

25. Ampleforth Abbey I.* Pl. 27*b*.
26. Castle Bromwich, Warw.
27. Cromer, Norf.
28. Paston, Norf.
29. Preston, Rutl.
30. Weston-on-Trent, Staff.

Details

12. I, 8, p. 13. II, 4, p. 14. II, 6, p.
15. I. Round centre ✠ DEXTRA DEI.
16. I. Depression in the form of a square in a quatrefoil.
17. I. 18. II, 8, p. 19. II, 4, e. 20–25. II, 6, p. 26. II, 6. e.
27. II, 6, p. 28. I. 29. I. 30. II, 6, e.

SACRED MONOGRAM, IHS OR IHC

1450–1540

31. Beeston-next-Mileham, Norf.
32. Beswick, Yorks.
33. Bishop's Sutton, Hants.
34. Bristol, All Saints.
35. British Museum (from Berwick St. James, Wilts.).
36. Buckhorn Weston, Dorset.
37. Challow, Berks.
38. Corsley, Wilts.
39. Dronfield, Derbys.
40. Farcet, Hunts.
41. Lord Hatherton.* Pl. 20.
42. Ratcliffe-on-the-Wreake, Leics.
43. Runton, Norf.
44. Sall, Norf.
45. Teffont Magna, Wilts.
46. Tuttington, Norf.
47. Walmer, Kent. Pl. 29*b*.
48. Wield, Hants.
49. Wood Dalling, Norf.
50. Woughton-on-the-Green, Bucks.

See also nos. 51, 67, 68, 123.

Details

31. II, 6, e. 32. I. 33. II, 6, p. 34. II, 7, e. 35. I.
36. II, 6, e. Maker's mark, *cross between four pellets* (*J*.G. 474).
37. I. 38. II, 6, e.
39. II, 6, e. Rim inscribed: BENEDICTVS DOMINVS DEVS ISRAEL QVIA.
40. II, 6, e.
41. II, 6, e. Rim inscribed: Sancta trinitas unus deus miserere nobis.
42. I. 43. II, 6, e. 44–45. I. 46. II, 6, e.
47. I. Embossed with a double rose.
48. Has been hammered inside out. 49. II, 6, e.
50. II, 6, e. Rim inscribed: Miserere mei deus secundam magnam misericordiam tuam.

VERNICLE

1450–1540

Hall-marked

51. Nettlecombe,* Som. Pl. 30*a*. 1479. Maker's mark, *grasshopper* (*J.G.* 92, 'a jug').
52. Stow Longa, Hunts. 1491. Maker's mark, *fish* (*J.G.* 93).
53. Shirley, Derbys. 1943. Maker's mark, *cross fleury*.
54. Clifford Chambers,* Glos. 1494. Maker's mark, *eagle's head* (*J.G.* 92).
55. Llanmaes, Glam. 1495. Maker's mark, *fish hook* (?)
56. Childrey, Berks. 1496. Maker's mark, *leaf* (*J.G.* 93).
57. Cossey, Norf. 1496. Maker's mark, *rosary*.
58. Hartshorne, Derbys. 1498–1513. Maker's mark, *B in dotted circle*.
59. Happisburgh, Norf. 1506. Maker's mark, *horse* (*J.G.* 93).
60. Orcheston St. Mary, Wilts. 1506. Maker's mark, *leaf* (*J.G.*) 93.
61. Corpus Christi College,* Oxford. Pl. 36*a*. 1507. Maker's mark, *fleur-de-lis* (*J.G.* 93).
62. West Drayton,* Middx. 1507. Maker's mark, *Vernicle* (*J.G.* 93, 'a maidenhead').
63. Hockham, Norf. 1509. Maker's mark, *two links* (*J.G.* 93).
64. Scremby, Lincs. 1512. Maker's mark, *fish* (*J.G.* 93).
65. Gissing, Norf. 1514. Maker's mark, *heart* (*J.G.* 94).
66. Heworth, Durham. Pl. 35*b*. 1514. Maker's mark, *gemini* (*J.G.* 93).
67. Kirk Hammerton, Yorks. (Rev. Thos. Staniforth in 1866). 1517. Maker's mark, *sheep* (*J.G.* 94).
68. Victoria and Albert Museum* (Bedingfield family, &c.). 1518. Maker's mark, *fish* (*J.G.* 93).
69. Moorlinch, Som. 1518. Maker's mark, *sceptre* (*J.G.* 94).
70. Wolston, Warw. 1518. Maker's mark, *orb* (*J.G.* 94).
71. Hamsterley, Durham. 1519. Maker's mark, *scorpion* (?) (*J.G.* 94).
72. Great Waltham, Essex. 1521. Maker's mark, *two links* (*J.G.* 94).
73. Beechamwell, Norf. 1523. Maker's mark, *sceptre* (*J.G.* 94).
74. Trinity College,* Oxford, Pl. 31*a*. 1527. Maker's mark, *female head* (*J.G.* 94).
75. Victoria and Albert Museum.* Pl. 35 *e*, *f*. 1527. Maker's mark, *Tau cross* (*J.G.* 95).
76. Morval, Cornwall. 1528. Maker's mark, *sceptre* (*J.G.* 94).
77. Midgham, Berks. 1531. Maker's mark, *millrind*.
78. Salisbury, St. Edmund. 1533. Maker's mark, *TW* (*J.G.* 95).

Without marks

79. Arundel Castle,* Sussex.
80. Bacton, Heref.
81. Banningham, Norf.
82. Barnetby-le-Wold, Lincs.
83. Bedingfield, Suff.
84. Beeston Regis, Norf. Pl. 35*c*.
85. Bierton, Bucks.
86. Brancaster, Norf.
87. Brasenose College,* Oxford.
88. Brasenose College,* Oxford.
89. Brushford, Devon.
90. Caston, Norf.

91. Cofton Hacket, Warw.
92. Colby, Norf.
93. Combpyne,* Devon.
94. Donnington, Sussex.
95. Fawley, Hants.
96. Great Easton, Leics.
97. Great Witley, Worcs.
98. Hanworth, Norf. Pl. 35*a*.
99. Hockering, Norf.
100. Holkham, Norf.
101. Jackson,* Heirs of Sir Chas.
102. Kirk Malew, I.O.M.
103. Leominster,* Heref.
104. Lessingham, Norf.
105. Lyng, Norf.
106. Melksham Forest, Wilts.
107. Mundham, Norf.
108. Narford, Norf.
109. Norton Canon, Heref.
110. Oulton, Norf.
111. Parson's Drove, Cambs.
112. Pilton, Som.
113. Pyke,* Col. E. J.
114. Saham Tony, Norf. Pl. 35*d*.
115. Sawston Hall, Cambs.
116. Shernebourne, Norf.
117. Thurgarton, Norf.
118. Tittleshall, Norf.
119. North Tuddenham, Norf.
120. Tugby, Leics.
121. Victoria and Albert Museum.*
122. Wootton, Berks.

Details

51. II, 6, e, with medallion of the *Sacred Monogram* on the underside.
52–57. II, 6, e.
58. II, 6, e. No date-letter, but leopard's head is of the type used 1498–1513.
59. II, 6, e. Rim inscribed: ✠ **accipite ex hoc omnes hoc est enī corpus meū quod pr vobis tradetur.**
60. II, 6, e. An extra rim has been added.
61–66. II, 6, e.
67–68. II, 6, e, with medallion of the *Sacred Monogram* on the underside.
69. II, 6, e.
70. I.
71. II, 6, e.
72. I. Rim inscribed: ✠ **Benedicamus patrem et filium cum sancto spiritu.**
73. II. 6, e.
74. II, 6, e. Rim inscribed: ✠ **CALICIM SALVTARIS ACCIPIAM ET NOMINE DOMINE IN VOCABO.**
75–77. II, 6, e.
78. I. Rim inscribed ✠ **Benedicamus patrem et filium cum sancto.**
79–95. II, 6, e.
96. I. The depression embossed in the form of an eight-petalled flower.
97–101. II, 6, e.
102. II, 6, e. Rim inscribed: ✠ **Sancte lupe ora pro nobis.**
103–11. II, 6, e.
112. II, 6, e. Rim inscribed: **JD** (monogram) **orate pro bono statu d. j. dier vicarius hius loci.**
113–22. II, 6, e.

THE MAJESTY

c. 1260

123. Cardiff, National Museum.* Pl. 25*b* (Dolgelley find, 1890).

Details

II, 6. Inscribed round centre: ✠ **IN NOMINE PATRIS ET FILII ET SPIRITVS SANCTI AM.** Symbols of the Evangelists on four of the spandrels.

THE TRINITY

1450–1540

Hall-marked

124. Edinburgh, Royal Scottish Museum.* Pl. 31*b*. 1527. Maker's mark, *sceptre* (*J.G.* 94).

Without marks

125. Birmingham, Oscott College. Pl. 28.
126. Cliffe-at-Hoo, Kent. Pl. 29*a*.

Details

124. I. Rim inscribed: ✠ **bENEDICAMVS PATREM ET FILEVM CVM SANCTO SPERE.**

125. II, 6, e. Rim inscribed: ✠ **Benedicamus patrem et filium cum sancto spiritu.** With medallion with the Sacred Monogram on the underside.

126. II, 6, e. Rim inscribed: ✠ **Benedicamus patrem et filium cum sancto spiritu.**

CHRIST OF THE DOOM

(seated on rainbow showing His wounds)

1450–1540

127. Claughton-on-Brock,* Lancs., R.C. church. Pl. 36*b*.
128. London, St. Magnus the Martyr.

Details

127. II, 6, e. Rim inscribed: **Salvum me fac Deus in nomine tuo.** Has been hammered inside out so as to serve as the lid of a ciborium.

CHRIST THE SAVIOUR

(standing with right hand raised in benediction and left hand holding orb)

1480–1500

129. Earl's Colne, Essex. Pl. 36*c*.

Details

II, 6, e.

CROSS

1450–1540

Hall-marked

130. Magdalen College,* Oxford, 1527. Maker's mark illegible.

Without marks

131. Noble,* heirs of Sir John.
132. Pentrobin, Flint. Pl. 34*d*.
133. Ringland, Norf.

Details

130. II, 4, e. 131. I. 132. II, 6, e. 133. II, 6, e.

SAINTS

1200–50

A bishop

134. Lincoln Cathedral★ (from grave of Bishop Grosseteste, d. 1253).

1480–1500

St. Margaret

135. Felbrigge, Norf. Pl. 36*e*.

Details

134. II, 4, p. 135. II, 6, e.

PLAIN

1180–1300

136. St. David's Cathedral I★ (from grave of a bishop).
137. York Minster I (from grave of an archbishop).

1300–50

138. Bushbury, Staffs. (from grave of Hugh de Bushbury, parson 1316–36).

1450–1500

139. Ampleforth College II★.

Details

136. I. Depression in the form of a square in a quatrefoil.
137. I, 4. 138–9. I.

PLAIN (central medallion lost)

1180–1300

140. York Minster II.★

1450–1540

141. Barsham, Suff.

Details

140. I. Medallion with *Holy Dove* has been lost.
142. II, 6, e.

APPENDIX II

LIST OF EDWARDIAN COMMUNION CUPS

(References to Jackson's *Goldsmiths* are prefaced *J.G.*; G = gilt.)

	Maker's mark	*Paten or paten-cover*
A. COMMONEST DESIGN		
1549 St. James Garlickhithe I. G.	*FB* (*J.G.* 96)	Paten
1549 St. Michael, Wood Street (now at St. Andrew and St. Michael, Greenwich). G.	None	None
1551 Beddington, Surrey. Pl. 49	*RD* (*J.G.* 96)	Paten
1551 Hunstanton, Norfolk. G.	*Crowned hand* (*J.G.* 96)	Paten
1551 Totnes, Devon	*AK* (*J.G.* 97)	None
1552 St. James Garlickhithe II. G.	*TL* (*J.G.* 97)	None
1552 Alan Burr (ex Wakefield Colln.)	*RD* (*J.G.* 96)	None
1553 Present location unknown (Christie's, 21.vi.1910, lot 22; Christie's, 6.v. 1924, lot 126). G. Variant of above design.	*Crowned hand* (*J.G.* 96)	None
1549 Present location unknown (formerly at St. Mildred, Bread Street). G.	*FB* (*J.G.* 96)	Paten
B. ALTERNATIVE DESIGN		
1549 St. Mary Aldermary. G. Pl. 50. Variant of the above design.	*W* (*J.G.* 111)	Paten-cover
1550 All Saints, Bristol	*High boot* (*J.G.* 96)	None
1551 St. Margaret, Westminster (pair). G.	*Stag's head* (R. Taylboyes) (*J.G.* 97)	None
C. ECCENTRIC DESIGNS		
1548 St. Lawrence Jewry. G. Pl. 51*a*	*Covered cup* (*J.G.* 96)	None
1549 St. Peter-upon-Cornhill, G. Pl. 51*b*	*RD* (*J.G.* 96)	None
1551 St. Michael, Southampton, G. Pl. 52*a*	*Swan's head erased* (*J.G.* 97)	Paten-cover
1552 Battle, Sussex. Pl. 53*a*	*Stalked daisy* (*J.G.* 96)	None
1552 Owslebury, Hants. Pl. 52*b*	*Bird* (*J.G.* 97)	None
1553 Great Houghton, Northants. Pl. 53*b*	*RM* (*J.G.* 98)	None

I have rejected the claims for inclusion in this list of the cup of 1550 at St. Michael, Cornhill (Freshfield, *City*, 78, pl. 1) on the grounds that it was probably made for secular use. It forms a pair with one made in 1608 and is inscribed: SAINCTE MICHAELS IN CORNHILL 1608. I have accepted the inscription at its face value because it does not seem possible to identify this piece with either of the communion cups mentioned in the 1552 inventory (Walters, 500), one of which we know (H. Overall, *Churchwardens' Accounts of St. Michael, Cornhill*, 1876, 92–93) weighed 20¾ ounces.

I have taken exactly the opposite course with regard to the cup at St. Peter-upon-Cornhill, which is inscribed: 'THE GIFT OF THOMAS SYMONDS TO YE PARISH CHURCH OF S. PETER IN CORNHILL 1625. I have assumed that by a mistake the engraver inscribed both this cup and the new one which bears the 1625 hall-mark. My reason for supposing that the 1549 cup never left the church is that in the 1552 inventory there were three communion cups, two of which with their patens weighed 67½ ounces. The present cup, which lacks a paten, weighs 27 ounces. Allowing it a paten weighing between 6 and 7 ounces, this would give a total of 33–34 ounces—half the 1552 figure for the pair.

I have rejected the claim of the flat cup at St. Mary, Sandwich, which bears an inscription, probably Edwardian: THIS IS THE COMVNION COVP, on the grounds that the cup is probably earlier and of secular origin.

I have rejected the cup at St. Clement, Oxford, which the Rev. J. T. Evans (*C.P. Oxon.* 124–5, pl. iv) claimed to have the 1550 mark. I am assured by Mrs. G. E. P. How that he must have misread the marks. She regards the piece as a remodelling by an Elizabethan goldsmith of an earlier cup of uncertain date.

I have also rejected the attractively decorated cup at Bridekirk, Cumberland (*C.P. Carlisle*, 73), because it appears to be a secular piece.

The unmarked and undated communion cup and paten at Gawsworth, Cheshire, I am inclined to assign to the beginning of the reign of Elizabeth I. As has already been remarked (p. 231), the fact that they are inscribed with a text from the Vulgate version of John VI, 63, indicates that they were made before Beza's translation came into general use. I am not prepared to exclude the possibility that they may have been produced towards the close of the reign of Edward VI.

APPENDIX III

QUANTITIES AND DISTRIBUTION OF COMMUNION CUPS AND PATEN-COVERS MADE BY THE GOLDSMITH *IP*

(Jackson, 98)

Only totals are given for the examples in Somerset. It should be remembered that some examples are no longer in the churches to which they originally belonged.

1563 ESSEX, Rainham.[1]

1564 KENT, Kemsing.

1565 HERTS. Aldenham. LINCS. Kirton-in-Lindsey.

1566 HERTS., Great Hormead. KENT, Westerham. SUFF., Little Glemham, Rendham. SURR. Dunsfold.

1567 SUFF. Horringer. SUSS. Aldingbourne, Eartham, Ticehurst.

1568 ESSEX, Mayland. LEICS., Catthorpe. HANTS, Chalton, Petersfield. PEMB., Hodgeston. SURR., Chessington. SUSS., Coldwaltham, Hastings (St. Mary), Iping, Terwick.
CHRISTIE'S I.

1569 BUCKS., Cranborough, Grendon Underwood, Little Horwood,[1] Oving, Padbury. HANTS, Deane, Kingsley. KENT, Isle of Grain. LEICS., Twyford. LINCS., Barlings, East Torrington, Walesby. RUTL., Barrowden. SURR., East Clandon, Tatsfield, Titsey.
GOLDSMITHS' HALL I, CHRISTIE'S I.

1570 DORSET, Bradpole. NORTHANTS, Thrapston.
CHRISTIE'S I.

1571 SOM., I., WORCS. White Ladies Aston.

1572 HANTS, Silchester. SOM., 22

1573 BERKS., Tilehurst. DEVON, Huntshaw. DORSET, West Chelborough. OXON, Over Worton, Westcot Barton. PEMB., Llanllawer. SOM., 71+2.[1]

1574 ANGL., Llanfflewin. DORSET, Lydlinch. OXON, Stokenchurch, Thame, Wootton. SOM. 2+I.[1]
CHRISTIE'S I.

1575 OXON, Cokethorp, Woodeaton.

1576 BRECON, Llanywern. GLOS., Littleton-on-Severn, Welford-on-Avon. HEREF., Leominster, Staunton-on-Wye. MON., Risca. OXON, Shennington, WILTS., Winterbourne Gunner.
NATIONAL MUSEUM, DUBLIN, I.

1577 CHRISTIE'S I.

1579 OXON, Swalcliffe.

TOTAL, 166 COMMUNION CUPS.
5 PATEN-COVERS (without communion cups).

[1] Paten-cover only.

APPENDIX IV

ANGLICAN SEVENTEENTH-CENTURY GOTHIC CHALICES

(References to maker's marks in Jackson's *Goldsmiths* are prefixed by *J.G.*)

Before 1620

Undated

1. St. John's College, Oxford. Pl. 80. Maker's mark, *FS in monogram* (*J.G.* 111).

1620

Hall-marked or dated

2. Southampton, St. Mary Extra. 1620. Maker's mark, *RB above star* (*J.G.* 117).

1630–41

Hall-marked or dated

3. Launton, Oxon, 1633. Maker's mark, *WR* (*J.G.* 118).
4. Llanavon,[1] Cards. Pl. 154*b*. 1633. Maker's mark, *WR* (*J.G.* 118).
5. Marston Bigot, Som. 1633. Maker's mark, *WR* (*J.G.* 118).
6. Kilkenny Cathedral.[2] 1636. Maker's mark. *Escallop* (*J.G.* 119).
7. Kilkenny Cathedral[2]. 1636. Maker's mark, *Escallop* (*J.G.* 119).
8. North Newton, Som.[1] 1636. Maker's mark, *BF over fleur-de-lis.*
9. Kenn,[1] Devon. 1638. Maker's mark, *FT in monogram* (*J.G.* 110).
10. Lambeth[2], St. Mary. 1638. Maker's mark, *GM above dove* (*J.G.* 120).
11. Lambeth, St. Mary. 1638. Maker's mark, *GM above dove* (*J.G.* 120).
12. Ashow,[2] Warw. 1638. Maker's mark, *Tb in monogram above dove* (*J.G.* 121).
13. Kenilworth,[2] Warw. Pl. 81. 1638. Maker's mark, *Tb in monogram above dove* (*J.B.* 121).
14. Leek Wootton,[2] Warw. 1638. Maker's mark, *Tb in monogram above dove* (*J.G.* 121).
15. Acton,[2] Middx. 1639. *Tb in monogram above dove* (*J.G.* 121).
16. Bradley,[2] Derbys. 1640. Makers' mark, *RP below fleur-de-lis.*
17. Kirk Langley,[2] Derbys. 1640. Maker's mark, *RP below fleur-de-lis.*
18. Kniveton[2], Derbys. 1640. Maker's mark, *RP below fleur-de-lis.*
19. Mugginton[2], Derbys. Pl. 82*a*. 1640. Maker's mark, *RP below fleur-de-lis.*
20. Osmaston-by-Ashbourne,[2] Derbys. 1640. Maker's mark, *RP below fleur-de-lis.*
21. Staunton Harold,[2] Leics. Pl. 83*a*. 1640. Maker's mark, *RB above star* (*J.G.* 116).
22. St. John's College, Oxford. Pl. 82*b*. 1641. Maker's mark, *FT in monogram* (*J.G.* 110).

Undated

23. Peterhouse, Cambridge. Maker's mark, *PB* (*J.G.* 118).
24. Southwell Cathedral. Maker's mark, *WC over scallop.*

[1] With cover. [2] With paten-cover.

25. Lambeth Palace.[2] Maker's mark, *PG* (*J.G.* 119).
26. Fulham Palace.[2] Pl. 83*b*. 1653. Maker's mark, *hound sejant* (*J.G.* 123).
27. Rochester Cathedral[2] (from Cobham Hall, Kent). 1653. Maker's mark, *hound sejant* (*J.G.* 123).
28. Rochester Cathedral[2] (from Cobham Hall, Kent). 1653. Maker's mark, *hound sejant* (*J.G.* 123).

Undated

29. Pendomer, Som. Maker's mark. *IP*.
30. Trinity College[2], Cambridge. No mark.
31. Trinity College,[2] Cambridge. No mark.
32. Jesus College, Cambridge. Maker's mark, *hound sejant* (*J.G.* 123).
33. Hawkden, Suff. Maker's mark, *hound sejant* (*J.G.* 123).
34. Liverpool, St. Francis Xavier[2] (R.C.). Maker's mark, *hound sejant* (*J.G.* 123).
35. Pembroke College,[1] Cambridge. Maker's mark, *hound sejant* (*J.G.* 123).
36. Staunton Harold,[2] Leics. Maker's mark, *hound sejant* (*J.G.* 123).
37. Wimpole,[2] Cambs. Maker's mark, *hound sejant* (*J.G.* 123).

1661–70

Hall-marked or dated

38. St. George's Chapel,[3] Windsor. Pl. 84*c*. 1661. Maker's mark, *WM over cinquefoil* (*J.G.* 125).
39. St. George's Chapel,[3] Windsor. 1661. Maker's mark, *WM over cinquefoil* (*J.G.* 125).
40. Welshpool, Montgomery. Pl. 87*a*. 1662. Maker's mark, *GW above two anulets.*
41. Southwell Cathedral. 1663. Maker's mark, *IP* (John Plummer of York, *J.G.* 289).
42. Southwell Cathedral. 1663. Maker's mark, *IP* (John Plummer of York, *J.G.* 289).
43. Ashburnham,[2] Sussex. 1666. Maker's mark. *S crowned* (C. Shelley, *J.G.* 135).
44. Hampton Court Palace. 1667. Maker's mark, *S crowned* (C. Shelley, *J.G.* 135).
45. Leicester, Wyggeston's Hospital. 1668. Maker's mark, *DG between two mullets.*
46. Lichfield Cathedral.[1] Pl. 89*a*. 1670. Maker's mark illegible.

Undated

47. Tower of London.[3] Maker's mark, *AS monogram* (*J.G.* 124), and *TV with bunch of grapes.*
48. St. James's Palace.[3] Pl. 85. Maker's mark, *IN above bird* (*J.G.* 128).
49. St. James's Palace.[3] Maker's mark, *IN above bird* (*J.G.* 128).
50. Private colln. in Glos.[2] (formerly Brownlow Colln). Maker's mark, *IN above bird* (*J.G.* 128).
51. Auckland Castle, Durham.[3] Pl. 84*a*. No mark.
52. St. George's Chapel, Windsor. Pl. 84*b*. Maker's mark, *AM in monogram* (*J.G.* 124).
53. Buckingham Palace. Pl. 86. Maker's mark, *S crowned* (C. Shelley, *J.G.* 135).

[1] With cover. [2] With paten-cover. [3] With paten (disc- or saucer-shaped).

54. Buckingham Palace.[3] Maker's mark, *S crowned* (C. Shelley. *J.G.* 135).
55. Buckingham Palace.[2] Maker's mark, *S crowned* (C. Shelley, *J.G.* 135).
56. Redlynch,[2] Som. Pl. 88*a*. Maker's mark, *S crowned* (C. Shelley, *J.G.* 135).
56*a*. Maddington, Wilts. Maker's mark *S crowned* (C. Shelley, *J.G.* 135).
57. Buckingham Palace. No mark.
58. St. James's Palace. No mark.
59. Caerhun, Caern. Maker's mark, *WH above cherub* (*J.G.* 128).

1671–88

Hall-marked or dated

60. Ingestre,[2] Staffs. Pl. 88*b*. 1672. Maker's mark, *IB above crescent* (*J.G.* 130).
61. Private colln. in Glos.[2] (formerly Brownlow Colln.). 1672. Maker's mark, *IB above crescent* (*J.G.* 130).
62. Private colln. in Glos.[2] (formerly Brownlow Colln.). 1672. Maker's mark, *IB above crescent* (*J.G.* 130).
63. Eglws Rhos, Caern. 1673. No mark.
64. Ashby-de-la-Zouch,[1] Leics. Pl. 89*b*. 1676. Maker's mark. *WW above fleur-de-lis* (*J.G.* 131).
65. Barking, Essex. 1680. Maker's mark, *IB above crescent* (*J.G.* 130).
66. Arksey, Yorks. 1682. Maker's mark, *HL* (*J.G.* 133).
67. Christ Church Cathedral, Dublin. 1683. Maker's mark, *S crowned* (C. Shelley, *J.G.* 135).

Undated

68. Kingswood, Surrey. Maker's mark, *IB above crescent* (*J.G.* 130).
69. Boughton Malherbe, Kent. Maker's mark, *V above CO.*

After 1688

70. Tower of London.[3] 1689 (?) No mark.

Hall-marked

71. Hampton, Middx. 1704. Maker's mark, *LE crowned* (G. Lewis, *J.G.* 159).

DETAILS

Bowls

With engraved band, 12–15, 24.
With engraved *Good Shepherd*, 1, 21–23, 35–37.
With engraved *Crown of Thorns*, 26.
With openwork calyx, 46, 50, 57–58, 64.
Bowl of later date, 5 (1636), 66 (1683).
The bowls of the remainder are mostly plain except for a few with coats-of-arms.

Stems and Knots

Hexagonal stem with lobed knot with six bosses, 1, 2, 6, 7, 10–23, 26–29, 32–42, 46, 61, 62, 64.

[1] With cover. [2] With paten-cover. [3] With paten (disc- or saucer-shaped).

Hexagonal stem with moulded hexagonal knot, 8, 9, 24, 25, 30, 31, 43, 44, 56, 60, 65.
Hexagonal stem with round knot, 3, 45, 56*a*, 59, 63, 71.
Baluster stem, 47, 52–55, 57, 58.
No stem, octagonal knot, 68.

Feet

Hexagonal, with incurved sides, 24, 25, 30, 31, 41, 42, 56*a*, 60–63, 65, 66, 71.
Hexagonal, with incurved sides and cherub knops, 1, 2, 6, 7, 9–23, 26–28, 32–37, 43, 44, 46 (cherubs upright), 53–55, 57, 58.
Octagonal, with incurved sides, 64 (cherubs upright), 68.
Sexfoil, 4, 5, 8, 29 (with upright cherubs between lobes), 38–40, 47, 56, 59, 70.
Octafoil, 3, 45, 52.
Decafoil, 48–51, 69.

APPENDIX V

IDENTIFIABLE GOLDSMITHS WHO WORKED FOR THE RECUSANTS BETWEEN 1558 AND THE INTRODUCTION OF THE *BRITANNIA STANDARD* IN 1697

Date	*Mark*	*Reference to Jackson,* Goldsmiths	*Examples*
c. 1570	*CH in monogram* (Christopher Hunton of York)	285	Paten, see p. 272.
c. 1610	*Unicorn's head*	112	Pyx, see p. 282.
H.M. 1633	*RM*	120	Chalices, see p. 269.
H.M. 1637–8	*WR*	118	Chalices, see p. 266–7.
H.M. 1639	*WT*	121	Chalice, see p. 270.
c. 1650–97	*AM in monogram* (?)	124	Chalices, see p. 270.
H.M. 1670	*IS crowned*	135	Ciborium, see p. 282.
c. 1670	*TP in monogram*	—	Cruet-tray, see p. 272.
c. 1670	*WB in shield with three-pointed top*	—	Chalice, Oscott, see p. 271.
H.M. 1675	*JC conjoined in script, beneath a coronet*	—	Candlesticks, see p. 275.
c. 1680	*HL above a lion passant in square-topped shield*	—	Chalice, Burchley, Lancs.
H.M. 1682	*S crowned* (Chas. Shelley)	137	Cruet, see p. 273.
c. 1685	*RH*	144	Chalice, Pluckley (C.E.), Kent.
c. 1685	*MP conjoined in square-topped shield*	141 (?)	Chalice, Burnfoot, Wigton, Cumberland.

INDEX OF PERSONS AND SUBJECTS

(Names and marks of goldsmiths are shown in italics. References to illustrations are in heavy type)

INDEX OF EXTANT PIECES OF PLATE TOPOGRAPHICALLY ARRANGED

(Pieces mentioned only in the appendixes are not included)

References to illustrations are in heavy type

C = chalice. CC = Communion cup. F = flagon. P = paten

PLATES

GROUP I

THE TREWHIDDLE CHALICE
Second half of 9th century
British Museum
H. 5½ in.

GROUP II

CHALICE. Parcel-gilt
From the grave of Archbishop Walter (d. 1205)
About 1160
Canterbury Cathedral
H. 5⅝ in.

a. CHALICE
From the grave of Bishop Swinfield (d. 1316)
1180–1280
Hereford Cathedral
H. $4\frac{3}{8}$ in.

b. CHALICE. Gilt
From the grave of Bishop Gravesend (d. 1279)
1180–1280
Lincoln Cathedral
H. $4\frac{7}{8}$ in.

GROUP IV

THE DOLGELLEY CHALICE. Gilt
About 1250
National Museum of Wales, Cardiff
H. $7\frac{1}{4}$ in.

GROUP IV

CHALICE. Gilt
About 1250
Dragsmark, Sweden
H. 6¾ in.

GROUP IV

CHALICE. Gilt
From the grave of an unidentified archbishop
About 1250
York Minster
H. $5\frac{3}{8}$ in.

GROUP IV

THE BØRSA CHALICE. Gilt
About 1250
Kunstindustrimuseum, Oslo
H. 5½ in.

a. CHALICE. Parcel-gilt
From the grave of Archbishop Melton (d. 1340)
About 1320
York Minster

b. CHALICE. Gilt
From a church in western Sweden
About 1320
Statens Historiska Museum, Stockholm

GROUP VI

CHALICE. Parcel-gilt
About 1360
Hamstall Ridware, Staffs.
(Lent to the Victoria and Albert Museum)
H. $4\frac{7}{8}$ in.

CHALICE. Gilt

About 1370

Aston-by-Sutton, Cheshire

H. $5\frac{1}{2}$ in.

GROUP VI

CHALICE
About 1410
Goathland, Yorks.
H. $5\frac{5}{8}$ in.

a. CHALICE. Gilt
Maker's mark, *a grasshopper*
Hall-mark for 1479
Nettlecombe, Som.

b. CHALICE. Gilt
Second half of 15th century
Ampleforth Abbey, Yorks.
H. $4\frac{5}{8}$ in.

a. CHALICE
About 1500
Stadarhraun, Iceland
H. 6 in.

b. CHALICE (one of a pair). Gilt
Maker's mark, *MW in monogram*
Hall-mark for 1498
Brasenose College, Oxford
H. $6\frac{7}{8}$ in.

GROUP VII

a. TRAVELLING CHALICE. Gilt
About 1500
R.C. church, West Grinstead, Sussex
H. 5 in.

GROUP VIII

b. CHALICE
About 1500
Colonel E. J. Pyke
H. 4½ in.

a. CHALICE. Parcel-gilt
About 1500
Coombe Keynes, Dorset
(Lent to the Victoria and Albert Museum)
H. $6\frac{3}{8}$ in.

b. CHALICE. Parcel-gilt
About 1500
R.C. church, Hornby, Lancs.
H. 7 in.

GROUP VIII

CHALICE. Gilt

About 1510

Leominster, Hereford

H. $8\frac{1}{2}$ in.

GROUP VIII

CHALICE. Gilt
About 1510
Calcena, Zaragoza, Spain
H. $8\frac{1}{2}$ in.

GROUP IX

CHALICE. Gold
Maker's mark, *fleur-de-lis*
Hall-mark for 1507
Corpus Christi College, Oxford
H. 6 in.

GROUP IX

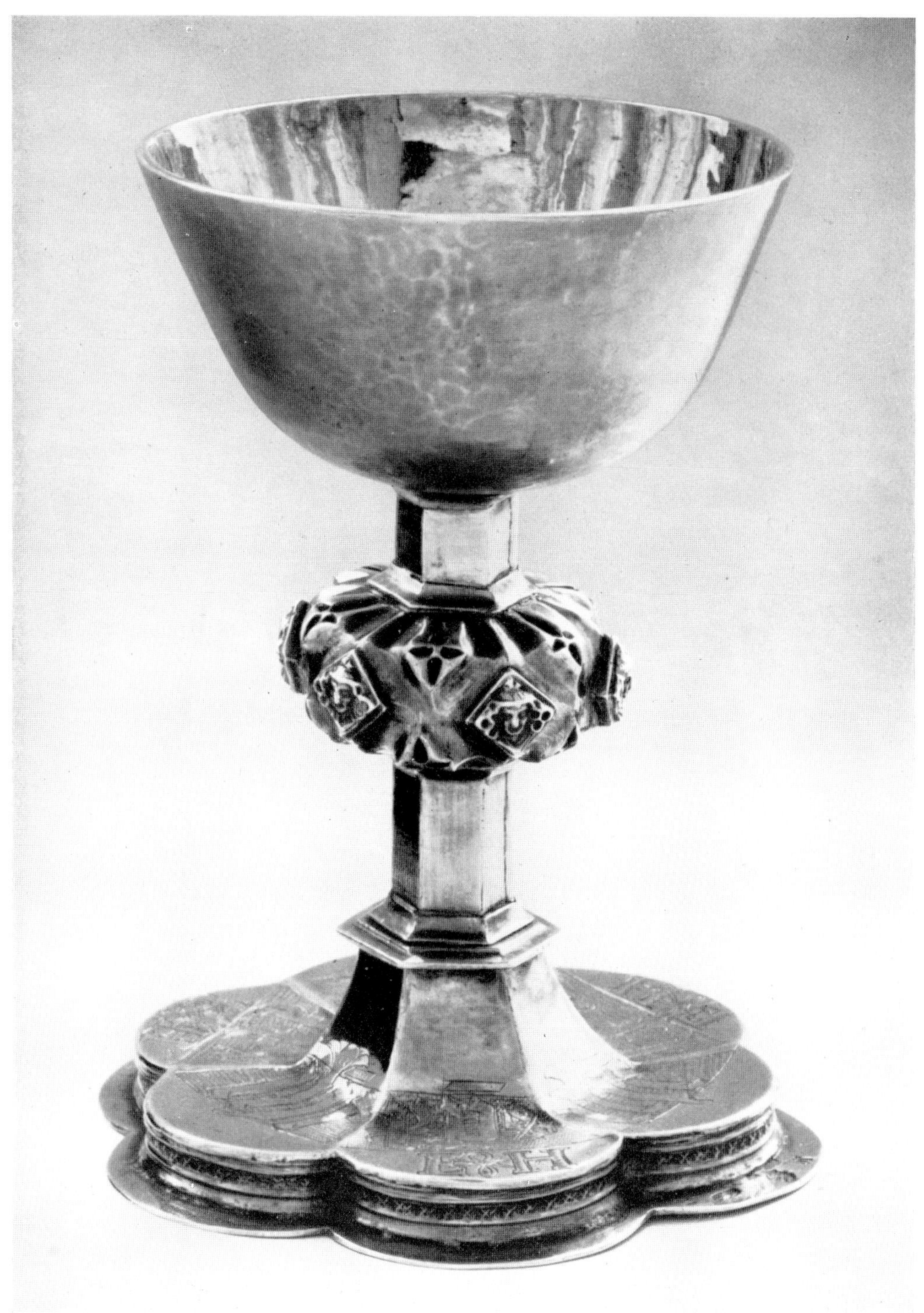

THE BEDINGFIELD CHALICE. Gilt
Maker's mark, *a fish*
Hall-mark for 1518
Victoria and Albert Museum
H. 6 in.

THE PILLATON HALL CHALICE AND PATEN. Gilt

About 1530

Lord Hatherton

(Lent to the City Museum and Art Gallery, Birmingham)

GROUP IX

CHALICE. Gilt
Maker's mark, *a sceptre*
Hall-mark for 1529
Westminster Cathedral
H. 6¾ in.

GROUP X

CHALICE. Gilt
Maker's mark, *a sceptre*
Hall-mark for 1525
Wylye, Wilts.
H. 6¾ in.

GROUP X

CHALICE. Gilt
Maker's mark, *a sceptre*
London hall-mark for 1527
Royal Scottish Museum, Edinburgh
H. 7½ in.

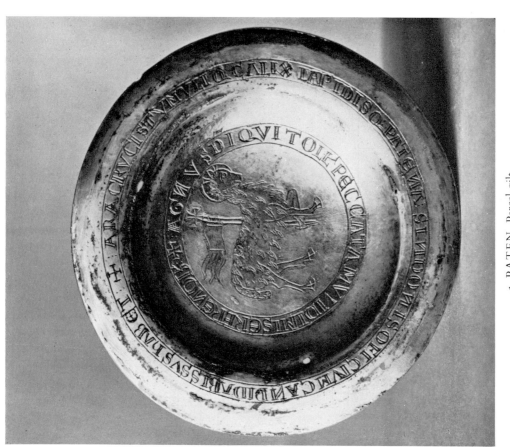

a. PATEN. Parcel-gilt
From the grave of Archbishop Walter (d. 1205)
About 1160
Canterbury Cathedral
Diam. 5½ in.

a. PATEN
Middle of 13th century
Wyke, Winchester, Hants
Diam. 5¾ in.

a. PATEN. Gilt
From the grave of Bishop Cantelupe (d. 1266)
About 1250
Worcester Cathedral
Diam. $4\frac{5}{8}$ in.

b. THE DOLGELLEY PATEN. Gilt
About 1250
National Museum of Wales, Cardiff
Diam. $7\frac{1}{4}$ in.

a. PATEN. Gilt
From the grave of Bishop Gravesend (d. 1279)
About 1250
Lincoln Cathedral
Diam. $4\frac{1}{2}$ in.

b. PATEN. Gilt
About 1250
Dragsmark, Sweden

a. PATEN. Parcel-gilt
About 1360
Hamstall Ridware, Staffs.
(Lent to the Victoria and Albert Museum)
Diam. $4\frac{5}{8}$ in.

b. PATEN. Gilt
About 1450
Ampleforth Abbey, Yorks.
Diam. 4 in.

Front

Back

PATEN. Gilt, with enamelled print

About 1510

Oscott College, Birmingham

Diam. $6\frac{3}{8}$ in.

a. PATEN. Gilt, with enamelled print
About 1520
Cliffe-at-Hoo, Kent
Diam. 6¼ in.

b. PATEN
About 1500
Walmer, Kent
Diam. 6⅛ in.

a. PATEN. Gilt, with enamelled print
Maker's mark, *a grasshopper*
Hall-mark for 1479
Nettlecombe, Som.
Diam. $4\frac{7}{8}$ in.

c. Print on back of *b*.
(full size)

b. THE BEDINGFIELD PATEN. Gilt, with enamelled print
Maker's mark, *a fish*
Hall-mark for 1518
Victoria and Albert Museum
Diam. $5\frac{1}{2}$ in.

a. PATEN. Gilt
Maker's mark, *a Vernicle*
Hall-mark for 1527
Trinity College, Oxford
Diam. 6¼ in.

b. PATEN. Gilt
Maker's mark, *a sceptre*
Hall-mark for 1527
Royal Scottish Museum, Edinburgh
Diam. 6 in.

PLATE 32

ICONOGRAPHY—CHALICES

Details (Saints Mary Magdalene, Jerome, Margaret, and Augustine) of the foot of the gold chalice of Bishop Foxe (cf. Pl. 18)

Corpus Christi College, Oxford

ICONOGRAPHY—CHALICES

The Crucified Christ

a. Foot of a chalice
About 1500
Old Hutton, Westmorland

b. Foot of a chalice
About 1500
Bacton, Hereford

a

b

c

d

ICONOGRAPHY

PATENS

a. Agnus Dei. About 1450. *Chewton Mendip, Som.*

b. Lamb of the Apocalypse. Hall-mark for 1521. *Milwich, Staffs.*

c. Agnus Dei. Hall-mark for 1537. *National Museum, Melbourne, Australia*

d. Cross. About 1450. *Pentrobin, Flint*

a b c d e f

ICONOGRAPHY—PATENS

The Vernicle

a. About 1500
Hanworth, Norf.

b. Hall-mark for 1514
Heworth, Durham

c. About 1450
Beeston Regis, Norf.

d. About 1480
Saham Tony, Norf.

e. Hall-mark for 1527
Victoria and Albert Museum

f. Hall-mark for 1528
Morval, Cornwall

a

b

c

d

ICONOGRAPHY

PATENS

a. The Vernicle
Hall-mark for 1507
Corpus Christi College, Oxford

b. The Christ of the Doom
About 1500
R.C. church, Claughton-on-Brock, Lancs.

c. The Saviour
1480–1500
Earl's Colne, Essex

d. St. Margaret
1480–1500
Felbrigg, Norf.

a

a. Gilt
Rhenish; about 1400
Aachen Münster
H. about 6 in.

b

CRUETS

b. Parcel-gilt
About 1480
Mrs. G. E. P. How
H. 3¼ in.

c

c. Parcel-gilt
About 1525
St. Peter Port, Guernsey
H. 6⅛ in.

b

a

c

PORTABLE ALTAR

Red porphyry, mounted in silver, parcel-gilt

b. Detail of top. *c*. Detail of top

First quarter of 11th century

Musée de Cluny, Paris

L. 10½ in.

HANGING RELIQUARY CROSS

Wood plated with gold, with ivory Christ and cloisonné enamel

About 1000

Victoria and Albert Museum

H. 7½ in.

a. PAX. Gilt
About 1480
Lee Collection, Hart House, University of Toronto
H. $4\frac{3}{8}$ in.

b. PAX. Parcel-gilt
About 1520
New College, Oxford
H. $5\frac{3}{8}$ in.

a. FOOT AND STEM OF A STANDING PYX. Gilt
Maker's mark, *HI crossed*
Hall-mark for 1507
St. Martin, Ludgate
(Lent to the London Museum)
H. 5 in.

b. CHRISMATORY. Crystal and silver-gilt
About 1520
British Museum
H. $2\frac{3}{4}$ in.

a. Inside of bottom

b. General view

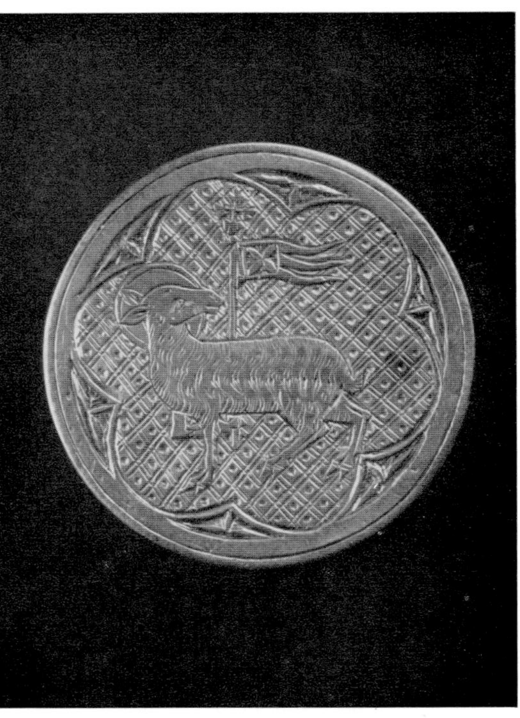

c. Outside of bottom

THE SWINBURNE PYX

Gilt, formerly enriched with enamel

About 1310

Victoria and Albert Museum

Diam. 2¼ in.

a. MS. Dd. 417
Cambridge University Library

b

c

THE SWINBURNE PYX
b. Outside of cover
c. Inside of cover

d. MS. Dd. 417
Cambridge University Library

BASIN FOR ABLUTIONS (one of a pair)
Gilt, with enamelled medallion
Maker's mark, *a horseshoe*
Hall-mark for 1493
Corpus Christi College, Oxford
Diam. $16\frac{3}{4}$ in.

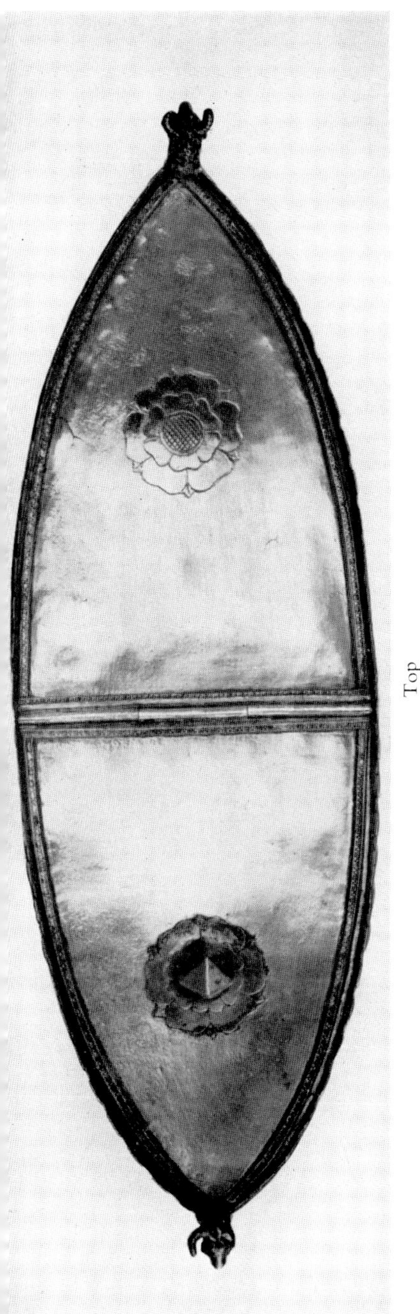

Top

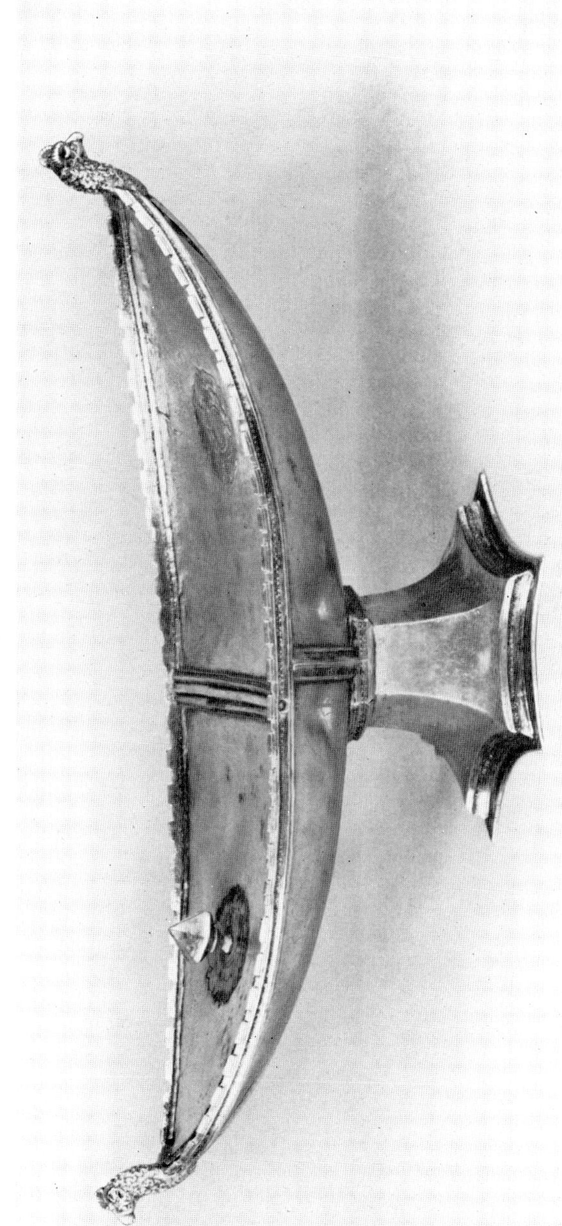

THE RAMSEY ABBEY INCENSE-BOAT

Parcel-gilt

Last quarter of 14th century

Victoria and Albert Museum

L. 11¼ in.

RELIQUARY OF ST. CUTHBERT'S ALTAR

Gilt

8th and 10th centuries

Durham Cathedral

L. $5\frac{1}{4}$ in.

RELIQUARY OF ST. THOMAS OF CANTERBURY

Parcel-gilt, with nielloed plaques

About 1180

Metropolitan Museum of Art, New York

W. $2\frac{3}{4}$ in.

SALT-CELLAR. Gilt

1494–1501

Corpus Christi College, Oxford

H. $11\frac{3}{4}$ in.

COMMUNION CUP AND PATEN

Maker's mark, *RD in monogram*

Hall-mark for 1551

Beddington, Surrey

H. 7¾ in.

COMMUNION CUP WITH PATEN-COVER. Gilt

Maker's mark, *W*

Hall-mark for 1549

[Inset, enamelled medallion of the arms of Edward VI on the foot of the paten-cover]

St. Mary Aldermary

(Lent to the Victoria and Albert Museum)

a. COMMUNION CUP. Gilt
Maker's mark, *a covered cup*
Hall-mark for 1548
St. Lawrence Jewry
H. $9\frac{1}{4}$ in.

b. COMMUNION CUP. Gilt
Maker's mark, *RD in monogram*
Hall-mark for 1549
St. Peter-upon-Cornhill
H. $9\frac{1}{2}$ in.

a. COMMUNION CUP WITH PATEN-COVER
Gilt
Maker's mark, *a bird's head erased*
Hall-mark for 1551
St. Michael, Southampton
H. (without cover) $7\frac{1}{8}$ in.

b. COMMUNION CUP
Maker's mark, *a bird*
Hall-mark for 1552
Owslebury, Hants
H. $8\frac{1}{4}$ in.

a. COMMUNION CUP
Maker's mark, *a daisy*
Hall-mark for 1552
Battle, Sussex
H. 8 in.

b. COMMUNION CUP
Maker's mark, *RM*
Hall-mark for 1553
Great Houghton, Northants
H. $6\frac{3}{4}$ in.

COMMUNION CUP WITH PATEN-COVER

Gilt

Hall-mark for 1558

St. Michael-le-Belfrey, York

H. 9 in.

COMMUNION CUP

Parcel-gilt

Maker's mark, *a bird*

Hall-mark for 1559

St. Botolph, Aldgate

H. $8\frac{3}{4}$ in.

a. COMMUNION CUP
Mark of Robert Taylboyes
About 1560
Victoria and Albert Museum
H. $7\frac{1}{2}$ in.

b. COMMUNION CUP
Maker's mark, *a wallet-hook*
Hall-mark for 1564
St. Michael, Oxford
H. $6\frac{1}{2}$ in.

a. COMMUNION CUP WITH PATEN-COVER
Maker's mark, *GK in a heart*
Hall-mark for 1562
Ashby-de-la-Zouch, Leics.
H. $9\frac{1}{2}$ in.

b. COMMUNION CUP WITH PATEN-COVER
Mark of Peter Carlill of Hull
Hall-mark for 1562
Beeford, Yorks.
H. $6\frac{5}{8}$ in.

a. COMMUNION CUP WITH PATEN-COVER
Maker's mark, *a bull's head erased*
Hall-mark for 1568
Reedham, Norf.
H. 8½ in.

b. COMMUNION CUP WITH PATEN-COVER
Maker's mark, *an orb with cross*
Norwich hall-mark for 1568
St. Martin-at-Palace, Norwich
H. 8½ in.

a. COMMUNION CUP WITH PATEN-COVER
Maker's mark, *an orb with cross*
Norwich; dated 1568
St. Andrew, Norwich
H. 10 in.

b. COMMUNION CUP WITH COVER
Maker's mark, *a slipped trefoil*
Norwich hall-mark for 1566
St. Lawrence, Norwich
H. 10 in.

a

a. COMMUNION CUP WITH PATEN-COVER

Mark of Thomas Buttell of Norwich

Dated 1569

Westley Waterless, Cambs.

H. $7\frac{1}{2}$ in.

b

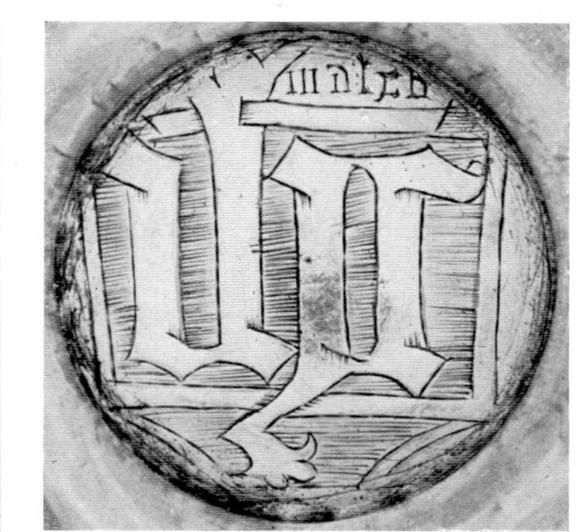

d

b. Interior of paten-cover of *a*, showing medieval paten design

d. Interior of *c*, showing medieval pyx design

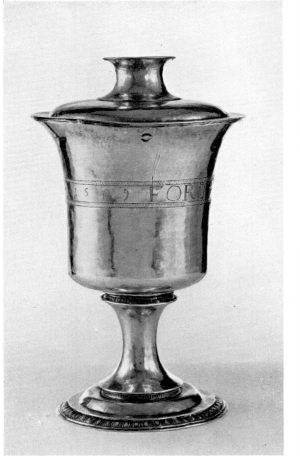

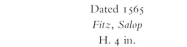

c. COMMUNION CUP WITH PATEN-COVER

Dated 1565

Fitz, Salop

H. 4 in.

THREE COMMUNION CUPS MADE BY THE GOLDSMITH *IP*

a. Hall-mark for 1568
Chessington, Surrey
H. $3\frac{3}{4}$ in.

b. Hall-mark for 1572
Wells Cathedral
H. $9\frac{3}{4}$ in.

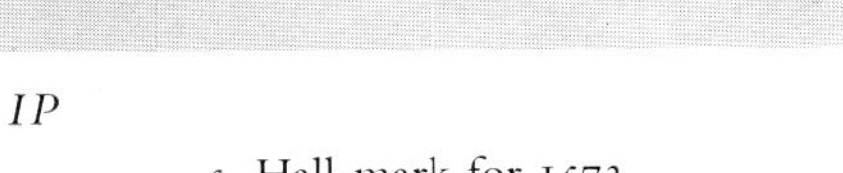

c. Hall-mark for 1573
Formerly Swaythling Collection
H. 8 in.

a. COMMUNION CUP WITH PATEN-COVER
Mark of Robert Taylboyes
Hall-mark for 1570
Cirencester, Glos.
H. 14 in.

b. COMMUNION CUP WITH PATEN-COVER
Maker's mark, *a rose*
About 1571
Barcheston, Warw.
H. 7 in.

a. COMMUNION CUP WITH PATEN

Maker's mark, *an animal's head*

Chester; about 1571

Great Budworth, Cheshire

H. $8\frac{1}{2}$ in.

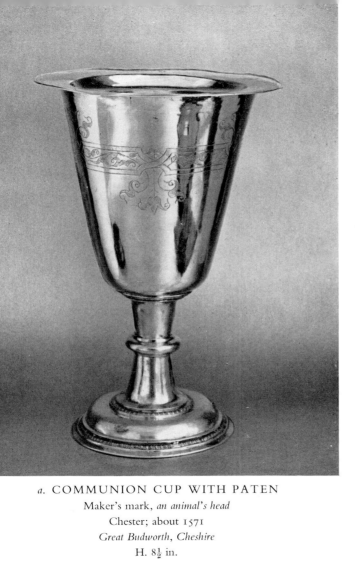

b. COMMUNION CUP WITH PATEN-COVER

Maker's mark, *an animal's head*

Chester; about 1571

St. Mary-without-the-Walls, Chester

H. $8\frac{1}{4}$ in.

COMMUNION CUP WITH PATEN
Maker's mark, *HB conjoined*
About 1570
Wombourn, Staffs.
H. 6 in.

a. COMMUNION CUP WITH PATEN-COVER
Marks, *NG and another*
About 1569
Walton-le-Wolds, Leics.
H. 5⅛ in.

b. COMMUNION CUP WITH PATEN-COVER
Maker's mark, *I over M* (John Morley?)
Lincoln; dated 1569
Mumby, Lincs.
(Lent to the Victoria and Albert Museum)
H. 5½ in.

COMMUNION CUP WITH PATEN-COVER
Mark of John Coton of Barnstaple
About 1572
Morwenstow, Cornwall
H. 7 in.

COMMUNION CUP WITH PATEN-COVER

Maker's mark, *IW*

Dated 1576

Bodmin, Cornwall

H. $7\frac{1}{2}$ in.

a. COMMUNION CUP WITH PATEN-COVER
Mark of John Jones of Exeter
About 1574
Victoria and Albert Museum
H. $7\frac{3}{4}$ in.

b. COMMUNION CUP
Mark of John Jones of Exeter
About 1574
Veryan, Cornwall
H. 7 in.

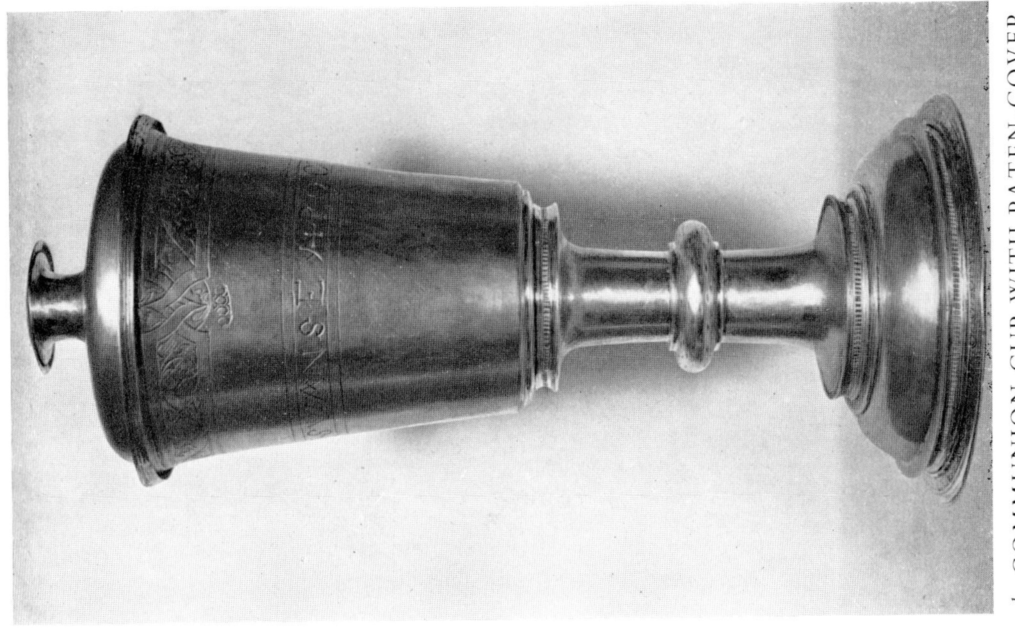

b. COMMUNION CUP WITH PATEN-COVER
Maker's mark, OOOO
About 1574
St. Mary, Swansea
H. $9\frac{3}{4}$ in.

a. COMMUNION CUP WITH PATEN-COVER
Mark of Lawrence Stratford of Dorchester
Dated 1574
Church Knowle, Dorset
H. $6\frac{1}{2}$ in.

a. COMMUNION CUP WITH PATEN-COVER
Maker's mark, *TS conjoined*
Hall-mark for 1580
St. Mary, Stockport, Cheshire
H. $9\frac{1}{2}$ in.

b. COMMUNION CUP WITH PATEN-COVER
Maker's mark, *RB in monogram*
Hall-mark for 1597
St. Mary, Reading
H. $9\frac{1}{2}$ in.

a. COMMUNION CUP WITH PATEN-COVER
Maker's mark, *JS interlaced*
Hall-mark for 1581
Worshipful Company of Goldsmiths
H. 7 in.

b. COMMUNION CUP
Maker's mark, *RW*
Hall-mark for 1589
Wendens Ambo, Essex
H. $4\frac{3}{4}$ in.

a. COMMUNION CUP
Maker's mark, *TS above an eagle*
Hall-mark for 1599
Brightwell, Berks.
H. 7 in.

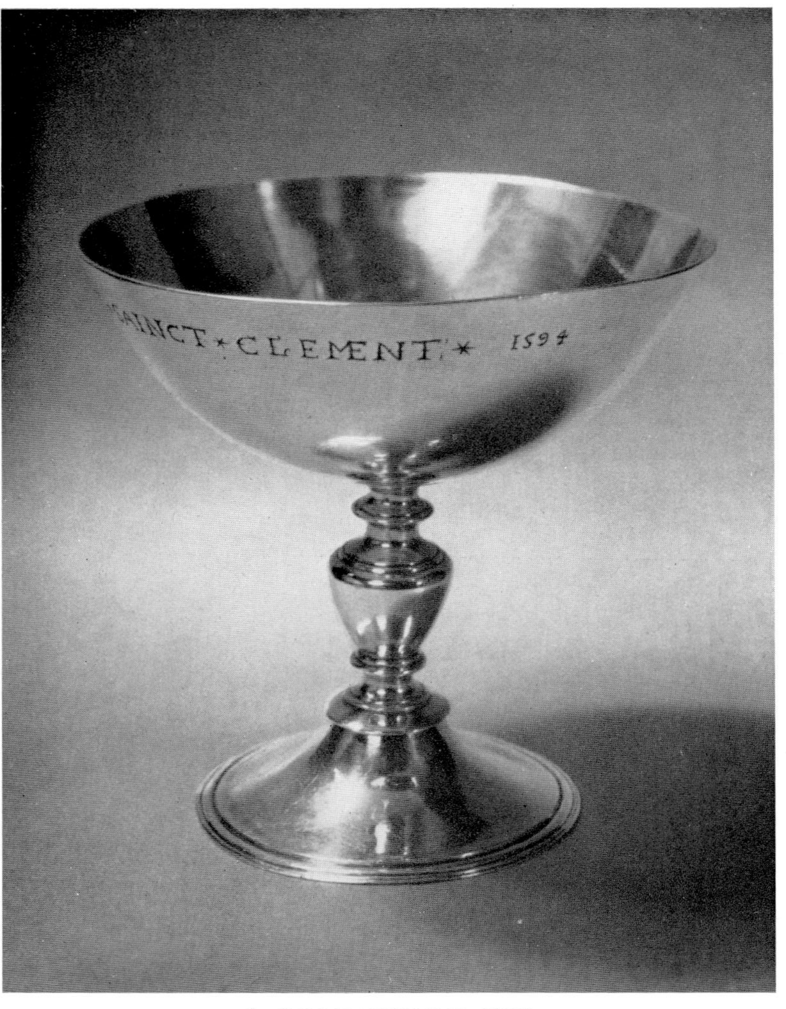

b. COMMUNION CUP
Dated 1594
St. Clement, Jersey
H. $5\frac{1}{4}$ in.

a *b*

a *b*

COMMUNION BOWLS

a. About 1600
Diam. 7 in.

b. Dated 1627
Diam. 7 in.

St. Brelade, Jersey

CHALICE AND PATEN-COVER

Maker's mark, *RS above a rose*

Hall-mark for 1610

Beddgelert, Caernarvon

H. 9 in.; paten-cover, H. 2½ in.

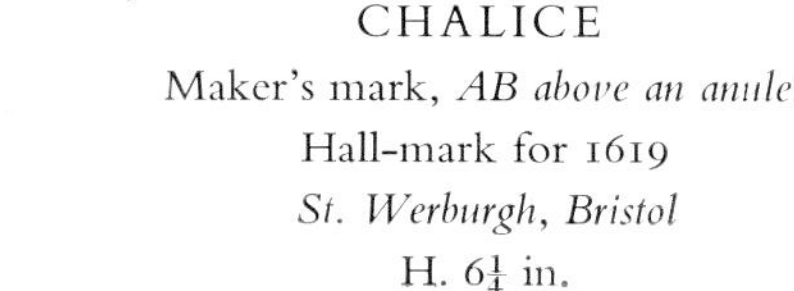

CHALICE

Maker's mark, *AB above an anulet*

Hall-mark for 1619

St. Werburgh, Bristol

H. 6¼ in.

a. CHALICE WITH COVER. Gilt
Maker's mark, *TE in monogram*
Hall-mark for 1622
St. Mary Aldermary
(Lent to the Victoria and Albert Museum)
H. $9\frac{3}{4}$ in.

b. CHALICE WITH PATEN. Gilt
Maker's mark, *HB in monogram*
Hall-mark for 1626
St. Mary, Woolnoth
H. $9\frac{3}{4}$ in.

a. CHALICE. Gilt
Maker's mark, *RC*
Hall-mark for 1629
Holy Trinity, Kensington Gore
(Lent to the Victoria and Albert Museum)
H. $8\frac{3}{4}$ in.

b. CHALICE WITH PATEN-COVER
Maker's mark, *WS with a bow*
Hall-mark for 1635
St. Botolph, Aldgate
H. 10 in.

THE ARUNDEL CHALICE

Gilt

Dated 1636

Canterbury Cathedral

H. 9 in.

CHALICE
Maker's mark, *TB in monogram*
Hall-mark for 1646
North Ockendon, Essex
(Lent to the Victoria and Albert Museum)
H. 10 in.

CHALICE WITH PATEN-COVER. Gilt

Maker's mark, *FS in monogram*

About 1615

St. John's College, Oxford

H. 11 in.

CHALICE WITH PATEN-COVER. Gilt
Maker's mark, *Tb in monogram above bird*
Hall-mark for 1638
Kenilworth, Warwick
H. 9 in.

a. CHALICE WITH PATEN-COVER. Gilt
Maker's mark, *RP below a fleur-de-lis*
Hall-mark for 1640
Mugginton, Derby
H. 10½ in.

b. CHALICE. Gilt
Maker's mark, *FT in monogram*
Hall-mark for 1641
St. John's College, Oxford
H. 9 in.

a. CHALICE WITH PATEN-COVER. Gilt
Maker's mark, *RB above a star*
Hall-mark for 1640
Staunton Harold, Leics.
(Lent by the National Trust to the Victoria and Albert Museum)
H. 16 in.

b. CHALICE WITH PATEN-COVER. Gilt
Maker's mark, *hound sejant*
Dated 1653
Fulham Palace
H. $15\frac{1}{2}$ in.

a. CHALICE WITH COVER. Gilt
About 1660
Auckland Castle, Durham
H. 13¼ in.

b. CHALICE WITH PATEN. Gilt
Maker's mark, *WM above a rose*
Hall-mark for 1661
St. George's Chapel, Windsor
H. 10¾ in.

c. CHALICE. Gilt
Maker's mark, *AM in monogram*
Before 1667
St. George's Chapel, Windsor
H. 9 in.

CHALICE WITH COVER AND PATEN. Gilt

Maker's mark, *IN above a bird*

About 1660

St. James's Palace

(Reproduced by gracious permission of Her Majesty the Queen)

CHALICE WITH PATEN-COVER. Gilt
Mark of Charles Shelley
About 1664
Buckingham Palace from Whitehall Palace
H. $11\frac{1}{2}$ in.
(Reproduced by gracious permission of Her Majesty the Queen)

a. CHALICE. Gold
Maker's mark, *GW*
Dated 1662
Welshpool, Montgomery
H. 9½ in.

b. CHALICE. Gilt
Mark of Michel Pohl the elder
Stockholm mark, 1667
Maria Kyrka, Stockholm

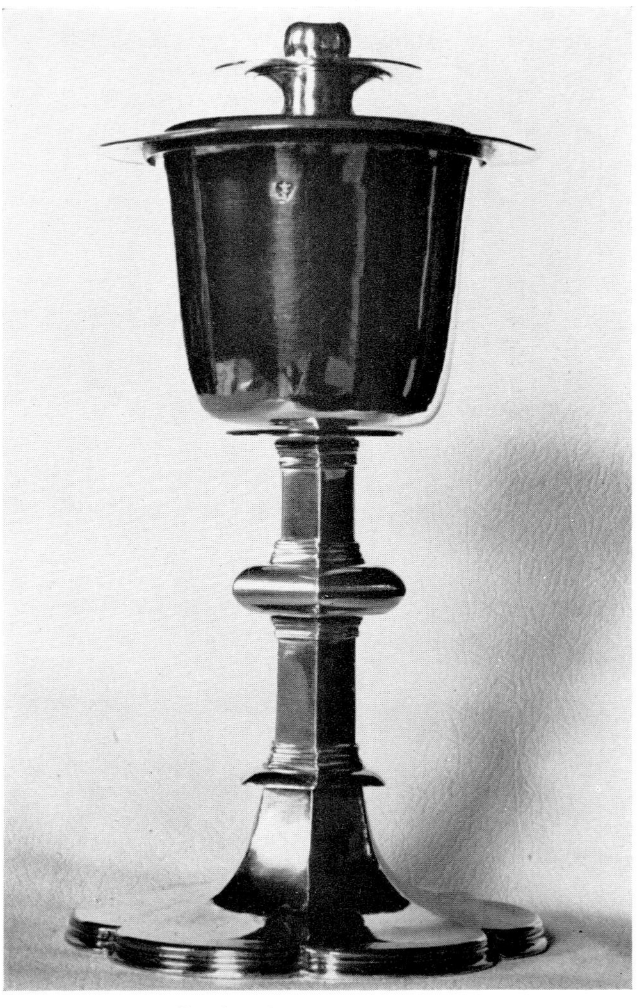

a. CHALICE WITH COVER
Mark of Charles Shelley
About 1675
Redlynch, Som.
H. 9 in.

b. CHALICE WITH PATEN-COVER. Gilt
Maker's mark, *IB above a crescent*
Hall-mark for 1672
Ingestre, Staffs.
H. $9\frac{7}{8}$ in.

a. CHALICE WITH COVER. Parcel-gilt
Hall-mark for 1670
Lichfield Cathedral
H. 33 in.

b. CHALICE WITH COVER. Parcel-gilt
Maker's mark, *WW*
Hall-mark for 1676
Ashby-de-la-Zouch, Leics.
H. $12\frac{1}{4}$ in.

a. CHALICE. Gilt
Maker's mark, *hound sejant*
Hall-mark for 1660
Gloucester Cathedral
H. $10\frac{7}{8}$ in.

b. CHALICE. Gilt
Maker's mark, *CS with an arrow*
Hall-mark for 1663
Bidford-on-Avon, Warw.
H. 10 in.

a. CHALICE. Gilt
Maker's mark, *IG within a heart*
Hall-mark for 1664
St. Augustine, from St. Faith-under-St. Paul's
(Lent to the Victoria and Albert Museum)
H. $9\frac{7}{8}$ in.

b. CHALICE WITH COVER. Gilt
Maker's mark, *EG*
Hall-mark for 1674
Oriel College, Oxford, from St. Mary Hall
H. $8\frac{3}{4}$ in.

a. CHALICE. Gilt
Maker's mark, *RL with a fleur-de-lis*
Hall-mark for 1683
St. James, Piccadilly
(Lent to the Victoria and Albert Museum)
H. $10\frac{5}{6}$ in.

b. CHALICE WITH COVER. Gilt
Maker's mark, *IH crowned*
Hall-mark for 1695
Wapping
H. $8\frac{3}{4}$ in.

a

b

a. CHALICE, PATEN, AND STRAINER-SPOON. Gilt
Maker's mark, *RL with a fleur-de-lis*
Hall-mark for 1688
Royal Hospital, Chelsea
H. 10$\frac{5}{6}$ in.

b. CHALICE WITH COVER
Maker's mark, *three storks*
Hall-mark for 1692
Swanage, Dorset
H. 10 in.

a. CHALICE
Mark of William Denny & John Bache
Hall-mark for 1697
St. Mary Abbots, Kensington
(Lent to the Victoria and Albert Museum)
H. $12\frac{5}{8}$ in.

b. CHALICE WITH COVER. Gilt
Mark of John Chartier
Hall-mark for 1699
Christ Church Cathedral, Oxford
H. $10\frac{1}{4}$ in.

a. CHALICE. Gilt
Mark of Paul de Lamerie
Hall-mark for 1720
Patshull, Staffs.
(Lent to the Victoria and Albert Museum)
H. 9 in,

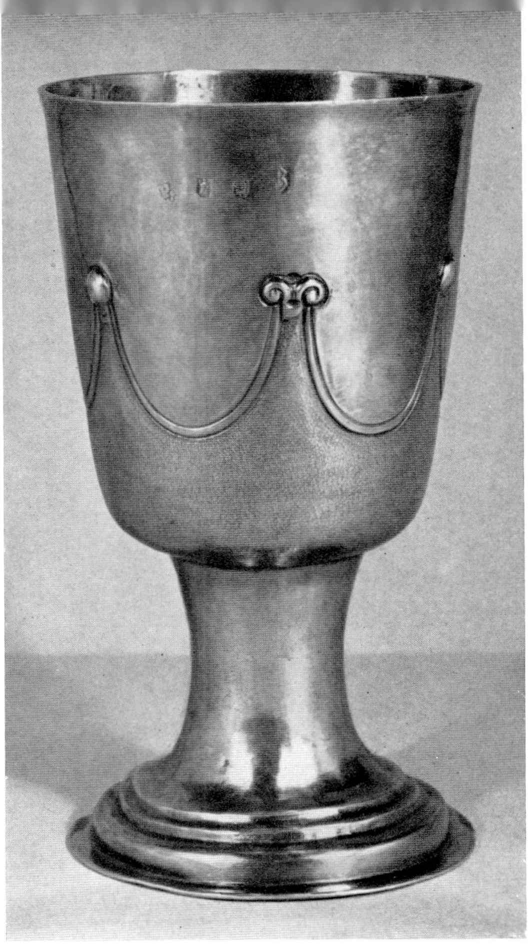

b. CHALICE. Gilt
Mark of Thomas Parr
Hall-mark for 1703
St. Nicholas Cole Abbey
H. 7¼ in.

c. CHALICE WITH PATEN-COVER. Gilt
From the design by Paul de Lamerie
Mark of Benjamin West
Hall-mark for 1747
Melbury Osmund, Dorset
H. 9¾ in.

a

b

a. CHALICE AND PATEN
Mark of William Cripps
Hall-mark for 1756
Stoke Climsland, Cornwall
H. $9\frac{7}{8}$ in.

b. CHALICE AND PATEN. Gilt
Mark of Thomas Heming
Hall-mark for 1766
St. Marylebone, from the Portland Chapel
(Lent to the Victoria and Albert Museum)
H. 9 in.

a

b

TWO CHALICES
Mark of Francis Butty
and Nicholas Dumee

a. Gilt
Hall-mark for 1766
Durham Cathedral
H. 9 in.

b. Hall-mark for 1772
Binley, Warw.
H. 11 in.

a. CHALICE. Gilt
Mark of Paul Storr
Hall-mark for 1821
St. Pancras
H. $9\frac{1}{2}$ in.

b. CHALICE
Mark of J. E. Terry & Co.
Hall-mark for 1821
Falmouth, Cornwall
H. $6\frac{1}{8}$ in.

a. CHALICE (copied from the gold coronation chalice of Charles II)
Mark of B. Preston
Hall-mark for 1827
St. Giles-in-the-Fields
H. $9\frac{1}{2}$ in.

b. CHALICE
Mark of John Bridge
Hall-mark for 1830
York Minster
H. $10\frac{7}{8}$ in.

b

CHALICE WITH COVER FOR THE COMMUNION OF THE SICK. Gilt

Mark of Samuel Wood

Hall-mark for 1743

St. Margaret Pattens

(Lent to the Victoria and Albert Museum)

a

CHALICE AND PATEN-COVER FOR THE COMMUNION OF THE SICK

Dated 1734

St. Edward, Cambridge

H. $3\frac{1}{2}$ in.

a. PATEN. Gilt
Maker's mark, *AT in monogram*
Hall-mark for 1608
St. Michael Paternoster Royal
Diam. $5\frac{5}{8}$ in.

b. PATEN
Maker's mark, *DG with an anchor*
Hall-mark for 1629
St. Michael Bassishaw
H. $3\frac{3}{4}$ in.

a. PATEN. Gilt
Maker's mark, *WS with a bow*
Hall-mark for 1633
All Hallows, Barking
$8\frac{3}{4}$ in. square

b. PATEN. Gilt
Maker's mark, *TF between two stars*
Hall-mark for 1617
St. Olave, Hart Street
H. $5\frac{1}{2}$ in.

a. PATEN. Gilt
Maker's mark, *IB below a stag*
Hall-mark for 1683
Withcote, Leics.
Diam. 6¼ in.

b. PATEN. Gilt
Maker's mark, *an escallop*
Hall-mark for 1629
Kingham, Oxon
Diam. 7½ in.

a. COVERED PATEN. Gilt
Maker's mark, *Tb in monogram above bird*
Hall-mark for 1638
Kenilworth, Warw.
H. 11 in.

b. COVERED PATEN. Gilt
Maker's mark, *hound sejant*
Dated 1653
Fulham Palace
H. $8\frac{1}{2}$ in.

a. COVERED PATEN. Gilt
Maker's mark, *CS with an arrow*
Hall-mark for 1663
Bidford-on-Avon, Warw.
H. $7\frac{7}{8}$ in.

b. COVERED PATEN. Gilt
Mark of John Plummer
York hall-mark for 1675
Ripon Cathedral
H. $9\frac{1}{2}$ in.

PATEN. Gilt
Mark of Francis Butty and Nicholas Dumee
Hall-mark for 1766
Durham Cathedral
Diam. $7\frac{3}{8}$ in.

a. FLAGON. Gilt
Maker's mark, *IP*
Hall-mark for 1572
Wells Cathedral
H. 12½ in.

b. FLAGON. Parcel-gilt
Maker's mark, *RH in monogram*
Hall-mark for 1577
Cirencester, Glos.
H. 13½ in.

a. FLAGON
Maker's mark, *SO*
Hall-mark for 1608
St. Michael Paternoster Royal, from All Hallows the Great
(Lent to the Victoria and Albert Museum)
H. 13 in.

b. FLAGON. Gilt
Maker's mark, *AB above an anulet*
Hall-mark for 1619
St. Mary Abbots, Kensington
(Lent to the Victoria and Albert Museum)
H. $12\frac{7}{8}$ in.

a. FLAGON
Maker's mark, *EL over a fleur-de-lis*
Hall-mark for 1619
Severn Stoke, Worcs.
H. 13 in.

b. FLAGON. Gilt
Maker's mark, *RC above a mullet*
Hall-mark for 1618
St. Andrew by the Wardrobe
H. 10½ in.

FLAGON. Gilt
Maker's mark, *AB*
Hall-mark for 1619
St. Werburgh, Bristol
H. $12\frac{3}{8}$ in.

a. FLAGON. Gilt
Maker's mark, *hound sejant*
Hall-mark for 1654
Staunton Harold, Leics.
(Lent by the National Trust to the Victoria and Albert Museum)
H. 10 in.

b. FLAGON. Gilt
Maker's mark, *PG with a rose*
Hall-mark for 1636
St. Anne and St. Agnes, from St. John Zachary
H. $11\frac{1}{2}$ in.

a. FLAGON. Gilt
Made by M. Houser
1660–1
Auckland Castle, Durham
H. 13 in.

b. FLAGON. Gilt
Mark of Charles Shelley
Hall-mark for 1664
Buckingham Palace, from Whitehall Palace
(Reproduced by gracious permission of Her Majesty the Queen)
H. 20 in.

a. FLAGON. Gilt
Maker's mark, *PB*
Hall-mark for 1661
Christ Church Cathedral, *Oxford*
H. 12 in.

b. FLAGON. Gilt
Maker's mark, *CS with an arrow*
Hall-mark for 1663
Bidford-on-Avon, *Warw*.
H. 13¼ in.

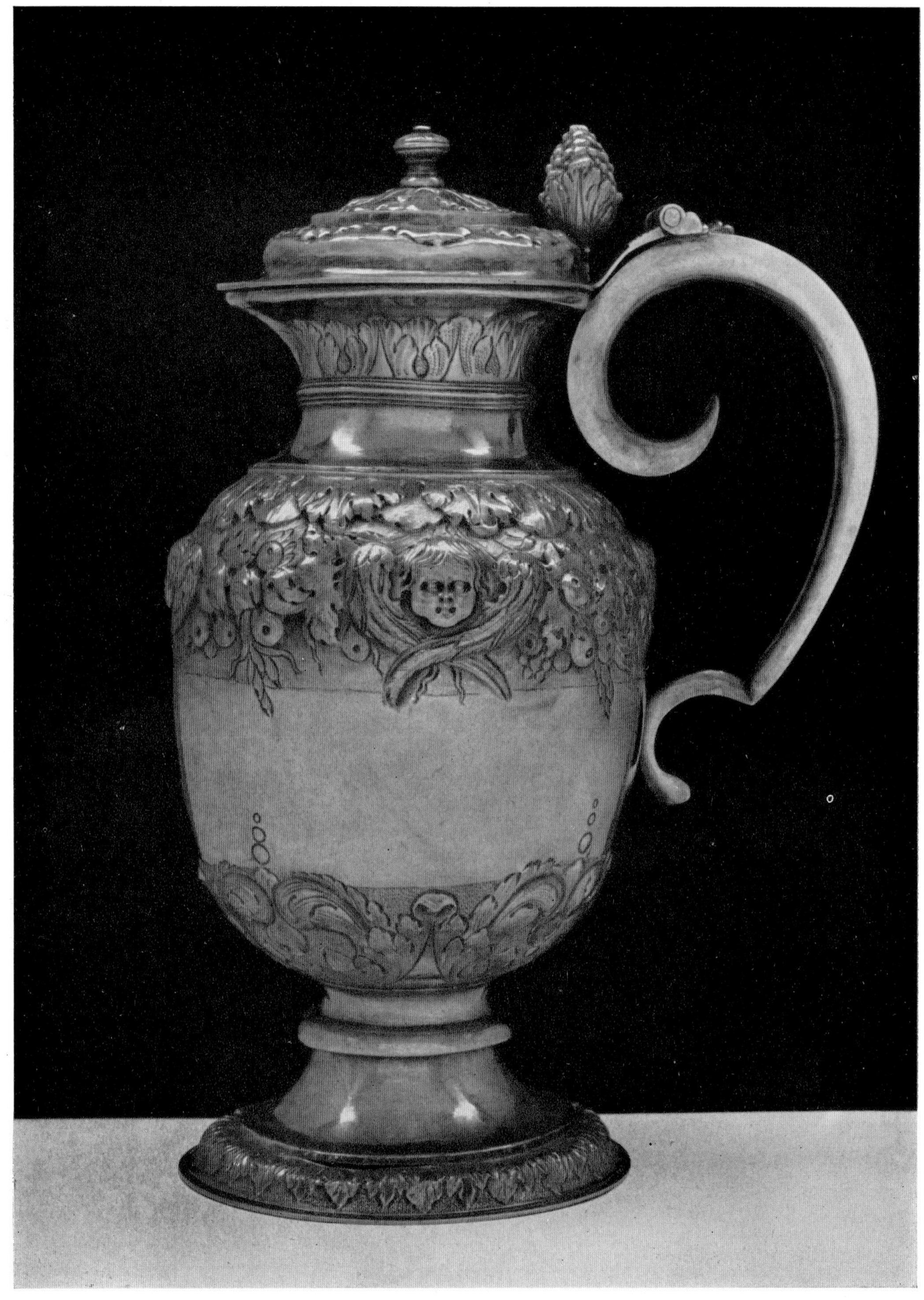

FLAGON. Gilt
Maker's mark, *ID in monogram*
Hall-mark for 1672
Easton Mauduit, Northants
(Lent to the Victoria and Albert Museum)
H. 13 in.

FLAGON. Gilt
Maker's mark, *RL with a fleur-de-lis*
Hall-mark for 1683
St. James, Piccadilly
(Lent to the Victoria and Albert Museum)
H. $14\frac{1}{2}$ in.

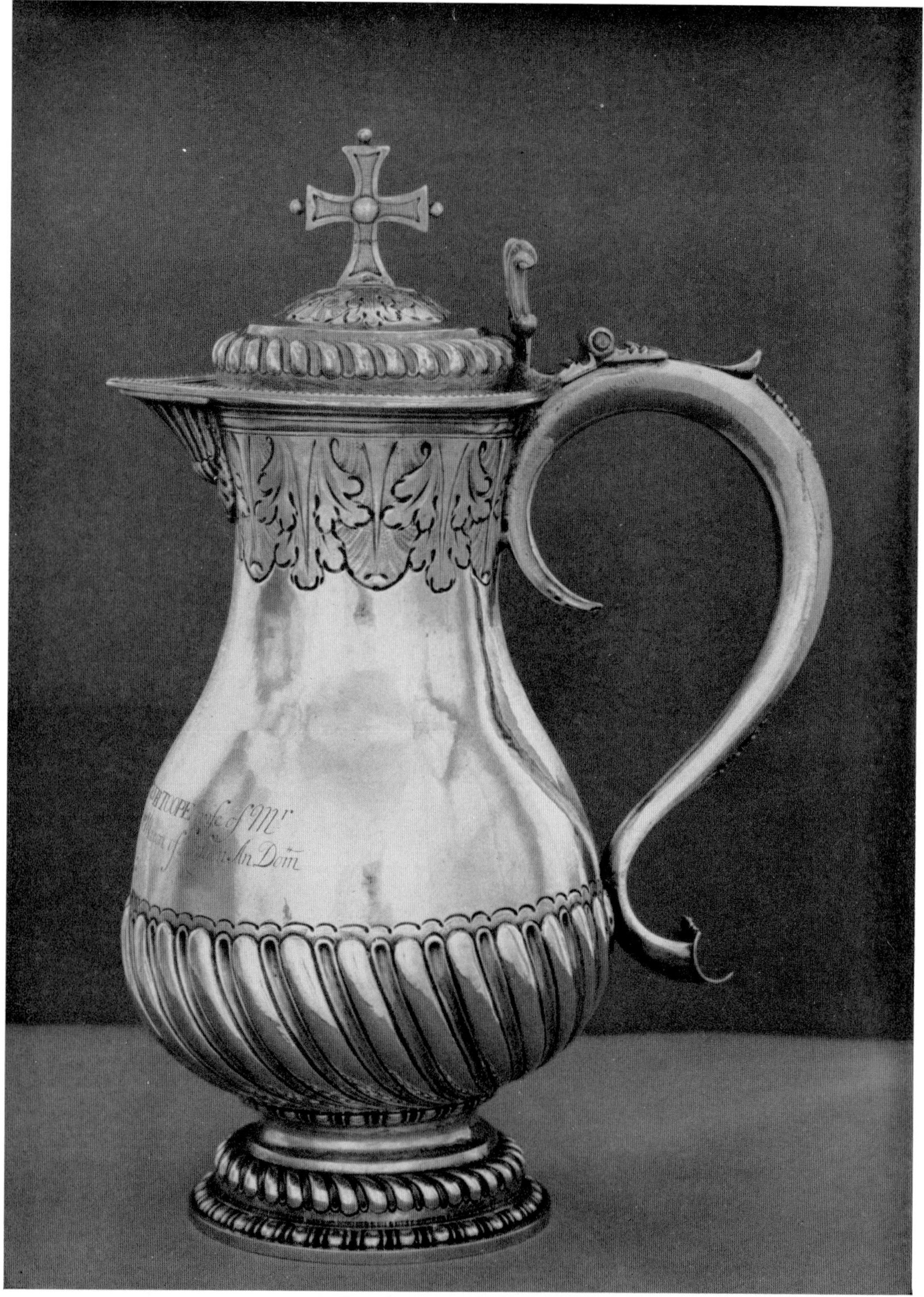

FLAGON. Gilt
Maker's mark, *three storks*
Hall-mark for 1692
Swanage, Dorset
H. 12 in.

a. FLAGON. Gilt
Mark of Timothy Ley
Hall-mark for 1709
St. Margaret Pattens
(Lent to the Victoria and Albert Museum)
H. 12 in.

b. FLAGON. Gilt
Mark of Paul de Lamerie
Hall-mark for 1727
West Drayton, Middlesex
(Lent to the Victoria and Albert Museum)
H. $11\frac{1}{4}$ in.

a. FLAGON. Gilt
Mark of Robert Cooper
Hall-mark for 1715
St. Nicholas Cole Abbey
H. 13½ in.

b. FLAGON. Gilt
Mark of Gabriel Sleath
Hall-mark for 1730
St. George, Bloomsbury
H. 13 in.

a. FLAGON. Gilt
Mark of Paul de Lamerie
Hall-mark for 1747
Melbury Osmund, Dorset
H. 12½ in.

b. FLAGON
Mark of Gabriel Sleath
Hall-mark for 1740
St. Mary, Woolwich
H. 11 in.

a. FLAGON
Mark of William Cripps
Hall-mark for 1756
Stoke Climsland, Cornwall
H. $14\frac{1}{4}$ in.

b. FLAGON. Gilt
Mark of Francis Butty and Nicholas Dumee
Hall-mark for 1766
Durham Cathedral
H. $11\frac{1}{4}$ in.

a. FLAGON
Mark of Edward Fennell
Hall-mark for 1791
Madron, Cornwall
H. 14 in.

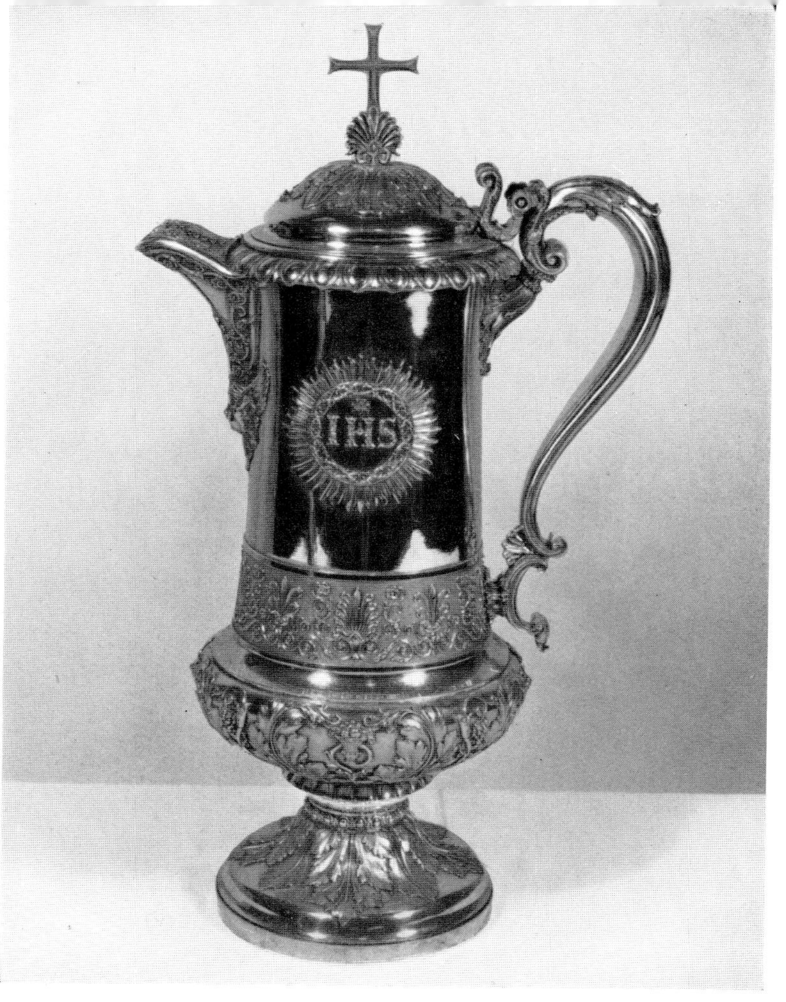

b. FLAGON. Gilt
Mark of Paul Storr
Hall-mark for 1821
St. Pancras
H. 18 in.

a. Design by A. W. Pugin for a FLAGON for the Chapel Royal, Brighton
Dated 1827
Victoria and Albert Museum

b. FLAGON. Gilt
Mark of John Bridge
Hall-mark for 1830
York Minster
H. $27\frac{1}{2}$ in.

ICONOGRAPHY

a. The Good Shepherd
Flagon. Hall-mark for 1619
Severn Stoke, Worcs.

b. The Good Shepherd
Chalice. Hall-mark for 1640
Staunton Harold, Leics.
(Lent by the National Trust to the Victoria and Albert Museum)

c. The Good Shepherd
Chalice. About 1655
Wimpole, Cambs.

d. Crucifix
Paten. Hall-mark for 1638
Kingerby, Lincs.
(Lent to the Victoria and Albert Museum)

ICONOGRAPHY

a. View of Cirencester
Flagon. Hall-mark for 1577
Cirencester, Glos.

b. The Crown of Thorns
Chalice. Hall-mark for 1640
Staunton Harold, Leics.
(Lent by the National Trust to the Victoria and Albert Museum)

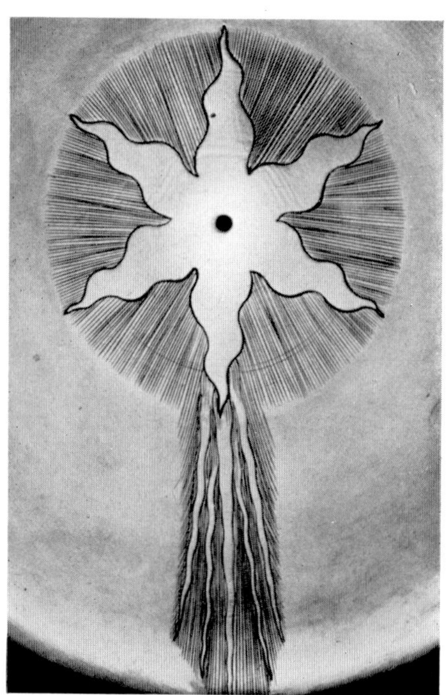

c. The Wise Men's Star
Covered paten. Dated 1653
Fulham Palace

d. The Sacred Monogram
From the account book of Benjamin Rhodes
Dated 1694
Hoare's Bank

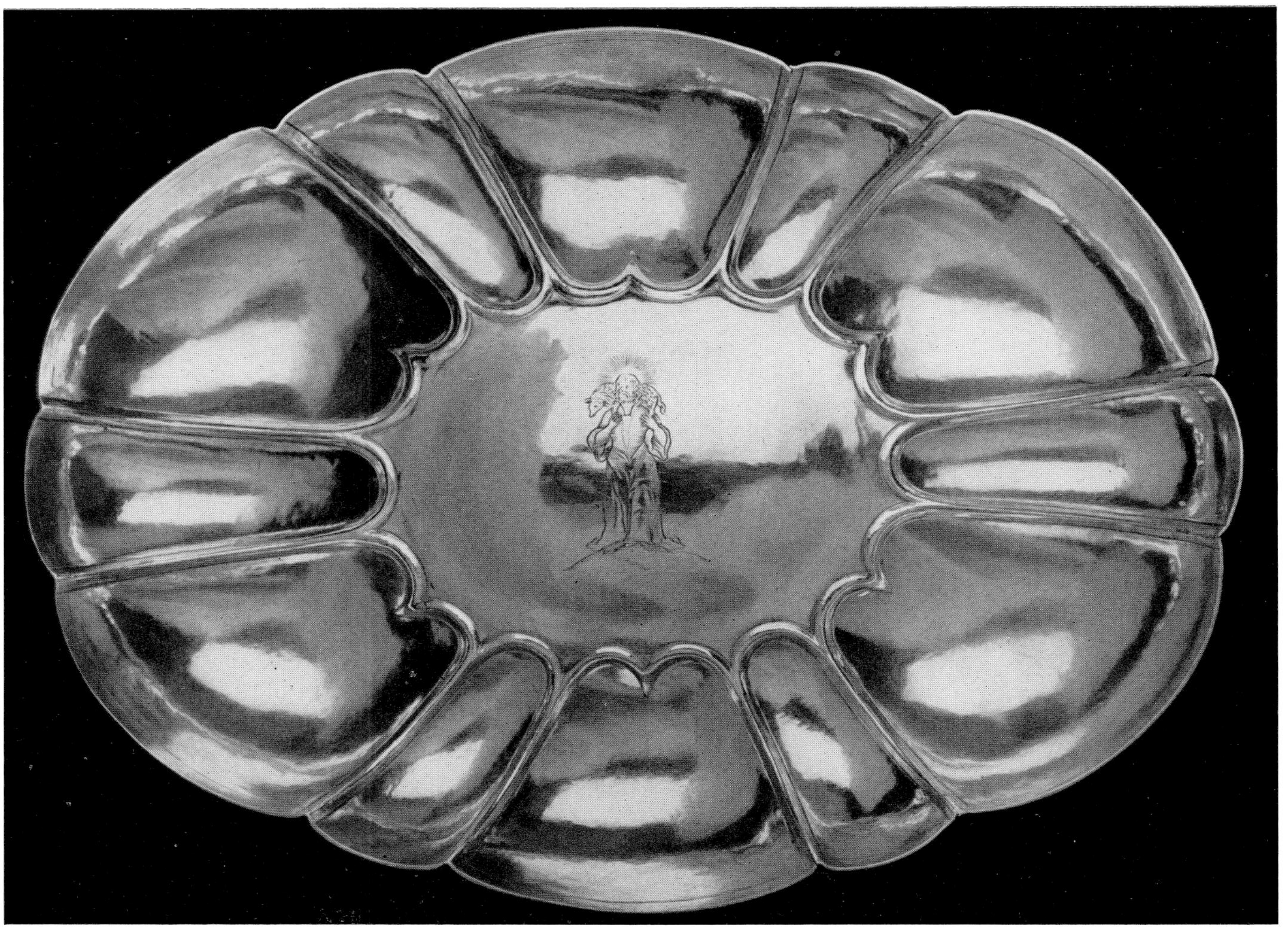

ALMS BASIN. Gilt
Maker's mark, *hound sejant*
About 1655
Wimpole, Cambs.
W. $15\frac{5}{8}$ in.

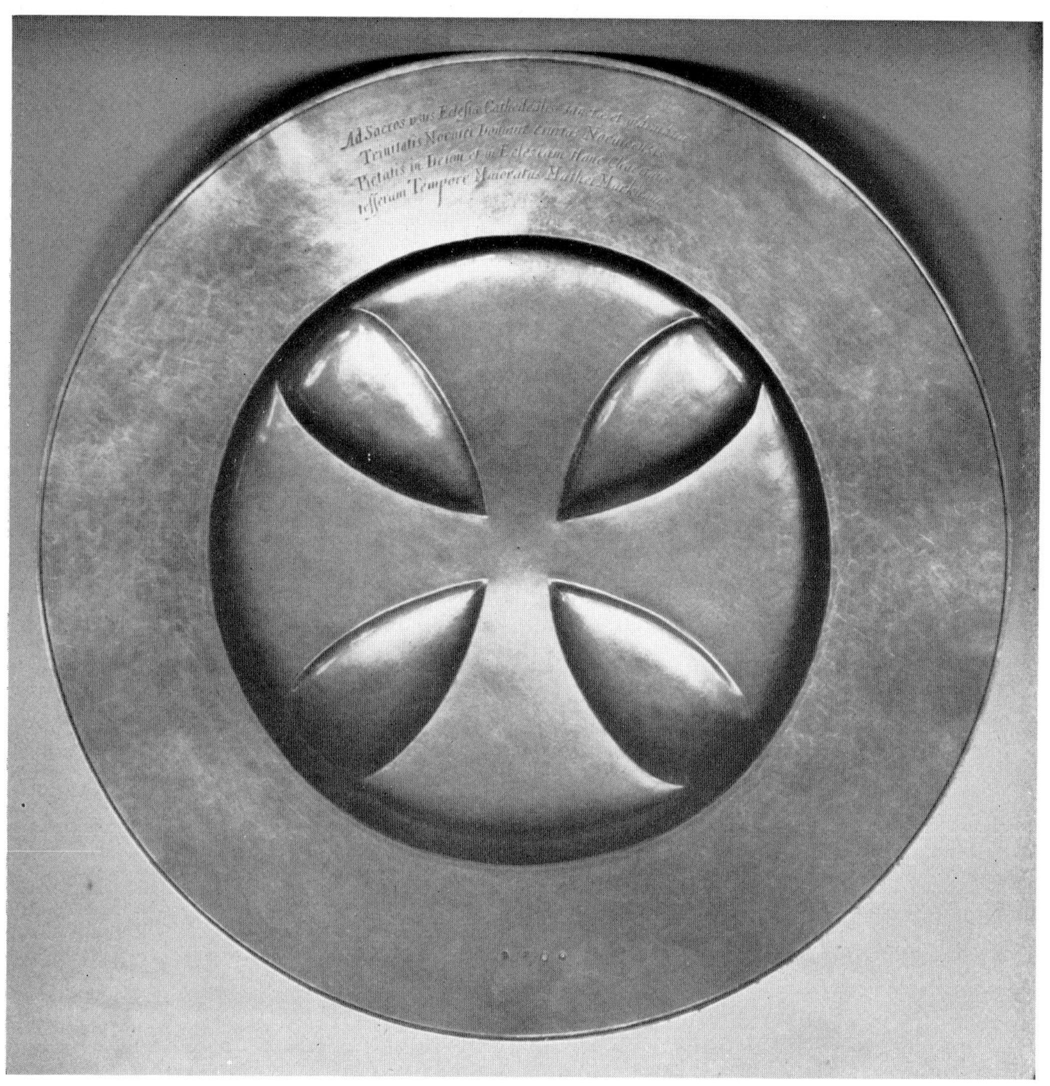

ALMS BASIN. Gilt
Maker's mark, *AF with a mullet*
Hall-mark for 1665
Norwich Cathedral
Diam. $21\frac{1}{2}$ in.

ALMS BASIN. Gilt
Embossed by M. Houser
1660–1
Auckland Castle, Durham
Diam. 21 in.

ALTAR DISH. Gilt
Probably embossed by M. Houser
Maker's mark, *HG with a mullet*
Hall-mark for 1664
Buckingham Palace from Whitehall Palace
(Reproduced by gracious permission of Her Majesty the Queen)
Diam. 37 in.

ALTAR DISH. Gilt
Probably embossed by M. Houser
1660
St. George's Chapel, Windsor
Diam. $28\frac{3}{4}$ in.

ALMS BASIN. Gilt

Maker's mark, *RL with a fleur-de-lis*

Hall-mark for 1683

(Below, detail showing the Nativity)

St. James, Piccadilly

Diam. $23\frac{1}{2}$ in.

a. ALMS BASIN. Gilt
Maker's mark, *PR in cypher*
Hall-mark for 1684
Westminster Abbey
Diam. 25 in.

b. ALMS BASIN
Maker's mark, *HR*
Hall-mark for 1685
St. Bartholomew the Less
Diam. $14\frac{7}{8}$ in.

a. ALMS BASIN
Maker's mark, *a water-bird in a circle*
Hall-mark for 1694
Trinity College, Oxford
Diam. $18\frac{1}{2}$ in.

b. ALMS BASIN. Parcel-gilt
Mark of Francis Garthorne
Hall-mark for 1710
Stoke Newington
Diam. 13 in.

Detail of ALMS BASIN

The Deposition

Engraved by Simon Gribelin after Annibale Carracci

Mark of Isaac Liger

Hall-mark for 1706

Dunham Massey Hall, Cheshire

a. Detail of ALMS BASIN
St. Paul
Hall-mark for 1710
St. Paul, Shadwell

b. Detail of ALMS BASIN. Gilt
The Last Supper
Mark of John Payne
Hall-mark for 1750
St. Lawrence Jewry

ALMS BASIN. Gilt
Mark of Thomas Heming
Hall-mark for 1765
St. Marylebone (from the Portland Chapel)
W. 19½ in.

ALMS BASIN. Gilt
Mark of Paul Storr
Hall-mark for 1821
St. Pancras
Diam. 24 in.

a

b

c

a. COLLECTING BOX
Maker's mark, *TC above a fish*
Hall-mark for 1677 (?)
H. $3\frac{3}{4}$ in.
St. Peter's Chapel, Tabley, Cheshire

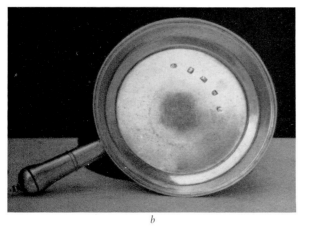

b. COLLECTING PLATE
Mark of John Babbage
Exeter hall-mark for 1743
St. Ives, Cornwall
Diam. 6 in.

c. COLLECTING TANKARD
Maker's mark, *IG crowned*
Dated 1750
St. Aubin, Jersey
H. 8 in.

a. BIBLE WITH SILVER MOUNTS

1634

York Minster

H. 17 in.

b. BIBLE WITH GILT MOUNTS

1638

Christ Church Cathedral, Oxford

H. 13½ in.

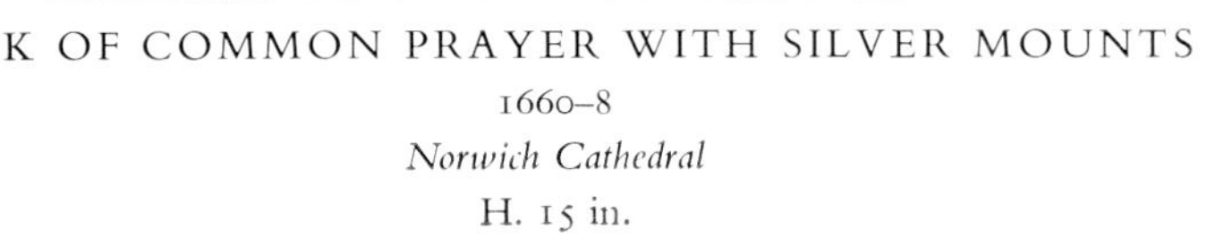

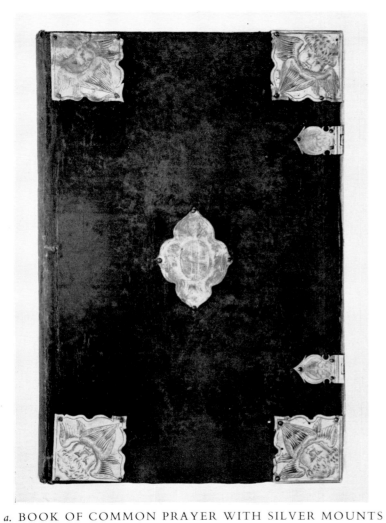

a. BOOK OF COMMON PRAYER WITH SILVER MOUNTS
1660–8
Norwich Cathedral
H. 15 in.

b. BIBLE WITH GILT MOUNTS
1660–72
Canterbury Cathedral
H. 15½ in.

a. CANDLESTICK. Gilt
Maker's mark, *HW above an escallop*
About 1655
Lambeth Palace
H. 17¼ in.

b. CANDLESTICK. Gilt
Maker's mark, *hound sejant*
Hall-mark for 1653
Staunton Harold, Leics.
(Lent by the National Trust to the Victoria and Albert Museum)
H. 22¾ in.

c. CANDLESTICK. Gilt
Maker's mark, *hound sejant*
Hall-mark for 1661
Gloucester Cathedral
H. 16½ in.

a. CANDLESTICK. Gilt
Maker's mark, *WM with a mullet*
Hall-mark for 1663
Salisbury Cathedral
H. 26 in.

b. CANDLESTICK. Gilt
Maker's mark, *FL with a bird*
1660
St. George's Chapel, Windsor
H. 28½ in.

c. CANDLESTICK. Gilt
Maker's mark, *IB above a crescent*
Hall-mark for 1676
Ingestre, Staffs.
H. 24 in.

CANDLESTICK. Gilt
Maker's mark, *IB above a crescent*
Hall-mark for 1675
Harthill, Yorks.
H. $13\frac{7}{8}$ in.

CANDLESTICK. Gilt
Maker's mark, *RL with a fleur-de-lis*
Hall-mark for 1688
Royal Hospital, Chelsea
H. 39 in.

a. CANDLESTICK. Gilt
Mark of Anthony Nelme
Hall-mark for 1694
St. George's Chapel, Windsor
H. 42 in.

b. CANDLESTICK
Mark of Gabriel Sleath
Hall-mark for 1712
Bristol Cathedral
H. 21¾ in.

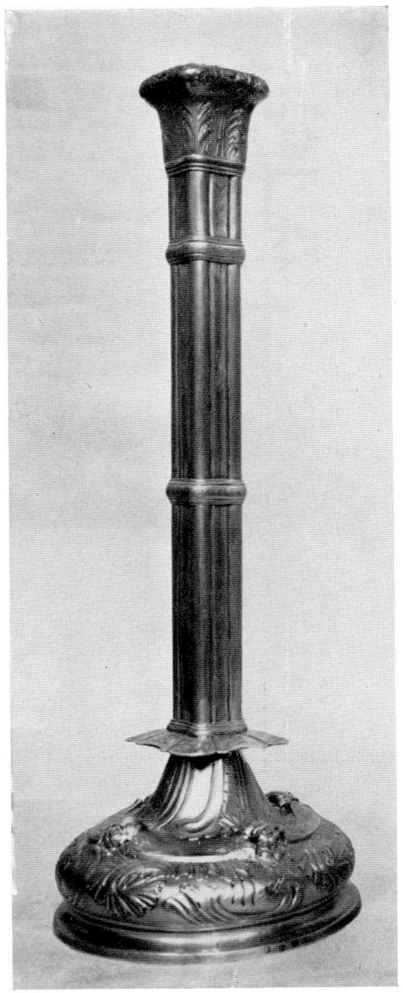

c. CANDLESTICK. Gilt
Mark of Paul de Lamerie
Hall-mark for 1738
Queen's College, Oxford
H. 23½ in.

a. CANDLESTICK
Maker's mark, *SW in Gothic script*
Hall-mark for 1759
Trinity College, Oxford
H. 26 in.

b. CANDLESTICK
Maker's mark, *IV*
Hall-mark for 1777
Christ Church Cathedral, Dublin
H. 30 in.

c. CANDLESTICK. Gilt
Mark of Francis Butty and Nicholas Dumee
Hall-mark for 1766
Durham Cathedral
H. 24 in.

a. BAPTISMAL BOWL
Mark of Richard Gurney and Thomas Cook
Hall-mark for 1730
St. Paul, Deptford
H. $4\frac{3}{8}$ in.

b. BAPTISMAL BOWL
Mark of David and Robert Hennell
Hall-mark for 1766
St. Mary, Reading
H. 6 in.

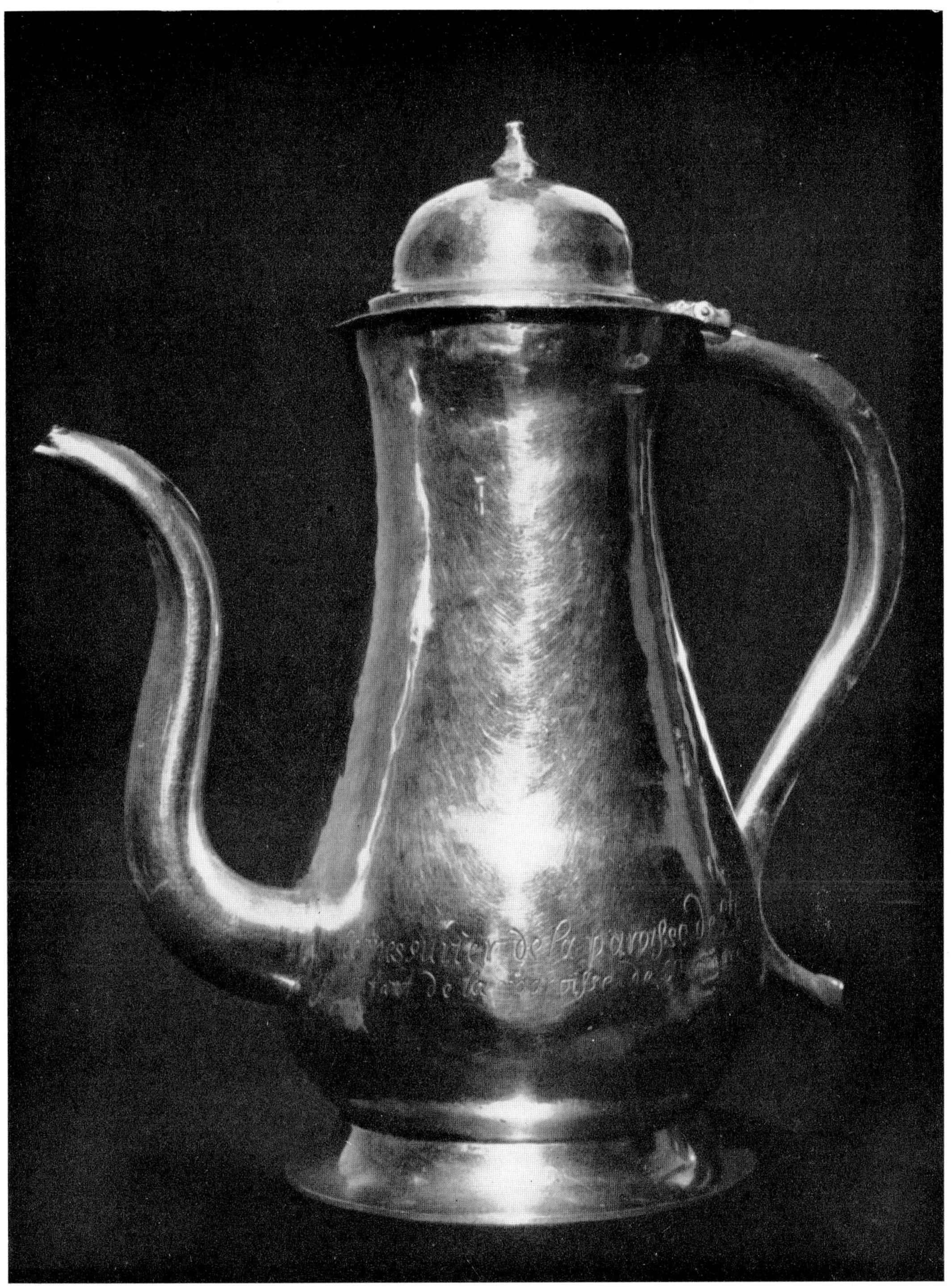

BAPTISMAL EWER

Maker's mark, *spearhead between IH*

Dated 1729

St. Andrew, Guernsey

H. 7 in.

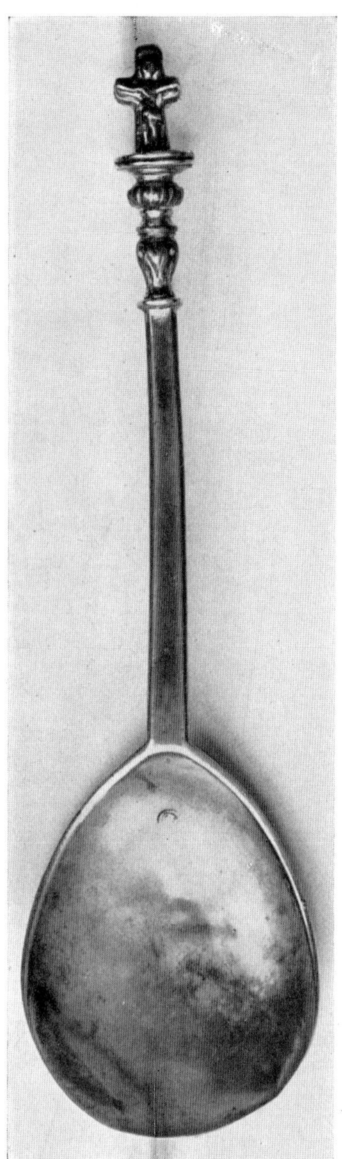

a. STRAINER SPOON. Gilt
Dated 1613
St. Peter-per-Mountergate, Norwich
L. 7¾ in.

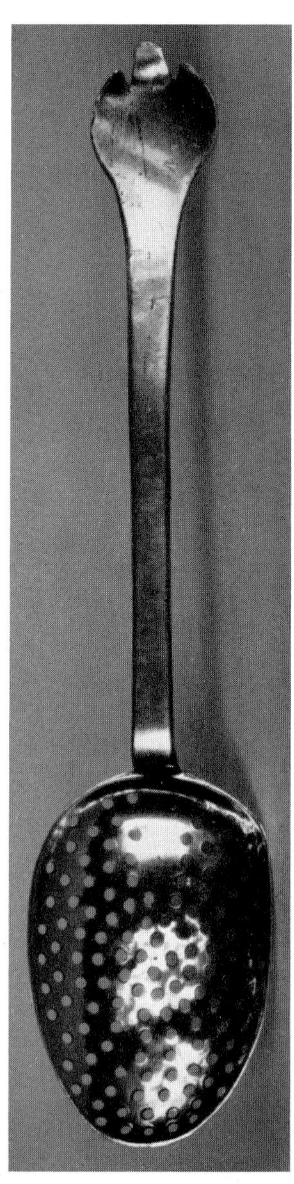

b. STRAINER SPOON
Maker's mark, *WM crowned*
Hall-mark for 1685
Bristol Cathedral
L. 5¾ in.

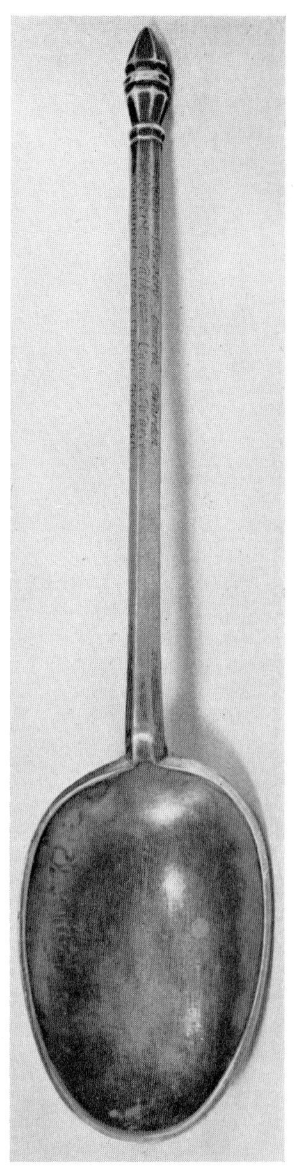

c. STRAINER SPOON
Maker's mark, *IW crowned above a star*
Hall-mark for 1693
St. Dunstan, Stepney
L. 8 in.

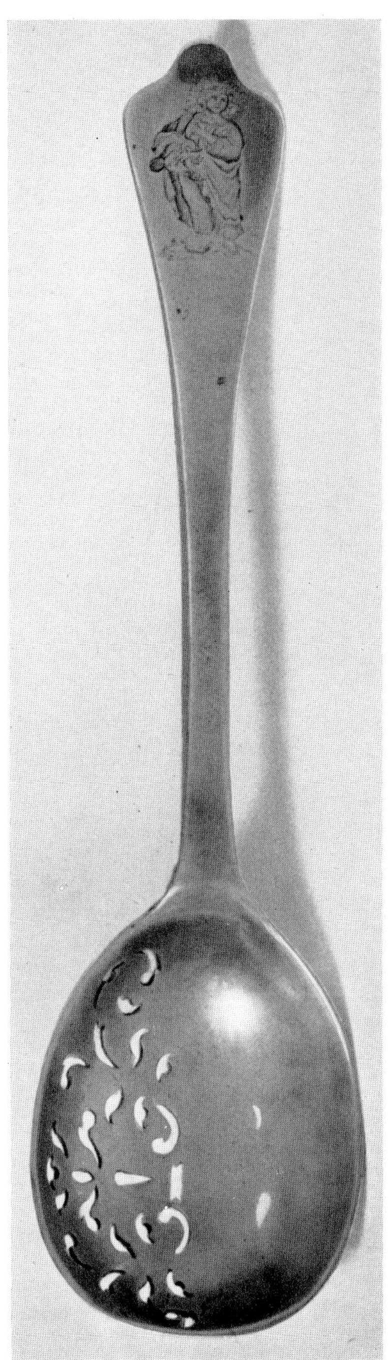

a. STRAINER SPOON. Gilt

Dated 1717

Wapping

L. 7¾ in.

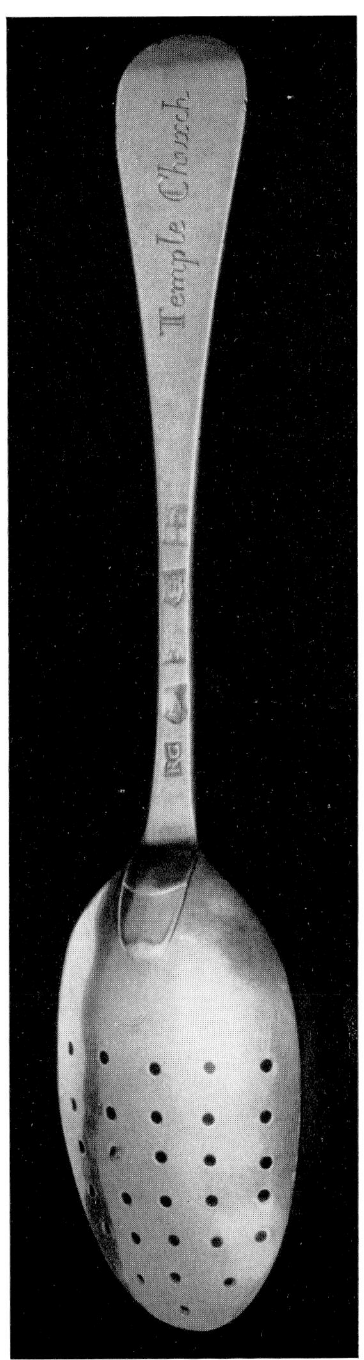

b. STRAINER SPOON

Mark of Ralph Good of Bristol

About 1730

Formerly at the Temple Church, Bristol

L. 7¾ in.

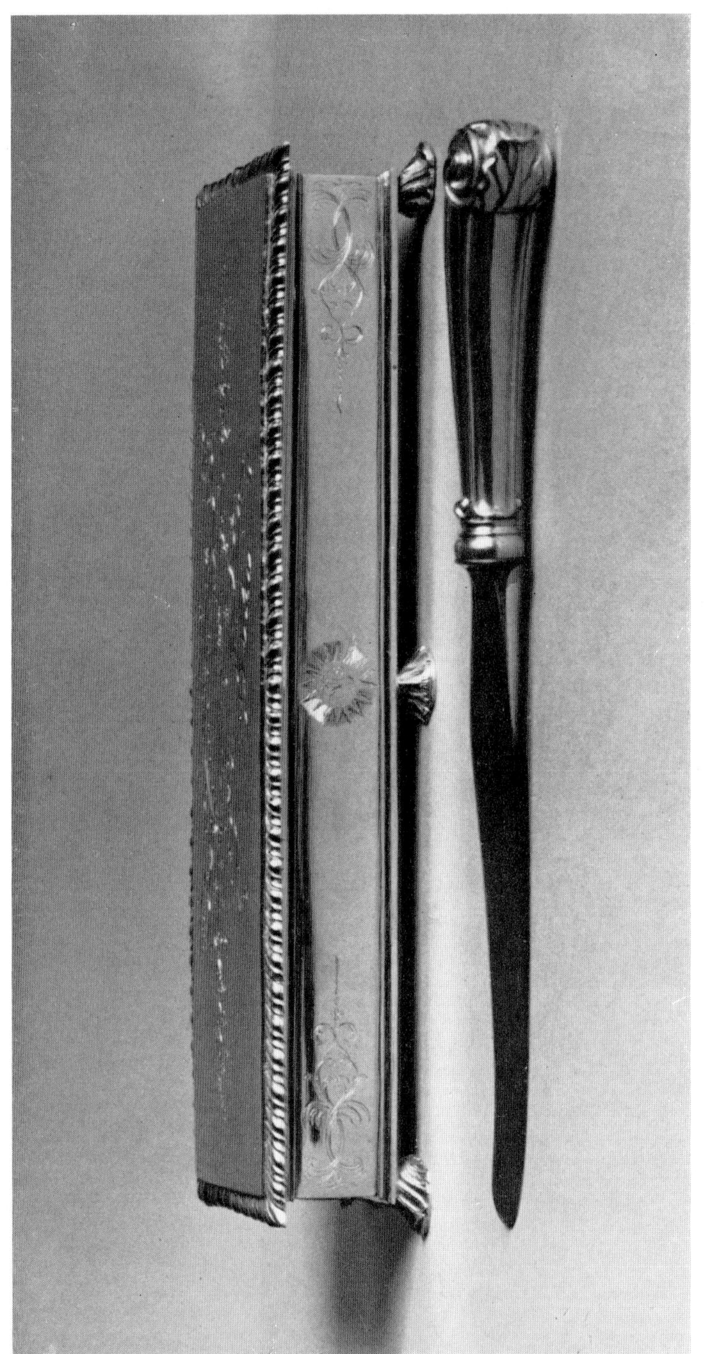

BREAD KNIFE WITH BOX. Gilt

Mark of James Shruder

Hall-mark for 1753

Melbury Sampford, Dorset

L. (box) $10\frac{3}{4}$ in.

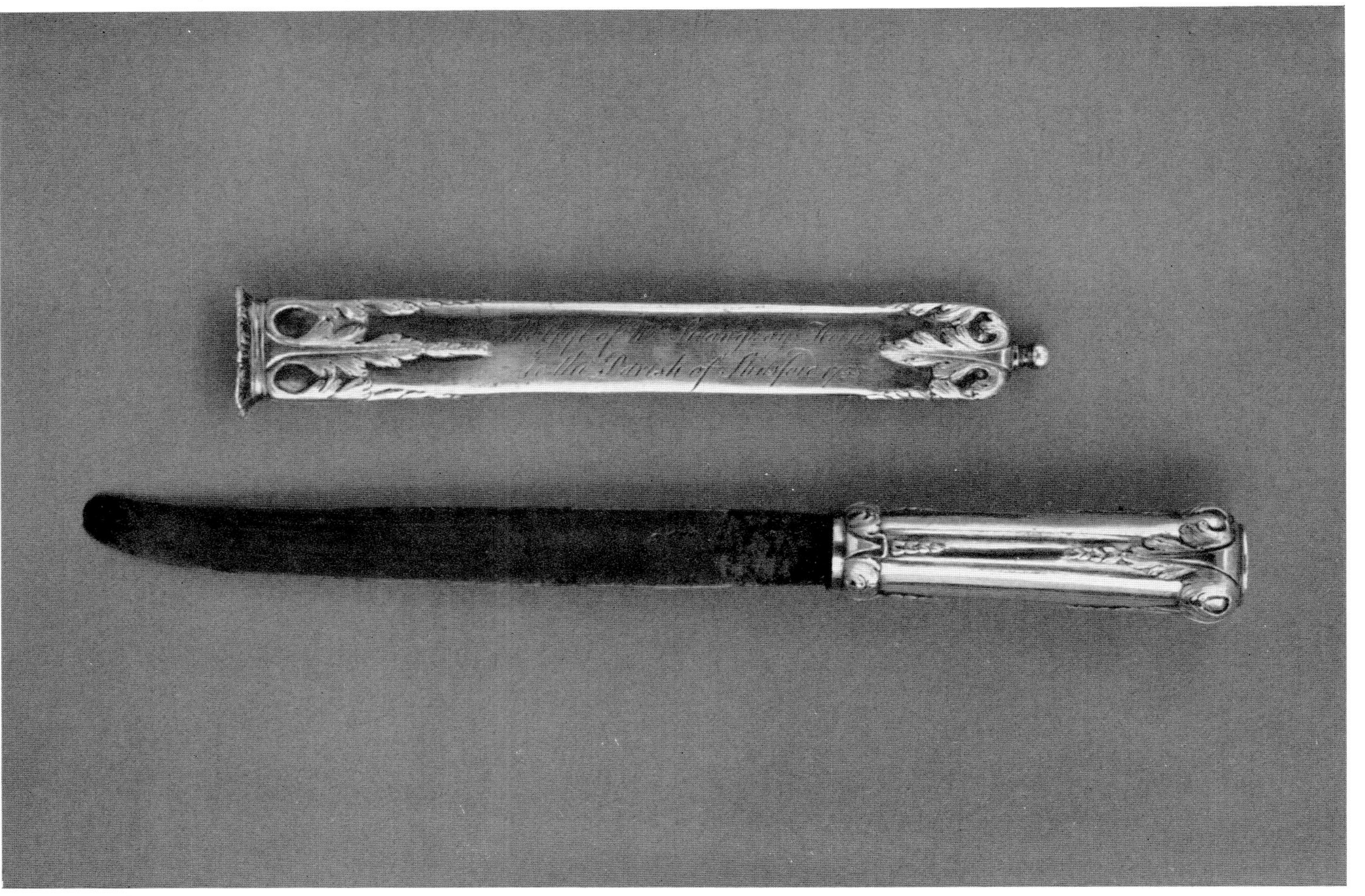

BREAD KNIFE AND SHEATH. Gilt

Dated 1755

Stinsford, Dorset

RECUSANT CHALICE AND PATEN

Early 17th century

R.C. church, Creswell, Staffs.

H. $5\frac{3}{4}$ in.

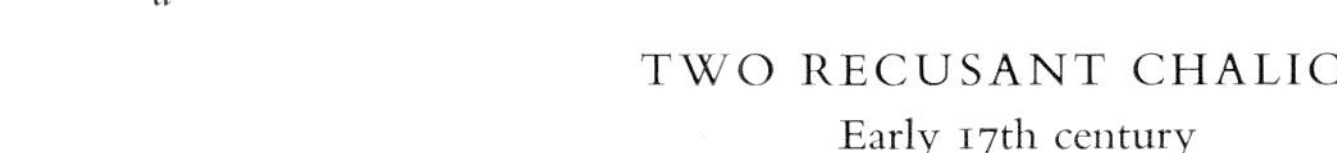

a

b

TWO RECUSANT CHALICES

Early 17th century

a. Lord Kenyon
H. $6\frac{1}{2}$ in.

b. Oscott College, Birmingham
H. $4\frac{3}{8}$ in.

GROUP CR. 2

a. RECUSANT CHALICE
About 1630
Bradoc (C.E.), Cornwall
H. 7 in.

b. ANGLICAN CHALICE WITH PATEN-COVER
Maker's mark, *WR below a bow*
Hall-mark for 1633
Llanafon (C.W.), Cardigan
H. 9½ in.

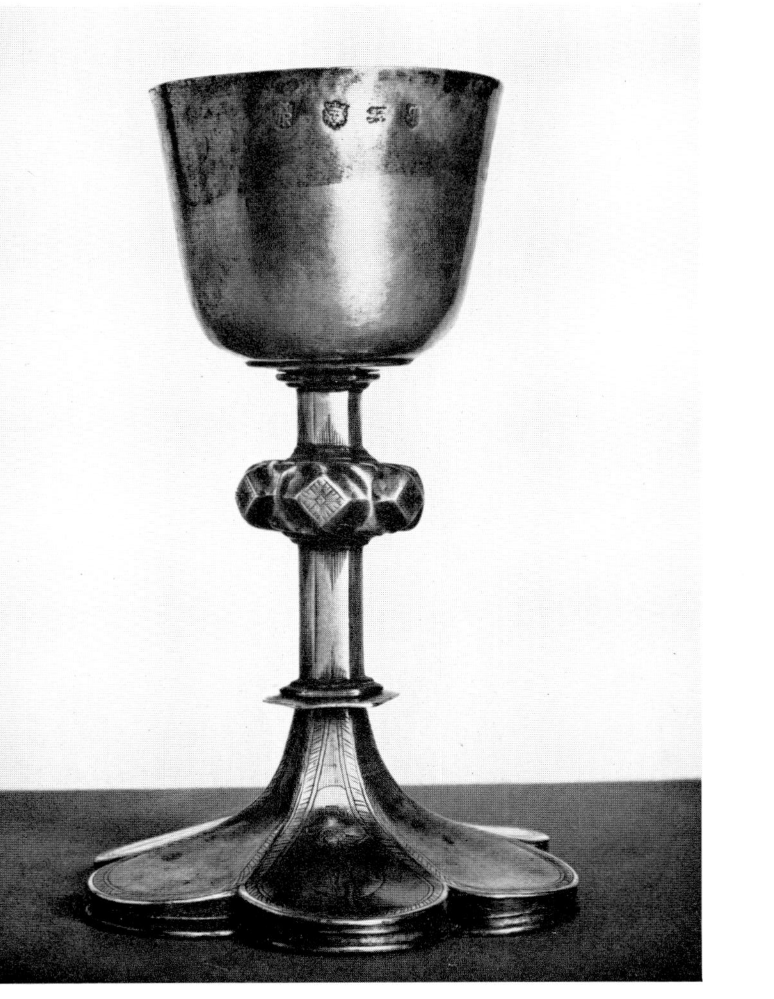

TWO RECUSANT CHALICES

a. Maker's mark, *WR below a bow*
Hall-mark for 1633
National Museum, Dublin
H. $6\frac{1}{2}$ in.

b. About 1630
Ampleforth Abbey, Yorks.
H. 7 in.

a

b

TWO RECUSANT CHALICES. Gilt

About 1630–40

Danby Hall, Middleham, Yorks.

a. H. $7\frac{5}{8}$ in. *b*. H. $7\frac{1}{4}$ in.

a. General view

b. Foot engraved with the *Instruments of the Passion*

RECUSANT CHALICE. Gilt

About 1630–40

Ashow (C.E.), *Warw.*

H. $8\frac{1}{2}$ in.

GROUP CR. 3

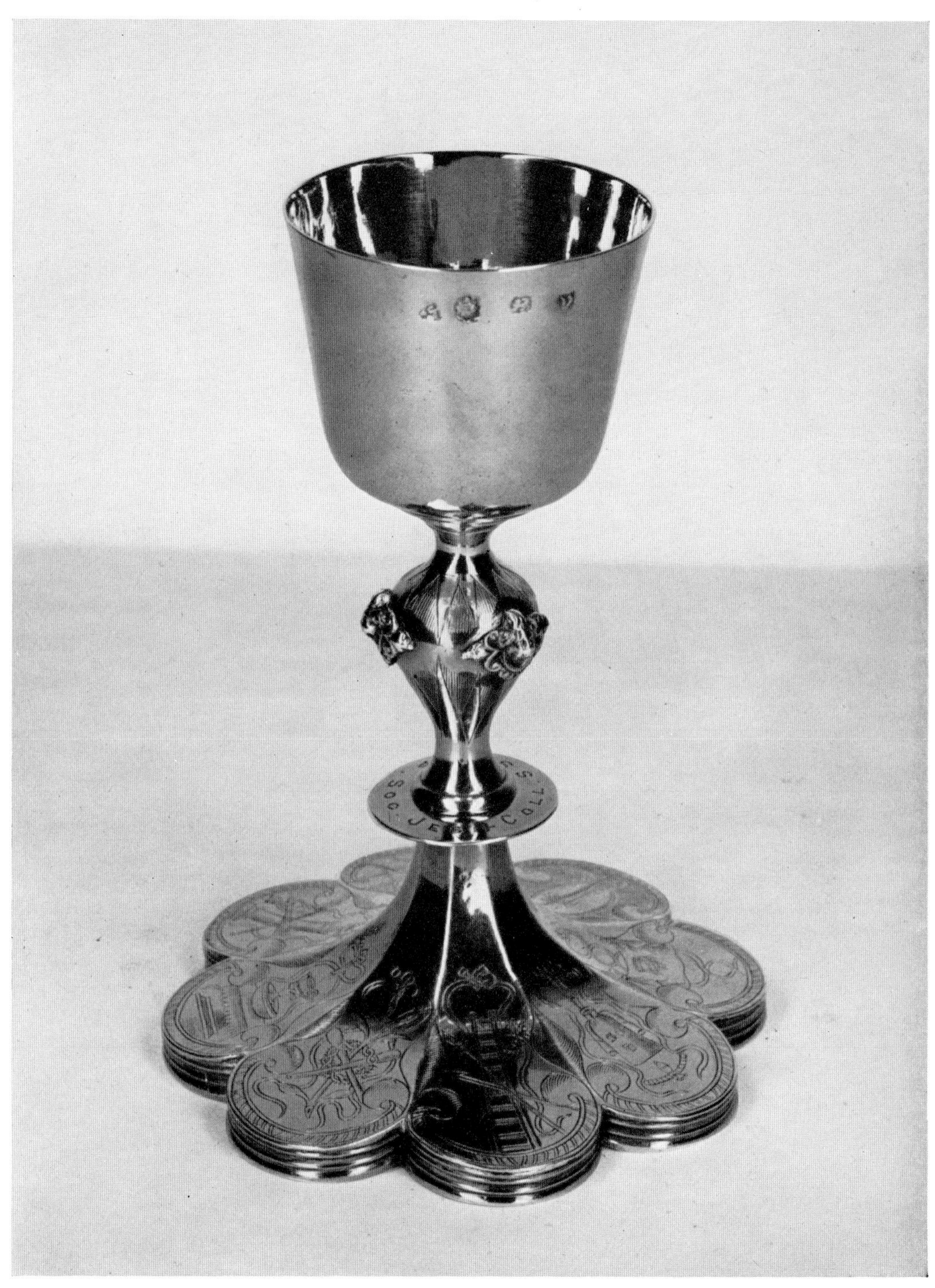

RECUSANT CHALICE. Gilt
Maker's mark, *RM above a rosette*
Hall-mark for 1637
St. Ignatius, South Tottenham
H. $7\frac{1}{2}$ in.

GROUP CR. 3

RECUSANT CHALICE AND PATEN. Gilt

Maker's mark, *RM above a rosette*

Hall-mark for 1638

Wardour Castle, Wilts.

H. $9\frac{1}{2}$ in.

a. General view

b. Detail of foot

RECUSANT CHALICE

Maker's mark, *RM above a rosette*

Hall-mark for 1639

Solihull (C.E.), *Warw.*

H. 8 in.

a *b*

TWO RECUSANT CHALICES

a. Maker's mark, *RM above a rosette*
About 1638
Stonyhurst College
H. 7 in.

b. Maker's mark, *WT below two anulets*
Hall-mark for 1639
St. Mary-on-the-Quay, Bristol
H. 7¼ in.

a

b

TWO RECUSANT CHALICES. Parcel-gilt

1650–70

a. Sawston Hall, Cambridge
H. 5 in.

b. Stonyhurst College
H. 6½ in.

a

b

TWO RECUSANT CHALICES

a. Parcel-gilt. 1650–70
R.C. church, Clitheroe, Lancs.
H. 8 in.

b. Maker's mark, *WB in a pointed-topped shield*
About 1690
Oscott College, Birmingham
H. 6½ in.

GROUP CR. 4

RECUSANT CHALICE. Gilt
Mark of Benjamin Pyne
Hall-mark for 1704
Lulworth Castle, Dorset
H. $9\frac{1}{2}$ in.

a

b

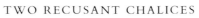

TWO RECUSANT CHALICES

a. Mark of Frederick Kandler
Hall-mark for 1739 (bowl remade about 1810)
R.C. church, Worcester
H. $8\frac{1}{2}$ in.

b. Mark of Wm. Pitts and Jos. Preedy
Hall-mark for 1791
Stonyhurst College
H. $10\frac{1}{2}$ in.

a

b

TWO RECUSANT CHALICES

a. Mark of Jean Quenault of St. Helier
1795
Société Jersiaise
H. 10 in.

b. Mark of Robert Hennell
Hall-mark for 1830
Westminster Cathedral
H. $10\frac{1}{8}$ in.

a

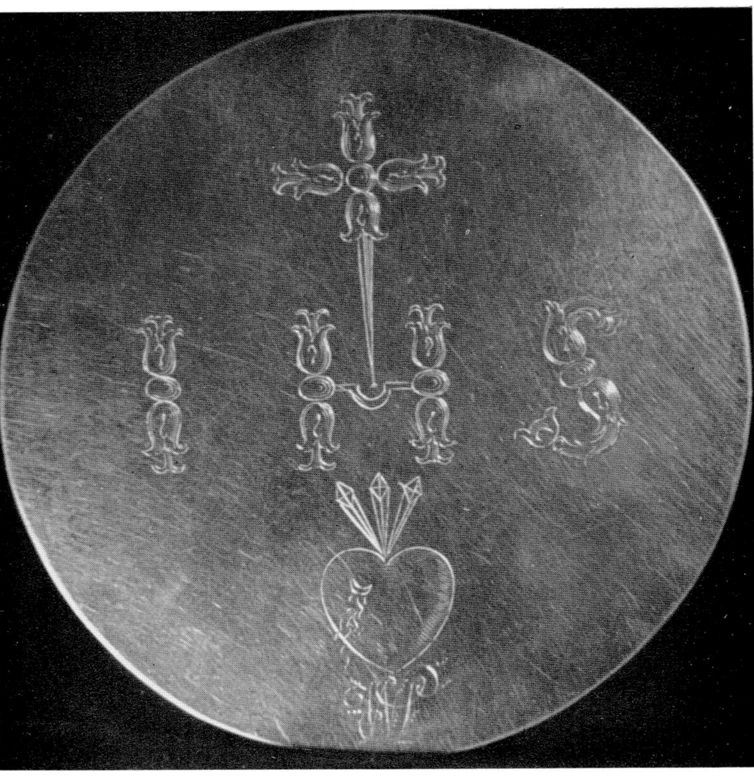

b

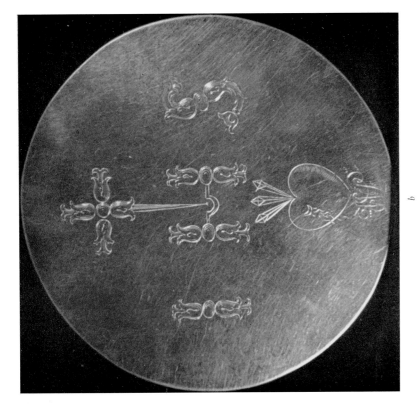

TWO RECUSANT PATENS

a. Parcel-gilt, 1650–70
Sawston Hall, Cambridge
Diam. $3\frac{1}{4}$ in.

b. 1650–70
Stonyhurst College
Diam. $3\frac{7}{8}$ in.

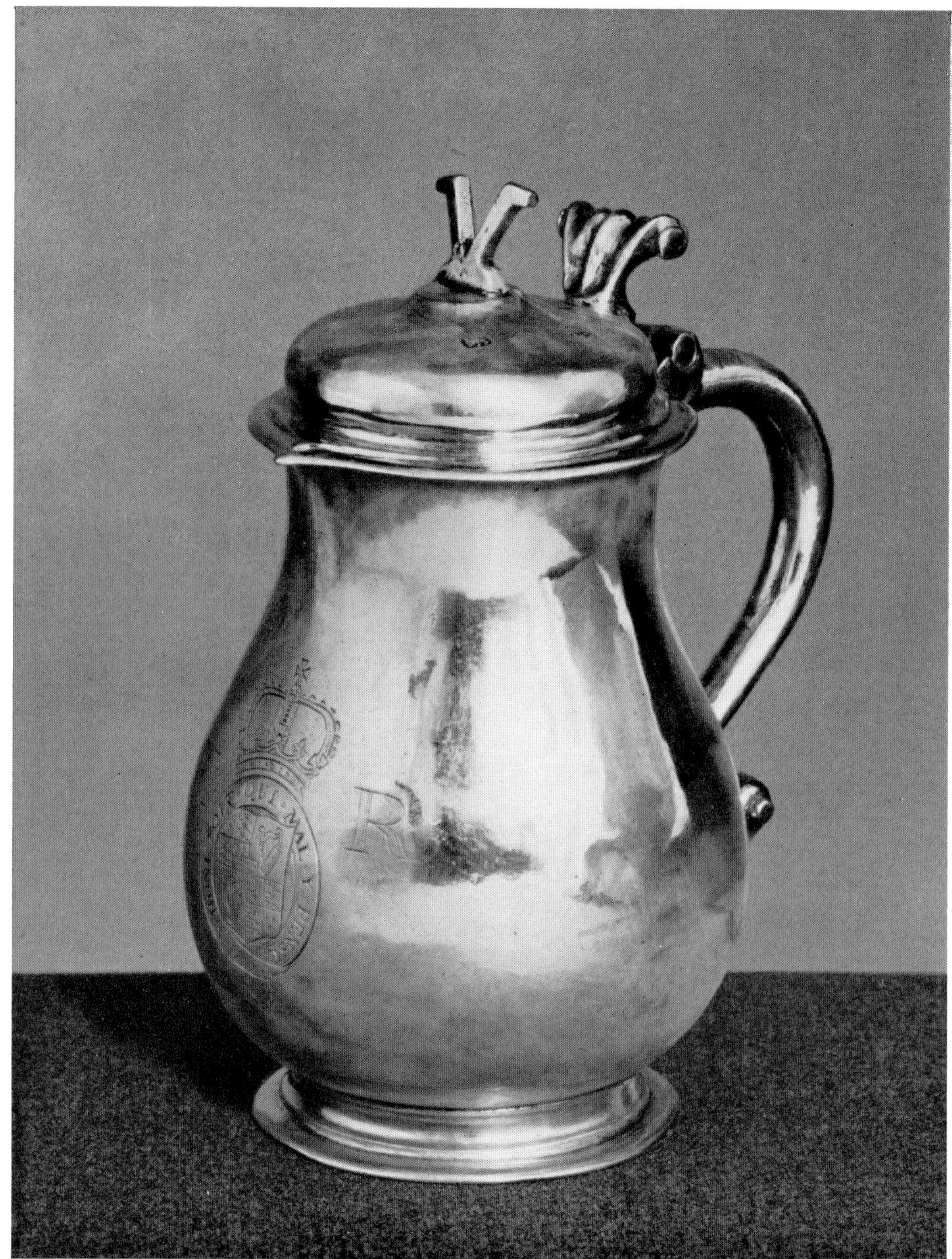

CRUET. Gilt
Mark of Charles Shelley
Hall-mark for 1682
The Earl of Lonsdale
H. 5½ in.

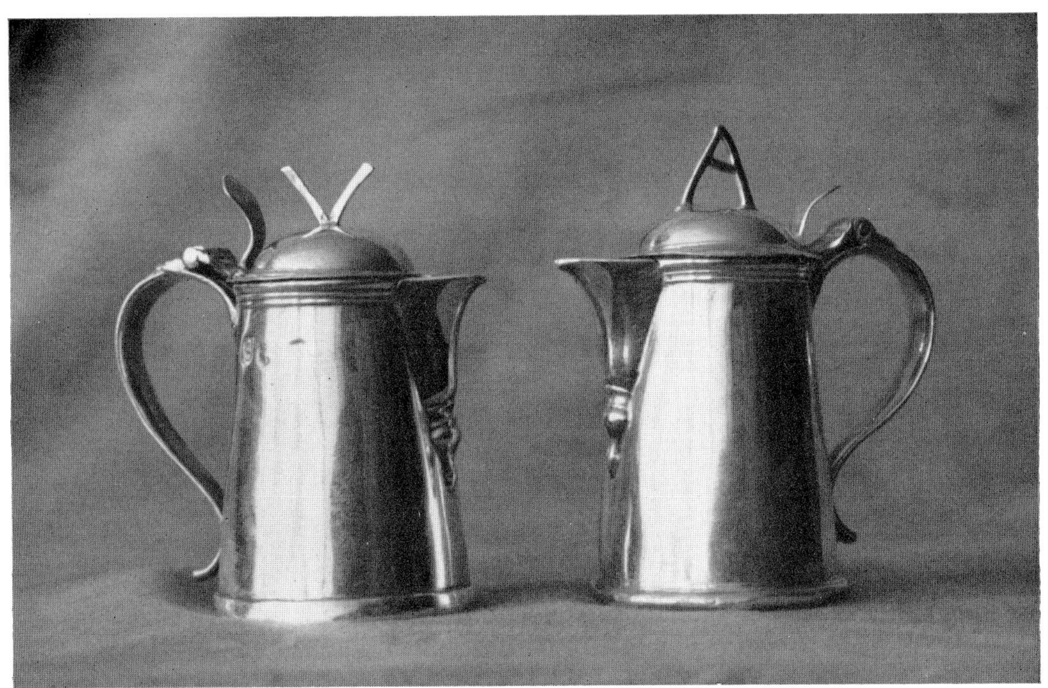

a. PAIR OF CRUETS
Mark of Benjamin Pyne
Hall-mark for 1707
York Minster
H. $3\frac{1}{2}$ in.

b. PAIR OF CRUETS
Mark of James Goodwin
Hall-mark for 1729
Stonyhurst College
H. $3\frac{1}{2}$ in.

PAIR OF CRUETS
Mark on tray (not shown) of Frederick Kandler
Hall-mark for 1776
Lulworth Castle, Dorset
H. 6¼ in.

PAIR OF CRUETS WITH TRAY
Mark of Philip Rundell
Hall-mark for 1820
Wardour Castle, Wilts.
H. 6 in.

PAIR OF CRUETS WITH TRAY. Gilt
Mark of John Angell
Hall-mark for 1823
Westminster Cathedral
W. (tray) 9 in.

RECUSANT CANDLESTICK (from a set of six)
Maker's mark, *JC in script crowned*
Hall-mark for 1675
H. 12 in.

a

b

RECUSANT CANDLESTICKS (from sets of six)

a. Mark of Ambrose Stevenson (?)
Hall-mark for 1710
Arundel Castle, Sussex
H. 16½ in.

b. Mark of Charles Kandler
Hall-mark for 1733
Wardour Castle, Wilts.
H. 14 in.

CENSER
Mark of Anthony Nelme
Hall-mark for 1703
Lord Rossmore
H. 6¾ in.

CENSER
Mark of Ann Tanqueray
Hall-mark for 1732
St. Dominic's Priory, Haverstock Hill
H. 8½ in.

CENSER
Maker's mark, *TK*
Hall-mark for 1742
Corby Castle, Cumberland
H. 8 in.

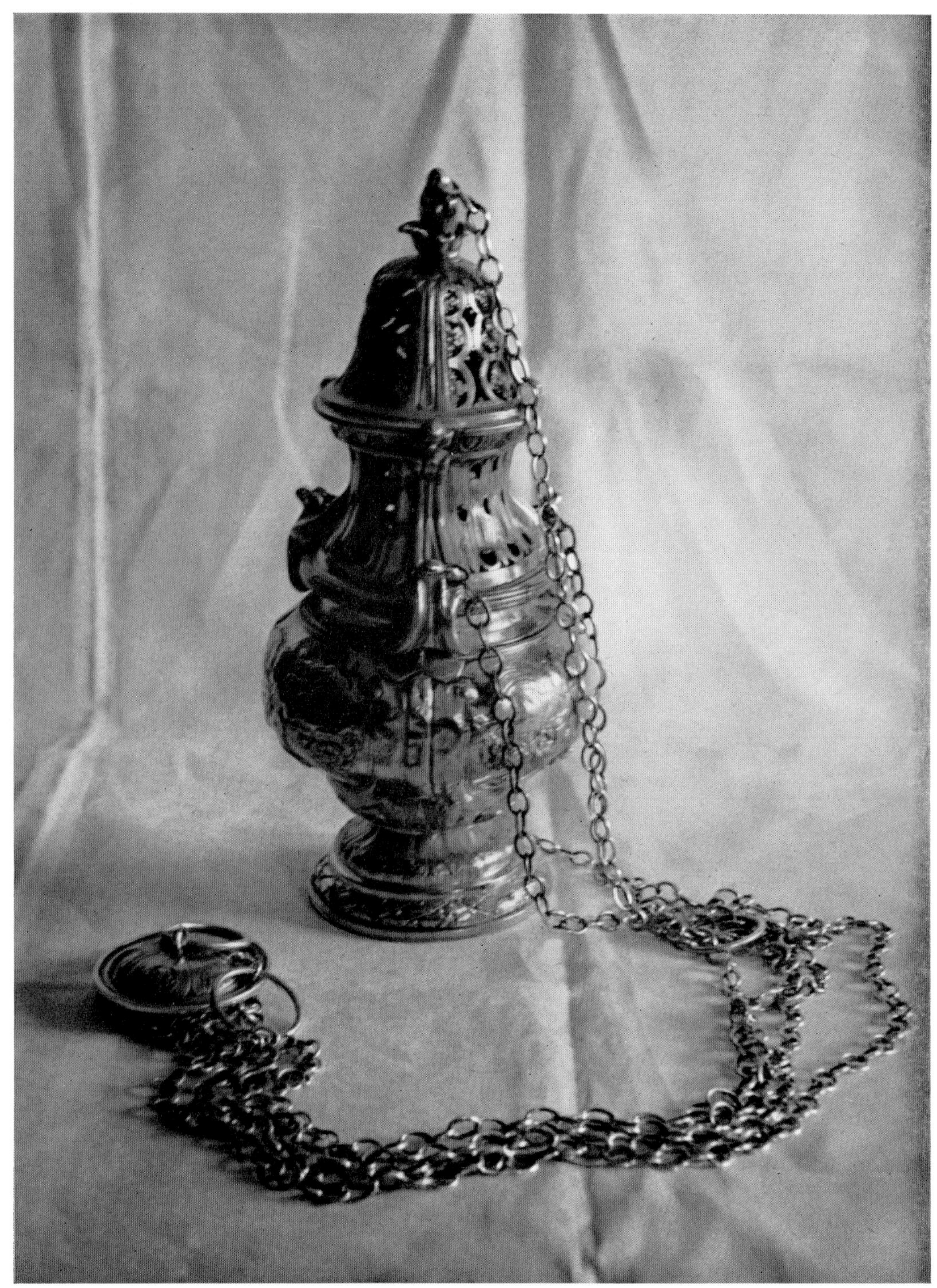

CENSER
Mark of Charles Kandler
Hall-mark for 1786
Wardour Castle, Wilts.
H. 8 in.

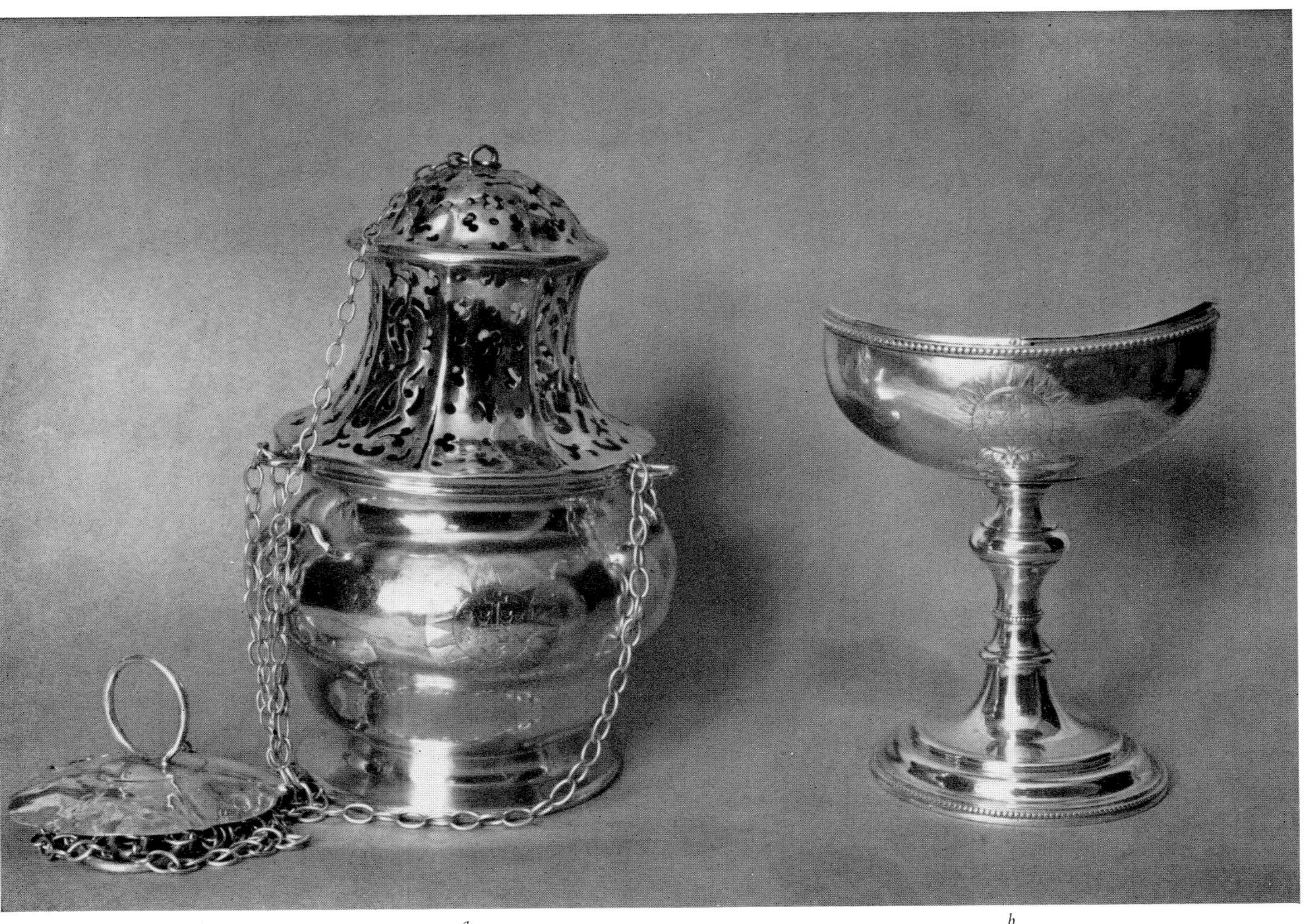

a

a. CENSER
Mark of Wm. Tuite
Hall-mark for 1772
Lulworth Castle, Dorset
H. 8 in.

b

b. INCENSE-BOAT
No marks
About 1790
Lulworth Castle, Dorset
H. 6 in.

INCENSE-BOAT
Maker's mark, *TK*
Hall-mark for 1742
Corby Castle, Cumberland
H. 5 in.

PROCESSIONAL CROSS
Made for Catherine of Braganza
Dated 1664
Palacio das Necessidades, Lisbon

a

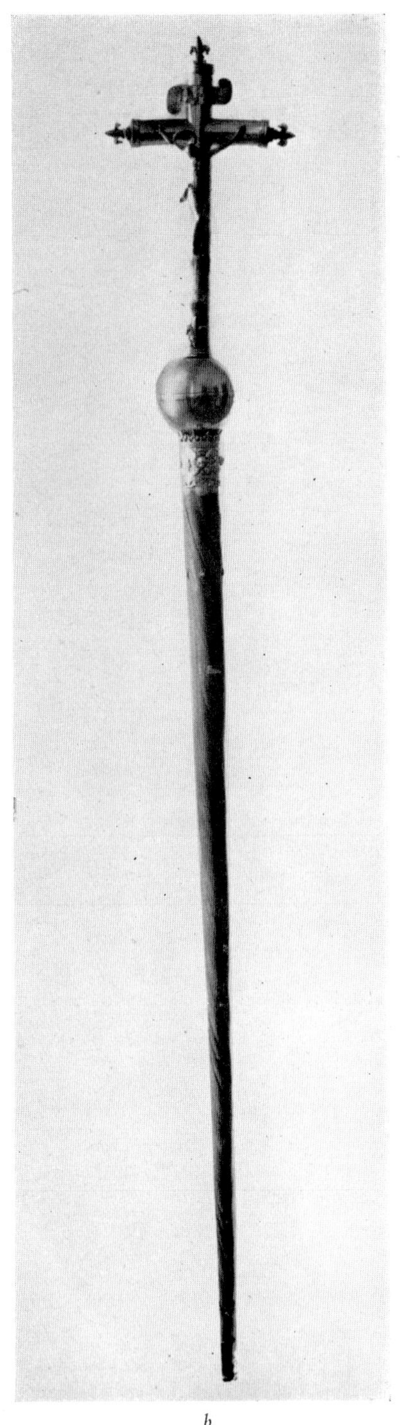

b

CROSS OF CATHERINE OF BRAGANZA

a. Back view, showing cavity for the relic

b. Full-length view, showing the unicorn's horn staff

H. 6½ ft.

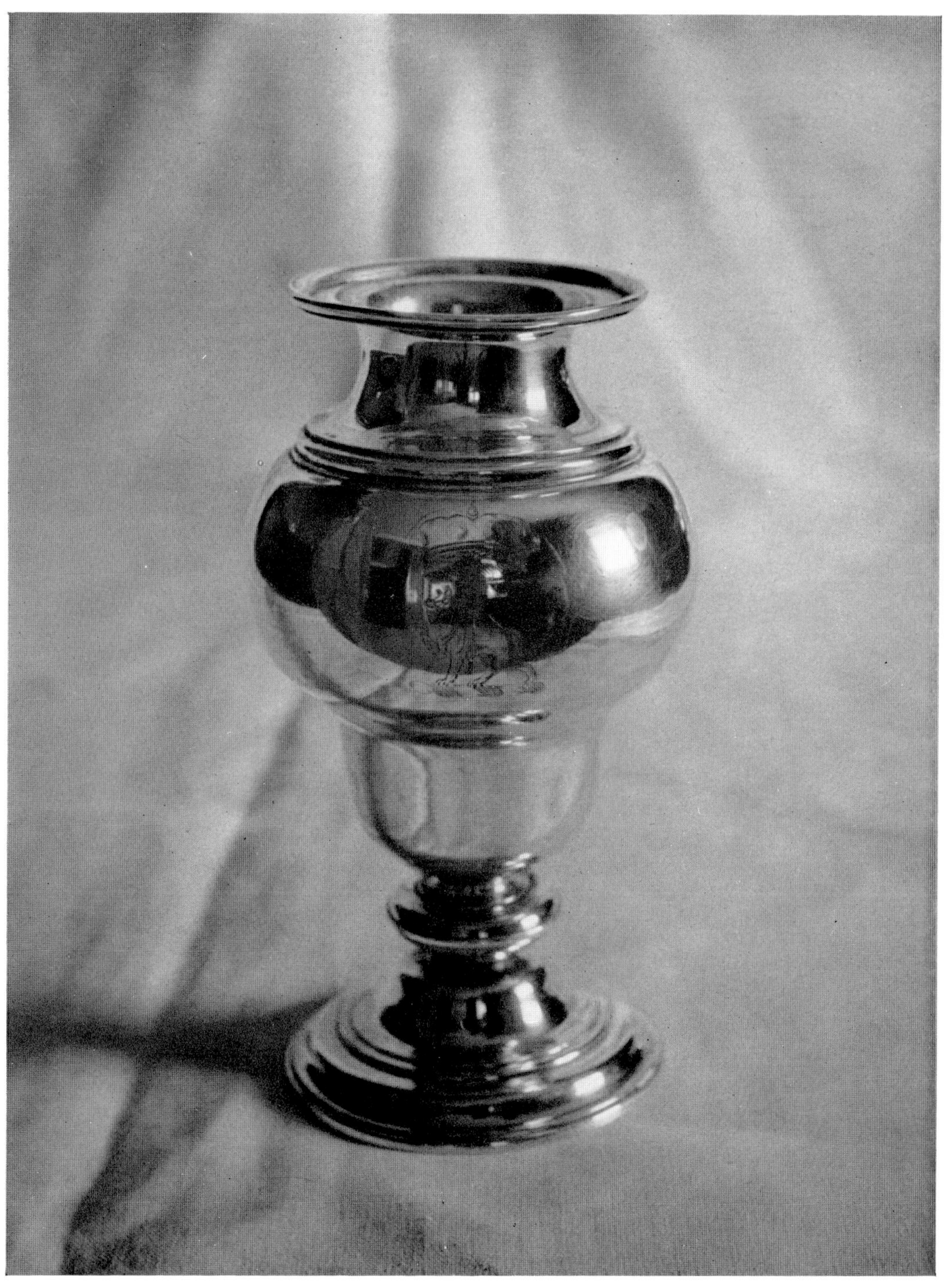

ALTAR VASE (from a set of four)
Hall-mark for 1725
Wardour Castle, Wilts.
H. $5\frac{1}{2}$ in.

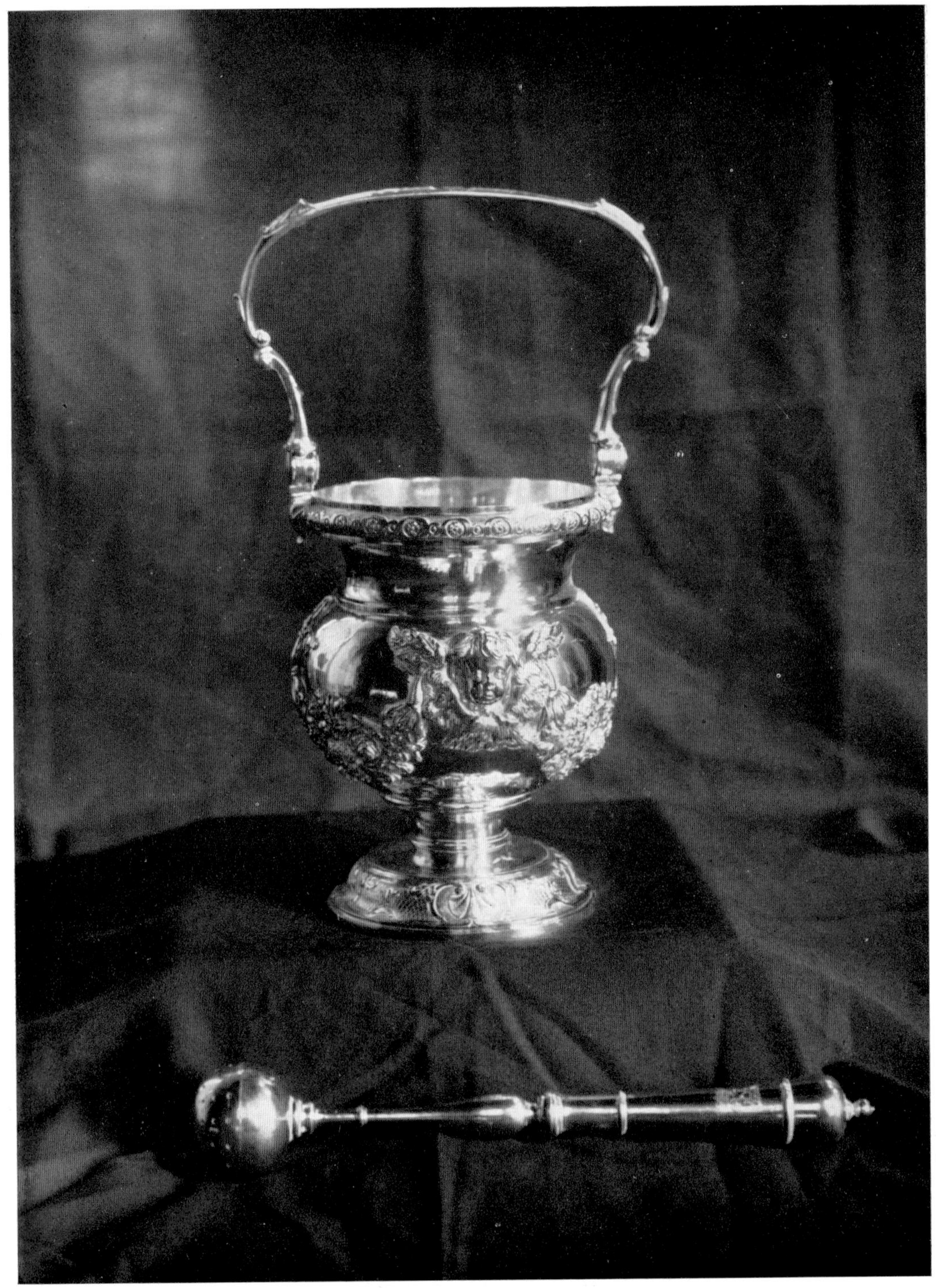

HOLY-WATER BUCKET WITH SPRINKLER

Mark of Frederick Kandler

Hall-mark for 1735

Arundel Castle, Sussex

H. 6½ in.

HOLY-WATER BUCKET
Mark of John Schofield
Hall-mark for 1793
Wardour Castle, Wilts.
H. 12 in.

HOLY-WATER STOUP
Mark of Joseph Barbitt
Hall-mark for 1719
Ashmolean Museum, Oxford
H. 10 in.

a

a. SANCTUARY LAMP. Gilt
Maker's mark, *SI* (?)
Hall-mark for 1700
Arundel Castle, Sussex
Diam. 12 in.

b

b. SANCTUARY LAMP
Hall-mark for 1789
Arundel Castle, Sussex
Diam. 6½ in.

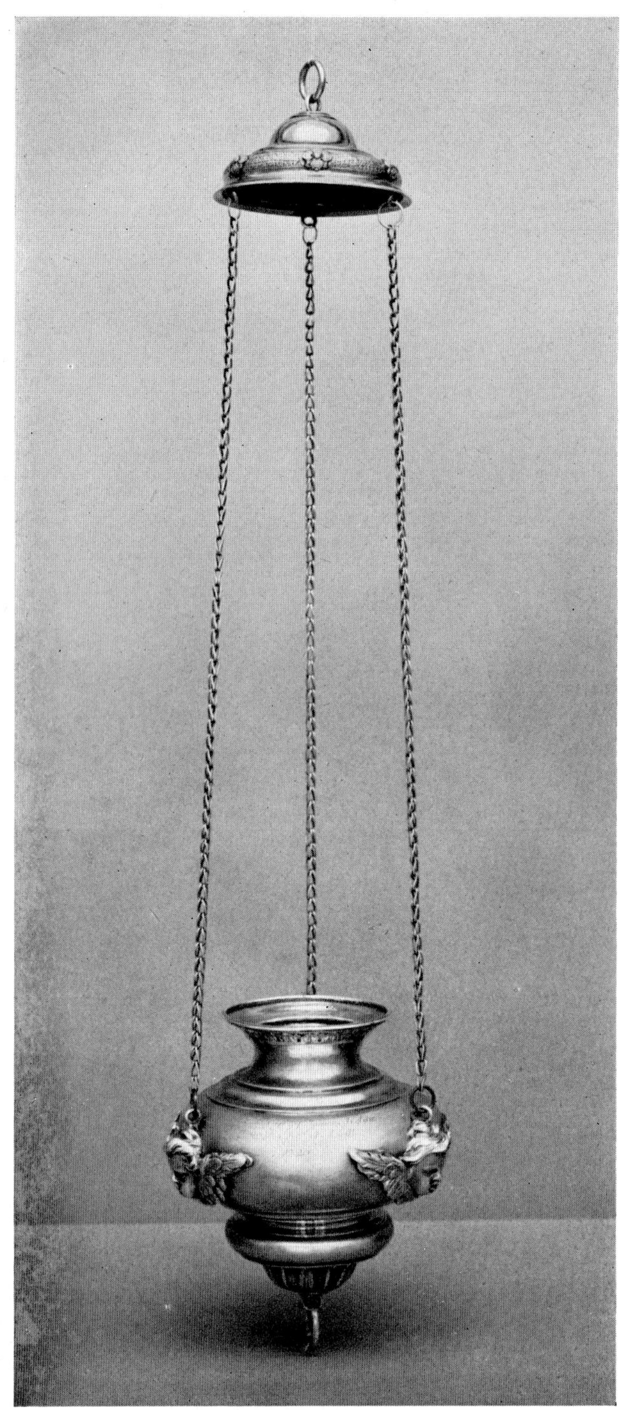

SANCTUARY LAMP
Mark of Charles Kandler
About 1727
Victoria and Albert Museum
Diam. $7\frac{1}{2}$ in.

CIBORIUM. Gilt
Maker's mark, *IS crowned*
Hall-mark for 1670
H. 9¾ in.

CIBORIUM
Mark of Benjamin Pyne
Hall-mark for 1712
Victoria and Albert Museum
H. 8½ in.

a

b

c

PYX. Gold
Maker's mark, *a unicorn's head*
About 1610
Westminster Cathedral
Diam. $2\frac{7}{8}$ in.

a. Open, showing inside of lid

b. Outside of lid
c. Bottom

a

b *c*

d

FOUR PYXES

a. About 1635. Diam. 2 in. *Oscott College, Birmingham*

b. About 1690. Diam. 2 in. ,, ,,

c. About 1635. Diam. $1\frac{3}{4}$ in. ,, ,,

d. About 1660. Diam. $1\frac{5}{8}$ in. *Stonyhurst College*

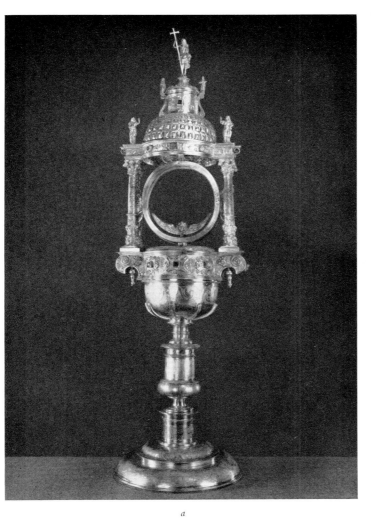

a

a. COMBINED CHALICE AND MONSTRANCE. Gilt
Portuguese, early 17th century
Victoria and Albert Museum
H. $27\frac{3}{8}$ in.

b

b. COMBINED CHALICE AND MONSTRANCE. Gilt
About 1670
Sizergh Castle, Westmorland
H. $14\frac{3}{4}$ in.

GLORY, CHALICE, AND PATEN. Gilt
Belonging to the Sizergh chalice-monstrance
H. (chalice) $7\frac{1}{2}$ in.

MONSTRANCE. Gilt
Hall-mark for 1693
National Museum, Dublin
H. 16 in.

MONSTRANCE
Mark of John Payne
Hall-mark for 1756
Mount St. Mary's College, Sprinkhill, Sheffield
H. 15 in.

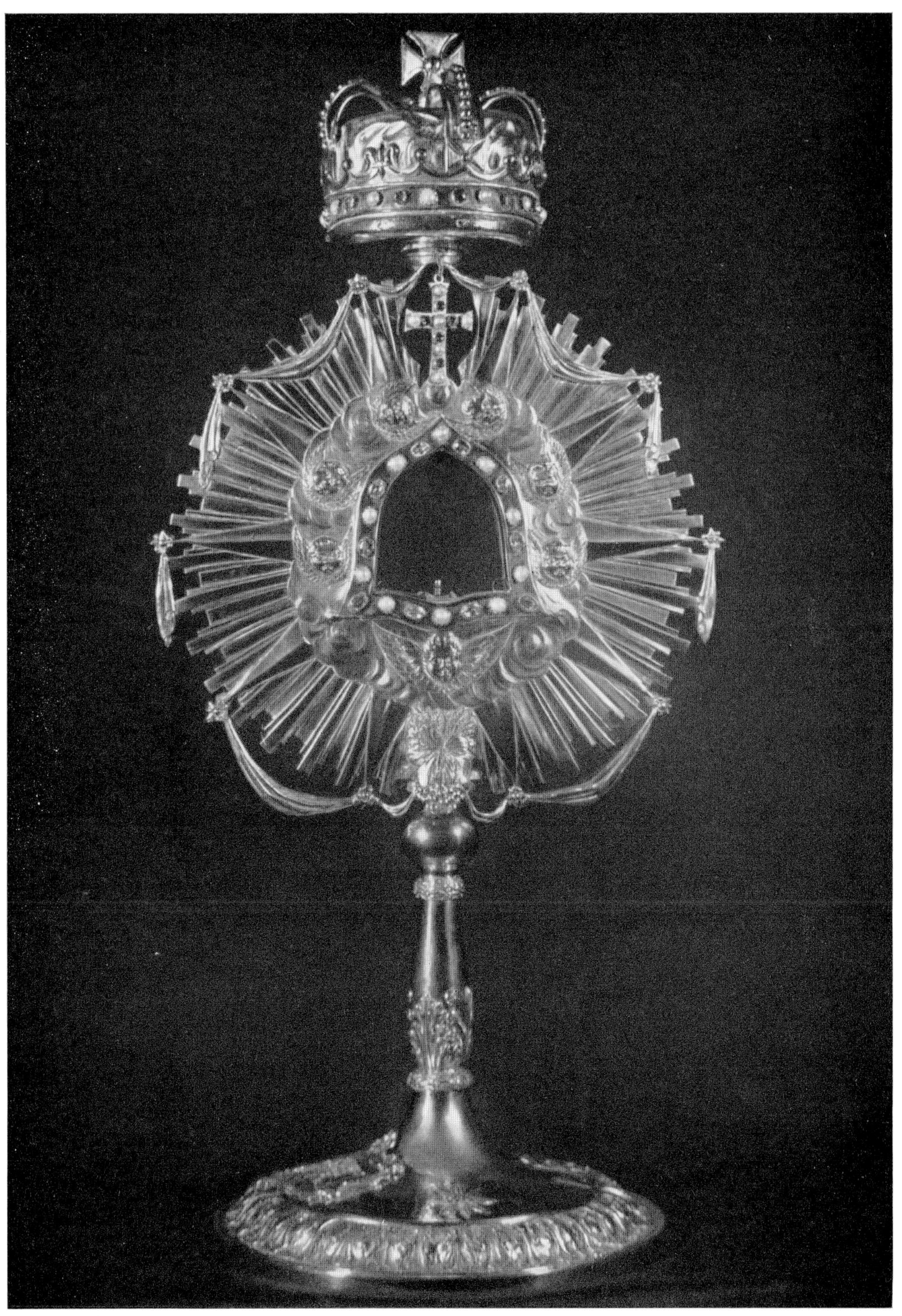

MONSTRANCE. Parcel-gilt
Mark of Samuel Hennell
Hall-mark for 1808
Stonyhurst College
H. 24 in.

RELIQUARY OF THE HOLY THORN
Enamelled gold
About 1600
Stonyhurst College
H. 6 in.

RELIQUARY OF THE HOLY THORN
Enamelled gold
About 1600
Sint-Michielskerk, Ghent
H. $7\frac{1}{2}$ in.

PRINTED IN GREAT BRITAIN
AT THE UNIVERSITY PRESS, OXFORD
BY CHARLES BATEY
PRINTER TO THE UNIVERSITY